BUSINESS FLUCTUATIONS

FORECASTING
TECHNIQUES
AND
APPLICATIONS

Dale G. Bails
Memphis State University

Larry C. Peppers
Creighton University

Prentice-Hall, Inc., Englewood Cliffs, New Jersey   07632

Library of Congress Cataloging in Publication Data

Bails, Dale.
   Business fluctuations.

   Bibliography: p.
   Includes index.
   1. Business forecasting.   2. Business cycles.
I. Peppers, Larry C. II. Title.
HB3730.B25   338.5′442   81-12098
ISBN 0-13-098400-0   AACR2

Editorial/Production supervision by Steven Young
Interior design by Lori E. Wieseneck
Cover design by R/D Graphics
Manufacturing buyer: Ed O'Dougherty

Printed in the United States of America

10 9 8 7 6 5 4 3 2

ISBN 0-13-098400-0

Prentice-Hall International, Inc., *London*
Prentice-Hall of Australia Pty. Limited, *Sydney*
Prentice-Hall of Canada, Ltd., *Toronto*
Prentice-Hall of India Private Limited, *New Delhi*
Prentice-Hall of Japan, Inc., *Tokyo*
Prentice-Hall of Southeast Asia Pte. Ltd., *Singapore*
Whitehall Books Limited, *Wellington, New Zealand*

To Fran, Marcia, Juloy, Dalene, Todd and Susan

Contents

Chapter 2   Macroeconomic Forces:
Shaping the Environment of the Business Sector   32

Chapter 3   The Great Recession of 1974–75:
Monitoring Econometric Forecasts   66

PART II   CLASSICAL TIME-SERIES DECOMPOSITION   99

Chapter 4   Forecasting, Time-Series Data Analysis, and Forecast Evaluation   101

PART III   THE TWO-VARIABLE REGRESSION MODEL   139

Chapter 5   Simple Linear Regression   141

Chapter 8   Case Studies of Multiple Regression Models   275

PART V   TIME-SERIES MODELS   331

Chapter 9   Time-Series Models   333

Chapter 10   Advanced Time-Series Models   365

PART VI   TRANSLATING THE FORECAST FOR MANAGEMENT   393

Chapter 11   Communicating Forecasts to Management   395

LIST OF APPENDICES   427

INDICES   473

Preface

The question of what material should be in a master's-level textbook in forecasting arose again and again as we talked with practitioners in the field, received comments from students and colleagues, wrote the manuscript, and discussed points of difference with reviewers. *Business Fluctuations* starts from the premises that students must become well acquainted with the broad institutional environment surrounding the business sector, that forecasting skills are best developed and retained by repeated exposure to real (as opposed to contrived) forecasting models, and that techniques and applications must accurately reflect the process of forecasting as actually carried out in the business sector.

For teachers of forecasting, a perennial source of frustration is that existing forecasting textbooks have tended to ignore institutional parameters such as the business cycle and the actual role of the business forecaster in facilitating management decision making. Forecasting textbooks have evolved into either advanced treatises in econometrics and time-series modeling, studies in macro-economic theory, or a smorgasbord of historical summaries and theories devoid of statistical interpretation. By way of contrast, our goal is to help students understand the activity of forecasting as performed by practicing business professionals.

The typical master's-level student will have had at least two semesters of economics and two or more semesters of statistical techniques and quantitative methods, and this is the background we assume in presenting the material. It is also true that graduate students invariably have educational gaps arising from differences in educational preparation and variability in knowledge retention. In Chapter 1, an overview of forecasting issues and concepts is presented in order to outline a general road map for the remainder of the book and to stimulate students to start thinking again about macroeconomic concepts such as recession and growth, about forecasting topics such as disaggregation and interdependence, and about the role the company forecaster plays in providing management personnel with the information needed to make decisions. Early in the book, we emphasize the functional division of labor that exists between commercial vendors that sell output from their large-scale econometric models and company-level forecasters who build statistical models designed to link the company's economic fortunes to national trends. The questions at the end of Chapter 1 are meant to familiarize students with basic data sources, such as the *Survey of Current Business*, which are to be found in the documents section of the library.

Although an elaborate review of macroeconomic theory is not presented in the book, Chapter 2 offers students a statistical profile of the business cycle that builds upon the historical legacies of Wesley Mitchell, Arthur Burns, and the National Bureau of Economic Research. The leading-indicator approach is studied, but the primary purpose of Chapter 2 is to heighten the student's awareness of the endogenous nature of cyclical forces and the transmission mechanism binding together all sections of the economy.

Chapter 3 is, we believe, a unique attempt to analyze how various sectors of the forecasting community—commercial forecast vendors, the Council of Economic Advisers, and the popular press as represented by *Fortune* magazine—anticipated and reacted to the events surrounding the worst recession of the postwar period, which occurred in 1973–75. Rather than attempting to determine which forecast group did the best job over the course of the recession, the study centers on the evolution of macroeconomic forecasts over that period, which Prof. Otto Eckstein has labeled *The Great Recession*.

Chapter 4 is a pivotal chapter, serving as a transition from macroeconomic concepts and cycle-related history to an introduction to time-series decomposition and techniques of forecast evaluation. Through a series of simple examples and problems, the student is guided through the basic steps involved in isolating the trend, cyclical, irregular, and seasonal components of a time series. A detailed printout of the Census X-11 seasonal-adjustment program's output is included.

Chapters 5, 6, 7, and 8 can be viewed as an integrated block of statistical methodology, empirical examples, and questions built around the least-squares regression model. Starting with the simple-regression model in Chapter 5, students are repeatedly taken through the steps involved in formulation and estimation of regression equations. Voluminous appendices contain the data used in the models, and the students are permitted, by Chapter 8, to follow the step-by-step development and testing of multiple-regression models. The material draws heavily upon the authors' own experiences as business forecasters and economic consultants. The applications purposely cover a wide range of industries and functional responsibilities—projections of quarterly air-miles traveled, retail sales of new passenger cars, installment-loan demand in Memphis, defense expenditures, sales revenues at Southern Airlines, and other models are estimated, corrected, and reestimated. After Chapter 6 introduces the complete multiple-regression model, Chapter 7 focuses on a series of special topics, such as stepwise regression, from which the instructor may pick and choose. Chapter 8, in turn, presents three complete regression cases designed to lead the student from theoretical formulation to tests for serial correlation, and to the development and interpretation of forecasts. The questions and exercises at the end of Chapters 5 through 8 focus the student's effort on activities that parallel the sequential development of topics such as simple- and multiple-regression models, tests of significance, and correction procedures.

Chapters 9 and 10 offer a two-chapter introduction to a variety of time-series models, such as single-moving-average techniques, Winters's seasonal exponential smoothing, and adaptive-response-rate exponential smoothing. Again, the models are presented in a sequential fashion from simple to complex and are illustrated with extended examples covering topics such as monthly demand for personnel in the airline industry, installment-loan demand in Memphis, turning-point accuracy of time-series models, projections of monthly steel shipments, and estimates of inventory levels for multiproduct companies. Although we judged Box-Jenkins time-series models to be beyond the scope of this book because of their inherent mathematical complexity and the substantial amount of judgment and experience required for successful implementation, we have nevertheless included a nonmathematical interpretation of the Box-Jenkins technique that can be used as a stepping stone to more mathematical presentations.

Chapter 11, the last chapter in the book, does not, in our view, contain optional material. Rather, we focus on several topics that are usually neglected in forecasting textbooks: how to interpret a request for a forecast; how to respond to a request with a series of questions that will identify the user's level of technical literacy and actual information needs; and how to translate a statistical outlook into a format that allows decision makers to fully integrate the forecaster's projections with other information flows. Stated differently, Chapter 11 focuses on the nonquantitative skills a forecaster must possess in order to bridge the gap from forecaster to advisor. The authors' experiences in business suggest that many forecasters misallocate their time by spending too many hours perfecting inherently fragile statistical models and too little time on the interpersonal skills needed to *sell* the forecast to management. The vast majority of the textbook is devoted to the critical job of learning how to forecast; Chapter 11 addresses the equally important task of communicating the forecast to management.

By now it should be evident that this book is pragmatic in nature. The most obvious example of this perspective lies in the extended examples, where real forecasting situations are studied. These extended examples are used not so much to get answers as to illustrate the process by which real forecasts are generated. In adopting this perspective, we have had to sacrifice coverage of advanced topics in macroeconomic theory and econometric modeling. This choice reflects our experience as corporate forecasters and our philosophy that people can become successful forecasters without becoming macroeconomic or statistical theoreticians. We do not believe that a master's-level forecasting book is the proper outlet for macroeconomic theory. Rather, we believe that practitioners spend the majority of their time in the eclectic world of macroeconomic analysis. To paraphrase Jude Wanneski, we believe our approach reflects the way the forecasting world works.

As is always the case, many people have contributed to the final version of this book, and to all of them we express our sincere gratitude. There are, however, several who warrant special mention. Dr. Robert A. Meyer of the University of California, Berkeley, offered innumerable suggestions for improvement. Indeed, at times, we felt that he was a joint author. Thanks also to Prof. E. J. Nosari of Florida State University and Prof. William C. Dunkelberg of Purdue University for reviewing the manuscript. Our editor, David Hildebrand, and our production editor, Steve Young, deserve mention because of their patience in dealing with first time authors. We also wish to thank Gerald Jernigan for typing the manuscript and Michael Athey for his proofreading skills. Finally we would like to thank Dean Jean Carrica of Creighton University and Dr. Thomas Depperschmidt of Memphis State University.

LARRY C. PEPPERS   DALE G. BAILS
Creighton University   *Memphis State University*
Omaha, Nebraska   *Memphis, Tennessee*

OVERVIEW
OF FORECASTING
AND
BUSINESS CYCLES

PART I

1

Business Forecasting: Economy, Region, Industry, and Company

INTRODUCTION

This chapter serves as an introduction to the world of business forecasting—an interesting and sometimes confusing arena that entails a high degree of technical specialization. The business forecaster combines expertise in business and economics with statistical training in order to analyze the behavior of a company or an industry over the course of the business cycle. To become a forecaster, a person must possess, in addition to a solid grounding in economics, statistics, and business, a basic understanding of postwar business cycles and such related concepts as peaks and troughs in economic activity, recession versus depression and prosperity, exogenous versus endogenous cycles, and macroeconomic or economywide cycles versus microeconomic or company-level cycles. It is also important to have a grasp of the broad range of activities actually performed by members of the forecasting profession—commercial forecasting companies that sell the output from their econometric models, business analysts responsible for translating general economic projections into specific sales estimates for their companies, industry and financial analysts making investment recommendations, and government forecasters trying to predict the course of prices and employment.

Although the prerequisites of forecasting can be neatly catalogued, the only sure way to develop the necessary skills is to become involved in repeated forecasting applications. This chapter provides a general overview of forecasting by examining the goals of forecasters, the business-cycle environment, industry-level disaggregation, and economic interdependence.

DECISION MAKERS: THE NEED FOR FORECAST INFORMATION

Before we become immersed in the milieu of forecasting tools and applications, it is worthwhile to discuss the purpose of forecasting from the perspective of a business organization. The goal of a business forecaster is to provide management with information that will facilitate the decision-making process. Although not always translatable into a profit-and-loss statement, a forecast, to be usable, must relate directly to the decisions facing management. This blunt appraisal of a forecast's worth is the standard for every projection presented to management. Forecasters do not know what will happen in the future, but they can work to reduce the range of uncertainty surrounding a business decision. Although surprises such as a natural calamity or an international political incident can overwhelm a well-thought-out projection, the forecaster's task remains one of analyzing historical data and institutional trends, studying the information needs of management, and generating detailed reports that focus on the decisions management must make.

Table 1-1 provides a sampling of the forecast users within a corporation, with specific forecast needs subdivided by functional responsibility. In essence, the categories listed in Table 1-1 represent general information requirements that are, in turn, linked to pending management decisions. For example, the production department has to schedule employment needs and raw-material orders for the next sixty days. Similarly, the finance department is required to arrange short-term financing for the next quarter to offset volatile cash-flow patterns. Key company executives must make capital-expenditure decisions in order to ensure that production capacity is adequate to meet forecasted market growth in the coming decade. Even traditional management support areas such as the law department are increasingly dependent on long-term projections related to social trends and environmental considerations. The demand for forecasts is, therefore, a derived demand based on management's constant decision-making activities. Although decision makers may be preoccupied with the immediate business environment, a forecaster's environment encompasses the broad social, political, and economic forces that shape the company's economic fortunes.

Table 1-1 Forecast users within the corporate structure and their forecast needs[a]

			Business Areas			
Personnel	Finance	Marketing	Production	Law	Purchasing	Top Management
General economic conditions	General economic conditions	General economic conditions	General economic conditions	General economic conditions	General economic conditions	General economic conditions
Labor demand	Total dollar sales	Total dollar sales	Labor demand	Environmental constraints	Labor demand	Total sales and cost
Wage rates	Production costs	Unit sales by product and region	Unit sales by product and region	Social trends	Product demand by region and customer	Environmental constraints
Economic trends and turning points	Economic trends and turning points	Economic trends and turning points	Plant production	Economic trends	Raw-materials demand	Social trends
Manpower projections	Product inventory	Product prices	Product inventory	New-product technology	Product backlog	Economic trends and turning points
Fringe benefits	Cash flow	Consumer preferences	Equipment expenditure		Economic trends and turning points	Capital expenditures
	Interest rates	New-product technology	Plant expansion		Interest rates	New-product technology
	Capital expenditures	Product inventory	Environmental constraints		Product prices	
			New-product technology		Capital expenditures	
					Environmental constraints	

[a]These are merely generalizations about the most obvious forecast needs of each functional area. Although the law department is not ordinarily seen as a user of manpower projections, such information could become very useful if a new pension law was being analyzed.

5

THE BUSINESS CYCLE:
PAST AND PRESENT

More than 65 years ago, Wesley Clair Mitchell brought forth his classic study, *Business Cycles and Their Causes*, which was designed both to describe the dynamic internal forces propelling the economy and to develop a comprehensive business-cycle theory.

> Much would be gained for the conduct of individual affairs and the guidance of legislation could we single out from the maze of sequences among business phenomena a few that are substantially uniform. For, with a degree of confidence that depends upon the regularity with which they recur, these sequences could be used as guides in forecasting the immediate business future.[1]

Although Mitchell regarded every business cycle as, literally, the product of a unique series of historical events, his quest was the development of a theory comprehensive enough to describe how one set of business conditions (for example, those to be found during a period of economic prosperity) transforms itself into another set (such as the economic conditions prevailing during a recession). Mitchell was searching for an endogenous theory of the cycle— that is, a theory that would explain the rhythmical ups and downs in the economy solely as a function of the internal workings of the free-enterprise or capitalist system. He felt that, although exogenous forces or propitious events such as bad weather, bumper crops, or labor strikes might retard or speed up these endogenous forces, exogenous factors were not by themselves sufficient to explain the cumulative processes that are at the heart of the business cycle.

Judged from a contemporary perspective, we can summarize Mitchell's achievements by saying that he succeeded admirably in finding a number of uniform patterns or sequences in business-cycle activity, but that he failed in his attempt to develop an endogenous theory of the cycle that could be used to accurately forecast the likely course of the economy. Mitchell was writing in 1913, and yet the following quotation from the *Wall Street Journal* in 1979 vividly illustrates the timelessness of his quest for an answer to the riddle of the business cycle:

> Will lights flash? Bells ring? Sirens wail? How will we know when the economy has entered a recession? We won't. Certainly not for many, many months. Probably not until any recession that comes along is more than half over.... Recessions are difficult to see arriving and can prove hard to detect long after they are firmly established.[2]

To illustrate the difficulty of diagnosing when a recession has occurred (which is different from forecasting when a recession will occur), consider

---

[1]Wesley C. Mitchell, *Business Cycles and Their Causes* (Los Angeles: University of California Press, 1963), p. x.

[2]*The Wall Street Journal*, "If a Recession Does Come, Experience Shows Its Arrival May Go Undetected for Months," May 16, 1979, p. 48.

Figure 1-1, which summarizes the movement of personal income and civilian employment since World War II. Can you spot the recessions that took place over this period? Economists call the onset of a recession the peak or upper turning point, and the end of a recession the trough or lower turning point. The turning points for the last five recessions are listed below:[3]

Peak	Trough
August 1957	April 1958
April 1960	February 1961
December 1969	November 1970
November 1973	March 1975
January 1980	July 1980
July 1981	

As outlined in Figure 1-1, the recession of 1973–75 was the most dramatic. Even in its January 1974 report to Congress (two months after the peak), however, the president's prestigious Council of Economic Advisers was still citing ". . . a number of factors tending to support the expansion of the economy . . ." in the remaining months of 1974.[4] Whether it was endogenous or exogenous forces that actually caused the upper turning point in economic activity in late 1973, forecasters clearly had not achieved Mitchell's initial goal of providing private individuals and public institutions with accurate advance warning concerning future turning points in the economy.

MEASURING ECONOMIC ACTIVITY
FROM PEAK TO TROUGH

Since the problems associated with economic fluctuations are still present, an attempt must be made to analyze the ebb and flow of economic activity in the economy. Return to Figure 1-1. These two series—personal income and civilian employment—are categorized as *macro* or aggregate measures for the entire economy. As an alternative, we might have chosen *micro* (partial) measures for, say, income and employment in Chicago or Pittsburgh over the same 25-year period. Such micro (or component) series often display different patterns of volatility from those of their macro counterparts.

Up to this point, we have purposely introduced a number of terms— *recession, prosperity, income, employment, business cycles,* and so on—with which you have some general familiarity. However, it is likely that the meanings you ascribe to these terms are not the same as the technical definitions accepted

[3]U.S. Department of Commerce, Bureau of Economic Analysis, *Business Conditions Digest* (Washington, D.C.: U.S. Government Printing Office, January 1981). August 1980 is the tentative trough date.
[4]*Economic Report of the President* (Washington, D.C.: U.S. Government Printing Office, January 1974), p. 23.

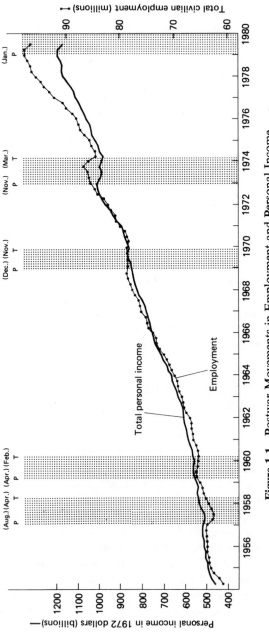

Figure 1-1 Postwar Movements in Employment and Personal Income.

Source: *Business Conditions Digest* and *Survey of Current Business.*

by the business-conditions analyst. For example, the term *profit* has a general meaning to the public, but it has a much more specific meaning to a team of accountants who have labored to prepare General Motors' income statement. And what, precisely, is the economic measure in Figure 1-1 labeled "Personal Income in 1972 Dollars"? The complete answer to this question can be found by consulting the *Survey of Current Business*. However, a less technical definition will serve to highlight the necessity of mastering a host of terms and concepts before moving on to the task of business-conditions analysis. First, this series is better described as *real* personal income in *constant* 1972 dollars. Because prices change from year to year, $100 of income in 1978 did not provide the same purchasing power as $100 in 1958. Thus, the income series shown in Figure 1-1 has been price-*neutralized* through a statistical procedure that holds prices constant at the level prevailing in 1972. But what is personal income? Stated roughly, it is the amount of income a person has to spend before deducting personal income tax payments.[5] If this measure is aggregated across all the people in the economy, we arrive at total personal income—a basic indicator of the consumers' ability to buy goods and services. This points out the necessity of becoming familiar with a host of divergent time series (measures of a given variable at different points in time) that quantify various facets of economic activity in the consumer, business, government, and international sectors.

One would, in fact, expect a high degree of correlation between employment and personal income—a fact that is supported by Figure 1-1. You may be surprised, however, by how little employment fell in the 1973–75 recession. Does that mean we were incorrect in labeling this a severe recession? Not really. A glance at Figure 1-2 illustrates that the unemployment rate reached 9 percent in 1975, more than double its prerecession level. Although some people were laid off or put on shorter work hours, the main reason for the climbing unemployment rate was that the growth in the number of new-job seekers entering the civilian labor force (see Figure 1-2) outpaced the number of new jobs generated by the economy. This dichotomy between employment and unemployment statistics points out one of the pitfalls associated with aggregate economic data.

ABSOLUTE VERSUS RELATIVE MEASURES OF ECONOMIC ACTIVITY

Of the many economic reports published each day concerning the health of the economy, no set of statistics is more widely heralded than the estimates for gross national product (GNP)—the dollar value of all the final goods and services produced in the economy for a specific period. GNP is the broadest

---

[5]See a recent issue of the *Survey of Current Business* for the exact accounting entries needed to derive personal income.

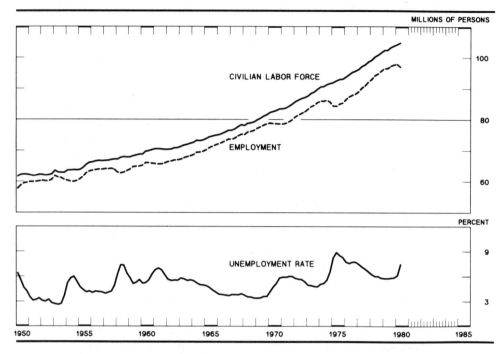

Figure 1-2 Labor Force, Employment, and Unemployment Movements, 1948–1980 (Seasonally Adjusted, Quarterly)

Source: Board of Governors of the Federal Reserve System, *Historical Chart Book*, 1980.

single measure of the economy's output of goods and services. Figure 1-3 contains a graphical summary of postwar GNP movements compiled by the Board of Governors of the Federal Reserve System. To the untrained eye, the upper half of the chart contains two relatively straight lines, whereas the lower displays an obviously erratic series. In fact, the upper and lower portions of the figure illustrate the same economic phenomena using different graphical techniques.

Look at the top portion of Figure 1-3. Along the right-hand side, we have billions of dollars of GNP. Note that a ratio scale is used so that the distance from $200 to $400 equals the distance from $400 to $800 and from $800 to $1,600—in other words, equal vertical distances measure equal percentage changes (this is known as semilogarithmic graph paper). Two quarterly GNP series are presented at seasonally adjusted annual rates (SAAR). The solid line measures GNP in actual prices, whereas the dashed line measures GNP in constant 1972 prices. Just as the dashed line has been statistically adjusted to eliminate the effect of changing prices, so both GNP series have been seasonally adjusted to statistically neutralize the normal ups and downs in the economy that are due to such seasonal GNP patterns as the pre-Christmas surge, the

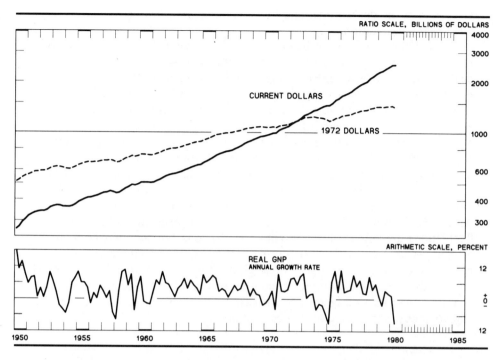

Figure 1-3 Gross National Product (Seasonally Adjusted Annual Rates, Quarterly)

Source: Board of Governors of the Federal Reserve System, *Historical Chart Book*, 1980.

postholiday winter decline, and numerous other institutional holidays such as Labor Day and Memorial Day, which regularly affect the production of goods and services.

Finally, the quarterly data have been annualized by multiplying the quarterly figures by a factor of 4. Just as you can report your earnings as $5 per hour, $200 per 40-hour week, or $10,400 per year, we can say that a GNP of $200 billion in this quarter is equivalent to an annualized rate of $800 billion. You must therefore internalize all the concepts above—ratio scale, current versus constant dollars, seasonal adjustment, annualization—before you can attempt to answer the most basic of questions: What is the secular or long-run pattern for postwar growth in GNP? By its nature, the upper portion of Figure 1-3 is designed so as to emphasize long-run movements (say, five or more years) as opposed to short-run fluctuations. When graphed using a ratio scale on the vertical axis, the slope of the line is a measure of relative or percentage change in GNP. Thus, the fact that the dashed line is nearly linear tells us that real GNP (GNP in 1972 dollars) has been growing at a steady percentage trend rate (roughly, 3 percent). Note that the slope of the current-dollar GNP line is steeper than the dashed line, and that the differential has been growing since 1970 owing to inflation.

Your focus should not be on the total or absolute level of GNP or company sales, but on quarter-to-quarter fluctuations; analysts work on the margin, dealing with the relative or percentage changes typified by the lower portion of Figure 1-3. Just as micro theory centers on marginal revenue, marginal cost, and marginal productivity, so forecasters dwell on rates of change rather than absolute levels. As compared to the upper section, the emphasis in the bottom half of Figure 1-3 is on the annualized, quarter-to-quarter percentage change in real, seasonally adjusted GNP (1972 dollars). In other words, the absolute or aggregate data embodied in the dashed line in the upper portion has been translated into a relative or percentage change in the bottom section. Notice how much easier it is now to identify the recessions beginning in August 1957, April 1960, December 1969, and November 1973. Investigators of past business fluctuations are often asked to synthesize the long-run or trend rates in the economy with short-run business-cycle movements. Whereas it is a comparatively easy task to predict next year's real GNP, it is much more demanding (and monetarily rewarding) to forecast monthly or quarterly GNP movements and translate these into disaggregated projections of rates of change for industry and company unit sales, dollar sales, and profit.

DISAGGREGATION: ECONOMY, REGION, INDUSTRY, AND COMPANY

There is a fundamental tradeoff between the desire to disaggregate or break series into their subcomponents and the need to minimize the cost of the economic resources required to produce a given industry- or company-level forecast. For example, producers of consumer products such as automobiles and beer could make, at best, crude industry forecasts if they were forced to rely on the aggregate projections for the quarterly employment and unemployment series shown in Figure 1-2. Since there is variation in consumer purchasing patterns for automobiles and beer based on age, race, and sex differentials, General Motors and Miller Brewing Company would be much more interested in having disaggregated unemployment (and income) projections similar to those shown in Figure 1-4. The payoff from disaggregation is the increased forecasting precision stemming from the ability to more accurately predict how many automobiles and gallons of beer will be purchased by males versus females, the over-35 age group versus the under-35 segment, and minority versus nonminority consumers.

As the end users of business projections demand more disaggregation, a host of new questions arise: Where, for example, has the most rapid growth come from in the personal-income series discussed previously in Figure 1-1?

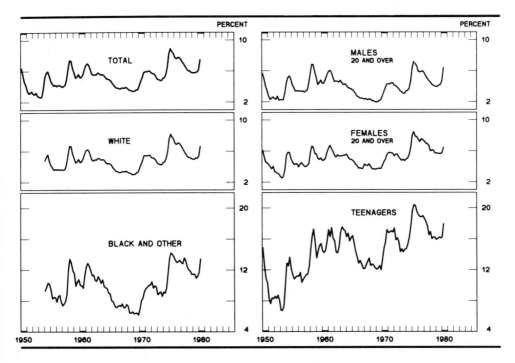

Figure 1-4   Unemployment Rates (Seasonally Adjusted, Quarterly)

Source: Board of Governors of the Federal Reserve System, *Historical Chart Book*, 1980.

As shown in Figure 1-5, much of the recent growth in personal income has come from transfer payments—nonwage payments by the government to individuals—which include unemployment compensation, Social Security benefits, welfare payments, and other income redistribution schemes. A billion-dollar increase in personal income arising from augmented transfer payments does not have the same effect on beer and automobile sales that a billion-dollar increment from wage and salary disbursements does. If you overlook this structural shift in the composition of personal income, you are likely to overestimate automobile sales and underestimate beer sales! Beer sales appear to be countercyclical; as the economy moves into a recession, unemployment rises, transfer payments increase, consumers switch from high-priced liquor to cheaper substitutes such as beer, and people devote more time to such nonwork activities as beer consumption. In the case of automobiles, however, injections of transfer payments because of rising unemployment are not as likely to increase new-car sales.

The very process of disaggregation will lead to a series of follow-up questions: Which component of GNP was responsible for the decline? Which group in the economy bore the greatest burden of the increase in unemploy-

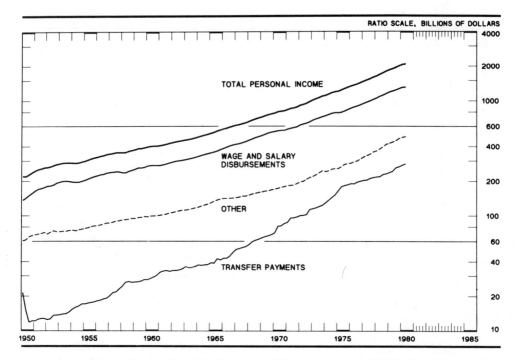

Figure 1-5 Personal Income (Seasonally Adjusted Annual Rates, Quarterly)

Source: Board of Governors of the Federal Reserve System, *Historical Chart Book*, 1980.

ment? What part of the increase in personal income was simply due to higher Social Security benefits? Which automobile producer experienced the smallest relative decline in unit sales? Which region of the country has the fastest growth rate? Which company in the beer industry is predicted to have the sharpest increase in market share? The questions are innumerable, but they all lead in the direction of more and more disaggregation. The movement from aggregate demand for goods and services to industrial output is one such form of disaggregation.

DISAGGREGATION BY INDUSTRY

Even though we speak about the need for constant disaggregation, the sheer size of the economy prohibits us from becoming intimately familiar with all its sectors. Although each industry and company poses unique questions, it is still true that the forecaster's kit of tools is largely transferable from job to job. We have chosen, therefore, to analyze throughout the text industries that will provide a cross section of forecasting topics and will arouse your interest. In this chapter, we will briefly introduce several industries (some of which are covered in detail in later chapters), discuss their unique forecasting characteristics, and try to get you to think about how you would approach, say, a six-quarter volume or sales forecast for any industry or firm.

THE AUTOMOTIVE INDUSTRY: DOMESTIC VERSUS FOREIGN PRODUCTION

Figure 1-6 illustrates quarterly sales of domestic and foreign automobiles at seasonally adjusted annual rates (SAAR). Note that domestic auto sales, which had been running at an annual rate of over 10 million units early in 1973, fell to a rate of close to 6 million units in 1975 before the turnaround in automobile sales was achieved. Equally noteworthy is the divergent path followed by foreign sales during the same period.

The issue of disaggregation appears as soon as you begin to ponder the logical steps to follow in preparing a business outlook for the automobile industry. Although foreign sales (see Figure 1-6) could be ignored in 1955,

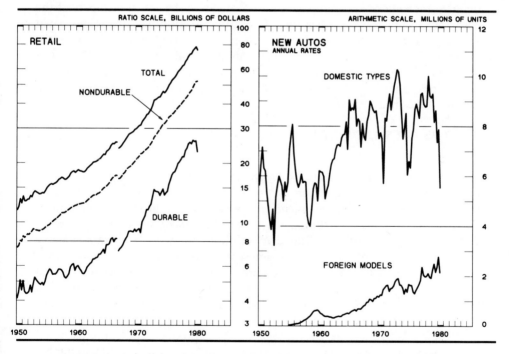

Figure 1-6   Sales of Consumer Goods (Seasonally Adjusted, Quarterly Averages)

Source: Board of Governors of the Federal Reserve System, *Historical Chart Book*, 1980.

their market share is now a critical determinant of profits and employment in the domestic automobile industry. And even if you had accurately forecasted the drop in total unit car sales during the 1980 recession, if you also assumed equal percentage declines for imports and domestics, the result would have been a foreign sales projection that was far too low and a domestic sales forecast that was much too high.

Recognizing the fundamental need to differentiate between domestic and import sales, what further disaggregation is justified? The correct answer to this question depends on the end users of the forecast. The optimum degree of forecast disaggregation (for an automobile forecast, or for any sector) is dependent upon the time horizon of the user. A brokerage house might want to forecast the expected earnings per share for a selected number of domestic automobile producers over the next six to eighteen months; alternatively, the same company might want a 10-year outlook. Suppose you have been hired as a business-conditions analyst by a major sparkplug manufacturer that supplies both the new-car and replacement-parts markets. Leaving aside the replacement market, you would obviously want to disaggregate domestic car sales by size of vehicle and type of engine—four, six, or eight cylinder. Literally hundreds of different individuals and companies (not to mention the actual members of the automotive industry) are, therefore, forecasting a multitude of disaggregated variables—earnings per share, steel consumption, sparkplug demand, advertising expenditures, new-car loan volume, automobile air-conditioner sales, new-car insurance-policy volume, rustproofing and wax sales, rail freight volume, and so on—linked to the short-run and long-run fortunes of the automotive industry described in Figure 1-6.

THE BEER INDUSTRY AND PRODUCT PROLIFERATION

Whereas automobiles are expensive and durable consumer products that provide the owner with a stream of transportation service far into the future, the beer industry provides a low-priced, perishable product that is consumed shortly after its purchase. But the generalization made about the degree of disaggregation is equally applicable to the beer industry. For example, beer producers have always produced premium and low-priced beers, but now they have branched out into a variety of differentiated offerings in order to broaden their market. Given its nondurable nature and its relative cheapness—the cost per ounce of beer being competitive with that of soda pop—one would not expect beer sales to exhibit the cyclical sensitivity of automobiles.

Figure 1-7 traces the level of postwar beer production. Again, as noted earlier, beer sales have been pushed along steadily by a host of demographic forces—absolute size of the population, relative growth in the beer-drinking segment of the population owing to the postwar baby boom, and so on—which are, in large part, impervious to short-run cyclical fluctuations in the economy. This does not necessarily yield a cycle-free industry, or a placid life for the

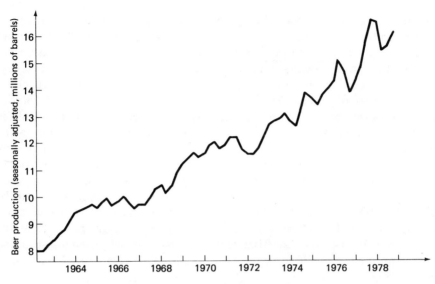

Figure 1-7 Postwar Beer Production

Source: *Survey of Current Business*

industry analyst trying to forecast the market share of the top ten manufacturers. If you are a beer drinker, or a sports fan inundated with beer commercials, you know that there has been an intense marketing battle waged in the beer industry over the last ten years. Utilizing historical trends in per capita beer consumption and a demographic profile of the population, you could put together a reasonably accurate projection for next year's total beer sales (this simple method will not, unfortunately, work for automobile sales). Having aggregate or total beer sales, however, you would still have to face the arduous task of predicting company-level beer sales in an industry that has experienced rather vigorous advertising campaigns, price competition, and a proliferation of new products.

Both automobiles and beer are subject to intense advertising, but the auto industry displays relatively greater sales volatility over the course of the cycle and comparatively fewer fluctuations in company-level market share. Although both beer and automobiles are tied to the consumer sector, the questions asked and the investigative methods used by the business-conditions analyst differ dramatically.

THE RAIL FREIGHT INDUSTRY
AND REGIONAL DISAGGREGATION

Many of you have never ridden on a passenger train, and you may not think of your lives as being touched by the freight segment of this industry. In a sense, you are correct. Railroads provide a service, not a tangible product such as beer or automobiles. More important, they provide an intermediate service to other businesses in the economy rather than a final or retail service to consumers. (By way of contrast, haircuts are a final service sold to consumers.) But even though you do not have a direct interface with the railroad industry, you do indirectly demand rail freight transportation service when you buy a new car, a loaf of bread, electricity, a can of beer, or any of the numerous commodities that make up your market basket of goods and services. Only in an abnormal situation such as a railroad strike does your dependence on the railroad industry surface. When you purchase a new car, you are not only indirectly demanding freight transport of the new car from, say, Detroit to your hometown; you are also indirectly causing hundreds of raw products and intermediate products—coal, steel, rubber, aluminum, glass, sand—to be transported. Directional flows become an important factor for the forecaster, since raw materials such as coal and soda ash increasingly move from the mines of the West to the industrial centers of the East, while semifinished and finished products fan out from the eastern industrial centers to all sections of the economy.

From a forecasting standpoint, the railroad industry poses a number of problems that are not faced in the automobile and beer industries. First, rail freight customers are shippers, not individuals in the consumer sector. Second, individual railroads such as Union Pacific, Southern Pacific, and ConRail do not traverse the entire U.S. rail network. General Motors, Ford, Miller, and Schlitz offer their product in every town and hamlet, but the railroad companies are balkanized or limited to certain regions. Regional analysis represents another dimension of disaggregation that must be considered when the rail freight sector is being investigated. To be sure, you can ship your freight from Los Angeles to Omaha via Union Pacific, Omaha to Chicago via Chicago and Northwestern, and Chicago to New York via ConRail, but this regional structure represents a unique institutional characteristic that must be given due weight.

Table 1-2 contains a tabular summary of the aggregate and regional tonnage of revenue freight originated on Class I railroads over the postwar period. Note, for example, that total tonnage originated by all railroads has been roughly flat during the last thirty years, in spite of the fact (see Fig. 1-3) that GNP in 1972 dollars had more than doubled during the same period. Also shown in Table 1-2 are regional figures. Even without a detailed analysis of the states in each region, you can see some very dramatic regional trends that must be factored into a future estimate of freight tonnage. Note that the Eastern District (largely comprising the major old industrial cities of the East Coast) has actually experienced a serious and prolonged decline in tonnage, whereas the Southern District (mainly the southeastern portion of the United States) has witnessed sustained growth and the Western District relatively modest growth. The relative stagnation in rail freight can be linked to the spectacular success of the railroad's main competitor—the trucking industry. What this

Table 1-2 Total tonnage handled by class I railroads, 1951–1978 (millions of tons)

	United States	Eastern District	Southern District	Western District
1951	1,477	699	244	533
1955	1,396	631	246	518
1964	1,354	565	285	503
1965	1,387	578	297	511
1966	1,448	585	313	550
1967	1,407	568	328	510
1968	1,431	574	330	526
1969	1,473	572	340	560
1970	1,484	557	351	575
1971	1,390	495	348	547
1972	1,447	507	367	573
1973	1,532	527	380	624
1974	1,530	520	387	622
1975	1,395	463	353	578
1976	1,406	452	362	591
1977	1,393	430	374	588
1978	1,389	384	366	637

Source: Association of American Railroads, *Yearbook of Railroad Facts*, 1979 edition.

suggests is that by focusing just on rail freight tonnage, we have already made an error in disaggregation. We should have first analyzed total freight demand for all transport modes and then devised a predictive technique for estimating the fraction that could be systematically disaggregated into the total rail share, the regional rail components, and finally, the portion accruing to the individual railroads in each region.

THE AIR PASSENGER TRANSPORTATION INDUSTRY: DISAGGREGATION BY CUSTOMER AND REGION

The United States has largely abandoned rail passenger transportation and has substituted air transportation. Numerous factors contributed to this switch, the most obvious of which is the opportunity cost of time—the economic value of time saved by choosing airline transportation over other modes. The relative price of different transport modes is also a factor: How many dollars does a family of four spend to travel from Chicago to Disneyland by car vis-à-vis by airline? The most obvious demand disaggregation is the separation of business travel from family or pleasure travel, the former being much more sensitive to time costs and less sensitive to dollar costs than is the family on vacation. As was the case with rail freight, airlines are regionalized, thereby experiencing different demand and growth patterns according to the particular routes they have secured—for example, New York to Miami versus Denver to Phoenix. The process of deregulation that has been initiated in the airline industry, most notably the easing of entry conditions into different regional markets, will provide new institutional dimensions for the business-conditions analyst to ponder. A key determinant of family travel demand is family income, whereas the level of business travel demand must depend, to a certain extent, on the level of profit and production in the business sector. This suggests that just as the level of steel production will be a cyclical determinant of rail freight demand, the magnitude of personal income, employment, industrial production, and profits should have cyclical links to air travel demand.

In Figure 1-8, we have graphed quarterly air passenger demand against quarterly real GNP for the postwar period. The growth of airlines vis-à-vis the economy is dramatic. In part, we can explain the spectacular growth of the airline industry as being due to its comparative infancy after World War II. Starting from a base of nearly zero, any growth is bound to look dramatic. But this ability to outpace growth in the economy has (see Figure 1-8) continued right through the 1960s and 1970s. In fact, an initial conclusion drawn from Figure 1-8 might be that the airline passenger sector is recession-proof. Certainly, this is true relative to the fortunes of the automobile industry. Even a high-growth sector can, however, have a *growth recession;* that is, a period of decline in the percentage rate of increase in air passenger traffic may be just as traumatic to the airline sector as an absolute decrease to the railroad industry.

THE STEEL INDUSTRY
AND DISAGGREGATION BY END USE

The steel industry is closely interrelated with two of the four sectors so far examined—automobiles and railroads being important direct users of steel for car bodies, railroad equipment, and railroad track. How do you analyze the economic factors affecting the steel industry? To begin with, you must, as we explained above with automobiles, break total sales into the domestic and foreign components. In turn, steel demand must be decomposed into the major end-use categories. A listing of major steel users is shown in Table 1-3.

The process of disaggregation leads in a widening circle. To predict steel demand accurately, you have to predict automobile sales, new highway construction, the volume of rail freight, the level of new orders for business machinery, and so forth. In other words, to assess the future course of output for the steel industry, it is necessary to project demand for all the major industrial sectors of the economy! This is not meant as a defeatist conclusion; rather, it is a reflection of the interdependence of the economy. In a broad sense, every forecast for a company or industry requires a macroeconomic forecast of the economy. You may forecast future steel output incorrectly if you are not cognizant of such economic phenomena as increased imports from Japan,

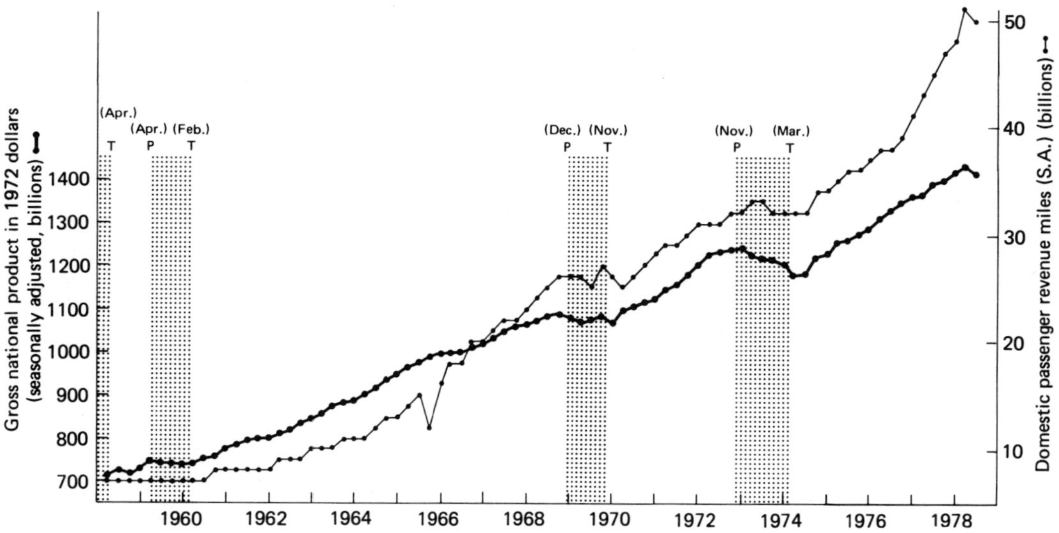

Figure 1-8 Comparative Growth of Airline Passenger Revenue Miles and Real GNP, 1959–1979

Source: *Survey of Current Business*

Table 1-3 Steel-consuming industries and related time-series measures of economic activity

Industry	Economic Time Series
Railroads	Deliveries of new freight cars
Oil and gas construction	Total oil-well footage drilled
Automotive	Domestic production of cars and trucks
Mining	Bituminous coal production
Shipbuilding	Deliveries of large commercial and naval vessels
Construction (other than oil and gas)	New-construction value put in place
Machinery	FRB indexes of production for electrical, nonelectrical, and farm machinery
Appliances	Shipments of appliances
Furniture	FRB indexes of production for furniture, fixtures, and furnishings
Ordnance	Department of Defense requirements

Source: U.S. Department of Commerce, *Statistical Abstract of the U.S.*; *Survey of Current Business;* and *Current Industrial Reports.*

government-mandated mileage standards, technological progress in the development of high-impact plastics, the demise of eastern railroads, changes in building codes, environmental guidelines for waste disposal, and numerous other factors that directly and indirectly alter both the demand for steel and the ability of the steel industry to produce or supply its product. All these phenomena are institutional manifestations of interdependence.

INTERDEPENDENCE

The rising demand for people who can put together cogent analyses of economic conditions is tied to the complex maze of interdependent problems facing businesses, the nonprofit sector, and government. The underlying forces producing this heightened sense of interdependence (simultaneous business peaks in numerous Western economies, inflation, uncertainty arising from government policies, the shortage of capital, and many other factors) have made the task of business-conditions analysis more hazardous.

Interdependence is not a new phenomenon. In Wesley Mitchell's classic study of cycles, he saw the diffusion of economic activity as proceeding along the "lines of interconnection among business enterprises" that lead backward to industries providing raw materials and forward to enterprises such as railroads that handle the increased output.[6] As pointed out above, however, Mitchell subscribed to an endogenous or internal theory of the business cycle. Exogenous or external factors could speed or slow cyclical movements, but it

[6]Mitchell, *Business Cycles*, p. 3.

was the basic profit motive that propelled Mitchell's economy from recession to prosperity and back to recession. For Mitchell, therefore, interdependence was primarily manifested in the linkages within the economic system—that is, endogenous forces.

You may or may not support the extended role of government in today's economy, but government policies (both domestic and foreign) are themselves a response to the public's growing awareness of interdependence. The political outgrowth has seen demands by the populace for action on a number of broad social goals in the energy and environmental arenas. In turn, this increase in external or exogenous instability has modified the endogenous or internal transmission mechanism of the economy outlined by Mitchell, and at the same time, it has significantly altered the task of the business-conditions analyst. In the Mitchellian world of endogenous cycles, the analyst's energy is devoted primarily to interpreting the signals of the marketplace—data on unit production costs, wage rates, interest rates, credit availability, product demand and company capacity, and other measures that quantify present and expected profitability. Today, however, you must construct a vast array of social and political assumptions dealing with the degree of government intervention in the economy. For example, will the Environmental Protection Agency (EPA) continue to close high-pollution steel plants, or will it make allowances for likely cyclical fluctuations in the economy? If it sticks to targeted long-run goals and ignores the consequences, it may exacerbate employment conditions during a recession. On the other hand, a number of steel companies will already have made substantial capital investments under the assumption that the output will be needed to make up for the anticipated void caused by the closing of high-pollution factories. Whether the EPA does or does not alter its prior time schedule, there will be economywide ripples spreading backward and forward via the "lines of interconnection among businesses."

Just as business analysts must have access to a complete forecast of the economy before attempting an industry or company forecast, they must also have a thorough understanding of the governmental and societal forces that shape the exogenous parameters. In addition to being well-informed observers of social and political trends, forecasters need an analytical framework capable of translating these exogenous assumptions into concrete recommendations that will serve as the basis for decisions by the users of the business-conditions output. It is the task of the next section, therefore, to illuminate how forecasters can keep abreast of economic, social, and political shifts and mold this information into a business outlook.

COMMERCIAL FORECAST VENDORS

Having read or heard numerous statements by business-conditions forecasters, one is quickly struck by the probabilistic nature of their projections. Rather than making absolute assertions concerning the likely course of GNP, corporate profits, the profitability of selected railroads, the prime rate, domestic steel output, or General Motor's market share, the projections are usually hedged with references to alternative scenarios that are possible, but less likely than the business forecasters' *best guess*. Thus, even though administration economists may argue that the most likely outcome for the coming year is 3 percent real GNP growth and 7 percent inflation, they will admit to an *outside chance* of 1 percent real growth and 9 percent inflation. Whether they are in the political or business sectors, all economic forecasters produce contingency projections based on a subjective probability assessment of likely exogenous assumptions: How rapidly will the Federal Reserve expand the money supply in the next twelve months? Will the government impose mandatory wage and price guidelines next year? Will an unstable foreign government nationalize the assets of a U.S. subsidiary supplying critical raw materials to the U.S. economy? All these questions require subjective probability assessments. The outlook for a particular company's economic fortunes over the next four quarters are summarized, as in Table 1-4, as *best guess*, *optimistic*, and *pessimistic*.

Table 1-4 The company outlook: A probabilistic assessment

Scenario	Best Guess	Optimistic	Pessimistic
Probability	50%	30%	20%
Company sales (000's of units)	125	150	95
Company employment (00's of workers)	10	13	7
Profit (millions of $)	1.2	1.8	(0.4)

The best guess is literally an estimate of the most likely outlook for the company after the state of the economy and the host of exogenous variables have been considered. In this case, there is a 50 percent chance that company sales will reach 125,000 units. The worst possible outlook—perhaps based on the assumption of a severe recession—entails company sales of only 95,000 units. This range of possible outcomes allows the company to formulate a contingency plan in the event that the best guess proves to be incorrect. Thus, instead of a single *point* forecast, a forecast *range* is compiled covering the entire spectrum from boom to bust for both the economy and disaggregated subcomponents such as company sales.

Forecasters are not able to devote a large percentage of their time to the task of forecasting such macro measures as GNP, industrial production, the consumer price index, or the prime interest rate. Instead, they buy economic projections from forecast vendors in much the same way that businesses buy labor or other needed raw materials and services. Having selected the macroeconomic projections that best fit their economic outlook, forecasters are then able to construct linkages between company or industry sales and the macroeconomic forecast variables and to translate the projections into an economic outlook that can serve as input to the decision-making process. At first, this division of labor may appear to be an abdication of responsibility, or even worse, a gross plagiarization of other forecasters' work. In reality, not even the largest corporation should attempt to produce a complete macroeconomic forecast. Anyone can make a *guess* of next year's real GNP and other key support measures such as industrial production, but this does not adequately meet the needs of today's interdependent economy.

To get a better initial appreciation of the range and depth of the forecast output produced by commercial forecast vendors, consider Table 1-5. As a simple summary of its monthly update on the economy, Data Resources Incorporated (DRI) compiled these data. Each month, DRI sends to its subscribers (as do Chase Econometrics, Wharton, and other commercial vendors) a review of the economy. Table 1-5 is merely a summary of the more important forecast variables compiled by DRI in January 1979. Forecasts become obsolete almost overnight, so it should be obvious that these DRI projections are of little current use. As you can see from perusing the table, the projections are grouped into major categories dealing with GNP, prices and wages, production, and money and interest rates. This was labeled DRI's *control*, or best guess, and was given a subjective probability of 50 percent; more pessimistic and optimistic outcomes were each given a 25 percent chance.

Each of the summary categories in Table 1-5 is, in turn, supported by detailed disaggregated analysis contained within the body of the *Monthly DRI Review*. For example, looking at the production section, you can see projected retail unit car sales falling from an annual rate of 10.9 million in the first quarter of 1979 to 9.3 million units in the fourth quarter before rebounding sharply to 11.1 million units in the first quarter of 1980. This is an example of a forecasted downturn and revival in the automobile industry. At the time of the forecast, you would certainly have wanted to move to the disaggregated DRI projections in order to see the effect on sales of big and small cars and on domestic versus foreign producers. This starting point could, depending on specific forecasting interests, lead to any of a number of different projections mentioned earlier— sparkplug demand, earnings per share, auto loans, and so on.

IS THE ECONOMY NEAR A TURNING POINT?

No matter how voluminous and disaggregated the forecast output provided by commercial vendors, there still remains a complex series of tasks for you to complete. First, given the vendor's best guess, optimistic outlook, and pessimistic outlook, what forecast alternatives should be integrated within the set of recommendations to top management? This is not a simple question, and it is not a task for those who wish to avoid taking a hard stand: Do you, or do

Table 1-5 DRI economic outlook, January 1979

	1978	1979				1980				Years			
	IV	I	II	III	IV	I	II	III	IV	1978	1979	1980	1981
GNP and Its Components—Billions of Dollars, SAAR													
Total consumption	1394.2	1429.2	1460.4	1485.4	1505.3	1552.3	1593.9	1641.7	1690.7	1337.7	1470.1	1619.7	1804.7
Nonres. fixed investment	234.6	240.9	245.8	248.5	247.7	255.2	262.0	271.9	281.5	222.0	245.7	267.6	303.4
Res. fixed investment	112.6	114.2	110.8	105.4	104.1	108.1	117.5	126.9	136.1	106.8	108.6	122.1	148.6
Inventory investment	13.3	14.0	17.9	10.5	-5.5	14.5	19.2	24.0	28.4	15.9	9.2	21.5	29.1
Net exports	-8.0	-6.7	-5.0	0.5	4.5	4.3	4.6	3.4	3.3	-12.1	-1.7	3.9	3.5
Federal purchases	159.2	162.3	165.2	167.9	173.5	176.7	179.7	182.7	189.8	153.0	167.2	182.2	199.5
State and local	293.9	301.8	309.6	316.2	322.4	329.7	337.2	345.2	353.6	280.6	312.5	341.4	376.0
Gross national product	2199.9	2255.7	2304.8	2334.4	2352.0	2440.7	2514.1	2595.8	2683.5	2103.9	2311.7	2558.5	2864.8
Real GNP (1972 dollars)	1405.6	1414.6	1420.0	1413.3	1399.2	1428.0	1446.0	1468.3	1489.9	1383.5	1411.8	1458.1	1524.5
Prices and Wages—Annual Rates of Change													
Implicit price deflator	8.0	7.8	7.3	7.3	7.3	6.9	7.1	6.9	7.7	7.4	7.7	7.1	7.1
Fixed weight deflator	8.2	7.7	7.3	7.1	7.3	6.9	7.0	7.0	7.9	7.8	7.7	7.1	7.2
CPI—all urban consumers	8.7	8.8	7.9	7.4	7.1	6.9	6.9	6.9	6.9	7.7	8.4	7.0	6.9
Wholesale price index	11.1	9.6	8.7	7.4	6.5	7.0	7.1	7.4	7.6	7.8	8.9	7.2	7.2
Compensation per hour	8.5	11.3	8.4	8.1	8.3	9.6	8.6	8.8	9.0	9.2	9.2	8.8	9.0
Production and Other Key Measures													
Industrial production (67 = 1)	1.493	1.504	1.501	1.471	1.415	1.486	1.512	1.538	1.572	1.450	1.473	1.527	1.621
Annual rate of change	6.6	2.9	-0.8	-7.7	-14.4	21.5	7.4	6.9	9.1	5.8	1.6	3.7	6.2
Housing starts (mil. units)	2.087	1.946	1.728	1.589	1.612	1.710	1.859	1.981	2.052	1.999	1.719	1.901	2.024
Retail unit car sales (mil. units)	11.1	10.9	10.6	10.2	9.3	11.1	10.8	10.9	11.1	11.3	10.2	11.0	11.1
Unemployment rate (%)	5.8	6.0	6.2	6.6	7.1	7.2	7.1	6.9	6.8	6.0	6.5	7.0	6.5
Federal budget surplus (NIA)	-21.1	-29.9	-32.5	-44.7	-58.2	-53.4	-48.1	-46.3	-41.3	-30.0	-41.3	-47.2	-27.0
Money and Interest Rates													
Money supply (M1)	361.3	365.0	368.9	373.9	379.3	386.0	393.4	400.7	408.4	361.3	379.3	408.4	436.9
Annual rate of change	4.6	4.1	4.4	5.5	5.9	7.3	7.9	7.6	7.9	7.3	5.0	7.7	7.0
New AA corp. utility rate (%)	9.47	9.92	10.04	9.73	9.58	9.51	9.70	9.85	9.90	9.12	9.82	9.74	9.89
New high-grade corp. bond rate (%)	9.21	9.60	9.69	9.37	9.23	9.16	9.34	9.49	9.54	8.87	9.47	9.38	9.52
Federal funds rate (%)	9.54	10.88	11.39	10.00	8.71	8.44	8.52	8.72	9.07	7.92	10.24	8.69	9.51
Prime rate (%)	10.79	12.23	12.64	11.54	10.74	10.07	10.14	10.35	10.52	9.05	11.79	10.27	10.88

Table 1-5 (Cont.)

| | 1978 | 1979 | | | | 1980 | | | | Years | | | |
	IV	I	II	III	IV	I	II	III	IV	1978	1979	1980	1981
					Incomes—Billions of Dollars								
Personal income	1784.5	1830.2	1875.9	1919.1	1949.8	2002.6	2061.1	2130.4	2200.8	1706.9	1893.7	2098.7	2342.8
Real disposable income (%Ch)	4.2	5.2	2.5	2.2	-0.4	5.0	4.6	6.6	6.0	4.2	3.4	3.7	4.1
Saving rate (%)	5.2	5.8	5.9	6.4	6.6	6.4	6.5	6.7	6.8	5.4	6.2	6.6	6.2
Profits before tax	209.3	210.1	210.3	201.7	188.4	215.0	224.2	235.8	245.4	198.1	202.6	230.1	262.0
Profits after tax	121.3	126.3	126.4	121.2	113.2	131.7	137.3	144.3	150.1	115.8	121.8	140.8	160.3
Four-qtr. percent change	16.2	23.7	4.9	1.7	-6.6	4.2	8.6	19.0	32.6	13.4	5.2	15.6	13.8
					Composition of Real GNP—Annual Rates of Change								
Gross national product	4.2	2.6	1.6	-1.9	-3.9	8.5	5.1	6.3	6.0	3.8	2.0	3.3	4.6
Final sales	4.2	2.6	1.1	-0.6	-1.4	5.1	4.5	5.7	5.5	3.7	2.4	2.9	4.4
Total consumption	3.7	2.4	1.4	-0.2	-1.5	6.0	4.2	5.6	5.4	3.7	2.3	3.1	4.5
Nonres. fixed investment	4.5	3.4	0.8	-3.2	-8.1	6.4	4.0	8.9	7.8	7.7	2.5	1.9	6.2
Equipment	4.4	3.6	0.9	-3.9	-10.1	12.9	2.9	9.4	8.8	6.4	1.6	2.8	6.6
Nonres. construction	4.8	2.9	0.8	-1.7	-3.9	-6.1	6.4	7.9	5.5	10.8	4.5	0.0	5.2
Res. fixed investment	2.8	-3.2	-18.6	-24.4	-11.7	6.4	28.0	24.8	21.0	3.7	-7.9	3.1	11.8
Exports	18.7	6.9	7.9	5.5	4.5	4.6	4.1	3.7	3.6	9.5	10.1	4.6	4.0
Imports	11.7	1.3	2.1	-3.3	-3.2	4.7	4.9	6.6	5.5	11.4	3.8	2.3	5.6
Federal government	2.0	1.0	1.2	0.9	1.1	1.0	1.2	0.7	1.6	-1.7	1.7	1.1	1.3
State and local	3.5	2.8	2.8	1.6	1.5	2.0	2.3	2.7	2.8	4.4	3.2	2.1	2.7

Source: *DRI Review* (Lexington, Mass.: Data Resources, Inc., January 1979).

you not, foresee a near-term recession (or, alternatively, recovery) in the economy? If you choose to assume that your industry faces a recession, you must quantify the transmission of this recession into the company's outlook. Such an outlook presumes that you have already carried out elaborate historical analyses of past recessions and have developed, through either statistical or qualitative means, an in-depth knowledge of how the company fares during a recession: Does the company lead or lag the economy? Does it rise or fall more or less sharply than the economy? Do all regional segments of the company move sequentially? These and other historical and cyclical insights provide invaluable background when the next recession is seen looming on the horizon. Although many unique factors surround each recession, researchers still rely on the pioneering work of Mitchell and his disciples at the National Bureau of Economic Research, which has shown that, even with an exogenous business cycle, there remains a basic continuity in the endogenous or internal patterns of economic activity within the business cycle.

There is no better way for you to grasp actual forecasting issues than to select a past period of economic uncertainty and read through historical accounts of leading business publications. Think back to June 1979. The 1975–79 business expansion had already proved to be one of the more durable and strong recoveries of the postwar period. A majority of the leading economists and business forecasters had, embarrassingly, missed the 1973 upper turning point in the economy; but the same experts had, by June 1979, once again reached a consensus. This time, however, the consensus called for a recession. As pointed out earlier, recessions are, in many ways, unique historical events differing in both duration and severity. "The Outlook" in the June 11, 1979, issue of *The Wall Street Journal* stated that although a majority of business forecasters foresaw a mild recession, some expected a severe decline:

> This diversity of views partly reflects the fact that the leading indicators, while useful in helping forecasters glimpse a future downturn, are next to useless in gauging a recessions' eventual severity. . . . Gauging the eventual severity of a recession can be far trickier than simply determining whether one is on the way.[7]

Consider the range of fundamental macroeconomic questions faced by the forecaster in June 1979. Had the recession already started? If not, was a near-term recession inevitable? If a recession was expected, would it be mild or severe? If an actual decline in real GNP was not seen as likely, would there be a reduction in the rate of growth? All these questions were paralleled by a similar set of industry and company forecasting issues. As a business-conditions analyst searching for a *leading indicator* or predictor of future economic conditions, you could have found a host of conflicting signals on which to base your own projections. Such an assessment of the economic scoreboard was contained in the June 12, 1979, issue of *The Wall Street Journal*, in the

---

[7] *The Wall Street Journal*, "The Outlook," June 11, 1979, p. 1.

front-page article entitled "Recession Now?"[8] Citing analysts' concern over erratic quarter-to-quarter growth in real GNP during 1979, the article pointed out that similar movements had been incorrectly interpreted as prerecession signals in 1976, 1977, and 1978! In fact, in June 1979, an examination of other measures for employment, housing, industrial production, and interest would have yielded a host of such contradictory signals.

For institutional investors trying to predict which industry groups would do well and which would perform poorly, the key issue was the cyclical sensitivity of various sectors. In other words, an institutional investor had to predict which industries would rise and fall faster than the economy during the prosperity and recession phases, respectively, of the business cycle. The task at hand for a financial forecaster was clear—put together a comprehensive set of industrial projections that would allow his or her company's portfolio to outperform that of the average investor in the long-heralded recession.

PREPARING THE FORECAST

You may have done a thorough job of studying the outlook, selecting the appropriate economic scenario, translating this into total industry demand, and finally, forecasting the company's total unit sales, but you cannot simply confront managers with a detailed computer printout. Ultimately, you will be asked to prepare a report that effectively focuses on the issues facing decision makers. The credibility of your projections will, most likely, be appraised by users possessing only a modest technical background; rather, the typical user will have a "forecasting literacy level" below that of the preparer of the business outlook. In essence, you should view the forecast report as an educational tool used to translate a scientific language into standard English.

In a broader sense, the framework of this book is designed to accomplish the same translation process. Just as you must master a host of technical terms and concepts, so you will be required to provide forecast summaries that integrate these concepts in a clear manner. As you work through the successive chapters in this book dealing with the tools utilized by the business-conditions analyst, and as you become immersed in the application of these tools to actual forecasting topics, you should also keep in mind some broader normative questions: What tasks ought (ought not) business forecasters to be doing? What are their professional limitations? What standards or norms should be used to evaluate the business forecaster's output? How does the business-conditions analyst fit into the broader corporate planning system? In general, how has the business-conditions analyst's role been modified by the events of the postwar era? All these are important issues that may otherwise tend to be pushed aside as you attempt to master the technical side of forecasting. They

[8] *The Wall Street Journal,* "Recession Now?" June 12, 1979, p. 1.

cannot, however, be sidestepped when you attempt to actually carry out the day-to-day functions of the business-conditions analyst.

QUESTIONS FOR DISCUSSION AND ANALYSIS

1. Go to the library, locate the monthly Department of Commerce publication entitled *Survey of Current Business*, copy down the GNP estimates in current and constant dollars for each of the last 16 quarters, calculate the quarter-to-quarter percentage change in both series, and write a short summary describing the behavior of the GNP over the last four years.

2. How would you describe the economy during the four-year span analyzed in question 1? Was there a recession? If not, did the economy grow steadily or erratically? Did inflation improve or worsen during this period? When is it better to use the quarterly percentage change in constant-dollar GNP than the quarterly percentage change in current-dollar GNP?

3. Using past issues of the *Survey of Current Business*, find, for 1973, 1974, and 1975, quarterly data (SAAR) for constant- and current-dollar GNP, monthly data (SAAR) for retail sales of motor vehicles (millions of units), quarterly estimates of ton-miles of freight hauled by Class I railroads, monthly estimates of air carriers' domestic passenger-miles, monthly estimates of beer production (millions of barrels), and monthly data for raw steel production (thousands of short tons).

4. a. The data collected in problem 3 cover the worst postwar recession in the U.S. economy and provide basic economic data on real growth in the economy as well as the five key industrial sectors. Calculate quarter-to-quarter or month-to-month percentage changes for the data.

   b. When does the upper turning point in the economy appear? the lower turning point? Which GNP series best describes the course of the recession? Why?

5. a. Write a short paragraph for each of the five industrial sectors describing its economic fortunes over the course of the 1973–75 recession. Although your GNP and automotive data are seasonally adjusted and annualized, the data you collected for the other three industries are not. Does this matter?

   b. Which industries appear to have been least (most) affected by the recession? Does this make economic sense?

   c. Which industries turned down before the economy, after the economy, or at the same time?

6. Locate the annual *Economic Report of the President* published in January 1974—two months after the November 1973 upper turning point in the economy. Study the Council of Economic Advisers' 1974 outlook contained in this report and compare its 1974 forecast with the actual results for the economy contained in the data you gathered in problem 3.

7. Do you know how many people there are in the U.S. economy, how many civilians are working, and how many are unemployed? You can get the answer to these and other employment-related questions by looking in the section labeled "Labor

Force, Employment, and Earnings" in the *Survey of Current Business*. In particular, put together a summary for the last two years that illustrates the total population, the size of the civilian labor force, the number of people unemployed, the aggregate unemployment rate, and the disaggregated unemployment rates for males 20 years and over, women 20 years and over, both sexes 16 to 19 years old, whites, blacks and other racial minorities, and white-collar and blue-collar workers. As a business-conditions analyst, what conclusions can you draw about the incidence of unemployment in the U.S. economy?

8. The most widely recognized measure of the increase (or decrease) in the cost of living is the consumer price index (CPI), which is calculated by the U.S. Department of Labor and is reproduced in the *Survey of Current Business*. Locate this section on prices, collect data for the last two years, and analyze which of the major components—food, housing, apparel, transportation, and medical care—experienced the greatest and smallest changes over this period.

9. Make up a list of important exogenous forecast variables and explain how shifts in such variables could occur. Are any predictable? What is meant by the profit motive, and how is business profitability affected by exogenous variables listed in the preceding question?

10. Forecasts of the economy inevitably incorporate discussions about the stock market. What groups are on the supply and demand sides of the stock market? As a business-conditions analyst interested in future price movements of steel-company stocks, present a qualitative assessment of the factors that you would wish to incorporate in your forecast.

11. Analyze the 1980 downturn in the economy by collecting data for 1979, 1980, and 1981 and repeating the steps listed in problems 3, 4, and 5.

12. How does your analysis in problem 11 compare with the outlook contained in the *Economic Report of the President* published in January 1980?

REFERENCES FOR FURTHER STUDY

"Business Roundup" in *Fortune*.

Economic Report of the President. Washington, D.C.: U.S. Government Printing Office.

"The Outlook" in the *Wall Street Journal*.

"What Businessmen Expect," *Dun's Review*.

2

Macroeconomic Forces: Shaping the Environment of the Business Sector

INTRODUCTION

Because business decision making takes place in a macroeconomic or economy-wide setting, it is important to understand the forces that shape the business environment at the national, regional, industrial, and company levels. Long-term trends, seasonal patterns, cyclical movements, and irregular factors combine to generate widely divergent growth paths for the industries and companies within the economy. The present chapter traces the cyclical linkages that bind the economy together during a typical recession. The business-cycle research of the National Bureau of Economic Research is studied in order to develop an understanding of the endogenous nature of cycles. Finally, a review of economic fluctuations during the entire span of the 1900s provides historical perspective and offers a clearer picture of the ongoing evolution of the institutional framework that plays such a critical role in altering the trend, seasonal, cyclical, and irregular forces at work in the economy.

ECONOMIC FORCES AT WORK
IN THE BUSINESS SECTOR

The list of forecast needs viewed earlier, in Table 1-1 of Chapter 1, can be better understood within the framework of the general forces shaping the economy. The growth or decline in company sales can be attributed to trend, seasonal, cyclical, and irregular forces in the economy. In the long run (five years or longer), the growth or decline in company sales is generated by trend forces propelling the economy. Shifts in trend forces represent fundamental alterations arising from factors such as:

Changes in consumer tastes and preferences
Changes in the distribution of income
Population shifts
Technological advances or constraints
Changes in tax policies

When these are related to Table 1-1, it is the presence of trend forces that gives rise to decisions concerning capital expenditures and the requisite need for long-run forecasts.

Cyclical fluctuations, or business-cycle movements, are nonperiodic, repeating oscillations around the long-run trend that arise from endogenous forces and exogenous shocks. Whereas long-run trend forecasts are required for capital planning purposes, it is the presence of cyclical instability that creates the need for one- to two-year projections for business volume and for the capacity-utilization rate for existing production facilities. A myriad of production decisions will be made based on the cyclical outlook for company sales. For example, the personnel and production departments need to know whether product demand will be strong enough to support one, two, or three work shifts.

Seasonal variations occur within a year and repeat from year to year, although not necessarily in an identical pattern. Seasonal fluctuations result from customs, such as spring purchases and holidays, and from institutional factors, such as model-year changes in the automobile industry and inventory sales in anticipation of tax dates. With respect to the forecast needs outlined in Table 1-1, production planners desire quantitative estimates of the daily, weekly, and monthly seasonal factors that cause company sales to fluctuate even in the absence of cyclical movements.

Irregular or nonrepeating factors also affect company fortunes; these forces arise from a host of unpredictable disturbances such as strikes, hurricanes, and international political incidents. All decision makers are affected by these erratic surprises. Although the exact timing of these exogenous disturbances is usually not predictable, forecasters can help to evaluate their effects in order to allow decision makers to take compensatory actions.

All these forces—trend, seasonal, cyclical, and irregular—must be incorporated in any model used to develop forecasts for business decision makers. Chapter 4 will explore in detail the specific statistical procedures used by forecasters to quantify the effect of each of these forces. The remainder of this chapter will focus on the business-cycle research that has been carried out by the National Bureau of Economic Research. The macroeconomic or aggregate forces propelling the economy having been dealt with, subsequent chapters will detail the actual techniques utilized by forecasters to analyze data and develop forecasting models.

THE BUSINESS CYCLE: AN OVERVIEW

In their seminal 1947 work, Arthur Burns and Wesley Mitchell introduced the most widely accepted definition of business cycles:

> Business cycles are a type of fluctuation found in the aggregate activity of nations that organize their work mainly in business enterprises; a cycle consists of expansions occurring at about the same time in many economic activities, followed by similarly general recessions, contractions and revivals which merge into the expansion phase of the next cycle; this sequence of changes is recurrent but not periodic. . . .[1]

This definition highlights several important characteristics of business cycles. The recurring sequence of changes that constitute a business cycle— expansion, downturn, contraction, and recovery—are not periodic. Although the phases of business cycles repeat themselves, their duration (time span), intensity (rate of change), and scope vary considerably. Although business cycles are generally found only in modern industrialized nations whose economic activities are organized through market-oriented business enterprises, this does not necessarily imply that the market system is the sole cause of business cycles. Indeed, even a cursory examination of the literature on business cycles reveals a diversity of opinion as to their cause(s).[2] Whatever its cause, the business cycle does affect the entire system of commerce—the formation and disappearance of firms, the level of prices, the volume of employment, the demand for labor, business costs and profits, income flows, spending and borrowing patterns, and credit conditions.

Table 2-1 provides a chronology of business cycles in the United States from 1900 to 1980, documenting the lack of cyclical periodicity. Published in

[1] Arthur Burns and Wesley Mitchell, *Measuring Business Cycles* (New York: NBER, 1947), p. 3.

[2] See, for example, Carl A. Dauten and Lloyd M. Valentine, *Business Cycles and Forecasting* (Cincinnati, O.: Southwestern Publishing Company, 1974), pp. 39–108; or American Economic Association, *Readings in Business Cycle Theory*, Vol. III (Homewood, Ill.: Richard D. Irwin, 1965).

Table 2-1 Chronology of business cycles in the United States 1900–1980

Business-Cycle Reference Dates		Duration in Months			
		Contraction	Expansion	Cycle	
Trough	Peak	(Trough from Previous Peak)	Trough to Peak	Trough to Trough	Peak to Peak
December 1900	September 1902	X	21	X	X
August 1904	May 1907	23	33	44	56
June 1908	January 1910	13	19	46	32
January 1912	January 1913	24	12	43	36
December 1914	August 1918	23	44	35	67
March 1919	January 1920	7	10	51	17
July 1921	May 1923	18	22	28	40
July 1924	October 1926	14	27	36	41
December 1927	August 1929	13	21	40	34
March 1933	May 1937	43	50	64	93
June 1938	February 1945	13	80	63	93
October 1945	November 1948	8	37	88	45
October 1949	July 1953	11	45	48	56
May 1954	August 1957	10	39	55	49
April 1958	April 1960	8	24	47	32
February 1961	December 1969	10	106	34	116
November 1970	November 1973	11	36	117	47
March 1975	January 1980	16	58	52	74
July 1980	July 1981	7		65	
Average, all cycles					
17 cycles, 1900–1975		16	37	52	53[c]
7 cycles, 1945–1975		11	48[a]	63	58[a]
3 cycles, 1960–1975		12	71[b]	68	82[b]

Source: *Business Conditions Digest.*
[a]Six cycles.
[b]Two cycles.
[c]Sixteen cycles.

the Commerce Department's *Business Conditions Digest*, these reference dates reflect the consensus reached by experts at the NBER concerning the upper and lower turning points (called peaks and troughs, respectively) in economic activity. A peak is designated by the NBER as the month that marks the end of an economic expansion and the beginning of a recession, whereas just the reverse is true of a trough. For example, looking at Table 2-1, you can see that the peak associated with the Great Depression of the 1930s occurred in August 1929, or prior to the October stock-market crash that is popularly used to date the beginning of the economic contraction. Also, notice that there was not a continuous decline throughout the 1930s. Rather, a trough or low point in March 1933 was followed by a peak in May 1937 and another trough in June

1938. Looking down the last column in the table labeled "Peak to Peak," you can see that the average duration from one peak to the next varied from as few as 17 months to as many as 116 months.

Business cycles are not merely fluctuations in aggregate activity; they are widely diffused throughout the economy and produce cyclical movements that we will call industry and company cycles. Although related to and influenced by aggregate cycles, they have their own distinctive features. Some economic activities—beer production, for example—appear to bear little relation in time to business cycles in aggregate activity.

Figure 2-1 illustrates the lack of cyclical conformity in beer production for the most recent business cycles. Even though the trough in aggregate activity occurred in the fourth quarter of 1970, the beer industry bottomed in the third quarter. Even more striking, the economy peaked in the fourth quarter of 1973, but the beer industry exhibited sustained growth throughout the 1974–75 recession.

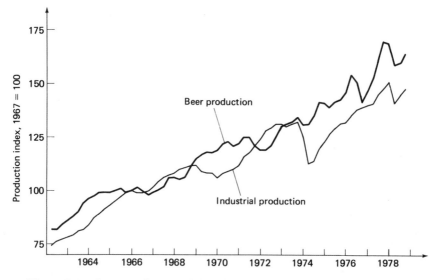

Figure 2-1 Comparative Cyclical Performance of the Index of Beer Production and the Index of Industrial Production, 1963–1979

Source: *Survey of Current Business*

Other economic sectors also display unique cyclical patterns. The growth in revenue passenger miles for airlines, illustrated in Figure 2-2, indicates that the airline industry has been able to expand despite the downturns in economic activity that occurred in 1969–70 and 1974–75. Figure 2-3, net tonnage shipments of Inland steel, documents the existence of *extra* cycles at the level of the individual company. The cyclical performance of the beer, airline, and steel

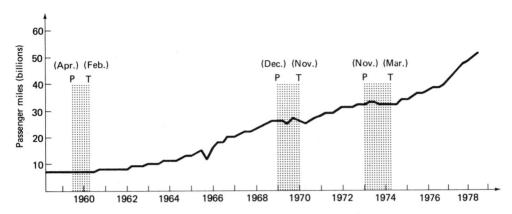

Figure 2-2 Business Cycles and Revenue Passenger Miles of Airlines, 1959–1979

Source: *Survey of Current Business*

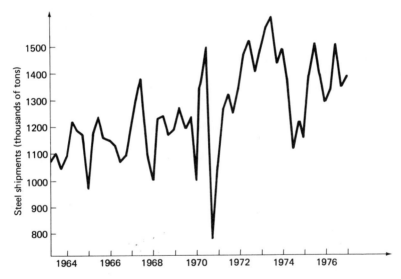

Figure 2-3 Volatility of Steel Shipments

Source: Inland Steel Company

sectors emphasizes the need to carry out statistical analyses to segregate the unique factors affecting industry production and company sales.

As explained in the first section of this chapter, time series (such as monthly steel production, daily stock prices, weekly auto sales, or quarterly GNP) are the product of four forces. Seasonal patterns and long-run trends are comparatively easy to analyze and predict because of their relative stability.

Endogenous cyclical forces may be partially or entirely responsible for the upper and lower turning points in business activity, but irregular factors are literally unpredictable. The explanation of when and why a firm's sales or production will stop declining (or expanding) will incorporate all these endogenous factors, as well as a host of external or exogenous variables. Further, advance knowledge of an upcoming expansion or recession may be worth millions of dollars for profit-oriented firms.

The diversity of movement in various sectors of the economy means that expansion in some sectors, whether firms or industries, is concurrent with contraction in others. This phenomenon occurs whether business as a whole is depressed or prospering. Turning points in industrial activity are not, however, randomly distributed. They come in clusters. Table 2-2 summarizes the indus-

Table 2-2 A cyclical comparison of employment patterns, 1957 vs. 1960

	Cyclical Peak August 1957		Cyclical Peak April 1960	
Number of	April 1957	7	November 1959	17
industries	May 1957	9	December 1959	22
experiencing an	June 1957	8	January 1960	20
increase in	July 1957	11	February 1960	19
employment over	August 1957	12	March 1960	13
prior month[a]	September 1957	11	April 1960	16

[a]For example, 12 industries experienced employment gains in August 1957.

trial employment expansion data centered around the peaks of August 1957 and April 1960. As compared to April 1960, the employment expansion prior to August 1957 was more gradual and less diffused (fewer industries were reporting expanding employment); the largest number of expanding industries actually occurred at the peak in August 1957. During the 1960 expansion, the largest number of expanding industries was recorded in December 1959, fully four months before the peak in aggregate economic activity. Further, the fact that more industries were affected during the 1960 expansion leads to the hypothesis that the amplitude of a business cycle is related to the degree of diffusion. This term, *diffusion*, refers to the extent to which the cycle *spreads outward* to affect some or all phases of the production/consumption network of business activity. Widespread expansions or contractions are apt to have a greater percentage growth from trough to peak or peak to trough—that is, greater amplitude. Thus, business-cycle severity is commonly measured by analyzing both duration and diffusion. Additional analysis of the two cycles noted in Table 2-2 revealed that (1) from the trough in May 1954 to the peak in August 1957, industrial production rose by 21.8 percent; (2) from the trough in April 1958 to the peak in April 1960, industrial production rose by 23.8

percent. Thus, even though the latter expansion was shorter in duration, the increase in industrial output was larger as well as more diffused.

THE ANATOMY OF THE 1970–75 CYCLE

The economic crosscurrents that are present in all phases of the cycle serve as a reminder of the problems involved in speaking of a typical business cycle. The degree of clustering and the precise sequence of the cyclical turns of individual sectors vary from one cycle to the next. Nevertheless, there is enough uniformity to warrant sketching what characteristically happens during the successive phases of a business cycle. This description will focus on the endogenous facets of the cycle during the 1970–75 period.

As will be detailed later, the 1974–75 recession was, in fact, largely the product of external or exogenous shocks that destabilized the economy. To get started, assume that the economy was stimulated by an appreciable increase in spending on automobiles. The impetus for this increase may have been either endogenous (an increase in consumer income) or exogenous (a shift in the relative price of American automobiles vis-à-vis Japanese automobiles). An example of this can be seen on line 1 of Table 2-3; retail sales of automobiles increased from $4.9 billion in the fourth quarter of 1970 to $6.1 billion in the first quarter of 1971. This stimulus set in motion a chain reaction. As seen on line 2 of Table 2-3, manufacturers' inventories declined up to the second quarter of 1972. Clearly, part of the increase in sales was met by running down inventories. Eventually, however, auto firms hired additional labor, disbursed larger sums in wages, increased overtime pay, utilized more fully existing plant capacity, and, in general, increased production. Lines 3 through 7 of Table 2-3 document these trends, *but not all these increases occurred simultaneously*. Both production and employment (lines 4 and 3, respectively) moved up sharply in early 1971 from their depressed levels at the trough in the fourth quarter of 1970.

With automobile workers spending their larger incomes on various commodities, retail sales increased (see lines 1 and 2 in Table 2-4). Thus, the initial expansion in the automobile industry spread slowly throughout the entire economy. The balance between expanding and contracting enterprises shifted toward aggregate expansion, and the index of industrial production (line 3 in Table 2-4) began to rise in the first quarter of 1971. This diffusion caused secondary firms (suppliers to the automobile industry) to revise their production plans, which in turn led to production and employment gains in tertiary firms (see lines 3 and 4, Table 2-4). Each expanding firm and industry stimulated activity elsewhere. With the scope of the expansion gradually becoming wider, retailers, wholesalers, and manufacturers augmented orders from their suppliers. Indeed, all the way through 1972, net new orders (line 6, Table 2-4) rose. Although business viewed in the aggregate was still operating below capacity

Table 2-3 Effect of the 1970–75 business cycle on the automobile industry (Data seasonally adjusted)

	1970	1970 Trough	1971	1971	1971	1971	1972	1972	1972	1972
	Q3	Q4	Q1	Q2	Q3	Q4	Q1	Q2	Q3	Q4
1. Retail sales, automobiles (billions of dollars)	5.4	4.9	6.1	6.3	6.6	7.1	6.9	7.2	7.3	8.2
2. Manufacturers' inventories, constant dollars (billions)	10.99	10.93	10.78	10.68	10.58	10.55	10.43	10.49	10.59	10.62
3. Employees on payrolls, transportation equipment (thousands)	1,819	1,582	1,741	1,729	1,721	1,709	1,710	1,747	1,741	1,799
4. Industrial production index, automobiles (1967 = 1.000)	0.850	0.699	1.161	1.123	1.178	1.189	1.190	1.244	1.325	1.404
5. Rate of capacity utilization, automobiles, percent	65	84	91	92	92	92	94	94	98	102
6. Average weekly hours, transportation	40.5	40.0	41.4	40.9	39.4	40.9	41.4	42.2	41.5	42.1
7. Average hourly earnings, transportation	4.10	4.09	4.40	4.39	4.37	4.47	4.61	4.70	4.71	4.90

Table 2-3 (continued)

| | 1973 | | | Peak | 1974 | | | | 1975 | Trough |
	Q1	Q2	Q3	Q4	Q1	Q2	Q3	Q4	Q1	Q2
1. Retail sales, automobiles (billions)	8.1	7.7	7.7	7.6	6.9	7.3	7.7	6.9	7.3	7.7
2. Manufacturers' inventories, constant dollars (billions)	10.70	10.74	11.93	11.22	11.51	12.94	12.46	12.80	12.83	12.50
3. Employees on payrolls, transportation equipment (thousands)	1,895	1,910	1,904	1,907	1,810	1,836	1,848	1,790	1,637	1,647
4. Industrial production index, automobiles (1967 = 1.000)	1.409	1.395	1.327	1.350	0.954	1.084	1.200	1.090	0.742	0.980
5. Rate of capacity utilization, automobiles, percent	104	107	99	91	83	87	92	70	73	80
6. Average weekly hours, transportation	42.6	42.3	41.5	41.3	40.5	39.6	40.2	40.0	39.4	39.8
7. Average hourly earnings, transportation	4.98	5.02	5.06	5.21	5.27	5.35	5.52	5.78	5.79	5.90

Source: *Business Conditions Digest* and *Business Statistics*

Table 2-4 Aggregate economic activity during the 1970–75 cycle
(Data seasonally adjusted)

	1970		1971				1972	
	Q3	Trough Q4	Q1	Q2	Q3	Q4	Q1	Q2
1. Retail sales, current dollars (billions)	31.8	31.6	32.8	33.6	34.5	35.1	35.6	36.8
2. Retail sales, constant dollars (billions)	34.6	33.9	34.8	35.1	35.8	36.1	36.0	37.0
3. Industrial production index, manufacturing (1967 = 1.000)	1.081	1.058	1.080	1.091	1.097	1.115	1.155	1.182
4. Employees on payrolls of nonagricultural establishments (millions)	70.9	70.5	70.8	71.1	71.3	71.7	72.6	73.4
5. Expenditures for plant and equipment, constant dollars (millions)	89.3	84.5	84.0	85.3	83.7	85.5	87.8	87.6
6. New orders, net, total (billions)	52.5	53.9	55.2	55.2	56.2	59.0	61.1	64.2
7. Rate of capacity utilization, manufacturing	79	80	80	81	80	80	82	82
8. Net profit after taxes, all industries (billions)	7.0	6.7	7.0	8.5	7.5	8.0	7.9	9.6
9. Index of consumer sentiment (1966 = 100)	77.1	75.4	78.2	81.6	82.4	82.2	87.5	89.3
10. New business incorporations, vendor performance (thousands)	75.6	66.2	66.5	71.3	73.3	76.5	76.6	79.1
11. Percent of companies reporting slower deliveries	47	37	43	52	48	50	54	59
12. Unfilled orders, all industries, constant dollars (billions)	118.6	115.1	115.0	111.7	109.0	109.9	110.0	111.6
13. Implicit price deflator (1972 = 100)	91.7	93.0	94.4	95.7	96.5	97.3	98.8	99.4
14. Index of labor cost per unit of output, manufacturing (1967 = 100)	112.8	112.6	113.3	113.3	113.2	112.4	113.4	113.5
15. Index of labor unit cost, private sector (1967 = 100)	119.1	120.6	120.1	121.8	122.2	122.8	124.9	124.5

		1973				1974				1975	
					Peak					Trough	
Q3	Q4	Q1	Q2	Q3	Q4	Q1	Q2	Q3	Q4	Q1	Q2
37.7	39.1	41.0	41.4	42.0	42.8	43.2	44.1	45.6	44.9	46.0	47.5
37.6	38.5	39.8	39.5	39.4	39.3	38.8	38.6	38.8	37.1	37.0	37.7
1.206	1.245	1.275	1.293	1.306	1.316	1.298	1.310	1.318	1.246	1.132	1.142
74.0	74.8	75.9	76.7	77.2	77.9	78.2	78.5	78.7	78.3	76.9	76.5
87.4	90.7	93.5	93.4	94.7	96.3	96.4	100.0	96.9	96.0	92.2	89.3
67.1	71.2	75.9	76.1	75.8	79.7	84.0	88.5	90.4	81.7	79.0	83.5
83	85	86	86	85	85	84	84	84	78	75	75
8.8	10.1	10.5	13.0	11.6	13.2	13.5	16.3	15.5	13.4	9.3	12.4
94.0	90.8	80.8	76.0	71.8	75.7	60.9	72.0	74.5	58.4	58.0	72.9
80.3	81.5	85.5	84.8	80.4	78.4	80.0	82.4	80.6	76.0	73.6	79.4
64	73	83	90	89	90	87	80	64	33	17	24
114.2	118.3	124.9	133.6	139.0	145.1	152.0	157.5	163.4	158.9	148.2	140.1
100.3	101.4	102.9	104.7	106.6	109.0	111.3	114.3	117.6	121.1	124.2	126.0
113.0	113.1	115.2	116.5	117.2	119.5	122.9	124.5	126.7	135.2	145.2	144.5
124.9	125.4	127.6	129.8	132.1	141.8	147.1	152.2	157.3	160.9	161.0	159.8

Table 2-4 (continued)

	1970		1971				1972	
	Q3	Trough Q4	Q1	Q2	Q3	Q4	Q1	Q2
16. Index of net business formation (1967 = 100)	105.2	105.7	106.6	110.1	112.6	114.7	115.4	117.9
17. Claims for unemployment insurance (thousands)	248	314	292	289	303	282	263	271
18. Composite index of four coincident indicators	1.084	1.058	1.075	1.084	1.086	1.102	1.136	1.158

Source: *Business Conditions Digest* and *Business Statistics*

(line 7, Table 2-4) some firms (the automobile industry, line 5, Table 2-3) were operating at close to full capacity throughout the second half of 1972. Moreover, as production expanded, profits improved (line 8, Table 2-4). With profits and consumer incomes climbing, with capacity levels being pressed (line 5, Table 2-3), with delivery periods lengthening, and with interest rates, machinery, and equipment prices and factor costs still relatively favorable, expenditures for capital goods (line 5, Table 2-4) began to rise one year after the trough. Finally, as the expansion spread, it generated a feeling of confidence about the future (line 9, Table 2-4), new firms began operations (line 10, Table 2-4), and even marginal firms remained in business as they were pulled along by the overall surge in prosperity.

As the expansion widened in scope, the slack in the economy was reduced. Idle or excess capacity diminished in a growing number of industries (line 7, Table 2-4) and firms. In the automobile industry (line 5, Table 2-3), capacity utilization actually exceeded 100 percent (no downtime for repairs) for the three quarters ending in the second quarter of 1973. Delivery time, as measured by vendor performance (line 11, Table 2-4) began to stretch out. As the 1973 peak approached, fully 90 percent of the reporting firms felt the pinch of slower service. Analyzing the change in unfilled orders (line 12, Table 2-4), we find the percentage rate increasing despite the fact that employment levels and overall industrial production were climbing. Clearly, the demands placed on the producing sectors in 1973 could not be fully satisfied. Rising sales in particular firms or industries still released forces of expansion elsewhere, but their effects were negated, since an ever-increasing number of firms had to contend with production bottlenecks—supply-side constraints. The monetary expression of these bottlenecks was an acceleration of price changes. In the first six quarters of the 1970–72 expansion, while overall prices were increasing, the rate of

		1973				1974				1975	
					Peak					Trough	
Q3	Q4	Q1	Q2	Q3	Q4	Q1	Q2	Q3	Q4	Q1	Q2
118.5	119.8	119.9	118.9	117.0	115.9	113.4	116.0	114.8	105.5	102.5	106.3
250	245	225	235	240	260	314	297	328	457	548	500
1.179	1.215	1.248	1.259	1.269	1.283	1.262	1.256	1.252	1.198	1.124	1.120

increase was declining. However, as the supply-side constraints became more and more significant, this process reversed itself and the rate of inflation increased (line 13, Table 2-4).

The description above of the expansionary phase following the trough in 1970 was meant to emphasize the cyclical variation between various sectors in a highly interdependent economy. Although postwar business forecasters tend to emphasize exogenous shocks—monetary policy, fiscal policy, weather, or international political turmoil—when explaining *why* an expansion or contraction took place, this description of the 1970–73 expansion examines *how* changes spread throughout the economy. That is, whether the cycle is endogenously or exogenously determined, the economy's internal transmission mechanisms need to be understood.

As the expansion in economic activity advanced, declining productivity, rising labor costs, and falling profit margins became of greater and greater concern to investors (lines 14 and 15, Table 2-4). Even though these cost increases were offset by increased selling prices, there were some firms whose prices failed to rise enough to maintain desired profit margins, and their number grew as the expansion approached its peak. In some industries, sales had expanded to the point of saturation. Other industries had overestimated future sales, and as a result, more output led to higher inventories. New businesses were constantly being formed, but marginal firms, which were previously being pulled along by the overall prosperity, began to fail. Thus, in late 1973 the number of failures exceeded new formations (line 16, Table 2-4).

These developments—the rise in labor costs, financing costs, and the cost of capital goods; the spread of these cost increases throughout the economy; falling profit margins and expected profits; and the decline in the number of business firms experiencing growth—were all present when the economy peaked in the third quarter of 1973. With retail sales falling (line 2, Table 2-4), businesses attempted to reduce inventories, and as a result, materials orders (line 6, Table 2-4) softened. Unit production costs (line 15, Table 2-4) still increased as over-head costs were adjusted to lower sales levels. Further pressures were put on already-tight profit margins. Given these developments, many firms and con-sumers became concerned about future prospects (line 9, Table 2-4). New capital commitments (line 5, Table 2-4) became less numerous. As the decline was transmitted to other sectors, the economy entered into the contractionary phase of the business cycle.

Normally, a contraction does not cumulate in the same manner as an expansion. In the United States, the factors causing a contraction are countered by institutionalized forces of growth and by government policies designed to diminish the scope of any recession (even though other government policies may have been initially responsible for the contraction). Businessmen and consumers are accustomed to economic growth, and they expect the govern-ment to undertake specific countercyclical programs—increase transfer pay-ments, cut taxes, augment expenditure programs, provide more job-training funds—in the event of a recession. Consumers themselves are reluctant to lower their living standards, and they reduce spending less than they would if recession was seen as permanent. As a result, consumer spending is maintained in the face of declines in income that are judged to be transitory. An exami-nation of retail sales in constant dollars (line 2, Table 2-4) reveals that from the peak, fourth quarter 1973, to the trough, first quarter 1975, the decline in retail sales was a modest 5.7 percent in real terms; current-dollar retail sales continued to expand. Further, both inter-firm and interindustry competition intensify as profit margins are squeezed. Successful enterprises are able to expand their markets, and hence their sales, even while aggregate activity is declining. A comparison of the retail sales of automobiles (line 1, Table 2-3) with overall retail sales (line 1, Table 2-4) empirically documents this phenome-non. Indeed, by the third quarter of 1974, auto sales were actually higher than they had been for the five preceding quarters. This expansion of sales came at the expense of less-efficient firms and industries. Some of these less-efficient firms are apt to move rapidly to counteract their ever-declining market shares. This involves purchasing new equipment, modernizing plants, and developing new and improved products as businesses operating at or close to capacity expand in anticipation of the upcoming recovery.

The endogenous developments that naturally grow out of a recession help to moderate most downturns. As the recession proceeds, these endogenous factors cause interest rates to fall, credit to become more readily available, inventories to come into better alignment with sales, and unit costs (line 15, Table 2-4) to moderate even prior to the trough in aggregate economic activity. Thus, even before the trough in March 1975, an ever-increasing number of firms found their profit margins improving. With the prospect of profits looming brighter, existing firms expanded and new companies were formed (line 10,

Table 2-4). Investment projects that had been postponed were now undertaken, and unwanted inventories (line 2, Table 2-3) continued to lessen as the recovery of aggregate production (line 3, Table 2-4) got underway.[3]

The summary above of the cycle from the trough in 1970 to the trough in 1975 was meant to reveal the general patterns operating in a business cycle. The cyclical process is full of economic crosscurrents. While some firms are failing, new companies are entering the same industry. While the economy is expanding, the pace of advance differs from company to company. Average industry performance may be a poor indicator of individual company achievement. We have not looked into the actual cause of the 1973 peak; rather, we have described the cyclical processes and their historical continuity with past troughs and peaks. In Chapter 3, we will delve into the analysis of the peak in 1973 and look at the forecasting community's record in predicting the downturn. First, however, you must be acquainted with the statistical techniques developed by the NBER to measure cyclical activity and the actual mechanics of developing forecast models.

STATISTICAL MEASUREMENT: THE NATIONAL BUREAU OF ECONOMIC RESEARCH

THE NATIONAL BUREAU OF ECONOMIC RESEARCH

The National Bureau of Economic Research (NBER)—a private, nonprofit research organization—has served as the leading source of information related to the tracking and measurement of business cycles since its inception in 1920. Its expressed purpose is:

> ... to ascertain and to present to the public important economic facts and their interpretation in a scientific and impartial manner.[4]

The NBER's pioneering business-cycle studies date back to the 1850s and, by common consent of government and private economists, it performs the task of dating business-cycle turning points (peaks and troughs) and provides the *official* definition of contractionary and expansionary periods. In addition to many NBER publications dealing with cycles, the *Business Conditions Digest* (*BCD*), published by the Department of Commerce, Bureau of Economic Analysis, contains a monthly update of the NBER's work and offers a wealth of quarterly and monthly time series.[5]

---

[3]Arthur Burns, *The Business Cycle in a Changing World* (New York: NBER, 1969), pp. 25–75.

[4]National Bureau of Economic Research, Inc., *55th Annual Report* (New York: NBER, September 1975).

[5]U.S. Department of Commerce, Bureau of Economic Analysis, *Business Conditions Digest* (Washington, D.C.: U.S. Government Printing Office, January 1979), pp. 1–5.

In 1938, 25 years after Wesley Mitchell had put forth his classic treatise, the NBER, under the guidance of Mitchell and Arthur Burns, published its first list of business-cycle indicators.[6] Updated in 1950, 1960, 1966, and 1975, these barometers are among the most heralded and misunderstood statistics published by the popular news media.[7]

INDICATORS, DIFFUSION INDICES, AND TURNING POINTS

The continuous evolution of business conditions necessitated the development of both a consistent method of isolating and dating business cycles and measuring cyclical activity and a rigorous basis for defining a myriad of forecasting-related terms such as *trough, recovery, peak,* and *recession.* Earlier in the chapter, you were introduced to the peaks and troughs in economic activity as they have been recorded by the NBER (see Table 2-1). These turning points mirror, as closely as possible, the cycle in aggregate economic activity. However, because no single measure captures the economy's diverse movements, the NBER analyzed many areas of economic activity before developing the reference dates shown in Table 2-1. Figure 2-4 contains an idealized conception of a simplified cyclical pattern in which you can readily identify the initial trough

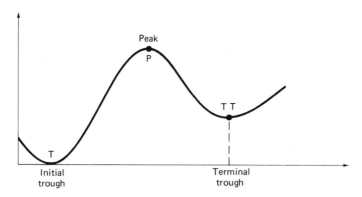

Figure 2-4   Simplified Cyclical Pattern

[6]See Wesley C. Mitchell and Arthur F. Burns, *Statistical Indicators of Cyclical Revivals,* Bulletin No. 69 (New York: NBER, May 28, 1938); Geoffrey H. Moore, *Statistical Indicators of Cyclical Revivals and Recessions,* Occasional Paper 31 (New York: NBER, 1950); Julius Shiskin, *Indicators of Business Expansions and Contractions,* Occasional Paper 103 (New York: Columbia University Press for NBER, 1967).

[7]Victor Zarnowitz and Charlotte Boschan, "Cyclical Indicators: An Evaluation and New Leading Indexes," *Business Conditions Digest,* May 1975; V. Zarnowitz and C. Boschan, "New Composite Indexes of Coincident and Lagging Indicators," *Business Conditions Digest,* November 1975.

(*T*), the upper turning point or peak (*P*), and the terminal trough (*TT*). As stated in the *Business Conditions Digest*:

> There are three composite indices of particular significance: Thus there is an index of leading indicators, series which historically reached their cyclical peaks and troughs earlier than the corresponding business cycle turns. There is an index of roughly coincident indicators, consisting of series which historically reached their turning points at about the same time as the general economy, and an index of lagging indicators, which includes series that typically reached their peaks and troughs later than the corresponding business cycle turns.[8]

The composite index of twelve leading indicators includes the following series (identification number in parentheses): average workweek, production workers (1): layoff rate per 100 employees in manufacturing (3); new orders, consumer goods and materials (8); new business formations (12); stock prices, 500 common stocks (19); contracts and orders, plant and equipment (20); new building permits, private housing (29); vendor performance (32); changes in inventories on hand and on order (36); change in sensitive prices (92); change in total liquid assets (104); and Ml, the money supply (105).

The composite index of coincident indicators is comprised of four roughly coincident indicators: employees on nonagricultural payrolls (41); industrial production (47); personal income less transfer payments (51); and manufacturing and trade sales (57).

The composite index of lagging indicators is for those activities that respond only slowly to changing business conditions or that reflect the pressures created during the immediately preceding expansion or contraction. This index has six components: labor cost per unit of output (62); manufacturing and trade inventory (70); commercial and industrial loans outstanding, weekly reports from large commercial banks (72); average duration of unemployment (91); ratio of consumer installment debt to personal income (95); and average prime rate charged by banks (109).

It should be emphasized that the composites have variable leads and lags at the turning points. Additionally, the forecaster must be aware of the limitations of these indices. Specifically, these aggregates have a propensity to generate false signals.[9] For example, the leading index fell for more than three months in 1950, 1951, 1962, and 1966, but in no case did a national recession follow. Consider a point made by Geoffrey Moore:

> It is important to be clear what these results do not mean as well as what they do mean. They do not mean that one can get much advance notice that a general

[8] *Business Conditions Digest*, January 1979.

[9] For detailed discussions, see D.J. Daly, "Forecasting with Statistical Indicators," in B.G. Hickman, ed., *Econometric Models of Cyclical Behavior*, Vol. 2 (New York: Columbia University Press, 1971), pp. 1159–94; and S.H. Hymans, "On the Use of Leading Indicators to Predict Cyclical Turning Points," and "Comments and Discussion," *Brookings Papers on Economic Activity* (Washington, D.C.: The Brookings Institution, 1973), 2, pp. 389–94.

business contraction is beginning or is coming to an end. They do help to recognize these events at about the time they occur. Even then there is some risk of error.[10]

INDICATORS: THEORETICAL UNDERPINNING AND EMPIRICAL RELIABILITY

The difficulties of indicator forecasting are compounded by the simplistic analyses that most often accompany the presentation of indicator-related statistics in newspaper and television coverage. You may share the popular misconception that the leading-indicators approach is a mechanistic compilation of economic data. But even though it is based on exhaustive statistical analysis of data patterns for numerous economic series, the interpretation of these statistics is highly judgmental (that is, nonmechanistic) and involves a sophisticated cataloguing of significant changes, false signals, exogenous shifts, structural alterations in endogenous patterns, and errors arising from actual data measurement. To engage in indicator forecasting, you need to look at the cyclical process as the outgrowth of numerous divergent crosscurrents that must be synthesized. Whether you use this method as your major tool of cyclical analysis or treat it as a supplement to an econometric model, it provides a logical framework for both diagnosis and prognosis of the economy's dynamic movements.

It is still necessary to critically appraise the theoretical underpinnings of the timing classifications. That is, as the economy moves from revival to prosperity, prosperity to recession, and recession to revival, do the individual leading, lagging, and coincident indicator series continue to display patterns consistent with their historical behavior? Out of the twelve leading series listed earlier, consider the average workweek of production workers (1), changes in inventories on hand and on order (36), contracts and orders for plant and equipment (20), and Standard & Poor's index of stock prices for 500 common shares (19). Three of these series (1, 36, and 20) represent the interplay of sales and production, whereas the stock-price index (19) is a barometer of the public's interpretation of profit prospects for the business sector. Depending on the profit expectations of businessmen, they can make marginal economic adjustments by altering hourly overtime, adjusting their desired inventory levels, or modifying future commitments for machinery and nonresidential construction. Similarly, the investing public will, depending on its optimism or pessimism, alter its portfolio of assets. But why should each of these four series lead aggregate activity at peaks and troughs? There is really no satisfactory answer to this question unless you adopt the expected-profits model used by Wesley C. Mitchell to explain the cyclical process:

[10]G.H. Moore, *Business Cycle Indicators*, I (Princeton, N.J.: Princeton University Press, 1961), p. 79.

> ... The critical point [upper turning point] is reached and a crisis precipitated as soon as a decline of present or prospective profits has occurred in a few leading branches of business and *before that decline has become general.*[11]

As Mitchell described the process, profit calculations are extremely sensitive to both the psychological forces of optimism and pessimism. Marginal employment adjustments such as a reduction in overtime grow out of a firm's inability to offset declining marginal productivity and climbing wage rates by raising product prices—that is, the inability to maintain desired profit margins on a per-unit basis. Major employment adjustments are most likely to occur when either recession or renewed prosperity have already arrived, but marginal reductions or additions in overtime (which can be quickly reversed if conditions change) represent an initial employment shift that is most probable in the period of uncertainty preceding upper or lower turning points in cyclical activity. Similarly, it is a revised outlook for expected profits that leads businesses to alter inventory investment (36) and orders for new plant and equipment (20). Given the gestation period for equipment and plant construction, changes in expected profit may alter capacity needs far into the future. It is necessary to distinguish between the leading series, which measures changes in inventories on hand and on order (36), and the lagging series, which represents the total book value of manufacturing and trade inventories (71). As expected profit declines or becomes less certain during the latter stages of prosperity, firms respond by making marginal reductions in their desired rate of inventory change. The total dollar value of inventories often continues to rise after the upper turning point, owing to unexpected declines in sales volume.

According to the studies carried out by the NBER, Standard & Poor's index of stock prices for 500 common shares (19) received the highest rating of the twelve series making up the composite leading index in terms of its ability to foreshadow changes in economic activity. As shown in Table 2-5, the composite index of leading indicators reached a peak of 143.6 (1967 base of 100) in October 1978, and it had fallen to 136.6 by November 1979—a decline of over twelve months that exceeded the nine-month lead prior to the 1973–75 recession. This consistent downward trend of the composite index took place despite a strong upward surge in Standard & Poor's index of stock prices. The latter measure moved from 100.58 in October 1978 to 107.69 in December 1979—a 7.2 percent increase, in direct contrast to the 4.9 percent decline in the composite index. Clearly, the highly touted stock-price index was contradicting the composite index.

By the end of 1979, a critical question in the minds of most forecast analysts was whether stock prices were still a valid leading indicator. Following the 1979 run-up in the prices of gold and other precious metals, it was felt that investors were now placing their money in the last *underpriced* asset, common

---

[11]Wesley C. Mitchell, *Business Cycles and Their Causes* (Los Angeles: University of California Press, 1963), p. 63.

Table 2-5 Composite indices and their components

| | | | | *Composite Indexes* | | | | | | |
| | | | | *Leading Indicator Subgroups* | | | | | | |
Year and Month	910, Index of 12 Leading Indicators (Series 1, 3, 8, 12, 19, 20, 29, 32, 36, 92, 104, 106) (1967=100)	920, Index of 4 Roughly Coincident Indicators (Series 41, 47, 51, 57) (1967=100)	930, Index of 6 Lagging Indicators (Series 62, 70, 72, 91, 95, 109) (1967=100)	913, Marginal Employment Adjustments (Series 1, 2, 3, 5) (1967=100)	19, Index of Stock Prices, 500 Common Stocks u (1941–43=100)	915, Inventory Investment and Purchasing (Series 8, 32, 36, 92) (1967=100)	105, Money Supply (M1) in 1972 Dollars (Bil. dol.)	917, Money and Financial Flows (Series 104, 106, 110) (1967=100)	940, Ratio, Coincident Index to Lagging Index (1967=100)	77, Ratio, Constant-dollar Inventories to Sales, mfg. and Trade (Ratio)
1977										
January	131.9	126.3	120.2	95.9	103.81	102.3	225.4	141.2	105.1	1.57
February	133.0	127.6	121.0	96.6	100.96	102.7	224.5	142.2	105.5	1.56
March	135.6	129.7	121.7	98.0	100.57	104.1	224.4	143.3	⊞106.6	1.55
April	136.0	130.0	122.3	97.3	99.05	105.0	224.7	143.3	106.3	1.57
May	135.8	130.6	123.1	97.1	98.76	104.7	224.5	142.2	106.1	1.57
June	135.5	131.3	125.0	97.2	99.29	103.8	224.5	142.5	105.0	1.57
July	135.0	131.7	125.2	96.7	100.18	103.0	226.0	144.8	105.2	1.57
August	136.9	131.9	126.5	96.2	97.75	103.3	226.4	146.9	104.3	1.57
September	138.0	132.6	127.8	97.0	96.23	103.8	227.2	148.2	103.8	1.58
October	139.1	133.8	129.4	97.4	93.74	104.3	227.9	148.8	103.4	1.57
November	139.4	134.7	131.1	98.0	94.28	103.8	227.4	148.8	102.7	1.57
December	140.2	135.7	131.7	98.7	93.82	104.3	227.8	148.5	103.0	1.56
1978										
January	139.1	134.0	134.1	97.6	90.25	104.8	⊞228.4	148.5	99.9	1.61
February	140.3	135.0	135.9	97.2	88.98	105.9	227.2	148.0	99.8	1.58
March	140.3	136.9	137.2	98.3	88.82	106.3	226.0	147.4	99.8	1.57
April	141.5	139.3	137.8	99.0	92.71	106.9	227.2	147.5	101.1	1.55
May	141.8	139.5	140.0	98.0	97.41	107.2	227.1	147.8	99.6	1.56
June	142.5	140.1	142.0	97.8	97.66	106.9	226.3	148.5	98.7	1.57
July	141.2	140.5	143.5	97.4	97.19	105.2	226.2	148.9	97.9	1.58
August	142.0	141.4	144.5	97.3	103.92	105.8	226.3	149.1	97.9	1.56
September	142.9	141.4	146.4	98.5	103.86	105.8	226.9	149.9	96.6	1.57
October	⊞143.6	143.0	148.1	98.7	100.58	106.1	225.4	150.6	96.6	1.55

Table 2-5 (Continued)

Composite Indexes

Leading Indicator Subgroups

Year and Month	910, Index of 12 Leading Indicators (Series 1, 3, 8, 12, 19, 20, 29, 32, 36, 92, 104, 106) (1967=100)	920, Index of 4 Roughly Coincident Indicators (Series 41, 47, 51, 57) (1967=100)	930, Index of 6 Lagging Indicators (Series 62, 70, 72, 91, 95, 109) (1967=100)	913, Marginal Employment Adjustments (Series 1, 2, 3, 5) (1967=100)	19, Index of Stock Prices, 500 Common Stock u (1941–43=100)	915, Inventory Investment and Purchasing (Series 8, 32, 36, 92) (1967=100)	105, Money Supply (M1) in 1972 Dollars (Bil. dol.)	917, Money and Financial Flows (Series 104, 106, 110) (1967=100)	940, Ratio, Coincident Index to Lagging Index (1967=100)	77, Ratio, Constant-dollar Inventories to Sales, mfg. and Trade (Ratio)
November	142.8	144.3	152.7	98.8	94.71	106.2	223.7	Ⓗ151.1	94.5	1.55
December	143.0	145.5	155.2	Ⓗ99.1	96.11	106.7	222.6	150.2	93.8	1.55
1979										
January	142.5	144.8	157.5	98.5	99.71	107.4	219.7	148.3	91.9	1.57
February	142.7	144.9	158.5	98.4	98.23	108.1	216.5	146.3	91.4	1.58
March	143.2	Ⓗ146.6	158.5	98.0	100.11	Ⓗ108.6	214.6	144.8	92.5	1.54
April	139.7	144.1	161.9	94.6	102.07	107.7	215.4	144.8	89.0	1.62
May	140.1	145.6	162.5	97.3	99.73	107.1	213.2	144.3	89.6	1.58
June	r140.5	145.0	163.9	96.6	101.73	106.3	213.8	145.8	88.5	1.62
July	r140.0	145.2	165.1	96.3	102.71	r105.4	213.5	146.8	87.9	Ⓗ1.63
August	r139.7	r144.9	r166.8	95.4	107.36	r105.0	212.5	146.9	86.9	1.62
September	140.3	144.8	r170.8	r96.3	Ⓗ108.60	104.0	212.2	146.5	r84.8	r1.61
October	a138.4	144.6	176.2	r96.7	104.47	r103.0	210.6	r145.6	r82.1	p1.62
November	b136.6	c144.9	d182.1	p95.7	103.66	p102.7	p208.7	p145.0	p79.6	(NA)
December					107.69					

NOTE: Series are seasonally adjusted except those series that appear to contain no seasonal movement. Unadjusted series are indicated by Ⓤ. Current high values are indicated by Ⓗ, for series that move counter to movements in general business activity, current low values are indicated by Ⓗ. Series numbers are for identification only and do not reflect series relationships or order. The "r" indicates revised, "p", preliminary, "e", estimated, "a", anticipated, and "NA", not available.

aExcludes series 12 for which data are not yet available.
bExcludes series 12 and 36 for which data are not yet available.
cExcludes series 57 for which data are not yet available.
dExcludes series 70 and 95 for which data are not yet available.
Source: *Business Conditions Digest*, December 1979

stocks. If this was true, then the financial motive was more akin to commodity speculation than to investment. In turn, if such a behavioral alteration (which was thought to have been occasioned by changing expectations concerning inflation) had occurred, it would have meant that stock-market prices were no longer a reliable barometer of future changes.

This historical example illustrates the pitfalls of blindly accepting the NBER's (or anyone's) indicator framework. Instead of assuming structural constancy, investigate to see whether monthly movements in a particular series are related to traditional cyclical patterns, to structural shifts, or to temporary exogenous fluctuations.

INTEGRATING TECHNICAL INDICATORS: DEVELOPING AN OUTLOOK

There is no prescribed set of steps to follow in preparing an indicator forecast. Even though disaggregation from the composite indexes to their individual components is a logical first step, where you go from this point depends upon the actual empirical situation confronting you and upon your own forecast interests. If, as was the case during 1979, the composite leading index is steadily pointing downward while an individual series (say, stock prices) is moving upward, the initial thrust of your research might focus on the determinants of the individual series. For example, in 1979 it would have been necessary to point out that most indicators making up the composite leading index are not measured in current dollars. Rather, they are either in constant-dollar units, such as the money supply in 1972 dollars, or in nonmonetary units, such as hours worked or housing units started. Stock prices are indexed on a current basis, so it is possible to get a distortion in economic behavior that is not *netted out* by inflation adjustments. Thus, there are always unique circumstances present that must be investigated at the first opportunity.

Since the unique course of cyclical events always shapes the relevant path for indicator analysis, let us return to December 1979 and use this as the period for study. Table 2-5, taken from the December 1979 issue of the *Business Conditions Digest*, contains information for the composite index of twelve leading indicators (series 910). Following the peak in October 1978, the composite leading index remained on a plateau through March 1979, fell by 3.5 percentage points in April, and remained roughly stable through September. Notice in the second column of Table 2-5 that the composite index of coincident indicators peaked in March 1979. Since the NBER usually dates the upper turning point soon after the peak in the coincident index, we might have argued, in December 1979, that a peak occurred in March 1979. Note, however, that over the entire period from November 1978 to November 1979, the composite index fluctuated in a rather narrow band around a value of 145. It might also have been argued, late in 1979, that rather than reaching a peak in March 1979, the economy had merely plateaued.

In order to decide whether the economy was at a plateau or in the initial phases of a recession, a forecast analyst in December 1979 would also have looked at both the composite index of lagging indicators and the ratio of the coincident index to the lagging index (series 930 and 940, respectively, in Table 2-5). Although the coincident index exhibited little movement in 1979, the lagging index surged ahead steadily. As listed earlier, the individual components of the lagging index reflect activities that respond slowly to changing business conditions or mirror cyclical imbalances created during the preceding expansion or contraction—unit labor costs (62), total inventories (70), commercial and industrial loans outstanding (72), average duration of unemployment (91), consumer installment debt as a percent of personal income (95), and average prime interest rate (109). As documented above under "Economic Forces at Work in the Business Sector," the endogenous forces that propel the economy also create imbalances that lead to rising labor cost per unit and tightness in the short-term money market. Since these imbalances grow stronger as coincident measures of economic activity are declining, the ratio of the composite coincident to the composite lagging index is itself a leading indicator of cyclical activity:

> The ratio of coincident to lagging series gives concrete expression to the notion of cyclical imbalance or maladjustment. On each of the occasions when the leading indicators entered upon a general decline, the ratio of coincident to lagging series showed substantial declines paralleling, if not preceding, the declines in the leaders.[12]

As pointed out above by Geoffrey H. Moore, this ratio has performed admirably as a leading indicator in its own right. In fact, the ratio had an average lead of more than nineteen months for the recessions in 1953–54, 1957–58, 1960–61, 1969–70, and 1973–75. By way of comparison, the composite index of leading indicators had an average lead of less than twelve months. Looking at Table 2-5, you can see that this ratio peaked in March 1977, nineteen months before the leading series. Further, it had fallen by over 25 percentage points by November 1979. Since the severity of the ratio's decline preceding the peak has historically been correlated with the subsequent severity of the recession, a forecaster writing in late 1979 might have legitimately concluded that a recession was forthcoming. When compared to the actual peak in January 1980, the ratio led the downturn by 34 months.

Depending on the unique characteristics of the cyclical environment and one's forecasting responsibilities, you would, as a forecast analyst in December 1979, have tried to support a recession prediction by analyzing a number of individual indicator series. For example, a monetarist would have looked at the money supply (M1) in 1972 dollars (series 105 in Table 2-5) and noted that

[12]Geoffrey H. Moore, "Generating Leading Indicators from Lagging Indicators," *Western Economic Journal*, VII, No. 2 (June 1969), 144.

this leading indicator peaked in January 1978. Unfortunately, this indicator's reliability has been clouded by recent financial-market innovations (structural changes) such as money-market funds. In other words, these financial innovations may have distorted the relationship between real GNP and the real money supply.

Because of the unprecedented surge in interest rates and commodity prices, a money-related indicator, even one corrected for inflation, might not have served the forecaster well in late 1979. Instead, the forecaster might have tried to anticipate the unemployment picture by studying an employment-sensitive leading barometer known as the index of marginal employment adjustments (series 913 in Table 2-5). This index is composed of the layoff rate in manufacturing (3), the average workweek of production workers (1), the accession rate in manufacturing (2), and the number of people filing first claims for state unemployment insurance (5). The marginal employment adjustments index peaked at 99.1 in December 1978 and had fallen to 95.7 by November 1979. Again, this would have served as confirmation that a recession was under way.

One final series illustrated in Table 2-5 is a lagging indicator that measures the ratio of constant-dollar inventories to sales in manufacturing and trade (77). Traditionally, the severity of a recession has been related to the degree of inventory imbalance. As seen in Table 2-5, the inventory-to-sales ratio did not move upward dramatically during 1979, and it peaked at 1.63 months' sales in July 1979.

Thus far we have only touched the surface of the indicator data available to the forecast analyst in late 1979. In addition to the composite indices, detailed support data are presented for each of the major and minor economic sectors. For example, the "Money and Credit Process" was covered in the December 1979 issue of *BCD* by 27 time series. These series focused on such processes as velocity of money, credit flows, credit difficulties, bank reserves, interest rates, and outstanding debt. Some, or possibly all, of these minor processes would have figured into a forecaster's subjective interpretation of economic cross-currents late in 1979. This interpretation might have been augmented by one of the diffusion indices prepared by the NBER.

As the name implies, diffusion indices attempt to measure the spreading out of what Wesley Mitchell referred to as the "cumulative forces" of economic activity. Mathematically, diffusion indices (see Table 2-6) measure the percent of series components that are rising (half the unchanged components are counted as rising). During the initial stages of an economic expansion, we would conceptually expect the leading-indicator diffusion index to be increasing. This increase should reflect the fact that more and more economic activities are pushed forward by the cumulative forces of growth in an interdependent economy. Conversely, as the expansion approaches its end, the diffusion index for leading indicators is likely to decline in value. As illustrated in Table 2-6, the composite diffusion index of the leading indicators, series 950, measured over a one-month span, displayed erratic movements during 1979, but in general,

Table 2-6 Diffusion indices and rates of change

Diffusion Indexes

Year and Month	950. Twelve Leading Indicator Components (Series 1, 3, 8, 12, 19, 20, 29, 32, 36, 92, 104, 106)		951. Four Roughly Coincident Indicator Components (Series 41, 47, 51, 57)		952. Six Lagging Indicator Components (Series 62, 70, 72, 91, 95, 109)		961. Average Workweek of Production Workers, Manufacturing (20 Industries)		966. Index of Industrial Production (24 Industries)		963. Number of Employees on Private Nonagricultural Payrolls (172 Industries)	
	1-Month Span	6-Month Span	1-Month Span	6-Month Span	1-Month Span	6-Month Span	1-Month Span	9-Month Span	1-Month Span	6-Month Span	1-Month Span	6-Month Span
1977												
January	45.8	91.7	25.0	100.0	66.7	83.3	10.0	80.0	58.3	83.3	73.0	86.3
February	50.0	79.2	100.0	100.0	75.0	83.3	97.5	90.0	72.9	91.7	67.2	84.6
March	83.3	70.8	100.0	100.0	91.7	100.0	32.5	80.0	68.8	91.7	72.4	84.0
April	50.0	58.3	75.0	100.0	75.0	100.0	52.5	82.5	70.8	83.3	71.5	82.3
May	41.7	83.3	75.0	100.0	83.3	100.0	57.5	82.5	72.9	87.5	70.3	79.1
June	58.3	54.2	100.0	100.0	100.0	100.0	72.5	90.0	83.3	83.3	65.1	77.6
July	45.8	62.5	75.0	100.0	75.0	100.0	22.5	45.0	68.8	89.6	70.3	75.3
August	70.3	58.3	75.0	100.0	91.7	100.0	55.0	72.5	75.0	87.5	57.8	76.7
September	54.2	70.8	75.0	100.0	83.3	100.0	67.5	10.0	66.7	83.3	67.2	79.7
October	75.0	66.7	100.0	100.0	91.7	100.0	80.0	25.0	72.9	75.0	64.2	80.5
November	70.8	75.0	100.0	100.0	100.0	100.0	40.0	67.5	66.7	79.2	73.3	84.0
December	58.3	66.7	100.0	100.0	75.0	100.0	45.0	90.0	72.9	75.0	75.3	82.3
1978												
January	45.8	58.3	25.0	100.0	100.0	100.0	0.0	82.5	39.6	83.3	68.3	83.1
February	62.5	54.2	75.0	100.0	100.0	100.0	77.5	70.0	47.9	79.2	69.2	79.1
March	41.7	58.3	100.0	100.0	91.7	100.0	92.5	55.0	85.4	91.7	69.5	77.6
April	66.7	54.2	100.0	100.0	66.7	100.0	75.0	45.0	87.5	87.5	68.0	73.5
May	54.2	50.0	50.0	100.0	100.0	83.3	15.0	65.0	54.2	87.5	57.8	72.7
June	62.5	58.3	75.0	100.0	91.7	83.3	52.5	95.0	83.3	85.4	66.6	71.2
July	45.8	62.5	75.0	100.0	83.3	100.0	50.0	87.5	70.8	87.5	64.5	73.0
August	50.0	83.3	100.0	100.0	83.3	100.0	42.5	50.0	83.3	87.5	60.5	77.3
September	62.5	66.7	62.5	100.0	83.3	100.0	65.0	42.5	70.8	91.7	62.5	79.7
October	54.2	66.7	100.0	100.0	66.7	100.0	47.5	60.0	66.7	87.5	73.0	82.3

Table 2-6 (Continued)

| | 950. Twelve Leading Indicator Components (Series 1, 3, 8, 12, 19, 20, 29, 32, 36, 92, 104, 106) | | 951. Four Roughly Coincident Indicator Components (Series 41, 47, 51, 57) | | 952. Six Lagging Indicator Components (Series 62, 70, 72, 91, 95, 109) | | 961. Average Workweek of Production Workers, Manufacturing (20 Industries) | | 966. Index of Industrial Production (24 Industries) | | 963. Number of Employees on Private Nonagricultural Payrolls (172 Industries) | |
| | Diffusion Indexes | | | | | | | | | | | |
Year and Month	1-Month Span	6-Month Span	1-Month Span	6-Month Span	1-Month Span	6-Month Span	1-Month Span	9-Month Span	1-Month Span	6-Month Span	1-Month Span	6-Month Span
November	37.5	66.7	100.0	100.0	100.0	100.0	70.0	65.0	79.2	77.1	75.9	82.3
December	66.7	50.0	100.0	100.0	83.3	83.3	52.5	5.0	87.5	81.3	74.4	80.5
1979												
January	58.3	33.3	25.0	75.0	83.3	100.0	55.0	20.0	54.2	58.3	70.3	74.1
February	50.0	33.3	75.0	100.0	75.0	83.3	37.5	7.5	52.1	58.3	65.1	67.4
March	58.3	33.3	100.0	50.0	75.0	100.0	60.0	15.0	66.7	50.0	60.5	61.9
April	20.8	37.5	12.5	75.0	91.7	83.3	0.0	10.0	16.7	56.3	44.8	58.1
May	41.7	29.2	75.0	50.0	58.3	100.0	90.0	r30.0	64.6	r54.2	54.7	50.3
June	50.0	33.3	62.5	25.0	83.3	100.0	32.5	r25.0	66.7	45.8	57.0	46.8
July	50.0	a40.9	100.0	75.0	66.7	100.0	62.5	p32.5	45.8	r62.5	61.6	r56.7
August	29.2	b40.0	50.0	c66.7	83.3	d100.0	35.0		45.8	p54.2	48.8	p58.7
September	58.3		r62.5		66.7		r72.5		r41.7		r46.8	
October	a22.7		37.5		83.3		r50.0		r56.3		r67.7	
November	b30.0		c66.7		d62.5		p42.5		p54.2		p65.4	
December												

aExcludes series 12 for which data are not yet available.
bExcludes series 12 and 36 for which data are not yet available.
cExcludes series 57 for which data are not yet available.
dExcludes series 70 and 95 for which data are not yet available.

NOTE: Figures are the percent of series components rising (half of the unchanged components are counted as rising). Data are centered within the spans. 1 month indexes are placed on the 2nd month, 6 month indexes on the 4th month, and 9 month indexes on the 6th month of the span. Diffusion indexes 961, 962, and 963 are computed from seasonally adjusted components, indexes 950, 951, and 952 are computed from the components of the composite indexes. The "r" indicates revised, "p", preliminary, and "NA", not available.

Source: *Business Conditions Digest*, December 1979

its behavior was consistent with expectations for a period of declining economic activity. The diffusion index based on a six-month span of leading indicators smooths out month-to-month fluctuations and presents a picture of deterioration from the third and fourth quarters of 1978 to the first and second quarters of 1979.

Support for the recession hypothesis can be seen by scanning the six-month diffusion index of industrial production in 24 industries (series 966, Table 2-6). Table 2-7, in turn, provides a monthly cross section of the industries making up series 966 and illustrates both the level of production via the production index and the direction of change via the sign (+, −, or 0). For example, an examination of the April column in Table 2-7 reveals that only 17 percent of the industries experienced increases in production—namely, chemicals and products, petroleum products, coal mining, and metal mining. In May 1979, however, there was a strong rebound, with 65 percent of the industries expanding. By looking across a row for a specific industry, you can quickly determine which industries are faring relatively well (say, coal mining) and which are performing below average (transportation equipment). Clearly, to the forecaster interested in analyzing firm- or industry-level cycles, these disaggregated measures are preferable.

THE 1980 DOWNTURN: CONFIRMATION OR REJECTION OF THE INDICATOR APPROACH

Based on the leading indicator data that we have gathered and interpreted from the perspective of a forecast analyst working in December 1979, the strongest evidence in support of the recession hypothesis was the sharp and sustained decline in the series that measured the ratio of the composite coincident index to the composite lagging index. On the other hand the relative stability of both the composite leading and lagging indices during 1979 seemed inconsistent with the prediction of a deep recession. Similarly, the data on inventory-to-sales ratios appeared to rule out the inventory imbalances historically associated with severe recessions in the postwar period. Neither the coincident measures of industrial production nor the leading marginal employment series helped to clarify the confusing signals that were present in December 1979. Consider this quote from a forecaster in March 1980, two months after the actual downturn in the economy:

> The progression has been marvelously painless. Inflation at 5 percent becomes inflation at 10 percent becomes inflation at 15 percent and so on upward. And yet—mirabile dictu—there is no pain. A record high percentage of working age population works. A recession that is supposed to arrive doesn't. Reaching birthday number five this month, the longest peacetime expansion grows longer. Inflation where is your sting?[13]

[13]*The Wall Street Journal*, March 10, 1980, p. 1.

Table 2-7 Industrial diffusion indices

Selected Diffusion Index Components: Basic Data and Directions of Change

Diffusion Index Components	1979							
	April	May	June	July	August	September[r]	October[r]	November[p]
966. INDEX OF INDUSTRIAL PRODUCTION[a] (1967=100)								
All industrial production	− 150.8	+ 152.4	+ 152.6	+ 152.8	− 151.6	+ 152.4	O 152.4	− 151.6
Percent rising of 24 components[b]	(17)	(65)	(67)	(46)	(46)	(42)	(56)	(54)
Durable manufactures								
Primary and fabricated metals								
Primary metals	− 121.7	− 121.0	+ 124.3	+ 127.1	− r121.0	+ 121.9	− 118.9	− 116.9
Fabricated metal products	− 148.8	+ 150.3	− 149.3	O 149.3	− 147.0	− 146.5	+ 146.9	− 146.4
Machinery and allied goods								
Nonelectrical machinery	− 161.8	+ 164.3	+ 164.5	+ 165.3	+ r166.2	− 165.3	− 161.7	− 161.6
Electrical machinery	− 170.6	+ 174.7	+ 175.1	− 174.4	− r171.7	+ 176.3	O 176.3	+ 176.6
Transportation equipment	− 131.6	+ 141.9	− 139.4	− 135.5	− 124.7	+ 131.5	+ 133.2	− 126.5
Instruments	− 176.3	− 174.7	+ 175.9	− 174.0	− 173.9	− 172.9	+ 174.3	+ 175.0
Lumber, clay, and glass								
Clay, glass, and stone products	− 161.2	+ 163.8	− 162.7	+ 163.3	− r161.4	− 161.0	+ 162.0	(NA)
Lumber and products	− 137.2	− 136.1	+ 136.8	− 135.2	+ r138.0	+ 138.6	− 136.6	(NA)
Furniture and miscellaneous								
Furniture and fixtures	− 159.4	+ 159.6	O 159.6	− 159.5	+ 161.7	− 161.2	+ 162.1	(NA)
Miscellaneous manufactures	− 152.3	− 150.7	+ 152.7	+ 155.7	O 155.7	− 153.5	+ 155.7	+ 156.0
Nondurable manufactures								
Textiles, apparel, and leather								
Textile mill products	− 141.2	+ 141.5	+ 144.6	− 143.0	+ r144.1	+ 146.9	+ 147.2	(NA)
Apparel products	− 130.8	− 128.2	+ 132.0	− 129.7	+ r130.1	+ 131.2	(NA)	(NA)
Leather and products	− 69.6	+ 72.3	− 70.1	− 69.7	O 69.7	+ 70.8	− 70.1	(NA)

Table 2-7 (Continued)

	Selected Diffusion Index Components: Basic Data and Directions of Change							
	1979							
Diffusion Index Components	April	May	June	July	August	September[r]	October[r]	November[p]
966 INDEX OF INDUSTRIAL PRODUCTION[a] (1967=100)								
Paper and printing								
Paper and products	− 148.7	− 147.9	+ 148.0	+ 154.0	− 153.9	+ 155.3	− 153.2	+ 154.3
Printing and publishing	− 135.7	+ 136.8	+ 136.9	− 135.6	+ 137.7	− 137.1	+ 138.5	+ 139.4
Chemicals, petroleum, and rubber								
Chemicals and products	+ 207.7	+ 209.7	− 207.8	+ 210.5	+ r213.1	− 211.7	+ 213.8	(NA)
Petroleum products	+ 145.4	− 142.4	+ 143.9	○ 143.9	− r143.0	− 141.9	− 141.4	+ 141.6
Rubber and plastics products	− 265.5	+ 270.0	○ 270.0	+ 278.0	− r275.7	− 272.9	+ 273.7	(NA)
Foods and tobacco								
Foods	− 147.0	+ 149.2	+ 149.5	− 149.4	− r148.1	+ 148.4	− 148.3	(NA)
Tobacco products	− 120.0	+ 120.2	− 118.3	+ 118.9	− 107.5	+ 117.4	(NA)	(NA)
Mining								
Coal	+ 130.1	+ 133.4	+ 137.5	− 137.1	+ 144.1	− 142.6	+ 145.7	− 143.8
Oil and gas extraction	− 118.6	○ 118.6	+ 119.6	+ 120.4	+ r121.6	− 121.0	+ 122.7	+ 124.0
Metal, stone, and earth minerals								
Metal mining	+ 128.9	− 123.1	+ 123.2	+ 128.6	− 126.5	− 121.9	+ 123.1	(NA)
Stone and earth minerals	− 135.3	+ 137.8	− 137.3	− 136.4	+ 138.3	− 137.5	− 136.8	(NA)

NOTE: Series direction is indicated by sign (+, −, or ○) in front of production index.
[a]Data are seasonally adjusted by the source agency.
[b]Where actual data for separate industries are not available, estimates are used to compute the percent rising.
Source: *Business Conditions Digest*, December 1979

The recession of 1980 was unique in terms of the economic vacillations which preceded the peak, but it will also be remembered for the severe decline in both housing starts and consumer expenditures for automobiles that took place between the peak in January and the trough in August. Whereas peak-to-trough spending on cars fell 29.4 percent from November 1973 to March 1975, the decline was 29.1 percent from January 1980 to August 1980. Similarly, housing starts fell 63.0 percent in the recession of 1973–75, but the drop was 58.5 percent in 1980.

The housing and automobile sectors have been repeated victims of the cyclical adjustment process, but the recession of 1980 did not leave the usual legacy of a healthy economic climate that would serve as foundation for the subsequent recovery. As first explained by Wesley Mitchell and as illustrated earlier in this chapter, the endogenous adjustment process which takes place as the economy plummets from peak to trough is supposed to correct the cyclical imbalances that have built up during the prior period of prosperity. These imbalances include both high unit labor costs resulting from rising wage rates and declining productivity and high interest rates arising from the excesses of business optimism and tightness in short-term money markets. While interest rates did fall dramatically between March and August 1980, the prime rate had soared to 21 percent by the middle of the following December. As a result a forecast analyst looking at the economy at the end of 1980 found many of the same problems that he had seen in December 1979—high inflation; record interest rates; stagnation in the automobile, steel, and housing sectors; and a great degree of economic uncertainty among private and governmental forecasters. While steel and automobile demand was weak in the fourth quarter of 1980, wage rates and prices in these two key industrial sectors continued to remain "sticky." Instead of falling, as might be expected in the free-market model of supply and demand, wage rates and prices continued to display their postwar pattern of rigidity.

As a novel and desperate attempt to force unions to accept lower real wage rates, Chrysler Corporation, in December 1980, asked workers to forego 1981 cost-of-living increases which had already been agreed upon in a prior contract. To a forecaster, this bizarre attempt at wage adjustment served as both an affirmation of the traumatic structural shift which had taken place in the new-car market and as a harbinger of continued changes in the government's role in the automobile industry.

Forecasters were arguing in December 1979 about the probability of an upper turning point in 1980, but in December 1980 the forecasting community was worried about the possibility of a double-dip, the euphemistic expression for successive recessions in 1980 and 1981. Turning points have always been difficult to recognize, but there is increasing evidence that not only has inflation distorted investor and consumer decision making processes, but that it has also started to affect the reliability of official government statistics of economic activity. This reflects in no small part the growing presence of the subterranean or underground economy. As more workers are pushed into higher marginal tax brackets, the disincentives of dealing in the money economy begin to outweigh the traditional benefits. Consumers turn to the cash-only or barter transactions which do not appear in the official statistics. (This phenomenon is brilliantly described in Jude Wanniski's book *The Way the World Works*.[14])

The evolution of the subterranean economy typifies the on-going process of institutional change. No forecasting system can be regarded as final in such an environment. Chapter 3 will examine the process by which forecasts are modified in response to alterations in the institutional fabric of the economy.

QUESTIONS FOR DISCUSSION AND ANALYSIS

1. Among the many ways to quantify the severity of a recession, three closely monitored statistics are the percentage change in the GNP deflator, the percentage drop in industrial output, and the peak jobless rate. Using the *Survey of Current Business*, the *Business Conditions Digest*, *Business Statistics*, the *Statistical Abstract of the United States*, or other government publications found in the documents and reference section of the library, estimate the peak-to-trough magnitudes for the deflator, output, and unemployment for the business slumps listed in Table 2-1. For example, how much did industrial output fall between August 1929 and March 1933? How did the 1980 recession compare to earlier declines?

2. Prepare a summary contrasting the slump of 1969 with the downturn of 1980. In addition to the aggregate statistics from problem 1, construct tables that illustrate quarterly changes in the major GNP components and highlight cyclical imbalances through the use of indicator series such as the ratio of inventories to sales. Bring in actual assessments made by forecasters just prior to the reference peaks in 1969 and 1980. In addition to government publications, most libraries have indexes available for past publications of such major newspapers as the *New York Times* and offer access to historical accounts via microfiche.

3. Pick two industries of particular interest to you and analyze their cyclical experiences over the peak-to-trough periods following the downturns in 1969 and 1980. For example, what happened to unit sales, dollar sales, and employment? Did these industries lead or lag? In addition to production indexes in the *Federal Reserve Bulletin*, consult government publications such as *Current Industrial Reports*, financial sources such as *Moodys* and *Standard & Poor's*, and publications prepared by industry trade associations.

4. Locate a local company in your city and collect sales or production data (ideally, in nonmonetary units or in real, inflation-adjusted units) over the period from the trough in 1970 to the trough in 1975. Did this company seem to be affected by the economy's surge in 1971 and 1972, and did its sales match the decline in 1974's real GNP? If you are unable to secure such data from a private company, try the local public utility or telephone company.

14Jude Wanniski, *The Way the World Works* (New York: Simon & Schuster, 1978).

5. Consult a private or public company in your city, interview the person(s) who prepares the company's annual budget, and write a report discussing how this company incorporates forecasts of short-term business conditions in its budgetary review. For example, does it monitor the leading, coincident, and lagging indicators? Does it reestimate the budget monthly to incorporate changing economic conditions? Does it know whether the company or its industry leads or lags cyclical turning points? Does it subscribe to commercial forecasting services?

6. The indicator forecast carried out at the end of the chapter was based on the December 1979 issue of *Business Conditions Digest* and concluded that a recession was forthcoming. With the advantage of historical hindsight, evaluate this conclusion. That is, was the hypothetical forecaster too reliant on the series that measures the ratio of the composite coincident index to composite lagging index? What happened to this ratio in 1980? What happened to the real money supply (M1) in 1980 following the rapid run-up in interest rates during the last half of 1979?

7. Using the latest available issue of the *Business Conditions Digest*, prepare an indicator outlook for the economy. Are there any unique circumstances dominating the current outlook? Is the economy mainly responding to endogenous forces, or are exogenous factors playing an unusually large role? Do you foresee a turning point? What are the strengths and weaknesses of the indicator approach?

8. Ask several friends to read a local newspaper report concerning the leading indicators. Did they interpret the information correctly? How might both the local and national news media improve their coverage of movements in the composite index of leading indicators?

9. Prepare a two-page summary of the current outlook of the economy over the next twelve months, based on analysis of the information contained in the latest issues of business-oriented publications such as *The Wall Street Journal, Fortune, Business Week,* and *Forbes.* The reference librarian can help you compile a complete listing of such publications. Take the most optimistic and most pessimistic appraisals of the outlook and try to explain why experts could have such varying interpretations concerning the future course of the economy.

10. Using the latest issue of the *Economic Report of the President,* analyze how its appraisal of the economy differs from those of the optimists and pessimists. Is the President's Council of Economic Advisers likely to be optimistic or pessimistic?

11. An important characteristic of the free market system is business freedom to enter and exit an industry, with business failure being the most common method of exit for those unable to earn a profit. Utilizing the section labeled, "Industrial and Commercial Failures," in the *Survey of Current Business,* locate the monthly series that measures the business failure rate per 10,000 during 1980. Did this recession impose a severe economic penalty on business firms? When might a business-conditions analyst be interested in forecasting the business failure rate? How could it be used by decision makers?

12. Business-conditions analysts often discuss countercyclical stabilization actions that can be taken by the federal government. How are these related to fiscal and monetary policy? What position concerning the proper degree of countercyclical economic intervention is taken by the neo-Keynesians and by the monetarists?

REFERENCES FOR FURTHER STUDY

Bretzfelder, Robert B., "Variations in National Output," *Survey of Current Business,* November 1960, pp. 14–20.

McKenna, Joseph P., *Aggregate Economic Analysis,* 5th ed. Hensdale, Ill.: Dryden Press, 1977.

Mitchell, W. C., *What Happens During Business Cycles: A Progress Report.* New York: National Bureau of Economic Research, 1951.

Moore, Geoffrey, ed., *Business Cycle Indicators,* Vol. I and II. Princeton, N.J.: Princeton University Press, 1961.

Smith, Walter Buckingham, and Arthur Harrison Cole, *Fluctuations in American Business, 1790–1860.* Cambridge, Mass.: Harvard University Press, 1935.

Stekler, O., and M. Schepsman, "Forecasting With an Index of Leading Indicators," *Journal of the American Statistical Association,* Vol. 68 (1973), 291–95.

U.S. Department of Commerce, Office of Business Economics, "The Economic Accounts of the United States: Retrospect and Prospect," a supplement to *Survey of Current Business,* 50th Anniversary Issue, July 1971.

3

The Great Recession of 1974-75: Monitoring Econometric Forecasts

INTRODUCTION

The 1974–75 recession provides insights concerning the actual evolution of macroeconomic forecasts over the course of the business cycle, the uses and limitations of macroeconometric models, and the implications for business-conditions analysts preparing industry-level projections. Comparisons will be made between statistical projections and qualitative assessments done before, during, and after the recession in an attempt to develop an understanding of how the ongoing forecasting process is shaped by exogenous alterations in the institutional environment, internal structural changes in the economy, and modifications in underlying econometric models. By investigating how past forecasts have changed over the course of the cycle, analysts can begin to formulate perceptions concerning the sensitivity of the forecasting process to exogenous and endogenous forces and to appreciate the necessity of combining the scientific approach with nonstatistical judgments.

EX POST FORECAST ANALYSIS: EVALUATING
CHANGING ECONOMIC SCENARIOS

Even though all business forecasters pay lip service to the ritual of *ex post* or after-the-fact comparisons between actual and forecasted economic performance, the results of such studies are most often voluntarily published only when the forecast has been reasonably accurate. It is instructive to take a recent turbulent economic period in the postwar era—specifically, the 1974–75 recession—and critically appraise the successes and failures of forecasters during this time.

The forecasting fraternity is composed of both individuals and large organizations, and it ranges over a wide spectrum, which includes the Council of Economic Advisers as the representatives of the official or administration position, columnists who publish their projections in newspapers and magazines, and commercial forecast services that provide a forecast for a fee. Each of these groups must answer the same harsh question: How accurate were past forecasts? That is, how good a job was done in predicting the timing, duration, and severity of the 1974–75 recession?

This is not a simple question to answer, even with the added advantage of historical hindsight. It is not just a matter of going back in the archives to December 1973 and digging out each forecaster's outlook for 1974 and 1975. Rather, one has to look at forecast dynamics—how and why did each forecaster modify his economic projections as the hectic events of 1974–75 unfolded? It is from this comparative study that you will begin to understand why forecasts differ, when they are likely to diverge or converge, how projections are altered to reflect changing exogenous events, the role of economic theory in model building, and the practical constraints that operate to limit the usefulness of many analytical forecasting approaches. Further, this process serves to highlight the significance of the reasoning or theory underlying all forecasts. In many respects, the reasoning is more important than the figures that emerge from the forecasting process.

Of the innumerable forecasts, this chapter will focus on the evolution of the annual forecasts of the Council of Economic Advisers (CEA), which are contained in the *Economic Report of the President;* the monthly outlook found in the "Business Roundup" section of *Fortune* magazine; and the monthly projections of Data Resources Incorporated (DRI), located in its *Review*.[1] Ideally, we would have an official monthly CEA outlook to contrast with that of the commercial vendor (DRI) and the public forecaster ("Roundup"), but no such publication exists. The myriad of monthly economic pronouncements by the chairman of the CEA, the Treasury secretary, the president, the chairman of the Federal Reserve System, and other public officials are simply too frag-

---

[1]These three groups were selected as being representative of the partisan, public, and private components of the forecasting community.

mented and disorganized to be utilized as a monthly barometer or official forecast. Since the *Economic Report* appears in January of each year, however, it serves as an official outlook for that year and can be conveniently compared with that of DRI and "Roundup." It should be restated that the main purpose in carrying out analyses of forecasts done by DRI, the CEA, and "Roundup" over the 1974–75 recession is not to ascertain which group has done the best job; rather, this study is designed to promote a better understanding of the actual nature of the forecasting process before you start to build statistical forecasting models. Before turning to the actual record of the forecasting fraternity during the recession, we will review the general forecasting approaches currently in vogue.

ALTERNATIVE MACROECONOMIC FORECASTING TECHNIQUES

MACROECONOMIC MODELS: INTRODUCTION

If you have even a casual interest in the stock market, you know that there appear to be an infinite number of ways of forecasting a stock's future price performance. Since future movements in stock prices are usually predicted on an assumption concerning the likely changes in the economy, it should not be surprising that there are so many different views (forecasts) concerning next year's GNP, price level, interest rates, exchange rates, and all the other parameters of an economy's performance. No attempt will be made here to catalog the diverse collection of guessing techniques used to predict the course of the economy; rather, as a means of setting the stage for the inquiry concerning the forecasting community's experience during the 1974–75 recession, we will briefly describe those analytical methods most widely used by the forecasting profession.

As stated earlier, the goal or purpose of this text is to improve your ability to engage in near-term and short-term forecasting (one month to eight quarters) at the aggregate, industrial, and company levels. To develop a macroeconomic forecast, as opposed to an undocumentable hunch or guess, you will need to make use of one or more of the major forecasting techniques: the NBER's indicator or barometric approach; the opportunistic, eclectic, or component approach; and the econometric approach. We have already discussed in detail the NBER approach and pointed out that it is primarily useful as a signal of directional change in the economy, not as a quantitative predictor of absolute change in the GNP components. In addition, the diffusion indices serve to measure the spreading (diffusion) of the cumulative forces of prosperity and recession throughout the economy.

The leading-indicator and component techniques are really two different versions of the qualitative or nonstatistical approach to forecasting. By labeling an approach eclectic or opportunistic, we do not mean to imply that it is unacceptable or less rigorous than more formalized statistical approaches. The best way to illustrate the component method is to simply restate the following national-income accounting identity:

$$\text{GNP} = C + I + G + X_n \qquad (3\text{-}1)$$

where:

GNP $=$ gross national product
$C =$ personal consumption expenditures
$I =$ gross private domestic investment
$G =$ government expenditures for goods and services
$X_n =$ net exports of goods and services

A component forecaster carries out separate analyses for each of the subcategories of these major components and then combines the pieces in order to derive a GNP estimate. For a projection of gross private domestic investment, for example, investment is disaggregated and segmented projections are prepared for inventory investment, residential construction, nonresidential construction, and business expenditures for new equipment (all of which may, in turn, be further disaggregated). These components may be estimated statistically, but adherents of this approach generally subscribe to rigorous, noneconometric methods. For example, rather than attempting to build a statistical forecasting model for business fixed investment (plant and equipment expenditures), they are more likely to make use of the McGraw-Hill or Commerce Department surveys, which summarize businesses capital plans for the coming year.[2] The major distinguishing characteristic of the component approach is that the expenditure categories are estimated individually, not simultaneously as part of an aggregate GNP model.

Economic forecasting at the macroeconomic level may be thought of as an attempt to construct a general equilibrium model of the economy. Rather than looking separately at each of the expenditure components, econometricians combine economic theory, mathematics, and statistical techniques as a means of constructing empirical models of the economy. The solution values or forecasts yielded by these models for C, I, and X_n are simultaneous; that is, the forecast magnitudes are jointly determined at the same time rather than being individually or independently estimated. The field of econometric modeling can be traced to Jan Tinbergen's models of the U.S. and Dutch economies during the 1930s.[3] In the United States, model building after World War II

---

[2]For a discussion of such investment surveys, see Morris Cohen, "Surveys and Forecasting," in *Methods and Techniques of Business Forecasting*, 2nd ed., ed. William F. Butler and others (Englewood Cliffs, N.J.: Prentice-Hall, 1974), pp. 76–96.

[3]Jan Tinbergen, *Selected Papers* (Amsterdam: North Holland, 1959).

can be linked to the work of Lawrence Klein, who attempted to develop Keynesian expenditure models that would explain movements in real expenditure categories such as C and I once postulated exogenous values had been determined for G and X_n.[4] It is beyond the scope of this book to attempt to present an 800-equation model, but it is necessary that you have a general understanding of what an econometric model is and how it might be used by an industry forecaster so that you can better comprehend the twists and turns experienced by econometric-model builders during the 1974–75 recession.

Econometric-model building may be viewed as an attempt to combine the insights of economic theory, the precision of statistical techniques such as multiple regression, and the "number-crunching" power of computers, in order to develop an empirical model of the economy. If, in fact, it is possible to develop a series of statistical equations that adequately track the ups and downs of the economy, forecasters will have at their disposal a tool that will serve as Mitchell's fabled *Guide in Forecasting the Immediate Business Future*. Consider the following model, put forth by Daniel Suits in 1962 to explain to the economics profession the nature and use of econometric models:[5]

$$C = 20 + 0.7(Y - T) \tag{3-2}$$

$$I = 2 + 0.1\,Y_{-1} \tag{3-3}$$

$$T = 0.2\,Y \tag{3-4}$$

$$Y = C + I + G \tag{3-5}$$

where:

$C =$ personal consumption expenditures by households
$Y =$ personal income, which in turn equals GNP
$T =$ taxes
$I =$ business investment
$(Y - T) =$ disposable income
$G =$ government expenditures
$Y_{-1} =$ lagged income

Suits provided the following concise summary:

> This econometric model approximates the economy by a system of equations in which the unknowns are those variables—income, consumption, investment, and tax yield—whose behavior is to be analyzed. The *knowns* are government expenditures and lagged income. When projected values for the knowns are inserted in the equations, the system can be solved to forecast the values of the unknowns.[6]

[4]Lawrence R. Klein and Arnold S. Goldberger, *An Econometric Model of the United States, 1929–1952* (Amsterdam: North Holland, 1955).
[5]Daniel B. Suits, "Forecasting and Analysis with an Econometric Model," *American Economic Review*, March 1962, pp. 104–32.
[6]Suits, "Forecasting," p. 599.

This system should be viewed, therefore, as an extremely simple econometric model of the economy, developed for pedagogical purposes.

As to the economic theory incorporated in the model, equation (3-2) represents the Keynesian consumption function, in which consumption (C) depends on disposable income ($Y - T$)—that is, the income actually available to consumers after taxes. Equation (3-3) incorporates the theoretical insight that business investment is a function of past income movements in the economy. Equation (3-4) states that the tax yield depends on income, and equation (3-5) is a definitional equation showing that personal income (which also equals GNP in this model) is equal to the sum of C, I, and G. With the exception of the foreign or rest-of-the-world sector, the model contains most of the aggregate expenditure categories (notice, however, the glaring omission of money, prices, and interest rates) focused on by the business-conditions analyst. This model has four equations and six variables. The *knowns*—income last period (Y_{-1}) and government expenditures (G)—are exogenous variables. As a forecast analyst, you would have a preliminary estimate of Y_{-1} and you would have to make a best estimate of G based on a host of budgetary data and your own expectations for major expenditure programs. If, for example, you assume that $G = \$20$ and preliminary data indicates that $Y_{-1} = \$100$, you would substitute these values into the model, solve for the unknown or endogenous variables, and find that $C = \$86.2$, $I = \$12$, $T = \$23.7$, and $Y = \$118.2$. These forecast values would, in turn, serve as the starting point for more disaggregated projections of industry and company sales. For example, you might wish to link gross private domestic investment (I) to industry sales of drill presses and to your own company's share of the drill-press market.

Although an accurate forecasting model would be a powerful tool for any business forecaster, a four-equation model is too aggregative, and as a result, it cannot deal with the complexity and interdependence of the U.S. economy. Starting with the basic insights of these early econometric models, specialized forecasting companies have evolved in the last fifteen years whose sole purpose is to develop larger and more disaggregated macroeconometric models of the economy. Imagine an 800-equation model as a substitute for Suits's four-equation system. In place of equation (3-2), for example, we might have fifteen statistical equations that would disaggregate personal consumption expenditures into durables, nondurables, and services and further subdivide these components into automobiles, refrigerators, furniture, doctors' services, food, clothing, and a myriad of other consumer-expenditure categories. Three of the leading commercial forecast vendors are Chase Econometrics, Wharton Econometric Forecasting Associates, and Data Resources Incorporated. These vendors sell a service—aggregated and disaggregated economic scenarios stretching fifteen years into the future.

The power of an econometric model is that it can consider a host of *What if*? questions. For example, what if government fiscal policy is more expansionary than previously assumed? What if Arab oil supplies are cut by 20 percent? Even with the simple four-equation model used earlier, we can pose hypothetical questions concerning fiscal policy. What if government expenditures are actually $21 rather than $20? If you resolve the model, you will find that Y rises by $2.273, C moves upward by $1.273, and T increases by $0.455. Because tax receipts grow with the economy, a $1 increase in G actually reduces the budgetary surplus by only $0.545 ($23.7 — $20 = $3.7, versus $24.155 — $21 = $3.155). If you wished to carry out the same simulation (that is, resolve the model using an alternative assumption for an exogenous variable such as G) with a large-scale econometric model, you would also be able to determine the projected effect on the consumer price index, the likely increase in car sales (part of C), the incremental impact on the demand for business loans (needed to finance I), the number of new housing starts indirectly stimulated (part of I), the dollar value of increased imports, and a great many other highly disaggregated measures of economic activity.

Because econometric models can provide finely disaggregated forecasts of national economic measures, they can be used as the starting point for firm and industry forecasts.

MACROECONOMETRIC MODELS: EQUATION FORMULATION

Even though we cannot enumerate and analyze the full range of equations contained in contemporary econometric models, it is instructive to proceed past Suits's pedagogical model. Equation (3-2) in Suits's model was built around the Keynesian theory of the consumption function, in which consumption (C) is a function of disposable income (DI). You could collect quarterly data on C and DI and estimate an empirical consumption function using the regression techniques explained in Chapter 5, but it would be of little use to forecast users and industry- or firm-level decision makers. These users need disaggregated measures of consumption—new-car sales, gasoline consumption, appliance and furniture sales, food, clothing, travel, services, ad infinitum—depending on their particular situation. In order to expand the macroeconomic theory of consumption, you have to rely upon the microeconomic theory of consumer behavior. One such model of a consumption function for new-car sales is given by:[7]

$$CS = f(DI, Cp, S_c, U, N, Gp, CRED, Ep) \qquad (3-6)$$

where:

> CS = new-car sales
> DI = disposable income

---

[7]Of the many forecasting models that have been developed, a particularly good explanation is provided by Robert J. Eggert and Jane R. Lockshin, "Forecasting the Automobile Market," in Butler et al., *Methods and Techniques of Business Forecasting*, pp. 420–53.

Cp = price of a new car relative to all other consumer goods
S_c = stock of automobiles
U = unemployment rate
N = demographic measure of car-buying population
Gp = relative price of gasoline
$CRED$ = availability of credit
Ep = consumer price expectations for Cp

Economic theory plays a critical role in the initial stages of econometric-model building. It is in these stages that causal relationships are hypothesized. However, these theoretical relationships may prove to be less than satisfactory when you begin to estimate an empirical model of the demand for new cars. For example, should you use income from the current period, a prior period, or an average of past periods to explain current-period car sales? All these measures are theoretically justifiable. Thus, it is likely to be a pragmatic consideration (which variant works the best) that determines the income variable that is finally selected for inclusion in the model. If an empirical version of equation (3-6) is to be incorporated into a large-scale econometric model, it follows that in other sections of this model there must be separate forecast equations for disposable income, car prices, the unemployment rate, and all the remaining variables listed as determinants of new-car sales. Each of these equations will, in turn, contain a host of different variables that must be determined (estimated) within the system. The model's size can escalate rapidly if all the disaggregated information required by industry- or firm-level decision makers is to be available.

A MONETARIST MODEL
OF THE ECONOMY

Although it is impossible to present an 800-equation model here, it is still worthwhile to examine a contemporary macroeconomic model of the economy. Table 3-1 contains a seven-equation, quarterly model of the U.S. economy estimated in the monetarist tradition by William Dewald over the period from the first quarter of 1953 to the third quarter of 1979.[8] This is not a system in which all equations are solved simultaneously; rather, it is a recursive system in which each equation is solved individually or sequentially. We will concentrate on the intuitive or theoretical content of these equations, reserving the statistical interpretation for later chapters.

The first equation in Dewald's model might initially have been formulated as:

$$\dot{Y}_t = f(\dot{M}_{t-i}, \dot{EF}_{t-i}, \dot{EX}_t) \tag{3-7}$$

[8]William G. Dewald, "Fast vs. Gradual Policies in Controlling Inflation," *Economic Review*, Federal Reserve Bank of Kansas City, January 1980, pp. 16–25.

Table 3-1 A monetarist model of the U.S. economy

Equations:

1. $\dot{Y}_t = 2.38 + \sum\limits_{i=0}^{4} m_i \dot{M}_{t-i} + \sum\limits_{i=0}^{6} e_i \dot{EF}_{t-i} + .04 \dot{EX}_t$
   $\quad$ (3.28) $\qquad\qquad\qquad\qquad\qquad$ (2.34)
   $\qquad\qquad \sum m_i = 1.03 \ \sum e_i = .02$
   $\qquad\qquad\quad$ (6.19) $\qquad\quad$ (.22)

$\qquad\qquad\qquad\qquad\qquad\qquad\qquad\qquad$ $R^2 = .52$
$\qquad\qquad\qquad\qquad\qquad\qquad\qquad\qquad$ $SE = 3.28$
$\qquad\qquad\qquad\qquad\qquad\qquad\qquad\qquad$ $DW = 1.90$

2. $D = \ln(Y/P^a) - \ln(XF)$

3. $\dot{P}_t^a = \sum\limits_{i=1}^{2} d_i D_{t-i} + \sum\limits_{i=1}^{12} p_i \dot{P}_{t-1} + \sum\limits_{i=1}^{7} w_i \dot{W}_{t-i}$
   $\qquad\quad \sum d_i = .01 \ \sum p_i = 1.00 \ \sum w_i = .00$
   $\qquad\qquad$ (.20)

$\qquad\qquad\qquad\qquad\qquad\qquad\qquad\qquad$ $R^2 = .81$
$\qquad\qquad\qquad\qquad\qquad\qquad\qquad\qquad$ $SE = 1.33$
$\qquad\qquad\qquad\qquad\qquad\qquad\qquad\qquad$ $DW = 2.06$

4. $\dot{P}_t = \dot{P}_t^a + .04 D_t$
   $\qquad\quad$ (1.28)

$\qquad\qquad\qquad\qquad\qquad\qquad\qquad\qquad$ $R^2 = .81$
$\qquad\qquad\qquad\qquad\qquad\qquad\qquad\qquad$ $SE = 1.20$
$\qquad\qquad\qquad\qquad\qquad\qquad\qquad\qquad$ $DW = 2.03$

5. $\dot{X} = \dot{Y} - \dot{P}$

6. $U_t = UF_t - .20 D_t - .16 D_{t-1}$
   $\qquad\quad$ (-7.82) $\ $ (-6.38)

$\qquad\qquad\qquad\qquad\qquad\qquad\qquad\qquad$ $R^2 = .72$
$\qquad\qquad\qquad\qquad\qquad\qquad\qquad\qquad$ $SE = .28$
$\qquad\qquad\qquad\qquad\qquad\qquad\qquad\qquad$ $DW = 2.05$
$\qquad\qquad\qquad\qquad\qquad\qquad\qquad\qquad$ $\rho = .73$

7. $R_t = 4.28 + \sum\limits_{i=0}^{11} b_i \dot{P}_{t-i}$
   $\qquad\quad$ (.04)
   $\qquad\qquad \sum b_i = .37$
   $\qquad\qquad\quad$ (5.18)

$\qquad\qquad\qquad\qquad\qquad\qquad\qquad\qquad$ $R^2 = .26$
$\qquad\qquad\qquad\qquad\qquad\qquad\qquad\qquad$ $SE = .18$
$\qquad\qquad\qquad\qquad\qquad\qquad\qquad\qquad$ $DW = 1.42$
$\qquad\qquad\qquad\qquad\qquad\qquad\qquad\qquad$ $\rho = 1.00$
$\qquad\qquad\qquad\qquad\qquad\qquad$ Dates: 1953:I–1979:III

Definitions of Symbols:

Y	= GNP	R	= Moody's corporate Aaa bond rate
M	= money stock (M1)	t	= quarter
EF	= high-employment federal government spending	$\ln$	= natural logarithm
		$\cdot$	= annual rate of change
EX	= exports	a	= anticipated
D	= demand pressure	Lowercase letters = coefficients	
P	= GNP deflator	Uppercase letters = variables	
XF	= high-employment real GNP	R^2	= coefficient of determination
W	= imports deflator	SE	= standard error of estimate
X	= Y/P = real GNP	DW	= Durbin-Watson statistic
U	= unemployment rate	ρ	= serial correlation coefficient
UF	= high-employment unemployment rate	t-values are in parentheses	

Source: Federal Reserve Bank of Kansas City, *Economic Review*, January 1980

That is, the monetarist theory of GNP (Y) determination would lead one to postulate that the rate of change in current-dollar GNP ($\dot{Y}_t$) is a function of past percentage changes in the money supply ($\dot{M}_{t-i}$), federal spending adjusted for full employment ($\dot{EF}_{t-i}$), and current exports ($\dot{EX}_t$). The model actually utilizes the percentage change in the money supply for the current quarter ($i = 0$) and the prior four quarters ($i = 1$ to 4). Although lagged values of the percentage change in the money supply are suggested by the monetarist's theoretical model, the actual lag pattern selected is, again, largely determined by pragmatic testing of alternative lag models. In other words, even though there may be a theoretical reason for a lagged relationship between real GNP and the money supply, there is no reason to suppose that a four-quarter lag is theoretically correct. Notice, the first equation in Table 3-1 tells us that the percentage change in the current quarter GNP is largely determined by economic forces in previous quarters. Also, $\dot{Y}_t$ is forecastable only after you make a series of assumptions regarding the exogenous factors of monetary and fiscal policy. We cannot make an estimate of $\dot{Y}_t$ without assessing the actions political decision makers are likely to pursue. Thus, the forecasted level of next year's GNP depends upon what scenario you expect to prevail. Indeed, you may want to postulate alternative scenarios.

The second equation in Dewald's model is definitional—demand pressure on prices and unemployment is based on the difference between anticipated real GNP and full-employment or potential real GNP. In turn, the third equation tells us that anticipated price changes ($\dot{P}_t^a$) depend on previous changes in demand pressure (D_{t-i}), the GNP deflator ($\dot{P}_{t-i}$), and the imports deflator ($\dot{W}_{t-i}$). Simply stated, price expectations are formed from past experiences. Similarly, the fourth equation provides the monetarist link between current price changes, anticipated price changes, and demand pressures.

Logically, you would first solve the third equation to find $\dot{P}_t^a$, then solve the second equation to get D_t, and then substitute into the fourth equation to estimate $\dot{P}_t$. Having current-dollar GNP ($\dot{Y}_t$) and the GNP deflator ($\dot{P}_t$), you could then substitute into the last three equations to find the percentage change in real GNP ($\dot{X}$), the unemployment rate (U_t), and Moody's corporate Aaa bond rate (R_t).

If we compare this monetarist model with the simple Keynesian model formulated by Suits, given earlier, the significance of alternative theories becomes readily apparent. We cannot hope to present either theory in its entirety, but a comparison is worthwhile. Keynesian theory relies on demand-side forces (consumer spending, investment plans, government budget policy) to explain changes in GNP. Thus, their alternative for equation 1 might be:

$$Y_t = f(C, I, G) \tag{3-8}$$

The absence of a money-market measure is the most obvious difference. Further, one of the predictions of Keynesian theory is that easy-money policies are likely to lead to low interest rates. Monetarist theory predicts just the opposite reaction—that is, easy-money policies result in high interest rates. To grasp the significance of this disagreement, let us postulate the following interest-rate equation:[9]

[9]Robert S. Pindyck and Daniel L. Rubinfeld, *Econometric Models and Economic Forecasts* (New York: McGraw-Hill, 1976), pp. 118–19.

$$R_t = f(DI_t, MAM_t, MAP_t) \qquad\qquad (3\text{-}9)$$

where:

R_t = three-month Treasury-bill rate
DI_t = disposable income
MAM_t = three-month moving average of changes in the money supply
MAP_t = three-month moving sum of the rate of change in the price level

The monetarists would postulate a positive relationship between R_t and MAM_t, whereas a Keynesian would expect a negative relationship. Such theoretical distinctions can lead to fundamental differences in actual forecasts, and this should be kept in mind when examining the events of the 1973–75 recession.

AN OVERVIEW OF THE GREAT RECESSION: THE ECONOMY FROM 1973 TO 1975

SETTING THE STAGE

In evaluating the forecasts of the CEA, DRI, and "Roundup" over the 1974–75 recession, there is an obvious need to preface these projections with general background information concerning the state of the economy during the years prior to the recession. But how far back in time does one need to go before having an adequate base of historical reference? Wesley Clair Mitchell struggled with essentially the same question in 1913 when he was writing *Business Cycles and Their Causes:*

> Since the processes of a nation's business life never cease or begin afresh, no natural starting point for the descriptive analysis to which we are committed exists. It is necessary to plunge in *medias res* by breaking into the unceasing processes at some arbitrarily chosen point.[10]

You may wish to refresh your memory of the events prior to 1973 by referring back to Chapter 2's chronology of cycles in the twentieth century. Following the mini-recession of 1969–70, the economy surged ahead in 1971 and 1972 and experienced a banner year in 1973. Real GNP was up 5.9 percent in 1973; industrial production soared by 9 percent; housing starts moved past 2.0 million units; retail car sales reached 11.5 million units; unemployment averaged only 4.9 percent; current-dollar profits (after tax) rose by 26.5 percent; and consumer prices rose by 6.2 percent (low by present standards, but high by 1973 criteria). Judged by either the record output of goods and services, the low unemployment rate, the escalating rate of inflation, rising interest rates, or the high capacity-utilization rates in manufacturing, it was painfully clear both

---

[10]Wesley C. Mitchell, *Business Cycles and Their Causes* (Los Angeles: University of California Press, 1963), p. xii.

to forecasters inside the Nixon administration and to independent business analysts that the economy was overheating as a result of strong growth in aggregate demand and a host of supply-side constraints.

Forecasting in 1973–74 was complicated by the uncertain effects of Nixon's Phase III voluntary price controls enacted in January 1973, the Phase III½ 60-day price freeze initiated in June 1973, the Phase IV selective mandatory price controls implemented in July 1973, and the OPEC oil embargo that was thrust upon the world economy in late 1973. Table 3-2 vividly delineates the severity of the 1974–75 recession that followed so closely on the heels of 1973's full-employment economy. Real GNP, which had grown from 1971 to 1973, fell sharply in both 1974 and 1975. Unemployment, which had averaged less than 5 percent in 1973, reached an average of 8.5 percent in 1975. Consumer prices escalated by 11 percent in 1974 and 9.1 percent in 1975. This was a marked difference from the 6.3 percent rate in 1973. Similarly, housing starts, as seen in Table 3-2, were cut nearly in half between 1973 and 1975.

In his path-breaking cliometric study (a statistical analysis of historical data) of this recession, Dr. Otto Eckstein dubbed the 1974–75 economic experience the Great Recession—"a name chosen to assert that it was an episode, not a turning point":[11]

> In the years 1973–76, the world economy passed through its most dangerous adventure since the 1930s. There is no way to tell whether those years were just bad luck, or a turning point. But exciting times do offer fertile material for the historian. Calm times teach few lessons. The true characteristics of economic and social systems can only be discovered in periods of stress.[12]

We now turn to the task of investigating the projections and analyses of economic forecasters during the 1974–75 recession, because, to paraphrase Dr. Eckstein, such a period of stress is apt to reveal the true characteristics of the forecasting process.

THE FORECAST ASSESSMENT
AT THE OUTSET OF 1974

Since the economy peaked in November 1973, one might expect to discover that forecasts made by the CEA, DRI, and "Roundup" in January 1974 would contain gloomy assessments of the forthcoming decline of the economy. But as often occurs at turning points in the business cycle, none of these three forecasting groups was willing to predict that a "Great Recession" was the most likely outcome for the economy of the United States in 1974. By far the most optimistic of the forecasts was "Roundup's" January 1974 headline, which assured us that "ZERO GROWTH IS HERE, BUT NOT FOR LONG."[13]

[11]Otto Eckstein, *The Great Recession* (Amsterdam: North Holland, 1978), p. i.
[12]Ibid.
[13]Sanford S. Parker, "Business Roundup," *Fortune*, January 1974, p. 13.

Table 3-2 Summary of the U.S. economy, 1964–75

	Years											
	1964	1965	1966	1967	1968	1969	1970	1971	1972	1973	1974	1975
GNP and Its Components—Billions of Dollars												
Gross national product	632.4	684.9	749.8	793.9	864.2	930.3	977.1	1054.9	1158.0	1294.9	1397.4	1477.5
Real GNP (1958 dollars)	581.0	617.8	658.1	675.2	706.7	725.6	722.5	746.3	792.5	839.2	821.2	797.7
Inventory investment	5.9	9.7	14.8	8.2	7.1	7.8	4.5	6.3	8.6	15.4	14.2	-14.8
Net exports	8.5	6.9	5.3	5.2	2.5	1.9	3.6	-0.1	-6.0	3.9	2.2	12.9
Prices and Wages—Annual Rates of Change												
Implicit price deflator	1.6	1.8	2.8	3.2	4.0	4.8	5.5	4.5	3.4	5.6	10.3	8.8
Consumer price index	1.3	1.6	3.0	2.8	4.2	5.4	5.9	4.3	3.3	6.2	11.0	9.1
Wholesale price index	0.2	2.0	3.3	0.2	2.5	3.9	3.6	3.2	4.5	13.1	18.8	9.2
Average hourly earnings index	2.7	3.7	4.1	4.9	6.2	6.6	6.7	7.1	6.5	6.4	8.2	8.8
Key Economic Measures												
Unemployment rate (percent)	5.2	4.5	3.8	3.8	3.6	3.5	5.0	6.0	5.6	4.9	5.6	8.5
Industrial production (67=1)	0.816	0.890	0.977	0.998	1.055	1.105	1.067	1.067	1.151	1.254	1.243	1.134
Annual rate of change	6.9	9.1	9.8	2.1	5.8	4.7	-3.5	0.0	7.9	9.0	-0.9	-8.7
Housing starts (millions)	1.54	1.47	1.17	1.28	1.50	1.49	1.43	2.04	2.36	2.05	1.34	1.17
Unit car sales (millions)	8.1	9.4	9.1	8.3	9.6	9.6	8.5	10.3	10.9	11.5	9.0	8.7
Federal budget surplus (NIA)	-3.0	1.2	-0.2	-12.4	-6.5	8.1	-11.9	-21.9	-17.5	-5.6	-8.1	-72.9
Money and Interest Rates												
Money supply (M1)	160.2	167.1	174.7	181.6	194.3	206.5	215.7	230.7	245.6	263.8	278.7	290.5
Annual rate of change	4.0	4.3	4.5	3.9	7.0	6.3	4.5	7.0	6.4	7.4	5.7	4.2
New high-grade corp. bond rate (percent)	4.40	4.54	5.44	5.77	6.48	7.67	8.50	7.36	7.16	7.65	8.96	9.01
Federal funds rate (percent)	3.50	4.07	5.11	4.22	5.66	8.21	7.18	4.66	4.43	8.73	10.50	5.82
Prime rate (percent)	4.50	4.54	5.63	5.63	6.28	7.95	7.91	5.70	5.25	8.02	10.80	7.86

Table 3-2 (Continued)

					Years							
	1964	1965	1966	1967	1968	1969	1970	1971	1972	1973	1974	1975
					Incomes—Billions of Dollars							
Personal income	497.5	538.9	587.2	629.3	688.9	750.9	808.3	864.1	944.9	1055.0	1150.5	1239.7
Real disposable income	408.1	434.8	458.9	477.6	499.0	513.5	534.7	555.4	580.5	619.5	602.9	610.4
Annual rate of change	7.0	6.5	5.5	4.1	4.5	2.9	4.1	3.9	4.5	6.7	-2.7	1.3
Saving rate (percent)	6.0	6.0	6.3	7.4	6.7	6.0	8.1	8.1	6.5	8.2	7.9	8.6
Profits after tax (percent change)	16.3	20.8	7.5	-6.6	2.4	-6.2	-12.5	17.5	25.1	26.5	16.6	-9.9
					Details of Real GNP—Annual Rates of Change							
Gross national product	5.4	6.3	6.5	2.6	4.7	2.7	-0.4	3.3	6.2	5.9	-2.1	-2.9
Total consumption	5.8	6.4	5.1	2.9	5.3	3.6	1.8	4.0	6.2	4.7	-2.3	0.7
Business fixed investment	11.3	14.8	11.7	-1.1	3.3	5.9	-3.6	-0.6	9.1	12.8	-0.4	-13.2
Equipment	13.7	13.8	13.7	0.9	3.3	6.9	-4.1	-0.0	11.8	15.3	-1.7	-15.3
Nonresidential construction	6.7	16.8	7.6	-5.7	3.3	3.9	-2.4	-2.0	2.7	6.4	3.4	-7.8
Residential construction	-2.4	-1.3	-10.6	-4.5	13.9	2.0	-6.1	30.6	18.1	-4.1	-26.9	-21.4
Federal government	-2.4	-0.3	12.9	14.1	4.6	-5.9	-12.4	-5.4	0.2	-6.1	-1.4	3.5
State and local governments	6.0	6.9	7.6	7.3	6.2	4.0	3.5	4.6	4.7	6.0	2.8	1.8

Source: Otto Eckstein, *The Great Recession* (Amsterdam: North Holland, 1978), p. 4

Although expecting real GNP to plateau at near zero growth in the first quarter of 1974, the "Roundup" outlook envisioned that the economy would resurge by mid-1974, experience 2.4 percent real growth for the full calendar year, and continue to advance at nearly a 6 percent real growth rate through mid-1975.[14] Overall, it was a projection calling for a one-quarter pause followed by renewed strength in the economy. Table 3-3 summarizes calendar-year 1974 scenarios

Table 3-3 Alternative forecast scenarios at the outset of 1974

1974 Outlook	CEA[a]	DRI[b]	"Roundup"[c]	Actual[d]
(1) GNP—current $ (billions)	$1,390.0	$1,392.7	$1,400	$1,412.9
(2) Percent change from 1973	+8.0%	+8.1%	+8.5%	+8.1%
(3) Real GNP—% change from 1973	+1%	+1%	+2.4%	−1.4%
(4) Implicit GNP deflator (% change)	+6.9%	+7%	+6.0%	+9.7%

[a]*Economic Report of the President*, 1974. Since only percentage-change forecast magnitudes were given in the *Report*, they have been converted to absolute magnitudes using the preliminary 1973 GNP data published in the *Report*.
[b]Data Resources Incorporated, *DRI Review*, January 1974.
[c]*Fortune*, "Business Roundup," January 1974.
[d]*Economic Report of the President*, 1976. Estimates have since been revised.

envisioned by "Roundup," DRI, and the CEA in January 1974 and contrasts them with the actual results for the economy.

If a forecast analyst had only the current-dollar GNP figures shown in the first row of Table 3-3, he would be led to the erroneous conclusion that "Roundup," with an error of only 0.9 percent, had most closely approximated the course of the economy in 1974. In terms of relative performance, it is clear from a subsequent examination of rows 2 to 4 that "Roundup" was far too high in its real GNP growth projection and much too low in its inflation forecast when compared to the 9.7 percent increase in the GNP deflator. When "Roundup's" overoptimistic real-GNP estimate is combined with its low deflator forecast, however, it produced the *best* current-dollar projection! Ultimately, economic prognosticators must be judged on their ability to discern when real-GNP growth rates will shift from positive to negative (the upper turning point) or from negative to positive (the lower turning point). Applying this standard to the annual real-GNP projections in row 3 of Table 3-3, we must judge all three sets of projections as deficient, in that they called for continued modest growth when, in fact, the economy was to be plagued by recession (a negative real-GNP growth rate throughout 1974).

Annual projections may mask quarter-to-quarter shifts that are particularly volatile at cyclical turning points. Even if a forecaster had correctly projected a real-GNP decline of 1.4 percent in 1974, his quarter-to-quarter growth-rate estimates might have been more misleading to a forecast user than the quarterly figures prepared by "Roundup," the CEA, or DRI. Table 3-4

[14]Ibid.

Table 3-4 Quarterly growth rates for real GNP in 1974
(Seasonally adjusted annualized rates)

| | Percentage Increase in Real GNP | | | | |
	1974:1	1974:2	1974:3	1974:4	Full Year 1974
(1) Actual[a]	−6.6	−1.6	−1.9	−9.6	−1.4
(2) CEA[b]	0.0	0.0	1.3	1.3	1.0
(3) DRI[c]	−3.9	2.4	2.8	5.9	1.0
(4) Fortune[d]	0.0	3.0	6.0	6.0	2.4

[a]*Economic Report of the President*, 1976. Estimates have since been revised.
[b]*Report*, 1974. Based on a verbal assessment on page 28 of the *Report* that real output would be flat in the first half of 1974 and grow in the second half so as to attain a 1% calendar-year gain.
[c]Data Resources Incorporated, *DRI Review*, January 1974.
[d]*Fortune*, "Business Roundup," January 1974. Based on a projection of 2.4% for calendar year 1974, zero growth in the first quarter, and graphical displays of quarterly growth curves.

compares actual quarterly growth rates for real GNP with one set of specific projections prepared by DRI and two general assessments made by "Roundup" and the CEA. As shown in row 1 of Table 3-4, the slide experienced in 1974 was both precipitous and erratic; the steep decline in the first quarter was followed by moderate dips in the second and third quarters and a sharp drop in the fourth. "Roundup" had foreseen a flat first quarter and the CEA a flat first half, but DRI forecasted a substantial decline in the first quarter, to be followed by a surge in the last three quarters of 1974. Two questions naturally arise: Why were these reputable forecast groups not able, at the outset of 1974, to more fully discern the outline of the coming recession, and when did the CEA, DRI, and "Roundup" begin to appreciate the full magnitude of the Great Recession? To completely answer these questions, it is necessary to look at the month-by-month evolution of each group's forecasts over the course of the 1974–75 recession, examine what role exogenous events played in the modification of the forecast scenarios, and focus on both the contribution and the limitations of economic theory and econometric modeling in a period of economic turbulence.

DIAGNOSING THE GREAT RECESSION: A MONTHLY CHRONICLE

INTRODUCTION

If a forecast for the economy is based on the most current information available, then today's forecast literally becomes outmoded by tomorrow. This fact is seen most dramatically in the daily price fluctuations (the market system's translation of changing information) in grain, stock, and precious-metal exchanges, but it is no less true for GNP estimates, projections of monthly steel output, or forecasts of a railroad's weekly carloadings of freight. Although it is true that, most of the time, today's forecast of the economy will be little changed from yesterday's, you must keep in mind the rapid rate of obsolescence inherent in forecasting when you critically evaluate either a current or a past projection for the economy or for a company. Lacking definitive information about future exogenous variables such as monetary and fiscal policy, international political stability, domestic political programs, strikes by labor, and abnormal weather conditions, the accuracy of today's forecast, no matter how well thought out its analytical foundation, will be largely determined by the degree to which unforecastable surprises overwhelm the forecaster's assumptions. In an analysis of the month-to-month projections, therefore, expect to find constant change, not stability.

"ROUNDUP'S" OPTIMISM:
NO MORE CYCLES?

The forecaster's world is dominated by lengthy computer printouts containing a seemingly infinite number of rows and columns of pertinent data; however, a concise tabular display is a more effective means of communicating critical information to the user. Table 3-5 provides such a summary of "Roundup's" forecasts for real GNP and inflation as taken from the January and July issues of *Fortune* magazine for each year from 1973 to 1975. Listed at the bottom of Table 3-5 are the lead titles from the respective "Roundup" forecasts.

If ever a feeling of optimism was expressed by a forecaster, it was in January 1973, when the "Roundup" headline declared that the economy was "set on the best of all possible courses."[15] "Roundup's" outlook was based on steady but slightly slower growth for real GNP and industrial production over the 18-month period from January 1973 to June 1974. The economy would, according to "Roundup":

> . . . sail fairly smoothly between the rocks of a mini-recession and the rocks of reheated inflation.[16]

As detailed in Table 3-5, this optimism specifically translated into 6.8 percent real growth for GNP and a 3.0 percent increase in the GNP deflator during 1973, dropping to a real growth rate of 5.0 percent for GNP by early 1974.[17] As seen in the table, "Roundup's" outlook dated July of 1973 (which encompassed the remainder of 1973 and all of 1974) was slightly less optimistic than its January 1973 scenario, but "Roundup" was still able to conclude firmly that:

[15]Sanford S. Parker, "Business Roundup," *Fortune*, January 1973, p. 21.
[16]Ibid.
[17]Ibid.

Table 3-5 "Roundup's" forecasts for GNP and the GNP deflator, 1973–1975

"Roundup" Forecast Date	1973				1974				1975			
	Real GNP % Change	GNP Def. % Change	GNP % Change	GNP (Billions)	Real GNP % Change	GNP Def. % Change	GNP % Change	GNP (Billions)	Real GNP % Change	GNP Def. % Change	GNP % Change	GNP (Billions)
Jan. 1973[b]	+6.8%	+3.0%	+10.0%	$1,265								
July 1973[c]	+6.3%	+4.4%	+11.0%	$1,280								
Jan. 1974[d]					+4.2%	+3.6%[a]	+8.0%	$1,390				
July 1974[e]					+2.4%	+6.0%	+8.5%[a]	$1,400	+3.5%	+5.7%	+9.4%	$1,532
Jan. 1975[f]					+0.5%	+8.2%	+8.8%	$1,400	−2.9%[a]	+8.8%	+6.0%	$1,480
July 1975[g]									−3.9%	+8.4%	+4.3%	n.a.

[a]Implicit number derived from "Roundup" projections but not explicitly presented.
[b]Roundup headline: "SET ON THE BEST OF ALL POSSIBLE COURSES."
[c]Roundup headline: "SLOWER GROWTH, YES; RECESSION, NO."
[d]Roundup headline: "ZERO GROWTH IS HERE, BUT NOT FOR LONG."
[e]Roundup headline: "A RETURN TO GROWTH—ON A SLOW TRACK."
[f]Roundup headline: "A STUNNING DECLINE, A LONG ROAD BACK."
[g]Roundup headline: "A VIGOROUS BUT NOT EXPLOSIVE RECOVERY."
Source: *Fortune*, "Business Roundup," selected issues

... the economy will avoid both the dangers often cited of late—overheating this year [1973], overcooling next year [1974].[18]

Even though "Roundup" foresaw a decline in home building and a cooling off in consumer demand in 1974, its July 1973 picture continued to envisage a relatively painless transition to a period of smooth growth.

Despite the Arab oil embargo and the relatively flat performance of the economy in the last quarter of 1973, "Roundup" in January 1974 could confidently argue against a recession. Indeed, it went out on a forecasting limb when it stated that ". . . in the spring [1974] the economy will begin to expand again."[19] Not only would it grow, but, according to "Roundup," the sustained strength in investment, when combined with a rebound in automobile and housing demand, would propel real GNP at nearly a 6 percent growth rate from mid-1974 to mid-1975.[20] As seen in Table 3-5, the inflation forecast contained in the January 1974 outlook had been ratcheted upward to 6.0 percent, but real GNP, reflecting the first-quarter pause, was to move upward by only 2.4 percent in 1974. Although "Roundup" voiced concern over the softness in housing and consumer durables and over the possibility of unexpected inventory buildups, it was felt that the economy's adjustments in January 1974 were ". . . not really anything like a true recession. . . ."[21]

During the first six months of 1974, the economy was buffeted by declines in real GNP and soaring prices. As outlined in Table 3-5, "Roundup" had by July 1974 reduced its forecast to 0.5 percent real growth in 1974 and raised the 1974 increase in the GNP deflator to 8.2 percent, but still clung to its no-recession scenario by predicting an 18-month surge in the economy that could yield a 3.5 percent increase in real GNP and a 5.7 percent increase in inflation during 1975.[22] Much of this optimism in July 1974 can be linked to preliminary GNP figures for the second quarter of 1974, which indicated that real GNP and the GNP deflator had gone from a 6 percent decline and a 11.5 percent rise, respectively, in the first quarter of 1974 to rises of 3 percent and 7.5 percent, respectively, in the second quarter.[23] Unfortunately, these preliminary statistics for the second quarter of 1974 were both too optimistic. Although second-quarter results were improved, the final record shows that real GNP declined at an annual rate of 1.6 percent in the second quarter after falling at a 7.0 percent rate in the first. Similarly, the GNP deflator moved from an annual rate of increase of 12.3 percent in the first quarter to 9.4 percent in the second quarter.[24] Both the rate of decline in real GNP and the rate of increase in prices did moderate, but the economy, based on its real GNP performance, had not rebounded

[18]Sanford S. Parker, "Business Roundup," *Fortune*, July 1973, p. 9.
[19]Sanford S. Parker, "Business Roundup," *Fortune*, January 1974, pp. 13–14.
[20]Ibid.
[21]Ibid.
[22]Sanford S. Parker, "Business Roundup," *Fortune*, July 1974, p. 7.
[23]Ibid.
[24]It should be pointed out that large adjustments in preliminary statistical estimates by the government are quite commonplace. See Eckstein, *Recession*, pp. 206–7.

in the second quarter! "Roundup" was not unmindful of the uncertainties in the forecast; in particular, its predicted 1975 housing recovery was predicated on the assumption of supportive monetary policy by the Federal Reserve. In addition, the forecasted rebound assumed that consumer demand would pick up with the abatement in inflation, that there would not be a severe inventory adjustment, and that there would be sustained strength in business capital-goods spending.[25]

"ROUNDUP'S" CAUTION:
RECOGNIZING A RECESSION

In July 1974, "Roundup" stated that "the economy appears to have weathered the turbulent events of the past half year," but it subsequently cited excessive inventories in the August outlook, continued softness in consumer buying in September, the slow housing recovery in October, the imminence of a recession in November, and the collapse of capital-goods spending in the December issue.[26] Of particular interest to the student of business-cycle history is the quandary voiced by "Roundup" in the November 1974 issue of *Fortune*. Not only was there an argument between President Ford (who denied the existence of a recession) and Arthur Burns (who felt a recession was in progress), but "Roundup" itself pointed out the statistical aberration of a situation in which the economy had lost nearly 3 percent in real GNP but had experienced very little decline in the index of industrial production. Indeed, "Roundup" concluded in its November 1974 outlook not only that a recession was on the way, but that it might be worse than the recession of 1957–58, owing to:

> ... Washington's likely unwillingness to provide the usual stimulus to a recession-weakened economy. . . .[27]

In November 1974, one year after the actual upper turning point in the economy, "Roundup" could finally conclude that:

> ... the day of reckoning for inventories and industrial production—in short, for the economy—is at hand.[28]

"ROUNDUP" CATCHES UP
WITH THE GREAT RECESSION

Even though "Roundup's" November 1974 outlook was still mulling the dimensions of the forthcoming recession, by the January 1975 issue it could dramatically conclude that:

---

[25]Parker, "Roundup," July 1974, p. 12.
[26]Sanford S. Parker, "Business Roundup," *Fortune*, July 1974, August 1974, September 1974, October 1974, and November 1974.
[27]Parker, "Roundup," November 1974, p. 32.
[28]Ibid.

... the worst U.S. recession since the Depression has lately struck with such stunning speed and severity that it has already run more than half of its course.[29]

After dipping moderately in the second and third quarters, real GNP plummeted at an annual rate of close to 10 percent in the last quarter of 1974 and the deflator moved upward at an annual rate in excess of 14 percent. Although "Roundup's" January 1975 forecast called for a decline of 2.9 percent in real GNP and an increase of 8.8 percent in the GNP deflator which was almost identical to the full-year 1975 results, the 1975 quarter-to-quarter pattern in real GNP growth rates was so volatile that neither "Roundup" nor any of the other leading forecasters was able to foresee a 12.5 percent annual rate of decline in the first quarter of 1975 followed by real-GNP gains of 1.9, 13.4, and 4.6 percent, respectively, in the last three quarters.

No well-known or established forecasting group accurately projected, with even the crudest degree of precision, the economy's path from the peak in November 1973 to the trough in March 1975. That is, those forecasters most readily relied upon by corporations and the general public were not able to delineate the true severity of the Great Recession until late 1974 or early 1975. There may have been less well known individuals or groups that accurately predicted a severe recession, but it is fair to conclude that, from a pragmatic viewpoint, their forecasts did not count, since they were ignored by the general public.

It is important to understand why the forecasting community failed so completely in predicting the Great Recession. As summarized earlier in Table 3-3, neither "Roundup," the CEA, or DRI were willing, in January 1974, to predict it. We have already traced "Roundup's" monthly outlook, and we now turn to examine that of the CEA and DRI in order to explain why the Great Recession slipped past the forecasting community.

DRI'S *EX POST* ANALYSIS
OF THE GREAT RECESSION

DRI'S OUTLOOK

Prof. Otto Eckstein's book, *The Great Recession*, "uses the Data Resources (DRI) Econometric Model of the U.S. economy to try to reconstruct just how the Great Recession came about."[30] As such, it is an invaluable aid in our attempt at explaining why the forecasting community, including DRI, found the task of forecasting so difficult during the Great Recession. Professor Eckstein's cliometric study makes use of DRI's model to retrace or simulate the course of the U.S. economy under a number of assumptions that incorporate alternative shocks to the economy. Having the full advantage of historical

[29]Sanford S. Parker, "Business Roundup," *Fortune*, January 1975, p. 9.
[30]Eckstein, *Recession*, p. i.

hindsight concerning such exogenous variables as monetary and fiscal policy, the Vietnam War, the food crises in 1972–74, and the Arab oil embargo, Eckstein first demonstrates that the current DRI model reproduces with a high degree of precision the actual ups and downs of the Great Recession. Next, he removes these shocks one at a time in order to calculate the relative importance of each of these different exogenous variables in terms of the Great Recession and to estimate what underlying changes have taken place in the U.S. economy.[31]

Before we look at DRI's *ex post* analysis of the Great Recession, it will be useful to summarize the monthly DRI forecasts actually sent to customers during the course of the recession. Table 3-6 contains a monthly chronicle of DRI's projections for annualized growth rates for real GNP and the GNP deflator. For example, the DRI projection dated January 30, 1974, called for real GNP to fall at an annual rate of 3.9 percent in the first quarter of 1974, to turn upward in the second quarter, to accelerate in the third and fourth quarters, and then to approach a trend rate of roughly 4.0 percent throughout 1975. Although this was less optimistic than "Roundup's" January 1974 forecast, the thrust of DRI's forecast was also far wide of the actual course to be followed by the economy during the Great Recession.

Table 3-6 can be read two ways. By looking across any given row, you can see DRI's forecast at a particular time for future movements in the economy. By looking down each column, you get multiple forecasts done at varying points for a particular future-time segment. For example, look at the forecast column labeled "1974: 4" (fourth quarter 1974). Although GNP actually fell in the fourth quarter of 1974 at an annual rate of nearly 10 percent, the DRI forecasts shown in the January 1974 and July 1974 *Reviews* called for positive rates of 5.9 percent and 2.6 percent, respectively, in that quarter. Even the forecast dated September 23, 1974—a scant week before the fourth quarter began—was calling for a very modest decline in real GNP of 0.6 percent. Nor was the inflation forecast significantly better. The GNP deflator moved upward at roughly a 14 percent rate in the fourth quarter of 1974, but DRI's forecasts of January 30, 1974, and July 31, 1974, called for increases of only 6.3 and 8.0 percent, respectively.

It is tempting to draw strong conclusions concerning the relative forecast accuracy of DRI vis-à-vis "Roundup" by studying the summaries in Tables 3-5 and 3-6; yet such an attempt is doomed to failure. To determine comparative forecast accuracy, you would have to carry out an elaborate statistical investigation, which is far beyond the scope of this book.[32] It is, however, worth your time to analyze these forecasts, compare them with the actual results, and ponder the reasons for the forecasting community's inability to call the Great Recession. Table 3-7 provides a short statistical summary of the Council of Economic Advisers' (CEA's) annual outlooks in January 1974 and 1975,

---

[31] Eckstein, *Recession*, p. 5.

[32] See Stephen K. McNees, "The Forecasting Record for the 1970's," *New England Economic Review*, Federal Reserve Bank of Boston, September/October 1979, pp. 33–53.

Table 3-6 Monthly evolution of DRI's forecast for real GNP and the implicit GNP deflator: January 1974 to December 1975 (Annual rate of change)

DRI Forecast Date[a]	1974:1		1974:2		1974:3		1974:4		1975:1		1975:2		1975:3		1975:4		1974		1975	
	(1) Real GNP	(2) GNP Def.	(3) Real GNP	(4) GNP Def.	(5) Real GNP	(6) GNP Def.	(7) Real GNP	(8) GNP Def.	(9) Real GNP	(10) GNP Def.	(11) Real GNP	(12) GNP Def.	(13) Real GNP	(14) GNP Def.	(15) Real GNP	(16) GNP Def.	(17) Real GNP	(18) GNP Def.	(19) Real GNP	(20) GNP Def.
1-30-74	-3.9	6.9	2.4	7.1	2.8	6.3	5.9	6.3	4.6	5.1	4.1	4.9	3.9	4.7	4.2	5.0	1.0	7.1	4.3	5.5
3-29-74	-4.5	9.7	2.4	7.8	4.0	5.9	5.5	6.2	4.6	4.8	4.7	4.4	3.4	4.3	4.9	4.4	1.0	8.0	4.5	5.2
5-21-74	-6.3	11.5	2.5	8.7	4.5	7.4	4.9	7.5	4.1	5.7	3.2	6.3	3.4	6.3	4.1	6.3	0.6	8.9	3.9	6.7
7-31-74	-7.0	12.3	-1.2	8.8	1.9	7.4	2.6	8.0	2.6	7.9	3.1	7.3	3.6	7.1	4.0	7.1	-0.9	9.2	2.6	7.7
9-23-74	-7.0	12.3	-1.6	9.4	0.4	9.6	-0.6	10.0	0.6	9.9	1.7	8.9	2.7	8.9	4.5	8.2	-1.3	9.8	0.9	9.4
11-18-74	-7.0	12.3	-1.6	9.4	-2.1	11.8	-7.7	11.7	-0.5	7.9	1.0	7.4	4.6	6.9	5.4	7.1	-2.1	10.2	0.9	8.9
12-28-74	-7.0	12.3	-1.6	9.4	-1.9	11.9	-8.8	11.9	-4.7	10.4	1.6	7.7	2.6	6.8	6.0	6.3	-2.1	10.2	2.3	9.5
1-25-75							-9.1	13.7	-6.9	10.7	0.3	10.7	3.5	8.1	5.1	7.6	-2.2	10.3	-3.1	10.8
3-12-75									-10.9	9.5	-0.4	7.4	4.9	6.7	8.3	5.8	-2.2	10.3	-3.9	9.6
5-27-75									-11.3	8.5	1.2	6.6	7.0	5.6	7.0	6.4	-2.1	10.3	-3.6	9.2
7-29-75									-11.4	8.5	-0.3	5.1	7.9	5.8	7.6	6.4	-2.1	10.3	-3.7	8.9
9-26-75									-11.4	8.5	1.9	5.1	8.6	7.4	6.8	8.5	-2.1	10.3	3.3	9.2
12-31-75															4.6	7.8	-2.1	10.3	-2.9	8.8

[a]Data Resources Incorporated, *Data Resources Review*, monthly, January 1974 to December 1975.

Table 3-7 Annual forecasts by the Council of Economic Advisers (Percentage changes)

	Jan. 1974[a]	Jan. 1975[b]
Real GNP	+1%	−2%
Current $ GNP	+8	+8
GNP deflator	+7	+10
Consumer goods (current $)	+8	+8.9
Capital spending	+12	+9.4
Gov't purchases	+10	+11.7
Housing starts	−20	−19.6
Unemployment rate (level)	5.5	6.6
Consumer spending (real)	+1	−2.3
Money supply (M2)	+8	+8

[a]*Economic Report of the President*, January 1974.
[b]*Economic Report of the President*, January 1975.

which can be cross-checked with those of DRI and "Roundup." Needless to say, the CEA fared little better in the task of predicting the recession.

It is tempting also to ridicule the error-plagued forecasts produced during the Great Recession, but it is more productive to isolate, if possible, the factors that led to these erroneous forecasts and ponder their implications for current forecasters. Prof. Otto Eckstein's research of the Great Recession provides some very powerful—and humbling—conclusions for today's forecaster. In Figure 3-1, the actual behavior of real GNP and the implicit GNP deflator is

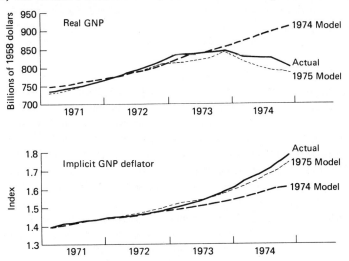

Figure 3-1 Simulation Performance of Successive Generations of Econometric Models.

Source: Otto Eckstein, *The Great Recession*, (Amsterdam: North Holland, 1978), p. 7.

contrasted with the simulations generated by the old, 1974 version of the DRI model and a new, improved model developed in 1975. The results are both startling and sobering. Using all the information currently available about exogenous variables and simulating the old DRI model, the simulation of the 1974 econometric model (dashed line) misses the decline in real GNP and the acceleration of inflation experienced during the Great Recession. Using the technologically superior 1975 version of the DRI econometric model, the simulation closely approximates the inflation path and catches the actual features of the downturn in real GNP. If we assume for the moment that the 1974 version of the DRI econometric model represented state-of-the-art technology, we are forced to conclude that the Great Recession was not forecastable! If, in fact, this conclusion is valid, it leaves two additional questions we must answer. First, what unique factors were present in the Great Recession, and what were their related forecasting implications? Second, should we expect that contemporary econometric models will serve us any better?

THE GREAT RECESSION:
LEGACY FOR THE FORECASTER

If the Great Recession was not forecastable by standard econometric methods, the implications for the forecaster vary greatly, depending on whether the cycle was endogenous or exogenous in nature. That is, was the recession caused by the natural internal workings of the U.S. economic system, or was it the result of one or more external shocks? Shocks are unforecastable surprises that are beyond the purview of the economist or any business forecaster. From the historical perspective of the cliometrician dissecting the root causes of business fluctuations, Professor Eckstein states that the Great Recession was spawned by the "unhappy coincidence of the energy and food shocks, and by extreme and unstable monetary policies."[33]

In other words, this was a purely exogenous cycle that was exacerbated by the simultaneous compounding of widely divergent shocks—weather conditions leading to the grain crisis, international political turmoil producing the oil embargo, and domestic political and socioeconomic factors yielding a set of destabilizing monetary policies. Not only was each exogenous shock unforecastable, the simultaneous presence of all of them was extremely unlikely.

Tables 3-8 and 3-9 summarize Professor Eckstein's cliometric study by decomposing the relative contributions of these exogenous shocks to both the inflation rate in 1974 and unemployment in 1975. Looking at Tables 3-8 and 3-9, you can see that the combined influence of these six exogenous factors was to add 6.4 percentage points to the inflation rate in 1974 and 4.5 percentage points to the unemployment rate in 1975. Viewed differently, these conclusions imply an endogenous or underlying inflation rate of 3.9 percent (10.3 percent

[33]Eckstein, *Recession*, p. 142.

Table 3-8 Impact of shocks on the inflation rate in 1974
(Percentage points)

Contributing Factor	Contribution to Inflation Rate[a]
(1) Energy crisis	1.7
(2) Agricultural price explosion	1.5
(3) Devaluation of dollar	1.2
(4) Monetary policies, 1964–74	0.9
(5) Price decontrol	0.8
(6) Fiscal policies, 1969–74	0.3
Sum of (1) through (6)	6.4
Rate of inflation, 1974	10.3

[a]Inflation rate is the historical tracking solution of the Data Resources Model minus the inflation rate in the alternative solution with the respective shock removed.
Source: Otto Eckstein, *The Great Recession* (Amsterdam: North Holland, 1978), pp. 139–40.

Table 3-9 Impact of shocks on unemployment in 1975
(Percentage points)

Contributing Factor	Contribution to Unemployment Rate[a]
(1) Energy crisis	1.9
(2) Monetary policies, 1964–75	1.6
(3) Agricultural price explosion	0.9
(4) Price controls	0.2
(5) Fiscal policies, 1969–74	0.1
(6) Devaluation	−0.2
Sum of (1) through (6)	4.5
Unemployment rate, 1975	8.5

[a]Unemployment rate is historical tracking solution minus unemployment rate in the alternative solution with the respective shock removed.
Source: See Table 3-8.

less 6.4 percent) in 1974 and an endogenous unemployment rate of 4.0 percent (8.5 percent less 4.5 percent) in 1975—magnitudes that certainly would have been consistent with price stability and full employment during 1974 and 1975. As shown in Table 3-8, over half the 6.4 precentage-point increase in prices in 1974 could be traced to the energy crisis and the agricultural price explosion. Similarly, the energy crisis and monetary policy were responsible for over three-fourths of the 4.5 percentage-point jump in the 1975 unemployment rate. Thus, we can answer the question raised earlier by concluding that, based on Eckstein's cliometric simulations of the economy, the Great Recession was purely exogenous in nature. This still leaves unanswered the question of whether contemporary econometric models will serve us better.

ECONOMETRIC MODELING:
ADAPTATION TO STRUCTURAL CHANGE

Each forecaster attempts to sift through the welter of forecast information and focus on those variables that are most critical at the current stage of the business cycle. For Wesley Clair Mitchell and his disciples at the National Bureau of Economic Research, this led to a detailed examination of underlying endogenous forces.

Increasingly since World War II, forecasters have augmented this endogenous information network with a myriad of domestically related exogenous variables—for example, measures of monetary and fiscal policy, information about planned labor strikes, and changes in the domestic price controls. Since the Great Recession, however, forecasters have had to add yet another tier of exogenous factors—namely, those related to international economic and political conditions. Thus, the forecaster's realm, which was originally built upon analytical models of endogenous processes, has been expanded by a host of noneconometric and highly subjective assessments concerning a wide range of exogenous factors in both the domestic and international spheres. Affirming this change in the tenor of the forecaster's analytical procedures are Professor Eckstein's twelve discoveries and rediscoveries, drawn from the Great Recession:

1. The economy is vulnerable to shocks, and they are an important source of business-cycle fluctuations.
2. There are various mechanisms in the private economy that amplify the impacts of shocks and convert them into business cycles.
3. The financial condition of the country has deteriorated because of the history of instability.
4. Consumer expectations are volatile and inflation-sensitive.
5. Business expectations can be wrong, and occasional periods of massive error are a major factor in the business cycle.
6. The stability of government institutions does matter to the economy.
7. Extreme fluctuations in monetary policy have accentuated the economy's instability.
8. But no simple rule is sufficient to guide monetary policy.
9. The Keynesian theory of fiscal policy received strong support during the Great Recession.
10. Government expenditures proved a far less effective instrument than tax reduction.
11. Price and wage controls produce little benefit in peacetime, cannot survive for long, and can do considerable harm.
12. The nature of the world economic system matters keenly to the United States, and the changes it is now undergoing are of great importance to our own prosperity.[34]

[34]Eckstein, *Recession*, pp. 146–50.

Each of these discoveries and rediscoveries has a direct effect on one's ability to accurately forecast at both the macroeconomic and microeconomic levels, and you should try to categorize these findings in terms of monetary and fiscal policy, changes in endogenous mechanisms, alterations in society's institutional structure or social fabric, or shifts in the transmission mechanism of exogenous shocks. The specific effect on forecasting techniques will be discussed later, but first consider some more general econometric implications of Professor Eckstein's discoveries.

The simple econometric model examined earlier in this chapter was constructed by Prof. Daniel Suits as a pedagogical or teaching device, but it is also crudely illustrative of what Eckstein has called the first generation of econometric models, which were designed to explain the major expenditure aggregates and were built in the 1940s and 1950s.[35] The second-generation models, of which the 1974 DRI model is representative, were larger in absolute size (150 to 300 equations) and theoretical complexity, and they were expanded to mesh with such techniques as input-output analysis. The third-generation models might be labeled post–Great-Recession models, since they were built in the wake of the second generation's inability to predict the economic events of 1974–75. As shown in Figure 3-1, the 1974 or second-generation model was not able to accurately track the economy in 1974 and 1975, whereas the 1975 or third-generation model was. The latest generation approaches 900 equations in size, and improvements may be traced to seven major innovations:

1. Modeling-sector flows of funds, balance sheets, and financial real interactions
2. Stage-of-processing approach to prices
3. More elaborate modeling of supply conditions, and their effects on prices and inventory behavior
4. Inventory behavior and the inventory-production price loop
5. Modeling expectations and error
6. Modeling consumer confidence and uncertainty
7. A disaggregated foreign-trade sector[36]

Compare this list of innovations with Eckstein's list of twelve discoveries. Because of the instability in the financial sector (discoveries 2, 3, and 7 in the prior list) it was necessary to model the key financial parameters (innovation number 1) contained in each sector's balance sheet. For example, the amount of consumer debt for installment purchases is a critical balance-sheet item related to future durable expenditures by households, just as the relative quantity of short- to long-term debt in the business sector is an important determinant of capital spending. The expanded modeling of supply-side conditions (innovation 3) is a direct response to the first- and second-generation models' inordinate focus on demand estimation and the resulting failure to

[35]Eckstein, *Recession*, p. 186.
[36]Eckstein, *Recession*, pp. 191–99.

consider exogenous supply-side shocks (discoveries 1, 11, and 12). Similarly, innovations 5 and 6 are an attempt to quantify the volatility of both consumer and business expectations (discoveries 4 and 5).

THE GREAT RECESSION'S LEGACY: MICROECONOMIC FORECAST IMPLICATIONS

Now that we have extensively documented the failure of the large-scale, second-generation models (as well as the less statistical approaches in use prior to 1975) in terms of such basic forecast parameters as real GNP, the GNP deflator, and unemployment, how does this affect the industrial and company-level forecaster and forecasts? Projected revenue for an individual company is derived in a series of steps that begin with GNP, move to industrial production, and arrive at company-level demand. If, as we have documented for the Great Recession, the initial macroeconomic outlook has been misdiagnosed in terms of such basic forecast parameters as growth rates for real GNP and the GNP deflator, then the derivative projections of company volume and revenue are also likely to be misleading. Regardless of the time and effort that has gone into the development of company-level forecasts, the forecast output will be no better than the accuracy of the macroeconomic projections it builds upon.

Although individual businesses represent the microeconomic dimension of business activity, an economic forecast for a firm is still a disaggregated macroeconomic forecast developed from a *top-down* forecasting methodology. For example, in the case of the automotive sector, the linkages go from GNP to personal consumption expenditures for automobiles; from automobile expenditures to domestic and foreign new-car production; from domestic production to regional production in Michigan, Missouri, and California; and from regional car production to company-level forecasts.

In attempting to set out the logical steps to be followed in disaggregating from GNP projections to industry and company estimates, we have been using a simple paradigm or model of top-down economic analysis. We could have reasoned just as cogently for a bottom-up paradigm involving successive aggregation from company to industry to economy, or from city to region to economy. Because the economic system is simultaneous, any of the paradigms above may be looked upon as artificial attempts to analyze one level of economic activity while holding the other dimensions constant. Given the present state of forecasting technology, however, a top-down approach realistically meshes with the capability of econometric forecasting models.

Obviously, if the scale of econometric forecasting models was grandiose enough, you would not have to settle for a sparse set of industry forecast statistics. Rather, these would be augmented by projections of domestic unit sales by company, by state, and by Standard Metropolitan Statistical Area

(SMSA). But even though all the major commercial econometric models are producing greater and greater industrial disaggregation by commodity (that is, decomposing output statistics into finer subcategories), interregional disaggregation (state, city, SMSA) of commodity production and consumption is in a state of relative infancy. True, you can apply last year's interregional ratios (for example, California automobile production as a percent of a domestic output) to this year's aggregate production to split out estimates of this year's regional production, but this is not comparable to a fully simultaneous econometric system that models the economic interaction between aggregate and interregional sectors.

It is the absence of a fully developed theoretical model of aggregate and interregional interaction that has increasingly led company forecasters to adopt a variety of pragmatic empirical approaches in an attempt to bridge the gap from macroeconomic projections to microeconomic scenarios. In the ensuing chapters, these methods will be laid out so that you can both grasp the procedure and wrestle with the actual application. Chapter 4 attempts to fill in any gaps in your prior statistical training related to the decomposition of time-series data. Subsequent chapters explore the use of simple-regression, multiple-regression, and autoregressive techniques in bridging the chasm from total to disaggregated projections. These forecasting procedures can be adapted to extremely short-run projects, such as developing estimates of next month's raw-material requirements at a manufacturing company, a one-year projection for labor requirements at an employment agency, a two-year budget review, or a ten-year outlook for capacity planning. Although all these forecast projects are unique in scope and duration, they can be approached consistently and intelligently if you keep in mind the conceptual paradigm of top-down forecasting and the experiences of the forecasting profession in the Great Recession of 1974–75.

QUESTIONS FOR DISCUSSION AND ANALYSIS

1. In Table 3-3, we compared the January 1974 outlooks for DRI, "Roundup," and the CEA. Using the January 1974 issue of the *Business Conditions Digest* (*BCD*), would you have predicted a recession? A complete answer to this question requires that you assimilate the data in a manner similar to the example given in Chapter 2, using the December 1979 issue of the *BCD*. We now know the upper turning point took place in November 1973, but would you have been able to draw such a conclusion using the January 1974 issue of the *BCD*? Did the indicators give adequate advance warning? Was the severity of the Great Recession forecastable?

2. Using the January 1975 issue of the *BCD*, would you have been willing to forecast a lower turning point (trough) in March? What leading-indicator series most clearly signaled an imminent upturn? Which leading indicators were providing

mixed or contradictory signals? With the advantage of historical hindsight, can you explain why some of the leading indicators were still signaling a continued recession?

3. Whether forecasting for the entire economy, an industry, or an individual company, you must be aware of the relationship between sales and inventories. Collect monthly data for the two-year period centered on the 1973 upper turning point for time-series numbers 70 (manufacturing and trade inventories, constant dollars), 71 (manufacturing and trade inventories, current dollars), 57 (manufacturing and trade sales, constant dollars), 56 (manufacturing and trade sales, current dollars), 52 (personal income, constant dollars), and 223 (personal income, current dollars). Calculate the following information:
   a. Annualized rates of change for each series
   b. Inventory-to-sales ratios for both current-dollar and constant-dollar measures
   c. The ratio of current- (constant-) dollar sales to current- (constant-) dollar personal income
   d. The ratio of current- (constant-) dollar inventories to current- (constant-) dollar personal income
   Present the data in tabular form and prepare an analysis of the effect of the 1973 downturn on sales and inventories.

4. The management of a steel company has asked you to select one or more economic time series that can be used as leading indicators for steel shipments. What economic measures would you consider? How well did your indicators perform in the Great Recession? Do they currently indicate a likely turning point in steel shipments?

5. Resolve Suits's four-equation model assuming government expenditures of $21 rather than $20. What is the numerical value of the Keynesian expenditure multiplier? Is the tax yield (T) endogenous or exogenous? Is this realistic? Resolve the model using alternative values of $20 and $21 for government expenditures in conjunction with a marginal tax rate of 0.3 (in place of 0.2). Explain your findings.

6. Explain how a company-level forecaster could make use of Professor Dewald's econometric model in Table 3-1. That is, how might the forecast output be used to complement the conclusions derived from a leading-indicator projection?

7. Examine the third equation in Dewald's model, which focuses on anticipated price change ($\dot{P}_t^a$). What is the value of such an equation to a purchasing agent wrestling with the decision of whether to make purchase commitments now or defer them to the future? What exogenous events might distort the predictive ability of this equation?

8. Reexamine Professor Eckstein's twelve discoveries and rediscoveries listed in Chapter 3. Write a short paragraph amplifying each of these points; draw upon events surrounding the Great Recession or upon contemporary events in the economy.

9. Locate two forecasts prepared in January 1974 by other prominent forecasters. Were these projections any more prescient than those of DRI, "Roundup," or the CEA?

10. What forecasting lessons/insights have you drawn from the events surrounding the Great Recession?

REFERENCES FOR FURTHER STUDY

Christ, Carl F., "Judging the Performance of Econometric Models of the U.S. Economy," *International Economic Review*, Vol. 16, No. 1 (February 1975), 54–74.

Cole, A. H., "Statistical Background of the Crisis of 1857," *Review of Economic Statistics*, November 1930, pp. 170–80.

Fels, Rendigs, and C. Elton Hinshaw, *Forecasting and Recognizing Business Cycle Turning Points.* New York: National Bureau of Economic Research, 1968.

Pindyck, Robert S., and Daniel L. Rubinfeld, *Econometric Models and Economic Forecasts.* New York: McGraw-Hill, 1976.

Rezneck, S., "Distress, Relief, and Discontent in the United States during the Depression of 1873–78," *Journal of Political Economy*, December 1950, pp. 494–512.

Roose, K.D., "The Recession of 1937–38," *Journal of Political Economy*, June 1948, pp. 239–48.

"The Current Recession in Perspective," *Federal Reserve Bulletin*, May 1975, pp. 273–79.

CLASSICAL TIME-SERIES DECOMPOSITION

PART II

4

Forecasting, Time-Series Data Analysis, and Forecast Evaluation

INTRODUCTION

Given the macroeconomic overview presented in Chapters 1 through 3 of the forces shaping the environment of the business sector, it is now time to turn to the actual techniques employed by forecasters to analyze time-series data, develop projections, and evaluate the results. Whereas Chapters 2 and 3 provided an in-depth analysis of the cyclical volatility of the business sector, this chapter isolates the statistical techniques used to quantify trend, seasonal, cyclical, and irregular forces in specific data series. Thus, the emphasis is shifted to the microeconomic factors that enter into forecasting at the industry and company levels.

FORECASTING AND FORECASTING TECHNIQUES

OBJECTIVES OF FORECASTING MODELS

The first objective in constructing business forecasting models is to improve managerial decision making by organizing and analyzing existing knowledge so as to reduce uncertainty. Second, a forecasting model must be capable of simulating the consequences of uncertain future events and quantifying the effects of alternative management decisions. Thus, the central problem facing the practicing forecaster is how to most effectively utilize current data so as to provide maximum benefit to managers faced with decisions linked to all dimensions of company profit.

Business forecasts should be viewed as the end result of an evolutionary process: First, the problem to be solved by the forecaster must be identified; second, provision must be made to obtain the data relevant to the problem; third, the appropriate forecasting method must be determined; and fourth, the results of the forecast must be interpreted and integrated into the decision-making process.

CLASSIFICATION OF FORECASTING TECHNIQUES

The seemingly endless variety of situations in which forecasts are prepared has dictated the evolution of an equally divergent collection of techniques, which can be grouped into two general categories—qualitative and quantitative. Qualitative techniques, sometimes referred to as judgmental, nonstatistical, nonscientific, or technological methods, generally rely on expert opinion. Since these techniques require little or no statistical analysis of historical data, experts are called upon to present intuitive judgments and to assign subjective probabilities to the alternative scenarios. The more common of these approaches make use of the Delphi Method, decision matrices, S-curves, game theory, and systems analysis.

This text concentrates on the second of these two forecasting approaches—namely, the quantitative or statistical approach—because the basic techniques are more readily learned and because the qualitative approach cannot be formalized into a systematic series of steps. Although expert opinion and judgment are invaluable, they represent the end result of years of study and on-the-job training, which cannot be duplicated in a textbook.

Fortunately, the quantitative approach can be grasped quickly and does provide the forecaster with objective results. To utilize this approach, you must have a historical data bank that furnishes a "chronological snapshot" of economic activity in the form of time-series data—weekly sales, monthly production, quarterly profits, annual costs of production, and so forth. Thus, no matter how complex or sophisticated, all quantitative techniques are based on the assumption of constancy or historical continuity. The underlying economic patterns in the historical data file must continue into the future. This need not imply that economic activity is static or unchanging, but it does assume that the pattern or structure of institutional relationships that exists in the historical data continues into the future. This process of projecting historical patterns is referred to as *extrapolation*.

We can further subdivide the various quantitative forecasting methods into *time-series* and *regression* techniques. This choice of titles, while commonplace, is unfortunate, since it seems to imply that only the former category utilizes time-series data. In fact, both techniques rely on time-series data when utilized for purposes of forecasting. Time-series models, or, more correctly, autoregressive models, forecast future values of a variable based entirely on the historical observations of that variable. For example, a simple time-series model for retail sales might be formulated as:

$$RS_{t+1} = c_0 + c_1 RS_t + c_2 RS_{t-1} \qquad (4\text{-}1)$$

RS_t refers to retail sales in the current period, RS_{t-1} to last period's sales, and RS_{t+1} to sales in the next period. All autoregressive time-series models, from simple moving averages to advanced Box-Jenkins techniques, are extensions of equation (4-1). Since the forecast of retail sales is based solely on historical observations, this type of model is most satisfactory when cyclical conditions are expected to remain the same. Our simple model may indeed provide a reliable forecast of retail sales, but it is of little value in predicting the sales effect of alternative prices, management policies, or advertising schemes.

Regression or causal models are based on insights from economic theory. For example, in place of the autoregressive model for retail sales in equation (4-1), a regression model might take the form:

$$RS_t = b_0 + b_1 DI_t + b_2 CPI_t \qquad (4\text{-}2)$$

Here, retail sales in the current period (RS_t) are linked to disposable income (DI_t) and the current value of the consumer price index (CPI_t). The goal in fitting a regression equation is to find the exact form of the relationship between sales, income, and prices—that is, we want to derive estimates of the regression coefficients (b_0, b_1, b_2) that embody the historical or structural relationship among the three variables. A retail sales model similar to equation (4-2) can be used to provide management with, say, an estimate of the change in sales resulting from a change in prices. The variable to be estimated, retail sales, is referred to as the dependent variable, and the other variables (disposable income and prices) are called independent or causal variables.

TECHNIQUE SELECTION

Proper selection of a forecasting technique is a two-step process. In addition to a working knowledge of the available forecast methodologies, a selection procedure must encompass the following factors:

1. The time frame
2. Data patterns
3. Costs
4. Desired accuracy
5. Availability of data
6. Ease of implementation
7. Accuracy and reliability of technique

Time frame or *time horizon* refers to the length of time into the future for which the forecast is desired. Typically, the forecaster is interested in one of the following time frames:

Immediate term—less than one month
Short term—one to six months
Intermediate term—six months to two years
Long term—longer than two years

For one firm, a two-year period may be long term, whereas to another firm, it may be a short or intermediate term. Additionally, the meaning of these time frames depends upon the individual decision maker's position in the firm. Thus, to a production-line supervisor, immediate-term planning may mean an hour or day and long-term a six-month time horizon. Conversely, for the board of directors or the chief executive officer, six-month forecasts may be immediate term.

Additionally, the appropriate time frame depends upon which component of the time series decision makers deem to be significant. Long-term forecasts tend to be related to trend factors such as the demand for the product, the general economic and political environment, technological change, and the competitive structure of the industry. Thus, one might develop a ten-year projection of regional demand patterns that are to be used to determine where warehouses are to be constructed. Intermediate-term forecasts are tied to the cyclical factor and focus on the allocation of resources among the competing activities within a firm; they are used to revise long-term plans in the light of cyclical developments. Thus, the marketing department is interested in the cyclical nature of sales and the proper pricing strategy. Similarly, the production department needs cost estimates, budget allocations, and cyclical employment forecasts. Financial decision makers must plan cash flows over the course of the business cycle.

Short-term forecasts are required to deal with seasonality and minor cyclical variations. Within a six-month period, turning points can occur, but monthly projections are dominated by seasonal characteristics. Short-term marketing forecasts might involve the evaluation of a promotional campaign or a price change. Production departments must have forecasts of seasonal demand patterns to schedule work shifts. Immediate-term forecasts are generally concerned with the irregular variations in time-series data. Thus, in the immediate term, management might be interested in forecasting daily inventory expenses, or in allocating its fleet of trucks to various sectors of the market area.

In general, the longer the time frame, the more useful regression models become and the less valuable are autoregressive schemes. In part, this is due to the much more critical role that the assumption of constancy plays in autoregressive models. As the time horizon lengthens, uncertainty increases, as does the need for a theoretical foundation.

Technique selection is affected by the pattern of the data. Quite frequently, this pattern is representative of characteristics inherent in the activity being studied. The relation between the data pattern and the time frame becomes obvious when one notes that trend patterns are long-term tendencies, but seasonal variation represents data patterns that repeat themselves within one year. Regression methods can deal with virtually all patterns that can be identified, but stationary or horizontal data patterns present problems. Autoregressive schemes, on the other hand, are better adapted to stationary and random variations.

Technique selection is also influenced by the costs associated with each of the forecasting alternatives. Specifically, there are three types of costs that warrant consideration. First, there is the cost associated with formulating and developing the forecasting model. Included in this category would be items such as the labor cost for expert advice in model building, the costs of writing and testing the necessary computer programs, and the cost of internal data generation for use in the model. Regression models must be constructed by people who have expertise in the areas of economic theory and statistical estimation. Further, firm- and industry-level regression models must often be augmented by commercial forecast services. Autoregressive schemes have development costs of from several hundred dollars for simple moving averages and exponential smoothing methods to several thousand dollars for Box-Jenkins and adaptive filtering techniques.

Second, the costs of collecting and storing the necessary data must be recognized. The major items here are the costs of storing the model and the data. On balance, autoregressive schemes result in larger data-storage costs. Additionally, program-storage costs tend to range from minimal in the simple schemes to extensive in the case of Box-Jenkins. Regression models involve somewhat more sophisticated computer programs and hence imply higher costs. Data-storage costs for regression models depend on the complexity of the system being constructed.

The third category is the cost of simulating alternative scenarios, updating the model, and selecting the appropriate parameters. Most of this cost is for computer time. Regression models tend to have the advantage here, because autoregressive techniques require constant updating and experimentation toward selection of the best smoothing parameters.

The concept of desired accuracy has many facets; however, it is virtually impossible to set forth its dimensions until the forecaster has closely evaluated the project under consideration. For example, in many situations a rough approximation of future trend patterns will provide sufficiently accurate projections. When a major television network negotiates an advertising contract for a future sporting event, the company purchasing the advertising time may be satisfied with a simple trend estimate of the number of households that will hear the commercial. At the other extreme, a forecast of future demand for electricity must be very refined since the cost of building an excessively large nuclear plant will be borne by utility customers. Likewise, an underestimate of electricity demand will result in inadequate capacity and a potential power shortage. For a utility, therefore, the desired degree of accuracy is tied directly to the negative consequences arising from both underestimates and overestimates. Whether a specific economic forecast turns out to be too high or too low is a matter of concern, but it is equally important that the theoretical premises upon which the numerical estimate is based are clearly articulated by the forecaster when he or she selects a forecasting technique.

Desired accuracy also incorporates the concepts of timeliness and sensitivity. Since a forecaster must meet the deadlines set by the decision maker, accuracy must be related to availability. The sensitivity of the forecast to random disturbances must also be considered since some forecasting techniques are easily influenced by temporary fluctuations. For example, if a company utilizes a naive model in which next month's sales are estimated to exceed last month's sales by a constant growth factor, a temporary one month spurt or drop in sales will generate distorted estimates of future sales. Desired accuracy is never simply a matter of specifying a set percentage, because all of the above factors act to constrain the actual level of achievable accuracy.

The availability of data may further complicate the selection of a technique. In particular, the availability of accurate, consistent, and timely historical data is a prerequisite for any model. Generally, the analyst relies upon data that have previously been collected in an attempt to minimize data-collection costs. Data that are outdated or subject to significant revisions may dictate the elimination of certain techniques.

Ease of implementation and understanding become significant factors because managerial decisions are based on forecast output, and decision makers must be able to comprehend the projections yielded by alternative techniques. It is imperative, therefore, that the forecaster fully comprehend the technique selected in order to present the forecast to management in a readily understandable format, as well as to evoke an understanding by management of the probabilistic nature of many forecasts.

Ultimately, the majority of decisions regarding technique selection hinges on the ability of the various methods to forecast accurately. Accuracy includes not only forecast reliability, but also adherence to the conceptual assumptions underlying the technique. In addition to several basic measures of accuracy presented in this chapter, some of the more commonly used measures will be presented in later chapters in conjunction with actual forecasting models. The appraisal of forecast accuracy remains, however, a topic of controversy.

TIME-SERIES ANALYSIS

We can begin our discussion by examining a company's production data for cameras. Recently, production has been approaching capacity, and the question facing management is: Should the production facilities be expanded? The engineering department has provided the figures in Table 4-1. The distinguishing feature of such data is that they consist of a sequence or ordering of observations on a particular variable, camera production, recorded over successive increments of time. Given these data, management might be interested in answers to some or all of the following questions:

1. When can we expect the demands on production capacity to be highest or lowest?
2. Under what economic circumstances will these highs and lows occur?
3. Are we going to have sufficient working capital to finance finished inventories, work in process, and accounts receivable during peak periods?
4. What contingency plans must be made in the case of a prolonged shutdown of one of our plants?
5. What is our estimate of the likely occurrence, timing, and severity of a recession?

The observations recorded in Table 4-1 are, in reality, a composite of a number of factors that must be disentangled prior to the development of meaningful forecasts. Classical time-series analysis attempts to segregate and analyze these factors in a systematic fashion. This process involves not only decomposition into component parts but also an analysis of the manner in which these forces interact.

The most widely relied upon model for time-series data is:

$$Y_t = T_t \cdot C_t \cdot S_t \cdot I_t \qquad (4\text{-}3)$$

The practical significance of this model is that it identifies the integral components of many economic time series. Further, equation (4-3) illustrates the fact

Table 4-1 Production of cameras

Year	Quarter	Camera Production (Millions)
1975	1	.740
	2	.959
	3	.841
	4	1.131
1976	1	1.242
	2	1.368
	3	.976
	4	1.306
1977	1	1.373
	2	1.534
	3	.976
	4	1.378
1978	1	1.325
	2	1.510
	3	1.057
	4	1.394

that these components interact in a multiplicative fashion. The components of this model are:

Y_t = the observed value of the series in period t

T_t = trend component in period t

C_t = cyclical component in period t

S_t = seasonal component in period t

I_t = random component in period t

Implicit in the multiplicative model is the assumption that percentage changes best describe the observed fluctuations in the data, a fact that approximates reality in a great number of economic activities. In addition to the multiplicative model, an alternative additive formulation is available:

$$Y_t = T_t + C_t + S_t + I_t \qquad (4\text{-}4)$$

Before proceeding, let us repeat what each of these components represents and how they all fit into the forecasting process. The trend component, T_t, is the general upward or downward tendency that characterizes all economic activity in a dynamic economy and represents the long-run growth or decline in time-measured economic phenomena. From a theoretical standpoint, this growth or decline reflects permanent shifts in either supply-side factors or demand-side determinants. A representative listing of these factors would be:

Changes in consumer preferences
Changes in income
Population shifts
Technological advances/constraints
Industrial expansion
Changes in tax policies

Cyclical fluctuations, C_t, in time-series data are nonperiodic, recurring oscillations around a long-run trend. As documented in Chapters 2 and 3, these fluctuations arise from endogenous forces and exogenous shocks.

Seasonal variation, S_t, occurs within a year and repeats (although not necessarily in an exact manner) in the following year. Seasonal variation may be related to noneconomic factors such as customs (spring purchases), holidays, and weather, or to institutional factors such as model-year changes in the automobile industry and inventory sales in anticipation of tax deadlines.

Random variation, I_t, is the erratic and irregular movement in time-series data that is left over after we have isolated the seasonal, cyclical, and trend components. It is the residual effect of a myriad of unpredictable disturbances, such as strikes, hurricanes, or foreign government's actions.

This process of isolating time-series components is commonly referred to as the decomposition of a time series. In this chapter, we are primarily interested in isolating the trend (T_t) and seasonal (S_t) components. We will focus on the statistical process involved in constructing stationary (detrended data) and the steps involved in moving from raw to seasonally adjusted data. Although this decomposition process is somewhat tedious, an understanding of the historical movements of a time series is a necessary prerequisite to forecasting. In fact, an understanding of why a specific activity behaved as it did sharpens our insight into its future behavior.

SEASONAL ADJUSTMENT

There are many alternative approaches to decomposing any set of time-series data, but all of them strive to isolate trend, seasonal, and cyclical factors, with the irregular factor left as a residual. Empirically, these procedures consist of first removing seasonality, then trend, and finally cyclical influences. The most relied-upon decomposition method has been developed by the Census Bureau and is known as the Census II or X-11 method. This section illustrates, as simply as possible, the concepts involved in decomposition of time-series data. Upon completion of the simplified explanation, a scaled-down version of the census technique will be presented. Although it is possible to prepare forecasts with these techniques, their actual use in developing projections will be presented in later chapters.

Identification and isolation of seasonal fluctuations are a necessary first step in utilizing time-series data for forecasting. The basic assumption underlying isolation of seasonal forces is that there is a repetitive pattern in the data. Further, it assumes that this pattern repeats in cycles, each of which is the same number of periods (quarters, months, weeks). If an extended time series of, say, quarterly data exhibits a seasonal pattern, the series value in each quarter will be inflated or deflated by this factor. For example, retail sales are typically very high in the fourth quarter, owing to the Christmas rush, and very low in the first quarter.

Patterns similar to this are estimated via a set of index numbers. These index numbers measure the percentage of the average value that typically occurs in that period. Thus, if the cycle has a length of four periods (a quarterly time series) before it repeats, seasonal analysis will generate four index numbers. Each of these numbers measures the relation between a specific quarter and the average quarter. A value of 100 implies that this quarter tends to be equal to the average quarter; a value of 115 implies that this quarter is typically 15 percent above average; and conversely, a value of 90 percent implies that the quarter under consideration is 10 percent below the average quarter. Thus, the purpose of seasonally adjusting time-series data is to compensate for the effect of seasonality.

The seasonal patterns in the airline industry are illustrated in Figure 4-1 and Table 4-2. Looking at the original or raw data, notice that the first-quarter travel via airlines is often lower than that in the other quarters of the same year, and that the third quarter is consistently the highest-volume quarter within a given year. This is certainly suggestive of a strong seasonal pattern. Although seasonal patterns can occur within a week or day (for example, weekly utility demand or peak demand within a day for electricity), this chapter concentrates on seasonal cycles over a one-year span. The techniques presented here can be extended to any time period. Thus, the goal is to illustrate a procedure whereby a time series similar to that pictured in Figure 4-1 can be seasonally adjusted.

One of the most popular seasonal techniques is the ratio-to-moving-average method. The raw data in column 1 of Table 4-2 contain four components: T, C, S, and I. To isolate the first two components ($T \cdot C$), calculate the four-quarter moving average shown in column 4. Columns 2 and 3 are simply intermediate steps in the derivation of the moving average. Since each moving average spans an entire year, the seasonal and irregular ($S \cdot I$) factors have been averaged or smoothed out of the data. If we now divide the raw data (column 1) by the moving average (column 4), we obtain the seasonal and irregular factors inherent in the series. To obtain the first-quarter index, average all first-quarter raw seasonals. The final seasonal index values are listed in column 6 of Table 4-2.

A specific illustration will serve to clarify this seemingly complex process. Let us focus our attention on the first quarter of 1970. Actual revenue passenger miles flown (column 1) were 24.49 million, whereas the four-quarter moving average (column 4) was 25.93.

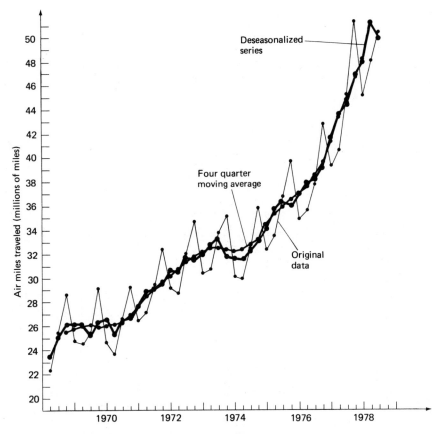

Figure 4-1 Passenger Air Miles Traveled (Millions)

Source: *Survey of Current Business*

An alternate, one-step procedure (circumventing columns 2 and 3) can be used:

Moving average for 1970:1

$$= \frac{(\tfrac{1}{2})(1969:3) + (1969:4) + (1970:1) + (1970:2) + (\tfrac{1}{2})(1970:3)}{4}$$

$$= \frac{(.5)(28.78) + (24.70) + (24.49) + (25.54) + (.5)(29.23)}{4}$$

$$= 25.93 \text{ million passenger miles} \tag{4-5}$$

The four-quarter moving averages are plotted along with the actual data in Figure 4-1. Since the moving average eliminates the seasonal and irregular components, these factors $(S \cdot I)$ were responsible for the fact that the actual value (24.49) was below the four-quarter moving average. Similarly, when we

Table 4-2 Ratio to moving average and seasonal adjustment for quarterly revenue passenger miles for airlines

Date		(1) Revenue Passenger Miles (Millions)	(2) Four-Quarter Moving Total	(3) Sum of Two Successive Four-Quarter Totals	(4) Four-Quarter Moving Average	(5) Original Series as a Percent of Moving Average	(6) Seasonal Index	(7) Deseasonalized Series
1969	I	22.20	—	—	—	—	94.20	23.57
	II	25.47	101.15	—	—	—	101.23	25.16
	III	28.78	103.44	204.59	25.58	112.51	109.92	26.18
	IV	24.70	103.51	206.95	25.87	95.48	94.65	26.10
1970	I	24.49	103.96	207.47	25.93	94.45	94.20	26.00
	II	25.54	103.58	207.54	25.95	98.42	101.23	25.23
	III	29.23	102.98	206.56	25.83	113.16	109.92	26.59
	IV	24.32	104.28	207.26	25.91	93.86	94.65	25.69
1971	I	23.89	104.41	208.69	26.09	91.57	94.20	25.36
	II	26.84	106.39	210.80	26.35	101.86	101.23	26.51
	III	29.36	109.59	215.98	27.00	108.74	109.92	26.71
	IV	26.30	112.17	221.76	27.72	94.88	94.65	27.79
1972	I	27.09	115.24	227.41	28.43	95.29	94.20	28.76
	II	29.42	118.11	233.35	29.17	100.86	101.23	29.06
	III	32.43	119.88	237.99	29.75	109.01	109.92	29.50
	IV	29.17	122.56	242.44	30.30	96.27	94.65	30.82
1973	I	28.86	124.99	247.55	30.94	93.28	94.20	30.64
	II	32.10	126.30	251.29	31.41	102.20	101.23	31.70
	III	34.86	128.31	254.61	31.83	109.52	109.92	31.71
	IV	30.48	129.96	258.27	32.28	94.42	94.65	32.20
1974	I	30.87	130.21	260.17	32.52	94.93	94.20	32.77
	II	33.75	129.84	260.05	32.51	103.81	101.23	33.34
	III	35.11	128.92	258.76	32.34	108.57	109.92	31.94
	IV	30.11	127.81	256.73	32.09	93.83	94.65	31.81

Table 4-2 (continued)

Date		(1) Revenue Passenger Miles (Millions)	(2) Four- Quarter Moving Total	(3) Sum of Two Successive Four-Quarter Totals	(4) Four- Quarter Moving Average	(5) Original Series as a Percent of Moving Average	(6) Seasonal Index	(7) Desea- sonalized Series
1975	I	29.95						31.79
	II	32.64						32.24
	III	36.78	129.48	257.29	32.16	93.13	94.20	33.46
	IV	32.34	131.71	261.19	32.65	99.97	101.23	34.17
1976	I	33.63	135.39	267.10	33.39	110.15	109.92	35.70
	II	36.97	139.72	275.11	34.39	94.04	94.65	36.52
	III	39.71	142.65	282.37	35.30	95.27	94.20	36.13
	IV	34.96	145.27	287.92	36.00	102.69	101.23	36.94
1977	I	35.78	147.42	292.69	36.59	108.53	109.92	37.98
	II	38.59	149.04	296.46	37.06	94.33	94.65	38.12
	III	42.96	152.29	301.33	37.67	94.98	94.20	39.08
	IV	39.27	156.60	308.89	38.61	99.95	101.23	41.49
1978	I	40.77	161.59	318.19	39.77	108.02	109.92	43.28
	II	45.31	168.31	329.90	41.24	95.22	94.65	44.76
	III	51.45	176.80	345.11	43.14	94.51	94.20	46.81
	IV	45.13	182.66	359.46	44.93	100.85	101.23	47.68
1979	I	48.13	190.02	372.68	46.58	110.46	109.92	51.09
	II	50.35	195.06	385.08	48.14	93.75	94.65	49.74
			—	—	—	—	94.20	
			—	—	—	—	101.23	

Source: *Survey of Current Business*

divide the actual value of 24.49 ($T \cdot C \cdot S \cdot I$) by 25.93 ($T \cdot C$), the resulting value of 94.45 percent tells us that seasonal and irregular forces were depressing first-quarter air miles by 5.55 percent. Table 4-3 contains the raw seasonals taken from column 5 of Table 4-2. The value of 94.45 for the first quarter of 1970 reappears as the 1970 entry in the column labeled "Winter" in Table 4-3. The

Table 4-3   Seasonal indices for revenue passenger miles

	Quarter			
Year	Winter	Spring	Summer	Fall
1969	—	—	112.51	95.48
1970	94.45	98.42	113.16	93.86
1971	91.57	101.86	108.74	94.88
1972	95.29	100.86	109.01	96.27
1973	93.28	102.20	109.52	94.42
1974	94.93	103.81	108.57	93.83
1975	93.13	99.97	110.15	94.04
1976	95.27	102.69	108.53	94.33
1977	94.98	99.95	108.02	95.22
1978	94.51	100.85	110.46	93.75
1979	—	—	—	—
Mean	94.16	101.18	109.87	94.61
Final Seasonals	94.20	101.23	109.92	94.65

Source: Table 4-2

irregular component contained in these raw seasonals is averaged out by calculating the mean for each quarter. These means—94.16, 101.18, 109.87, and 94.61—are shown at the bottom of each column in Table 4-3. Since these figures total 399.82, rather than 400.00, the following adjustment for the winter quarter must be made:

$$\frac{400}{399.82} \, 94.16 = 94.20 \tag{4-6}$$

Similar calculations are made for the three remaining quarters. These figures then become the final seasonal factors illustrated in the last row of Table 4-3 and column 6 of Table 4-2. In place of actual air miles of 24.49 million, the seasonally adjusted or deseasonalized magnitude is 26.00 million miles.

Seasonally adjusted figures are listed in column 7 of Table 4-2. Conceptually:

$$\text{Deseasonalized value} = \frac{Y_t}{\text{Seasonal index}}$$

$$= \frac{T_t \cdot C_t \cdot S_t \cdot I_t}{S_t}$$

$$= T_t \cdot C_t \cdot I_t \tag{4-7}$$

For example:

$$\text{Deseasonalized value for winter } 1970 = \frac{24.49 \text{ million miles}}{.9420}$$

$$= 26.00 \text{ million miles} \qquad (4\text{-}8)$$

or:

$$\text{Deseasonalized value for spring } 1979 = \frac{50.35}{1.0123}$$

$$= 49.74 \text{ million miles} \qquad (4\text{-}9)$$

Thus, the final column in Table 4-2 contains the seasonally adjusted series for revenue passenger miles. As before, this series is graphically illustrated in Figure 4-1. The line based on this series contains only the trend, cyclical, and irregular elements of the time series.

In reporting these figures to management, it is common practice to use one of two approaches. The first method would be:

Revenue passenger miles for the second quarter of 1979 were 49.74 million on a seasonally adjusted basis.

The second approach utilizes the concept of a seasonally adjusted annualized rate (SAAR). To obtain the SAAR, simply take the seasonally adjusted quarterly figure and multiply it by a factor of 4. Thus, for the second quarter of 1979, the SAAR is 198.96 (49.74 × 4). In other words, air passenger volume was running at an annualized rate of 198.96 million miles. With a monthly series, take the seasonally adjusted monthly value and multiply by 12 to obtain the seasonally adjusted annualized rate. Alternatively, if you were given an SAAR for a specific quarter, you would derive the quarterly figure by dividing the SAAR by 4. Thus, if SAAR equals 198.96, the quarterly value is 49.74 (198.96/4).

TREND ISOLATION

Even though the primary purpose of seasonally adjusting data is to compensate for seasonality, it is also the starting point for cyclical analysis. In terms of the classical time-series model:

$$\text{Detrended value} = \frac{\text{Deseasonalized } Y_t}{T_t}$$

$$= \frac{T_t \cdot C_t \cdot I_t}{T_t}$$

$$= C_t \cdot I_t \qquad (4\text{-}10)$$

Once the data are deseasonalized and detrended, only the cyclical and irregular components remain.

There are a number of trend patterns that occur frequently in time-series data. The more common patterns are illustrated in Figure 4-2. The trend illustrated in 4-2(a) is linear. Figure 4-2(b) illustrates a growth curve, whereas the S-curve in 4-2(c) corresponds to many industry or firm growth paths in which rapid initial growth is followed by a slowing as the industry or firm matures. The particular shape of the trend in any economic activity can be determined by studying a scatter diagram. The familiar parabolic or second-degree equation is noted in Figure 4-2(d).

A scatter diagram of deseasonalized revenue passenger miles is provided in Figure 4-3, and the scatter indicates a linear trend line. A popular procedure for fitting a linear trend line involves finding an equation of the form:

$$Y_t = a + bX \qquad (4\text{-}11)$$

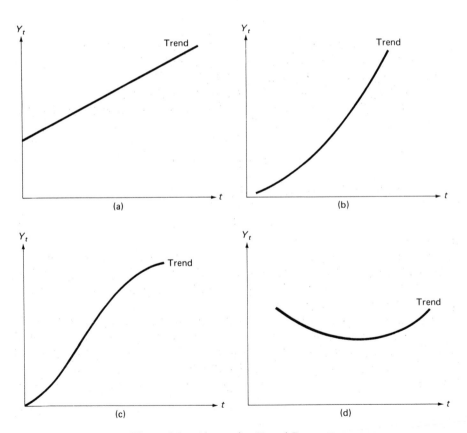

Figure 4-2 Alternative Trend Patterns

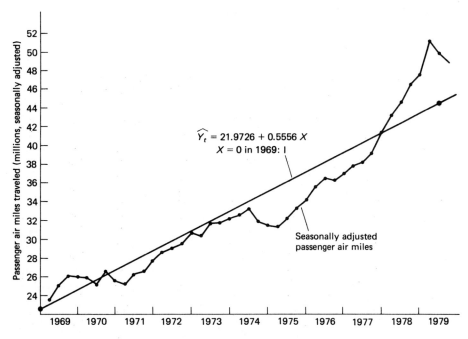

Figure 4-3 Trend Isolation for Air-Miles Traveled

where:

$$Y_t = \text{value of the dependent variable in time period } t$$

$$X = \text{time variable, } X = 0, \text{ in the first quarter of 1969}$$

$$a, b = \text{coefficients to be derived}$$

The coefficients, a and b, are obtained by the method of least squares, which yields the following normal equations:[1]

$$a = \bar{Y}_t - b\bar{X}$$
$$b = \frac{\sum XY_t - n\bar{X}\bar{Y}_t}{\sum X^2 - n\bar{X}^2} \qquad (4\text{-}12)$$

Strictly speaking, this method implies that the passage of time causes the trend, a claim that is dubious. Nonetheless, this approach can be rationalized by arguing that we are using time as a proxy variable for other determining variables (income, preferences, economic growth or similar phenomena).

[1] The proof and exact derivation of these definitions will be presented in the chapter covering regression analysis.

In the case of the revenue passenger miles (column 7 of Table 4-2):

$$\bar{Y}_t = 33.3838 \text{ million miles}$$

$$n = 42 \text{ quarters}$$

$$\sum XY_t = 32{,}178$$

$$\bar{X} = 20.5$$

$$\sum X^2 = 23{,}821$$

Therefore:

$$a = 21.9726$$

$$b = 0.5556$$

$$Y_t = 21.9726 + 0.5556X$$

$$X = 0 \text{ in the first quarter 1969} \tag{4-13}$$

The trend value for the first quarter of 1969 is 21.9726, and passenger revenue miles, Y_t, increase by 0.5556 million miles per quarter. Figure 4-3 presents a comparison of the actual data with the trend line. Once the equation is derived and the origin for X is specified, you can extrapolate by simply picking a future time period, determining X and calculating Y_t from equation (4-13). Thus, the value of Y_t for the first quarter of 1990 would be 68.64 million miles ($X = 84$). Even though it is dangerous to extrapolate a trend far into the future, it is often done.

Not all time series are characterized by linear trend. In many time series, Y_t changes at an increasing or decreasing rate. Industries or firms that are expanding rapidly will typically have exponential trend lines as shown in Figure 4-2(b). In this case, the trend value of Y_t will be increasing at an increasing rate. Figure 4-4 presents a graphical picture of annual operating revenues for Southern Airlines. For these data, a more probable trend equation is:

$$Y_t = ab^x \tag{4-14}$$

Here, b is a positive constant raised to the power x, which measures the number of time periods beyond the base year; and a is a constant multiple. Whenever the series has a negative exponential pattern, the appropriate equation will be:

$$Y_t = ab^{-x} \tag{4-15}$$

where the minus sign indicates that Y_t is decreasing over time.

Taking the logarithm of both sides of equation (4-14), the result is:

$$\log Y_t = \log a + x \log b \tag{4-16}$$

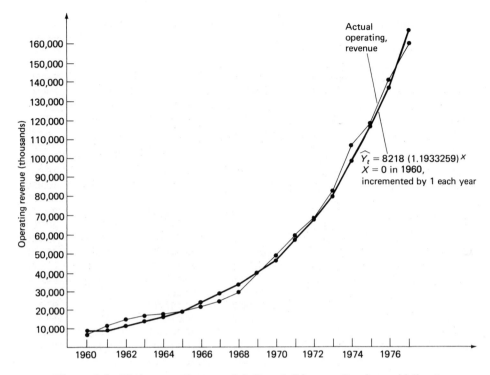

Figure 4-4 Fitting an Exponential Trend Line to Southern Airlines' Operating Revenue

The advantage of this transformation is that the equation is linear in the logs and can be estimated in the following fashion:

$$\log a = \frac{\sum \log Y_t}{n} - \bar{x} \log b$$

$$\log b = \frac{\sum x \log Y_t - \bar{x} \sum \log Y_t}{\sum x^2 - n\bar{x}^2} \quad (4\text{-}17)$$

The procedure for Southern Airlines' operating revenue is illustrated in Table 4-4. Substituting the relevant values into equation (4-17):

$$\log b = \frac{735.9705 - (8.5)(82.209499)}{1785 - (18)(8.5)^2}$$

$$= 0.07675905$$

$$\log a = \frac{82.209499}{18} - (8.5)(0.07675905)$$

$$= 3.9147425 \quad (4\text{-}18)$$

Table 4-4 Exponential trend line computations: Southern Airlines' operating revenue

Year	Years Beyond Base Period x	Operating Revenue Y_t	$\log Y_t$	$x \log Y_t$	x^2	Trend Value
1960	0	7,032	3.487080	0	0	8,218
1961	1	10,718	4.030114	4.030114	1	9,806
1962	2	14,033	4.147150	8.294301	4	11,702
1963	3	15,582	4.192623	12.577870	9	13,964
1964	4	16,835	4.226213	16.904852	16	16,664
1965	5	19,888	4.298591	21.492956	25	19,886
1966	6	22,054	4.343487	26.060924	36	23,730
1967	7	24,256	4.384819	30.693734	49	28,318
1968	8	29,300	4.466868	35.734941	64	33,792
1969	9	37,836	4.577905	41.201147	81	40,325
1970	10	49,447	4.694140	46.941399	100	48,121
1971	11	60,334	4.780562	52.586183	121	57,424
1972	12	68,637	4.836558	58.038700	144	68,525
1973	13	84,609	4.927417	64.056415	169	81,773
1974	14	108,352	5.034837	70.487717	196	97,582
1975	15	117,950	5.071698	76.075469	225	116,447
1976	16	140,167	5.146646	82.346332	256	138,959
1977	17	159,511	5.202791	88.447441	289	165,824
	153	986,541	82.209499	735.970500	1,785	

$n = 18$ $\sum x = 153$ $\sum \log Y_t = 82.209499$

$\bar{x} = 8.5$ $\sum x \log Y_t = 735.9705$ $\sum x^2 = 1,785$

Source: *Moody's Transportation Manual*

The logarithmic trend line becomes:

$$\log Y_t = 3.9147425 + 0.07675905x \qquad (4\text{-}19)$$

The values for a and b may be obtained by taking the antilogs of these coefficients:

$$a = \text{antilog } 3.9147425 = 8,218$$
$$b = \text{antilog } 0.07675905 = 1.1933259$$

Thus, the exponential trend line may be expressed as:

$$Y_t = 8,218(1.1933259)^x$$
$$x = 0 \text{ at } 1960 \qquad (4\text{-}20)$$

In computing trend values, equation (4-19) is commonly used because of computational ease. For example, to find the trend value for 1977, plug

$x = 17$ into equation (4-19):

$$\log Y_{17} = 3.9147425 + .07675905(17)$$
$$= 5.2196474$$
$$Y_{17} = \text{antilog } 5.2196474$$
$$= 165,824 \tag{4-21}$$

This exponential trend line is plotted alongside the actual line in Figure 4-4. Since equation (4-20) assumes a constant growth rate, the value of b, 1.1933259, furnishes the rate of growth. That is, if we subtract 1.00 from this value and convert it to a percentage, it yields a growth rate of 19.33 percent. Southern Airlines' revenue is growing at a long-run trend rate of 19.33 percent. We have not attempted to separate price increases from volume growth.

Another common, although less frequent, trend line is a second-degree polynomial of the form:

$$Y_t = a + bX + cX^2 \tag{4-22}$$

The graph of such an equation takes a shape similar to that in Figure 4-2(d). Since X increases by one unit for each successive time period, the X values can be transformed by subtracting the mean value from each observation. That is, $x = X - \bar{X}$. This simplifies the computations when we simultaneously solve the following three definitional equations for a, b, and c:

$$\sum Y_t = na + c \sum x^2$$
$$\sum x^2 Y_t = a \sum x^2 + c \sum x^4$$
$$b = \frac{\sum xY}{\sum x^2} \tag{4-23}$$

In selection of the appropriate trend line, extensive reliance was placed on visual inspection of a scatter diagram. There is, however, an additional method for assessing the appropriate trend line. The technique of differencing allows one to ascertain whether a linear equation, a second-degree polynomial, or a higher-degree equation should be selected. First-order differences are defined as:

$$\Delta Y_t = Y_t - Y_{t-1} \tag{4-24}$$

If the difference between successive observations is relatively constant, a linear trend is appropriate. This concept of a stationary time series can best be seen by deriving the first differences of the simple time series: 2, 4, 6, 8, 10. The first differences are 2, 2, 2, 2. This new series is stationary, indicating a perfectly linear trend. It is, however, highly unlikely that an actual time series will correspond to this ideal.

First differences for revenue passenger miles are tabulated in Table 4-5. Although the differenced series in the last column contains a cyclical component as well as trend, the data do suggest a linear trend. For a perfectly linear trend line, the first differences can be shown to be equal to the b coefficient in equation (4-11).

Table 4-5 Computation of first differences for revenue passenger miles

Year	Revenue Passenger Miles (Millions)	First Differences	Year	Revenue Passenger Miles (Millions)	First Differences
1966	57	0	1972	118	12
1967	75	18	1973	126	8
1968	88	13	1974	130	4
1969	101	13	1975	132	2
1970	104	3	1976	145	13
1971	106	2	1977	157	12
			1978	183	26

Source: Table 4-2

The second difference of a series is:

$$\Delta^2 Y_t = \Delta Y_t - \Delta Y_{t-1} \tag{4-25}$$

Calculation of second differences is illustrated in Table 4-6. In this instance, the second differences are stationary, indicating that a second-degree polynomial best describes the trend.

Table 4-6 Computation of second differences

Y_t	First Differences	Second Differences
16		
29	13	
46	17	4
67	21	4
92	25	4
121	29	4
154	33	4
191	37	4
232	41	4
277	45	4

CYCLICAL FLUCTUATIONS

To the forecaster, cyclical fluctuations are the most perplexing. Whereas seasonal variation and trend are relatively easy to isolate, cyclical fluctuations are neither periodic nor systematic. Peaks and troughs can occur at any time during the calendar year, and from cycle to cycle the effect on particular sectors varies.

Isolation of the cyclical component can be achieved via a technique similar to that utilized for seasonal segregation:

1. Symbolically, the deseasonalization process can be expressed as:

$$\frac{Y_t}{\text{Seasonal index}} = \frac{T_t \cdot C_t \cdot S_t \cdot I_t}{S_t} = T_t \cdot C_t \cdot I_t \qquad (4\text{-}26)$$

Seasonally adjusted data are shown in column 7 of Table 4-2.

2. Similarly, trend removal is illustrated as:

$$\frac{T_t \cdot C_t \cdot I_t}{T_t} = C_t \cdot I_t \qquad (4\text{-}27)$$

This procedure of isolation is frequently referred to as the residual method.

Separation of the cyclical component for revenue passenger miles is illustrated in Table 4-7. The deseasonalized quarterly data and the trend values derived in the previous sections are detailed in columns 1 and 2, respectively, and the cyclical-irregular component as a percentage of trend is in column 3.

The irregular component can be eliminated via a moving-average calculation that smoothes these irregular variations out of the data. So as to avoid losing too much information in the smoothing process, it is common practice to assign weights to the data. The values selected for the weights in this example were 1, 2, 1—the current quarter has twice the weight of the succeeding and preceding quarters. Thus, for the second quarter of 1971, the weighted moving total of 389 in column 4 is obtained by summing $(96 \cdot 1) + (98 \cdot 2) + (97 \cdot 1)$. The cyclical component is derived by dividing the weighted three-quarter moving total by the sum of the weights. Returning to the second quarter of 1971, the cyclical component value is 97 ($389 \div 4$). The cyclical components are noted in column 5 of Table 4-7. Numbers in excess of 100 imply that cyclical forces are boosting economic activity above trend levels. For example, the trend value for revenue passenger miles for the first quarter of 1979 was 44.23 million; however, the cyclical-component value of 113 implies that because of the influence of the business cycle, the actual value exceeds the long-term trend value by 13 percent. Conversely, a cyclical value of 97 implies that actual passenger miles in the second quarter of 1971 were being depressed by 3 percent because of recessionary forces. One of the principal goals in forecasting is to determine what causal factors can be found to explain these variations around the long-term trend.

Table 4-7 Computational procedure for isolating the cyclical component for revenue passenger miles

Year and Quarter	Deseasonalized Quarterly Revenue Passenger Miles (1)	Trend Y_t (2)	Cyclical-Irregular Component as a Percent of Trend (3)	Weighted Three-Quarter Moving Total (4)	Cyclical Component (5)
1969 I	23.57	21.97	107	—	—
II	25.16	22.53	112	444	111
III	26.18	23.08	113	448	112
IV	26.10	23.64	110	440	110
1970 I	26.00	24.20	107	426	107
II	25.23	24.76	102	416	104
III	26.59	25.31	105	411	103
IV	25.69	25.87	99	399	100
1971 I	25.36	26.43	96	389	97
II	26.51	26.98	98	389	97
III	26.71	27.54	97	391	98
IV	27.79	28.10	99	395	99
1972 I	28.76	28.65	100	398	100
II	29.06	29.21	99	397	99
III	29.50	29.71	99	397	99
IV	30.82	30.32	102	402	100
1973 I	30.64	30.87	99	402	100
II	31.70	31.44	100	398	100
III	31.71	31.99	99	397	97
IV	32.20	32.54	99	396	99
1974 I	32.77	33.11	99	396	99
II	33.34	33.66	99	390	97
III	31.94	34.21	93	386	96
IV	31.81	34.78	91	365	91
1975 I	31.79	35.33	90	361	90
II	32.24	35.89	90	362	90
III	33.46	36.45	92	366	91
IV	34.17	37.00	92	371	93
1976 I	35.70	37.55	95	378	94
II	36.52	38.12	96	380	95
III	36.13	38.67	93	376	94
IV	36.94	39.22	94	376	94
1977 I	37.98	39.78	95	378	94
II	38.12	40.34	94	379	95
III	39.08	40.89	96	386	96
IV	41.49	41.46	100	399	100
1978 I	43.28	42.01	103	411	103
II	44.76	42.56	105	422	105
III	46.81	43.12	109	432	108
IV	47.68	43.60	109	449	112
1979 I	51.09	44.23	115	450	113
II	49.74	44.80	111	—	—

CENSUS METHOD OF DECOMPOSITION

The most commonly utilized method of seasonally adjusting and decomposing a time series was developed by the National Bureau of Economic Research during the 1920s. This technique has been refined and expanded by the Bureau of the Census. For a detailed explanation of this procedure, the reader should consult the Bureau of the Census Technical Paper No. 15, "The X-11 Variant of the Census Method II Seasonal Adjustment Program."[2]

The X-11 version of this program consists of four distinct phases. In the first phase, monthly time-series data are adjusted to account for variations in trading days. Trading-day adjustments are necessary because a given month may not have the same number of working, or trading days from year to year. In certain sectors—for example, retail sales—this factor can significantly alter the observed value in different years. This adjustment process is shown for May retail sales in Memphis, in Table 4-8. The number of actual trading days in May for the years 1966–79 is detailed in column 2. These values are averaged and then divided into each of the individual monthly values to obtain the adjustment factor in column 3. Finally, the actual series in column 1 is divided

Table 4-8 Trading-day adjustment for Memphis retail sales

Year	May Retail Sales (000) (1)	Trading Days (2)	Adjustment Factor[a] (3)	Adjusted Data[b] (4)
1966	$102,307	22	.990354	$103,404
1967	103,290	23	1.035370	99,761
1968	122,132	23	1.035370	117,960
1969	131,366	22	.990354	132,646
1970	135,325	21	.945338	143,150
1971	161.981	21	.945338	171,347
1972	177,492	22	.990354	179,221
1973	204,786	23	1.035370	197,790
1974	222,757	23	1.035370	215,147
1975	228,127	22	.990354	230,349
1976	235,671	21	.945338	249,298
1977	264,922	22	.990354	267,502
1978	296,458	23	1.035370	286,330
1979	323,186	23	1.035370	312,145
Average		22.214286		

[a]Trading days divided by average.
[b]May sales divided by adjustment factor.

[2]U.S. Department of Commerce, Bureau of the Census, "The X-11 Variant of the Census Method II Seasonal Adjustment Program," Technical Paper No. 15, 1967 revision (Washington, D.C.: U.S. Government Printing Office, 1967).

by the adjustment factor to obtain the adjusted series in column 4. Trading-day adjustments are not needed in the case of quarterly data.

The second phase of the X-11 system encompasses preliminary estimates of seasonal factors and adjustments of the raw data for seasonality, using a centered, five-term moving average of the seasonal component for monthly series and a four-term average for quarterly data. A monthly version, for example, would average five Januaries, five Februaries, and so on. In this phase, adjustments can be made for extreme values caused by unusual events. The determination of extreme values is made via standard deviation computations.

In the third phase, the seasonal factors calculated at the beginning of phase 2 are recomputed as a result of the extreme adjustments. The adjustment process is accomplished by utilizing a Spencer 15-point formula.[3] Additionally, the trend and cyclical components are estimated via a centered moving average of the original series. The X-11 version also provides the analyst with a forecast of the seasonal factors one year into the future.

The final phase of the census method generates summary statistics that can be utilized by the analyst to determine how successfully the technique has isolated the seasonal factors and to develop future estimates of the trend-cycle factor. Appendix A contains a computer printout of the output from the census program for seasonal adjustment for retail sales in Memphis.

FORECASTS AND FORECAST ACCURACY

CONCEPT OF A FORECAST

A forecast or prediction can be defined as a statement concerning future events. Forecasts are made because organizations must have information regarding the occurrence of future economic events. Even though these future events are unknown, explicit assumptions about future activity levels enter into present decisions. For example, a manager at a steel factory may be interested in obtaining automobile sales forecasts for the next six months so as to plan for the needed volume of specialty steel products. A government planner wants to determine the potential effect of a policy shift (more or less taxes) on the economy prior to its actual implementation. Financial managers require cash-flow forecasts in order to arrange short-term financing. The president of a university needs enrollment projections so as to plan staffing requirements.

Forecasts may be either put forth in the form of a single number or stated over a range as an interval estimate. Unfortunately, point forecasts have a tendency to become accepted as certain because they are stated in a definitive fashion: *Next year, we project university enrollment of* 22,598 *students.* Interval forecasts, however, offer a range of values within which the true value of the

---

[3]Census Bureau, "The X-11 Variant."

variable is apt to fall: *Next year, university enrollment should be between 22,000 and 23,000 students.* In this case, *should be* might be translated as 90 percent confidence in the prediction.

SIMPLE FORECASTING TECHNIQUES

Three of the simplest forecasting techniques are the mean forecast, the naive forecast, and trend extrapolation. The first of these, the mean forecast, implies:

$$\hat{Y}_{t+1} = \bar{Y} \qquad (4\text{-}28)$$

where $\hat{Y}_{t+1}$ is the estimated value of Y in time period $t + 1$. As an example, Table 4-9 contains quarterly data on revenue passenger miles from 1970 to mid-1979. Given these data, the mean point forecast for the third quarter of 1979 would be 34.24 million revenue passenger miles (the average value of Y over the nine-year period). Assume that we are interested in a 95 percent confidence level estimate:

$$\bar{Y} - t_\alpha s \le \hat{Y}_{t+1} \le \bar{Y} + t_\alpha s \qquad (4\text{-}29)$$

where:

$t = t$ value taken from the t table in Appendix B
$\alpha =$ confidence level, 95%
$s =$ standard deviation
$\quad = \sqrt{\dfrac{\sum(Y_i - \bar{Y})^2}{n - 1}}$
$\quad = \sqrt{1{,}841.8/37}$
$\quad = 7.06$

Plugging in the t and s values, the projection for revenue passenger miles in the third quarter of 1979 becomes:

$$34.24 - 2.04\,(7.06) \le \hat{Y}_{t+1} \le 34.24 + 2.04\,(7.06)$$
$$19.84 \le \hat{Y}_{t+1} \le 48.64 \qquad (4\text{-}30)$$

with 95 percent confidence. In other words, instead of a mean point estimate of 34.24 million miles, the interval estimate falls between 19.84 and 48.64 million miles—a very imprecise forecast. Indeed, one method of evaluating a forecast is the width of this interval.

Naive forecasting techniques are of the form:

$$\hat{Y}_{t+1} = c\,Y_t \qquad (4\text{-}31)$$

where c is a constant factor. This constant factor can take on any value specified by the analyst. Once this value is specified, the naive model becomes a specific

Table 4-9 Error computations for mean forecast and naive forecast of revenue passenger miles

Date	Revenue Passenger Miles (Millions)	Mean Forecast[a] e_t	Mean Forecast[a] e_t^2	Mean Forecast[a] $(e_t/y_t) \times 100$	Naive Forecast[b] e_t	Naive Forecast[b] e_t^2	Naive Forecast[b] $(e_t/y_t) \times 100$
1970 I	26.00	−8.24	67.89	−32	—	—	—
II	25.23	−9.01	81.18	−36	−0.77	0.59	−3.1
III	26.59	−7.65	58.52	−29	1.36	1.85	5.1
IV	25.69	−8.55	73.10	−33	−0.90	0.81	−3.5
1971 I	25.36	−8.88	78.85	−35	−0.33	0.11	−1.3
II	26.51	−7.73	59.75	−29	1.15	1.32	4.3
III	26.71	−7.53	56.70	−28	0.20	0.04	0.7
IV	27.79	−6.45	41.60	−23	1.08	1.17	3.9
1972 I	28.76	−5.48	30.03	−19	0.97	0.94	3.4
II	29.06	−5.18	26.83	−18	0.30	0.09	1.0
III	29.50	−4.74	22.46	−16	0.44	0.19	1.5
IV	30.82	−3.42	11.69	−11	1.32	1.74	4.3
1973 I	30.64	−3.60	12.96	−12	−0.18	0.03	−0.6
II	31.70	−2.54	6.45	−8	1.06	1.12	3.3
III	31.71	−2.53	6.40	−8	0.01	0.00	0.0
IV	32.20	−2.04	4.16	−6	0.49	0.24	1.5
1974 I	32.77	−1.47	2.16	−4	0.57	0.32	1.7
II	33.34	−0.90	0.81	−3	0.57	0.32	1.7
III	31.94	−2.30	5.29	−7	−1.40	1.96	−4.4
IV	31.81	−2.43	5.90	−7	−0.13	0.02	−0.4
1975 I	31.79	−2.45	6.00	−8	−0.02	0.00	−0.0
II	32.24	−2.00	4.00	−6	0.45	0.20	1.4
III	33.46	−0.78	0.60	−2	1.22	1.49	3.6
IV	34.17	−0.07	0.00	0	0.71	0.50	2.1
1976 I	35.70	1.46	2.13	4	1.53	2.34	4.3
II	36.52	2.28	5.19	6	0.82	0.67	2.2
III	36.13	1.89	3.57	5	−0.39	0.15	−1.1
IV	36.94	2.70	7.29	7	0.81	0.66	2.2
1977 I	37.98	3.74	13.98	10	1.04	1.08	2.7
II	38.12	3.88	15.05	10	0.14	0.02	0.4
III	39.08	4.84	23.42	12	0.96	0.92	2.5
IV	41.49	7.25	52.56	17	2.41	5.80	5.8
1978 I	43.28	9.04	81.72	21	1.79	3.20	4.1
II	44.76	10.52	110.67	24	1.48	2.19	3.3
III	46.81	12.57	158.00	27	2.05	4.20	4.8
IV	47.68	13.44	180.63	28	0.87	0.75	1.8
1979 I	51.09	16.85	283.92	33	3.41	11.62	6.7
II	49.74	15.50	240.25	31	1.35	1.82	−2.7
Absolute Sum		211.93	1,841.8	618	34.60	50.53	97.24

[a]Error is defined as $e_t = (Y_t - \bar{Y}_t)$. Mean forecast is defined in equation (4-28)
[b]Error is defined as $e_t = (Y_t - Y_{t-1})$. Naive forecast is defined in equation (4-32)

form of autoregressive model. Continuing with the revenue-passenger-miles illustration, if we let $c = 1$, equation (4-31) simplifies to:

$$\hat{Y}_{t+1} = Y_t \tag{4-32}$$

Therefore, $\hat{Y}_t$ for 1979: III $= Y_t$ for 1979: II, or $\hat{Y}_t$ for 1979: III $= 49.74$. It is technically incorrect to construct an interval around this point estimate, because we have no method of calculating a measure of variability. However, one frequently used approach is to compare the predicted value to the historical observations, calculate the quarterly errors, and find the standard deviation of these errors (see Table 4-9).

A variant of this approach is to postulate that the time series being studied grows by a constant percentage rate. For example, in the case of operating revenues for Southern Airlines, the forecasting equation could be presented as:

$$\hat{Y}_{t+1} = 1.1933 Y_t \tag{4-33}$$

Thus, the point forecast for 1978 would be:

$$\hat{Y}_{1978} = 1.1933(159,511)$$
$$= 190,344 \tag{4-34}$$

As in the previous case, there is no technically correct methodology for developing an interval forecast, but a year-by-year inspection of forecast error still provides insight concerning historical accuracy.

Linear trend equations can also be utilized to prepare forecasts. In the case of revenue passenger miles, the estimated trend equation was:

$$\hat{Y}_t = 21.9726 + 0.5556X$$
$$X = 0 \text{ at } 1969: I \tag{4-35}$$

To obtain a forecast for, say, the third quarter of 1979, we must use $X = 42$, because the third quarter of 1979 is 42 time periods beyond the base quarter. From the trend equation, the projection of revenue passenger miles is:

$$\hat{Y}_{79:III} = 21.9726 + 0.5556(42)$$
$$= 45.31 \text{ million passenger miles} \tag{4-36}$$

Because of the mathematical properties of the least-squares technique used to fit the trend line, an error measure known as the standard error of the estimate can be calculated, but it will be delayed until chapter 5. The forecast value of 45.31 is based on the assumption that the forces that propelled airline volume in past quarters will continue.

The utility of these techniques must not be overlooked because of their relative simplicity. Frequently, they provide more accurate forecasts than the more sophisticated techniques do. Indeed, one of the purposes behind the presentation of these methods is to provide you with a norm. Since these simple methods tend to be less costly and easier to implement and understand, it is possible that the cost and complexity of more sophisticated models may outweigh any gains in accuracy. It is clear, therefore, that an analysis of forecasting error is critical to technique selection.

ERROR ANALYSIS

The forecast error in period t can be defined as the actual value (Y_t) less the predicted value ($\hat{Y}_t$):

$$e_t = Y_t - \hat{Y}_t \tag{4-37}$$

In the section on trend isolation, the importance of matching the estimated trend value to the actual data pattern was noted. A similar procedure can be utilized with forecasts. Specifically, an examination of forecast errors can frequently indicate whether the forecasting technique being used accurately mirrors the pattern exhibited by the data. An evaluation of the reliability of any technique necessarily involves the specification of criteria. Unfortunately, there is no generally accepted *best measure*. Rather, a great many measures have evolved for assessing forecast accuracy, and they will be introduced gradually throughout the text. The reason for this is straightforward: Some of the evaluation techniques are more applicable to certain forecasting models than to others.

One method of determining the reliability of a forecasting technique is a simple graphical inspection of the error terms. If a particular technique forecasts accurately, the error terms should be randomly distributed. This random distribution corresponds to the irregular component of time-series data and is illustrated in Figure 4-5(a). Contrast quadrant 4-5(a) with the remaining illustrations, which exemplify scatter diagrams of forecast errors with very distinct patterns. Frequently, when the forecasting technique does not fit the data pattern, the error terms themselves will follow a systematic pattern. In Figure 4-5(b), the error terms appear to lie about an upward sloping linear trend, and in Figure 4-5(c), the quarterly error terms suggest that the seasonal pattern has not been eliminated properly. Finally, the graph illustrated in Figure 4-5(d) indicates that the cyclical pattern has been overlooked.

Example 4-1: Airline Revenue Passenger Miles

In the section of fitting a trend line, we derived the trend equation:

$$\hat{Y}_t = 21.9726 + 0.5556X$$

$$X = 0 \text{ at } 1969:I \tag{4-38}$$

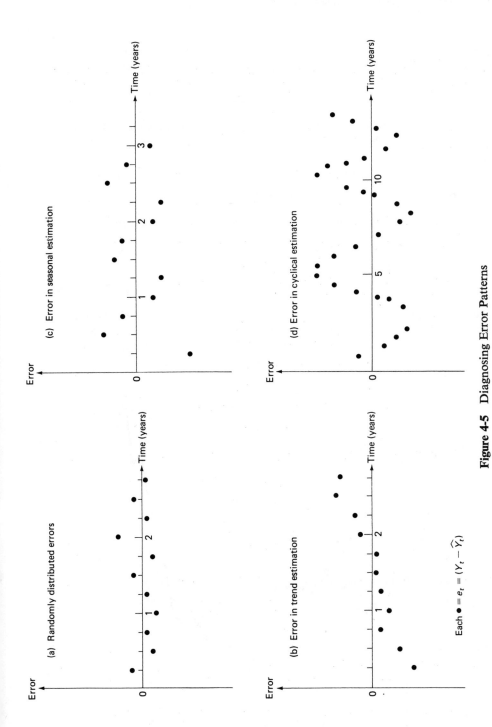

Figure 4-5 Diagnosing Error Patterns

This equation can be utilized to develop a historical forecast for revenue passenger miles. Thus, to obtain the estimated values, $\hat{Y}_t$, at a particular point—say, the first quarter of 1969—simply substitute the appropriate value for X—0 in this case—to obtain:

$$\hat{Y}_t = 21.9726 \tag{4-39}$$

Since this value has been seasonally adjusted, we must incorporate the seasonal factor for the first quarter, 94.20. The estimated value (ignoring cylical effects) would thus be:

$$(\hat{Y}_t)(\text{Seasonal factor}) = \text{Estimate}$$
$$(21.9726)(.9420) = 20.70 \tag{4-40}$$

To derive the error implicit in this estimated value, we proceed as follows:

$$e_t = Y_t - \hat{Y}_t$$
$$= 22.20 - 20.70$$
$$= 1.50 \tag{4-41}$$

The remaining values for e_t would be derived in a similar fashion. Figure 4-6 presents the scatter diagram of these error terms based on the trend equation for revenue passenger miles. A comparison of this figure with Figure 4-5(d) reveals a close similarity;

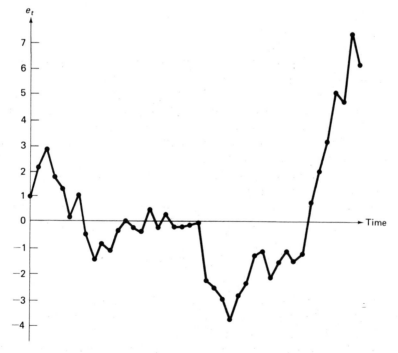

Figure 4-6 Error Pattern for Airline Passenger Miles

Source: Equation (4-38) and Table 4-2

the trend equation fails to account for the cyclical pattern in the data and therefore yields a nonrandom error pattern.

Although the graphical approach has merit, it also has certain disadvantages. First, quite frequently, a scatter diagram of the error terms exhibits no discernible pattern. Second, it is virtually impossible to compare the reliability of alternative forecasting models via a visual inspection of scatter diagrams. Finally, if the model is to be used to forecast future behavior, the analyst will not know if the model has missed some systematic pattern (for example, cyclical factors) until after the fact. For these reasons, numerous quantitative criteria are used in conjunction with scatter diagrams.

Quantitative measures can be used to aid the analyst in selecting a forecast technique. Typically, the analyst is faced with choosing among several forecasting techniques. One of the factors influencing the choice is the comparative accuracy of the alternative models. A simulation of historical data is undertaken. In this simulation process, we act as if the values of the historical data were unknown. Then each of the alternate forecasting techniques is used to produce estimates $(\hat{Y}_t)$ of the historical data. After these estimates are compared with the actual values and their reliability in estimating the historical data is determined, the models can be ranked in terms of cost, data availability, and ease of implementation so that a final selection can be made.

Accuracy measures can also be used to monitor a forecasting method in order to detect fundamental changes in the activity being modeled. Suppose, for example, that interest rates are being monitored and that the Federal Reserve Board decides to change its policy to one of slower growth in the money supply. Unfortunately for the analyst, the Federal Reserve Board's actions are kept secret. In order to take account of these actions as soon as possible, the forecaster might utilize one of the accuracy measures to monitor forecast error. This process can provide valuable signals when the forecast error becomes large relative to past behavior.

One such accuracy measure is the mean square error, or MSE:

$$\text{MSE} = \frac{\sum\limits_{t=1}^{n} (e_t^2)}{n} = \frac{\sum\limits_{t=1}^{n} (Y_t - \hat{Y}_t)^2}{n} \tag{4-42}$$

Table 4-9, shown earlier, contains the data needed for calculation of the MSE for both the mean forecast and the naive forecast. For the former, the forecast is equal to the mean value—that is, $\hat{Y}_t = \bar{Y} = 34.24$.

$$\text{MSE}_{\text{mean}} = \sum_{t=1}^{38} (Y_t - \hat{Y}_t)^2 / n$$

$$= \frac{1,841.80}{38}$$

$$= 48.469 \tag{4-43}$$

$$\begin{aligned} \text{MSE}_{\text{naive}} &= \sum_{t=1}^{37} (Y_t - \hat{Y}_t)^2/n \\ &= \frac{50.532}{37} \\ &= 1.366 \end{aligned} \tag{4-44}$$

Thus, the naive forecast generates more reliable simulated forecasts for revenue passenger miles according to the MSE criteria.

The principal drawback to the MSE criterion is that it penalizes a forecasting technique much more for large errors than for small ones. For this reason, the mean absolute deviation (MAD) may be preferable:

$$\begin{aligned} \text{MAD} &= \sum_{t=1}^{n} |e_t|/n \\ &= \frac{\sum_{t=1}^{n} |Y_t - \hat{Y}_t|}{n} \end{aligned} \tag{4-45}$$

Again, Table 4-9 contains the error data for the two forecasting techniques presented here.

$$\begin{aligned} \text{MAD}_{\text{mean}} &= \frac{\sum_{t=1}^{38} |e_t|}{n} \\ &= \frac{211.93}{38} \\ &= 5.58 \\ \text{MAD}_{\text{naive}} &= \sum_{t=1}^{37} |e_t|/n \\ &= 34.60/37 \\ &= 0.94 \end{aligned} \tag{4-46}$$

In this instance, the mean forecast is in error by 5.58 million miles, whereas the naive forecast errors by an average of 0.94 million miles. The naive forecast once again performs better.

The next measure presented in this chapter is the mean absolute percentage error, MAPE. The advantage of this measure is that it relates the size of the error to the actual observation:

$$\text{MAPE} = \sum_{t=1}^{n} \frac{|e_t/Y_t \times 100|}{n} \tag{4-47}$$

The appropriate calculations for the mean and naive forecasts are:

$$MAPE_{mean} = \sum_{t=1}^{38} \frac{\left| \frac{e_t}{Y_t} \times 100 \right|}{n}$$

$$= 618/38$$

$$= 16.26\%$$

$$MAPE_{naive} = \sum_{t=1}^{37} \frac{\left| \frac{e_t}{Y_t} \times 100 \right|}{n}$$

$$= 97.24/37$$

$$= 2.63\% \tag{4-48}$$

The mean forecast has an average error of 16.26 percent, and the naive forecast has an average error of only 2.63 percent. In terms of simulating the historical data, the naive forecast performs better by all three measurement standards.

The final measure presented here is the Theil U statistic, which is based on a comparison of the predicted change with the observed change, as shown by:[4]

$$U = \frac{\sqrt{\frac{1}{n} \sum_{i=1}^{n} (Y_i - \hat{Y}_i)^2}}{\sqrt{\frac{1}{n} \sum_{i=1}^{n} \hat{Y}_i^2} + \sqrt{\frac{1}{n} \sum_{i=1}^{n} Y_i^2}} \tag{4-49}$$

where the $\hat{Y}_i$ are the forecasts for each period, the Y_i are the actual values in each period, and n is the number of periods being compared. If the technique forecasts perfectly ($Y_i - \hat{Y}_i = 0$ for all i), $U = 0$. Alternatively, if $U = 1$, the technique is generating *erroneous forecasts*. In Figure 4-7, actual changes in the data are measured along the vertical axis, and forecast changes are measured along the horizontal axis. The diagonal line represents perfect forecasts—that is, $U = 0$. Zones IB and IIIB are zones of underprediction of observed changes ($\Delta Y_t - \Delta \hat{Y}_t > 0$). Similarly, zones IA and IIIA are zones of overprediction of observed changes ($\Delta Y_t - \Delta \hat{Y}_t < 0$). If, as is generally the case, most of the points fall in these regions, then $0 < U < 1$. Zones II and IV are zones of turning-point error; that is, the model predicted increases when in fact there was a decrease (IV), and vice versa (II). If there are a large number of points in these quadrants, U approaches 1, implying that the technique employed to generate the predicted changes is not very satisfactory. As is the case with all these measures, the Theil U statistic is impossible to evaluate in isolation. Returning to the forecasts prepared in Table 4-9, the U statistic for the mean forecast is 0.62, as compared to $U = 0.12$ for the naive forecast.

The usefulness of these simple forecasting techniques must not be ignored

[4]H. Theil, *Economic Forecasts and Policy* (Amsterdam: North Holland, 1965), pp. 32–38.

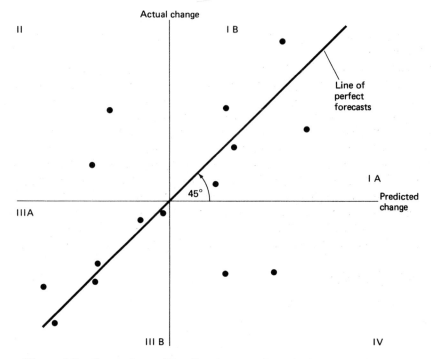

Figure 4-7 Comparison of Predicted Versus Actual Changes in the Forecast Variable

by the analyst. Indeed, their very simplicity gives them merit. In the example used throughout this section, the naive forecasting technique performs extremely well on an average basis. More complex and sophisticated models must therefore be compared to this simple technique. Selection of a more complex technique should be made only if the marginal gain in accuracy is worth more than the marginal cost of the complex method.

MODELS AND FORECASTING

Business and economic forecasts, if properly constructed and presented, are an integral part of decision making. Although the primary goal of forecasting is to assist management in understanding the implications of currently available courses of action (choices) on the future success of the organization, forecasting models are abstractions from reality. A complete listing of all factors affecting the outcome of a firm's decisions would be overwhelming. Models focus on a few characteristics that best represent the real system in a way that is simple enough to understand and manipulate, yet similar enough to reality to permit satisfactory results whenever the model is used in decision making. The acid test of a model's utility is whether or not it provides reliable predictions. Since models must be continually revised, modeling implies a learning process in which the original model is formulated and the parameters (measurable relationships) are estimated from real-world (empirical) data. Once they are estimated, this model provides decision makers with the likely outcomes of alternative choices. The decisions, once made, lead to actual outcomes that are then compared with the predicted outcomes. If the predicted result varies widely from the actual outcome, a critical appraisal must first be made to see if the underlying set of forecast assumptions has been seriously violated. If the assumptions are fallacious, the model should be resimulated to determine whether the *ex post* forecast is accurate given the proper set of assumptions. On the other hand, if the predictions are still at variance with actual results, the model must be either revised or replaced. Thus, forecasting is a continuous process of technique selection, model construction, and forecast evaluation.

QUESTIONS FOR DISCUSSION AND ANALYSIS

1. Suppose you had collected retail sales data for a department store located in Phoenix, a furniture manufacturer in North Carolina, and an apple grower in Washington State. Categorize the trend, seasonal, cyclical, and irregular forces you would expect to affect sales for each of these businesses. For example, what are the trend forces affecting apple sales or furniture sales?

2. Using current and past issues of the *Survey of Current Business*, collect monthly data for the production of electric power (millions of kilowatt hours) for the last ten years, convert to a quarterly series, and estimate the final seasonal factors for each quarter, using the techniques described in Tables 4-2 and 4-3. Explain precisely the meaning of each quarterly index. Focusing on just the seasonality of power production, by what percentage does the third quarter differ from the first quarter?

3. Fit a linear trend line to electric-power data as illustrated by equations (4-11) and (4-12); let $X = 0$ in the first quarter of your observation period. Reestimate your trend equation using the single-log transformation outlined in equations (4-14), (4-15), and (4-16). Graph the two trend equations against the raw data. Which appears to fit best?

4. Set up a table in which column 1 contains the actual or raw observations for power production for the last eight quarters, column 2 contains the appropriate seasonal factors, column 3 the seasonally adjusted series, column 4 the quarterly trend forecast, column 5 the cyclical irregular residual, and column 6 the cyclical component. Explain your findings concerning the relative contributions of trend, seasonal, cyclical, and irregular components over this period.

5. Calculate and interpret the MSE, MAD, MAPE, and Theil U statistics for the two trend equations in problem 3.

REFERENCES FOR FURTHER STUDY

Burman, J. P., "Moving Seasonal Adjustments of Economic Time Series," *Journal of the Royal Statistical Society*, Series A, Vol. 128 (1965), 534–58.

Butler, William F., Robert A. Kavesh, and Robert B. Platt, eds., *Methods and Techniques of Business Forecasting*. Englewood Cliffs, N.J.: Prentice-Hall, 1976.

Chambers, J. C., et al., "How to Choose the Right Forecasting Techniques," *Harvard Business Review*, July–August 1971, pp. 45–74.

Dauten, Carl A., and Lloyd M. Valentine, *Business Cycles and Forecasting*, 5th ed. Cincinnati, O.: South-Western Publishing, 1978.

Kuznets, Simon, *Seasonal Variations in Industry and Trade*. New York: National Bureau of Economic Research, 1933.

THE TWO-VARIABLE REGRESSION MODEL

PART III

5

Simple Linear
Regression

INTRODUCTION

In the discussion of trend estimation and cyclical isolation in the preceding chapter, we implicitly assigned a causal role to the passage of time. However, in many circumstances, the analyst has access to economic data that display a cause-and-effect relationship. For example, the analyst may believe that sales are determined by income levels, or that the demand for steel is in part influenced by automobile production. Thus, instead of relying on a simplistic notion of time, we will develop models that focus on the changes in sales as income varies, or on the fluctuations in automobile production as they relate to the demand for steel. Further strengthening the use of causal relationships in forecasting models are the factors noted in the discussion of the NBER's indicators and the business cycle. For example, inventory levels are related to sales, plant construction is related to financing costs, manpower requirements are related to production levels.

Regression analysis is the most widely used technique for quantifying the behavioral relationships between two or more economic factors. In this chapter, we begin our study with the simplest possible case: the two-variable linear regression model. Even though this model oversimplifies reality, the results can be easily extended to more complex and realistic regression models.

The starting point in regression analysis is an equation (model) that postulates a causal relationship between a dependent variable and one or more independent variables. For example, we might want to estimate automobile sales, on either an industry or a firm level, based on disposable income or, alternatively, predict steel production as a function of automobile output. These relationships are quantified by means of an equation such as:[1]

$$\hat{Y} = \hat{\beta}_0 + \hat{\beta}_1 X \qquad (5\text{-}1)$$

This equation provides estimates of an unknown variable, $\hat{Y}$ (sometimes referred to as the dependent variable), when the value of another variable, X (the independent or causal variable), is known and the parameters, $\hat{\beta}_0$ and $\hat{\beta}_1$, have been specified. We have assumed that a basic relationship between X and Y exists, that it can be represented by a particular mathematical form, and that the relationship is linear.[2] The unknown parameters, $\hat{\beta}_0$ and $\hat{\beta}_1$, are estimated with available sample data, and a fitted equation is obtained. Since we cannot be certain about the reliability of $\hat{Y}$, predictions based on the regression equation must be gauged for accuracy and checks made as to the validity of the underlying assumptions. Additionally, the characteristics (slope, accuracy) of the estimated line are evaluated by subjecting the estimated equation to statistical tests of significance.

LINEAR-REGRESSION MODEL

STATISTICAL FORMULATION

The linear-regression model is a shorthand mathematical way of expressing the statistical relationship that we believe exists between the two variables. The principal elements of this statistical relationship are (1) the tendency of the dependent variable, Y, to vary in a systematic way with the independent variable, X; and (2) the dispersion of points about the line that represents the relationship between X and Y. The objective is to specify the model that produces the *best* straight line relating X and Y.

To illustrate, suppose we wish to determine if consumer expenditures are related to income. If expenditures (Y) and income (X) are plotted on a scatter

---

[1] In fact, the linear regression model is but a special case of the general linear model. For a detailed treatment, see F.A. Graybell, *Theory and Application of the Linear Model* (North Scituate, Mass.: Duxbury Press, 1976).

[2] This assumption is not as restrictive as it might appear. It will become evident that the majority of business and economic data approximate linearity either directly or by some form of transformation.

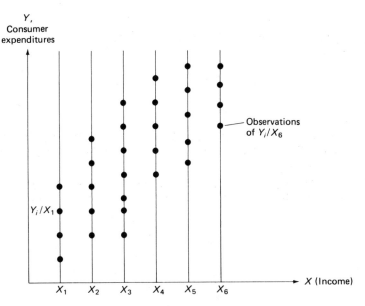

Figure 5-1 Scatter Diagram for Expenditures and Income

Note: Y_i/X_i denotes the alternative values Y can take for a given value of X.

diagram, something similar to Figure 5-1 might be observed. From this diagram, it is clear that consumer expenditures are positively related to income. Moreover, it should be possible to quantitatively estimate an equation describing this relationship. Geometrically, this could be accomplished by simply drawing a line through the scatter of points. However, in the great majority of cases, this method is not likely to be satisfactory, either because of the large number of observations or because there is no obvious *best* line. What is needed is a means of estimating the values of the parameters, $\hat{\beta}_0$ and $\hat{\beta}_1$ in equation (5-1), in such a way that the line estimated represents the *best* line. One best-fit line is known as the least-squared regression of Y on X.

As an example, let us consider the simple, but likely, situation of an analyst who feels that automobile sales are related to the real disposable income of individuals. He obtains the 16-year sample detailed in Table 5-1 and Figure 5-2.[3] Many straight lines can be chosen to fit the plotted data points. For example, one could connect the points from the lowest X value to the highest X value (G_1 in Figure 5-2), or one could simply draw a line that appears to fit the full scatter of data points (G_2 in Figure 5-2). Let us define the best line as the line with the least total error. These errors are generally referred to as deviations

[3]In order to reduce sampling error, a sample larger than sixteen ought to be obtained. The small number used here is only for ease in showing calculations. In fact, the example used throughout this section must be regarded as illustrative.

Table 5-1 Automobile sales and real disposable income, 1962–1977

Year	X Real Disposable Income (Billions of 1972 $)	Y Retail Sales of Passenger Cars (Thousands)
1962	$522	6,700
1963	539	7,316
1964	577	7,658
1965	613	8,784
1966	644	8,408
1967	670	7,583
1968	695	8,600
1969	713	8,442
1970	741	7,158
1971	769	8,683
1972	801	9,317
1973	855	9,675
1974	842	7,542
1975	860	7,084
1976	890	8,612
1977	926	9,119

Source: *Survey of Current Business*

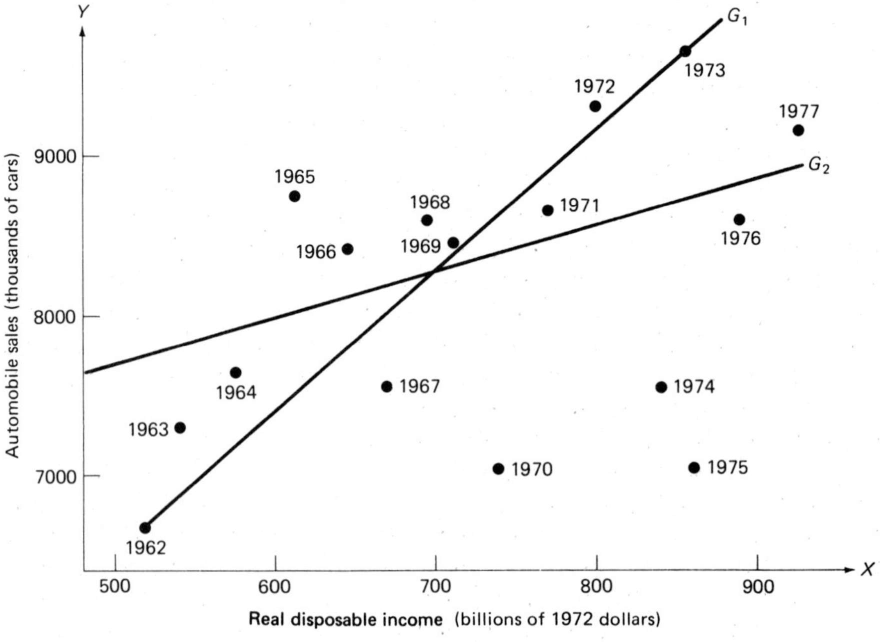

Figure 5-2 Scatter Diagram for Automobile Sales and Disposable Income 1962–1977

or residuals about the regression line. There are many possible ways to minimize error, but the most frequently relied upon criterion is the least-squares model, which minimizes the sum of the squared deviations about the regression line.

Formally, the objective is to find the line, $\hat{Y} = \hat{\beta}_0 + \hat{\beta}_1 X$, in which the values $\hat{\beta}_0$ and $\hat{\beta}_1$ ensure that the squared deviations from the data points to the line are minimized. That is, we want to find values for $\hat{\beta}_0$ and $\hat{\beta}_1$ that minimize:

$$\sum_{i=1}^{n} (Y_i - \hat{Y}_i)^2 = \sum (\text{errors})^2 \qquad (5\text{-}2)$$

where $\hat{Y}_i = \hat{\beta}_0 + \hat{\beta}_1 X_i$ is the fitted (estimated) value of Y_i corresponding to a particular observation on X_i, n is the total number of observations, and $(Y_i - \hat{Y}_i)$ is the regression error.

Figure 5-3 graphically illustrates the regression error as the vertical distance from $\hat{Y}_i$ to Y_i. We are interested in finding values for $\hat{\beta}_0$ and $\hat{\beta}_1$ that will minimize the sum of the squares of these vertical deviations. β_0 and β_1 (without "hats") are the unknown regression parameters contained in the *true* regression line describing Y and X. Since β_0 and β_1 are not known in advance (*a priori*) in a regression problem, they must be estimated from sample data similar to those in Table 5-1; these values are referred to as the regression coefficient estimates and are denoted by $\hat{\beta}_0$ and $\hat{\beta}_1$—our best statistical guess

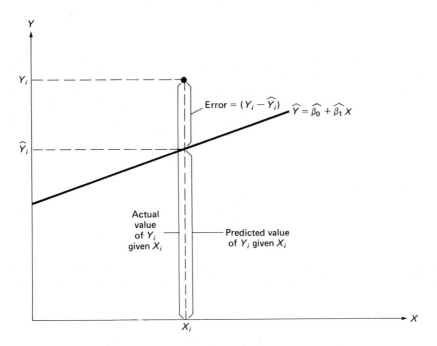

Figure 5-3   Fitting Points with a Regression Line: Error Analysis

of the unknown parameters, β_0 and β_1. This is analogous to taking a random sample of sixteen 13-year-olds, calculating their average weight ($\bar{X}$), and using this as an estimate of the average weight (μ) of all 13-year-olds in the United States.

Mathematically, it may be shown that the estimated values of $\hat{\beta}_0$ and $\hat{\beta}_1$ must simultaneously satisfy the following expressions, referred to as the normal equations:[4]

$$\sum Y_i = n\hat{\beta}_0 + \hat{\beta}_1 \sum X_i \tag{5-3}$$

$$\sum X_i Y_i = \hat{\beta}_0 \sum X_i + \hat{\beta}_1 \sum X_i^2 \tag{5-4}$$

Solving equations (5-3) and (5-4) we get the following definitional formulas:[5]

$$\hat{\beta}_1 = \frac{n \sum X_i Y_i - \sum X_i \sum Y_i}{n \sum X_i^2 - (\sum X_i)^2} \tag{5-5}$$

$$\hat{\beta}_0 = \frac{\sum Y_i}{n} - \hat{\beta}_1 \frac{\sum X_i}{n}, \text{ or} \tag{5-6}$$

$$\hat{\beta}_0 = \bar{Y} - \hat{\beta}_1 \bar{X} \tag{5-7}$$

In these three equations (5-5, 5-6, and 5-7), the symbols are defined as follows:

$$n = \text{number of sample observations}$$
$$\sum = \text{summation of observations}$$
$$X_i = \text{independent variable}$$
$$Y_i = \text{dependent variable}$$
$$\bar{Y} = \text{arithmetic mean of } Y$$
$$\bar{X} = \text{arithmetic mean of } X$$

[4]Formally, this process is as follows:
a. Substitute into equation (5-1) the definition of $\hat{Y}$, obtaining:

$$\sum (Y_i - \hat{\beta}_0 - \hat{\beta}_1 X_i)^2$$

b. To minimize this expression, we take the partial derivatives with respect to $\hat{\beta}_0$ and $\hat{\beta}_1$ and set them equal to zero:

$$\frac{\partial}{\partial \hat{\beta}_0} \sum (Y_i - \hat{\beta}_0 - \hat{\beta}_1 X_i)^2 = -2 \sum (Y_i - \hat{\beta}_0 - \hat{\beta}_1 X_i)$$

$$\frac{\partial}{\partial \hat{\beta}_1} \sum (Y_i - \hat{\beta}_0 - \hat{\beta}_1 X_i)^2 = -2 \sum X_i(Y_i - \hat{\beta}_0 - \hat{\beta}_1 X_i)$$

Equating these to zero yields:

$$\sum (Y_i - \hat{\beta}_0 - \hat{\beta}_1 X_i) = 0$$
$$\sum X_i(Y_i - \hat{\beta}_0 - \hat{\beta}_1 X_i) = 0$$

c. Rewriting these, we obtain equations (5-3) and (5-4).
[5]If one is forced to compute a significant number of regression equations, shorthand formulas are available. See R.J. Wonnacott and T.H. Wonnacott, *Econometrics* (New York: John Wiley, 1970), pp. 6–9.

STATISTICAL ESTIMATION

Calculations for $\hat{\beta}_0$ and $\hat{\beta}_1$ are carried out in the first four columns of Table 5-2 (the remaining columns may be ignored for the present). The regression equation can now be stated as:

$$\hat{Y}_i = 5{,}807 + 3.24X_i \tag{5-8}$$

This estimated line is graphed, along with the actual data points, in Figure 5-4. Historical estimates of automobile sales for any given income level are easily obtainable from equation (5-8). For example, if disposable income of $801 billion were used, the estimate of automobile sales would be:

Table 5-2 Least-square calculations: demand for automobiles
(Data from Table 5-1)

(1)	(2)	(3)	(4)	(5) $\hat{Y}_i =$ 5,807 + 3.24$X_i{}^c$	(6)	(7)
$X_i{}^a$	$Y_i{}^b$	$\sum X_i Y_i$	X_i^2		$(Y_i - \hat{Y}_i)$	$(Y_i - \hat{Y}_i)^2$
522	6,700	3,497,400	272,484	7,498	− 798	637,344
539	7,316	3,943,324	290,521	7,553	− 237	56,366
577	7,658	4,418,666	332,929	7,677	− 19	343
613	8,784	5,384,592	375,769	7,793	991	981,761
644	8,408	5,414,752	414,736	7,894	514	264,612
670	7,583	5,080,610	448,900	7,978	− 395	155,891
695	8,600	5,977,000	483,025	8,059	541	292,869
713	8,442	6,019,146	508,369	8,117	325	105,532
741	7,158	5,304,078	549,081	8,208	−1,050	1,102,201
769	8,683	6,677,227	591,361	8,299	384	147,785
801	9,317	7,462,917	641,601	8,402	915	836,774
855	9,675	8,272,125	731,025	8,577	−1,098	1,205,174
842	7,542	6,350,364	708,964	8,535	− 993	986,205
860	7,084	6,092,240	739,600	8,593	−1,509	2,278,274
890	8,612	7,664,680	792,100	8,691	− 79	6,176
926	9,119	8,444,194	857,476	8,807	312	97,205

$\sum X_i =$ 11,657 $\quad$ $\sum Y_i =$ 130,681 $\quad$ $\sum X_i Y_i =$ 96,003,315 $\quad$ $\sum X_i^2 =$ 8,737,941 $\quad$ $\sum (Y_i - \hat{Y}_i)$ ≈ 0 $\quad$ $\sum (Y_i - \hat{Y}_i)^2 =$ 9,154,513

$$\bar{X} = \frac{\sum X_i}{n} \qquad \bar{Y} = \frac{\sum Y_i}{n} \qquad \hat{\beta}_1 = \frac{n\sum X_i Y_i - \sum X_i \sum Y_i}{n\sum X_i^2 - (\sum X_i)^2}$$

$$\bar{X} = \frac{11{,}657}{16} \qquad \bar{Y} = \frac{130{,}681}{16} \qquad = 3.24$$

$$\bar{X} = 728.56 \qquad \bar{Y} = 8{,}167.6$$

$$\hat{\beta}_0 = \bar{Y} - \hat{\beta}_1 \bar{X}$$
$$= 8{,}167.6 - (3.24)(728.56)$$
$$= 5{,}807$$

$^a X =$ real disposable income (billions of 1972 dollars)
$^b Y =$ retail sales of passenger cars (thousands)
^{c}Estimated regression values have been rounded to nearest integer.

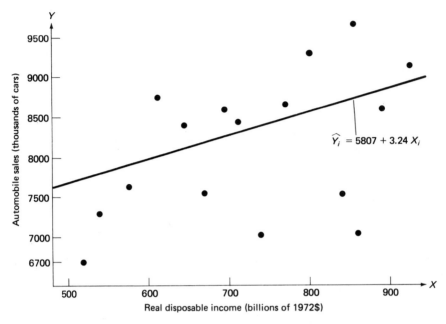

Figure 5-4 Regression Line of Automobile Sales and Real Disposable Income

Source: Tables 5-1 and 5-2; equation (5-8)

$$\hat{Y}_i = 5{,}807 + 3.24X_i$$
$$= 5{,}807 + 3.24(801)$$
$$= 8{,}402$$

That is, if we input the actual value of income ($801) in 1972, we would estimate sales at 8.402 million cars, compared to the actual value of 9.317—an underestimate of 915 thousand cars.

What, precisely, do the regression coefficients tell us? The slope of the line, $\hat{\beta}_1$, is an estimate of the change in Y resulting from a one-unit change in X. That is, for every $1 billion change in disposable income, automobile sales will change by 3,240 units. The interpretation of the intercept, $\hat{\beta}_0$, depends entirely on whether observations near $X = 0$ are available. If so, $\hat{\beta}_0$ may be interpreted as the estimate of Y when X equals zero. Strictly speaking, we would predict sales of 5.807 million cars when disposable income equals zero! However, if sufficient observations near $X = 0$ are not available (generally true in business and economic data, and clearly true in this case), then the intercept is simply the height of the least-squares regression line. The majority of computer programs simply refer to $\hat{\beta}_0$ as the constant; in most cases, therefore, it has no meaningful economic interpretation. To utilize the regression line, one must distinguish between interpolation and extrapolation. The former uses the regression equation to estimate Y based on an X value within the data-base range, whereas extrapolation produces an estimate based on an X value falling outside the actual data base.

The estimate of 8.402 million units for automobile sales was based on income of \$801 billion, an income level actually contained within the data base. If, however, we were to estimate automobile sales based on an income level of 0, we would obtain:

$$\hat{Y}_t = 5,807 + 3.24X$$
$$= 5,807 + 3.24(0)$$
$$= 5,807 \qquad\qquad (5\text{-}9)$$

The reliability of this estimate is questionable both statistically (we have no sample observations with which to compare) and logically (we would not expect people to buy almost 6 million automobiles without income).

MATHEMATICAL MODEL

PROPERTIES OF THE LEAST-SQUARES MODEL

In the introductory section, concern was directed toward the mechanics of estimating the parameters $\hat{\beta}_0$ and $\hat{\beta}_1$. In this section, the focus will be on the statistical validity of the least-squares regression model. The principal statistical advantage of regression analysis (as compared to the other techniques presented in this book) is that it is based on a model that yields a number of statistical measures designed to check its validity. Initially, we will discuss the underlying assumptions of the two-variable model, analyze the statistical properties of the least-squares estimators, and examine the usefulness of the estimated regression line as a predictive device.

To comprehend the probabilistic nature of the least-squares model, we must note that for a given observed value of X, we would observe many possible values of Y.[6] In our example, consider the expenditures on automobiles by different people, each of whom receives \$50,000 each year. Even though income (X) is the same, we would not observe exactly the same expenditures by each person. Instead, there would be fluctuations in the Y values, with a clustering about the central value or mean expenditure. In the absence of additional information, we will assume that for each X value, observations on

---

[6]For a more thorough discussion, see Wonnacott and Wonnacott, *Econometrics*; and R.S. Pindyck and D.L. Rubinfeld, *Econometric Models and Economic Forecasts* (New York: McGraw-Hill, 1976).

Y will vary in a random fashion. Formally, this situation can be described by adding an error term and expressing the theoretical model as:

$$Y_i = \beta_0 + \beta_1 X_i + \epsilon_i \qquad (5\text{-}10)$$

where for each observation, Y_i is a random variable, X_i is fixed, and ϵ_i is a random error term.[7] Equation (5-10) is the equation for the theoretical or unknown true regression line linking Y_i to X_i. When we gather data and estimate the coefficient, the "hat" symbol ($\frown$) is used to denote a sample estimate.

Equation (5-10) is the formal model of the relationship that we believe exists. We begin by assuming that the least-squares method is a valid model for the problem being analyzed, and then we statistically test this hypothesis based on the output of our regression statistics. The statistical power of the least-squares regression model is built upon a series of critical assumptions, all of which were implicitly assumed to hold in the automobile-sales regression line. Figure 5-5 illustrates the assumptions of the classical linear model, which are formally listed below.[8] In particular, Figure 5-5 implies that

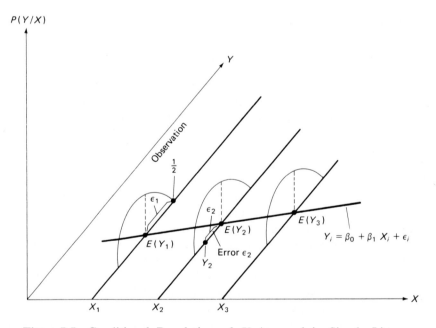

Figure 5-5   Conditional Population of *Y* Assumed in Simple Linear Regression

[7]Following standard procedure, we will use Greek letters with a "hat," $\frown$, to denote estimates.

[8]For proof of these assumptions, as well as for many of the mathematical characteristics noted in this section, see footnote 6.

for every X_i there exists a probability distribution of the Y_is, $P(Y_i|X_i)$, that meets the following conditions:

1. The relationship between X_i and Y_i is linear.
2. The X_is are nonrandom variables whose values are fixed.
3. The error term has constant variance for all X_i. This variance is denoted by $E(\epsilon_i^2) = \sigma^2$.
4. The random variables, Y_i, are statistically independent. That is, Y_2 is not affected by Y_1 or by Y_3.
5. The error term has an expected value of zero.

These assumptions may be summarized more concisely as: The random variables, Y_i, are statistically independent, with:

$$E(Y) = \text{Mean} = \beta_0 + \beta_1 X_i$$
$$V(Y) = \text{Var} = \sigma^2 \qquad (5\text{-}11)$$

Additionally, it is occasionally useful to describe the model in terms of the error term. In this case, the model and its assumptions may be written as:

$$Y_i = \beta_0 + \beta_1 X_i + \epsilon_i \qquad (5\text{-}12)$$

where the ϵ_i are independent random variables with:

$$\text{Mean} = E(\epsilon_i) = 0$$
$$\text{Var} = V(\epsilon_i) = \sigma^2$$

These alternative formulations highlight four significant facets of the model. First, the distributions of Y_i and ϵ_i are identical, except that their means differ. Second, no assumption is made regarding the shape of the distribution of ϵ_i. All that is required is a finite variance. Third, the variance, σ^2, is an unknown parameter and must be estimated as part of the regression model. Finally, before the models developed by the forecaster are actually used, the validity of the assumptions must be checked.

The error term, ϵ_i, may be regarded as the sum of two components:

1. Specification errors appear because a regression model is a simplification of reality. For example, we assumed that income was the sole determinant of automobile sales. In fact, we have omitted such determinants as prices and population. The effect of all these omitted variables is captured by the error term. In addition, it is highly unlikely that any postulated relationship is perfectly linear.
2. The second source of error is measurement error. Typically, economic and business data are difficult to measure with complete accuracy. Rounding error, recording error, and missing data points are all potential causes of measurement error.

These errors are inherent in the theoretical model—that is, the population regression line. They do not occur because we are estimating a regression line.

STATISTICAL PROPERTIES

In the estimation of the regression equation for automobile sales, a significant distinction was glossed over. This is the relationship between the true regression line, denoted by equation (5-10):

$$Y_i = \beta_0 + \beta_1 X_i + \epsilon_i$$

and the estimated regression line denoted by equation (5-13):

$$\hat{Y}_i = \hat{\beta}_0 + \hat{\beta}_1 X_i + e_i \qquad (5\text{-}13)$$

The true regression line is generally unknown to the forecaster; thus, the task is one of determining the best estimate. As previously noted, this is achieved by using equation (5-13), the least-squares line, as the best estimate of equation (5-10). Figure 5-6 highlights this distinction. In all likelihood, the estimated regression line will differ from the true regression line. This difference occurs because of the impossibility of reproducing economic phenomena perfectly, even in a random sample.

Return to the estimated least-squares equation, (5-13). The most important theoretical justification for use of this least-squares criterion is the Gauss-Markov theorem, which we state without formal proof:

> Within the class of linear unbiased estimates of β_0 and β_1, the least-squares estimators have minimum variance.

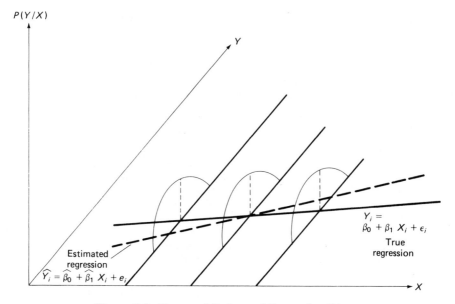

Figure 5-6   True and Estimated Regression Lines

There are several features of this theorem that are noteworthy. First, the theorem requires no assumption about the shape of the distribution of the error term. Further, the theorem applies only to linear estimators. It is possible that a nonlinear estimator may be unbiased and have lower variance than the least-squares estimators. Despite the fact that we will not prove the theorem, it is worthwhile noting some of its corollaries:

1. The estimators, $\hat{\beta}_0$ and $\hat{\beta}_1$, are unbiased; i.e.:

$$E(\hat{\beta}_0) = \beta_0 \text{ and } E(\hat{\beta}_1) = \beta_1 \qquad (5\text{-}14)$$

2. The least-squares estimators are both efficient and consistent. An efficient estimator is an estimator whose variance is smaller than the variance of any other unbiased estimator. In informal terms, a consistent estimator is one that concentrates completely on its target (β_0 and β_1, in our case) as sample size increases.

3. The variance of the two estimators can be shown to be:

$$V(\hat{\beta}_0) = \frac{\sigma^2(\sum X_i^2)}{n(\sum (X_i - \bar{X})^2)} \qquad V(\hat{\beta}_1) = \frac{\sigma^2}{\sum (X_i - \bar{X})^2} \qquad (5\text{-}15)$$

where σ^2 is the variance of the error term.

4. Since σ^2 is unknown, it is estimated by s^2 where:

$$s^2 = \frac{1}{n-2} \sum (Y_i - \hat{Y}_i)^2$$

$$= \frac{\sum (Y_i - \hat{Y}_i)^2}{n-2} \qquad (5\text{-}16)$$

where $\hat{Y}_i = \hat{\beta}_0 + \hat{\beta}_1 X_i$, so

$$s^2 = \frac{\sum e_i^2}{n-2}$$

where $e_i = (Y_i - \hat{Y}_i)$.

5. It can be shown that s^2, the residual variance, is also an unbiased and consistent estimator. The reader might wonder why the sum of the squares, $\sum (Y_i - \hat{Y}_i)^2$, is divided by $n - 2$. This divisor is technically referred to as the degrees of freedom. In our example, two degrees of freedom (d.f.) are lost by using $\hat{\beta}_0$ and $\hat{\beta}_1$ to estimate β_0 and β_1. The sample or residual variance is often referred to as a mean square.

6. $\hat{\beta}_1$ is a linear combination of the random variable, Y_i.

7. If we now add, for the first time, the assumption that the Y_i are normally distributed, it follows that $\hat{\beta}_1$ is normally distributed. This assumption is *not* required in forming the point estimates, $\hat{\beta}_0$, $\hat{\beta}_1$, and s^2, but it is required for the statistical testing of the model.

STATISTICAL VALIDATION

HYPOTHESIS TESTING

Having obtained estimates of the parameters, $\hat{\beta}_0$ and $\hat{\beta}_1$, the next step is to statistically evaluate the usefulness of the model. This involves the computation and interpretation of summary statistics. The meaning and use of these statistics are especially valuable in applied regression analysis. Textbook problems in which the model is correctly specified and the data are clean are rarely encountered in real-world forecasting. Thus, applied regression requires a great deal of judgment at various stages of research, utilizing summary statistics and tests to feel one's way through the data. Since regression estimates are mathematically derived, it is possible to make statistical statements regarding the significance and accuracy of estimated regression equations. The use of these statistical properties, along with our knowledge of $\hat{\beta}_0$ and $\hat{\beta}_1$ and the normality assumption, will also allow us to make statements about the likelihood that future values will vary from the forecast (estimate), the confidence that we place in having estimated the best straight line, and finally, the accuracy of the coefficients. At this juncture, remember that the estimated regression line is based on a sample; hence, sampling error exists. The primary goal of all these statistical tests is to take this sampling error into consideration.

Classical hypothesis testing involves a five-step procedure. What follows is a brief review of these steps. A detailed examination of each step will be made for the automobile-sales example. We will concentrate on the slope coefficient, $\hat{\beta}_1$, since $\hat{\beta}_0$ has no economic importance.[9]

1. Statement of the null hypothesis, H_0, and the alternative hypothesis. In general, the null hypothesis is established so as to permit either acceptance or rejection. The most frequently tested null hypothesis is that the slope coefficient, β_1, is equal to zero. That is:

$$H_0: \quad \beta_1 = 0 \qquad (5\text{-}17)$$

$\beta_1 = 0$ implies that there is no statistically observable relationship between Y and X. If H_0 is true, then our estimated regression line is of no use to us as a predictive device. Equation (5-17) implies that if disposable income has no influence on automobile sales, the slope coefficient, in the population regression line, will equal zero. That is, is the regression coefficient, $\hat{\beta}_1$, significantly different from zero, or did our estimated value, $\hat{\beta}_1 = 3.24$, occur by chance? What we should like to do, statistically, is to say, if the true value of β_1 is zero, what is the chance that we could have obtained our specific value of $\hat{\beta}_1$? The alternative hypothesis, H_1, follows from the null hypothesis:

$$H_1: \quad \beta_1 \neq 0 \qquad (5\text{-}18)$$

Equations (5-17) and (5-18) imply a two-tailed test, since no direction is specified; that is, $\beta_1 > 0$ or $\beta_1 < 0$.[10]

[9]Suffice it to say that if the intercept had some economic significance, it would be necessary to undertake the statistical tests for β_0.

[10]We could have chosen a null hypothesis that was more specific. For example, we could have used any of the following in our example:

$$H_0: \quad \beta_1 > 0$$
$$H_0: \quad \beta_1 < 0$$
$$H_0: \quad \beta_1 < 1$$

The first two specifications present no particular difficulties, since the only significant difference between these and our test specification is the use of a one-tailed test in the former case; the latter specification is common when similar models are available and there is some reason to expect β_1 to exceed 1.

2. The second step is the selection of a level of significance. The most common levels of significance (denoted by α) are .01, .05, .10. For our example, we will arbitrarily select an α level of .05. In effect, we are stating that we are willing to incorrectly reject H_0 5 percent of the time.

3. The statistical test utilized in accepting or rejecting H_0 is the t test.[11] This is the relevant distribution because σ^2 is unknown. t_e is calculated as:

$$t_e = (\hat{\beta}_1 - \beta_1)/S_{\beta_1} \qquad (5\text{-}19)$$

where t_e has $n - 2$ degrees of freedom, and t_e is the calculated t value based on sample results:

$$t_e = \frac{\hat{\beta}_1 - 0}{S_{\beta_1}} \quad \text{or} \quad t_e = \frac{\hat{\beta}_1}{S_{\beta_1}} \qquad (5\text{-}20)$$

$$\hat{\beta}_1 = 3.24$$

$$t_e = \frac{3.24}{1.634}$$

$$t_e = 1.98$$

$$S_{\beta_1} = \frac{s}{\sqrt{\sum (X_i - \bar{X})^2}} \qquad (5\text{-}21)$$

$$s^2 = \frac{\sum (Y_i - \hat{Y}_i)^2}{n - 2}$$

$$s^2 = \frac{9{,}154{,}513}{14} \quad \text{(Table 5-2)}$$

$$s^2 = 653{,}894 \qquad (5\text{-}22)$$

$$s = 809$$

$$\sum (X_i - \bar{X})^2 = 245{,}091$$

$$S_{\beta_1} = \frac{809}{\sqrt{245{,}091}}$$

$$S_{\beta_1} = 1.634$$

4. The decision rule specifies the appropriate interval over which we will accept or reject H_0. This involves a determination of a critical value of t, denoted by t_{cr}. For our example:

$$t_{cr}, .05, 14 = 2.145$$

$$\alpha = .05 \text{ and d.f.} = n - 2 \text{ or } 14$$

Thus, the decision rule is: If $(-2.145 \leq t_e \leq 2.145)$, accept H_0; if $t_e \leq -2.145$ or $t_e \geq 2.145$, reject H_0.

5. The final step is to either accept or reject the null hypothesis. This is accomplished by comparing t_e and t_{cr}.

$$t_e = 1.98$$

$$t_{cr} = \pm 2.145$$

Since 1.98 is less than 2.145, the decision is to accept H_0. Therefore, we can conclude that the relationship between disposable income and automobile sales is not statistically significant.

---

[11]Technically speaking, we do not accept H_0; we simply cannot reject it.

Since we specified the level of significance at $\alpha = 0.05$, there is a 5 percent chance that we will err in rejecting H_0. That is, there is a 5 percent possibility that we will reject H_0 when it is true. We can say, however, that we will make the statistically correct decision 95 percent of the time. The arbitrary selection of the level of significance is subject to criticism. This criticism can be avoided by utilizing the Prob-Value approach.[12]

The important issue is not whether statistical significance is achieved, but rather at what level it is achieved. The level at which we cross over from insignificance to significance is referred to as the critical confidence level. To determine this value, calculate the t_e value as before, locate this value in Appendix B, and find the appropriate α level. For our problem, a calculated t_e of 1.98 and 14 degrees of freedom implies a Prob-Value of approximately 0.07. In other words, if disposable income is unrelated to automobile sales, there are less than 7 chances out of 100 that we would observe a $\hat{\beta}_1$ value as large as 3.24 when H_0 is true. Although we could utilize the same procedure to test a hypothesis about β_0, the intercept, it is generally not done, because β_0 has no economic significance.

POINT AND INTERVAL ESTIMATES

By applying the method of least squares, we have estimated β_1 from a sample of 16 observations and determined that $\hat{\beta}_1 = 3.24$. This is the best point estimate of β_1. Similarly, the best point estimate of β_0 is $\hat{\beta}_0 = 5,807$. The difficulty with these numbers is that we do not have a means of measuring the accuracy of the estimates. Confidence intervals, or simply interval estimates, provide us with a measure of the reliability of these estimates. They provide a range of values within which the true values of β_0 and β_1 are likely to fall. As before, we will concentrate on the slope coefficient, $\hat{\beta}_1$. The confidence interval for β_1 is given by:

$$\beta_1 = \hat{\beta}_1 \pm t_{cr} S_{\beta_1} \qquad (5\text{-}23)$$

where t_{cr} denotes the critical value determined by the degree of significance we would be satisfied with. It is possible to calculate confidence intervals for any level of significance. As previously noted, confidence intervals provide us with a statement about the range within which the parameter, β_1, will fall. Equation (5-23) states that, if we repeat this experiment over and over, an interval of (t_{cr}) standard deviations on either side of the estimated slope value, $\hat{\beta}_1$, has a probability of 0.90 (assuming that 0.10 has been selected as our α level of significance) of containing the true slope, β_1. For our example, the 90 percent confidence interval for β_1 is computed as follows:

[12]R.J. Wonnacott and T.H. Wonnacott, *Introductory Statistics* (New York: John Wiley, 1972), pp. 189–93.

$$\beta_1 = \hat{\beta}_1 \pm t_{cr}S_{\beta_1}$$
$$= 3.24 \pm 1.761(1.634)$$
$$= 3.24 \pm 2.877$$
$$0.363 < \beta_1 < 6.117 \qquad (5\text{-}24)$$

We can be 90 percent confident that the true value of β_1 falls within this range, a span wide enough to expose the lack of precision in the model.

As an interesting corollary, this can be used to check H_0. Once we have determined the confidence interval for β_1, we do not have to go through the lengthy process of hypothesis testing. The simplest procedure is to examine the confidence interval for β_1 and see if it contains the hypothesized value— that is, $\beta_1 = 0$. If it does, then H_0 cannot be rejected. Since equation (5-24) does not contain zero, we can reject the null hypothesis that there is no statistical relationship between disposable income and automobile sales.

To further illustrate this point, let us postulate that $H_0: \beta_1 = 0$ and use an α level of .05 and repeat the process:

$$\beta_1 = \hat{\beta}_1 \pm t_{cr}S_{\beta_1}$$
$$= 3.24 \pm 2.145(1.634)$$
$$= 3.24 \pm 3.505$$
$$-0.265 < \beta_1 < 6.745 \qquad (5\text{-}25)$$

In this case, we would accept H_0 at the .05 level of significance. The reason is that the confidence interval contains the postulated value of zero.

STANDARD ERROR OF THE ESTIMATE

Because a regression estimate represents a type of average, we do not expect all the actual values to lie on this average line. This claim is analogous to the fact that the arithmetic mean, 10, of the numbers 4, 6, 14, and 16 is not one of the elements in the data set. Knowing this, we are interested in determining the average regression error.

The statistic that enables us to measure regression error is the standard error of the estimate:

$$\text{SEE} = \sqrt{\frac{\sum (Y_i - \hat{Y}_i)^2}{n - 2}} \qquad (5\text{-}26)$$

As can be seen from this formulation, the SEE focuses on deviations about the regression line. Hence, it should be interpreted as the average error in guessing $\hat{Y}_i$. Returning to the automobile-sales example, the average error is computed as follows:

$$SEE = \sqrt{\frac{9,154,513}{16 - 2}}$$

$$SEE = 809 \text{ thousand automobile units} \qquad (5\text{-}27)$$

Although the standard error of the estimate may be utilized to gauge the reliability of estimates, it has several deficiencies. First, it can be shown that the SEE depends upon the unit of measurement of the dependent variable. This occurs because the SEE relies on the residual term, $Y_i - \hat{Y}_i$, to measure goodness of fit. This residual is not unit-free. If we divide all values of Y by 100, this yields a different result for SEE. Second, the standard error is a measure of single-period error; it does not provide us with any measure of the error in future multiperiod forecasts. Finally, the SEE is calculated based on known values of the independent variables. This certainly is not the situation that prevails in the future periods for which estimates are desired.

ANALYSIS OF VARIANCE

Analysis of variance, hereafter called AOV, focuses on the ability of a regression line to explain or account for the variation in Y. This can best be seen by concentrating our attention on Figure 5-7. Assume, again, that you

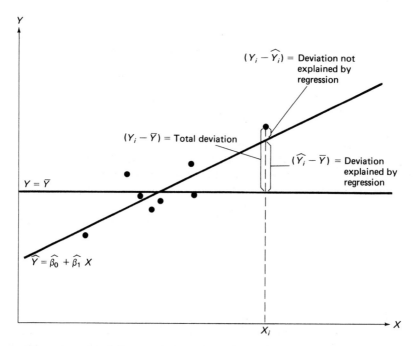

Figure 5-7   Explained and Unexplained Deviation: Simple Regression

are a business-conditions analyst interested in predicting automobile sales. Further assume that you are doing this in the absence of any knowledge about income levels. In this case, your best guess will be the average observed value of automobile sales—that is, $\bar{Y}$. In Figure 5-7, this guess ($\bar{Y}$) involves a large estimating error. This error can be depicted as $(Y_i - \bar{Y})$, the deviation in Y_i from its mean. Estimation of the regression line allows us to obtain another, perhaps better, estimate of Y. That is, instead of estimating automobile sales as $\bar{Y}$, we use $\hat{Y}$, which is derived from the regression line. Figure 5-7 presents this comparison.

A large part of the deviation, $(\hat{Y}_i - \bar{Y})$, is now explained by the regression. This leaves only a relatively small portion of the deviation unexplained, $Y_i - \hat{Y}_i$. Formally, the total deviation in Y can be regarded as the sum:

$$
\begin{array}{ccc}
(Y_i - \bar{Y}) = & (\hat{Y}_i - \bar{Y}) + & (Y_i - \hat{Y}_i) \\
\text{Total} & \text{Explained} & \text{Unexplained} \\
\text{deviation} & = \text{deviation} + & \text{deviation}
\end{array}
\tag{5-28}
$$

which holds for all i. It therefore follows that:

$$
\sum (Y_i - \bar{Y}) = \sum (\hat{Y}_i - \bar{Y}) + \sum (Y_i - \hat{Y}_i)
\tag{5-29}
$$

Furthermore, it can be shown that this same equality holds when these deviations are squared. Thus:

$$
\begin{array}{ccc}
\sum (Y_i - \bar{Y})^2 = & \sum (\hat{Y}_i - \bar{Y})^2 + & \sum (Y_i - \hat{Y}_i)^2 \\
\text{Total} & \text{Explained} & \text{Unexplained} \\
\text{variation} & = \text{variation} + & \text{variation}
\end{array}
\tag{5-30}
$$

where variation is defined as the sum of squared deviations. It is occasionally convenient to rewrite equation (5-30) as:

$$
\begin{array}{ccc}
\sum (Y_i - \bar{Y})^2 = & \hat{\beta}_1^2 \sum (X_i - \bar{X})^2 + & \sum (Y_i - \hat{Y}_i)^2 \\
\text{Total} & \text{Variation} & \text{Unexplained} \\
\text{variation} & = \text{explained} + & \text{variation} \\
& \text{by } X &
\end{array}
\tag{5-31}
$$

This formulation highlights the role of X in accounting for variations in Y.

The components noted in equations (5-30) and (5-31) are commonly presented in an AOV table similar to Table 5-3.

The goal in regression analysis is to derive a regression line that will assist us in predicting Y. If we can link the variation in Y to variations in X, we can use our knowledge of changes in disposable income to predict changes in automobile sales. The AOV table incorporates the F test of the regression equation's significance. The F test may be viewed as a test that $\beta_1 = 0$, or a

Table 5-3 Analysis-of-variance table for linear regression

Sources of Variation	Variation	Degrees of Freedom[b]	Variance[c]	F_e[d]
Explained by regression[a]	$\sum (\hat{Y}_i - \bar{Y})^2$ or $\hat{\beta}_1^2 \sum (X_i - \bar{X})^2$	1	$\dfrac{\sum (\hat{Y}_i - \bar{Y})^2}{1}$	
Unexplained residual or error[a]	$\sum (Y_i - \hat{Y})^2$	$n - 2$	$s^2 = \dfrac{\sum (Y_i - \hat{Y}_i)^2}{n-2}$	$\dfrac{\sum (\hat{Y}_i - \bar{Y})^2}{s^2}$
Total	$\sum (Y_i - \bar{Y})^2$	$n - 1$		

[a]See equations (5-30) and (5-31).
[b]Based on a sample of size n. If used for a multiple regression equation with a sample of size N and K regression coefficients, the corresponding degrees of freedom would be K, $N - (K + 1)$, and $N - 1$. The K value does not include the constant.
[c]Variation divided by degrees of freedom.
[d]See equations (5-33) and (5-34). This is the actual or observed F value. It is compared to the theoretical or critical F value in order to determine the significance of the regression.

test that $r^2 = 0$.[13] Analysis of variance focuses on the first of these two tests. The issue under consideration is whether or not the ratio of the explained variance to unexplained variance is sufficiently large to reject the hypothesis that Y is unrelated to X. Specifically, the test statistic and the hypothesis are:

$$H_0: \beta_1 = 0$$

$$F_e = \frac{\text{Variance explained by regression } (X)}{\text{Unexplained variance}} \tag{5-32}$$

Formally:

$$F_e = \frac{\hat{\beta}_1^2 \sum (X_i - \bar{X})^2}{s^2} \tag{5-33}$$

or:

$$F_e = \frac{\sum (\hat{Y}_i - \bar{Y})^2}{\sum (Y_i - \hat{Y}_i)^2/(n - 2)} \tag{5-34}$$

A .05 significance test involves finding the critical F value that leaves 5 percent of the distribution in the right-hand tail. Thus, the decision rule can be formulated as: If the calculated value of F_e exceeds the critical value of F_{cr}, reject H_0. Table 5-4 illustrates the AOV table for the automobile-sales example.[14]

To test the null hypothesis, calculate F_e:

$$F_e = \frac{2,572,539}{653,894}$$

$$F_e = 3.93 \tag{5-35}$$

[13]The observant reader will notice that this is identical to the situation of testing H_0: $\beta_1 = 0$ with the t test. However, this equality is not true in general (in multiple regression); therefore, both are presented here. Further, the F test has a special applicability in the case of stepwise regression. This use will be noted in Chapter 7.

[14]Some computer software packages will refer to variation as sum of squares and variance as mean square or mean square error.

Table 5-4 Analysis-of-variance table for automobile sales and income

Source of Variation	Variation	d.f.	Variance
Explained by regression	$\hat{\beta}_1^2 \sum (X_i - \bar{X})^2 =$ (3.240)^2(245,091)	1	2,572,539
Unexplained	$\sum (Y_i - \hat{Y}_i)^2 =$ 9,154,513	14	653,894
Total	11,727,050	15	$F_e = 3.93$

Source: Table 5-2 and equation (5-35)

Since F_e is less than 4.60 (the critical value of F taken from Appendix C), we accept H_0. Therefore, knowledge of the level of disposable income does not provide a statistically reliable estimate of automobile sales.

COEFFICIENTS OF DETERMINATION AND CORRELATION

Correlation coefficients can also be used to specify the degree of relationship between variables. Simple correlation analysis yields a number designed to give us a picture of how closely two variables move together. In correlation analysis we need not be concerned with causal relationships. This is the primary distinction between regression and correlation. Correlation techniques do not involve any implicit assumptions of causality; regression techniques do. Generally, forecasters find correlation to be a less powerful technique; hence, our interest is in utilizing correlation as one of several measures of goodness of fit.

There are a variety of formulas for calculating and interpreting the simple correlation coefficient, r. The most convenient method follows from the development of AOV. Let us first define the coefficient of determination as:

$$r^2 = \frac{\sum (\hat{Y}_i - \bar{Y})^2}{\sum (Y_i - \bar{Y})^2}$$
$$= \frac{\text{Explained variation}}{\text{Total variation}} \qquad (5\text{-}36)$$

This formulation permits a clear interpretation. The coefficient of determination is the proportion of the total variation in Y that is explained by a regression line. Since the explained variation cannot exceed the total variation, the maximum value of r^2 is 1—that is, 100 percent. The coefficient of correlation (r) is the square root of the coefficient of determination. That is:

$$r = \sqrt{r^2} \qquad (5\text{-}37)$$

The sign of r depends on the sign of the regression coefficient $(\hat{\beta}_1)$; hence its limits are ± 1. Returning to the example in Table 5-2:

$$r^2 = \frac{\sum (\hat{Y}_t - \bar{Y})^2}{\sum (Y_t - \bar{Y})^2}$$

$$= \frac{2{,}572{,}539}{11{,}727{,}050}$$

$$r^2 = .22$$

$$r = .47 \qquad\qquad (5\text{-}38)$$

Thus, we have explained approximately 22 percent of the variation in Y by variation in X, further evidence that our simple model is an inadequate explanatory model. Although it is a common practice to associate high values of r and r^2 with a good fit and low values with a poor fit, this interpretation can be misleading if not supported by other summary statistics. It can be shown that these measures are somewhat dependent upon the number of independent variables in the regression.

CONCLUDING COMMENTARY

Prior to the presentation of more realistic examples and the use of regression for forecasting, several concluding remarks are in order. First, the reader is reminded that the example utilized throughout this section was selected for illustrative purposes. In the majority of cases, the forecaster will have access to computers. The formulas, calculations, and tests previously noted were presented and analyzed so as to develop a conceptual understanding.

Second, we have not verified the assumptions of the classical linear model.

Finally, and most significantly for our purposes, we have not evaluated the usefulness of regression as a predictive device. The tests presented here are designed primarily to measure the statistical reliability of regression. Although there is some relation between statistical reliability and achievement of forecasting accuracy, they are not the same thing. In order to evaluate regression equations as forecasting techniques, we need to develop additional concepts and tools.

Example 5-1: Air-Miles Traveled

The head of the forecasting division received a request from a senior vice-president of purchasing to provide a quarterly estimate that can be used to plan crude-oil purchases so as to minimize costs. The firm is a major supplier of fuel to the airlines, and advance estimates of fuel demand are critical because of erratic fluctuations in both the price and the supply of crude oil. The goal is to develop a model that will provide a quarterly estimate of the demand for airline fuel.

The preparation of a forecast presupposes several items. The first item of concern is the selection of a variable that can be used to measure the demand for high-octane airplane fuel. After a review of past research, it was decided to use air miles flown as a proxy variable. The advantage of this variable is that there is a fairly stable relationship between miles flown and fuel consumption. Once estimated, the mileage can simply be used to determine the probable demand for fuel.

Since total miles flown is related to economic activity on a national level, real gross national product was selected as the independent or causal factor that best measures aggregate activity. The model becomes:

$$\widehat{AM}_t = \hat{\beta}_0 + \hat{\beta}_1 \, RGNP_t + e_t \tag{5-39}$$

where:

$\widehat{AM}_t$ = quarterly air-miles traveled in time period t; seasonally adjusted; billions of miles

$RGNP_t$ = real gross national product in quarter t; seasonally adjusted; billions of dollars

$\hat{\beta}_0, \hat{\beta}_1$ = regression coefficients to be estimated

We would logically expect the slope coefficient, $\hat{\beta}_1$, to have a positive value, implying that as real gross national product increases, air-miles traveled increases. Additionally, we have no *a priori* expectation regarding the intercept, $\hat{\beta}_0$. That is, since we do not have any observations on AM_t when $RGNP_t$ is equal to zero, we cannot assign any economic interpretation to the value or sign of $\hat{\beta}_0$.

Time-series data were collected on a quarterly basis for the period from the first quarter of 1961 (1961: I) to the third quarter of 1979 (1979: III). The actual data utilized in this example are documented in Appendix D, Table D-1. As an initial step, a scatter diagram was plotted, and the clustering in Figure 5-8 verified the belief that there was a positive relationship between air-miles traveled and RGNP. That is, as RGNP increases, air miles traveled increases.

Based on the inspection of Figure 5-8, we decide to proceed with fitting a regression equation and investigating its statistical reliability. The results of fitting a linear regression to the data (Table D-1) were:

$$\widehat{AM}_t = -41.824 + 0.061130223 \, RGNP_t \tag{5-40}$$

Standard error	(0.0011757541)
t_e	51.99
95% C.I.	±0.002304478
Range of data:	1961 : I to 1978 : IV
Degrees of freedom:	70
$r^2 = 0.975$	$F_{1,70} = 2,703$
$r = 0.987$	SEE = 1.82183

This output is typical of the cryptic summarization of regression information provided by computer-generated statistical programs. A business-conditions analyst

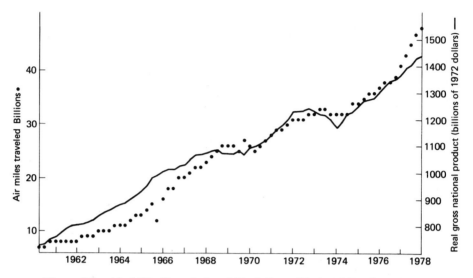

Figure 5-8 Air Miles Traveled and Real Gross National Product, 1961–1978

Source: *Survey of Current Business;* Table D–1

interested in forecasting applications must squeeze the maximum possible information from each of the regression statistics. Looking first at the regression coefficients, the intercept value, −41.824, provides no meaningful information; interpreted literally, it implies that if GNP equals zero (that is, if we have no economic activity), we will have a negative level of air travel! The slope coefficient implies that a $1 billion increase in real GNP will lead to an increase of approximately 61 million air passenger miles traveled.

Immediately below the regression coefficient associated with RGNP are the statistics used to evaluate its reliability. The standard error of the coefficient is used in calculating the t statistic and in computing the confidence interval. To check the null hypothesis that the observed slope of 0.061130223 is significantly different from zero (that is, it did not occur by chance), we can use either of the following two procedures:

1. A comparison of the calculated t statistic, t_e, with the critical value of this statistic, t_{cr}, can be used to accept (or reject) $H_0: \beta_1 = 0$. In this case, the fact that t_e (52) exceeds t_{cr} (2) implies that we can reject H_0.
2. The information needed to construct a 95 percent confidence interval is presented immediately below the t statistic. In this case, the actual confidence interval is:

$$0.058779 \leq \beta_1 \leq 0.063480 \qquad (5\text{-}41)$$

Since the interval does not contain zero, we reject H_0. Given these test results, we can be reasonably confident that the observed slope coefficient, 0.061130223, is significantly different from zero. Thus, the equation can be used to estimate air miles traveled.

Continuing with the analysis, note that the regression equation explained approximately 98 percent of the variation in the dependent variable. Alternatively, we could have relied upon the analysis-of-variance table, Table 5-5, to test the statistical

Table 5-5 Analysis of variance for air miles traveled

Source of Variation	Variation	d.f.	Variance
Explained	8,972.11	1	8,972.11
Unexplained	232.33	70	3.3191
Total	9,204.44	71	$F_e = 2,703$

Source: Equations (5-40) and (5-42)

reliability of the regression equation. This is accomplished by computing the F statistic as follows:

$$F_e = F_{1,70} = \frac{\text{Explained variance}}{\text{Unexplained variance}}$$

$$= 8,972/3.32 \text{ (Table 5-5)}$$

$$F_e = 2,703 \qquad (5\text{-}42)$$

Since F_e exceeds the critical value of 4, we conclude that the regression equation is statistically significant. That is, the observed regression relationship will provide a better estimate of AM_t than could be obtained by simply relying on the mean of air miles traveled.

As a final check on the average precision of the regression estimates, we can use the standard error of the estimate (SEE). As noted earlier, the SEE is the average error $(AM_t - \hat{AM}_t)$ one would have made by mechanically plugging the historical values of RGNP into the regression equation. Since it is futile to interpret this average quarterly error without reference to the actual values of AM_t, a simple comparative ratio is given by:

$$\text{Average percentage regression error} = \frac{\text{SEE}}{\text{AM}_t}$$

$$= \frac{1.82183}{23.7778}$$

$$\text{APE} = 7.66\% \qquad (5\text{-}43)$$

On average, regression estimates have been in error by 7.66 percent.

Example 5-2: Retail Sales of New Passenger Cars

Suppose you are the credit manager for a firm whose primary line of business is the provision of short-term financing for inventories of retail automobile dealers. In order to determine the demand for cash to finance these inventories, you decide to develop quantitative estimates of automobile sales.

To assist in the analysis of quarterly sales of automobiles, let us postulate the following model for dollars-sales of new cars:

$$\widehat{RSAUTO}_t = \hat{\beta}_0 + \hat{\beta}_1 YPLTP_t + e_t \qquad (5\text{-}44)$$

where:

$\widehat{RSAUTO}_t$ = quarterly retail sales of automobiles in millions of dollars; seasonally adjusted at annual rates

$YPLTP_t$ = personal income less transfer payments; billions of dollars; seasonally adjusted at annual rates

Demand theory tells us that retail sales should be positively related to income levels; thus, the coefficient associated with $YPLTP$ should be positive. As before, we have no reason to analyze $\hat{\beta}_0$.

The data base is a quarterly tabulation for the period from 1956: I to 1979: IV and is presented in Table D-2 (Appendix D). The scatter diagram in Figure 5-9 provides initial verification that high values of income are indeed associated with high sales levels. The results of fitting a regression line to the scatter diagram are:

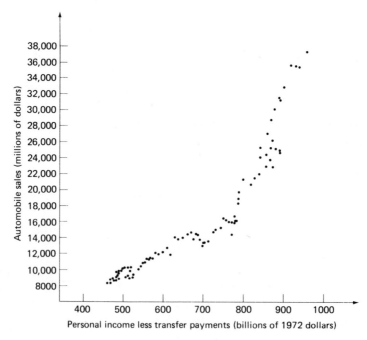

Figure 5-9 Retail Sales of Automobiles and Personal Income Less Transfer Payments, 1956–1977

Source: Table D-2

$$\widehat{RSAUTO}_t = -14{,}956 + 45.98248 YPLTP_t \qquad (5\text{-}45)$$

Standard error	(2.116788)
t_e	21.72
99% C.I.	±5.45
Range of data: 1956:I to 1977:IV	
Degrees of freedom: 86	
$r^2 = 0.846$	$F_{1,86} = 472$
$r = 0.920$	SEE = 3,030

The 99 percent confidence interval for β_1

$$40.532 \le \beta_1 \le 51.432 \qquad (5\text{-}46)$$

does not contain zero, indicating that we can reject the hypothesis that $\beta_1 = 0$. The observed relationship between auto sales and income is statistically significant at the .01 confidence level. The coefficient itself indicates that if income changes by \$1 billion, automobile sales increase by \$45.98 million.

The analysis-of-variance table, Table 5-6, presents the necessary information to evaluate the reliability of the entire equation. The F statistic from Table 5-6 is:

$$F_{1,86} = \frac{4{,}331{,}967{,}780}{9{,}180{,}269}$$

$$= 472 \qquad (5\text{-}47)$$

This F value, together with the fact that we have been able to explain 85 percent of the variation in automobile sales, means that the regression equation passes the statistical tests of reliability. The average percentage error (APE) is, however, high:

$$APE = \frac{SEE}{\overline{RSAUTO}_t}$$

$$= \frac{3{,}030}{16{,}620}$$

$$APE = 18\% \qquad (5\text{-}48)$$

Table 5-6   Analysis of variance for retail sales of automobiles

Source of Variation	Variation	d.f.	Variance
Explained by regression	4.3319677 E 09	1	4.3319677 E 09
Unexplained	7.8950312 E 08	86	9,180,269 $F_e = 472$

Source: Equation (5-45)

Many computers will present the numbers in the AOV table, Table 5-6, in scientific form because of their magnitude. Therefore, rather than printing 4,331,967,780, they will print 4.331967780 E 09. The E 09 tells us to move the decimal point nine places to the right of its current position. If the number had been 4.3319E-04, we would have moved the decimal point four places to the left.

FORECASTING WITH SIMPLE LINEAR REGRESSION MODELS

TYPES OF FORECASTS

Previous sections of this chapter have focused on fitting a regression line and on how to evaluate the statistical reliability of this model. We now turn to the task of using regression models in forecasting.

A forecast is a numerical estimate concerning the probability of future events based on past and current information. The estimated regression equation contains all the past and current information at our disposal. By extending our models beyond the reference period, we can utilize this information to obtain quantitative guesses about future values of specific variables. Specifically, our concern is to obtain estimates of the changes in certain variables, given information about the changes in other variables.

Forecasts of future values of Y involve a two-step process. First, we must derive a point estimate of Y based on a specific value of X; second, we must derive a confidence interval around this point. Formally, the first step can be stated as:

$$\hat{Y}_{t+1} = \hat{\beta}_0 + \hat{\beta}_1 X_{t+1} \qquad (5\text{-}49)$$

Once we have estimated $\hat{\beta}_0$ and $\hat{\beta}_1$ by the least-squares procedure and have estimated a value for X_{t+1}, we can obtain a forecast value for Y_{t+1}. In the unit-car-sales example, assume that $X_{t+1} = \$800$ billion. Thus, the best point estimate can be obtained as follows, based on equation (5-8):

$$\begin{aligned}
\hat{Y}_{t+1} &= \hat{\beta}_0 + \hat{\beta}_1 X_{t+1} \\
&= 5{,}807 + 3.24 X_{t+1} \\
&= 5{,}807 + 3.24(800) \\
\hat{Y}_{t+1} &= 8{,}399 \text{ million}
\end{aligned}$$

Construction of a confidence interval for this point estimate requires a measure of the forecasting error. It can be shown that the variance involved in this process is:

$$V_f = \sigma^2 \left[\frac{1}{n} + \frac{(X_{t+1} - \bar{X})^2}{\sum (X_i - \bar{X})^2} + 1 \right] \qquad (5\text{-}50)$$

Since the variance for the population, σ^2, is generally unknown, it is estimated by s^2, the sample variance. Equation (5-50) is of immediate interest because it tells us that the forecast error is sensitive to (1) sample size, (2) variance of X, and (3) the distance between X_{t+1} and $\bar{X}$. This latter point deserves further clarification. The best forecasts for Y can be made for values of X close to $\bar{X}$. In fact, when $X_{t+1} = \bar{X}$, the latter term in equation (5-50) disappears, and the error is simply a function of sample size. Thus, the farther we extend X_{t+1} away from $\bar{X}$, the larger the error becomes and the less reliable the forecast is likely to be. The confidence interval for the point estimate, equation (5-49), can be shown to be equal to:[15]

$$Y_{t+1} = \hat{Y}_{t+1} \pm t_\alpha s \sqrt{\frac{1}{n} + \frac{(X_{t+1} - \bar{X})^2}{\sum (X_i - \bar{X})^2} + 1} \qquad (5\text{-}51)$$

When $X_{t+1} = 800$ and $\alpha = .10$, the calculations are:

$$Y_{t+1} = 8{,}399 \pm 1.761(809) \sqrt{\frac{1}{16} + \frac{(800 - 729)^2}{245{,}091} + 1}$$

$$= 8{,}399 \pm 1{,}483 \qquad (5\text{-}52)$$

$$6{,}916 \le Y_{t+1} \le 9{,}882 \qquad (5\text{-}53)$$

The forecaster has 90 percent confidence that the true value of Y_{t+1} falls somewhere in this confidence interval. Furthermore, we can obtain 90 percent confidence intervals for all other values of X. This permits the derivation of confidence bands—a confidence interval for all values of X. Figure 5-10 illustrates the 90 percent confidence band for the unit-car-sales example. The principal usefulness of this diagram is to highlight the fact that the greater the distance between X and $\bar{X}$, the larger our confidence interval becomes. Thus, once we attempt to extrapolate too far into the future, we are likely to encounter ever-larger forecast errors.

It is useful to differentiate among (1) *ex post* and *ex ante* forecasts, and (2) conditional and unconditional forecasts. Both *ex post* and *ex ante* forecasts provide estimated values of the dependent variable beyond the time period for which the model has been fitted. However, in an *ex post* forecast, the forecast period is such that observations on both the dependent and independent variables are known with certainty. *Ex post* forecasts can be compared with existing data for Y, thereby providing a means of evaluating the forecasting

---

[15]Technically, this confidence interval is for small samples. The interval for large samples ($n > 30$) is given by:

$$Y_0 = \hat{Y}_0 \pm t_\alpha s$$

For details, see, for example, H. Theil, *Principles of Econometrics* (New York: John Wiley, 1971), Chap. 8.

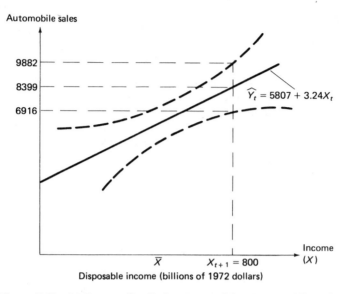

Figure 5-10   90 Percent Prediction Interval for Automobile Sales

reliability of the model. Indeed, as we shall see in the next section, one of the best techniques for evaluating forecasts from regression models is *ex post* forecasting. This distinction can be clarified by referring to Example 5-1, the air-miles-traveled model given in equation (5-40). An examination of the data reveals that the fourth quarter of 1978 was the last data point included in the estimating equation. An *ex post* forecast can be prepared for the first quarter of 1979 because the actual values for real GNP ($1,431 million) and air miles traveled (51 billion miles) are available. Thus, the *ex post* forecast value is:

$$\widehat{AM}_t = -41.824 + 0.061130223 RGNP_t \tag{5-40}$$

$$\widehat{AM}_{1979:1} = -41.824 + 0.061130223 RGNP_{1979:1}$$
$$= -41.824 + 0.061130223(1,431)$$
$$= 46 \text{ billion miles} \tag{5-54}$$

The critical feature in this computation is that the estimate of 46 billion miles can be compared with the actual value of 51 billion miles. Furthermore, this *ex post* forecast is based on an actual value for real GNP (1,431).

Whereas an *ex post* forecast is made with certain knowledge as to the values of both the independent and dependent variable, an *ex ante* forecast is made without any knowledge regarding the value of the actual dependent variable. The value of the independent variable may or may not be known with certainty.

Continuing with the air-miles-traveled example, an *ex ante* forecast would be of the form:[16]

$$\widehat{AM}_{1979:IV} = -41.824 + 0.061130223RGNP_{1979:IV} \qquad (5\text{-}55)$$

or:

$$\widehat{AM}_{1986:III} = -41.824 + 0.061130223RGNP_{1986:III} \qquad (5\text{-}56)$$

An unconditional forecast implies that the values for all the independent variables in the regression equation are known. Equation (5-55) is an unconditional forecast, because the 1979: IV value of RGNP is known with certainty. All *ex post* forecasts are unconditional, but *ex ante* forecasts may also be unconditional. For example, it is possible that we would know the exact value of RGNP in the third quarter of 1982 but would not have the exact value for AM_t for the same period. *Ex post* forecasts require certain knowledge for both dependent and independent variables. Unconditional forecasts require that only independent variables be known with certainty. In a conditional forecast, values for one or more independent variables are not known with certainty. The implication is that with conditional forecasts, we must have a method of forecasting (estimating) values for the independent variables. Equation (5-56) exemplifies a conditional forecasting equation.

The practicing forecaster is apt to rely upon all four of these classifications at various stages of research. For example, *ex post* forecasts are made with the intention of evaluating forecast reliability (see the next section). Alternatively, development of *ex ante* forecasts, which focus on estimating unknown values for the dependent variable, is the primary point of interest throughout this text. The previous discussion pointed out the distinction between conditional and unconditional forecasts; the former utilizes projections for the independent variables, whereas the latter incorporates known values. Even though in most cases future values of the independent variables are not known, many variables can be estimated with a high degree of accuracy. Because conditional forecasting requires a high level of mathematical sophistication, many business forecasters utilize estimates of the independent variables prepared by commercial forecast vendors. One way to circumvent the problem of predicting values for the independent variable is to have lagged independent variables. In Example 5-2, we could have postulated that retail sales of automobiles in the current period are related to income levels in the previous period. That is:

$$\widehat{RSAUTO}_t = \hat{\beta}_0 + \hat{\beta}_1 YPLTP_{t-1} \qquad (5\text{-}57)$$

[16]At the time this was written, the value of air miles traveled in the fourth quarter of 1979 was not tabulated. However, the value for real GNP was known for this quarter. By way of contrast, neither value was known for equation (5-56).

The alternative is to construct models in such a manner that the independent variables can be predicted with near perfection. The most efficient way of accomplishing this goal involves reliance on commercial forecast vendors; that is, in applied work, the independent variables selected for inclusion in the model should be variables that the commercial vendors themselves forecast with a high degree of historical accuracy.

FORECAST EVALUATION

Although it is important to develop a regression equation that minimizes error, it is equally important that the forecaster understand that the sources of forecast error associated with a linear regression result from a combination of four distinct sources.

First, the random nature of the linear regression model literally guarantees that the forecast values will differ from the actual values even if we have the equation of the true unknown regression line. Second, the actual process of estimating the sample regression coefficient (which was discussed at length in this chapter) gives rise to sampling errors. Third, in the case of a conditional forecast, errors occur becaues predictions must be made for the independent variables; to the extent that forecast scenarios for independent variables such as real GNP are incorrect, the projections for the dependent variable (Y) will thus be in error. Finally, errors may be introduced because the equation is mathematically misspecified; that is, the least-squares assumption of linearity may be incorrect.[17]

Prior to preparing unconditional forecasts, we need to further develop techniques for evaluating the forecasting reliability of regression estimates. This is a quite different problem from statistical evaluation. In all previous examples, we have highlighted the t, F, r^2, SEE, and confidence intervals. A single-equation regression model may have a high t and F, yet may fail as a forecasting device. This can occur because of inherent volatility in the forecast variable being analyzed. For example, if we estimate a monthly equation, the irregular component can dominate and produce low t and F statistics. However, if the errors in estimating tend to offset each other, it may be a satisfactory forecasting equation. Conversely, a high SEE or a low r^2 does not guarantee a bad forecasting equation. This could occur when our dependent variable exhibits little variation—that is, changes slowly over time.

As has been pointed out several times, the best test of the reliability for any model is its *ex ante* forecasting performance. However, if this were the only test, forecasting as we know it would cease to exist. Some pretesting on actual data is essential to an evaluation of models. Included in this pretesting

---

[17]The distinctions and definitions in this section draw on R. S. Pindyck and D. L. Rubinfeld, *Econometric Models and Economic Forecasts* (New York: McGraw-Hill, 1976), pp. 156–80.

are computation and validation of the t and F statistics. The most common measure of goodness of fit is the correlation coefficient (r) or its counterpart, the coefficient of determination (r^2). This is unfortunate, because, to quote Michael Evans:

> In all of the thousands of equations which I have estimated for predictive purposes, probably less than five percent of those selected for forecasting were those with the highest $\bar{R}^2$. The reason is simple. If one calculates several regression equations in order to determine the best one, it is likely that certain variables will appear to be significant when in fact they have only a spurious correlation. If one leaves these variables in the equation, he is likely to generate a very poor forecast.[18]

If this is true, how do we exclude those variables that do not belong? Once again, we quote Evans:

> Part of the answer to this question goes back to my earlier remarks about the importance of choosing a reasonable theory as a guide toward estimating the best forecasting equation.[19]

The other part of the answer involves computation and interpretation of measures specifically devised to measure and test the forecasting reliability of models. Virtually all practitioners test their empirical work by estimating an equation, looking at the size of the error terms, and then re-estimating the equation in an attempt to reduce the error terms. Although this approach is a reasonable part of empirical work, there are other facets of this process that must be noted. These include the autocorrelation of the residuals, the signs ($+$ or $-$) and significance of the estimated coefficients, the reliability at turning points, intuitive judgements as to the size of the coefficients, and the overall fit of the equation. The specific criteria most commonly relied upon are: (1) the mean absolute deviation (MAD), (2) mean square error (MSE), (3) mean absolute percentage error (MAPE), (4) Theil U statistic, (5) *ex post* forecasts, and (6) turning point error graphs and computations. The first four criteria were presented in Chapter 4; hence, they require no additional elaboration.

Ex post forecasts are the other commonly relied upon evaluative technique, and these *ex post* forecasts can then be used to examine the reliability of the estimated equation outside the sample period. To perform this test, the following steps are undertaken:

1. The regression equation is estimated based on a truncated sample period (i.e., the entire data base is not used). Although there is no magic number of data periods to omit, we will generally omit the last three or four.

---

[18]Michael K. Evans, "Econometric Models," in William F. Butler, Robert A. Kavesh, and Rǫbert B. Platt, *Methods and Techniques of Business Forecasting* (Englewood Cliffs, N.J.: Prentice-Hall, 1974), pp. 172–73.

[19]Ibid., p. 173.

2. The known values for the independent variables are utilized to develop uncon-ditional *ex post* forecasts for the dependent variable.
3. These forecast values are then compared to the actual values.
4. If the equation is deemed to be satisfactory, the equation is rerun using all available data points.

Another set of widely used tests is the various turning-point error tests. All of these tests are based on a comparison of the equation's ability to correctly predict turning points and involve a comparison of the signs or amounts of predicted changes and actual changes. For example, suppose we have a series that rises, declines, and then rises again in three successive periods. Further-more, suppose that the forecast method predicts three increases. In this situation, we have missed one turning point; thus we have made one turning-point error. That is, the pattern in the actual series was $+ - +$, whereas in the predicted series it was $+ + +$. We have missed the directional change between periods 1 and 2. Further, quoting Zarnowitz:

> In evaluating turning point errors, two questions must be asked: (1) How often do turning points occur that have not been predicted? (2) How often do pre-dicted turns actually occur? Accordingly, there are two basic types of error: missed turns and false signals.[20]

False signals would be exemplified by a pattern of $+ + +$ for actual values, as opposed to a predicted pattern of $+ - +$.

By way of contrast, there are two types of correct forecasts. In one, a turning point was predicted and it actually occurred; in the other, no turning point was predicted and none occurred. Again, quoting Zarnowitz:

> Thus there are four basic possibilities, which can be arranged in a 2 × 2 table as follows. (*N* refers to the absence, *T* to the presence of a turning point. The first letter refers to actual values, the second to forecasts.)

Actual \ Forecast	No TP	TP
No TP	*NN*	*NT*
TP	*TN*	*TT*

The number of correct forecasts is the sum of the diagonal frequencies: *NN* + *TT*. False signals are represented by *NT* and missed turns by *TN*.[21]

To compute the proportion of false signals, we use the ratio:

---

[20]Victor Zarnowitz, *An Appraisal of Short Term Economic Forecasts* (New York: National Bureau of Economic Research, 1967), pp. 51–59.
[21]Ibid., p. 52.

$$\bar{E}_{T1} = \frac{NT}{NT + TT} \qquad (5\text{-}58)$$

whereas the missed signals are given by:

$$\bar{E}_{T2} = \frac{TN}{TN + TT} \qquad (5\text{-}59)$$

In addition to computing the false and missed signal values, analysts rely heavily upon graphs similar to Figure 5-7 in which comparisons between actual and predicted values of the dependent variable are made. The pragmatic empiricist utilizes all of these tests when developing his or her model. Due to space limitations, we will not attempt to present all tests with all models. Nevertheless, in real forecasting situations, you should, at various stages of your analysis, rely on these measures in conjunction with the standard statistical and theoretical considerations. Indeed, they are all integral parts of any successful forecasting effort.

Example 5-3: Air-Miles Traveled, Continued

In Example 5-1, the primary purpose was to check the statistical validity of the regression equation. We now turn to the task of appraising the forecasting reliability of the estimated equation. In order to gauge the reliability, we need to check the performance of our regression equation relative to the simple models introduced earlier. Specifically, we will compare the regression equation with the naive forecast that $\hat{Y}_{t+1} = Y_t$.

As previously noted, one of the conventional methods of evaluation is to analyze *ex post* forecasts. Once the regression equation has been estimated, it can be utilized to conduct numerous simulations. There are three time periods over which this testing can be conducted. Simulation over the period in which the model has been estimated is referred to as the *ex post* or historical simulation. The advantage of this simulation is that actual values of the dependent variable are known and hence can be compared with the estimated values to test the equation's validity. These after-the-fact estimations are invaluable in developing empirical models. *Ex post* forecasting implies that the model is simulated beyond the estimation period but not beyond the last date for which actual data are available for all variables. Thus, in an *ex post* forecast, observations on both the dependent and independent variables are known with certainty. This can be assured by the omission of several of the data points from our series. In equation (5-40), the last observation actually used was the fourth quarter of 1978. However, the data base (Table D-1) contains observations for three succeeding quarters—1979: I, II, and III. Equation (5-40) can be utilized to prepare *ex post* forecasts for these three periods. These forecasts can then be compared with the actual observed values.

Actual values for real gross national product (the independent variable) and air miles traveled (the dependent variable) are listed in the first and second columns of Table 5-7.

Table 5-7 Predicting air miles traveled: regression vs. naive forecasting models

		Real GNP (Billions of $) (1)	Air Miles Traveled (Billions) (2)	*Ex Post* Estimates from Regression[a] (3)	Forecast Error from Regression (4)	*Ex Post* Estimates from Naive Model[b] (5)	Forecast Error from Naive Model (6)
1979:	I	1,431	51	45.66	5.34	48	3
	II	1,422	50	45.11	4.89	51	−1
	III	1,433	52	45.78	6.22	50	2

[a]Based on equation (5-40).
[b]Based on naive model: $\hat{Y}_{t+1} = Y_t$.

The naive-model's *ex post* forecasts are presented in column 5 of Table 5-7. A comparison of columns 4 and 6 reveals that the naive model performs significantly better than the regression model. The former involves an average percentage error of 4 percent, and the latter has a percentage error of almost 11 percent. Further, the regression model consistently underestimates the actual number of air miles traveled. Based solely on this appraisal, the regression equation has less forecasting reliability than the simple naive model. This is true despite the fact that the former passed all our statistical tests. However, it is still possible that the relative performance of the regression equation is superior according to other criteria. For example, the regression equation may perform better at picking up turning points. This becomes especially significant with regard to the turning points that occur at the peaks and troughs of a business cycle.

To test for turning point accuracy, the equation was re-estimated:

$$\widehat{AM}_t = -43.818 + 0.063165461\,RGNP_t \tag{5-60}$$

Standard error	(0.0012364472)
t_e	51.09
95% C.I.	±0.0024729
Range of data:	1961:I to 1979:III
d.f. = 73	$F_{1,37} = 2,610$
$r^2 = 0.973$	SEE = 2.056
$r = 0.986$	

The reliability of this equation can be related to the naive model via a comparison of the four remaining criteria noted in the preceding section, "Forecast Evaluation." Table 5-8 presents the results of this comparison.

According to all criteria, save one, the naive forecasting model performs better than the estimated regression equation. The naive technique misses 35 percent of the turning points, whereas the regression equation misses only 14 percent.

The principal implication of these results is that, as specified, the regression equation is not particularly useful as a forecasting device. There are numerous explana-

Table 5-8 Alternative evaluations of regression and naive models for air miles

	MAD[a]	MSE[a]	MAPE[a]	Turning-Point Errors[b]	
				Missed TP	False TP
	(Billions of air miles)	(Billions of air miles)	Percent		
Regression model[c]	1.55	4.12	9.35%	14%	33%
Naive model[d]	0.81	1.37	3.63%	35%	27%

[a]MAD, MSE, and MAPE error calculations based on the mean absolute deviation, the mean square error, and the mean absolute percentage error, respectively. See Chapter 4 for a discussion of the computational formulas.
[b]See equations (5-58) and (5-59).
[c]Based on equation (5-60).
[d]Assumes $\hat{Y}_{t+1} = Y_t$.

tions for this. We may be violating one or more of the assumptions of the linear model, or we may have misspecified the equation.

Example 5-4: Retail Sales of Automobiles, Continued

Two additional factors deserve mention at this stage of our analysis. The forecasting equation for retail sales of automobiles, equation (5-45), was estimated utilizing seasonally adjusted quarterly data. This implies that any estimates obtained from the equation will also be seasonally adjusted. The relationship between seasonally adjusted and nonadjusted data is given by:

$$\text{Seasonally adjusted data} = \frac{\text{Unadjusted (raw) data}}{\text{Seasonal factor}} \qquad (5\text{-}61)$$

For our example, the predicted value for the third quarter of 1974 is:

$$\widehat{\text{RSAUTO}}_{1974:\text{III}} = -14,956 + 45.98248\text{YPLTP}_{1974:\text{III}}$$
$$= \$23,945 \text{ million} \qquad (5\text{-}62)$$

This value must be multiplied by the seasonal factor associated with the third quarter, 1.06, yielding the estimated value of $25,382 million in retail sales. In order to obtain any raw quarterly figure, a similar procedure would be undertaken.

A second factor that merits consideration is that in some situations, we can assess the probable usefulness of a regression model by scanning a plot of the error terms. The advantage of this approach is that the majority of computer packages automatically provide this graph. For example, Figure 5-11 presents the plot of error terms for the retail-sales illustration. The error terms form a consistent pattern, and this violates the assumption of randomly distributed errors. In Chapter 6, techniques will be developed for measuring and correcting nonrandom error patterns, and it is to these more advanced techniques that we turn.

Figure 5-11 Error Pattern from Regression of Retail Sales of Automobiles on Disposable Income

Source: Equation 5-45

QUESTIONS FOR DISCUSSION AND ANALYSIS

1. Take the data for real disposable income and automobile sales in Table 5-1 and perform the following operations:

   a. Plot the data in a scatter diagram and analyze the linearity assumption.

   b. Estimate, by hand and via the university computer, the least-squares line; the standard error of each of the regression coefficients (S_{β_0} and S_{β_1}); the actual t values; the coefficient of determination (r^2); the standard error of estimate (SEE); the total, explained, and unexplained variation in the dependent variable (as per the AOV table); the actual F value; the average (mean) values of income and automobile sales, as well as their standard deviations; and the average percentage regression error.

   c. Write a two-page report summarizing and interpreting all the information conveyed by the regression statistics above. You should explain the precise meaning of each statistic.

   d. Construct a 99% confidence interval estimate for the true regression slope (β_1) and interpret your findings.

   e. Carry out the following hypothesis test:

   $$H_0: \quad \beta_1 = 0$$
   $$H_1: \quad \beta_1 \neq 0$$

   Use $\alpha = .01$, and specify the degrees of freedom, the critical t value, the actual t value, and your decision.

   f. Construct a 90 percent confidence-level estimate of automobile sales when disposable income reaches $1 trillion. Is this a precise estimate?

2. A refrigerator manufacturer is interested in obtaining forecasts of unit production of its economy and deluxe models. The following data have been collected and are presented to you for analysis:

		Unit Production of Economy Refrigerators (Not Seasonally Adjusted)	Unit Production of Deluxe Refrigerators (Not Seasonally Adjusted)
1966	Q1	697,311	8,199
	Q2	638,470	7,378
	Q3	252,466	4,361
	Q4	614,511	5,000
1967	Q1	457,643	8,206
	Q2	552,976	6,898
	Q3	312,313	1,647
	Q4	510,755	7,017
1968	Q1	490,668	7,078
	Q2	624,301	8,978
	Q3	369,236	7,713
	Q4	640,117	8,701
1969	Q1	585,833	8,706
	Q2	492,640	2,826
	Q3	419,509	7,586
	Q4	474,956	7,802
1970	Q1	457,396	7,978
	Q2	573,096	5,852
	Q3	279,048	5,713
	Q4	172,456	3,043
1971	Q1	647,165	8,355
	Q2	623,545	7,061
	Q3	451,624	4,813
	Q4	571,524	6,611
1972	Q1	586,175	7,304
	Q2	678,073	7,613
	Q3	393,580	5,316
	Q4	614,568	7,143
1973	Q1	661,661	8,573
	Q2	622,686	8,478
	Q3	449,334	6,846
	Q4	567,816	8,719
1974	Q1	464,021	9,537
	Q2	589,834	10,889
	Q3	366,043	4,167
	Q4	460,983	9,276
1975	Q1	326,120	11,666
	Q2	435,165	12,617
	Q3	379,463	10,684
	Q4	492,758	10,999
1976	Q1	516,226	12,064
	Q2	526,694	12,079
	Q3	414,577	12,058
	Q4	507,102	11,224

(continued)

	Unit Production of Economy Refrigerators (Not Seasonally Adjusted)	Unit Production of Deluxe Refrigerators (Not Seasonally Adjusted)
1977 Q1	515,577	11,490
Q2	583,581	12,193
Q3	438,462	11,159
Q4	551,977	11,503

a. Prepare a scatter diagram for each of the series.

b. Illustrate the distinction between cyclical fluctuations and seasonal variation, using your scatter diagram.

c. Can you think of any explanation for the relative stability of production for the deluxe model as compared to the economy model?

d. Where might measurement error occur in these data?

e. Would income lead, lag, or be coincident with production? Why?

f. Would your answer to *e* change if you were forecasting dollar sales? Why?

3. As a business-conditions analyst interested in constructing quarterly production projections, you have decided to build separate forecast equations for economy and deluxe refrigerators.

a. Seasonally adjust both series and discuss the seasonal patterns exhibited by the two series.

b. Alternative techniques for handling exogenous disturbances will be developed in Chapter 7; however, one method often used is to drop those data points that are obviously distorted by past historical shocks. Which points would you delete?

c. If your goal is to link the seasonally adjusted production series to independent measures of aggregate economic activity that can logically be said (in the jargon of forecasters) to drive the dependent series, you must select independent variables that, theoretically, can be expected to cause the observed changes in refrigerator production. Regress each of the production series against national income, personal income, and disposable income. Are the results satisfactory?

d. Based on the three regression equations for each production series, construct alternative point estimates for production of economy and deluxe refrigerators in the first quarter of 1977. Are these conditional or unconditional projections?

e. For the same quarter, construct 95 percent confidence interval estimates and compare the ranges. Did they catch the actual production values?

f. Develop multiple regression models for both series; you are free to select any independent variables, to use the actual data values or transform them by differencing, and to make any other statistical adjustments you deem appropriate. Prepare a formal report that analyzes the strengths and weaknesses of your model.

4. Explain the difference between an *ex post* and *ex ante* forecast; between conditional and unconditional forecasts.

5. Based on your results in question 3:
   a. Prepare an *ex post* forecast for the fourth quarter of 1977.
   b. Prepare an *ex ante* forecast for the second quarter of 1984.
   c. Is your forecast in *b* conditional or unconditional? Why?
   d. Use the five methods introduced in the chapter to evaluate your equations' forecasting reliability.
6. The model estimated for retail sales of automobiles, equation (5-45), was fitted for a data base that ended in the fourth quarter of 1977. Re-estimate the model by dropping the last eight observations. Analyze the reliability of the forecasting equation by comparing *ex post* forecasts to actual values, using the turning-point criterion.
7. Prepare an unconditional forecast for air miles traveled, equation (5-60), for the third quarter of 1981.
8. Derive the 95% confidence interval for equation (5-60).

REFERENCES FOR FURTHER STUDY

Chisholm, Roger K., and Gilbert R. Whitaker, Jr., *Forecasting Methods.* Homewood, Ill.: Richard D. Irwin, 1971.

Granger, C.W.J., *Forecasting in Business and Economics.* New York: Academic Press, 1980.

Klein, L.R., *An Essay on the Theory of Economic Prediction.* Chicago: Markham, 1971.

Neter, John, and William Wasserman, *Applied Linear Statistical Models.* Homewood, Ill.: Richard D. Irwin, 1974.

Wonnacott, R.J., and T.H. Wonnacott, *Econometrics.* New York: John Wiley, 1970.

THE
MULTIPLE
REGRESSION
MODEL

———————

PART IV

6

Multiple Regression Models

INTRODUCTION

Few forecasters rely completely upon simple regression models because the pattern exhibited by economic variables is a product of numerous factors. The more information we have, the better the predictions should be. Equations that utilize more than one independent variable are referred to as multiple regression equations. Such equations will serve as the focus of this chapter. Since the assumptions underlying both the simple linear model and the multiple regression model are often violated, this chapter also presents the procedures needed to test the assumptions that are made in estimating a regression equation and to correct the model if the assumptions have been violated.

MULTIPLE REGRESSION

THE MULTIPLE REGRESSION MODEL

In any modeling effort, the forecaster has to make a choice: to construct a model similar to the simple linear model, or to build a highly sophisticated and complex model in which an effort is made to include all independent variables influencing Y. This latter case is generally referred to as multiple regression analysis. Multiple regression analysis, merely an extension of simple regression, attempts to link changes in the dependent variable (Y) to changes in two or more independent variables $(X_1, X_2, X_3,$ and so on).

In general, there are three reasons why multiple regression is preferable to simple regression:

1. To reduce stochastic error, thereby strengthening the statistical tests
2. To eliminate the bias that results when we ignore variables that have a significant impact on Y
3. To reduce forecasting error by more fully utilizing all the information at our disposal

However, the construction of a multiple regression model does involve added costs. First of all, the more sophisticated the model, the larger the amount of data the forecaster has to collect and analyze. The second cost results from use of the regression equation as a forecasting device. The forecaster has to have future values for the X_i's, and highly sophisticated models are apt to require more reliance on estimated values. There is a greater likelihood of forecasting error because of errors made in estimating values for the X_i's. Thus, the tradeoff is between greater accuracy and higher cost.

In general terms, we can write the multiple regression model as

$$Y_i = \beta_0 + \beta_1 X_{1i} + \beta_2 X_{2i} + \ldots + \beta_k X_{ki} + \epsilon_i \qquad (6\text{-}1)$$

where Y_i and ϵ_i are as before, and the X_{ki}'s denote the independent variables and k the number of regressors. For example, X_{2i} represents the ith observation on the independent variable X_2. In comparison with the simple linear model, one assumption must be modified and two assumptions added. The modification is as follows: The dependent variable (Y) is a linear function of a number of independent variables rather than being linearly related to one independent variable. The two additional assumptions are:

1. The X's must be independent of each other. That is, X_1 does not significantly influence X_2, X_3, etc., and X_3 is independent of X_2.
2. The number of observations, n, must exceed the number of regressors, k. That is, $n > k$.

In deriving the least-squares estimators, it is convenient to consider the special case of $k = 2$—that is, two independent variables.

$$\hat{Y}_i = \hat{\beta}_0 + \hat{\beta}_1 X_{1i} + \hat{\beta}_2 X_{2i} + e_i \qquad (6\text{-}2)$$

Paralleling the development of estimators in the simple model, the general coefficients for the multiple regression model may be derived by solving a set of three normal equations in three unknowns:

$$\sum Y_i = n\hat{\beta}_0 + \hat{\beta}_1 \sum X_{1i} + \hat{\beta}_2 \sum X_{2i}$$
$$\sum X_{1i}Y_i = \hat{\beta}_0 \sum X_{1i} + \hat{\beta}_1 \sum X_{1i}^2 + \hat{\beta}_2 \sum X_{1i}X_{2i}$$
$$\sum X_{2i}Y_i = \hat{\beta}_0 X_{2i} + \hat{\beta}_1 \sum X_{1i}X_{2i} + \hat{\beta}_2 \sum X_{2i}^2 \qquad (6\text{-}3)$$

Solving these three equations simultaneously yields values for $\hat{\beta}_0$, $\hat{\beta}_1$, and $\hat{\beta}_2$. Finally, all the comments with respect to bias, consistency, and reliability noted in the case of simple linear regression hold here. That is, it can be shown that these estimators are also BLUE (best linear unbiased estimators). This implies that the procedures of hypothesis testing and interval estimation, as well as calculations of SEE, AOV, and correlation coefficients, are conceptually identical to those developed for simple linear regression.

The objectives and procedures in fitting a multiple regression equation are essentially the same as they were in the earlier simple linear regression case. We want to obtain estimates for the regression coefficients, $\hat{\beta}_0$, $\hat{\beta}_1$, and $\hat{\beta}_2$; test the statistical reliability of these coefficients; test the validity of all regressors (independent variables) taken together; use the regression equation to estimate Y given values for X_1 and X_2; measure the error involved in the estimations; and assess the model's efficiency as a forecasting device. Although the objectives and procedures remain similar, the calculations become more complex, and the interpretations of several of the measures change.

To illustrate the complexity of the computations, let us estimate the regression equation for the sales data noted in Table 6-1. In order to solve the normal equations for the regression coefficients, it is convenient to translate X_1 and X_2 into deviations from their respective means; that is, $x_1 = X_1 - \bar{X}_1$ and $x_2 = X_2 - \bar{X}_2$. The normal equations can then be restated as:

$$\hat{\beta}_0 = \bar{Y}$$
$$\sum x_{1i}Y_i = \hat{\beta}_1 \sum x_{1i}^2 + \hat{\beta}_2 \sum x_{1i}x_{2i}$$
$$\sum x_{2i}Y_i = \hat{\beta}_1 \sum x_{1i}x_{2i} + \hat{\beta}_2 \sum x_{2i}^2 \qquad (6\text{-}4)$$

Based on the calculations in Table 6-1, the regression equation is:

$$\hat{Y}_i = 995.4 + 4.090x_{1i} + 0.9740x_{2i} \qquad (6\text{-}5)$$

In terms of the original data (X_1 and X_2),

$$\hat{Y}_i = 995.4 + 4.09(X_1 - \bar{X}_1) + 0.974(X_2 - \bar{X}_2)$$
$$\hat{Y}_i = 995.4 + 4.09(X_1 - 198.35) + 0.974(X_2 - 679.05)$$
$$\hat{Y}_i = -477.2 + 4.09X_1 + 0.974X_2 \qquad (6\text{-}6)$$

Table 6-1 Least squares estimates for multiple regression of final sales (Y) on population (X_1) and disposable income (X_2)

Final Sales in '72 Dollars (Billions) Y_i	Population (Millions) X_{1i}	Disposable Income in '72 Dollars (Billions) X_{2i}	$x_{1i} = X_{1i} - \bar{X}_1$	$x_{2i} = X_{2i} - \bar{X}_2$	$x_{1i}Y_i$	$x_{2i}Y_i$	x_{1i}^2	x_{2i}^2	$x_{1i}x_{2i}$
$ 681	174	459	−24.35	−220.05	−16,582	−149,854	593	48,422	5,358
714	177	477	−21.35	−202.05	−15,244	−144,264	456	40,824	4,314
732	181	487	−17.35	−192.05	−12,700	−140,581	301	36,883	3,332
752	184	501	−14.35	−178.05	−10,791	−133,894	206	31,702	2,555
791	187	522	−11.35	−157.05	− 8,978	−124,227	129	24,665	1,783
823	189	539	− 9.35	−140.05	− 7,695	−115,261	87	19,614	1,309
867	192	577	− 6.35	−102.05	− 5,505	− 88,477	40	10,414	648
915	194	612	− 4.35	− 67.05	− 3,980	− 61,351	19	4,496	292
964	197	644	− 1.35	− 35.05	− 1,301	− 33,788	2	1,229	47
996	199	670	0.65	− 9.05	647	− 9,104	0	82	−6
1,043	201	695	2.65	15.95	2,764	16,636	7	254	42
1,068	203	712	4.65	32.95	4,966	35,191	22	1,086	153
1,071	205	742	6.65	62.95	7,122	67,419	44	3,963	419
1,101	207	769	8.65	89.95	9,524	99,035	75	8,091	778
1,162	209	801	10.65	121.95	12,375	141,706	113	14,872	1,299
1,218	210	855	11.65	175.95	14,190	214,307	136	30,958	2,050
1,210	212	842	13.65	162.95	16,516	197,170	186	26,553	2,224
1,212	214	860	15.65	180.95	18,968	219,311	245	32,743	2,832
1,264	215	891	16.65	211.95	21,046	267,905	277	44,923	3,529
1,324	217	926	18.65	246.95	24,693	326,962	348	60,984	4,606
19,908	3,967	13,581	0	0	50,035	584,931	3,286	442,758	37,564

Table 6-1 (continued)

Computations:

$$\bar{Y} = \frac{\sum Y_i}{n} \qquad \bar{X}_1 = \frac{\sum X_{1i}}{n} \qquad \bar{X}_2 = \frac{\sum X_{2i}}{n}$$

$$= \frac{19{,}908}{20} \qquad = \frac{3{,}967}{20} \qquad = \frac{13{,}581}{20}$$

$$= 995.4 \qquad = 198.35 \qquad = 679.05$$

Formulas:

(1) Confidence Intervals

$$\beta_1 = \hat{\beta}_1 \pm t_{cr} S_{\beta_1}$$
$$\beta_2 = \hat{\beta}_2 \pm t_{cr} S_{\beta_2}$$

(2) Standard Errors of Coefficients

$$S_{\beta_1} = \frac{s}{\sqrt{\sum x_{1i}^2 - (\sum x_{1i}x_{2i})^2/\sum x_{2i}^2}} = 1.21$$

$$S_{\beta_2} = \frac{s}{\sqrt{\sum x_{2i}^2 - (\sum x_{1i}x_{2i})^2/\sum x_{1i}^2}} = 0.104$$

$$s^2 = \sum(Y_i - \hat{Y}_i)^2/(n-3)$$

$$= 145.3$$

$$\hat{\beta}_0 = \bar{Y} = 995.4$$

$$\left.\begin{array}{l} 50{,}035 = 3{,}286\hat{\beta}_1 + 37{,}564\hat{\beta}_2 \\ 584{,}931 = 37{,}564\hat{\beta}_1 + 442{,}758\hat{\beta}_2 \end{array}\right\} \begin{array}{l}\text{Based on substitution} \\ \text{into equation (6-4)}\end{array}$$

Solution: $\hat{\beta}_0 = 995.4$
$\hat{\beta}_1 = 4.09$
$\hat{\beta}_2 = 0.974$

(3) Standard Error of the Estimate

$$\text{SEE} = S_{Y|x_1x_2} = \sqrt{\frac{\sum(Y_i - \hat{Y}_i)^2}{n-3}} = 12.06$$

(4) t Distribution

t has $n - (k+1)$ degrees of freedom = 17

(5) Estimated Values, $\hat{Y}_i$; $i = 20$

$$\hat{Y}_{20} = -477.2 + 4.09X_{1,20} + 0.974X_{2,20}$$
$$= -477.2 + 4.09(217) + 0.974(926)$$
$$= \$1{,}312.3 \text{ billion}$$

(6) $e_{20} = Y_{20} - \hat{Y}_{20}$
$$= 1{,}324 - 1{,}312.3$$
$$= 11.7$$

The formulas necessary for computing confidence intervals, standard errors of the regression coefficients, and the SEE are noted at the bottom of Table 6-1.

A perusal of Table 6-1 reveals the difficulties of carrying out multiple regression computations by hand. In fact, the sheer drudgery and likelihood of error associated with hand calculation necessitates the use of matrix algebra in cases where we have more than two independent variables. While a conceptual understanding of regression analysis is an important by-product of manual calculations, it is much more efficient, once the regression concepts have been mastered, to carry out computations on the computer. The appendix at the end of this chapter details the matrix algebra approach to regression analysis that is utilized in computer-based computations.

INTERPRETATION OF THE MODEL

The first difference in interpretation between simple and multiple regression centers on the regression coefficients. In the former situation, $\hat{\beta}_1$ referred to the change in Y, the dependent variable, as a result of a one-unit change in the independent variable, X. In the two-variable model:

$$\hat{Y}_i = \hat{\beta}_0 + \hat{\beta}_1 X_{1i} + \hat{\beta}_2 X_{2i} + e_i \tag{6-2}$$

$\hat{\beta}_0$'s interpretation is unchanged, while $\hat{\beta}_1$ measures the change in Y associated with a unit change in X_1 when all other independent variables remain constant. In economics terminology, this corresponds to the *ceteris paribus* assumption (Latin for "all other things being equal"). In calculus, these coefficients correspond to partial derivatives. A similar interpretation follows for $\hat{\beta}_2$. The terms $\hat{\beta}_1$ and $\hat{\beta}_2$ are sometimes referred to as partial regression coefficients and can be shown to be systematically related to partial correlation coefficients. These interpretations follow from the assumption that the independent variables are unrelated. For example, if X_1 and X_2 vary systematically, the *ceteris paribus* assumption no longer holds.

The analysis-of-variance table for a multiple regression equation is identical to that for the simple regression equation, except for the degrees-of-freedom column. Note that this implies different divisors in the variance column. In the case of multiple regression, the null and alternative *hypotheses* being tested by the F test are:

$$H_0 : \beta_1 = \beta_2 = 0$$

and

$$H_1 : \beta_1, \beta_2 \neq 0 \tag{6-7}$$

That is, the F test analyzes the joint effect of X_1 and X_2 on Y and measures the combined statistical significance of $\hat{\beta}_1$ and $\hat{\beta}_2$, whereas the t test looks at the significance of the coefficients taken one at a time. The F test involves testing the significance of the coefficients all at one time; that is:

$$F_{cr} = F_{\alpha, k, n-(k+1)} \tag{6-8}$$

The prediction interval for a multiple regression equation is defined by:

$$Y_{t+1} = \hat{Y}_{t+1} \pm t_{cr}s\sqrt{\frac{1}{n} + \frac{(X_{1t+1} - \bar{X}_1)^2}{\sum (X_{1i} - \bar{X}_1)^2} + \frac{(X_{2t+1} - \bar{X}_2)^2}{\sum (X_{2i} - \bar{X}_2)^2} + 1} \tag{6-9}$$

where $\hat{Y}_{t+1}$ is the point estimate. Conceptually, the confidence band for a multiple regression equation is identical to the simple regression band illustrated in Figure 5-10.

MULTIPLE AND PARTIAL CORRELATION

One of the more significant areas of difference between simple and multiple regression is in the interpretation of the coefficients of determination and correlation. In simple regression, the simple correlation coefficient and the coefficient of determination were denoted by r and r^2, respectively. In the case of a multiple-regression equation, it is common practice to refer to these terms as the multiple correlation coefficient and the multiple coefficient of determination, symbolized by R and R^2, respectively. As would be expected, the coefficient of determination measures the variation in Y explained by the combined influence of X_1 and X_2. That is:

$$R^2 = \frac{\sum (\hat{Y}_i - \bar{Y})^2}{\sum (Y_i - \bar{Y})^2} \tag{6-10}$$

where $\hat{Y}_i = \hat{\beta}_0 + \hat{\beta}_1 X_{1i} + \hat{\beta}_2 X_{2i} + e_i$, and:

$$R = \sqrt{R^2}$$

At this juncture, a word of caution concerning the correlation coefficient is in order. R is dependent upon the number of independent variables included in the regression equation. The addition of more independent variables can never lower R (or R^2) and will generally increase it. For this reason, it is necessary to correct R^2 for the number of regressors utilized—that is, degrees of freedom. These corrected coefficients, $\bar{R}^2$ and $\bar{R}$, can be found by using the formulas in equation (6-11). As n becomes larger, $\bar{R}^2$ approaches R^2.

$$\bar{R}^2 = 1 - (1 - R^2)\left(\frac{n-1}{n-k}\right)$$

$$\bar{R} = \sqrt{\bar{R}^2} \tag{6-11}$$

In addition to the multiple correlation coefficients, it is possible to calculate the correlation between each independent variable and the dependent variable. Specifically, we may want to see how the dependent variable and any one independent variable are related after netting out the effect of all other independent variables in the model. It can be shown that:

$$r_{YX_2 \cdot X_3} = \frac{r_{YX_2} - r_{YX_3}r_{X_2X_3}}{\sqrt{1 - r_{X_2X_3}^2}\sqrt{1 - r_{YX_3}^2}}$$

$$r_{YX_3 \cdot X_2} = \frac{r_{YX_3} - r_{YX_2}r_{X_2X_3}}{\sqrt{1 - r_{X_2X_3}^2}\sqrt{1 - r_{YX_2}^2}} \qquad (6\text{-}12)$$

where:

$r_{YX_2 \cdot X_3}$ = partial correlation coefficient between Y and X_2, controlling for X_3

$r_{YX_3 \cdot X_2}$ = partial correlation coefficient between Y and X_3, controlling for X_2

r_{YX_2} = simple correlation between Y and X_2

r_{YX_3} = simple correlation between Y and X_3

$r_{X_2X_3} = r_{X_3X_2}$ = simple correlation between X_2 and X_3

$r_{X_2X_3}^2$ = simple coefficient of determination between X_2 and X_3, equal to $r_{x_3x_2}^2$

$r_{YX_2}^2$ = simple coefficient of determination between X_2 and Y

$r_{YX_3}^2$ = simple coefficient of determination between X_3 and Y

These partial correlation coefficients are especially useful when estimating a regression line via the stepwise procedure, which will be covered in Chapter 7.

BETA COEFFICIENTS AND ELASTICITIES

The relative importance of the independent variables in a multiple-regression model can be measured by the beta coefficient. Beta coefficients are determined by estimating a regression equation wherein each variable is *normalized* by subtracting its mean and dividing by its standard deviation. It can be shown that the following relationship exists:

$$\hat{\beta}_i^\alpha = \hat{\beta}_i \frac{S_{x_i}}{S_y} \qquad (6\text{-}13)$$

The beta coefficient, $\hat{\beta}_i^\alpha$, is equal to the estimated regression slope, $\hat{\beta}_i$, multiplied by the ratio of the standard deviation of the independent variable, S_{x_i}, to the standard deviation of the dependent variable. The value computed from equation (6-13) has a straightforward interpretation. A beta coefficient of 0.5 implies that a change of one standard deviation in the independent variable leads to a change of 0.5 standard deviations in the dependent variable.

Elasticity coefficients measure the percentage change in one variable relative to the percentage change in some other variable. For example, the elasticity of Y with respect to X_3 is defined as the percentage change in Y divided by the percentage change in X_3. In general, elasticities change along a regression line; thus, computer-tabulated elasticities are measured at the means of each of the independent variables. The elasticity of Y with respect to X_i is defined by:

$$E_i = \hat{\beta}_i(\bar{X}_i/\bar{Y}) = \frac{\% \Delta Y}{\% \Delta X_i} \qquad (6\text{-}14)$$

If $E_i = 2.0$, then about the means of the variables X_i and Y, a 1 percent change in X_i will lead to a 2 percent change in Y. The principal advantage of these coefficients is that they are unit-free—their values are independent of the units in which the variables are measured. If X_i and Y values are measured far from their respective means, such interpretations are apt to lead to erroneous conclusions.

FORECASTING AND EXPLANATORY EQUATIONS

The use of a multiple regression equation for forecasting must be distinguished from its use in explanatory models. In the latter case, the independent variables are selected from a theoretical model. The primary purpose of this type of analysis is to test the validity of the theory. For this reason, future values of the independent variables are of minor interest.

By the very nature of a forecasting equation, the primary goal in developing it is to obtain reliable forecasts for future values of the dependent variable. Hence, its success in satisfying this goal depends crucially on our ability in obtaining future values for the independent variables with a reasonable degree of accuracy. It is of little consolation to a forecaster to find that he or she has developed an equation that explains historical movements of the dependent variable accurately but is useless for forecasting because future values of the independent variables are impossible to obtain.

As an example of this difference, suppose a forecaster wishes to develop an equation to forecast disposable real income, $YD72$. Economic theory reveals that a person's real income ($YD72$) is apt to depend on, among other things, the wage rate (WR), hours worked (AHW) and the rate of inflation (CCPI). Formally:

$$\widehat{YD72}_t = \hat{\beta}_0 + \hat{\beta}_1 \text{WR}_t + \hat{\beta}_2 \text{AHW}_t + \hat{\beta}_3 \text{CCPI}_t + e_t \qquad (6\text{-}15)$$

Although this equation might fit well historically, it is extremely difficult to obtain reliable forecast values for wage rates and average hours worked; hence, the equation's usefulness in forecasting is minimal. Thus, instead of using equation (6-15), the forecaster might formulate the following equation, using lagged values for the independent variables:

$$\widehat{YD72}_t = \hat{\beta}_0 + \hat{\beta}_1 WR_{t-1} + \hat{\beta}_2 WR_{t-2} + \hat{\beta}_3 AHW_{t-1} + \hat{\beta}_4 CCPI_{t-1} + e_t \quad (6\text{-}16)$$

The advantage of this formulation is obvious. Reliable estimates for the independent variables are readily available and accurate. The selection of independent (explanatory) variables should be based on the degree of confidence with which future values can be projected and the strength of the relationship between the independent variables and the dependent variable. Obtaining future values for the independent variables is one of the most perplexing problems facing the forecaster. The use of lagged values for the independent variables, as per equation (6-16), is one of the more popular approaches. Closely allied with simple lag models are more complex distributed lag models. For example, one might postulate that aggregate consumption (C) is a function of disposable income in the prior quarter ($YD72_{t-1}$). The specific lag structure utilized is dependent upon the time units of the data, that is, monthly, quarterly, annually. In general, we would expect the interrelationship between consumption and income to be spread out over a long time horizon ($YD72_{t-2}$, $YD72_{t-3}$, . . .). Advertising dollars spent this month may affect sales for an extended period, and distributed lag models attempt to capture this time adjustment process. For example, this month's sales (S_t) might be linked to advertising expenditures over a twelve-month period ($A_t, \ldots, A_{t-11}$). Alternative distributive lag models are presented in Chapter 7.

Forecasters also derive future values of the independent variables by utilizing multiple-equation models that allow the analyst to account for interrelationships among economic phenomena. In Chapter 7 we will examine some of the more common multiple-equation techniques such as two-stage least squares and recursive systems. From the standpoint of the industry or firm level analyst, the ready availability of purchasable forecasts of economic variables from commercial forecast vendors is a cost-effective substitute for internally developed multiple-equation models. Thus, for many business forecasters, the selection of independent variables is as heavily weighted by the array of economic variables available from commercial vendors as it is by theoretical considerations.

Example 6-1: Automobile Sales Revisited

In the first attempt at modeling the cyclical fluctuations of automobile sales (Example 5-2), the simple least-squares regression equation, equation (5-45), passed all the statistical tests of significance.

$$\widehat{RSAUTO}_t = -14,956 + 45.98248 YPLTP_t \quad (5\text{-}45)$$

where:

$\widehat{\text{RSAUTO}}_t$ = estimated quarterly retail sales of automobiles in millions of dollars; seasonally adjusted

YPLTP_t = personal income less transfer payments; billions of dollars; seasonally adjusted at annual rate

However, when evaluated in terms of its performance in forecasting (Example 5-4), the results were less than satisfactory. Here we reconsider the development of a forecasting model by investigating more complex multiple-regression models.

To briefly restate the situation, the goal is to develop a forecasting model for automobile sales. In turn, this forecast will be used to determine cash needs for financing the inventories of retail automobile outlets. In the original formulation, the dependent variable, RSAUTO, referred to seasonally adjusted retail sales of automobiles in current dollars, and this can lead to serious estimation problems. Consider the following equation:

$$\widehat{\text{RSAUTO}}_t = \hat{\beta}_0 + \hat{\beta}_1 \text{YPLTP}_t + \hat{\beta}_2 U_t + e_t \qquad (6\text{-}17)$$

The theoretical relationship between RSAUTO and YPLTP has been covered in previous discussions. Automobile sales should be inversely related to the unemployment rate, (U_t) since, as the rate of unemployment increases, purchases of automobiles decline. However, an initial empirical estimate of equation (6-17) yielded a positive relationship; that is, the sign attached to U_t was positive. Clearly, this contradicts our *a priori* reasoning. In order to explain the empirical results, remember that although the number of automobiles sold should decline as unemployment increases, the dollar value of the units sold may very well increase as a result of higher prices. That is, the dollar value of automobile sales can increase if the decline in unit sales is more than offset by price increases. Fortunately, this difficulty can be overcome by using unit sales of automobiles (UNITSAL) as the dependent variable. Having forecast values for this variable, we can simply multiply these figures by the price level of automobiles to obtain cash needs for financing. The first step in this process is to reestimate the simple regression model with UNITSAL substituted for RSAUTO (all variables are seasonally adjusted):

$$\widehat{\text{UNITSAL}}_t = 1.53466 + 0.0098837134\,\text{YPLTP}_t$$

Standard error	(0.00068837301)
t_e	14.58

$(6\text{-}18)$

Range of data: 1960:I to 1979:IV	
Degrees of freedom: 78	
$r = 0.85176$	SEE = 0.93372
$r^2 = 0.72550$	$F_{1,78} = 206.1544$
	$U = 0.050044$

(Data for this equation and all equations in this example are detailed in Appendix E, Table E-1). The equation and the coefficient are significant at the .01 level. Figure 6-1(a) traces the efficiency of equation (6-18) in simulating the historical pattern in unit

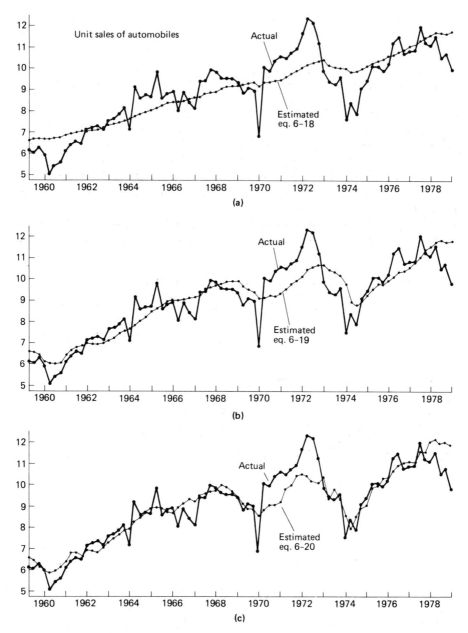

Figure 6-1 Efficiency of Regression Equations in Simulating Automobile Sales

sales of automobiles. Although the equation is statistically significant, the fit, as shown graphically in Figure 6-1(a), leaves much to be desired. Further highlighting this point is the fact that the average percentage error (APE) of 10.33 percent is relatively large.

In an attempt to overcome these deficiencies, the unemployment rate was added as a determining factor in automobile sales. The results of this reestimation are:

$$\widehat{\text{UNITSAL}}_t = 2.82832 + 0.010672546\text{YPLTP}_t - 0.3447252U_t$$

Standard error	(0.00063270161)	(0.073062897)	
t_e	16.87	4.718	(6-19)

Range of data: 1960: I to 1979: IV
Degrees of freedom: 77
$R = 0.8872$ $U = 0.044296$
$R^2 = 0.78706$ SEE $= 0.8277$
$\bar{R}^2 = 0.78153$ $F_{2,77} = 142.3049$

Both coefficients are significant at the .01 level, and the R statistics are satisfactory. The F statistic indicates the significance of the equation when both coefficients are considered simultaneously. The average percentage error has fallen from 10.33 percent (in the simple regression) to 9.16 percent, and equation (6-19) tracks the historical data more closely than did equation (6-18). This latter point can best be appreciated by comparing Figure 6-1(a) with Figure 6-1(b).

Consumers' expectations regarding the state of the economy are likely to affect their willingness to commit themselves to large purchases such as automobiles. In general, the better people expect the economy to perform, the more willing they are to purchase automobiles. The Index of Consumer Sentiment (JATTC) is tabulated and published by the University of Michigan; the advantage of using this measure is that forecast values are available through the major commercial vendors, such as Data Resources, Inc., and Chase Econometrics.

Table 6-2 presents the correlation matrix for the automobile-sales example; it contains the simple correlation coefficients between all combinations of the dependent

Table 6-2   Correlation matrix for unit automobile sales

Coefficient	UNITSAL[a]	YPLTP[b]	JATTC[c]	U[d]
UNITSAL	1.0000	0.8518	-0.3239	-0.0142
		(.001)	(.002)	(.450)
YPLTP	0.8518	1.0000	-0.6270	0.2643
	(.001)		(.001)	(.009)
JATTC	-0.3239	-0.6270	1.0000	-0.3816
	(.002)	(.001)		(.001)
U	-0.0142	0.2643	-0.3816	1.0000
	(.450)	(.009)	(.001)	

[a]unit sales of automobiles
[b]personal income less transfer payments
[c]index of consumer sentiment
[d]unemployment rate
Source: Appendix E, Table E-1; values in parentheses indicate level of significance.

and independent variables. The correlation between each variable and itself is 1; that is, UNITSAL is perfectly correlated with UNITSAL. The correlation between personal income and automobile sales is positive, and there is a negative relationship between UNITSAL and the unemployment rate. The negative correlation between consumer expectations and automobile sales is unexpected, but these are simple correlation coefficients between the dependent variable (UNITSAL) and the independent variables (JATTC and U), and they do not take into consideration other economic factors that influence automobile sales. Consequently, the numbers in the first row are of limited value in selection of reliable independent variables. The high correlation between YPLTP and JATTC and between JATTC and U is fairly typical when one is working with time-series data; they indicate the presence of multicollinearity (covered in a later section of this chapter). However, the problem is not particularly distressing in light of the significance of the t statistics associated with the regression in equation (6-20), below.

Table 6-3 details the information pertinent to the estimated regression equation (6-20):

$$\widehat{\text{UNITSAL}}_t = -3.186461 + 0.012494969 \text{YPLTP}_t +$$
$$0.047822402 \text{JATTC}_t - 0.2583437 U_t \qquad (6\text{-}20)$$

A comparison of the calculated t statistics (t_e) with the critical values obtained from Appendix B for 76 degrees of freedom implies that all the coefficients taken individually are statistically significant at the .01 level, which means that the null hypothesis of no relationship ($H_0: \beta_2 = 0; \beta_3 = 0; \beta_4 = 0$) can be rejected. There is less than one chance in 100 that these values (0.012494969, 0.047822402, and -0.2583437) would be observed if H_0 were true. Additionally, all the coefficients conform to *a priori* theoretical expectations. Interpreting these coefficients is a straightforward procedure. For example, unit sales of automobiles will decline by 258,344 units for every 1 percentage point increase in the unemployment rate, assuming that all other things (specifically, personal income and consumer sentiment) remain the same.

The sixth column contains the list of partial correlation coefficients, and columns 7 and 8 present the beta and elasticity coefficients, respectively. The partial coefficient of 0.4490 attached to the expectations variable implies that 20 percent (0.4490^2) of the variance of UNITSAL *not* accounted for by the other independent variables is explained by the variation in expectations. The beta of 1.0768 for personal income means that an increase of 1 standard deviation in income will lead to a 1.0768 standard deviation increase in unit sales of automobiles. By examining the elasticities, the sensitivity of unit sales to a given percentage change in any specific independent variable can be computed. For example, if unemployment were to rise by 1 percent, unit sales would decrease by slightly more than 0.15 percent. Conversely, if personal income were to fall by 1 percent, unit sales would decline by 1.05 percent.

Table 6-4 presents the analysis of variance for equation (6-20). A comparison of the calculated F statistic (124) with the critical value (Appendix C) implies that the equation is significant at the .01 level. Thus, the regression equation should provide us with better forecasts for UNITSAL than would be obtained by relying on a mean forecast. In terms of *ex post* forecast reliability, the estimated equation tracks the historical data pattern reasonably well as is seen by examining Figure 6-1(c). Further, the Theil U statistic declines as we move from equation (6-18), $U = 0.050044$, to equa-

Table 6-3 Regression results for unit sales of automobiles

Variable	Regression Value ($\hat{\beta}_i$) (1)	Standard Error ($S_{\hat{\beta}_i}$) (2)	t Statistic (t_e) (3)	Mean ($\bar{X}_i$) (4)	Standard Deviation (S_{x_i}) (5)	Partial Correlation Coefficient (6)	Beta Coefficient (β) (7)	Elasticity at Mean (E_i) (8)
Personal income less transfer payments (YPLTP)	0.012494969	.00070491125	17.725592	759.19951172	152.609146118	0.8973 (.001)	1.076798	1.0495443
Index of consumer sentiment (JATTC)	0.047822402	0.010917083	4.3805137	86.92500305	10.2817935944	0.4490 (.001)	0.2776646	0.45992364
Unemployment rate (U)	-0.2583437	0.068607687	-3.7665146	5.489997711	1.3215456089	-0.3965 (.001)	-0.1927964	-0.15692056
Constant ($\hat{\beta}_0$)	-3.186461							

Summary Statistics

Durbin-Watson	1.01499	Coefficient of determination (R^2)	0.82999
Mean of auto sales ($\bar{Y}$)	9.03837490082	Multiple correlation coefficient (R)	0.91104
Standard deviation of Y (S_Y)	1.7708473206	Corrected for degrees of freedom ($\bar{R}^2$)	0.82328
Standard error of estimate	0.7443		$F_{3,76} = 123.6763$

Missed turning points = 44%
False turning points = 17%

APE = 8.2%

U = 0.03948

Range of data: 1960:I to 1979:IV

Source: Equation (6-20) and Appendix E, Table E-1

Table 6-4 Analysis of variance for unit sales of automobiles

Source of Variation	Variation	Degrees of Freedom	Variance	F Statistic
Explained	205.61796	3	68.539321	
Unexplained	42.117917	76	0.55418311	123.6763
Total	247.73588	79		

Source: Equation (6-20)

tion (6-19), $U = 0.044296$, to equation (6-20), $U = 0.039482$. Since a U value of zero implies a perfect forecast, the last model estimated, equation (6-20), is preferable to the preceding models. There are, however, three disturbing factors. First, the APE of 8.2 percent is relatively high. Secondly, equation (6-20) missed 44 percent of the turning points and predicted false turning points 17 percent of the time. Finally, the Durbin-Watson statistic of 1.01499 is so low as to lead one to expect positive autocorrelation; that is, the error terms (e_t) are positively related. Identifying and correcting this situation is the subject of a later section of this chapter, "Autocorrelation."

Example 6-2: Installment-Loan Demand in Memphis

Market-share forecasting is one of the forecaster's principal activities. Generally, this involves a prediction of demand for the firm's product or products. A common approach to this type of forecasting is to:

1. Develop an industrywide forecast, which in turn is used to
2. Develop specific company and/or product forecasts.

In this example, attention will be focused on developing a methodology for predicting installment-loan demand for an individual bank in Memphis, Tennessee.

Consider the following theoretical model:

$$\widehat{\text{INST}_t} = \hat{\beta}_0 + \hat{\beta}_1 \text{PINST}_{t-n} + \hat{\beta}_2 U_t + \hat{\beta}_3 \text{MEMIND}_t + e_t \qquad (6-21)$$

where:

INST_t = installment loan demand in Memphis in time period t; monthly data in millions of dollars

PINST_{t-n} = installment loan demand lagged n months

U_t = unemployment rate in the Memphis SMSA; monthly percentage rate, seasonally adjusted

MEMIND_t = index of economic activity in Memphis, 1967 = 1.000 (100%); monthly, seasonally adjusted

A priori there should be a negative relationship between U_t and INST_t; and a positive relationship between INST_t and the remaining independent variables. Since the majority of installment loans have a maturity date of greater than one month, a portion of the demand for installment loans this month is dependent upon the demand (level) in previous months. There is no theoretical basis for arguing that the demand in month t is more closely related to demand in month $t - 1$ than it is to month $t - 2$.

Time lags of from one to twelve months were estimated for equation (6-21), and the best empirical results were obtained with a one-month time lag.

After estimating and testing the model for loan demand in Memphis, the results were (all data utilized for this estimation can be found in Appendix E, Table E-2):

$$\widehat{INST_t} = -56.08784 + 0.9635235PINST_{t-1} -$$

$$1.249709U_t + 0.6060539MEMIND_t \qquad (6\text{-}22)$$

The complete regression output is presented in Table 6-5. Equation (6-22) passes all statistical tests of significance, and all coefficients are significant at the .01 level. The estimated model had an average percentage error of 1.38 percent; the individual monthly errors were well within acceptable limits.

The turning-point efficiency of the model can be judged by examining the actual-versus-predicted change diagram shown in Figure 6-2. In this figure the vertical axis measures actual changes in the dependent variable, installment loans ($\Delta INST_i = INST_t$

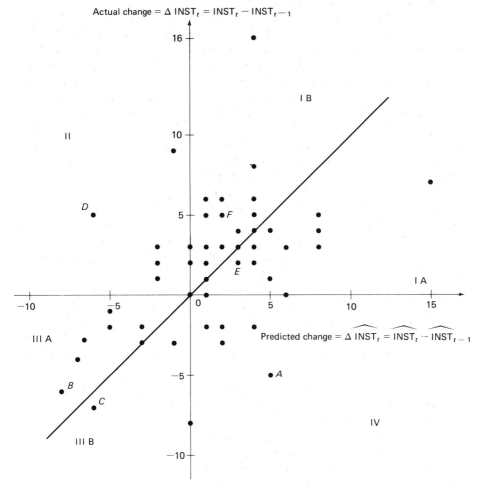

Figure 6-2   Predicted Versus Actual Loan Demand in Memphis

Table 6-5 Regression analysis for installment loan demand in Memphis

Variable	Regression Value ($\hat{\beta}_i$) (1)	Standard Error ($S_{\hat{\beta}_i}$) (2)	t Statistic (t_e) (3)	Mean ($\bar{X}_i$) (4)	Standard Deviation (S_{x_i}) (5)	Partial Correlation Coefficient (6)	Beta Coefficient (β) (7)	Elasticity at Mean (E_i) (8)
$PINST_{t-1}$	0.9635235	0.016592415	58.07	246.3167	46.9524	.9918	0.932522	0.9560842
U_t	−1.249709	0.8366640	1.50	6.196834	0.9022202	−.1957	−0.023409	0.0311974
$MEMIND_t$	0.6060539	0.2010512	3.01	123.31166	4.70967	.3736	0.05883401	0.3010616
Constant	−56.08784							

Summary Statistics

Coefficient of determination (R^2) 0.995

Correlation coefficient:
(R) 0.998
$\bar{R}^2$ 0.995
$F_{3,56}$ 3,892

APE = 1.38

D.W.	2.025	Range of data = 1975:1 to 1979:12
$\bar{Y}$	248.2333	
S_Y	48.51326	
SEE	3.44044	

Source: Equation (6-22) and Appendix E, Table E-2

$- \text{INST}_{t-1}$), while the horizontal axis measures predicted changes in installment loans ($\widehat{\Delta \text{INST}}_t = \widehat{\text{INST}}_t - \widehat{\text{INST}}_{t-1}$). The 45° line represents the line of perfect forecasts, $\Delta \text{INST}_t = \widehat{\Delta \text{INST}}_t$; thus, if the model forecasts well, we should observe a clustering of points about the 45° line. Quadrants IA and IIIA represent periods in which the model overestimated changes in installment loans. Thus, between June and July of 1976, point E, the actual change in installment loans was $2 million while the predicted change was $3 million. Alternatively, at point B, February–March of 1975, the actual change was a decline of $6 million while the model predicted a decline of $8 million. Underestimates are shown in Quadrants IB and IIIB. At point F, November–December 1976, the actual and predicted changes in installment loan demand were $5 and $2 million, respectively. Turning point errors are noted in Quadrants II and IV. Points in Quadrant II, for example, point D, indicate periods in which actual installment loans increased and the model predicted a decline. By way of contrast, points such as point A in Quadrant IV represent months in which actual installment loans declined and the estimated model, equation (6-22), predicted an increase. The final model missed several turning points; however, in the majority of these months, the error was relatively minor (close to the origin).

Once aggregate estimates for installment loans in the Memphis area have been derived, a simple procedure can be employed to project loan demand for one bank. In this case, the individual bank consistently had 46 percent of the total market for installment loans in Memphis. Actual values for the independent variables in the first month of 1980 were 343 for PINST_{t-1}, 5.52 for U_t, and 125.4 for MEMIND_t. Substituting these values into equation (6-22), the results are as follows:

$$\widehat{\text{INST}}_{t=1980:1} = -56.08784 + 0.9635235\text{PINST}_{1979:12}$$
$$- 1.249709 U_{1980:1} + 0.6060539\text{MEMIND}_{1980:1}$$
$$= -56.08784 + 0.9635235(343) - 1.249709(5.52)$$
$$+ 0.6060539(125.4)$$

$$\widehat{\text{INST}}_{t=1980:1} = 343.5 = \text{Aggregate loan demand of \$343.5 million} \qquad (6\text{-}23)$$

This figure is then multiplied by .46 (the firm's share), yielding forecasted installment-loan demand of $158.01 million for the bank in January 1980. The assumption of constant market share is, of course, challengeable, and the forecaster will have to carry out an ongoing analysis of competitive factors to determine the legitimacy of this procedure for forecasts that extend farther into the future. Even on a monthly basis, promotional programs and exogenous factors could disturb this apparently stable market-share measure.

VALIDATION OF THE MODEL

INTRODUCTION

Up to this point, no attempt has been made to check the validity of the underlying assumptions of the regression model. The next step is to determine those situations in which the assumptions are violated and to investigate the proper techniques for correction.

The assumptions of the linear model are these:

1. The relationship between the X_i's and Y is linear.
2. The X_i's are nonrandom variables whose values are fixed.
3. The error term has constant variance.
4. The random variables, Y_i, are statistically independent.
5. The error term has an expected value of zero.
6. The independent variables, X_i, must be independent of each other.
7. The number of observations, n, must exceed the number of regressors; i.e., $n > k$.

Note than an assumption of normality is not included in the preceding list. Even without the normality assumption, it can be shown that the least-squares estimators are BLUE (best linear unbiased estimators). Although the assumption of normality is needed to perform the t and F tests, the central-limit theorem provides the rationale of using statistical tests without a normality assumption when the sample size is large.[1]

The assumption that the error term has an expected value of zero is insignificant for purposes of forecasting. The reason is that if the error has a nonzero expected value, the slope parameters remain unchanged, but the intercept ($\hat{\beta}_0$) reflects this effect. Although this implies that the true intercept cannot be accurately estimated, the intercept generally has no economic interpretation; thus, this assumption can be disregarded.

Thus far we have implicitly assumed that the independent variables are fixed and under the control of the forecaster. It must be obvious that this condition rarely holds in the problems being analyzed by the business analyst. Fortunately, the majority of the results and their interpretations remain valid whether the X_i's are fixed or random if the error terms are normally distributed and independent of the X_i's.[2] Both these assumptions are reasonable; hence, we will continue to pursue development of the least-squares model. The first assumption, that the model is correctly specified—that is, the relationship is linear—is an important one. However, any discussion regarding linearity will be delayed until the next section. The remaining assumptions will be considered in some detail in the following paragraphs.

MULTICOLLINEARITY

Whenever more than one independent variable appears in a regression equation, it is possible that the variables are related to or are dependent upon each other. If either of these conditions are present, multicollinearity among the variables is said to exist. In general, when two or more independent variables are related to each other, they are redundant—they contribute overlapping

[1] Ronald J. Wonnacott and Thomas H. Wonnacott, *Econometrics* (New York: John Wiley, 1970), pp. 15–34.
[2] Ibid., pp. 38–40.

information. Although it is possible to obtain least-squares estimators, the use, testing, and interpretation of the regression equation and its coefficients is troublesome when multicollinearity is present.

It can be proved that the presence of multicollinearity results in an overstatement of the standard errors of the regression coefficients. Thus, even though the independent variables are related to Y, their statistical significance may be masked. Additionally, if the standard errors are overstated, the t test and confidence intervals are adversely affected, the process of partitioning the regression sum of squares is invalid, and the F test cannot be employed in statistically checking the regression equation.

With regard to interpreting the regression coefficients, the effect of multicollinearity can be illustrated by examining a multiple regression equation of the form:

$$\hat{Y}_i = \hat{\beta}_0 + \hat{\beta}_1 X_{1i} + \hat{\beta}_2 X_{2i} + e_i \tag{6-24}$$

In this equation, the coefficients, $\hat{\beta}_1$ and $\hat{\beta}_2$, were given specific meanings. For example, $\hat{\beta}_1$ measures the change in Y due to a change in X_1, other things (specifically X_2) remaining the same. However, if X_1 and X_2 are related to each other, this interpretation is no longer valid. That is, we cannot isolate the effect of X_1 on Y because X_1 also influences X_2, which in turn affects Y.

Methods of detecting the presence of multicollinearity follow from an understanding of the problem and its effects. There are two relatively simple schemes employed. The first method involves examining the values of the regression coefficients, their standard errors, and/or t statistics to see if they are sensitive to changes in the specification of the model. For example, consider the following model:

$$\widehat{FS}_t = \hat{\beta}_0 + \hat{\beta}_1 INC_t + \hat{\beta}_2 POP_t + e_t \tag{6-25}$$

where:

$$FS_t = \text{final sales; annual data;}$$
$$\text{billions of '72 dollars}$$
$$INC_t = \text{disposable personal income;}$$
$$\text{annual data; billions of '72 dollars}$$
$$POP_t = \text{population; annual data; millions}$$

To check for multicollinearity, first estimate:

$$\widehat{FS}_t = \hat{\beta}_0 + \hat{\beta}_1 INC_t + e_t \tag{6-26}$$

The data needed to estimate these equations are documented in Table E-3, Appendix E. In estimating equation (6-26), we obtain:

$$\widehat{FS}_t = 98.299 + 1.321112 INC_t$$
$$S_{\hat{\beta}_i} \qquad (0.0227824)$$
$$t_e \qquad \qquad 57.99 \tag{6-27}$$

Now, if INC_t and POP_t are independent of each other, inclusion of POP_t into equation (6-27) should not change the value of $\hat{\beta}_1$ (1.32112) or the values of the standard error or t statistic. Rerunning equation (6-27) with the second independent variable, POP_t, included yields:

$$\widehat{FS}_t = -477.16672 + 0.9742 INC_t + 4.08888 POP_t$$
$$S_{\hat{\beta}_i} \qquad\qquad\qquad (0.1040551) \quad (1.207746)$$
$$t_e \qquad\qquad\qquad\qquad 9.35 \qquad\quad 3.38 \qquad\qquad (6-28)$$

Clearly, the regression coefficient for income was altered by the inclusion of POP_t in the model. Therefore, one could reasonably conclude that multicollinearity between income and population exists and is likely to adversely affect the equation's ability to estimate future values of final sales accurately.

The second method of detecting multicollinearity involves the calculation and examination of a correlation matrix. A correlation matrix documents the simple correlation coefficients among all combinations of the dependent and independent variables. A correlation coefficient (r) can be calculated between every pair of variables of a given set of m variables, each with n observations, using the equation:

$$r = \frac{\sum_{i=1}^{n}(X_i - \bar{X})(Y_i - \bar{Y})}{\sqrt{\sum_{i=1}^{n}(X_i - \bar{X})^2 \sum_{i=1}^{n}(Y_i - \bar{Y})^2}} \qquad (6-29)$$

where X_i and Y_i are variables. The correlation matrix gives the correlation coefficient, r_{jk}, for the pairs of variables $j = 1, 2, \ldots, n$ and $k = 1, 2, \ldots, n$.

The format of a correlation matrix is given in Table 6-6. In that table, $r(Y_1 Y_1)$ can be interpreted as the correlation between Y_1 and Y_1; $r(Y_1 X_1)$ as

Table 6-6 Correlation matrix for three variables[a]

Variable \\ Variable	Y_1	X_1	X_2
Y_1	$r(Y_1 Y_1)$	$(rY_1 X_1)$	$r(Y_1 X_2)$
X_1	$r(X_1 Y_1)$	$r(X_1 X_1)$	$r(X_1 X_2)$
X_2	$r(X_2 Y_1)$	$r(X_2 X_1)$	$r(X_2 X_2)$

[a]See equation (6-29) for definition of r.

the correlation between Y_1 and X_1; $r(X_1 X_2)$ as the correlation between X_1 and X_2; and so on. The assumption that the independent variables are unrelated implies that $r(X_1 X_2)$ and $r(X_2 X_1)$ are zero.

Continuing with the final sales example, in equation (6-28), the correlation matrix is shown in Table 6-7. In this table, the cross diagonal represents the correlation between each variable and itself. As expected, $r(FS, FS)$, $r(POP, POP)$, and $r(INC, INC)$ all equal 1.000. The remaining elements in the first row represent the relationship between the dependent variable, FS_t, and the independent variables, POP_t and INC_t. These correspond to the simple correlation coefficients noted in the preceding chapter. The astute reader will note that $r(FS, POP) = r(POP, FS)$; $r(FS, INC) = r(INC, FS)$; and so on.

Table 6-7 Correlation matrix for final sales example

Variable \ Variable	$FS_t{}^a$	$POP_t{}^a$	$INC_t{}^a$
FS_t	$r(FS, FS) =$ 1.000	$r(FS, POP) =$ 0.99016	$r(FS, INC) =$ 0.99733
POP_t	$r(POP, FS) =$ 0.99016	$r(POP, POP) =$ 1.000	$r(POP, INC) =$ 0.98473
INC_t	$r(INC, FS) =$ 0.99733	$r(INC, POP) =$ 0.98473	$r(INC, INC) =$ 1.000

[a]Final Sales, Population and Income as defined in equation (6-25).

The only elements of present interest are $r(POP, INC)$ or $r(INC, POP)$. The r statistic represents the relationship—that is, correlation—between the two independent variables. The classical linear model assumes that there is no relationship. That is, it assumes $r(INC, POP) = r(POP, INC) = 0$. For all practical purposes, it is impossible to obtain a value of zero in real-world calculations. Therefore, a good rule of thumb is that the correlation between the independent variables should be less than $\pm.50$. Since the correlation coefficient between income and population, $r(INC, POP)$, equals 0.98473, the assumption that population and income are independent of each other has clearly been violated.

Whenever the problem of multicollinearity is severe, the forecaster should generally take steps to correct the situation. Many textbooks and forecasters suggest dropping one of the related variables from the equation. There are two drawbacks to this recommendation. First, which one should be dropped, and second, if there is a theoretical reason for including the variable, omitting it will inject bias into the results. Fortunately, there are several alternative methods of minimizing the effects of multicollinearity. One common practice is to redefine the variables. The two most popular methods of accomplishing this are via aggregation or transformation. These procedures are easier to illustrate than to explain; hence, we will return to the final sales example.

In equation (6-28), both population and income are statistically significant and are theoretically sound. Unfortunately, they are also interrelated. We can transform final sales and income by simply dividing them by population. These computations yield figures for per capita final sales ($PCFS_t$) and per capita income ($PCINC_t$). The equation to be estimated now becomes:

$$\widehat{PCFS_t} = \hat{\beta}_0 + \hat{\beta}_1 PCINC_t + e_t \tag{6-30}$$

Implicitly, we have taken the effect of population on both these variables into account. Empirically, this yields:

$$\widehat{PCFS_t} = 673.69388 + 1.268399PCINC_t \tag{6-31}$$

The important facet of this process is that we have eliminated the existence of multicollinearity without ignoring information that is obviously relevant.

In large-scale regression equations, some minimal levels of multicollinearity must be tolerated. In preceding paragraphs, this minimal level (rule-of-thumb value for r) was postulated to be ± 0.5. There is nothing particularly magical about this cutoff point. Indeed, the only plausible justification for disregarding correlation coefficients outside these boundaries is that, *as long as the multicollinearity can be expected to continue*, short-run forecasts will be reasonably accurate.

HETEROSCEDASTICITY

The third basic assumption in regression analysis is that of constant variance of the error terms, often referred to as the homoscedasticity assumption. Thus if we do *not* have constant variance, we have heteroscedasticity.

The occurrence of heteroscedasticity is generally due to changes in the background conditions not included in the specification of the model. For example, changes in laws, customs of people, and government policies can alter the underlying structure of the economy. With regard to time-series data, a common reason for heteroscedasticity is a change in the accuracy of measurement. That is, it is possible that recent data are measured more accurately than earlier data.

The effect of heteroscedasticity can best be seen by looking at the graphs in Figure 6-3. Figure 6-3(a) illustrates the case of constant variance. Note that the observations of Y given X fall within a constant band around the regression line. Thus, variance is not dependent on the X value specified. In Figures 6-3(b), (c), and (d), the variance fluctuates as the size of X changes. In (b), the variance increases as X increases; in (c), it decreases; and in (d), it varies over the entire range of X. To see the effect on future values of Y, assume that the pattern illustrated in (b) prevails, and observe that the difference between the observed values and the estimated values increases over time. If the regression

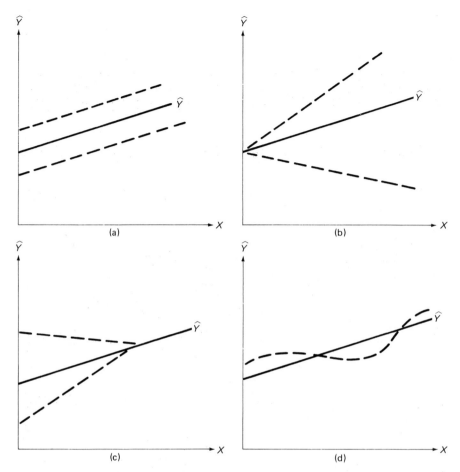

Figure 6-3 Constant and Heteroscedastic Variance in the Residuals[a]

[a]Dashed lines indicate pattern of actual Y values about the estimated regression values ($\hat{Y}$).

equation is used to forecast, it is likely to continually misrepresent Y, and the confidence intervals will be less and less likely to contain the true value of the dependent variable.

There are several statistical tests that have been developed to test for the existence of heteroscedasticity. Specifically, both Bartlett's test and the Goldfeld-Quandt test are designed to check the validity of constant variance. Unfortunately, most computer packages do not print these statistics; hence, they will not be covered here.[3] For the forecaster, the method of detection most commonly utilized is a plot of e_t, where $e_t = Y_t - \hat{Y}_t$.

[3]Robert S. Pindyck and Daniel L. Rubinfeld, *Econometric Models and Economic Forecasts* (New York: McGraw-Hill, 1976), pp. 102–6.

To illustrate this procedure, a simple example relating military expenditures (MILEXP) to gross national product follows.

In order to relate expenditures on national defense to gross national product for the years 1940 to 1950, a regression model was constructed, with the results noted in Table 6-8 and Figure 6-4. The existence of heteroscedasticity can be seen by the systematic error pattern in Figure 6-4. MILEXP and e_t vary

Table 6-8 National defense expenditures and GNP regression

Year	$MILEXP_t$	GNP_t	$\widehat{MILEXP}_t$	$e_t =$ $MILEXP_t - \widehat{MILEXP}_t$
1940	1.5	99.7	26.2	−24.7
1941	6.1	124.5	27.4	−21.3
1942	24.0	157.9	29.0	− 5.0
1943	63.2	191.6	30.6	32.6
1944	76.8	210.1	31.5	45.3
1945	81.3	211.9	31.6	49.7
1946	43.2	208.5	31.4	11.8
1947	9.0	232.8	32.6	−23.6
1948	10.7	259.1	33.9	−23.2
1949	13.2	258.0	33.8	−20.6
1950	14.0	286.2	35.2	−21.2

$$\widehat{MILEXP}_t = 21.33866 + 0.048330458 GNP_t$$

Std. error 0.1715563

t_e 0.2818

Range of data: 1940–1950

$R^2 = 0.09$ Data in billions of dollars

SEE = 31.22826

in a nonrandom fashion. For the years 1940–42 and 1947–50, the equation underestimates military expenditures. The effect of World War II on military expenditures represents a fundamental change in the underlying structure of our model.

The correction of heteroscedasticity requires the use of weighted least squares, transformed variables, or respecification of the model. One frequently employed tool is the specification of two equations, with one being applied whenever condition A (wartime, for example) prevails and the other applied when condition B (peacetime) prevails. In fact, this procedure is closely related to the use of dummy variables which will be presented in Chapter 7.

AUTOCORRELATION

The fourth basic assumption of the classical regression model is that the error terms, e_t, corresponding to different observations are unrelated to each other—they are randomly distributed. This assumption implies that e_t is

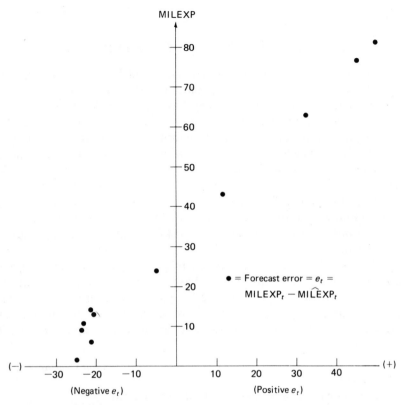

Figure 6-4 Heteroscedastic Variance in National Defense Expenditures Regression

independent of e_{t-1}, e_{t-2}, as well as e_{t+1}, e_{t+2}, and so on. Alternatively, the random variable Y_t in period t is assumed to be unrelated to Y_t in any other period. These statements are identical in terms of their implications for forecasting models, and for time-series data, both assumptions are frequently violated. For example, suppose disposable income is the dependent variable. Its value in 1980 is apt to be influenced by its value in 1979, which in turn is influenced by the 1978 value, and so on. Clearly, successive observations over time are related to each other. For such data, the error terms are said to exhibit autocorrelation or serial correlation. In fact, it is fair to say that autocorrelation is the most serious problem you are likely to incur in developing reliable forecasting models. Therefore, we will cover in some detail the tests and corrective procedures for this problem.

The major cause of autocorrelated error terms in economic models is misspecification of the model. In particular, whenever we have omitted one or more key explanatory variables, we are apt to observe a systematic pattern in the residual or error terms. For example, consider a demand equation for automobiles of the form:

$$\widehat{DAUTO}_t = \hat{\beta}_0 + \hat{\beta}_1 INCOME_t + \hat{\beta}_2 PRICE_t + e_t \qquad (6\text{-}32)$$

This specification ignores many variables, one of which is the driving-age population, that have a significant bearing on auto sales. Another common cause of autocorrelation is that the data may have been collected or tabulated in such a way that measurement errors are systematically built into the model.

Throughout this text, we will concentrate on the problem of first-order autocorrelation in which e_t is correlated with e_{t+1}. It is, of course, possible that e_t is related to e_{t+2} or e_{t+3}. These cases can be handled by the use of generalized least squares. In addition, although it is possible that autocorrelation can be negative, attention will be centered on positive autocorrelation (errors in one time period are positively correlated with errors in the next time period). Positive first-order autocorrelation is the most frequent occurrence in economic time-series data.

If the error terms in the regression model are positively autocorrelated, the use of ordinary least squares will have some important statistical consequences. As a general rule, the presence of autocorrelation will not affect the unbiasedness or consistency of the regression coefficients, but it does affect their efficiency. Specifically, the existence of positive autocorrelation will lead to the following problems:

1. The least-squares coefficients will no longer have minimum variance and will be inefficient.
2. The variance of the error term will be underestimated.
3. The standard errors of the regression coefficients, $S_{\hat{\beta}_i}$, will be underestimated.
4. The confidence intervals and tests using the t and F statistics are not applicable.

To illustrate these problems intuitively, examine Figures 6-5(a) and (b).

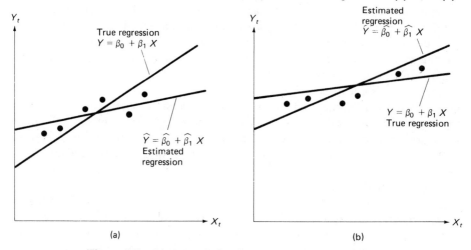

Figure 6-5 Autocorrelation Patterns in Regression Lines

Both graphs illustrate the presence of positive autocorrelation. This can best be noted by looking first at Figure 6-5(a). The error term associated with the first observation is positive. This leads to a series of error terms following a systematic pattern. The first four error terms are positive, and the last two are negative. Figure 6-5(b) illustrates the opposite case, where a series of negative errors is followed by a series of positive errors. In the first case, the estimated regression slope $(\hat{\beta}_1)$ is lower than the true slope (β_1), whereas in the second case, it is higher. Both cases are equally possible, implying that on the average, the estimates will be correct. In other words, they will be unbiased. However, in both cases, the least-squares regression lines fit the observed data points more closely than does the true regression line. This leads to an overstatement of the reliability of the least-squares regression line, which means that the estimate of the error variance, SEE, is smaller than the true error variance, σ^2. As before, this will cause the standard statistical tests to further overstate the reliability of any future estimates.

In a forecasting sense, the consequences of autocorrelated errors are equally adverse. If either of the situations pictured in Figure 6-5 prevails, the forecast error tends to increase (or decrease) in size over time. Given this occurrence, the forecasts themselves worsen over time. For example, if the forecast in time period $t + 1$ is in error by 10 percent, the error in $t + 2$ will be somewhat greater than 10 percent, with the effect being cumulative—10, 12, 15, 20 percent errors in $t + 1$, $t + 2$, $t + 3$, and $t + 4$, respectively.

Fortunately, in checking for the existence of autocorrelation, we have two readily accessible tools. The first of these tools involves an examination of either the signs of the error terms or a plot of the error terms. Once again returning to the example for final sales, equation (6-31), we can illustrate this technique. Table 6-9, column 3, documents the error terms obtained from the historical simulation for equation (6-31). In this case, the relevant information is derived by looking at the systematic sign pattern. The first four error terms have negative signs, the next eight have positive signs, then two negative, one positive, four negative, and one positive—in other words, a nonrandom error pattern. A similar conclusion could be reached via an examination of Figure 6-6.

A common procedure for testing for the presence of autocorrelation is based on the Durbin-Watson (DW or d) statistic. This statistic is defined by:

$$\text{DW} = d = \frac{\sum\limits_{t=2}^{n} (e_t - e_{t-1})^2}{\sum\limits_{t=1}^{n} e_t^2} \tag{6-33}$$

where:

$e_t = Y_t - \hat{Y}_t =$ actual error in period t
$\hat{Y}_t =$ estimated or forecasted value of the dependent variable
$Y_t =$ actual or observed value of the dependent variable

Table 6-9 Actual and observed values for per capita final sales

Year	Actual Real per Capita Final Sales (1)	Estimated Real per Capita Final Sales (2)	$e_t = \text{PCFS}_t - \widehat{\text{PCFS}}_t$ (3)	e_t^2 (4)	$(\Delta e_t)^2 = (e_t - e_{t-1})^2$ (5)
1958	3,914	4,017	−103	10,609	
1959	4,034	4,093	− 59	3,481	1,936
1960	4,044	4,095	− 51	2,601	64
1961	4,087	4,130	− 43	1,849	64
1962	4,230	4,220	10	100	2,809
1963	4,354	4,287	67	4,489	3,249
1964	4,516	4,490	26	676	1,681
1965	4,716	4,672	44	1,936	324
1966	4,893	4,826	67	4,489	529
1967	5,005	4,950	55	3,025	144
1968	5,189	5,067	122	14,884	4,489
1969	5,261	5,132	129	16,641	49
1970	5,224	5,264	− 40	1,600	28,561
1971	5,319	5,384	− 65	4,225	625
1972	5,560	5,540	20	400	7,225
1973	5,800	5,826	− 26	676	2,116
1974	5,708	5,713	− 5	25	441
1975	5,664	5,779	−115	13,225	12,100
1976	5,879	5,920	− 41	1,681	5,476
1977	6,101	6,091	10	· 100	2,601
				$\sum e_t^2 = 86{,}712$	$\sum(\Delta e_t)^2 = 74{,}483$

Source: Equation (6-31)

The test for autocorrelation assumes a first-order autoregressive error model of the form:[4]

$$Y_t = \beta_0 + \beta_1 X_{1t} + \beta_2 X_{2t} + \beta_3 X_{3t} + \beta_4 X_{4t} + \beta_5 X_{5t} + \mu_t$$
$$\mu_t = \rho\mu_{t-1} + \epsilon_t$$
$$|\rho| \leq 1 \qquad\qquad (6\text{-}34)$$

where:

μ_t = nonrandom error term in quarter t
ϵ_t = random error term
ρ = autocorrelation parameter

Since most business applications involve positive autocorrelation (a large positive [negative] error this quarter is followed by a large positive [negative]

[4]This model is consistent with the computational formula for the Durbin-Watson statistic in which the sum of the squared first differences in successive error terms in found.

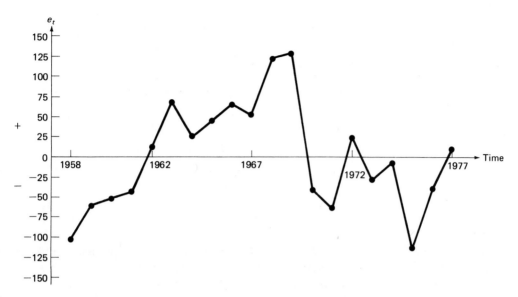

Figure 6-6   Error Pattern for Estimated Real per Capita Final Sales

Source: e_t shown in column 3 of Table 6-9

error next period), the test for autocorrelation is:

$$H_0: \rho = 0, \text{ there is no autocorrelation}$$

$$H_1: \rho > 0, \text{ there is positive autocorrelation}$$

The actual value of the DW statistic is computed and compared against the upper and lower bounds (d_u and d_l, respectively) as presented in Appendix F. This value is compared to the critical values (d_u and d_l) utilizing the following scheme (Pos. and Neg. indicate direction of the one-tail test):

Value of the Calculated DW(d)	Conclusion
$d < d_l$	Positive autocorrelation (Pos. test)
$d > (4 - d_l)$	Negative autocorrelation (Neg. test)
$d_l < d < d_u$	Indeterminate (Pos. test)
$(4 - d_u) < d < (4 - d_l)$	Indeterminate (Neg. test)
$d_u < d$	No autocorrelation (Pos. test)
$d < (4 - d_u)$	No autocorrelation (Neg. test)

The preceding scheme can be simplified by noting that values of DW (d) close to zero and 4 indicate autocorrelation, whereas values near 2 indicate a random pattern. Appendix F contains the d_l and d_u values based on sample size (n) and number of regressors excluding the intercept (k), and level of significance $(\alpha = .025)$.

For our example, $n = 20$, $k = 1$, and a 2.5 percent level of significance, the critical values are $d_l = 1.08$ and $d_u = 1.28$. Columns 4 and 5 of Table 6-9 furnish the calculations necessary for the Durbin-Watson statistic for our example:

$$\text{DW} = \frac{\sum\limits_{t=2}^{n} (e_t - e_{t-1})^2}{\sum\limits_{t=1}^{n} e_t^2}$$

$$= 74{,}483/86{,}712$$

$$= 0.859 \qquad\qquad (6\text{-}35)$$

Since the calculated value of d, 0.859, is less than the lower acceptance point, $d_l = 1.08$, we conclude that there is positive autocorrelation in the error terms. Several concluding comments with respect to this test are in order.

1. If we want to check for negative autocorrelation, the test statistic used is $4 - d_l$. The rest of the procedure is similar. That is, if the quantity $4 - d_l < d$, we conclude that negative autocorrelation exists, if $d < 4 - d_u$, **accept** H_0.
2. If the results are inconclusive, more observations are required.

Since autocorrelation is such a serious problem for the forecaster utilizing time-series data, techniques have been developed to overcome its existence. There are a great many schemes specifically designed to correct this situation. Among them we would find improved specification, use of generalized least squares, use of the Cochrane-Orcutt iterative procedures, differencing, and various autoregressive schemes. The first of these approaches, improved specification, has the most theoretical merit. However, it may not always be possible to improve the specification. For one thing, the missing variable, although known to us, may not be quantifiable. For example, while business investment in future periods is related to the optimism of investors, it is difficult to quantify this factor. Nevertheless, where possible, the model must be specified in accordance with theoretical insights. Blind application of any corrective technique to a theoretically unsound model *will not* solve the problem of autocorrelation.

Given the conclusion that the autocorrelation parameter is greater than zero for the model in Table 6-9, either an iterative approach or a first-differences approach may be utilized to transform the dependent and independent variables.[5] First, consider an iterative transformation of the model in equation (6-34) that builds upon a statistical estimate of ρ:

[5]The techniques of variable transformation are discussed in John Neter and William Wasserman, *Applied Linear Statistical Models* (Homewood, Ill.: Richard D. Irwin, 1974), pp. 123–30.

$$Y_t^* = Y_t - \rho Y_{t-1} \qquad (6\text{-}36)$$

$$X_{kt}^* = X_{kt} - \rho X_{kt-1} \qquad (6\text{-}37)$$

It can be shown that if we use these transformed variables, and if they are substituted into the old autoregressive model in equation (6-34), the new regression model will have independent error terms and retain the BLUE properties summarized in Chapter 5:[6]

$$Y_t^* = \beta_0^* + \beta_1^* X_{2t}^* + \beta_3^* X_{3t}^* + \beta_4^* X_{4t}^* + \beta_5^* X_{5t}^* + \epsilon_t \qquad (6\text{-}38)$$

The relationship between the old and new parameters can be shown to be equal to:

$$\beta_0 = \frac{\beta_0^*}{1 - \rho} \qquad (6\text{-}39)$$

$$\beta_i = \beta_i^* \qquad (6\text{-}40)$$

Alternatively, these relationships can be illustrated by rewriting equation (6-38) utilizing the definitional statements in equations (6-36), (6-37), (6-39), and (6-40):

$$Y_t = \rho Y_{t-1} + \beta_0(1 - \rho) + \beta_1(X_{1t} - \rho X_{1t-1}) + \beta_2(X_{2t} - \rho X_{2t-1}) +$$
$$\beta_3(X_{3t} - \rho X_{3t-1}) + \beta_4(X_{4t} - \rho X_{4t-1}) + \beta_5(X_{5t} - \rho X_{5t-1}) + \epsilon_t \quad (6\text{-}41)$$

Notice that if $\rho = 0$, we are back to the original model in equation (6-1). If $\rho = 1$—that is, if we have perfect positive autocorrelation—then we are taking first differences for all variables and dropping the constant term $(1 - \rho)$, since it equals zero. Variable transformation using either the iterative or first-difference method of correcting for autocorrelation should be viewed, therefore, as a choice between statistically estimating ρ or assuming that $\rho = 1$, respectively. Given a value for ρ, both procedures make use of the model summarized in equation (6-41).

Suppose, for example, a simple regression of Y on X is run:

$$\hat{Y}_t = \hat{\beta}_0 + \hat{\beta}_1 X_t + e_t \qquad (6\text{-}42)$$

Further, suppose the Durbin-Watson statistic indicates that autocorrelation exists. The autocorrelation coefficient ρ is estimated by r_t, as follows:

$$r_t = \frac{\sum\limits_{t=2}^{n} e_t e_{t-1}}{\sum\limits_{t=2}^{n} e_{t-1}^2} \qquad (6\text{-}43)$$

[6]To say that a model is BLUE (best linear unbiased estimator) does not guarantee that it will forecast well; it merely meets a series of statistical conditions that yield desirable properties for the estimators.

or:

$$r_t = \frac{\sum\limits_{t=2}^{n} (Y_t - \hat{Y}_t)(Y_{t-1} - \hat{Y}_{t-1})}{\sum\limits_{t=2}^{n} (Y_{t-1} - \hat{Y}_{t-1})^2} \tag{6-44}$$

The data are then transformed via equations (6-36) and (6-37), with the least-squares technique being applied to the transformed variables.

The regression equation then becomes:

$$\hat{Y}_t^* = \hat{\beta}_0^* + \hat{\beta}_1^* X_t^* \tag{6-45}$$

If $r_t = 1$, this equation is equivalent to first differences. After the regression is estimated, the Durbin-Watson statistic is again checked. If autocorrelation still exists, the process can be repeated. This iterative procedure, known as the Cochrane-Orcutt process, produces unbiased standard errors and reliable statistical tests. Further, many computer software packages have this routine built into them.

Both these techniques can be illustrated for our final sales example. To review, the original fitted equation was equation (6-31):

$$\widehat{PCFS}_t = 673.69388 + 1.268399PCINC_t$$
$$\text{Std. Error} \qquad (.028953739)$$
$$t_e \qquad\qquad 43.81$$

$r^2 = 0.991$	$F_{1,18} = 1,919$
SEE = 69.36	DW = 0.859
	$d_l = 1.06$
	$d_u = 1.28$

The Durbin-Watson value of 0.859 indicates the presence of positive autocorrelation. Table 6-10 contains the relevant transformations necessary to estimate both first differences and the Cochrane-Orcutt procedure of direct estimation of the autocorrelation coefficient, r_t.

Columns 2 and 5 of Table 6-10 contain first-differences for $PCFS_t$ and $PCINC_t$. The new regression is:

$$\widehat{PCFS}_t' = 14.6612 + 1.167PCINC_t' \tag{6-46}$$
$$\text{Std. Error} \qquad (0.2314)$$
$$t_e \qquad\qquad 5.04$$

$r^2 = 0.5995$	$F_{1,17} = 25.5$
$r = 0.7743$	DW = 2.12
SEE = 65.406	$d_l = 1.06$
	$d_u = 1.28$

Table 6-10 First differences and direct transformation for final sales estimation

Date: t	Real per Capita Final Sales in Thousands (PCFS$_t$) (1)	PCFS$_t'^a$ (2)	PCFS$_t^{*b}$ (3)	Real per Capita Disposable Income in Thousands (PCINC$_t$) (4)	PCINC$_t'^c$ (5)	PCINC$_t^{*d}$ (6)
1958	$3,914			$2,636		
1959	4,034	$120	$2,038	2,696	$ 60	$1,352
1960	4,044	10	1,987	2,697	1	1,322
1961	4,087	43	2,025	2,725	28	1,350
1962	4,230	143	2,146	2,796	71	1,406
1963	4,354	124	2,197	2,849	53	1,423
1964	4,516	162	2,296	3,009	160	1,556
1965	4,716	200	2,413	3,152	143	1,617
1966	4,893	177	2,488	3,274	122	1,666
1967	5,005	112	2,510	3,371	97	1,701
1968	5,189	184	2,636	3,464	93	1,745
1969	5,261	72	2,615	3,515	51	1,748
1970	5,224	−37	2,541	3,619	104	1,826
1971	5,319	95	2,655	3,714	95	1,868
1972	5,560	241	2,847	3,837	123	1,943
1973	5,800	240	2,964	4,062	225	2,105
1974	5,708	−92	2,750	3,973	−89	1,901
1975	5,664	−44	2,753	4,025	52	1,999
1976	5,879	215	2,990	4,136	111	2,083
1977	6,101	222	3,103	4,271	135	2,162

Source: Equations (6-36) and (6-37); $r_t = 0.51$ from equation (6-47) and Table 6-9
^{a}PCFS$_t'$ = PCFS$_t$ − PCFS$_{t-1}$
^{b}PCFS$_t^*$ = PCFS$_t$ − r_tPCFS$_{t-1}$
^{c}PCINC$_t'$ = PCINC$_t$ − PCINC$_{t-1}$
^{d}PCINC$_t^*$ = PCINC$_t$ − r_tPCINC$_{t-1}$

To determine if negative autocorrelation is now present, we test the null hypothesis, H_0: there is no autocorrelation. Since $d = 2.12 < 4 - d_u = 2.72$, the null hypothesis is accepted.

In order to use the Cochrane-Orcutt iterative procedure, we must first estimate ρ by the formulas given in either equation (6-43) or (6-44). For the original model in equation (6-31):

$$r_t = \frac{\sum_{t=2}^{n} e_t e_{t-1}}{\sum_{t=2}^{n} e_{t-1}^2}$$

$$= 0.51 \tag{6-47}$$

where r_t is the best estimate of ρ.

If r_t had been equal to 1, the direct approach would have yielded the same results as the first-differences procedure. Thus, one should estimate the autocorrelation coefficient prior to deciding which approach to utilize. Columns 3 and 6 of Table 6-10 present the figures based on transformations given by equations (6-35 and 37). For example, real per capita sales of $4,034 in 1959 is transformed in column 3 to $2,038, and real per capita disposable income of $2,696 becomes $1,352 in column 6:

$$Y_2^* = Y_2 - r_t Y_1$$
$$= 4,034 - .51(3,914)$$
$$= 4,034 - 1,996$$
$$Y_2^* = 2,038 \tag{6-48}$$

and:

$$X_2^* = X_2 - r_t X_1$$
$$= 2,696 - .51(2,636)$$
$$= 2,696 - 1,344$$
$$X_2^* = 1,352 \tag{6-49}$$

The remaining values are similarly transformed, and the resulting equation is:

$$\widehat{PCFS}_t^* = 391.443 + 1.236279 PCINC_t^*$$

Std. Error   (0.047735)

t_e 25.9   (6-50)

$r^2 = 0.975$	$F_{1,17} = 671$
$r = 0.987$	DW = 1.9
SEE = 55.01	$d_l = 1.06$
	$d_u = 1.28$

The results of the two correction procedures in equations (6-46) and (6-50) can be compared in terms of specific statistics.

If the Durbin-Watson statistic for equation (6-50) had indicated the presence of autocorrelation, another iteration would have been run by performing a second transformation, rerunning the regression equation, and again testing the same null hypothesis for positive autocorrelation. To utilize equation (6-50) for forecasting, all new data must be transformed. Once the forecast has been made, we must retransform the results back to their original form. For example, if PCINC in 1978 is equal to $4,600, then:

$$PCINC_t^* = 4,600 - .51(4,271)$$
$$= 2,422 \tag{6-51}$$

and:

$$\widehat{\text{PCFS}_t^*} = 391.443 + 1.236279\text{PCINC}_t^*$$
$$= 391.443 + 1.236279(2,422)$$
$$= 3,386 \qquad\qquad (6\text{-}52)$$

This value for $\widehat{\text{PCFS}_t^*}$ would then have to be added to the prior value for per capita final sales in 1977 to obtain our forecast value:

$$\widehat{\text{PCFS}}_{1978} = \widehat{\text{PCFS}^*}_{1978} + 0.51\text{PCFS}_{1977}$$
$$= 3,386 + 3,112$$
$$= 6,498 \qquad\qquad (6\text{-}53)$$

Example 6-3: Unit Sales of Automobiles; Correction for Autocorrelation

One of the disturbing features of equation (6-20):

$$\widehat{\text{UNITSAL}}_t = -3.186461 + 0.012494969\text{YPLTP}_t +$$
$$0.047822402\text{JATTC}_t - 0.2583437U_t \qquad (6\text{-}20)$$

was the presence of autocorrelation. The effect of this autocorrelation can be seen in Figure 6-7 by observing how the regression errors (e_t's) tend to be closely related. Because of autocorrelation, when the estimated value associated with one observation lies above (below) the true value, neighboring estimated values also tend to be above

$e_t = \text{UNITSAL}_t - \widehat{\text{UNITSAL}}_t$

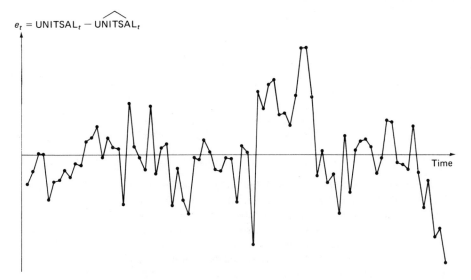

Figure 6-7   Error Pattern for Unit Sales of Automobiles

(below) the actual values. Especially discouraging to forecasters is the fact that the last six estimated or fitted values lie above the actual values, which implies that, without correction, future forecasts will overstate actual unit sales of automobiles.

To test for the existence of autocorrelation, set up the following hypothesis:

H_0: There is no positive autocorrelation, $p = 0$
H_1: There is positive autocorrelation, $p > 0$

where

if $d < d_l$, DW is significant; accept the alternative hypothesis, H_1.
if $d_u < d$, DW is not significant; accept the null hypothesis.
if $d_l < d < d_u$, the test is inconclusive.

The upper and lower bounds, d_u and d_l, are ($k = 3, n = 80, \alpha = .025$), 1.65 and 1.49, respectively. Since d is equal to 1.015, we can conclude, with 97.5 percent confidence, that the error in time period $t + 1$ is positively related to the error term in time period t.

In order for the forecasting reliability of the equation to be improved, it must be reestimated using the Cochrane-Orcutt iterative procedure, which directly estimates the autocorrelation coefficient. The estimated value of rho (p), based on the estimated values from equation (6-20), is 0.5023. Since perfect positive autocorrelation would yield $p = 1$, this estimate is roughly midway on the range of positive values; hence, first-differencing would be inappropriate. To remove the autocorrelation, transformations similar to that shown in equation (6-38) must be performed. The results of the reestimates on the transformed data are:

$$\widehat{UNITSAL}_t^* = -1.83433 + 0.01187233YPLTP_t^* +$$
$$0.04053523JATTC_t^* - 0.30470073U_t^* \qquad (6\text{-}54)$$

where the second iteration yields a rho value of 0.5023

$$\widehat{UNITSAL}_t^* = UNITSAL_t - 0.5023UNITSAL_{t-1}$$
$$YPLTP_t^* = YPLTP_t - 0.5023YPLTP_{t-1}$$
$$JATTC_t^* = JATTC_t - 0.5023JATTC_{t-1}$$
$$U_t^* = U_t - 0.5023U_{t-1}$$

$R^2 = 0.8638$	SEE $= 0.659$
$R = 0.9294$	$F_{3,75} = 38.06$
$\bar{R} = 0.9179$	DW $= 2.22$

The above statistics were generated by the time series processor (TSP) computer software package using the Cochrane-Orcutt iterative procedure in which the data is repeatedly transformed until the autocorrelation is eliminated. These results cannot be replicated unless one has access to a software package similar to TSP. The correction for autocorrelation significantly improved the historical fit of the original equation, and this can be verified by a visual examination of Figure 6-8. The estimated values in this figure are obtained from equation (6-54), with the numbers retransformed to their original levels.

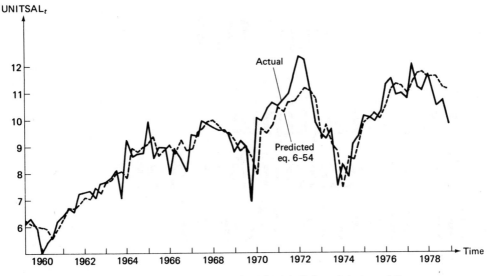

Figure 6-8 Actual Versus Predicted Unit Sales of Automobiles

CONCLUSION

In this chapter the basic multiple regression model has been presented, and the procedures required to validate the assumptions underlying this model have been outlined. As was the case in Chapter 5, the purpose has been to present these concepts in a relatively simple framework that facilitates understanding even as it abstracts from reality. Subsequent chapters will build upon this foundation by providing more advanced and specialized topics—such as stepwise regression, dummy variables, two-stage least squares, and simultaneous equation estimation. Additionally, the role of subjective interpretations and input will be analyzed. Techniques will be designed to link industry and firm models to national econometric models. All these real-world problems involve an integration of regression analysis, the theory and measurement of aggregate business cycles, and firm/industry business cycles.

APPENDIX 6.1

The Multiple Regression Model in Matrix Form

GENERALIZED MULTIPLE REGRESSION MODEL

The purpose of this appendix is to summarize, with the aid of matrix algebra, the generalized procedure for estimating regression coefficients. We will not present any new results, but shall only restate the results derived in Chapter 6 in matrix form. The reader is presumed to have some prior knowledge of linear algebra, and we will not attempt to describe or prove the basic theorems of matrix algebra that can be found in the econometrics textbooks noted in Chapters 6 and 7.

The basic regression model incorporates k regressors (including the constant) and can be stated as:

$$Y_1 = \beta_1 + \beta_2 X_{21} + \beta_3 X_{31} + \ldots + \beta_k X_{k1} + \epsilon_1$$
$$Y_2 = \beta_1 + \beta_2 X_{22} + \beta_3 X_{32} + \ldots + \beta_k X_{k2} + \epsilon_2$$
$$\ldots\ldots\ldots\ldots\ldots\ldots\ldots\ldots\ldots\ldots\ldots\ldots\ldots\ldots\ldots\ldots\ldots\ldots$$
$$Y_n = \beta_1 + \beta_2 X_{2n} + \beta_3 X_{3n} + \ldots + \beta_k X_{kn} + \epsilon_n \qquad \text{(A6-1)}$$

The corresponding matrix formulation of this model is:

$$\mathbf{Y} = \mathbf{X\beta} + \boldsymbol{\epsilon} \qquad (A6\text{-}2)$$

where

$$\mathbf{Y} = \begin{bmatrix} Y_1 \\ Y_2 \\ \cdot \\ \cdot \\ \cdot \\ Y_n \end{bmatrix} \qquad \mathbf{X} = \begin{bmatrix} 1 & X_{21} & \cdots & X_{k1} \\ 1 & X_{22} & \cdots & X_{k2} \\ \cdot & \cdot & \cdots & \cdot \\ \cdot & \cdot & \cdots & \cdot \\ \cdot & \cdot & \cdots & \cdot \\ 1 & X_{2n} & \cdots & X_{kn} \end{bmatrix}$$

$$\mathbf{\beta} = \begin{bmatrix} \beta_1 \\ \beta_2 \\ \cdot \\ \cdot \\ \cdot \\ \beta_k \end{bmatrix} \qquad \boldsymbol{\epsilon} = \begin{bmatrix} \epsilon_1 \\ \epsilon_2 \\ \cdot \\ \cdot \\ \cdot \\ \epsilon_n \end{bmatrix}$$

$\mathbf{Y}$ = an $n \times 1$ column vector of dependent variable observations
$\mathbf{X}$ = an $n \times k$ matrix of independent variable observations
$\mathbf{\beta}$ = a $k \times 1$ column vector of unknown parameters
$\boldsymbol{\epsilon}$ = an $n \times 1$ column vector of error observations

Within the X matrix, each element (X_{km}) has two subscripts. The first subscript signifies the appropriate column (variable), whereas the second subscript refers to the appropriate row (observation). All columns in X represent a vector of n observations on a given independent variable. Note that all observations associated with the intercept term are equal to one.

The assumptions of the classical linear model are:

1. The elements of $\mathbf{X}$ are fixed and have a finite variance
2. $\mathbf{X}$ has rank k, where k is less than n
3. $\boldsymbol{\epsilon}$ is normally distributed with $E(\boldsymbol{\epsilon}) = 0$ and $E(\boldsymbol{\epsilon\epsilon}') = \sigma^2\mathbf{I}$, where $\mathbf{I}$ is the identify matrix.

BASIC CALCULATIONS

The **X** and **Y** matrices for our example are:

$$\mathbf{Y} = \begin{bmatrix} 40 \\ 45 \\ 50 \\ 65 \\ 70 \\ 70 \\ 80 \end{bmatrix} \qquad \mathbf{X} = \begin{bmatrix} 1 & 100 & 36 \\ 1 & 200 & 33 \\ 1 & 300 & 37 \\ 1 & 400 & 37 \\ 1 & 500 & 34 \\ 1 & 600 & 32 \\ 1 & 700 & 36 \end{bmatrix} \qquad (A6\text{-}3)$$

Prior to deriving the least squares estimates, we need to compute:

$$\mathbf{X'X} = \begin{bmatrix} 1 & 1 & \dots & 1 \\ 100 & 200 & \dots & 700 \\ 36 & 33 & \dots & 36 \end{bmatrix} \begin{bmatrix} 1 & 100 & 36 \\ 1 & 200 & 33 \\ \cdot & \cdot & \cdot \\ \cdot & \cdot & \cdot \\ \cdot & \cdot & \cdot \\ 1 & 700 & 36 \end{bmatrix} \qquad (A6\text{-}4)$$

where $\mathbf{X'}$ is the transpose of $\mathbf{X}$, and $\mathbf{X'X}$ yields:

$$\mathbf{X'X} = \begin{bmatrix} 7 & 2{,}800 & 245 \\ 2{,}800 & 1{,}400{,}000 & 97{,}500 \\ 245 & 97{,}500 & 8{,}599 \end{bmatrix} \qquad (A6\text{-}5)$$

Additionally,

$$\mathbf{X'Y} = \begin{bmatrix} 1 & 1 & \dots & 1 \\ 100 & 200 & \dots & 700 \\ 36 & 33 & \dots & 36 \end{bmatrix} \begin{bmatrix} 40 \\ 45 \\ \cdot \\ \cdot \\ 80 \end{bmatrix} \qquad (A6\text{-}6)$$

$$\mathbf{X'Y} = \begin{bmatrix} 420 \\ 187{,}000 \\ 14{,}680 \end{bmatrix} \qquad (A6\text{-}7)$$

Finally, the inverse of $\mathbf{X'X}$ can be shown to be equal to:

$$(\mathbf{X'X})^{-1} = \begin{bmatrix} 7 & 2{,}800 & 245 \\ 2{,}800 & 1{,}400{,}000 & 97{,}500 \\ 245 & 97{,}500 & 8{,}599 \end{bmatrix}^{-1}$$

$$(\mathbf{X'X})^{-1} = \begin{bmatrix} 56.476 & -0.0042306 & -1.5611 \\ -0.0042306 & 0.0000037467 & 0.000078055 \\ -1.5611 & 0.000078055 & 0.043711 \end{bmatrix} \qquad (A6\text{-}8)$$

LEAST SQUARES ESTIMATION

The least squares estimates, $\hat{\boldsymbol{\beta}}$, can be shown to be equal to

$$\hat{\boldsymbol{\beta}} = (\mathbf{X'X})^{-1}(\mathbf{X'Y}) \qquad (A6\text{-}9)$$

$$\hat{\boldsymbol{\beta}} = \begin{bmatrix} 56.576 & -0.0042306 & -1.5611 \\ -0.0042306 & 0.0000037467 & 0.000078055 \\ -1.5611 & 0.000078055 & 0.043711 \end{bmatrix} \begin{bmatrix} 420 \\ 187{,}000 \\ 14{,}680 \end{bmatrix} \qquad (A6\text{-}10)$$

$$\hat{\boldsymbol{\beta}} = \begin{bmatrix} 12 \\ 0.06943 \\ 0.6127 \end{bmatrix} = \begin{bmatrix} \hat{\beta}_1 \\ \hat{\beta}_2 \\ \hat{\beta}_3 \end{bmatrix} \tag{A6-11}$$

Thus, the estimated regression equation is:

$$\hat{Y}_i = 12 + 0.06943X_{1i} + 0.6127X_{2i} \tag{A6-12}$$

The regression estimates of $\hat{\mathbf{Y}}$ are given by:

$$\hat{\mathbf{Y}} = \mathbf{X}\hat{\boldsymbol{\beta}} \tag{A6-13}$$

$$\begin{vmatrix} \hat{Y}_1 \\ \hat{Y}_2 \\ \hat{Y}_3 \\ \hat{Y}_4 \\ \hat{Y}_5 \\ \hat{Y}_6 \\ \hat{Y}_7 \end{vmatrix} = \begin{bmatrix} 1 & 100 & 36 \\ 1 & 200 & 33 \\ 1 & 300 & 37 \\ 1 & 400 & 37 \\ 1 & 500 & 34 \\ 1 & 600 & 32 \\ 1 & 700 & 36 \end{bmatrix} \begin{bmatrix} 12 \\ 0.06943 \\ 0.6127 \end{bmatrix} = \begin{bmatrix} 41 \\ 46 \\ 55 \\ 62 \\ 68 \\ 73 \\ 83 \end{bmatrix} \tag{A6-14}$$

STATISTICAL TESTS

To test whether Y_i is statistically related to X_1 and X_2, we must compute the F statistic. As was the case in the text, the total variation in Y_i may be partitioned into the explained and unexplained variation. If one assumes that the Y_i variable (which is defined as the sum of $\hat{Y}$ and $\hat{\epsilon}$) has a zero mean, we may derive the following relationship:

$$\mathbf{Y} = \mathbf{X}\hat{\boldsymbol{\beta}} + \boldsymbol{\epsilon} \tag{A6-15}$$

which can be shown to yield:

$$\mathbf{Y'Y} = \hat{\boldsymbol{\beta}}'\mathbf{X'X}\hat{\boldsymbol{\beta}} + \boldsymbol{\epsilon}'\boldsymbol{\epsilon}$$
$$\text{or} \quad \text{TSS} = \text{RSS} + \text{ESS} \tag{A6-16}$$

where

TSS = total sum of squares
RSS = variation explained by the regression
ESS = unexplained variation

Further,

$$R^2 = 1 - \frac{\boldsymbol{\epsilon}'\boldsymbol{\epsilon}}{\mathbf{Y'Y}} \frac{\hat{\boldsymbol{\beta}}'\mathbf{X'X}\hat{\boldsymbol{\beta}}}{\mathbf{Y'Y}} \tag{A6-17}$$

The F statistic is given by

$$F = \frac{(\hat{\boldsymbol{\beta}} - \boldsymbol{\beta})'\mathbf{X}'\mathbf{X}(\hat{\boldsymbol{\beta}} - \boldsymbol{\beta})}{\boldsymbol{\epsilon}'\boldsymbol{\epsilon}} \times \frac{(n - k)}{(n - 1)} \qquad \text{(A6-18)}$$

Finally, the standard error of the estimate is given by

$$s^2 = \frac{\boldsymbol{\epsilon}'\boldsymbol{\epsilon}}{n - k} \qquad \text{(A6-19)}$$

The use of matrix algebra allows one to condense the large system of equations given in (A6-1). Conceptually, the complex solution of a least squares regression problem translates into a routine computer task of matrix inversion and multiplication.

QUESTIONS FOR DISCUSSION AND ANALYSIS

1. Consider the following multiple-regression equation:

$$\widehat{PCFS}_t = \hat{\beta}_0 + \hat{\beta}_1 X_1 + \hat{\beta}_2 X_2 + e_t$$

where:

$PCFS_t$ = real per capita final sales in year t as given in column 1 of Table 6-10

X_i = independent variables selected by researcher

a. Estimate the model for the period 1958 to 1977, and calculate the following statistics: $\bar{R}^2$, SEE, $S_{\hat{\beta}_1}$, $S_{\hat{\beta}_2}$, DW, r_t, and F.

b. Test the statistical significance of the individual regression coefficients, $\hat{\beta}_1$ and $\hat{\beta}_2$, using an α level of 0.05. Explain precisely the economic interpretation of $\hat{\beta}_1$ and $\hat{\beta}_2$.

c. Carry out the F test for the equation using $\alpha = .05$.

d. Does the calculated value of DW suggest an autocorrelation problem? Test, using $\alpha = .025$.

e. Using the estimated value of r_t, transform the data and reestimate the transformed model.

f. Based on X_1 and X_2 values for 1978, estimate 1978 final sales using both the original equation and the transformed equation.

g. If available, obtain a computer estimate of the correlation matrix (as per Table 6-6) for the original model and interpret the results.

2. Using the same data, reestimate the original model using first differences. Carry out steps a, b, c, d, f, and g.

3. Equations (6-15) and (6-16) were presented as an example of the alternative specifications a forecaster might consider in developing a model to forecast real

income. Is equation (6-15) theoretically superior to (6-16)? How does your answer to this question change depending on whether annual, quarterly, or monthly data are used to estimate the model? Using a quarterly model that covers the last five years, develop empirical estimates of equations (6-15) and (6-16). Data can be found in the *Survey of Current Business* and the *Business Conditions Digest*. Some series may have to be aggregated from monthly to quarterly.

4. Equation (6-33) presents the formula for the Durbin-Watson statistic. Values close to 2 for the DW statistic are said to be consistent with the absence of auto-correlation. Why should values of DW less than 2 be associated with positive autocorrelation and values greater than 2 with negative autocorrelation? In other words, explain how equation (6-33) measures autocorrelation.

5. The sample autocorrelation coefficient, r_t, is calculated using equation (6-43). Explain to someone not familiar with statistical formulas how this formula measures autocorrelation.

6. "If $r_t = 1$, then the transformation outlined in equation (6-45) is equivalent to the first-differences approach." Explain.

7. Equations (6-46) and (6-50) represent the use of first differences and the Cochrane-Orcutt procedure, respectively, to deal with the autocorrelation found in equation (6-31). Contrast the summary statistics found in equations (6-46) and (6-50). Which correction yielded the best statistical fit?

8. Appendix E, Table E-1, contains the historical data used in estimating the automobile demand model in equation (6-20). Conduct an *ex post* evaluation of the model's forecasting precision by leaving out the last three data points.

9. The results of the installment-loan demand model in equation (6-22) are presented in Table 6-5, with the data listed in Appendix E, Table E-2. Carry out the following analyses:
   a. Leaving out the last four data points or observations, re-estimate the model in equation (6-22), and carry out an *ex post* evaluation.
   b. The variable MEMIND$_t$ represents the index of economic activity in Memphis. Your employer is particularly interested in understanding the effect of business activity on loan demand. Explain each of the row entries in Table 6-5 pertaining to MEMIND$_t$. Assume that your employer has had a course in statistics, but still wants a basic explanation of the statistical results.
   c. Should the variable U_t be left in the model? What statistical evidence is most pertinent?
   d. Test for autocorrelation, using $\alpha = .025$.
   e. As was done in Table 6-3, calculate the percentage of missed turning points and false turning points. Analyze the results.

10. The partial correlation coefficient for YPLTP in Table 6-3 is 0.8973. What does this mean?

11. In what sense is the transformed equation for unit sales of automobiles in equation (6-54) superior to the model developed in (6-20)?

12. Compute the Theil U statistic for equation (6-22).

13. Plot an actual change-predicted change diagram similar to Figure 6-2 for equation (6-20).

REFERENCES FOR FURTHER STUDY

Aaker, D.A., ed., *Multivariate Analysis in Marketing*. Belmont, Calif.: Wadsworth, 1971.

Brown, R.G., *Statistical Forecasting for Inventory Control*. New York: McGraw Hill, 1959.

Cochrane, D., and G.H. Orcutt, "Application of Least Squares Regressions to Relationships Containing Autocorrelated Error Terms," *Journal of the American Statistical Association*, Vol. 44 (1949), 32–61.

Draper, N., and H. Smith, *Applied Regression Analysis*. New York: John Wiley, 1966.

Farrar, D.E., and R.R. Glauber, "Multicollinearity in Regression Analysis: The Problem Re-visited," *Review of Economics and Statistics*, Vol. 49 (1967), 92–107.

Goldfeld, S.M., and R.M. Quandt, "Some Tests for Homoscedasticity," *Journal of the American Statistical Society*, Vol. 60 (1965), 539–47.

Lewis, Colin D., *Demand Analysis and Inventory Control*. Lexington, Mass.: Lexington Books, 1975.

Neter, John, and William Wasserman, *Applied Linear Statistical Models*. Homewood, Ill.: Richard D. Irwin, 1974.

Wonnacott, Ronald J., and Thomas H. Wonnacott, *Econometrics*, 2nd ed., New York: John Wiley & Sons, 1979.

7

Advanced Topics in Regression Analysis

INTRODUCTION

Forecasting with regression models is not as simple as it may have appeared in the preceding two chapters, where considerable time was spent estimating and studying the statistical properties of regression coefficients. These estimates were derived under the suppositions that the model was clearly and correctly specified and that the variables were well defined and measured. In many of the models, only the final regression results were presented, since a complete cataloging of all the intermediate models would have been tedious. Nonetheless, there are innumerable tricks of the trade that the researcher must master in order to become a successful forecaster. This chapter presents some of the more common techniques utilized by analysts to simplify the complex task of developing valid and reliable forecasts.

While proceeding through this chapter, remember that standard statistical tests may not be applicable at all stages of the analysis if an underlying assumption such as variable independence has been violated. Although the techniques presented in this chapter may not appear to be as scientific as the regression steps outlined in earlier chapters, these methods can help in minimizing the cost of an investigation. Additionally, they provide the hands-on experience that is necessary to carry out empirical research.

PROXY AND DUMMY VARIABLES

PROXY VARIABLES

A common plight facing the researcher is the lack of data. Least-squares estimators are unbiased only when all relevant independent variables are specified and included in the regression. Even when all the variables have been specified in a theoretical framework, the forecaster may run into a situation where one (or more) of the variables cannot be measured precisely. To avoid the bias that inevitably occurs when important variables are omitted, the pragmatist can frequently find variables that are close substitutes. For example, in agriculture-related business enterprises, the ability to accurately forecast next year's crop yield is of paramount importance. While weather is a significant independent variable, accurate one-dimensional measures of weather are all but impossible to obtain. Thus, forecasters use average rainfall or the number of sunny days as surrogate measures—*proxy variables*—for weather.

In Chapter 6, equation (6-20), two proxy variables—$YPLTP_t$ and $JATTC_t$—were used to project unit sales of automobiles:

$$\widehat{UNITSAL_t} = -3.186461 + 0.012494969 YPLTP_t +$$
$$0.047822402 JATTC_t - 0.2583437 U_t \quad (6\text{-}20)$$

Ideally, a forecaster would have an aggregate measure of individual income that netted out adjustments for taxes and transfer payments and that deducted expenditures for necessities such as food and shelter. Because automobiles are durable goods, a consumer can always postpone a new-car purchase by spending money to maintain his old car for one more year. No such deferral is possible for taxes, food, and shelter. Instead of the theoretically desirable income concept, equation (6-20) makes use of $YPLTP_t$—personal income less transfer payments. Pragmatically, $YPLTP_t$ works well, but it is merely an imperfect proxy for a theoretical concept that is otherwise impossible to obtain.

The second proxy variable used in developing the forecasting model for unit sales was consumer sentiment, $JATTC_t$. Economic theory reinforces the notion that expectations influence consumer decision making; however, an exact formulation of this variable is dependent upon the person making the decision to purchase a car. For example, some consumers may assign a high decision-making weight to the likelihood of future price changes, whereas others may feel that future income expectations are most relevant. In the present situation, the consumer-sentiment variable is an aggregate expression of consumer expectations that attempts to quantify the net effect of a seemingly infinite range of human perceptions. Microeconomic theory points out the hazards of interpersonal comparisons, but, once again, the justification for the proxy variable is pragmatic—JATTC$_t$ is the best real-world measure of consumer expectations at the forecaster's disposal.

DUMMY VARIABLES

Many important social phenomena such as wars, strikes, and other exogenous disturbances are not naturally quantifiable. One of the more common techniques of incorporating this information into regression models involves the creation of dummy variables. Three frequent applications of dummy-variable techniques involve the categorization of qualitative variables (married $= 1$, divorced $= 2$, single $= 3$), the estimation of time-series forces such as seasonality, and quantification of exogenous disturbances (war $= 1$ and peace $= 0$).

Suppose it is necessary to investigate how the level of military expenditures (MILEXP$_t$) is related to gross national product. A scatter diagram of annual observations for these two variables is shown in Figure 7-1. The relationship between military spending and GNP$_t$ is seen to follow two distinct patterns—one in wartime (1942–46, 1951–53, 1966–70), the other in peacetime. The normal relationship of MILEXP$_t$ to GNP$_t$ is shifted upward during wartime. MILEXP$_t$, therefore, is dependent upon both GNP$_t$ and another variable—the presence or absence of war (W_t). Unfortunately, war (W_t) is both a qualitative and a discrete variable. That is, we are either at war or we are not. In order to generate accurate forecasts, we must make a distinction between these two discrete possibilities.

Let the value of W_t be 1 for wartime and 0 for peacetime; that is, W_t is a 0,1 variable. The model to be estimated is:

$$\widehat{\text{MILEXP}}_t = \hat{\beta}_0 + \hat{\beta}_1 \text{GNP}_t + \hat{\beta}_2 W_t + e_t \tag{7-1}$$

W_t, the dummy variable, equals 1 during the war years (1942–46, 1951–53, and 1966–70) and zero for other years. The results of the least-squares regression were:

$$\widehat{\text{MILEXP}}_t = 10.93 + 0.05607901 \text{GNP}_t + 22.38869 W_t \tag{7-2}$$

Equation (7-2) yields the two estimated lines shown in Figure 7-1, where $\widehat{\text{MILEXP}}_1$ is the estimate of military spending in peacetime and $\widehat{\text{MILEXP}}_2$ is for wartime. The relationship between MILEXP$_t$ and GNP$_t$ cannot be properly estimated without W_t, but such a variable provides only crude results.

A second application of dummy variables involves the removal of seasonality from time-series data. In previous chapters and examples, data have

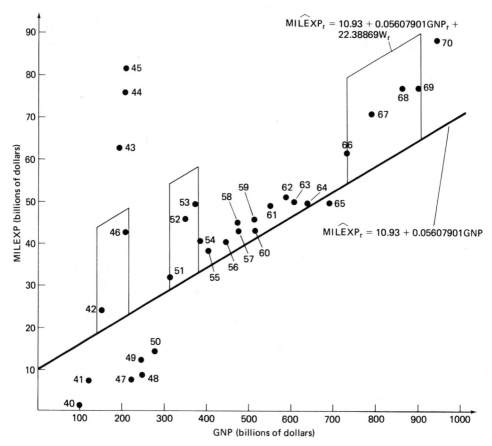

Figure 7-1 Military Expenditures and Real Gross National Product, 1940–1970

Source: *Business Statistics*

been seasonally adjusted via either the Census X-11 technique or a moving-average approach. A disadvantage of both these techniques is that they require a large number of data points. Since seasonal patterns are qualitative in nature, seasonality may be incorporated into regression models by using a set of dummy variables. Let Q_i be a dummy variable that takes the value 1 during the ith season (and 0 otherwise). The formal regression equation incorporating $m + 1$ seasonal variables is:

$$Y_t = \beta_0 + \beta_1 X_{1t} + \beta_2 X_{2t} + \beta_3 Q_1 + \beta_4 Q_2 + \ldots + \beta_m Q_m + \epsilon_t \quad (7\text{-}3)$$

where the $(m + 1)$th season is the excluded category. For example, if monthly data ($m + 1 = 12$) were used, there would be eleven values for Q_i, with the twelfth month excluded.

Consider how toy-store sales increase over time. The figures in column 1 of Table 7-1 outline the dramatic sales increase in the fourth quarter because of

Table 7-1   Toy sales and seasonal dummies

Date	Sales (000) (1)	Time (2)	Q_4 (3)	Q_3 (4)	Q_2 (5)
1976: I	21	0	0	0	0
II	25	1	0	0	1
III	25	2	0	1	0
IV	44	3	1	0	0
1977: I	21	4	0	0	0
II	26	5	0	0	1
III	25	6	0	1	0
IV	45	7	1	0	0
1978: I	21	8	0	0	0
II	26	9	0	0	1
III	27	10	0	1	0
IV	45	11	1	0	0
1979: I	22	12	0	0	0
II	27	13	0	0	1
III	29	14	0	1	0
IV	49	15	1	0	0

Christmas. If the forecaster is interested in isolating the trend increase in sales, the extreme seasonality evident in toy sales can be statistically neutralized by adding a dummy variable, Q_4, for the fourth quarter:

$$\hat{S}_t = \hat{\beta}_0 + \hat{\beta}_1 T + \hat{\beta}_2 Q_4 + e_t \qquad (7\text{-}4)$$

This model is not likely to be adequate, since explicit adjustments must also be made for seasonality in other quarters. For example, first-quarter toy sales will always be depressed relative to the high level of the fourth quarter. Seasonality can be completely estimated by adding dummies Q_2 and Q_3 for the second and third quarters respectively. Three dummy variables will suffice to measure quarterly seasonality (51 for weekly, and so on), because Q_2, Q_3, and Q_4 measure the seasonal shift from a first-quarter base. The complete model becomes:

$$\hat{S}_t = \hat{\beta}_0 + \hat{\beta}_1 T + \hat{\beta}_2 Q_2 + \hat{\beta}_3 Q_3 + \hat{\beta}_4 Q_4 + e_t \qquad (7\text{-}5)$$

The actual least-squares equation is:

$$\hat{S}_t = 19.825 + 0.2375T + 4.5125Q_2 + 4.775Q_3 + 23.7875Q_4$$
$$t_e \qquad\quad (4.36) \qquad (6.52) \qquad (6.84) \qquad (33.59) \qquad (7\text{-}6)$$

Each quarter, trend sales are augmented by $237.50, but this effect is always less than the seasonal effect. Equation (7-6) is presented graphically in Figure 7-2

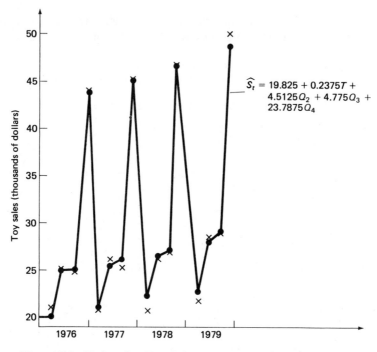

Figure 7-2 Estimating Toy Sales: Dummy Variable Technique

Source: Equation (7-6)

and the seasonality is exactly the same every year; that is, the same upward adjustments, $\hat{\beta}_2$, $\hat{\beta}_3$, and $\hat{\beta}_4$, occur in the fitted equation between the first and second, first and third, and first and fourth quarters, respectively. When first-quarter sales are estimated, the $\hat{\beta}$'s drop out and only the trend variable remains.

The final application of dummy variables, and the one of primary significance in forecasting, involves incorporation of exogenous influences such as prolonged strikes or severe weather into regression models. To see the effect of exogenous factors on car sales, refer to Appendix E, Table E-1, which contains raw data, and Figure 6-1(c), which depicts the accuracy of equation (6-20).

$$\widehat{UNITSAL}_t = -3.186461 + 0.012494969 YPLTP_t +$$
$$0.047822402 JATTC_t - 0.2583437 U_t \quad (6\text{-}20)$$

One of the best methods of evaluating the reliability of a forecasting equation is to use residual error analysis to identify any time periods that may have been unduly influenced by exogenous forces. For example, the error terms in Figure 6-1(c) are abnormally large in the following periods: 1966: QI; 1967: QIII and QIV; 1970: QIV; 1971: QI; 1973: QI, QII, and QIII; and 1976: QIII. As seen in Table E-1, the most precipitous declines in unit sales of automobiles are clustered around these dates. Historical analysis provides the missing link— these declines all occurred in conjunction with prolonged autoworkers' strikes. If a forecaster chooses to ignore this information, he not only produces bad estimates in these periods but also introduces bias into the model. The result is an overstatement of the standard error of the estimate and an understatement of the relevant statistics (F ratio, t statistics, R, and R^2).

Dummy variables can be introduced, but there are two complicating factors. In all previous examples with dummy variables, values of 0 or 1 have been assigned to particular periods. There is no reason to believe that these values accurately reflect the effect of an automobile strike. Further, if a value of 1 were assigned to different strike periods, all strikes would be unrealistically treated as equal in impact. If values of 0 or 1 are not to be adopted, what should be done? Ideally, dummy values would be selected such that the effect of the strike is completely negated. In other words, the value of the dummy variable would rise or fall just enough to offset the influence of the strike.

The second complicating factor arises because decision makers may take anticipatory actions designed to mitigate the effect of unusual events such as strikes. For example, if automobile producers anticipate a strike, a decision may be made to increase output prior to the strike so as to maintain sales at near-normal levels even though production has been curtailed. Alternatively, if economic agents do not anticipate these unusual events, adjustment decisions may be pushed into future time periods. For example, if consumers have not foreseen an automobile strike, their purchase plans may simply be delayed until after the strike is settled. Because events such as strikes not only influence sales during the strike but also alter sales in preceding and succeeding months, dummy values need to be created for periods surrounding the strike period. Dummy values for unit automobile sales will, ideally, provide a quantitative measure of the quarterly stimulus or drag generated by a strike. In this instance, the object is to evaluate past strikes so as to improve the historical fit of the regression model. Even though future strikes will differ qualitatively and quantitatively, owing to the unique characteristics of the economy, information about past strikes can provide a historical perspective concerning the likely spectrum of future outcomes.

Conceptually, the derivation of dummy values is based on *ex post* error analysis. For example, if the historical model starts to underestimate prior to a strike period, what part of this error is due to the strike? Similarly, what portion of the overestimate during the strike is strike-related? There is no reason for the total strike effect to equal zero; that is, the positive and negative influences on unit automobile sales need not cancel out. Theoretically, the adjustment process may span a long period before and after the strike, but it is necessary to truncate this process when estimating dummy values.

Commercial vendors are an excellent source of information regarding exogenous influences, and the dummy variable for automobile strikes

(DMYSTR$_t$) is based on analysis by Data Resources, Inc. These values are noted in Appendix G (which also contains data that will be used in other illustrations in this chapter), and when incorporated into the model, the results were:

$$\widehat{UNITSAL_t} = -1.09374523 + 0.00976276YPLTP_t +$$
$$t_e \qquad\qquad\qquad (8.20)$$

$$0.04401713JATTC_t - 0.14326459U_t - 0.00013734DMYSTR_t$$
$$t_e \quad (3.88) \qquad\qquad (1.71) \qquad\qquad (3.36) \qquad\qquad\qquad (7\text{-}7)$$

$\bar{R}^2$ = 0.615	SEE = 0.74
DW = 0.7731	1965 : I–1979 : IV

As was the case with the original equation, the error terms are autocorrelated, as indicated by the Durbin-Watson statistic of 0.77. The equation was re-estimated using the Cochrane-Orcutt iterative procedure on TSP:

$$\widehat{UNITSAL_t^*} = 1.25619221 + 0.00895512YPLTP_t^* +$$
$$t_e \qquad\qquad\qquad (3.75)$$

$$0.02788205JATTC_t^* - 0.21350163U_t^* - 0.00016181DMYSTR_t^*$$
$$t_e \quad (1.79) \qquad\qquad (1.43) \qquad\qquad (5.21) \qquad\qquad\qquad (7\text{-}8)$$

$\bar{R}^2$ = 0.78	DW = 2.2	SEE = 0.59

where the second iteration yields a rho (ρ) value of 0.661:

$$UNITSAL_t^* = UNITSAL_t - 0.661UNITSAL_{t-1}$$
$$YPLTP_t^* = YPLTP_t - 0.661YPLTP_{t-1}$$
$$U_t^* = U_t - 0.661U_{t-1}$$
$$JATTC_t^* = JATTC_t - 0.661JATTC_{t-1}$$
$$DMYSTR_t^* = DMYSTR_t - 0.661DMYSTR_{t-1}$$

As shown in Figure 7-3, after iterating and adding the dummy variable for automobile strikes, equation (7-8) performs better than did the original model in equation (6-20). Of course, this is always true of dummy variables, since a contrived variable has been incorporated to pull the predicted value closer to the actual observation. Indeed, a *perfect* dummy series could be constructed by merely using the error series as an explanatory variable. Except in the case of seasonality, dummy variables have values of zero in all future periods. That is, dummy variables have no effect on future predictions. The effect of the DMYSTR$_t$ variable in equation (7-8) is to shift the slope of equation (6-20)

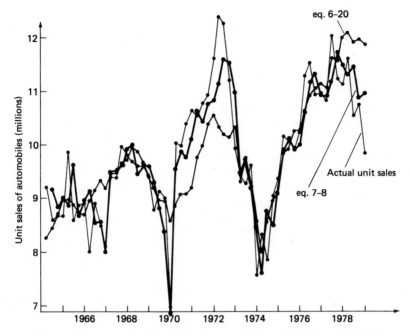

Figure 7-3 Automobile Sales, Quarterly from 1965: I to 1979:IV

downward during those historical periods when a strike occurred (see Figure 7-3).

LINEAR TRANSFORMATIONS

Implicit in all the estimated regression models has been the assumption of linearity, but this specification is not as restrictive as it might first appear. Indeed, the least-squares methodology can be applied to all systems that are *intrinsically linear*. A model is intrinsically linear if it can be expressed, by transformation of the variables, in a linear-form. This section presents, briefly, the intrinsically linear models that are frequently encountered by the practicing forecaster.

LOGARITHMIC TRANSFORMATIONS

A logarithmic transformation is useful when the underlying model is multiplicative:

$$Y = \beta_0 \beta_1{}^X \epsilon \qquad (7\text{-}9)$$

where β_0 and β_1 are the parameters to be estimated, X and Y are the two variables being studied, and ϵ is the error term. As it is formulated, this model is neither linear in the parameters (β_0 and β_1 are multiplied together), nor linear in X, since X appears as an exponent. However, equation (7-9) is said to be intrinsically linear because it can be expressed in linear form via a logarithmic transformation.

$$\log Y = \log \beta_0 + X \log \beta_1 + \log \epsilon \qquad (7\text{-}10)$$

The transformed error terms must satisfy all the conditions noted in conjunction with the error term in the standard model; for instance, error terms must be randomly distributed and independent of each other. Multiplicative models have been used in sales forecasting models. Examination of the scatter diagram for sales revenue at Southern Airlines, Figure 4-4, led to the conclusion that a a linear model was inappropriate. As illustrated in Chapter 4, a logarith ic transformation was used to link sales (Y) to time (X):

$$\log Y = 3.9147425 + 0.07675905X \qquad (4\text{-}29)$$

Additional models involving logarithmic transformations are:

$$Y = \beta_0 + \beta_1 \log X + \epsilon \qquad (7\text{-}11)$$

$$\log Y = \beta_0 + \beta_1 \log X + \log \epsilon \qquad (7\text{-}12)$$

Economists have used equation (7-12) when examining the relationship between the price of a commodity (X) and the quantity demanded (Y). In equation (7-12), the parameter β_1 can be interpreted as the price elasticity of demand. Additionally, this formulation can be utilized to determine the tax elasticity of various government revenue sources. This process will be examined in more detail in the example presented at the conclusion of this section.

RECIPROCAL TRANSFORMATIONS

A reciprocal transformation may be in order when a scatter diagram indicates the desirability of a curvilinear model similar to that shown in Figure 7-4. In this situation, the graph leads to a model of the form:

$$Y = \beta_0 + \frac{\beta_1}{X} + \epsilon \qquad (7\text{-}13)$$

By letting:

$$X' = 1/X \qquad (7\text{-}14)$$

equation (7-13) becomes:

$$Y = \beta_0 + \beta_1 X' + \epsilon \qquad (7\text{-}15)$$

which conforms to the simple linear model. Here, the forecaster is simply using the reciprocal of the independent variable in fitting the equation. The same type of transformation can be made on the dependent variable, Y. Thus, the model:

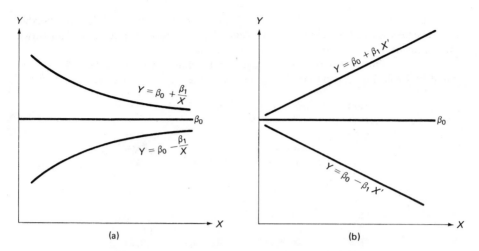

Figure 7-4 Reciprocal Variable Transformations

$$Y' = \beta_0 + \beta_1 X + \epsilon \tag{7-16}$$

is still linear when Y' is equal to $1/Y$.

COMMENTS ON TRANSFORMATION ISSUES

Whenever any of these transformations are employed, the estimators, $\hat{\beta}_0$ and $\hat{\beta}_1$, obtained by least squares are BLUE with respect to the transformed variable observations, not the original ones. Further, if a transformation is made, the forecaster must check the validity of the model's assumptions by applying the tests noted in Chapter 6 to the transformed variables and error terms.

Example 7-1: Sales Tax Revenue Elasticity

As a research analyst for the revenue department in Tennessee you receive a request to prepare a recommendation as to the most productive way to increase tax revenues to balance the state's budget. Conceptually, the revenue from any tax is the product of the tax rate and the tax base:

$$T_t = R_t B_t \tag{7-17}$$

where:

T_t = tax revenues in time t
R_t = tax rate in time t
B_t = tax base in time t

Thus, tax revenues can be increased by raising the tax rate or by expanding the taxable base. The task is to advise the tax commission about the revenue potential of these two options, or more specifically, the tax elasticity of each variable.

As a preliminary step, data on sales tax revenue have been collected and presented in Table 7-2. Preliminary examination of the data suggests the desirability of

Table 7-2   Sales tax revenues, tax rates, and retail sales, 1968–1979 (millions of dollars)

Year	Sales Tax Revenues (1)	Sales Tax Rate (2)	Retail Sales (3)
1968	$13,304	3.0	$1,393,157
1969	18,880	3.0	1,527,566
1970	20,797	3.0	1,595,879
1971	24,099	3.3	1,923,092
1972	27,040	3.5	2,162,719
1973	30,339	3.5	2,409,905
1974	33,343	3.5	2,594,179
1975	34,435	3.5	2,735,269
1976	36,559	4.3	2,944,422
1977	39,628	4.5	3,206,269
1978	44,361	4.5	3,576,321
1979	48,753	4.5	3,908,409

Note: Some retail sales are tax exempt.

using the general model noted in equation (7-12). First, the data in column 1 of Table 7-2 seem to follow an exponential pattern. Second, the state is interested in determining the responsiveness of tax revenues (ST) to changes in either the tax rate (STR) or the tax base (RS). Thus, the model to be estimated by least squares is:

$$\log \widehat{ST}_t = \log \hat{\beta}_0 + \hat{\beta}_1 \log STR_t + \hat{\beta}_2 \log RS_t + \log e_t \qquad (7\text{-}18)$$

where:

$$ST_t = \text{sales tax revenues in millions of dollars}$$
$$STR_t = \text{sales tax rate}$$
$$RS_t = \text{retail sales (tax base) in millions of dollars}$$

The results of applying this model to the data in Table 7-2 are:

$$\log \widehat{ST}_t = -3.841 - 0.562 \log STR_t + 1.352 \log RS_t$$
$$t_e \qquad\qquad\qquad (1.39) \qquad\qquad (7.00) \qquad\qquad (7\text{-}19)$$

$\bar{R}^2 = 0.96$	SEE = 0.032
$F_{2,9} = 143$	DW = 1.35

A brief response to the tax commission could be made as follows: (1) A 1 percent increase in the tax rate will lead to a 0.562 percent decrease in tax revenues; and (2) a 1 percent increase in the taxable base, retail sales, will increase revenues by 1.352 percent. The negative coefficient for the sales tax rate is probably due to the fact that several major cities in Tennessee are near the state border. Because of the small sample size, the model is sensitive to rounding; it is preferable, therefore, to enter the data as listed in Table 7-2 and have the computer carry out the logarithmic transformation (to the base 10 in Example 7-1). These results, while tentative, elicit some doubts about the ability of state government to rely on sales tax increases as means of raising tax revenue.

FINDING THE BEST SET
OF INDEPENDENT VARIABLES

INTRODUCTION

In the process of constructing forecasting models via least squares, the forecaster is faced with two conflicting options:

1. Include as many X's as possible so as to make the equation useful for predictive purposes.
2. Include as few X's as possible so as to minimize the costs involved in obtaining information and in monitoring the statistical model.

Theory can and should aid the analyst in selecting the independent variables (X's) to be employed. Typically, the number of X's in purely theoretical models is rather large. Variables may be deleted prior to statistical analysis if they are not fundamental to the problem being studied, if they are subject to unacceptable measurement errors, if they are intercorrelated with other variables, or if they are not directly measurable. Unfortunately, even after this initial screening, the number of variables is likely to be large. The forecaster needs to pare his model, because a regression model with a large number of independent variables is expensive to maintain. Further, the presence of a large number of independent variables presents the forecaster with the complicated problem of obtaining future values for all these variables when the equation is to be employed for prediction. Finally, the presence of numerous interrelated variables adds little to the predictive capabilities of a model and tends to detract from its simulative power.

The problem, then, is to shorten the list of independent variables so as to obtain a set of them that is small enough to have manageable maintenance costs, yet large enough to accurately represent the real-world situation and to predict well. The purpose of this section is to develop the more common approaches employed by practitioners to find the *best set* of independent variables.

ALL POSSIBLE REGRESSIONS

The all-possible-regressions procedure is just what its name implies. It literally entails an examination of all possible regression equations yielded by the list of potential independent variables and selection of the best equation(s).

A major disadvantage of this procedure is the amount of computational time required. Since each X_i can either be or not be in the equation, and since this is true for every X_i, $i = 1, 2, \ldots, k$, there are altogether 2^k possible equations. For example, if there are ten ($k = 10$) independent variables, then there are 1,024 possible (2^{10}) regression equations. Indeed, this approach is so costly that it has given way to other, more practical procedures.

STEPWISE REGRESSION

The stepwise regression technique does not require an examination of all possible regressions; rather, this search method computes a sequence of least-squares equations, and at each step of the sequence, independent variables are added or deleted according to a predetermined criterion.

First, the stepwise routine computes k simple regressions based on the k potential independent variables and calculates the F statistic in order to test whether or not the slope is significantly different from zero. Let this calculated F be symbolized by F_c^i, where i refers to the specific independent variable being used. Although there are criteria other than the F statistic upon which to judge regression equations, the majority of computer software packages rely on this statistic.

Recall that the F statistic is based on the following ratio:

$$F_c^i = \frac{\text{MSR}(X_i)}{\text{MSE}(X_i)} \tag{7-20}$$

$\text{MSR}(X_i)$ measures the reduction in total variation of Y associated with the inclusion of X_i in the regression, and $\text{MSE}(X_i)$ represents the mean square error. The independent variable with the largest F_c^i value is the first variable added to the model *if* this value exceeds a predetermined minimum referred to as F_L. F_L is simply a critical or limiting F value based on a given level of significance (α). Before the stepwise regression process is begun, the forecaster selects an α value—say, $\alpha = .01$—and uses the F table (Appendix C) to determine F_L. If F_c^i is greater than F_L when $\alpha = .01$, then the analyst can be 99 percent confident that he has found a statistically significant relationship. If no F_c^i exceeds F_L, the regression process terminates and the forecaster must conclude that no regression equation provides better estimates than the mean value of the dependent variable.

For illustrative purposes, assume that X_5 is the independent variable entered at step 1. The stepwise regression routine now computes all two-variable regressions in which X_5 is combined with one of the remaining variables. Each F_c^i is obtained and compared with F_L, and the equation that explains the largest percentage of the variation in Y becomes the next building block, provided that $F_c^i > F_L$. If none of the combinations meets this condition, the program terminates and Y is assumed to be only a function of X_5.

Suppose X_2 is added at the second stage, so that the model becomes:

$$\hat{Y}_t = \hat{\beta}_0 + \hat{\beta}_5 X_5 + \hat{\beta}_2 X_2 + e_t \qquad (7\text{-}21)$$

Now the stepwise routine investigates whether any of the variables incorporated in the model prior to the inclusion of X_2 should be deleted. In our example, only one other independent variable was in the model, X_5, so that only one conditional F statistic, $F_c(X_5/X_2)$ is obtained. At later stages there would be a number of these F_c statistics computed, one for each variable other than the last one added. The variable for which the F_c value is the smallest is a candidate for deletion if the value falls below F_L; otherwise, all variables are retained.

Suppose that X_5 is retained and the model remains as noted in equation (7-21). The routine now examines which independent variable is the next candidate for inclusion with X_5 and X_2, specifies whether any of the variables already in the equation should be deleted, and continues on until no more independent variables can be added or deleted; at this point, the search process terminates. It must be noted that a true stepwise regression procedure allows an independent variable, brought into the model at an earlier stage, to be subsequently deleted if it is no longer statistically significant in conjunction with variables added at later stages.

FORWARD STEPWISE SELECTION

This process is a simplified version of the stepwise procedure discussed in the preceding paragraphs, the principal difference being that once a variable enters into the regression equation, it is never deleted because of the introduction of additional variables. Thus, the main drawback of this technique is that it makes no attempt to evaluate the effect that insertion of a new variable has on the variables selected at earlier stages.

BACKWARD STEPWISE ELIMINATION

Whereas the forward selection procedure begins with the smallest regression model, the backward elimination technique begins with a regression model based on all variables and subsequently reduces the number until a decision is reached on the *best* equation. This process is accomplished by comparing F_L and F_c according to the following rules:

1. If $F_c < F_L$, remove the variable that gave rise to F_c and recompute the regression equation with the remaining variables.
2. If $F_c > F_L$, adopt the regression as computed.

COMMENTS ON SEARCH PROCEDURES

None of the search procedures can be proved to inevitably yield the best set of independent variables. Indeed, there may be no unique best set. The entire variable-selection process is pragmatic and relies on judgment. The principal advantage of automatic search procedures is that the time and cost elements of the search are minimized, thereby allowing the forecaster to spend his time on judgmental questions. One of the mistakes commonly made by practioners is to ignore economic theory and blindly accept the results of the search routine.

Finally, it is essential to comprehend fully the specific features and/or options of the computer package being used. For example, various packages have the following options:

1. Regression lines can be forced through the origin.
2. Variables can be inserted into the models and tested in pairs or groupings as desired.
3. The partial correlation coefficient can be used to decide whether variables should be inserted or deleted.
4. F limits for adding or deleting variables can be varied.
5. Certain variables can be forced into the regression if the forecaster has an *a priori* belief that they should be included.

In addition, the forecaster may want to experiment with lower (or higher) F_L levels, or may wish to compare the final equation obtained via one of the search procedures with an equation based on *a priori* expectations. The point of all of these comments is simple: *Do not use search procedures as a substitute for intelligent reasoning.*

Example 7-2: Unit Sales of Automobiles, Stepwise Analysis

Equation (7-8) was developed earlier to explain car sales:

$$\widehat{\text{UNITSAL}}_t^* = 1.25619221 + 0.00895512\text{YPLTP}_t^* + 0.02788205\text{JATTC}_t^* -$$
$$0.21350163U_t^* - 0.00016181\text{DMYSTR}_t^* \qquad (7\text{-}8)$$

In this equation, unit sales of automobiles (UNITSAL_t) is dependent upon personal income less transfer payments (YPLTP_t), the unemployment rate (U_t), the index of consumer sentiment (JATTC_t), and a dummy variable for automobile strikes (DMYSTR_t). Additionally, the equation was corrected for autocorrelation; that is, it contains transformed variables.

There are a number of variables that theoretically influence automobile sales: personal income less transfer payments (YPLTP_t); index of consumer sentiment (JATTC_t); unemployment rate (U_t); index of cost of car ownership (C_t); average miles per gallon of current model-year cars (AMPG_t); dummy variable for automobile strikes (DMYSTR_t); the depreciation rate of the stock of cars (DSTK_t); average price of a new car (P_t); the stock of automobiles (STK_t); and the interest rate on automobile loans (I_t).[1] If this list comprised all relevant variables, then the theoretical model would be:

$$\widehat{\text{UNITSAL}}_t = \hat{\beta}_1 + \hat{\beta}_2\text{YPLTP}_t + \hat{\beta}_3\text{JATTC}_t + \hat{\beta}_4U_t + \hat{\beta}_5C_t +$$
$$\hat{\beta}_6\text{AMPG}_t + \hat{\beta}_7\text{DMYSTR}_t + \hat{\beta}_8\text{DSTK}_t + \hat{\beta}_9P_t + \hat{\beta}_{10}\text{STK}_t + \hat{\beta}_{11}I_t + e_t \quad (7\text{-}22)$$

---

[1] Numerical values for many of these variables were obtained from Data Resources' national econometric model.

In all previous equations, $\hat{\beta}_0$ referred to the constant term, but in equation (7-22), $\hat{\beta}_1$ is the constant term. The reason for this change is that the BMDP computer software package utilized in the next example employs this notation.[2]

Figure 7-5 shows an abbreviated copy of the computer printout for the stepwise regression routine of UCLA's BMDP software package when applied to the unit car-sales example in equation (7-22). At the top of Figure 7-5, the control information is presented. In this program, the F statistic is used to decide whether to insert or delete specific variables (that is, the step algorithm is based on F). The maximum number of steps is 22 in order to allow each variable noted in equation (7-22) to be entered and deleted from the model. The dependent variable is $X1$, which refers to unit sales of automobiles. (For future edification, refer to the variable numbers as shown in equation (7-22) or to the column numbers in Appendix G, which contains the entire listing of the automobile data.) In this example, the F_L limit for adding or deleting variables was set at 2.00. This corresponds to a significance level of approximately 0.10 for a single variable. Now the stepwise process can be traced:

1. As a preliminary step, the stepwise routine computes the partial correlation coefficients and F_c values to enter for each variable, on the assumption that none of the variables are in the equation. This step serves two purposes. First, it is possible that none of the simple regression coefficients would be significantly different from zero. If this were true, the best estimate of UNITSAL would be the mean value of 9.828 (the $X1$-intercept). Second, this step presents the ranking of each of the variables in terms of the variation in Y that is explained. The largest F-to-enter, 36.907, is associated with $X2$(YPLTP).

2. Since the largest F-to-enter exceeds 2.00, X_2 becomes the first variable in the regression equation.

3. The results of $X2$'s inclusion are shown in step number 1 in Figure 7-5. The remaining statistics have the same interpretation as in previous examples.

4. Next, all regression equations containing $X2$ and another variable are computed and the F_c statistics calculated. These values are listed under the "F-to-enter" heading. $X11$ has the highest F_c, and it exceeds F_L, so $X11$ enters the model.

5. The results of including $X11$ with $X2$ are summarized at the beginning of step 2. Next, the routine tests whether $X2$ should be dropped. This test is shown in the "F-to-remove" column. Since F_c ($X2/X11$) exceeds F_L, $X2$ is not dropped from the equation.

6. Next, all regression equations containing $X2$, $X11$, and one more variable are tabulated and the F values computed and shown in step 2. Since $X5$'s F-to-enter value is the largest and exceeds F_L, $X5$ enters the equation.

7. The first portion of step 3 summarizes the results of the inclusion of $X5$. As before, the routine tests whether any of the previously entered variables ($X2$ and $X11$) have F-to-remove values less than 2. Neither of them does; hence, the equation has $X2$, $X11$, and $X5$ as independent variables. Additionally, the introduction of one more variable is considered.

8. Step 4 summarizes the results of including $X3$, the variable with the largest F-to-enter value in step 3. The test for removal is now conducted. $F_c(X11/X3)$ falls below the critical value of 2, so $X11$ is deleted, as shown at the beginning of step 5. Further, the routine now computes the F-to-enter values. Since $X7$ has the largest F_c value and exceeds F_L, $X7$ becomes the next candidate for inclusion.

[2]W.J. Dixon and M.B. Brown, eds., *BMDP-77* (Berkeley: University of California Press, 1977), pp. 399–417.

```
REGRESSION TITLE. . . . . . . . . . . . . .STEPWISE FOR AUTOS
STEPPING ALGORITHM. . . . . . . . . . . . .F
MAXIMUM NUMBER OF STEPS . . . . . . . .  22
DEPENDENT VARIABLE. . . . . . . . . .   1 X1 (Unit Sales of Automobiles)
MINIMUM ACCEPTABLE F TO ENTER . . . .  2.000,  1.999
MAXIMUM ACCEPTABLE F TO REMOVE. . . .  1.999,  1.999
MINIMUM ACCEPTABLE TOLERANCE. . . . .   .01000


STEP NO.   0

MULTIPLE R             .0000
MULTIPLE R-SQUARE      .0000
STD. ERROR OF EST.    1.1976

ANALYSIS OF VARIANCE
                    SUM OF SQUARES      DF    MEAN SQUARE    F RATIO
REGRESSION            .00000000         0    .0000000         .000
RESIDUAL            84.620392          59   1.434243

                 VARIABLES IN EQUATION
                              STD. ERROR    STD REG
VARIABLE        COEFFICIENT   OF COEFF      COEFF    F TO REMOVE

(Y-INTERCEPT       9.828 )
```

		VARIABLE	PARTIAL CORR.	F TO ENTER
Personal Income Less Transfer Payments	X2	2	.62360	36.907
Index of Consumer Sentiment	X3	3	.00537	.002
Unemployment Rate	X4	4	.17593	1.853
Index of Cost of Car Ownership	X5	5	.42179	12.552
Average Miles Per Gallon	X6	6	.36078	8.679
Dummy Variable for Strikes	X7	7	-.41147	11.821
Depreciation Rate	X8	8	.24432	3.682
Index of Average Price of New Car	X9	9	.51242	20.652
Stock of Cars	X10	10	.54128	24.035
Finance Rate on Automobile Loans	X11	11	.24843	3.815

VARIABLES NOT IN EQUATION

Figure 7-5 BMDP's Stepwise Regression Program Applied to Automobile Sales

STEP NO. 1
VARIABLE ENTERED   2 X2

MULTIPLE R   .6236
MULTIPLE R-SQUARE   .3889
STD. ERROR OF EST.   .9443

ANALYSIS OF VARIANCE

	SUM OF SQUARES	DF	MEAN SQUARE	F RATIO
REGRESSION	32.906876	1	32.906888	36.907
RESIDUAL	51.713515	58	.8916123	

VARIABLES IN EQUATION

VARIABLE	COEFFICIENT	STD. ERROR OF COEFF	STD REG COEFF	F TO REMOVE
(Y-INTERCEPT	4.178)			
X2 2	.007	.001	.624	36.907

VARIABLES NOT IN EQUATION

VARIABLE		PARTIAL CORR.	F TO ENTER
X3	3	.50626	19.644
X4	4	-.30668	5.917
X5	5	-.51791	20.893
X6	6	.00089	.000
X7	7	-.41487	11.851
X8	8	.54042	23.515
X9	9	-.26623	4.348
X10	10	-.39334	10.433
X11	11	-.55367	25.198

Figure 7-5 Continued

```
STEP NO. 2
VARIABLE ENTERED    11  X11

MULTIPLE R              .7591
MULTIPLE R-SQUARE       .5762
STD. ERROR OF EST.      .7932

ANALYSIS OF VARIANCE

                    SUM OF SQUARES    DF    MEAN SQUARE    F RATIO
REGRESSION          48.759781         2     24.37988       38.752
RESIDUAL            35.860611        57      .6291335

                    VARIABLES IN EQUATION
                                  STD. ERROR    STD REG
VARIABLE    COEFFICIENT OF COEFF   OF COEFF      COEFF     F TO REMOVE

(Y-INTERCEPT   6.908 )
X2     2      .013        .002      1.216        69.202
X11   11     -.784        .156      -.734        25.198


                              VARIABLES NOT IN EQUATION

            VARIABLE         PARTIAL CORR.        F TO ENTER

            X3     3            .25056             3.751
            X4     4           -.18652             2.018
            X5     5           -.49431            18.108
            X6     6           -.23847             3.377
            X7     7           -.33291             6.980
            X8     8            .36427             8.567
            X9     9           -.39501            10.353
            X10   10           -.32007             6.392
```

Figure 7-5 Continued

STEP NO. 3
VARIABLE ENTERED   5 X5

MULTIPLE R   .8245
MULTIPLE R-SQUARE   .6798
STD. ERROR OF EST.   .6956

ANALYSIS OF VARIANCE

	SUM OF SQUARES	DF	MEAN SQUARE	F RATIO
REGRESSION	57.522125	3	19.17404	39.624
RESIDUAL	27.098267	56	.4838976	

VARIABLES IN EQUATION

VARIABLE	COEFFICIENT	STD. ERROR OF COEFF	STD REG COEFF	F TO REMOVE
(Y-INTERCEPT	2.867)			
X2 2	.021	.002	1.919	84.254
X5 5	-3.126	.735	-.862	18.108
X11 11	-.660	.140	-.618	22.204

VARIABLES NOT IN EQUATION

VARIABLE	PARTIAL CORR.	F TO ENTER
X3 3	.52496	20.923
X4 4	-.04291	.101
X6 6	.31651	6.123
X7 7	-.40499	10.791
X8 8	.42882	12.393
X9 9	.25749	3.906
X10 10	-.14726	1.219

Figure 7-5 Continued

STEP NO. 4
VARIABLE ENTERED   3 X3

MULTIPLE R   .8764
MULTIPLE R-SQUARE   .7680
STD. ERROR OF EST.   .5974

ANALYSIS OF VARIANCE

	SUM OF SQUARES	DF	MEAN SQUARE	F RATIO
REGRESSION	64.989822	4	16.24745	45.521
RESIDUAL	19.630569	55	.3569194	

VARIABLES IN EQUATION

VARIABLE		COEFFICIENT	STD. ERROR OF COEFF	STD REG COEFF	F TO REMOVE
(Y-INTERCEPT		-7.025)			
X2	2	.023	.002	2.076	128.981
X3	3	.055	.012	.477	20.923
X5	5	-4.225	.675	-1.165	39.165
X11	11	-.163	.162	-.153	1.018

VARIABLES NOT IN EQUATION

VARIABLE		PARTIAL CORR.	F TO ENTER
X4	4	.09224	.463
X6	6	.07170	.279
X7	7	-.51882	19.889
X8	8	.15007	1.244
X9	9	.07888	.338
X10	10	.07271	.287

Figure 7-5 Continued

STEP NO. 5
VARIABLE REMOVED   11 X11

MULTIPLE R   .8739
MULTIPLE R-SQUARE   .7637
STD. ERROR OF EST. .5975

ANALYSIS OF VARIANCE

	SUM OF SQUARES	DF	MEAN SQUARE	F RATIO
REGRESSION	64.626282	3	21.54208	60.336
RESIDUAL	19.994064	56	.3570368	

VARIABLES IN EQUATION

VARIABLE		COEFFICIENT	STD. ERROR OF COEFF	STD REG COEFF	F TO REMOVE
(Y-INTERCEPT		-8.914)			
X2	2	.023	.002	2.056	127.966
X3	3	.063	.009	.547	49.991
X5	5	-4.486	.624	-1.237	51.718

VARIABLES NOT IN EQUATION

VARIABLE		PARTIAL CORR.	F TO ENTER
X4	4	.08793	.429
X6	6	.11363	.719
X7	7	-.53145	21.649
X8	8	.14944	1.256
X9	9	.12907	.932
X10	10	.09024	.452
X11	11	-.13483	1.018

Figure 7-5 Continued

STEP NO. 6
VARIABLE ENTERED   7 X7

MULTIPLE R   .9113
MULTIPLE R-SQUARE   .8305
STD. ERROR OF EST.   .5107

ANALYSIS OF VARIANCE

	SUM OF SQUARES	DF	MEAN SQUARE	F RATIO
REGRESSION	70.273499	4	17.56837	67.350
RESIDUAL	14.346897	55	.2608526	

VARIABLES IN EQUATION

VARIABLE	COEFFICIENT	STD. ERROR OF COEFF	STD REG COEFF	F TO REMOVE
(Y-INTERCEPT	-7.781)			
X2 2	.022	.002	1.972	158.910
X3 3	.058	.008	.506	57.583
X5 5	-4.390	.534	-1.210	67.687
X7 7	-.000	.000	-.263	21.649

VARIABLES NOT IN EQUATION

VARIABLE	PARTIAL CORR.	F TO ENTER
X4 4	.11421	.714
X6 6	.09814	.525
X8 8	.13039	.934
X9 9	.02557	.035
X10 10	.02026	.022
X11 11	-.00544	.002

Figure 7-5 Continued

STEPWISE REGRESSION COEFFICIENTS

VARIABLES STEP	0 Y--INTCPT	2 X2	3 X3	4 X4	5 X5	6 X6	7 X7	8 X8	9 X9	10
558 0	9.8277*	.0068	.0006	.1423	1.5302	.3483	-.0002	116.1522	.4961	
449 1	4.1784*	.0068*	.0535	-.2406	-3.8473	.0008	-.0002	208.1218	-.5798	
012 2	6.9077*	.0133*	.0280	-.1271	-3.1263	-.1951	-.0001	135.1025	-.7207	
444 3	2.8675*	.0210*	.0547	-.0267	-3.1263*	.3833	-.0001	138.2748	1.2593	
203 4	-7.0246*	.0227*	.0547*	.0502	-4.2254*	.0855	-.0001	52.8917	.3537	
251 5	-8.9139*	.0225*	.0627*	.0483	-4.4862*	.1281	-.0001	53.1538	.5258	
048 6	-7.7811*	.0216*	.0581*	.0531	-4.3902*	.0939	-.0001*	39.3943	.0901	

NOTE--
1) REGRESSION COEFFICIENTS FOR VARIABLES IN THE EQUATION ARE INDICATED BY AN ASTERISK
2) THE REMAINING COEFFICIENTS ARE THOSE WHICH WOULD BE OBTAINED IF THAT VARIABLE WERE TO ENTER IN THE NEXT STEP

Figure 7-5 Continued

```
                    STEPWISE REGRESSION COEFFICIENTS

  VARIABLES   11 X11
STEP
   0           .2654
   1          -.7840
   2          -.7840*
   3          -.6599*
   4          -.1635*
   5          -.1635
   6          -.0058


NOTE-
   1)  REGRESSION COEFFICIENTS FOR VARIABLES IN THE EQUATION ARE INDICATED BY AN ASTERISK
   2)  THE REMAINING COEFFICIENTS ARE THOSE WHICH WOULD BE OBTAINED IF THAT VARIABLE WERE TO ENTER IN THE NEXT STEP
SUMMARY TABLE
 5
```

STEP NO.	VARIABLE ENTERED	VARIABLE REMOVED	MULTIPLE R	MULTIPLE RSQ	INCREASE IN RSQ	F-TO-ENTER	F-TO-REMOVE	NUMBER OF INDEPENDENT VARIABLES INCLUDED
1	2 X2		.6236	.3889	.3889	36.9072		1
2	11 X11		.7591	.5762	.1873	25.1980		2
3	5 X5		.8245	.6798	.1035	18.1078		3
4	3 X3		.8764	.7680	.0882	20.9226		4
5		11 X11	.8739	.7637	-.0043		1.0184	3
6	7 X7		.9113	.8305	.0667	21.6489		4

Figure 7-5 Continued

9. The results of including $X7$ are shown in step 6. The test for removing and introducing variables is now conducted. No variable has a F-to-remove of less than 2 or an F-to-enter of greater than 2; thus, the routine terminates.

The least-squares regression for unit sales can now be stated as:

$$\widehat{\text{UNITSAL}}_t = -7.7811 + 0.0216\text{YPLTP}_t + 0.0581\text{JATTC}_t$$
$$S_{\beta_t} \qquad\qquad\quad (0.001713) \qquad (0.0076507)$$
$$t_e \qquad\qquad\qquad 12.61 \qquad\qquad 7.59$$

$$-4.3902\text{C}_t - 0.0001\text{DMYSTR}_t$$
$$(0.5336) \qquad (0.0000281)$$
$$8.23 \qquad\qquad 4.65 \qquad\qquad (7\text{-}23)$$

$F_{4,55} = 67.35$	DW = 1.74
SEE = 0.51074	APE = 5.2%
$R^2 = 0.831$	False Signals = 18%
$\bar{R}^2 = 0.82$	Missed Signals = 23%
	1965 : I–1979 : IV

Both the equation and the coefficients are significant at the .01 level. The coefficients are theoretically sound, since the signs match the *a priori* expectations. As a forecasting device, the equation tracks the historical data patterns reasonably well. The average percentage error on a quarterly basis is only 5.2 percent. Somewhat disturbing is the fact that the equation missed 23 percent of the quarterly turning points; but this factor is mitigated by the fact that only one turning point was missed over the last three years (twelve quarters). Also, on an annual basis, the equation missed only one turning point, and over the last seven years, the forecast errors were -0.7%, 3.4%, 1.5%, 0%, -1.4%, 0.67%, and -0.67%.

Another interesting facet of equation (7-23) is the Durbin-Watson statistic of 1.74. This value falls within the acceptable range, indicating no autocorrelation. In all previous automobile-sales equations, corrections for autocorrelation were necessary. The fact that no correction is needed for equation (7-23) serves to highlight a point made previously regarding the presence of autocorrelated error terms. When this situation exists, it may imply that the model has not been correctly specified. That is, related error terms are apt to imply that the analyst has ignored some variable(s) that are significant in explaining the data pattern inherent in the dependent variable. Therefore, whenever the analyst detects autocorrelation, the first check should relate to respecification of the model.

LAGGED INDEPENDENT VARIABLES

SIMPLE LAGGED RELATIONSHIPS

When an analyst sets out to construct a forecasting model, the choice of independent variables is influenced by theoretical considerations, statistical constraints, and data availability. Of particular interest is the last constraint, data availability. For example, a sales forecasting equation might be formulated as:

$$\hat{S}_t = \hat{\beta}_0 + \hat{\beta}_1 P_t + \hat{\beta}_2 Y_t + \hat{\beta}_3 \text{ADV}_t + e_t \qquad (7\text{-}24)$$

where S_t is current dollar sales, P_t is price, Y_t is income, and ADV_t is advertising expenditures. Even if this equation is statistically significant and judged to be theoretically sound, estimates of future sales cannot be determined unless the variables P_t, Y_t, and ADV_t are determinable for the period in question. One common method of overcoming this difficulty is to use lagged values for the independent variables. Thus, equation (7-24) might be restated as:

$$\hat{S}_t = \hat{\beta}_0 + \hat{\beta}_1 P_{t-1} + \hat{\beta}_2 Y_{t-1} + \hat{\beta}_3 \text{ADV}_{t-1} + e_t \qquad (7\text{-}25)$$

With this formulation, estimates of sales in period t can be made based on prior-period values $(P_{t-1}, Y_{t-1}, \text{ and } \text{ADV}_{t-1})$. Although the inclusion of lagged variables such as P_{t-1} present no special problems in terms of satisfying the least-squares criteria, the issue of the theoretical appropriateness of lagged variables still remains.

Reliance on lagged values, besides being helpful in forecasting, has some justification in theory. In time-series models of economic behavior, a substantial period of time may elapse between the moment when a decision is made and the period in which the final effect is measurable. People rarely change their behavior patterns immediately. Frequently, the response to a price change will be delayed as the consumers assess the permanence of the change. In the case of a price decline, potential buyers may delay purchases in the belief that prices will decline even further. A similar time-lag pattern may exist between a change in income and a measurable change in consumer spending. Further, there are situations where contractual or informal commitments may extend beyond one time period. Indeed, this was the primary justification for the inclusion of a lagged installment-loan variable in the earlier model for loan demand in Memphis (see equation (6-22)).

Finally, in certain cases, the existing stock of new or used commodities may influence both buyers' and sellers' responses. Consecutive years of record refrigerator sales may literally saturate the market and act as a drag on future sales. Alternatively, as sales of automobiles begin to increase toward the end of a recession, businesses may decide to hold down production in order to deplete existing inventories. Past analysis by the forecaster may have confirmed the existence of both consumer-response and producer-response lags, but the job of forecasting remains complicated because of the inherent variability of such lags. Other factors in the business environment are constantly changing response lags. For example, given a current surplus of raw materials, a forecaster might assume that raw material output would lag behind sales. This tendency for output to lag, however, might be offset by exogenous factors such as a fear that the future supply of the raw material would be interrupted.

Example 7-3: Estimation of Sales via Lagged Relationships

As an example of the technique of employing lagged variables, consider the following illustration, drawn from a model that forecasts the sales for a chain of men's stores located in Memphis, Tennessee. The first step, as always, is to formulate a theoretical model that expresses sales as a function of a number of factors. In conversations with the sales manager and the vice-president of finance, the most influential factors affecting their sales were said to be product prices, consumer income levels, credit availability, the company's advertising expenditures, and the advertising expenditures of competing firms. After the model has been conceptually formulated, the next step is to collect data for the five independent variables and the dependent variable (sales). The theoretical model becomes:

$$\hat{S}_t = \hat{\beta}_0 + \hat{\beta}_1 P_t + \hat{\beta}_2 Y_t + \hat{\beta}_3 CC_t + \hat{\beta}_4 ADV_t + \hat{\beta}_5 CADV_t + e_t \qquad (7\text{-}26)$$

where:

S_t = quarterly sales of men's clothing in millions of dollars
P_t = average price level of the company's product
Y_t = quarterly income of the Memphis SMSA population in millions of dollars
CC_t = new credit lines extended in the current quarter in thousands of dollars
ADV_t = quarterly advertising expenditures in thousands of dollars
$CADV_t$ = quarterly advertising expenditures of competitors in thousands of dollars

All data are listed in Appendix H.

The *a priori* expectations are for (1) negative relationships between price and sales and between sales and the advertising expenditures of competitors; and (2) positive relationships between sales and the remaining three independent variables, Y_t, CC_t, and ADV_t. The inclusion of the first four independent variables is easily justified. The last variable, $CADV_t$, was incorporated as a measure of regional competition generated by the special sales promotions held by competitors during various quarters throughout the year.

Because it would be difficult to derive future estimates for the explanatory variables, the first model tested was:

$$\hat{S}_t = \hat{\beta}_0 + \hat{\beta}_1 P_{t-1} + \hat{\beta}_2 Y_{t-2} + \hat{\beta}_3 CC_{t-1} + \hat{\beta}_4 ADV_{t-1} + \hat{\beta}_5 CADV_{t-1} + e_t \quad (7\text{-}27)$$

The $t-1$ subscript means that the variable has been lagged one quarter, and $t-2$ signifies a two-quarter lag. The longer lag for income incorporates the theoretical insight known as the permanent-income hypothesis. That is, changes in consumption expenditures are not likely to occur unless income changes are perceived as permanent; thus, consumers need not react immediately to a change in income.

The least-squares estimators for equation (7-27) are:

$$\hat{S}_t = 3.864 - 0.017676P_{t-1} + 0.005821\,Y_{t-2} + 0.001521CC_{t-1} +$$
$$\phantom{\hat{S}_t = 3.864 -}(0.00693)(0.000739)(0.000706)$$

$t_e 2.55 7.88 2.15$

$$0.007432ADV_{t-1} - 0.000598CADV_{t-1}$$
$$(0.001729)(0.000392)$$
$$4.30 1.53 (7\text{-}28)$$

Range of data: 1970:III to 1979:IV (Appendix H)	
$R = 0.89$	SEE $= 0.27839$
$R = 0.80$	$F_{5,32} = 25$
$\bar{R}^2 = 0.76$	DW $= 2.24$
	$U = 0.023$

The equation and its individual coefficients are statistically significant at the .05 level or better. The Durbin-Watson statistic of 2.24 falls within the acceptable range, and an examination of the forecast residuals indicates that the other least-squares conditions are satisfied. Theoretically, the signs of all the variables match the *a priori* expectations. In terms of forecasting performance, equation (7-28) is equally outstanding. The average percentage error is a relatively small (5 percent), as is the U statistic. Additionally, the turning-point performance is excellent in that only one actual turning point was missed and only two extra turning points were predicted. Finally, estimation errors exceeding 5 percent were recorded in only six quarters, and over the last two years, only one error in excess of 5 percent was observed.

DISTRIBUTED LAGS

A logical extension of simple-lag models is the development of distributed-lag models, which attempt to explain delays when the effects of the independent variables are spread out over a large number of periods. One way of estimating these lags is to include the value of the independent variable in each relevant period. For example, a new advertising campaign should generate a large sales increase the first month, with smaller and smaller increments in successive months. It is possible to express this theoretical model as:

$$\hat{S}_t = \hat{\beta}_0 + \hat{\beta}_1 P_t + \hat{\beta}_2 Y_t + \hat{\beta}_3 ADV_t + \hat{\beta}_4 ADV_{t-1} + \hat{\beta}_5 ADV_{t-2} +$$
$$\hat{\beta}_6 ADV_{t-3} + \hat{\beta}_7 ADV_{t-4} + \ldots \hat{\beta}_i ADV_{t-n} + e_t \quad (7\text{-}29)$$

Direct estimation of equation (7-29) is likely to be difficult, because of the high degree of multicollinearity among ADV_t, ADV_{t-1}, ADV_{t-2}, and so on. That is, there is an insufficient amount of variation among the independent variables to permit accurate estimation of the regression coefficients.

Since current economic behavior is predicated upon past values of certain variables, it is common practice for forecasters to include lags of different lengths for the same variable. The notion that the effect may be spread over several periods is the basis for the name *distributed-lag model*. In its most general form, the distributed-lag model can be written as:

$$Y_t = \beta_0 + \beta_1(w_0 X_t + w_1 X_{t-1} + w_2 X_{t-2} + \ldots) + \epsilon_t \qquad (7\text{-}30)$$

or:

$$Y_t = \beta_0 + \beta_1 \sum_{i=1}^{n} w_i X_{1i} + \beta_2 \sum_{j=1}^{m} w_j X_{2j} + \epsilon_t \qquad (7\text{-}31)$$

The only difference between these two equations is that in equation (7-31), Y_t is related to more than one independent variable. The distributed-lag effect of the variable X on the variable Y is described by the specification of the weights, ws. Different sets of values for the ws imply different distributed-lag schemes.[3]

The general form of the geometric lag model is:

$$Y_t = \beta_0 + \beta_1(X_t + w X_{t-1} + w^2 X_{t-2} + w^3 X_{t-3} + \ldots) + \epsilon_t$$
$$0 < w < 1 \qquad (7\text{-}32)$$

In this lag scheme, the weights decline, so that the effect of additional lagged variables is minimized. For example, the pattern where $w = 1/2$ is graphically illustrated in Figure 7-6. Further, in this pattern, one-half the effect of a

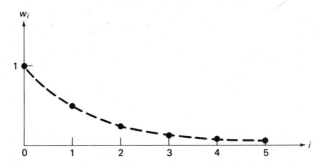

Figure 7-6   Geometric-Lag Weights[a]

[a]If w equals $\frac{1}{2}$, the weights become $1, \frac{1}{2}, \frac{1}{4}, \frac{1}{8}, \frac{1}{16}, \frac{1}{32}$, or simply $(\frac{1}{2})^i$. See equation (7-32)

change in X is registered in the first period. As formulated in equation (7-32), the model is difficult to estimate. This can be overcome by rewriting equation (7-32) as:

$$Y_{t-1} = \beta_0 + \beta_1(X_{t-1} + w X_{t-2} + w^2 X_{t-3} + \ldots) + \epsilon_{t-1} \qquad (7\text{-}33)$$

[3]Robert S. Pindyck and Daniel L. Rubinfeld, *Econometric Models and Economic Forecasts* (New York: McGraw-Hill, 1976), pp. 212–25.

The next step is to calculate values for $Y_t - wY_{t-1}$:

$$Y_t - wY_{t-1} = \beta_0(1 - w) + \beta_1 X_t + u_t \tag{7-34}$$

where $u_t = \epsilon_t - w\epsilon_{t-1}$. Rearranging, this becomes:

$$Y_t = \beta_0(1 - w) + wY_{t-1} + \beta_1 X_t + u_t \tag{7-35}$$

which can be more easily estimated with OLS.

To see how the analyst estimates a polynomial distributed-lag model, consider the example of a second-degree polynomial (parabola) with a two-period lag. The general specification of this model is:

$$Y_t = \beta_0 + w_0 X_t + w_1 X_{t-1} + w_2 X_{t-2} + \epsilon_t \tag{7-36}$$

The assumption of a second-degree polynomial for the weighting system implies that:

$$w_t = c_0 + c_1 i + c_2 i^2 \qquad i = 0, 1, 2 \tag{7-37}$$

Substituting this into equation (7-36) and rewriting yields:

$$Y_t = \beta_0 + c_0 X_t + (c_0 + c_1 + c_2)X_{t-1} + (c_0 + 2c_1 + 4c_2)X_{t-2} + \epsilon_t \tag{7-38}$$

or:

$$Y_t = \beta_0 + c_0(X_t + X_{t-1} + X_{t-2}) + c_1(X_{t-1} + 2X_{t-2})$$
$$+ c_2(X_{t-1} + 4X_{t-2}) + \epsilon_t \tag{7-39}$$

Equation (7-39) can be estimated using ordinary least-squares procedures. As long as the assumptions of the least-squares model are satisfied, the estimated cs are BLUE. Further, once the cs are estimated, the original lag weights, ws, can be determined by working backwards to equation (7-36).

Example 7-4: Capital Expenditures and Polynomial Distributed Lags

The original application of polynomial distributed lags was employed by Shirley Almon in 1965 to examine the relationship between the capital expenditures of the 1,000 largest manufacturing firms and capital appropriations. Her model specified that capital expenditures, E_t, were related to present and past values of appropriations, A, and a series of seasonal dummy variables, S_1, S_2, and S_3. In the Almon formulation there was a seven-period lag profile with a third-degree polynomial. The results of her estimation were:[4]

$$E_t = -283 + 13S_{1t} - 50S_{2t} + 320S_{3t} + .048A_t + .900A_{t-1} + 141A_{t-2} +$$
$$.165A_{t-3} + .167A_{t-4} + .146A_{t-5} + .105A_{t-6} + .053A_{t-7} \tag{7-40}$$

[4]Shirley Almon, "The Distributed Lag Between Capital Appropriations and Expenditures," *Econometrica*, Vol. 33 (1965), 178–96.

The lag coefficients follow an inverted U shape; that is, the coefficients first increase and then decrease. This particular model was statistically significant and fit the data pattern well.

TWO-STAGE LEAST SQUARES AND THE IDENTIFICATION PROBLEM

INTRODUCTION

The representation of an economic process may involve specification of multiple equations in a simultaneous-equation system. In such models, the variables being studied are simultaneously determined; that is, the variables must simultaneously satisfy all equations. Perhaps the simplest example of a simultaneous process is the interaction of supply and demand. Each side of the market represents a unique set of economic forces, and these sets interact to simultaneously yield market-clearing prices and quantities. The preparation of reliable forecasts requires knowledge about both equations, supply and demand. An example of a system of equations for a regional firm might be:

$$S = f(P, A, REA, COMP)$$
$$PC = g(UP, INV, W, E)$$
$$SC = h(A, L)$$
$$A = i(S, COMP, PR)$$
$$P = j(S, SC, PC, COMP, PR)$$
$$PR = k(S, P) \tag{7-41}$$

where:

$$S = \text{sales}$$
$$REA = \text{regional economic activity}$$
$$P = \text{price}$$
$$A = \text{advertising}$$
$$COMP = \text{competition}$$
$$PC = \text{production costs}$$
$$UP = \text{units produced}$$
$$INV = \text{inventory levels}$$
$$W = \text{wage rate}$$
$$E = \text{employment levels}$$
$$SC = \text{selling cost}$$
$$L = \text{sales personnel}$$
$$PR = \text{profits}$$

Thus, in place of a single equation to forecast sales, the preceding set of six simultaneous equations implies that sales are influenced by many factors. The conceptual advantage of this set of equations vis-à-vis a single-equation model is that the interdependencies of economic phenomena are highlighted.

The ordinary least-squares estimation procedure (OLS), discussed in previous chapters, can lead to biased and inconsistent estimators if incorrectly applied to variables that are part of an interdependent subsystem. Numerous techniques have been developed to deal with the identification problem that arises when single-equation models are incorrectly used in lieu of a simultaneous system. Five of the best known methods are (1) full information maximum likelihood estimators (FIML); (2) limited information maximum likelihood estimators (LIML); (3) two- and three-stage least squares (2SLS and 3SLS); (4) indirect least squares (ILS); and (5) recursive systems.[5] Only two-stage least squares will be discussed, but the fundamentals of other methods can be found in more advanced textbooks.[6]

THE IDENTIFICATION PROBLEM

The question of identification comes down to the forecaster's ability to correctly estimate the desired equation or equations from the empirical data. Suppose an analyst observes the price-quantity combinations shown in Figure 7-7. Although a regression line can be fitted to these points, it is not clear whether a demand or a supply equation has been estimated. Each of these data points represents an intersection of the supply and demand curves, but both curves may have shifted because of changes in other economic factors.

Although it does not lend itself to a simple treatment, the identification problem can be illustrated with a supply-and-demand model, as follows:

$$Q_t^D = \hat{\beta}_0 + \hat{\beta}_1 P_t + \hat{\beta}_2 Y_t : \quad \text{Demand} \qquad (7\text{-}42)$$

$$Q_t^S = \hat{\beta}_3 + \hat{\beta}_4 P_t \qquad : \quad \text{Supply} \qquad (7\text{-}43)$$

$$Q_t^D = Q_t^S = Q_t^e \qquad : \quad \text{Equilibrium} \qquad (7\text{-}44)$$

Considered together, these three equations yield the market-clearing prices and quantities noted in Figure 7-7. The variables, Q_t^D, Q_t^S, and P_t, are referred to as the endogenous variables, since they are determined within the system of equations. Variables such as Y_t, which are not determined directly within the system, are said to be exogenous. These three equations (7-42 through 7-44) are commonly called the *structural equations*. The endogenous variables can be defined

---

[5]We do not mean to imply that these techniques are applicable to all systems and will solve all problems. They are all formulated to handle simultaneous-equation systems.

[6]See J.L. Murphy, *Introductory Econometrics* (Homewood, Ill.: Richard D. Irwin, 1973); or R.J. Wonnacott and T.H. Wonnacott, *Econometrics* (New York: John Wiley, 1970); or Potluri Rao and Roger Leroy Miller, *Applied Econometrics* (Belmont, Calif.: Wadsworth, 1971).

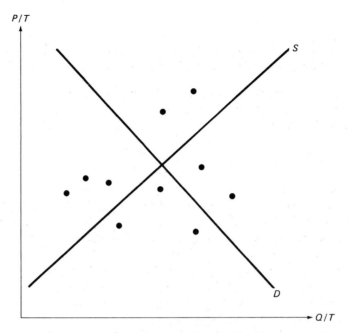

Figure 7-7 The Identification Problem

in terms of the exogenous variables by setting the right-hand side of equation (7-42) equal to the right-hand side of equation (7-43). That is, market clearing occurs when quantity supplied equals quantity demanded. Algebraically, this yields (for simplification, the error terms are omitted):

$$Q_t = \frac{\hat{\beta}_4\hat{\beta}_0 - \hat{\beta}_3\hat{\beta}_1}{\hat{\beta}_4 - \hat{\beta}_1} + \frac{\hat{\beta}_4\hat{\beta}_2}{\hat{\beta}_4 - \hat{\beta}_1}Y_t \qquad (7\text{-}45)$$

$$P_t = \frac{\hat{\beta}_0 - \hat{\beta}_3}{\hat{\beta}_4 - \hat{\beta}_1} + \frac{\hat{\beta}_2}{\hat{\beta}_4 - \hat{\beta}_1}Y_t \qquad (7\text{-}46)$$

Equations (7-45) and (7-46) are the reduced-form equations. The identification problem is based on the relationship between the reduced-form equations and the structural equations: Can estimates for the coefficients of the structural equations be derived once the coefficients of the reduced-form equations have been estimated? Technically, consideration of the identification problem precedes the empirical estimation process. That is, once the analyst has specified the structural model, he or she should check to see whether the equation or equations are identified. Formally, an equation is identified if a unique parameter value can be found, overidentified if more than one value is obtainable for some parameters, and underidentified if none of the structural equation parameters can be estimated from the reduced form. The necessary condition for identification is that the number of variables not contained in a particular equation but appearing elsewhere in the model must be one less than the number of endogenous variables.[7]

These concepts are less formidable than might at first appear. To see this, return to the simple supply-and-demand model previously postulated:

$$Q_t^D = \hat{\beta}_0 + \hat{\beta}_1 P_t + \hat{\beta}_2 Y_t \tag{7-47}$$

$$Q_t^S = \hat{\beta}_3 + \hat{\beta}_4 P_t + \hat{\beta}_5 C_t \tag{7-48}$$

$$Q_t^D = Q_t^S = Q_t^e \tag{7-49}$$

There are two endogenous variables, Q_t^e (or $Q_t^D = Q_t^S$) and P_t; thus, the model is identified if it is possible to find one variable $(2 - 1)$ excluded from each equation but contained elsewhere in the model. C_t is excluded from the demand function but included elsewhere; hence, equation (7-47) is identified. Likewise, the supply function is identified, because Y_t is excluded but appears in the demand equation.

Suppose, however, that the model had been specified as:

$$Q_t^D = \hat{\beta}_0 + \hat{\beta}_1 P_t + \hat{\beta}_2 Y_t \tag{7-50}$$

$$Q_t^S = \hat{\beta}_3 + \hat{\beta}_4 P_t \tag{7-51}$$

$$Q_t^D = Q_t^S = Q_t^e \tag{7-52}$$

In this model, the supply equation is identified, because Y_t is excluded but appears in the demand function. However, the demand equation is not identified, since there is no excluded variable. Since one equation is not identified, the system is not identified. If this situation prevails, the system is said to be under-identified.

The final possibility is overidentification. This occurs when the model is specified as:

$$Q_t^D = \hat{\beta}_0 + \hat{\beta}_1 P_t + \hat{\beta}_2 Y_t \tag{7-53}$$

$$Q_t^S = \hat{\beta}_3 + \hat{\beta}_4 P_t + \hat{\beta}_5 C_t + \hat{\beta}_6 X_t + \hat{\beta}_7 Z_t \tag{7-54}$$

$$Q_t^D = Q_t^S = Q_t^e \tag{7-55}$$

Here, the demand function is overidentified, because there are three variables— C_t, X_t, and Z_t—that are excluded but appear in the supply function. Conversely, the supply function is identified, because there is only one excluded variable, Y_t, that appears elsewhere.

At this stage, the identification problem may appear transparent, because ordinary least-squares (OLS) regression lines could be estimated directly for the structural equations in any of the models. However, because these models involve simultaneous variables, OLS estimators are biased and inconsistent

---

[7]This condition does not apply to equations such as $Q_t^S = Q_t^D$.

when applied directly to the structural equations. With an underidentified system, the analyst can simply determine which equation is underidentified, find another variable that influences the dependent variable, and use OLS techniques to estimate the reduced form. With overidentification, the solution is not so simple. Variables cannot be deleted, because if there was a theoretical justification for including them, there is no *a priori* reason for deletion. Fortunately, there is an alternative way of solving the problem of overidentification, using two-stage least squares (2SLS).

TWO-STAGE LEAST SQUARES (2SLS)

Two-stage least-squares procedures are particularly useful in obtaining the values of the structural-equation parameters in the presence of overidentification. The principal justification for 2SLS is that in simultaneous systems, all the exogenous variables influence each of the endogenous variables. For example, in equation (7-53), Q_t^p is directly related to P_t and Y_t and therefore indirectly related to C_t, X_t, and Z_t. Two-stage least squares takes this interdependence into consideration.

The general applicability of 2SLS can be seen by referring to the following supply-and-demand model, where, for convenience, we have expressed the variables in terms of deviations from their respective means:

Structural Equations

$$q_t^p = \hat{\beta}_1 p_t \tag{7-56}$$

$$q_t^s = \hat{\beta}_2 p_t + \hat{\beta}_3 y_t + \hat{\beta}_4 c_t \tag{7-57}$$

Reduced-Form Equations

$$p_t = \frac{\hat{\beta}_3}{\hat{\beta}_1 - \hat{\beta}_2} y_t + \frac{\hat{\beta}_4}{\hat{\beta}_1 - \hat{\beta}_2} c_t \tag{7-58}$$

$$q_t = \frac{\hat{\beta}_1 \hat{\beta}_3}{\hat{\beta}_1 - \hat{\beta}_2} y_t + \frac{\hat{\beta}_1 \hat{\beta}_4}{\hat{\beta}_1 - \hat{\beta}_2} c_t \tag{7-59}$$

In this model, the demand equation is overidentified; hence, OLS estimators are inappropriate. The two-stage least-squares procedures works as follows:

1. Estimation of the reduced-form equation for p_t is done with OLS techniques in the first stage. This means that p_t is separately regressed on all the exogenous variables. From this first-stage regression, the fitted values of $\hat{p}_t$ are obtained.
2. In the second stage, the demand equation of the structural model is estimated, once again with OLS, after replacing p_t with $\hat{p}_t$ (obtained from the first-stage OLS).

Thus, the name *two-stage least squares* is derived from a two-step application of ordinary least-squares techniques.

OLS VS. 2SLS: AN OVERVIEW

According to noted econometrician Michael Evans, estimation of a single structural equation by simultaneous-equation methods can cost between 50 and 1,000 times as much as estimating the same equation employing OLS. Further, these simultaneous methods may not produce better parameter estimates than does OLS. If the forecaster misspecifies one variable in a structural equation, the entire system of structural equations may be biased, causing distortions that are worse than with OLS. In addition, the number of observations must exceed the number of variables. With over 200 variables in the currently popular macroeconomic models, this would require at least fifty years of data! Finally, once estimated, these systems require constant monitoring and updating. These problems have led Michael Evans to conclude that "ordinary least squares has proven so useful and durable that it still accounts for the great majority of empirical work. . . ."[8]

This is high praise for the relatively simple OLS methodology. In most applications, OLS is superior to more complex regression models, which provide a small increase in statistical power and a large jump in cost.

MULTIPLE-EQUATION MODELS

INTRODUCTION

With the exception of the two-stage least squares procedure, all of the examples presented in the last three chapters have been single-equation models. These models have been estimated by applying the ordinary least squares methodology. Despite the general applicability and power of this technique situations do arise in which multiple-equation models are preferable. Multiple-equation models are specifically constructed to account for both the inter-relationships among the independent variables themselves and the feedback between the dependent variable and the independent variables. The present section serves as a general introduction to multiple-equation modeling, while Chapter 8 examines an actual multiple-equation, monetarist model of the national economy.

SIMULTANEOUS EQUATION SYSTEMS

Simultaneity occurs in models whenever at least one independent (explanatory) variable in one equation is simultaneously a dependent variable in another equation. In general, a simultaneous equation model has M equations

---

[8]Michael K. Evans, "Econometric Models," in *Methods and Techniques of Business Forecasting*, eds. William F. Butler, Robert A. Kavesh, and Robert B. Platt (Englewood Cliffs, N.J.: Prentice-Hall, 1974), pp. 161–90.

in which M endogenous variables are jointly determined. That is, multiple-equation models involve simultaneously solving a set of equations for a specific number of endogenous variables. In constructing the models, the analyst must ensure that the number of equations equals the number of endogenous variables. If the number of equations exceeds the number of endogenous variables, the model has an infinite number of solutions. Alternatively, no solution is possible if the number of equations is less than the number of endogenous variables.

Consider the following three-equation, macroeconomic model.

$$C_t = \beta_0 + \beta_1 Y_t + \beta_2 W_t + \epsilon_1$$
$$I_t = \beta_3 + \beta_4 Y_t + \beta_5 R_t + \epsilon_2$$
$$Y_t = C_t + I_t + G_t \qquad\qquad (7\text{-}60)$$

where

$C =$ consumption expenditures
$I =$ investment expenditures
$Y =$ gross national product
$R =$ interest rate
$W =$ wealth holdings
$G =$ government spending
$\epsilon_i =$ random error term, $i = 1$ to 2

The variables G_t, R_t, and W_t are exogenous (predetermined) variables in that they are determined outside of the model. Within the model, C_t, I_t and Y_t are the three endogenous variables. The simultaneous nature of the model can be seen by noting that C_t and I_t depend upon Y_t but, as shown in the third equation, Y_t depends upon C_t and I_t. This interrelationship or two-way causality dictates that all three equations be solved simultaneously.

RECURSIVE MODELS

In a recursive model, some of the endogenous variables are dependent upon others but the dependency flows in one direction—X_1 affects X_2, but X_2 does not affect X_1. Equations in a recursive model are solved sequentially rather than simultaneously. Thus, the value of the first endogenous variable is esti-mated. It is then combined with externally determined values of the exogenous variables in order to estimate the second endogenous variable, which in turn is utilized to solve the third endogenous variable, and so forth. Note that the third endogenous variable does not influence the second, nor does the second have any feedback to the first endogenous variable.

As an example of a recursive system, consider the following model.

$$P_G = \alpha_0 + \alpha_1 A + \epsilon_1$$
$$P_B = \beta_0 + \beta_2 P_G + \beta_3 T + \epsilon_2$$
$$Q_B = \sigma_0 + \sigma_1 A + \sigma_2 P_G + \sigma_4 P_B + \epsilon_3 \qquad\qquad (7\text{-}61)$$

where

$$P_G = \text{price of malt grain}$$
$$P_B = \text{price of beer}$$
$$Q_B = \text{quantity of beer sold}$$
$$A = \text{acreage planted}$$
$$T = \text{tax on beer}$$

In this specification, the price of grain is dependent upon the predetermined level of acreage planted. The price of beer is related to the price of grain and the predetermined tax rate levied on each barrel of beer produced. Finally, the quantity of beer sold is dependent upon the prices of malt grain and beer and acreage planted. Each of these equations is estimated individually using ordinary least squares, and the equations are then solved for the endogenous values in a sequential fashion beginning with the first equation. The mechanics of this recursive process are illustrated in Chapter 8 using a monetarist model of the economy.

Example 7-5: Testing the Structural Stability of Regression Models: The Chow Test[9]

Whenever time series data are used in conjunction with regression models, the analyst needs to consider whether the fitted model is structurally stable over time. To illustrate this situation, consider the final model estimated for installment loan demand in Memphis, equation (6-22).

$$\widehat{INST}_t = -56.08784 + 0.9635235 PINST_{t-1} - 1.249709 U_t + 0.6060539 MEMIND_t$$

Structural stability implies that the observed relationship between the unemployment rate (U_t), the Memphis Index ($MEMIND_t$), lagged installment loans ($PINST_{t-1}$), and installment loan demand has remained relatively constant over the period for which the model was estimated (January 1975 to December 1979). That is, the model builder implicitly assumes that throughout this entire time period a 1 percentage point increase in the unemployment rate will cause loan demand to fall by \$1.25 million, that a 1 percentage point change in Memphis Business Activity will change loan demand by \$606 thousand, and that a \$1 million jump in lagged installment loans will lead to a subsequent increase of \$963 thousand in current loan demand.

To test the structural stability of the equation, the following steps must be carried out: divide the data base into two sub-periods; estimate an equation for each sub-period; calculate the sum of squares from each regression; compute an actual F statistic and compare to a critical F value; and decide whether to accept or reject the assumption of structural stability.

---

[9]Gregory C. Chow, "Tests of Equality between Sets of Coefficients in Two Linear Regressions," *Econometrica*, vol. 28, (July, 1960), pp. 591–605.

To illustrate this procedure, the model in equation (6-22) was reestimated over the period from January 1975 to December 1976.

$$\widehat{INST}_t = -35.79947 + 0.8526677PINST_{t-1} - 1.349996U_t +$$
$$0.6348865MEMIND_t \quad (7\text{-}62)$$

The same model estimated from January 1977 to December 1979 is:

$$\widehat{INST}_t = -53.22729 + 0.9747280PINST_{t-1} - 0.9406547U_t +$$
$$0.5451388MEMIND_t \quad (7\text{-}63)$$

In order to test the structural stability of the coefficients in these two equations, (that is, to test whether or not the differences are the result of sampling error), the sum of squares of the residual (unexplained variation) was computed for equations (6-22), (7-62), and (7-63), with the results reproduced in Table 7-3.

Table 7-3 Installment loan demand in Memphis: analysis of structural stability

Data set I: January 1975—December 1976, Equation (7-62)

Analysis of Variance	Sum of Squares	d.f.	Mean Square	F Statistic
Explained by Regression	2,082.3090	3	694.10299	51.8666
Error Variation	267.64937	20	13.382469	

Data set II: January 1977—December 1979, Equation (7-63)

Analysis of Variance	Sum of Squares	d.f.	Mean Square	F Statistic
Explained by Regression	66,345.508	3	22,115.169	1,980.9703
Error Variation	357.24182	32	11.163807	

Data set III: January 1975—December 1979, Equation (6-22)

Analysis of Variance	Sum of Squares	d.f.	Mean Square	F Statistic
Explained by Regression	138,195.88	3	46,065.294	3,891.7629
Error Variation	662.85038	56	11.836614	

The test statistic for equality of coefficients is given by:

$$F_{(k,\, n_1+n_2-2k)} = \frac{(Q - Q_1)/k}{Q_1/(n_1 + n_2 - 2k)} \quad (7\text{-}64)$$

where

n_1 = number of observations in data set I, equation (7-62)
n_2 = number of observations in data set II, equation (7-63)
k = number of regressors, including constant
Q = error variation for equation (6-22)
Q_1 = combined error variation for equations (7-62) and (7-63)

Table 7-4 contains all of the data necessary to compute the F statistic.

Table 7-4 The Chow test for structural stability: installment loan demand

Residual or Error Variation	Sum of Squares	d.f.	Mean Square	F^a Statistic
Regression error for complete equation (6-22)	$Q = 662.85038$	56		
Combined error from equations (7-62) and (7-63)	$Q_1 = 624.89119$	52	12.017138	0.7897
Complete less combined error	$Q_2 = Q - Q_1$ $= 37.95919$	4	9.4897975	

^{a}The actual F statistic is based on equation (7-64). Statistics taken from Table 7-3. The null hypothesis of structural stability is accepted since the critical F equals 3.70 when $\alpha = .01$. Therefore, we can conclude that the regression coefficients in equation (6-22) exhibit structural stability.

The error variation, Q, measures the variation not explained by the regression model in equation (6-22), thus $Q = 662.85$ as shown in Table 7-4. The combined sum of squares, Q_1, measures the total unexplained variation in equations (7-62) and (7-63), thus $Q_1 = 624.89$ as shown in Table 7-4. As illustrated in the formula for the actual F value in equation (7-64), the greater the difference between Q and Q_1, the greater the evidence against the null hypothesis of structural stability in the regression coefficients for the original model in equation (6-22). A low F value implies that random forces have caused the observed differences in the regression coefficients for the equations analyzed in Tables 7-3 and 7-4. In the case of the installment loan demand model, the actual F of 0.7897 (see Table 7-4), is less than the critical value of 3.70 ($\alpha = .01$), hence the null hypothesis of structural stability is accepted.

In the example just completed, the dividing point between the two data sets was arbitrarily selected whereas in actual situations the analyst would attempt to pinpoint a potential structural turning point. For example the analyst might believe that the competitive structure of the shoe industry had been radically altered by the passage of a law allowing increased foreign imports. Similarly, a business analyst in the banking industry in Tennessee would certainly need to quantify the structural impact of NOW accounts on competition between savings and loans and commercial banks. Alternatively, we might have developed a model of installment loan demand which works well in one region of the country but which needs to be checked for structural stability before being applied to other regions. In the case of structural change arising from a new statute, the sub-periods for the test of structural stability may be self-evident. In other instances background research has to be carried out to assess the likely period of change. The Chow test illustrated in Tables 7-3 and 7-4 represents one method of validating the stability of a regression model before it is used for forecasting purposes.

QUESTIONS FOR DISCUSSION AND ANALYSIS

1. The use of proxy variables represents an attempt to formulate a variable to serve as a stand-in for an exogenous influence or as an imperfect surrogate for a theoretical concept. What proxy variables might be used to represent the following?
   a. Credit availability in a demand equation for housing starts
   b. Profit expectations in an equation that predicts capital expenditures
   c. The presence of import quotas in a demand model for domestic steel
   d. Consumer anticipations in a model for refrigerator demand
   e. Environmental pollution standards in a demand model for pollution-abatement equipment
   f. The effect of television on the demand for advertising space in newspapers

2. Equation (7-1) utilizes a 0, 1 dummy variable to incorporate the exogenous influence of war on military expenditures. What problems or defects are there in using such a dummy-variable technique? That is, what dimensions of the war-to-military-expenditures relationship are neglected by this dummy-variable approach? Collect quarterly, seasonally unadjusted data for toy sales (or any other sales series) for the last five years and fit a regression equation of the form illustrated in equation (7-5). That is, estimate the influence of the trend force (T) and the seasonal factors (Q_2, Q_3, and Q_4) on quarterly sales. Explain precisely the meaning of each of the regression coefficients.

3. Examine the error distribution for the regression equation that was estimated in problem 2. Is there any evidence of a volatile error pattern that might be ascribed to an exogenous shock? If not, fit a similar regression equation to a sales series of a company or industry (such as the coal industry in 1979) that has recently experienced a prolonged strike. Can you identify a prestrike residual from the error distribution and the known dates of the strike?

4. Appendix E, Table E-1, contains the historical data used in estimating the automobile-demand model in equation (6-20). Rerun this model in logarithmic form. That is, fit the following model:

$$\log \widehat{\text{UNITSAL}}_t = \hat{\beta}_0 + \hat{\beta}_1 \log \text{YPLTP}_t + \hat{\beta}_2 \log \text{JATTC} + \hat{\beta}_3 \log M_t + \log e$$

   a. How do the statistical results from this logarithmically modified equation differ from the summary for equation (6-20)?
   b. "The regression coefficient, $\hat{\beta}_2$, measures the elasticity of unit sales with respect to consumer sentiment." Explain. In particular, how can one simply glance at the equation above and know that $\hat{\beta}_1$, $\hat{\beta}_2$, and $\hat{\beta}_3$ are elasticity coefficients? Based on the empirical value found for $\hat{\beta}_2$, provide a specific interpretation for this elasticity coefficient.
   c. The equation listed above is linear in logarithms, but it was derived from a nonlinear formula. Working backwards from the formula above, find its nonlinear antecedent.

5. If a curvilinear model of the form presented in equation (7-13) is to be utilized for a simple regression equation, how might the scatter of observed points appear so as to be consistent with the model?

6. As stated in the chapter, an examination of the sales tax revenue in Table 7-2 leads

to the conclusion that the data follow an exponential pattern. What is meant by *exponential pattern*? Why was equation (7-18) suggested as the appropriate vehicle for use with an exponential data pattern? What is the nonlinear antecedent of equation (7-18)?

7. Collect data comparable to that in Table 7-2 for your state or municipality, fit the model shown in equation (7-18), and compare the results to equation (7-19), which was estimated for the State of Tennessee.

8. Based on the data in Appendix G, use a stepwise regression program to duplicate the results in equation (7-23).

REFERENCES FOR FURTHER STUDY

Fair, R., "A Comparison of Alternative Estimators of Macroeconomic Models," *International Economic Review*, Vol. 14, No. 2 (June 1973), 261–77.

————, "The Estimation of Simultaneous Equation Models with Lagged Endogenous Variables and First Order Serially Corrected Errors," *Econometrica*, May 1970.

Glasser, M., "Linear Regression Analysis with Missing Observations among the Independent Variables," *Journal of the American Statistical Association*, Vol. 59 (1964), 834–44.

Hertz, D.B., and K.H. Schaffir, "A Forecasting Model for Management of Seasonal Style Goods Inventories," *Operations Research*, Vol. 8, No. 2 (1960), 45–52.

Michael, G.C., "A Computer Simulation Model for Forecasting Catalog Sales," *Journal of Marketing Research*, May 1971, 224–29.

Wallis, K.F., "Lagged Dependent Variables and Serially Corrected Errors: A Reappraisal of Three-Pass Least Squares," *Review of Economics and Statistics*, Vol. 49 (1967), 555–67.

Wonnacott, Ronald J., and Thomas H. Wonnacott, *Econometrics*, 2nd ed., New York: John Wiley & Sons, 1979.

8

Case Studies of Multiple Regression Models

INTRODUCTION

As every researcher soon realizes, the *final* regression equation used to prepare forecasts represents only a fraction of the analysis that has been undertaken. In Chapters 4 through 7, we introduced the tools needed to apply regression models to economic phenomena. These tools were presented on a piecemeal basis. The advantage of this approach is that we were able to focus attention on one topic at a time and meticuously examine its theoretical underpinnings. The disadvantage is that analysis is actually based on a synthesis of all these tools. Therefore, the goal in this chapter is to present a complete economic and statistical analysis of actual situations in which regression forecasting models have been developed and used. Just as an artist must learn to synthesize diverse and separate bodies of knowledge pertaining to light, color, form, and technique, so you must master the art of integrating quantitative techniques, judgmental expertise, and theoretical logic.

A QUARTERLY MODEL
OF RAIL FREIGHT TON-MILES

THE HISTORICAL SETTING

Table 8-1 contains quarterly data for rail freight ton-miles (billions) handled by all Class I railroads in the United States from 1954 to 1979. Railroads provide a service rather than a tangible product, and the unit of measurement for this service is the ton-mile—the movement of one ton of freight over a distance of one mile. This table is a concise historical profile of an entire industry over the span of a quarter century. As such, Table 8-1 summarizes all past information as to how the railroad industry has been influenced in that period by exogenous and endogenous forces—economic growth, recession, intermodal competition, government regulations, energy prices, and demographic shifts. Despite the interaction of all these factors, a cursory examination of

Table 8-1   Quarterly rail ton-miles, 1954–1979 (Billions)

Year	First Quarter	Second Quarter	Third Quarter	Fourth Quarter	Total
1954	129.8	136.6	139.0	143.8	549.2
1955	139.9	156.1	163.1	163.9	623.0
1956	158.8	164.7	157.5	165.9	646.9
1957	153.0	159.3	158.1	147.9	618.3
1958	130.1	132.2	141.3	147.9	551.5
1959	140.6	155.5	134.9	144.6	575.6
1960	144.4	149.7	140.1	138.0	572.2
1961	128.9	140.4	144.8	149.2	563.3
1962	144.3	151.4	146.6	150.4	592.7
1963	144.3	161.5	154.8	160.3	620.9
1964	158.5	165.8	163.9	170.8	659.0
1965	162.6	178.2	175.6	181.9	698.3
1966	178.0	189.9	186.1	186.1	740.1
1967	177.2	184.0	174.9	182.6	718.7
1968	181.8	191.5	183.6	188.0	744.9
1969	184.6	196.5	188.8	197.9	767.8
1970	184.6	198.6	189.2	191.1	763.5
1971	185.0	197.8	179.3	177.3	739.4
1972	187.2	198.8	190.4	202.0	778.4
1973	203.6	218.0	211.2	218.2	851.0
1974	216.3	223.8	210.8	204.2	855.1
1975	186.9	189.6	182.4	196.2	755.1
1976	190.7	203.6	197.9	200.8	793.0
1977	195.6	216.0	205.3	208.6	825.5
1978	188.5	203.4	210.5	227.1	829.5
1979	207.6	236.8	223.9	—	668.3

Source: Interstate Commerce Commission

the raw data in Table 8-1 suggests the existence of a stable pattern of growth in the railroad industry. That is, the data seem to lend themselves to statistical analysis.

As a first step, we might ask who would be able to use an economic forecast of quarterly rail ton-miles. The most obvious users would be company forecasters within the rail industry, but there are other groups for whom rail ton-mile projections would prove valuable—for example, producers of railroad freight cars and locomotives, steel manufacturers, diesel-fuel suppliers, and financial analysts interested in the transportation sector. Each of these groups has specialized forecast needs that relate to differing levels of disaggregation. In the case of diesel-fuel suppliers and locomotive builders, projections of aggregate rail ton-miles might be more than adequate. A builder of rail freight cars, however, would want disaggregated ton-mile projections by specific commodity, in order to project demand for such diverse car types as covered hopper cars to move grain, refrigerated boxcars to haul fresh vegetables, tank cars to move oil products, and gondolas to transport coal.

TIME-SERIES ANALYSIS OF RAW DATA

The initial goal of time-series analysis is to obtain as much information as possible from the raw data concerning their time-series characteristics— trend, seasonal, cyclical, and irregular. The data in Table 8-1 were subjected to statistical analysis using the X-11 seasonal adjustment program of the Census Department, and were found to have stable seasonality present at the 1 percent significance level.[1] Table 8-2 contains the final seasonal factors that were generated by this program.

In addition to the historical seasonal factors, the X-11 program provides us with the seasonal factors one year—four quarters—into the future. An analysis of the data in Table 8-2 reveals several important facets of economic activity in the rail sector. First, whereas the simple procedure for estimation of seasonality outlined in Chapter 4 produced a single set of four quarterly seasonal indices, the seasonal indices in Table 8-2 fluctuate over time. In other words, although there is stable seasonality in a statistical sense, it is changing slowly over time.[2] For example, the first-quarter seasonal index started out at 95.996 in 1954, reached a peak of 97.948 in 1973, and declined rapidly to 95.644 in 1979. The third quarter, however, started at 101.667 in 1954, fell to 98.070 in 1972, and then climbed back to 99.471 by 1979. Between 1954 and 1972, therefore, there was an upward trend in the first-quarter seasonal index and a downward trend in the third quarter.

---

[1] For a detailed discussion of the X-11 seasonal adjustment program, see U.S. Department of Commerce, Bureau of the Census, "The X-11 Variant of the Census Method II Seasonal Adjustment Program," *Technical Paper No. 15* (Washington, D.C.: U.S. Government Printing Office, 1967).

[2] Although not discussed in the text, standard regression techniques can be used to estimate trend movements in the seasonal components.

Table 8-2 Final seasonal factors for quarterly rail ton-miles

Year	First Quarter	Second Quarter	Third Quarter	Fourth Quarter
1954	95.996	101.110	101.667	101.259
1955	95.998	101.008	101.709	101.335
1956	95.982	100.946	101.703	101.313
1957	96.118	100.968	101.478	101.357
1958	96.234	101.117	101.194	101.296
1959	96.430	101.358	100.764	101.316
1960	96.507	101.742	100.352	101.180
1961	96.721	102.051	99.922	101.217
1962	96.764	102.284	99.671	101.211
1963	96.854	102.347	99.521	101.258
1964	96.868	102.469	99.366	101.140
1965	97.107	102.526	99.176	101.045
1966	97.278	102.675	98.977	100.885
1967	97.490	102.817	98.817	100.709
1968	97.587	103.143	98.559	100.525
1969	97.704	103.454	98.316	100.392
1970	97.753	103.742	98.096	100.317
1971	97.838	103.787	98.071	100.280
1972	97.924	103.665	98.070	100.428
1973	97.948	103.344	98.246	100.666
1974	97.798	103.024	98.453	101.087
1975	97.408	102.693	98.840	101.477
1976	96.834	102.608	99.069	101.879
1977	96.263	102.600	99.308	102.084
1978	95.836	102.719	99.390	102.161
1979	95.644	102.776	99.471	102.199[a]
1980	95.548[a]	102.805[a]	99.512[a]	

[a]Forecasted values. Data were analyzed using the Census Bureau's X-11 seasonal adjustment program. Raw data taken from Table 8-1. Stable seasonality test produced an actual F value of 69.160, which is significant at the 1 percent level.

It is not unreasonable to assume that next year's seasonal pattern will be nearly the same as this year's—an assumption that is borne out if we make a year-by-year comparison of the seasonal factors—but the question of long-run trend patterns in the seasonal indices must be recognized and addressed. The task of explaining these changing seasonal patterns will, in all probability, entail identification of the economic variables that influence rail traffic. Remember that total rail ton-miles is an aggregate figure based on literally thousands of commodities. As the economy evolved in the postwar period, and as other freight modes (truck, barge, and pipeline) became increasingly competitive, the mix of commodities shipped by the railroads changed.[3] For example, farmers

[3]Data on the composition of U.S. railroad traffic can be found in *Moody's Transportation Manual* (New York: Moody's Investors Service, 1979).

traditionally shipped their grain to the market immediately upon harvesting it in the fall; now, they are able to store their grain and wait for the most propitious time to ship it to market. Shipments of coal, which formerly originated from mines in Appalachia or Illinois, are increasingly being transported from mines in Wyoming. Changing demographic patterns have caused lumber shipments to move to the Sunbelt via truck rather than by rail. These factors, plus others, have combined to produce the changing seasonal patterns observable in Table 8-2.

Table 8-3 Quarterly rail ton-miles, seasonally adjusted, 1954–1979 (Billions)

Year	First Quarter	Second Quarter	Third Quarter	Fourth Quarter	Total
1954	135.215	135.101	136.721	142.013	549.049
1955	145.733	154.543	160.359	161.741	622.375
1956	165.447	163.156	154.862	163.751	647.216
1957	159.180	157.773	155.797	145.920	618.671
1958	135.191	130.740	139.633	146.008	551.572
1959	145.805	153.416	133.877	142.722	575.820
1960	149.626	147.137	139.609	136.390	572.762
1961	133.270	137.579	144.913	147.407	563.169
1962	149.125	148.019	147.084	148.600	592.828
1963	148.987	157.797	155.545	158.308	620.637
1964	163.624	161.806	164.945	168.875	659.251
1965	167.443	173.810	177.058	180.018	698.330
1966	182.981	184.953	188.024	184.467	740.425
1967	181.762	178.959	176.994	181.314	719.028
1968	186.296	185.664	186.283	187.019	745.262
1969	188.939	189.939	192.034	197.128	768.040
1970	188.842	191.436	192.872	190.496	763.646
1971	189.088	190.582	182.827	176.805	739.303
1972	191.168	191.772	194.147	201.139	778.226
1973	207.865	210.946	214.971	216.755	850.537
1974	221.171	217.230	214.113	202.005	854.519
1975	191.873	184.628	184.541	193.344	754.386
1976	196.936	198.425	199.759	197.097	792.217
1977	203.193	210.527	206.730	204.342	824.793
1978	196.691	198.015	211.792	222.296	828.794
1979	217.056	230.404	225.090	—	672.549

Source: Tables 8-1 and 8-2

By dividing the raw data in Table 8-1 by the seasonal factors in Table 8-2, we can derive the seasonally adjusted rail ton-mile data shown in Table 8-3. As explained earlier in Chapter 4, when the raw data $(T \cdot S \cdot C \cdot I)$ are divided by the seasonal index (S), the result is a series containing trend, cyclical, and irregular factors $(T \cdot C \cdot I)$. Further, the data in Table 8-3 have been decomposed by the X-11 program into the trend-cycle component $(T \cdot C)$, Table 8-4, and the irregular factor (I), Table 8-5.

Table 8-4 Quarterly rail ton-miles, trend cycle, 1954–1979 (Billions)

Year	First Quarter	Second Quarter	Third Quarter	Fourth Quarter	Total
1954	135.059^L	135.102	137.253	141.141	548.554
1955	146.819	154.052	159.752	162.847	623.469
1956	164.478^H	163.167	160.280	159.361	647.285
1957	159.097	158.339	154.732	145.815	617.983
1958	135.600	133.183^L	139.089	145.399	553.271
1959	147.060^H	145.032	142.348^L	143.890	578.330
1960	147.974^H	146.666	140.631	135.548	570.819
1961	134.142^L	137.838	144.032	147.852	563.863
1962	148.751	148.071	147.453	148.156	592.431
1963	150.547	153.424	155.834	158.915	618.719
1964	161.662	162.814	165.093	167.640	657.208
1965	169.568	172.985	177.197	180.112	699.862
1966	182.754	185.672	186.901^H	185.084	740.410
1967	181.624	178.631	177.815^L	181.363	719.432
1968	185.325	186.250	186.123	187.253	744.951
1969	188.636	190.206	192.190	192.777^H	763.809
1970	191.628	191.611	192.171	190.812	766.223
1971	189.695	187.667	183.827	182.326^L	743.514
1972	186.224	190.778	195.099	201.029	773 130
1973	207.276	211.515	214.398	217.842	851.031
1974	219.537^H	218.542	212.597	202.743	853.419
1975	191.633	184.828^L	185.715	192.077	754.253
1976	197.016	198.847	198.540	198.595	792.998
1977	203.550	208.687^H	208.135	202.799	823.171
1978	197.528^L	199.602	210.206	220.225	827.561
1979	226.198	227.803^H	226.698	—	680.699

Source: Tables 8-1 to 8-3. Raw data in Table 8-1 have been adjusted to remove seasonal and irregular effects and are named by the Census X-11 program as a "five-term Henderson Curve." The letters H and L denote quarterly highs and lows, respectively, for rail ton-miles. Minor declines have been ignored.

Turning to the irregular factors in Table 8-5, we find a series of index numbers. These indices are interpreted in exactly the same fashion as seasonal index numbers. Analysis of irregular factors is a convenient way of identifying the historical occurrence of unpredictable exogenous influences.[4] As explained in Chapter 4, the irregular component measures the net effect of all random and nonrandom forces, and the mean effect of these non-time-series forces is expected to be zero. However, individual exogenous influences (for example, a strike or an abnormally severe winter) may produce a positive or negative effect on rail ton-miles in any specific quarter. An overview of the effect of the irregular force can be obtained by studying the last column of Table 8-5,

[4]Since the irregular component (I) is estimated as a time-series residual, it measures the net effect of all factors other than trend, seasonal, and cyclical. It remains for the researcher to pinpoint the source of the exogenous shock.

Table 8-5 Irregular Index for rail ton-miles, 1954–1979

Year	First Quarter	Second Quarter	Third Quarter	Fourth Quarter	Standard Deviation
1954	100.115	99.999	99.613	100.618	0.369
1955	99.260	100.319	100.380	99.321	0.560
1956	100.589	99.994	96.620	102.755	2.200
1957	100.052	99.643	100.689	100.072	0.390
1958	99.699	98.165	100.391	100.419	0.973
1959	99.146	105.781	94.049	99.188	4.190
1960	101.117	100.321	99.273	100.621	0.752
1961	99.351	99.812	100.612	99.699	0.480
1962	100.252	99.964	99.749	100.300	0.233
1963	98.964	102.850	99.815	99.618	1.531
1964	101.214	99.381	99.911	100.137	0.778
1965	98.747	100.477	99.922	99.948	0.672
1966	100.124	99.613	100.601	99.667	0.399
1967	100.076	100.183	99.538	99.973	0.252
1968	100.524	99.685	100.086	99.875	0.315
1969	100.160	99.859	99.919	102.257	1.134
1970	98.546	99.908	100.365	99.834	0.755
1971	99.680	101.554	99.456	96.972	1.731
1972	102.655	100.521	99.512	100.055	1.375
1973	100.284	99.731	100.268	99.501	0.344
1974	100.744	99.400	100.713	99.636	0.624
1975	100.125	99.892	99.368	100.659	0.464
1976	99.959	99.788	100.614	99.246	0.498
1977	99.825	100.882	99.325	100.761	0.679
1978	99.576	99.205	100.754	100.941	0.753
1979	95.958	101.141	99.291	—	2.459

Source: Table 8-1 and Census X-11 adjustment program

which contains the standard deviation of the four irregular index values for each year. The standard deviation was quite small in 1954 and 1955, but it jumped significantly in 1956. Looking in the row for 1956, we see that the irregular force pulled tonnage downward by 3.4 percent (1.000 less 0.966) in the third quarter and upward by 2.8 percent in the fourth quarter. Similarly, the biggest irregular effect was felt in the second and third quarters of 1959, when the index fell from 105.78 to 94.05. Even if there is no interest in continuing the analysis in order to determine the exact nature of the historical forces causing these shocks to rail tonnage, it is necessary to be aware of their existence, since a regression model is not likely to yield accurate estimates for these quarters. To the extent that the model cannot capture these shifts, it will inflate the standard error of estimate and reduce the apparent statistical significance of the findings.[5]

[5]Observations can, of course, be suppressed from the data set used in the regression analysis, or dummy variables can be created. Both techniques, however, rely on a method of locating these unusual observations.

Having analyzed the seasonal and irregular forces in Tables 8-2 and 8-5, respectively, our next step is to study the cyclical sensitivity of rail ton-miles. The time series presented in Table 8-4 summarizes the quarter-to-quarter movements in rail ton-miles attributable solely to trend and cyclical influences. An important forecasting question is whether the railroad industry tends to lead, lag, or coincide with upper and lower turning points in the economy. If a consistent timing pattern can be found for railroad ton-miles relative to the upper turning point in GNP and industrial production, it may be possible to predict the timing of the next rail downturn with greater accuracy. Further, if this consistent pattern exists, it may lead to identification of those economic forces that explain the pattern of change exhibited by rail ton-miles.

Table 8-6 summarizes the cyclical timing pattern exhibited by the rail sector; it was derived by comparing the trend-cycle series for rail ton-miles

Table 8-6   Timing of rail ton-miles at cyclical turning points, 1954–1979

Reference Cycle Peak[a]	Reference Cycle Trough[a]	Rail High[a]	Rail Low[a]
(Month and Year)		(Year and Quarter)	
July 1953	May 1954	N.A.	1954:I
August 1957	April 1958	1956:I	1958:II
		1959:I	1959:III
April 1960	February 1961	1960:I	1961:I
		1966:III	1967:III
December 1969	November 1970	1969:IV	1971:IV
November 1973	March 1975	1974:I	1975:III
January 1980	August 1980	1977:III	1978:I
		1979:II	

Source: Tables 2-1 and 8-4
[a]Reference cycle peaks and troughs as dated by the NBER. The highs and lows for rail ton-miles are derived by examining the entries in Table 8-4; the specification is judgmental rather than statistical. Some turns were left out if they appeared minor or if they lasted only one quarter. The reference trough in August 1980 is tentative.

in Table 8-4 with the NBER's business-cycle reference points, outlined in Chapter 2, Table 2-1. As explained in the footnote to Table 8-6, we have simply recorded highs and lows for the quarterly ton-mile figures contained in the table. Since an elaborate statistical dating procedure was not used, we refer to railroad highs and lows rather than peaks and troughs.

No simple summary concerning rail timing patterns can be drawn from Table 8-6. In 1954, the first-quarter low in rail ton-miles preceded the economy's trough in May, the first-quarter rail high in 1956 was far in advance of the August 1957 peak, and the second-quarter low in 1958 was roughly coincident with the April 1958 trough. In 1959, however, the rail sector experienced an extra cycle when it reached a high in the first quarter and a low in the third quarter. Since these highs and lows are based on the observed values, and since no further statistical tests are carried out, it might be argued that the two-quarter decline in rail ton-miles in 1959 was an insignificant drop rather than an extra cycle. Lending credence to this hypothesis are the abnormal values of the irregular series index (Table 8-5) for the second and third quarters of 1959 (105.78 and 94.05, respectively). This extra cycle may reflect an inadequate statistical adjustment for irregular forces.

Continuing with the chronology, the rail sector reached a first-quarter high in 1960, slightly in advance of the April 1960 peak; similarly, the first-quarter low in 1961 was roughly coincident with the trough in February 1961. Again, we see the possibility of an extra rail cycle with a high in the third quarter of 1966 and a low in the third quarter of 1967. A quick check of Table 8-5 confirms that irregular forces are not a likely explanation. In this case, there is, in fact, more solid ground to argue for an extra cycle related to the credit crunch that was generated late in 1966 by the Federal Reserve's attempt to cool the war-induced inflation. Although the Federal Reserve aborted this policy before it produced an upper turning point in the economy, it did generate near-recession conditions in the housing and construction markets, two major rail freight customers. This extra-cycle hypothesis is, therefore, apt to bear up under closer scrutiny. Looking at the 1973–75 cycle, note that the rail high was almost coincident with the cyclical peak in 1973, whereas the low lagged the cyclical trough by two quarters. The economy's peak in January 1980 was, again, preceded by an extra rail cycle in 1977–78.

To summarize, the rail timing data in Table 8-6 suggests a lack of consistency in relation to cyclical turning points, although there is a tendency to lead or to coincide rather than to lag. In addition, the 1966–67 and 1977–79 periods illustrate the presence of extra cycles during those times when economic dislocation is concentrated in areas that are of particular importance to railroads (lumber, construction materials, and other major bulk-commodity segments).

DEVELOPING A RAIL REGRESSION MODEL

Having isolated and studied the various time series factors at work in the rail sector, we next formulate a causal model to explain the quarterly movements in rail ton-miles. (All subsequent references to rail ton-miles should be interpreted as referring to seasonally adjusted data.) The model developed here takes the form of a theoretical demand function for rail ton-miles, which can be transformed to an empirical demand function by the use of multiple regression. Since rail freight demand is a derived demand based on final demand in the economy, it is logical to isolate the major commodity groups transported by railroads and then use production indices for these commodities as measures of derived freight demand. Farm products, coal, raw materials, lumber products, automobiles, and merchandise (a conglomeration of consumer-related products) are consistently the major generators of freight tonnage and revenue.[6] Any or all of these commodity classifications might be placed in a general multiple-regression (demand) model of the form:[7]

$$Y_t = \beta_0 + \beta_1 X_{1t} + \beta_2 X_{2t} + \beta_3 X_{3t} + \ldots + \beta_k X_{kt} + \epsilon_t \qquad (8\text{-}1)$$

where:

$Y_t =$ the value in quarter t of rail ton-miles; seasonally adjusted; billions

$X_{kt} =$ the value of the kth independent variable in quarter t

$\epsilon_t =$ the error term in quarter t; $E(\epsilon_t) = 0$; $V(\epsilon_t) = \sigma^2$

A complete listing of all factors affecting rail ton-miles would fill a book. Thus, we must develop a model that is a simplification of reality. Pragmatically, empirical tests of alternative demand formulations are necessary in order to isolate those independent variables that make sense theoretically and are statistically significant predictors of rail demand. There is, in most cases, no *a priori* method that will allow you to guess in advance which independent variables will work best as predictors. For example, even though lumber is one of the major commodities transported by the rail sector, it did not turn out to be a statistically significant determinant of quarterly rail ton-miles in any of the alternative versions that were run. To completely explain the reasons for its insignificance would require an in-depth study of both the lumber and rail sectors. Even a cursory examination of the lumber industry, however, reveals that there has been a structural shift in regional patterns, with production increasingly moving from the traditional western regions to the Southeast.[8] In addition, regional lumber demand has also shifted, owing to demographic movements. The net result is that railroads have experienced an increasing loss of traffic to intermodal competitors such as trucks. Because rail lumber traffic has not grown as rapidly as national lumber production, it is hard to statistically link shifts in rail demand to movements in lumber production.

Table 8-7 contains a statistical summary of an initial rail demand model for quarterly ton-miles of freight. Five independent variables have been chosen. After we discuss the independent variables and the general results, a diagnosis of the model's problems will be presented. The last three independent variables— COAL, CHEM, and STEEL—are seasonally adjusted FRB production indices for coal mining (FRB 12), chemicals and products (FRB 28), and basic steel and mill products (FRB 331), respectively. Steel production is a proxy for raw materials such as iron ore, semifinished steel products such as sheet steel, and final products such as automobiles and appliances. The second variable, FARMIN, measures farm proprietors' income (billions of dollars, seasonally

[6]For detailed railroad commodity tonnage figures, see *Moody's Transportation Manual*.

[7]This is one of many possible mathematical formulations. Other nonlinear versions (for example: $y = ax^b$) can be transformed into a linear relationship.

[8]This is easily seen in the regional commodity statistics in *Moody's Transportation Manual*.

Table 8-7 Model 1 : multiple regression model for quarterly ton-miles, 1954–1979 (Ordinary least squares)

Quarterly (1954:1 to 1979:3)   103 Observations
Dependent Variable: QTMFRT (Quarterly revenue ton-miles, billions, seasonally adjusted)

Coefficient	Std. Error	t_e	Independent Variable	
197.560	20.33	9.719	CONSTANT	
−115.893	18.44	−6.285	GNP RATIO	(ratio of potential to actual GNP, both in 1972 $)
0.290368	0.1215	2.390	FARMIN	(farm proprietors' income, billions, seasonally adjusted)
25.0140	5.151	4.856	COAL	(production index, coal mining, seasonally adjusted)
28.6462	2.239	12.80	CHEM	(production index, chemicals and products, seasonally adjusted)
38.1200	4.452	8.562	STEEL	(production index, basic steel and mill products, seasonally adjusted)

R-Bar Squared: 0.9672
Durbin-Watson Statistic: 0.9444
Standard Error of the Regression: 4.730   Normalized: 0.02691 (2.69% error)

	Partial Correlation	Mean	Standard Deviation	Elasticity at Mean
GNP RATIO	−0.537945	1.01055	0.0319576	−0.666340
FARMIN	0.235868	15.8553	6.61903	0.0261940
COAL	0.442247	0.963608	0.185838	0.137139
CHEM	0.792452	1.03599	0.514735	0.168849
STEEL	0.656080	0.968871	0.179635	0.210134

Source: Model developed to explain ton-mile fluctuations in Table 8-3

adjusted); it is included in the model to capture the effect of farm-related demand. Unfortunately, there are no readily available production indices for the agricultural sector that work as well as the FRB's production indices for manufacturing and mining.

The first variable, GNP RATIO, measures the ratio of full-employment GNP in 1972 dollars to actual GNP in 1972 dollars. In this case, the variable was specifically formulated to reflect detailed knowledge of the freight transportation industry. Historical analysis of the freight transportation sector revealed that the farther the economy moves from full employment, the greater is the traffic lost by the rail sector to the trucking industry. In essence, this is due to the much greater flexibility of the trucking sector as compared to the more regulation-constrained railroad industry. Conversely, as the economy approaches full employment, there is less need for the trucking sector to compete so intensively for rail business. At full employment, GNP RATIO equals 1. As the economy moves into a recession, the ratio moves upward and the rail sector loses business. As a result, we would expect to get a negative sign for this ratio variable.

With the use of t-statistic values of ± 2 as the standard for comparison with the actual t_e values, all the independent variables in Table 8-7 are statistically significant.[9] The $\bar{R}^2$ of 0.9672 means that 96.7 percent of the variation in rail ton-miles was explained by the five independent variables. The standard error of the regression (standard error of estimate) was 4.73, indicating that the average quarterly error using this demand equation over the 103 quarters from 1954 to the third quarter of 1979 was 4.73 billion ton-miles. When this error is normalized relative to the actual value of each quarter, it produces an average quarterly error of 2.69 percent.

The most disturbing statistic in Table 8-7 is the reported Durbin-Watson (DW) statistic of 0.9444. As explained in Chapter 6, we assume in constructing the model that the error in the present quarter (ϵ_t) is not correlated with the error in the preceding quarter (ϵ_{t-1}). In many time-series models, however, this assumption is violated, and the Durbin-Watson statistic provides a quick method of checking for autocorrelation of the error terms. If there is no autocorrelation present, the DW statistic should take a value near 2; positive correlation will yield a value less than 2, and negative correlation a value of more than 2. If the autocorrelation parameter, p, is greater than zero, the adjacent error terms will be similar in value, their difference will be small, and the DW statistic will be low. Thus, the question in the rail-ton-mile example is whether a DW of 0.944 is so low that we must conclude that there is positive autocorrelation. The upper and lower test bounds can be found in Appendix F once you have specified the sample size (n), the level of significance, and the number of independent variables in the regression model. In the quarterly rail

---

[9] With a large sample size, this rule of thumb for the t values is equivalent to a confidence level of approximately 95 percent.

model outlined in Table 8-7, $n = 103$ and there are five independent variables. If we use a level of significance of .025 and $n = 100$, we get:[10]

$$d_u = 1.72$$
$$d_l = 1.51$$

Since DW $= 0.944$, it is less than d_l, and we can conclude that there is positive autocorrelation; the next step is to correct the problem.

CORRECTING THE RAIL-TON-MILE MODEL FOR AUTOCORRELATION

Initial review of the quarterly ton-mile model in Table 8-7 raised the possibility of autocorrelation, and the subsequent test confirmed the presence of positive serial correlation. As previously noted, autocorrelation gives rise to the following complications:[11]

1. The standard errors of the regression coefficients are likely to be substantially below the true standard deviations of the estimated regression coefficients.
2. The t and F tests and interval estimates can no longer be correctly carried out.
3. Although the least-squares coefficients are still unbiased estimators, they are no longer minimum-variance estimators and they may be inefficient.
4. The mean squared error may substantially underestimate the variance of the error terms.

Although the model in Table 8-7 has a high $\bar{R}^2$, the presence of autocorrelation casts doubt on the statistical significance of the independent variables, since underestimates for the standard errors of the regression coefficients will produce actual t_e values that are inflated.

Given the conclusion that the autocorrelation parameter is greater than zero for the model in Table 8-7, either an iterative approach or a first-differences approach may be utilized to transform the dependent and independent variables.[12] Table 8-8 contains the results of this iterative procedure applied to the same set of five independent variables specified in Table 8-7. The statistical estimate of ρ, $r_t = 0.806197$, does signify a high degree of autocorrelation.

As explained earlier, one consequence of autocorrelation is the likely inflation of the t_e statistic for each regression coefficient. A comparison of the

[10]Since the table does not have upper and lower limits for $n = 103$, they have been approximated by using $n = 100$. It can be seen from Appendix F however, that as n increases, d_l is increasing. Thus, if the actual DW statistic is below d_l for $n = 100$, this would also be true for $n = 103$.

[11]For a more detailed discussion of autocorrelation, see Robert S. Pindyck and Daniel Rubinfeld, *Econometric Models and Economic Forecasts* (New York: McGraw-Hill, 1976), pp. 108–13.

[12]The techniques of variable transformation are discussed in John Neter and William Wasserman, *Applied Linear Statistical Models* (Homewood, Ill.: Richard D. Irwin, 1974), pp. 123–30.

Table 8-8 Model 2: revised version of Model 1, 1954–1979
(Ordinary least squares with first-order autocorrelation correction)

Quarterly (1954:1 to 1979:3)   103 Observations
Dependent Variable: QTMFRT

Coefficient	Std. Error	t_e	Independent Variable
189.401	34.35	5.515	CONSTANT
−88.3830	32.71	−2.702	GNP RATIO[a]
−0.00472005	0.1720	−0.02744	FARMIN[a]
10.9991	3.260	3.374	COAL[a]
38.7744	3.664	10.58	CHEM[a]
25.6241	3.083	8.311	STEEL[a]
0.806197	0.05946	13.56	RHO (estimate of ρ)

R-Bar Squared: 0.9831
Durbin-Watson Statistic: 2.1889
Standard Error of the Regression: 3.392   Normalized: 0.01930

[a]For variable definitions, see Table 8-7.

t_e statistics in Table 8-7 with those yielded by the first-order autocorrelation correction procedure in Table 8-8 reveals that the initial model did exaggerate the statistical significance of the regression coefficients. In fact, the second independent variable, farm proprietors' income (FARMIN), drops from a t_e value of 2.390 in Table 8-7 to a statistically insignificant level of −0.02744 in Table 8-8. Had we kept the original model in Table 8-7 and ignored the presence of autocorrelation, we would have unknowingly included an independent variable that was not a statistically significant determinant of quarterly rail ton-miles. This does not mean that our theory was invalid. Rather, we have not been able to accurately measure the effect of grain shipments on rail ton-miles.

The logical extension of the findings in Table 8-8 is to drop FARMIN as an explanatory variable and reestimate the multiple-regression relationship using the four remaining variables. The model in Table 8-9, called the "final model," embodies both a first-order autocorrelation correction and the four independent variables previously analyzed. Of the three remaining production indices, the chemicals index (CHEM) yields the biggest effect on rail ton-miles per unit change in the index: A rise from, say, 1.15 to 1.25 in CHEM (a change of one-tenth of a unit) produces, all other variables held constant, a jump in seasonally adjusted quarterly rail ton-miles of 3.87 billion (38.7 times 0.1).

The standard error of the regression and $\bar{R}^2$ in Table 8-9 provide overall or average measures of accuracy for the 103 quarterly observations encompassed by the model, but from a forecaster's perspective, they need to be augmented by quarter-to-quarter and annual error analyses. Table 8-10 contains absolute and percentage error terms generated by the model on an annual basis, and Table 8-11 provides comparable data on a quarterly basis. Should we describe this model as satisfactory or unsatisfactory? The answer is dependent upon

Table 8-9 Final model, quarterly ton-miles, 1954–1979
(Ordinary least squares with first-order autocorrelation correction)[a]

Quarterly (1954:1 to 1979:3) 103 Observations
Dependent Variable: QTMFRT

Coefficient	Std. Error	t_e	Independent Variable
189.438	33.91	5.586	CONSTANT
−88.4512	32.39	−2.731	GNP RATIO
11.0068	3.241	3.396	COAL
38.7194	3.135	12.35	CHEM
25.6306	3.067	8.358	STEEL
0.805372	0.05909	13.63	RHO (estimate of ρ)

R-Bar Squared: 0.9833
Durbin-Watson Statistic: 2.1888
Standard Error of the Regression: 3.374   Normalized: 0.01920

	Partial Correlation	Mean	Standard Deviation	Elasticity at Mean
GNP RATIO	−0.267187	1.01055	0.0319576	−0.508558
COAL	0.325955	0.963608	0.185838	0.0603449
CHEM	0.781880	1.03599	0.514735	0.228224
STEEL	0.647023	0.968871	0.179635	0.141287

[a]See Chapter 6 for a discussion of first-order autocorrelation correction techniques.

both the accuracy of the model and the needs of the forecast user. If the quarterly forecasts produced by the model in Table 8-9 are to be used for extremely sensitive facilities planning by a particular railroad, it is likely that this error analysis would have to be augmented by comparable figures from a series of satellite models that would disaggregate total ton-miles into commodity-related categories. The projections from the final model might be more than satisfactory, however, for a locomotive builder concerned with the yearly demand for railroad ton-miles relative to the potential supply of ton-miles that could be generated by the existing stock of locomotives owned by the railroad sector. Similarly, a financial analyst specializing in the transportation sector might find the level of quarterly forecast error in Table 8-11 to be very satisfactory. In other words, a given error pattern might be acceptable or unacceptable, depending on the actual requirements of the user.[13]

Apart from the issue of user needs, the other dimension of acceptability is the model's forecasting accuracy. In Table 8-10, the actual and estimated values of quarterly ton-miles have been annualized, with the annual percentage errors shown in the last column. The maximum absolute percentage error is

[13]That is, one user's error tolerance might be 5 percent on an annual basis, and another's might be 8 percent for a monthly system of projections.

Table 8-10 Accuracy of the final rail-ton-mile model

| Year | Billions of Ton-Miles | | | Percentage Error |
	Actual	Estimated	Error	
1954	549.2	548.3	− 0.9	−0.2%
1955	623.0	614.7	− 8.3	−1.4
1956	646.9^H	637.8^H	− 9.1	−1.4
1957	618.3	623.5	5.2	0.8
1958	551.5^L	555.5^L	4.0	0.7
1959	575.6^H	579.5^H	3.9	0.7
1960	572.2	578.9	6.7	1.2
1961	563.3^L	570.1^L	6.8	1.2
1962	592.7	594.1	1.4	0.2
1963	620.9	620.9	− 0.2	−0.0
1964	659.0	660.7	1.7	0.3
1965	698.3	691.4	− 6.9	−1.0
1966	740.1^H	740.4^H	0.3	0.0
1967	718.7^L	722.3^L	3.6	−0.5
1968	744.9	738.4	− 6.5	−0.9
1969	767.8^H	764.3^H	− 3.5	−0.5
1970	763.5	758.9	− 4.6	−0.6
1971	739.4^L	744.6^L	5.2	0.7
1972	778.4	777.4	− 1.0	0.1
1973	851.0	837.4	−13.6	−1.6
1974	855.1^H	848.2^H	− 6.9	−0.8
1975	755.1^L	759.2^L	4.1	0.5
1976	793.0	800.3	7.3	0.9
1977	825.5	828.3	2.8	0.3
1978	829.5	835.8	6.3	0.8
1979	668.3^a	669.0	0.7	0.1
Average absolute error			4.7	0.7%

Source: See final model in Table 8-9. Quarterly estimates were aggregated to get annual projections. Average error ignores sign. H and L denote highs and lows, respectively.
[a]Only three quarters were available in 1979.

1.6 percent, with an average absolute error of 0.7 percent. Equally impressive is the parallel pattern of actual versus forecasted highs (H) and lows (L) for annual ton-miles in Table 8-10. The model caught every turn in annual ton-miles and was also quite close on the absolute change in ton-miles experienced at each of the rail turning points.

A more critical test of the model's reliability can be carried out in Table 8-11 by examining the quarterly turning points in rail ton-miles. A complete diagnosis would require looking at all the 103 quarterly observations, but several turning points are suggestive of the model's performance. For example, look at the actual and estimated ton-mile figures in Table 8-11 over the span from the fourth quarter of 1969 to the first quarter of 1972. The rail high in the fourth quarter of 1969 was followed by a six-quarter plateau ending in the

Table 8-11 Actual vs. estimated quarterly rail
ton-miles (Seasonally adjusted)

| | Billions of Ton-Miles | | Percent |
Quarter	Actual	Estimated	Error
1954:1	135.2	137.0	1.322%
1954:2	135.1	133.9	−0.859
1954:3	136.7	137.9	0.839
1954:4	142.0	139.5	−1.742
1955:1	145.7	146.9	0.822
1955:2	154.5	150.9	−2.384
1955:3	160.4	157.7	−1.670
1955:4	161.7	159.2	−1.561
1956:1	165.4	159.4	−3.644
1956:2	163.2	162.9	−0.172
1956:3	154.9	153.9	−0.648
1956:4	163.8	161.6	−1.299
1957:1	159.2	161.1	1.222
1957:2	157.8	155.7	−1.304
1957:3	155.8	158.9	1.969
1957:4	145.9	147.8	1.334
1958:1	135.2	136.5	0.965
1958:2	130.7	134.6	2.940
1958:3	139.6	139.5	−0.122
1958:4	146.0	144.9	−0.778
1959:1	145.8	149.5	2.514
1959:2	153.4	153.4	−0.017
1959:3	133.9	132.9	−0.734
1959:4	142.7	143.7	0.677
1960:1	149.6	153.7	2.703
1960:2	147.1	144.1	−2.095
1960:3	139.6	144.8	3.687
1960:4	136.4	136.3	−0.102
1961:1	133.3	135.5	1.650
1961:2	137.6	140.4	2.031
1961:3	144.9	145.5	0.414
1961:4	147.4	148.7	0.878
1962:1	149.1	149.6	0.339
1962:2	148.0	146.7	−0.911
1962:3	147.1	149.0	1.307
1962:4	148.6	148.8	0.152
1963:1	149.0	151.7	1.831
1963:2	157.8	155.5	−1.432
1963:3	155.5	156.1	0.377
1963:4	158.3	157.4	−0.546
1964:1	163.6	161.1	−1.557
1964:2	161.8	165.6	2.337
1964:3	164.9	165.5	0.308
1964:4	168.9	168.5	−0.202
1965:1	167.4	171.9	2.633

Table 8-11 (continued)

| Quarter | Billions of Ton-Miles | | Percent Error |
	Actual	Estimated	
1965:2	173.8	169.6	−2.401%
1965:3	177.1	175.6	−0.847
1965:4	180.0	174.3	−3.168
1966:1	183.0	183.3	0.164
1966:2	185.0	182.9	−1.120
1966:3	188.0	187.3	−0.391
1966:4	184.5	186.9	1.294
1967:1	181.8	180.5	−0.668
1967:2	179.0	178.8	−0.104
1967:3	177.0	181.3	2.452
1967:4	181.3	181.7	0.187
1968:1	186.3	182.3	−2.138
1968:2	185.7	187.3	0.859
1968:3	186.3	183.7	−1.377
1968:4	187.0	185.1	−1.033
1969:1	188.9	190.7	0.923
1969:2	189.9	189.5	−0.222
1969:3	192.0	191.5	−0.270
1969:4	197.1	192.6	−2.312
1970:1	188.8	190.6	0.955
1970:2	191.4	187.9	−1.851
1970:3	192.9	191.4	−0.778
1970:4	190.5	189.0	−0.767
1971:1	189.1	190.5	−0.764
1971:2	190.6	189.7	0.762
1971:3	182.8	184.1	−0.453
1971:4	176.8	180.3	0.679
1972:1	191.2	188.1	2.003
1972:2	191.8	195.0	−1.598
1972:3	194.1	195.1	1.707
1972:4	201.1	199.2	0.515
1973:1	207.9	202.7	−0.945
1973:2	210.9	207.3	−2.488
1973:3	215.0	212.9	−1.733
1973:4	216.8	214.5	−0.954
1974:1	221.2	211.5	−1.023
1974:2	217.2	217.7	−4.387
1974:3	214.1	216.4	0.220
1974:4	202.0	202.6	1.085
1975:1	191.9	191.3	0.305
1975:2	184.6	188.1	−0.321
1975:3	184.5	189.3	1.873
1975:4	193.3	190.5	2.596
1976:1	196.9	199.9	−1.462
1976:2	198.4	199.7	1.514
1976:3	199.8	200.2	0.622

Table 8-11   (continued)

Quarter	Billions of Ton-Miles		Percent Error
	Actual	Estimated	
1976:4	197.1	200.5	0.221%
1977:1	203.2	200.2	1.709
1977:2	210.5	209.2	−0.629
1977:3	206.7	211.5	2.289
1977:4	204.3	207.4	1.488
1978:1	196.7	199.6	1.492
1978:2	198.0	210.6	6.334
1978:3	211.8	205.1	−3.159
1978:4	222.3	220.5	−0.813
1979:1	217.1	219.1	0.955
1979:2	230.4	218.9	−4.993
1979:3	225.1	231.0	2.646

Source: See final model in Table 8-9.

second quarter of 1971, a sharp drop in the third quarter, and a vigorous rebound in the first quarter of 1972. The estimated values parallel this pattern quite closely. Similarly, the model did reasonably well over the period from the last quarter of 1973 to the second quarter of 1975, a period of extreme volatility in the economy. The tremendous uncertainty in the economy during 1979 is captured by the model's erratic performance for the last four quarters of the data in Table 8-11, the period just before the peak in January 1980.

Again, the question is whether this model is accurate enough. Although no model is ever complete, this model appears to have captured the basic essence of the railroad's cyclical profile. The acceptability of the model is never known until the user specifies his needed standard of accuracy. Goodness of fit to historical data, however, does not guarantee an accurate forecast.

PREPARATION OF A FORECAST FOR RAIL TON-MILES

Once we have accepted the forecasting reliability of the model in Table 8-9, we can proceed to prepare forecasts for future periods. Actual preparation of a rail forecast necessitates quarterly projections for each of the independent variables. The choice is either to personally prepare the scenarios for the independent variables or to purchase the information from a commercial forecast vendor. In this situation, the forecast was based on output from a large-scale econometric model. The quarterly forecast for rail ton-miles through 1990 is presented in Table 8-12; Table 8-13 contains an annual summary for both ton-miles and the independent variables.

Following the actual ton-mile peak in the second quarter of 1979, the

Table 8-12 Forecast of rail ton-miles, 1979–1990
(Billions, seasonally adjusted)

	First Quarter	Second Quarter	Third Quarter	Fourth Quarter	Total
1979	217.1	230.4	225.1	221.2	893.8
1980	216.7	212.1	209.7	210.2	848.8
1981	213.5	216.5	219.7	222.9	872.6
1982	225.9	228.4	230.6	232.3	917.2
1983	234.8	235.8	234.5	234.8	939.9
1984	236.3	237.1	238.3	240.2	951.9
1985	243.1	246.7	250.5	254.2	994.5
1986	258.4	261.5	262.8	265.3	1,048.1
1987	268.7	271.1	272.8	273.9	1,086.5
1988	274.7	274.8	274.6	274.4	1,098.5
1989	275.2	276.2	277.1	279.1	1,107.6
1990	282.1	284.8	287.5	290.1	1,144.4

Source: Based on model in Table 8-9 and forecast assumptions in Table 8-13

Table 8-13 Annual forecast of rail ton-miles and assumed values of independent variables

	Ton-Miles (Billions)	COAL	CHEM	STEEL	GNP RATIO
1979	893.777	1.337	2.099	1.143	1.020
1980	848.752	1.247	2.025	1.003	1.070
1981	872.595	1.261	2.129	1.044	1.065
1982	917.211	1.282	2.319	1.131	1.051
1983	939.942	1.290	2.441	1.162	1.051
1984	951.907	1.296	2.528	1.162	1.056
1985	994.453	1.315	2.717	1.244	1.044
1986	1,048.070	1.346	2.948	1.342	1.026
1987	1,086.485	1.374	3.127	1.390	1.013
1988	1,098.484	1.384	3.210	1.383	1.015
1989	1,107.589	1.390	3.277	1.381	1.019
1990	1,144.437	1.409	3.451	1.453	1.014

Source: Rail forecast generated using the model in Table 8-9 and scenario above for independent variables. See Table 8-7 for variable definitions.

forecast in Table 8-12 calls for rail ton-miles to bottom out at 209.7 billion in the third quarter of 1980 and move onto a trend path that reaches 290.1 billion ton-miles by the fourth quarter of 1990. Although it is not likely that the railroads will actually move through the 1980s without a downturn, the current state of forecasting technology precludes accurate projections of cyclical peaks and troughs beyond a two- to three-year time horizon. The relative importance of unforeseeable exogenous shocks swamps the more predictable trend, cyclical, and seasonal influences as the time horizon is extended beyond two years. The simulation in Table 8-12 splices together a cyclical outlook for the rail sector through mid-1982, with a long-term trend projection for the remainder of the decade. If the rail model accurately transmits the effect of the economy on the rail sector, and if the forecast assumptions for the independent variables are correct, then the scenario envisioned for the rail industry in Table 8-12 is one of cyclical decline from mid-1979 to late 1980, followed by steady growth throughout the remainder of the decade.

This rail outlook is, of course, a statistical reflection of the divergent paths followed by the independent variables in Table 8-13. In particular, look at the values taken by GNP RATIO (the ratio of potential to actual constant-dollar GNP) over the forecast period. A value of 1 for this ratio indicates that actual GNP equals potential GNP—the economy is at full employment. The greater the ratio, the farther the economy is falling below its potential output. Starting from a 1980 index value of 1.07, the ratio falls to a two-year plateau of 1.051 in 1982–83, rises slightly in 1984, descends steadily through 1987, rises marginally in 1988 and 1989, and reaches 1.014 in 1990—a level indicating that potential GNP is only 1.4 percent above the actual GNP. Even though this is a trend forecast for the remainder of the decade, it should not be viewed as a simple-minded, straight-line extrapolation of economic growth off the 1980 base. Hidden behind the projections for the independent variables is a complex set of assumptions for growth in the labor supply, output per worker, and government fiscal and monetary policy, as well as numerous other exogenous assumptions that must be made before generating a macroeconometric forecast.

Between 1979 and 1985 (a period that includes a forecasted rail recession), the projections in Table 8-12 yield a compound growth rate for ton-miles of only 1.8 percent, but from 1982 to 1985, the rate jumps to 2.7 percent. For the entire span between 1979 and 1990, the compound rail growth rate is 2.3 percent, and for the post-recession years of 1982–90, the rate is 2.8 percent.

CAPITAL PLANNING FOR A LOCOMOTIVE BUILDER

A locomotive builder analyzing the data in Table 8-12 in the spring of 1980 with respect to future capacity needs might have been equally interested in the near-term recession and the ton-mile growth rate of 2.8 percent over the 1982–90 span. Should, for example, the locomotive supplier make a strategic decision to build past the recession by placing additional orders for new plant and equipment in the face of a mild downturn in rail ton-miles? The answer to this question depends partially on the behavior of strategic planners in the rail industry. If railroads collectively made plans for sharp retrenchment in capital expenditures in the face of a recession, locomotive builders would be hard-pressed to take the long view. Even here, a forecaster can assist decision makers by analyzing the cyclical sensitivity of locomotive orders in past recessions. A consistent pattern of cyclical moderation in locomotive orders in the midst of recession might raise the decision maker's subjective probability assessment of a similar occurrence in the next recession. Although rail ton-miles of freight are the prime determinant of locomotive demand, discretionary actions by rail management can generate alternative paths for locomotive orders in response to a near-term decline in the railroads' economic fortunes. Consider the following hypothetical outcomes:

1. Previous plans to augment capacity in late 1981 are retained, locomotive demand drops sharply, and locomotive builders experience significant excess capacity through 1985.
2. Previous plans to augment capacity are retained, locomotive demand grows at the historical trend rate, and capacity is adequate and efficiently used through 1985.
3. Previous capacity augmentation plans are scrapped, additional capacity is not forthcoming until 1984, locomotive demand falls sharply, and existing capacity is adequate to handle orders through 1984.
4. Previous plans are scrapped, the new target data for capacity additions is 1984, locomotive demand grows at the trend rate, and the locomotive industry experiences massive shortages owing to inadequate capacity.

Obviously, other demand-supply combinations are possible, but the capital planning process for the locomotive industry will still be based on the forecaster's projections. On top of these estimates are strategic assessments by management personnel in the locomotive sector and a myriad of financial projections (which also include forecasts of variables such as interest rates) for cash flow and net income. The end product of the demand analysis and capital planning is, therefore, a set of decision options—add capacity now or in five years—paired with profitability projections and subjective probability assessments of likely outcomes. It is not the job of the forecaster to make the final decision concerning massive capital expenditures, but it is his or her responsibility to articulate clearly the critical assumptions underpinning the numerical projections so that management is aware of the risks attending each outlook. Just how easily exogenous influences can overwhelm a forecast is demonstrated in the next section, on the trailer industry.

EXOGENOUS SAFETY SHOCKS: FORECASTING IN THE TRAILER SECTOR

Table 8-14 provides a historical summary for the years from 1960 to 1975 for retail sales of heavy-duty trucks and shipments of truck trailers.[14] Now that we

[14]Material in this section is based on H. Wade German and Larry C. Peppers, "Regulatory Spillovers in the Economy: An Analysis of the Trucking Industry," *Transportation Journal*, Winter 1977, pp. 65–74.

have investigated postwar cycles in Chapter 2 and the Great Recession of 1974–75 in Chapter 3, the behavior of annual truck sales and trailer shipments in Table 8-14 may not seem out of line with the cyclical experiences of other

Table 8-14 Retail sales of heavy-duty trucks and shipments of truck trailers, 1960–1975 (Thousands of units)

	Annual Truck Sales	Annual Trailer Shipments			Quarterly[a] Truck Sales	Quarterly[a] Trailer Shipments
1960	30.2	59.0	1973:	I	37.6	39.3
1961	30.2	51.8		II	39.2	41.9
1962	40.6	67.9		III	37.6	38.8
1963	50.1	73.8		IV	39.8	44.6
1964	59.3	84.6			154.2	164.6
1965	68.6	101.2	1974:	I	39.4	52.0
1966	83.8	110.7		II	39.3	53.1
1967	72.3	92.7		III	37.4	53.6
1968	79.9	109.8		IV	30.9	49.2
1969	99.0	135.9			147.0	207.9
1970	91.1	103.9	1975:	I	24.9	21.5
1971	98.7	102.1		II	20.2	20.2
1972	126.2	143.3		III	18.9	18.0
1973	154.6	164.6		IV	19.3	18.6
1974	147.5	207.9			83.3	78.3
1975	83.1	78.3				

[a]Seasonally adjusted.
Source: U.S. Department of Commerce, *Current Industrial Reports* and *Report M 37L*; Truck Trailers and Motor Vehicle Manufacturers Association, *FS20 Report*.

capital-goods suppliers. In particular, look at the data for annual trailer shipments. Following the recession in 1960–61, trailer shipments bottomed out in 1961 at 51.8 thousand units, grew steadily to a peak of 110.7 thousand units in 1966, fell to 92.7 thousand following the mini–credit crunch of late 1966, peaked again in 1969 owing to the 1970–71 recession, soared to a postwar high of 207.9 thousand units in 1974, and plummeted to 78.3 thousand in 1975. Although the annual data for truck sales displayed less cyclical volatility than did trailer shipments, truck sales are clearly sensitive to turning points in the economy.

The first inkling of an exogenous disturbance can be seen in the annual trailer figures for 1973 to 1975. Even though the economy peaked in late 1973 and fell sharply during 1974, trailer shipments grew by over 25 percent in 1974 and declined by over 60 percent in 1975. Evidence supporting the hypothesis of an exogenous shock can be gleaned from the quarterly-shipments data for trailers in the last column of Table 8-14. On a seasonally adjusted quarterly basis, trailer shipments fell from 49.2 thousand in the last quarter of 1974 to 21.5 thousand units in the first quarter of 1975. True, cyclical declines can be sharp, but this drop is so abrupt that it should immediately arouse any forecaster's suspicions. This is especially so in the light of the sustained surge in 1974 trailer shipments, which took place in an economy experiencing deteriorating growth and rising interest rates.

HISTORICAL BACKGROUND: TRUCK SAFETY GUIDELINES

Was the meteoric growth in 1974 trailer shipments and the ensuing collapse in 1975 forecastable? Before answering this question directly, consider the extenuating circumstances that helped to shape demand for truck trailers in 1974 and 1975. Effective January 1, 1975, the National Highway Traffic Safety Administration (NHTSA), through the imposition of Federal Motor Vehicle Safety Standard Number 121 (SS 121), required that an antilock, antiskid air-breaking system be installed on all new heavy-duty trucks, tractors, and truck trailers in order to prevent "jackknifing" by semitrailers. The direct cost in 1975 of implementing SS 121 was estimated by the American Trucking Association (ATA) as $2,800 for a typical five-axle tractor-trailer combination. This safety innovation was not well received by the trucking industry. In addition to obvious fuel diseconomies because of increased weight, it was argued that the SS 121 system complicated maintenance, increased downtime, and involved expensive replacement parts.[15] More fundamentally, representatives of the trucking industry doubted the efficacy of SS 121 and felt that it had not been proved an effective safety system under actual operating conditions.[16] Summarizing the industry position, the first vice-chairman of the American Trucking Association informed the House Consumer Protection and Finance Subcommittee that SS 121 and subsequent modifications resulted in "unbelievable instability in the [trucking] industry costing millions of dollars."[17]

FORECAST EVALUATION OF EXOGENOUS SHOCKS

The SS 121 safety guidelines were issued by NHTSA late in 1973. How could (should) a forecaster in the trucking sector have reacted to this exogenous change in the economic environment? Complicating the analysis of SS 121's impact was the breadth of the trucking industry. A safety innovation of this type could conceivably affect a wide-ranging group of participants in the economy—shippers, motor carriers, truck producers, trailer manufacturers,

[15]Unpublished information provided by the Engineering Department, American Trucking Association.

[16]American Trucking Association, *Truck Line*, No. 30, March 22, 1976, p. 1.

[17]Ibid., p. 2.

consumers, and intermodal freight competitors such as railroads. On the one hand, it might logically have been argued that the relatively modest cost of the SS 121 system ($2,800 per tractor-trailer unit) would easily be passed from equipment manufacturer to common carrier to consumer with minor competitive distortions in truck freight rates; the perceived superiority of truck service would easily offset the increase in truck rates. Reinforcing this analytical prediction would have been the surge in postwar freight ton-miles hauled by trucks. While rail ton-miles were growing from 596.9 billion in 1950 to 857.6 billion in 1973, truck ton-miles leaped from 172.9 billion to 505.0 billion in the same time span.[18] This strong secular surge in truck freight demand would, again, have reinforced a forecaster's conclusion, late in 1973, that the SS 121 system would have a negligible effect on the demand for truck freight. The issue, however, was whether this would also mean a negligible effect on the demand for the trucks and truck-trailers needed to haul freight.

We have already highlighted the bizarre pattern for trailer shipments in Table 8-14; the data in Table 8-15 further disaggregate trailer shipments by model type and illustrate quite vividly the dramatic result of SS 121. Although all sectors of the trailer industry were battered during 1975, those manufacturers that concentrated on the production of closed-top trailers, for example, found that their shipments fell by a rather phenomenal 72 percent between 1974 and 1975. Similarly, flat-bed-trailer shipments dropped by 53 percent over the same period.

Subsequent events have borne out the assessment that truck freight demand would be impervious to SS 121; however, the data in Tables 8-14 and

Table 8-15   Industry trailer shipments by model type
(Thousands of units)

	1960	1970	1973	1974	1975
Closed top	25.0	51.2	77.7	99.3	28.0
Insulated	5.5	11.7	15.0	16.8	9.5
Drop frame	1.8	3.4	5.6	4.2	1.3
Livestock	0.5	1.3	2.2	3.0	1.6
Open top	3.8	3.7	6.4	7.8	3.1
Tank	4.5	4.5	6.2	6.9	4.9
Bulkers	1.1	1.6	1.4	1.6	1.1
Pole	1.0	1.1	2.1	1.7	1.1
Flat	8.3	14.9	30.0	38.1	16.3
Low bed	2.1	3.5	5.0	5.2	3.6
Dump	2.3	4.3	6.0	7.9	4.1
Other	3.0	2.7	6.9	15.5	3.7
Total	59.0	103.9	164.4	207.9	78.3

Source: See Table 8-14.

[18] *Moody's Transportation Manual,* 1979.

8-15 certainly raise the possibility that SS 121 had a major demand-destabilizing influence in the trailer sector during 1974 and 1975. Consider the plight of a forecaster late in 1973 attempting to predict trailer shipments in 1974 and 1975. Given back-to-back years in 1972–73 of record industry shipments (see Table 8-14), the uncertainty concerning both diesel-fuel prices and availability following the Arab oil embargo, macroeconomic forecasts calling for a slow-down in the economy in 1974, and the historical instability of the capital-goods sector, a forecaster could have reasonably and persuasively projected that shipments of trailers would decline in 1974. There is little reason to believe, and certainly no published analyses have been put forth, that transportation analysts correctly foresaw the psychological reaction of motor carriers to the imposition of SS 121 by NHTSA.

Although no forecasters accurately predicted late in 1973 the boom-bust cycle that would follow in the trailer industry, this does not mean that the forecaster's role was one of passively recording actual results. On the contrary, as was illustrated in Chapter 3 for the macroeconomic forecasts carried out during the Great Recession, economic projections must be continually reassessed, modified, and reinterpreted for top management. If a forecast model yields an inaccurate projection for one month or quarter, the obvious task is to assess the source of the error and its implications for the next period. Given the advantage of historical insight, we can use a statistical forecasting model to carry out an *ex post* evaluation of SS 121 and its effect on trailer manufacturers.

QUANTIFYING SS 121'S EFFECT ON TRAILER DEMAND

A critical question facing trailer forecasters in 1973 was whether a structural change had occurred in the trailer market. Once a structural change has taken place, the multiple regression coefficients in an estimated demand function no longer capture current behavior; rather, they measure the relationship that used to exist. As soon as buyers of truck trailers became cognizant of the impending deadline for trailer safety equipment and reacted negatively to it, a structural change had been spawned, and prior regression formulations of demand could not measure this exogenous shock.

Based on analysis of the seasonally adjusted quarterly data for trailer shipments (last column of Table 8-14), it was felt that in the fourth quarter of 1973, motor carriers and private firms began to "pre-buy" trailers—that is, buy trailers ahead of the January 1, 1975, deadline in order to circumvent the need for safety equipment. The surge in this quarter, just as the economy was weakening, suggested that buyers had developed a strategy of stocking up on non-safety-equipped trucks. From a statistical standpoint, therefore, the structural change began to occur in the fourth quarter of 1973. A historical-demand equation was fitted to quarterly trailer-shipments data over the period from the first quarter of 1956 through the third quarter of 1973—that is, up to the point when the pre-buy began. It was felt that if an accurate historical model could be estimated, it could be simulated over 1974 and 1975, using actual values of the independent variables, in order to estimate what trailer shipments would have been if not for SS 121, and the difference between actual and estimated sales would then become a measure of the pre-buy that was due to SS 121. Equation (8-2) presents the trailer-demand equation:[19]

$$\widehat{TRS}_t = -7.06 + \underset{\substack{(35.70) \\ [2.31]}}{0.2905 BFI_t} - \underset{\substack{(-8.95) \\ [-0.45]}}{1.66 PR_{t-4}} \tag{8-2}$$

$\bar{R}^2 = 0.96$

SEE $= 1.53$

DW $= 1.74$

$(\ \ ) = t_e$ statistic

$[\ \ ] =$ elasticity at mean

where:

$TRS_t =$ quarterly trailer shipments, thousands of units, seasonally adjusted

$BFI_t =$ business fixed investment, billions of 1972 dollars, seasonally adjusted

$PR_{t-4} =$ prime interest rate lagged four quarters

The model explains 96 percent of the quarterly variation in trailer shipments and links the volume of current-quarter trailer shipments to fixed investment in constant dollars and the prime rate four quarters in the past. The t_e values are significant in equation (8-2), and the standard error of 1,530 trailers (1.53 units) is small when viewed relative to quarterly trailer volume in Table 8-14. Also included are measures of the elasticity at the mean for BFI_t and PR_{t-4}. A 1 percent increase in BFI_t yields a 2.31 percent increase in trailer shipments (TRS_t), and a 1 percent increase in the prime rate four quarters past produces a current-quarter decline of 0.45 percent in trailer shipments.

Given the trailer-demand formulation in equation (8-2), what might we have expected to happen in the period from the fourth quarter of 1973 through the end of 1975? Table 8-16 summarizes the effect of SS 121 on the trailer industry. Column 1 contains actual, seasonally adjusted trailer shipments; column 2 provides estimates derived from equation (8-2). The difference between actual and estimated trailer shipments is captured in column 3 as the pre-buy effect. In order to generate the estimated volume of quarterly trailer shipments, actual magnitudes for BFI_t and PR_{t-4} were substituted into equation (8-2).

[19]German and Peppers, "Regulatory Spillovers," p. 73.

Table 8-16 Quantifying the impact of SS 121
(Thousands of trailer units, seasonally adjusted)

		(1) Actual[a]	(2) Ex Post Est.[b]	(3) Pre- buy[c]	(4) Naive Est.[d]	(5) Naive Est.[e]
1973:	IV	44.6	39.1	5.5	—	—
1974:	I	52.0	36.9	15.1	42.1	44.6
	II	53.1	34.9	18.2	49.2	52.0
	III	53.6	28.5	25.1	43.4	53.1
	IV	49.2	23.3	25.9	43.8	53.6
Total		207.9	123.6	84.3	178.5	203.3
1975:	I	21.5	20.4	1.1	43.1	49.2
	II	20.2	15.5	4.7	16.3	21.5
	III	18.0	14.3	3.7	18.6	20.2
	IV	18.6	18.0	0.6	22.7	18.0
Total		78.3	68.2	10.1	100.7	108.9

[a]H.W. German and Larry C. Peppers, "Regulatory Spillovers in the Economy: An Analysis of the Trucking Industry," *Transportation Journal*, Winter 1977, p. 70.
[b]Based on equation (8-2) in text. Actual values were used for independent variables.
[c]Actual less estimated sales.
[d]Based on equation (8-3) in text.
[e]Based on equation (8-4) in text.

A forecaster utilizing this model late in 1973, however, would have known only some of the PR_{t-4} values, and would have had to forecast BFI_t separately, thereby introducing another source of uncertainty into the demand estimate. As discussed in Chapter 3, forecasters late in 1973 had an overoptimistic assessment of the outlook for 1974 and 1975. As a result, the error in the trailer forecast generated by reliance on contemporary expert opinion would have been lower than the *ex post* estimate in column 2 of Table 8-16. The overoptimistic assessment of BFI_t would have inflated projections of trailer shipments relative to the estimates in column 2, since the latter were based on actual recession-deflated magnitudes.

Look in more detail at columns 1 to 3 in Table 8-16; what do the figures tell us about the magnitude of the structural change in trailer demand that took place at the end of 1973? If SS 121 had not been promulgated, predicted trailer shipments would have been 123.6 thousand units in 1974, as compared to actual shipments of 207.9 thousand units. The differential is most dramatic in the third and fourth quarters, when the economy (and BFI_t) was declining rapidly while actual trailer shipments were maintaining their historic peak. The 1974 pre-buy is estimated at 84.3 thousand units. Since there was such a massive pre-buy in 1974, it would be logical to expect this to act as a drag on 1975 trailer demand and, therefore, for the trailer model to overestimate in 1975.

In fact, the trailer model continued to slightly underestimate in 1975. This may be taken as evidence that some of the estimated 84.3-thousand-unit pre-buy was, in fact, forecast error, or simply that the recession was so severe that the secondary drag in 1975 was suppressed. In any case, it is clear that the trailer model performed well in 1975 given the double shock of pre-buy and the Great Recession. This is best seen between the fourth quarter of 1974 and the first quarter of 1975—actual trailer shipments fell from 49.2 to 21.5 thousand units while estimated shipments fell 23.3 to 20.4 thousand units. Once the exogenous shock was removed and traditional cyclical forces again became predominant, the model tracked admirably.

Again, all models have their greatest forecast error at turning points. In this case, the model accurately predicted that trailer shipments would bottom in the third quarter of 1975, but it overestimated the severity of the decline.

DEMAND ANALYSIS: DEVELOPING AD HOC MODELS

Given this example of *ex post* forecast analysis of exogenous shocks to trailer demand, what insights can be gained? Returning to the unanswered question raised at the beginning of the section, "Historical Background," it does not seem likely that the actual volume of quarterly trailer shipments shown in column 1 of Table 8-16 was forecastable. Regression models such as that exhibited in equation (8-2) are built upon theoretical relationships that quantify the transmission of cyclical forces from aggregate to industrial levels. The SS 121 ruling by NHTSA is an example of an institutional surprise that may counteract, temporarily or permanently, normal economic forces. Clearly, such surprises are not forecastable, but how could a trailer-industry analyst have provided management with useful information during the spring of 1974? It is, of course, impossible to completely recapture the uncertainty of the past, but it is feasible to point out alternatives that might have been suggested by the trailer forecaster.

Typically, a trailer-industry analyst would have first prepared an industry demand projection and then translated it into a company-level volume projection that would have served as the basis for the company's annual budget and operating plan. This process would have been finalized in the fall of 1973, roughly the same time that the potential truck buyers were beginning to react to the SS 121 mandate. As shown in columns 1 and 2 of Table 8-16 for the fourth quarter of 1973, the *ex post* simulation underestimated actual trailer sales by 5.5 thousand units, or roughly 12 percent. It is likely, however, that historical forecast error by the trailer analyst would have been lower than this, since the analyst was working (as we saw in Chapter 3) with a relatively optimistic economic forecast. It can be hypothesized, therefore, that actual trailer shipments did not begin to exceed the analyst's historical estimates by a wide margin until the first quarter of 1974. Again, it is probable that the analyst's underestimate for the first quarter of 1974 was less than the 15.1 thousand units generated by the *ex post* simulation in column 3 of Table 8-16, but the error was likely to have been so large as to lead to a series of tough questions by management for the forecaster:

1. What went wrong with the first-quarter (1974) outlook?
2. Why was the trailer model so inaccurate?
3. How should the trailer forecast be modified for the remainder of 1974?
4. Should the company be reassessing its tentative capital plans for 1975?
5. How uncertain is the new outlook?
6. What are the long-run implications of SS 121?

What happens at this point to the trailer forecast is not just a function of the forecaster's technical expertise in econometric modeling; rather, it depends on his credibility with management, his willingness to critically and objectively analyze his own errors in an environment of uncertainty, and his ability to subsequently convince management that the new forecast is significantly better than the recently discredited projection. Faced with trailer shipments for the first quarter of 1974 that were far in excess of the model's estimates, the trailer forecaster would logically have had to ask whether his assumptions for the independent variables—in this case, business fixed investment (BFI_t)—were so pessimistic as to be the source of a major underestimate. Having looked at his model's historical sensitivity to alternative scenarios for the independent variable, he would probably have concluded quickly that some exogenous shock must have been influencing demand, and would have tried to isolate a probable cause. The best initial source of appraisal is likely to come from an internal source such as the head of the sales department, who is in more intimate contact with trailer buyers on a day-to-day basis. Sales personnel in 1974 would have been able to quickly pinpoint the source of demand as a pre-buy of trailers due to SS 121. In addition, it was common knowledge that the pre-buy effect could last no longer than January 1, 1975, the date set for the adoption of the antiskid braking system.

Having isolated the exogenous shock as a spinoff of SS 121, the trailer analyst would have been able to explain what happened in the first quarter of 1974 and why the model was unable to estimate trailer shipments within the historical standard of accuracy. Although the forecaster could not be faulted for missing an exogenous shock, his responsibility then became one of constructing shipment projections that incorporated both the cyclical outlook and the pre-buy effect. At this point, forecasting becomes relatively more subjective, since the model in equation (8-2) cannot be relied on so heavily. A number of sophisticated statistical alternatives might be suggested, but they are likely to be so heavily weighted with subjective input that it is better to present a simpler, more straightforward assessment to management, openly conveying the uncertainty attending SS 121's impact.

Two simple approaches that might have been used by a trailer forecaster early in 1974 are represented in equations (8-3) and (8-4):

$$\hat{Y}_t = \frac{(Y_{t-1})}{(\hat{Y}_{t-1}^e)} \cdot (\hat{Y}_t^e) \tag{8-3}$$

$$\hat{Y}_t = Y_{t-1} \tag{8-4}$$

where:

$\hat{Y}_t =$ projected quarterly trailer shipments, seasonally adjusted, thousands of units, in period t

$Y_{t-1} =$ actual trailer shipments in quarter $t - 1$, seasonally adjusted, thousands of units

$\hat{Y}_t^e =$ trailer shipments in quarter t estimated from the econometric model in equation (8-2), seasonally adjusted, thousands of units

In the time-series model analyzed in Chapter 4, each time-series observation was viewed as the product of trend, cyclical, seasonal, and irregular forces $(T \cdot C \cdot S \cdot I)$. The models outlined in equations (8-3) and (8-4) assume that the trend factor continues on its long-run path and that traditional seasonal patterns have not been distorted by SS 121. Equation (8-3) inflates the statistical estimate $(\hat{Y}_t^e)$ yielded by the econometric trailer model (see equation (8-2)) by a multiplicative error measure $(Y_{t-1}/\hat{Y}_{t-1}^e)$ for the prior quarter. Thus, equation (8-3) attempts to incorporate both cyclical and exogenous influences. Using the actual and *ex post* magnitudes for trailer shipments contained in Table 8-16, and adopting the model in equation (8-3), the forecast for trailer shipments in the second quarter of 1974 (column 4 in Table 8-16) would have been 49.2 thousand units $[(52.0 \div 36.9) \cdot (34.9)]$, or roughly 4 thousand units below the actual level of 53.1 thousand. The second model, equation (8-4), abstracts entirely from the econometric trailer model and its focus on cyclical forces; rather, equation (8-4) assumes that the level of seasonally adjusted sales in the current quarter is equal to that of the prior quarter. Using this technique, trailer sales would have been estimated as 52.0 thousand units in the second quarter of 1974, or only 1.1 thousand units below the actual level of 53.1 thousand units. Columns 4 and 5 of Table 8-16 provide estimates for 1974 and 1975 based on the forecasting models set forth in equations (8-3) and (8-4), respectively. Both sets of projections represent *ad hoc* responses to an exogenous jolt.

For shocks such as SS 121, equations (8-3) and (8-4) represent a legitimate attempt to quantify an unknown stimulus. They would, however, have been buttressed both by internal information based on constant contact with trailer customers and by weekly statistical analyses of new orders and shipments. That is, the *ad hoc* quarterly projections carried out in columns 4 and 5 in Table 8-16 would, in fact, have been produced on a weekly and monthly basis to generate as much information as possible for such near-term needs as production planning and cash-flow management. The entire process of trailer forecasting during 1974 would have taken on a spontaneous aura.

Although a naive model of trailer shipments might have worked adequately in providing management with quarter-to-quarter shipment projections in 1974, the basic cyclical forces in the economy could not have been ignored when management was asking, early in 1974, for a reassessment of both 1975 trailer shipments and the need for new capital equipment. Columns 1 to 5 in Table 8-16 contain the basic information a trailer forecaster would have been providing to management during the course of 1974. The original econometric model was not able to track actual 1974 sales, but the information it was providing became of increasing importance in terms of the extended outlook beyond January 1, 1975. As shown in column 2 of Table 8-16, there was a rapid deterioration of trailer demand in 1974, based on cyclical forces generated by the Great Recession. By the last quarter of 1974, actual trailer shipments of 49.2 thousand units were more than double the *ex post* estimate of 23.3 thousand shown in column 2. The pre-buy estimates in column 3 should have given an industry forecaster, late in 1974, a strong base upon which to argue for a drastic downturn in 1975 trailer sales. Clearly, employment would have to be reduced, inventory pared, raw-material orders canceled, and capital expansion plans shelved or delayed.

Even though the estimates shown in column 2 of Table 8-16 were based on an *ex post* simulation of trailer shipments using actual values for business fixed investment (BFI_t), which were unknown in 1974, the general picture of a massive pre-buy in 1974 and subsequent decline in 1975 should have been clear by the fall of 1974 when the industry analyst was preparing a 1975 outlook. Notice that the 1974 pre-buy was larger than the aggregate level of sales projected for 1975. Actual shipments in 1975 of 78.3 thousand units were above the level of 68.2 thousand predicted in column 2, yet they still registered a 62 percent decline! Thus, even though the original statistical model was overwhelmed by events in 1974, it could have played an invaluable role in clarifying the outlook for 1975. The role of forecasters might be expected to diminish during a period when exogenous events dominate normal time-series forces, but the SS 121 experience vividly illuminates the reason that the demand for business forecasters rises during periods of uncertainty.

QUANTIFYING THE SECONDARY EFFECTS OF SS 121

The SS 121 experience is not just a historical novelty; it is the type of exogenous disturbance that can produce secondary demand ripples, as well. If, in addition to a modified trailer-demand outlook for 1974 and 1975, a trailer-industry analyst had been asked in mid-1974 to produce a five-year trailer outlook, how would the SS 121 experience have been factored into the long-term outlook?

To answer this question completely, it is not enough to collect data for total trailer shipments; these figures must be disaggregated by trailer type, as shown earlier in Table 8-15. Dry-van trailers, which comprise the first five categories listed in Table 8-15 and which represent a major demand grouping, experienced a drop from 137.5 thousand trailers in 1974 to 43.6 thousand in 1975, a decline of 68 percent. Given an average dry-van trailer life of six or seven years, a forecast analyst might have wondered whether SS 121 would have held down sales in 1976 and 1977 and have led to a secondary bulge in replacement demand in 1980 and 1981 as the units stockpiled in 1974 began to wear out. Table 8-17 presents monthly shipments data for dry vans from 1960 through October 1979, and Tables 8-18 to 8-21 contain the final seasonal factors, seasonally adjusted time series, trend-cycle series, and irregular series, respectively, generated by the Census Bureau's X-11 seasonal adjustment program. Questions 7 to 9 at the end of the chapter direct you to carry out a complete time-series analysis of these data, and to investigate secondary effects of SS 121 via multiple-regression demand models. Evaluating other forecaster's models is a productive exercise, but it is more stimulating to develop your own!

SIMULATING ECONOMIC ACTIVITY WITH A MONETARIST MODEL

The models developed in Chapters 6 to 8 have been used to link macroeconomic forces to activity in the various sectors of the economy. Since measures such as industrial production and real GNP often serve as independent variables in demand equations, it is necessary to understand both the nature of past fluctuations in economic activity (as was done in Chapters 2 and 3) and the role economic theory plays in constructing future predictions of business conditions. Even though forecasts of real GNP, industrial production, and related macroeconomic variables can be readily purchased from commercial forecast vendors, they cannot be used effectively unless the basic parameters of the underlying theoretical framework are clearly delineated. It does make a difference, for example, whether forecasts have been generated by a macro-econometric model that is Keynesian, monetarist, or eclectic; the independent variables may be the same (GNP, prime rate, and so forth), but the theoretical framework of a monetarist model is radically different from that of income expenditure models.[20]

THE MONETARIST APPROACH

Table 8-22 summarizes the seven-equation monetarist model developed by Prof. William G. Dewald to analyze how long it might take the Federal Reserve to control inflation, and to estimate the associated sacrifice in employment and economic growth. To forecast the annual rate of change in GNP

[20]For an elaboration of this distinction, see Karl Brunner, "The Role of Monetary Policy," *Monthly Review*, Federal Reserve Bank of St. Louis, July 1968.

Table 8-17 Monthly shipments of dry-van truck trailers, 1960–1979

Year	January May September	February June October	March July November	April August December	Annual Total
1960	3,879	3,871	3,934	3,548	
	3,139	3,188	2,375	2,611	
	2,385	2,251	2,067	1,784	35,032
1961	1,764	1,844	2,540	2,135	
	2,377	2,565	2,417	3,020	
	2,955	3,562	3,492	3,050	31,721
1962	3,539	3,423	4,733	4,132	
	4,157	3,644	3,091	3,174	
	3,306	4,024	3,839	3,733	44,795
1963	3,715	3,422	4,065	3,659	
	3,832	3 792	3 514	3,879	
	3,736	4,556	4,311	4,139	46,620
1964	3,883	3,674	4,313	4,788	
	4,571	4,614	4,541	4,366	
	4,841	4,177	3,558	4,510	51,836
1965	4,536	4,613	5,659	5,753	
	5,923	5,544	5,261	5,627	
	5,533	5,716	5,684	6,060	65,909
1966	5,674	5,593	7,572	7,018	
	6,673	6,928	5,206	6,232	
	6,600	6,468	5,961	5,602	75,527
1967	5,275	5,253	6,309	4,829	
	5,376	3,999	3,684	4,336	
	4,619	5,549	5,161	4,757	59,147
1968	5,028	5,713	6,775	5,899	
	7,188	5,676	5,529	6,439	
	6,475	7,036	6,774	6,616	75,148
1969	6,739	7,405	8,581	7,910	
	7,935	8,942	7,941	7,554	
	8,730	8,761	7,754	6,556	94,808
1970	6,795	6,547	7,237	6,062	
	7,057	5,630	5,880	4,953	
	5,817	5,240	5,238	4,818	71,274
1971	4,187	4,256	4,748	4,897	
	4,415	5,244	5,260	5,367	
	6,353	7,315	6,483	7,260	65,785
1972	7,089	7,820	9,085	8,128	
	8,588	7,410	6,796	8,225	
	7,984	8,960	7,516	8,278	95,879
1973	7,524	8,612	9,599	8,950	
	9,222	9,002	8,792	8,690	
	8,441	10,384	10,290	9,434	108,940
1974	10,804	10,133	11,728	10,822	
	10,996	11,690	10,770	13,336	
	11,820	12,864	12,141	10,375	137,469
1975	4,810	3,954	3,424	3,682	
	3,725	2,851	3,126	2,879	
	3,432	4,944	2,965	3,804	43,596
1976	3,129	4,704	5,532	5,156	
	4,673	5,297	4,731	5,412	
	5,636	5,714	6,125	5,617	61,726
1977	5,516	7,005	8,364	8,200	
	8,163	8,507	7,284	9,528	
	9,654	9,592	9,312	8,226	99,351
1978	7,887	8,717	11,733	10,000	
	11,230	11,047	8,923	11,665	
	10,404	12,031	12,424	12,505	128,566
1979	10,321	10,907	13,833	12,326	
	13,191	10,693	10,523	13,548	
	11,444	11,785			118,571

Source: Table 8-14

Table 8-18 Final seasonal factors for dry-van shipments

Year	January May September	February June October	March July November	April August December
1960	95.468 103.827 95.159	93.241 102.412 107.567	117.112 87.281 102.014	103.258 98.687 94.069
1961	95.512 103.956 95.080	92.831 102.509 107.361	116.640 87.767 101.872	103.691 98.631 94.548
1962	95.304 104.649 94.765	92.185 102.022 106.930	116.138 88.735 101.523	104.273 98.409 95.797
1963	94.915 105.261 95.069	91.221 101.355 105.834	115.683 89.441 100.716	105.600 97.729 97.002
1964	94.806 106.018 95.781	91.367 99.967 105.210	115.692 89.783 100.146	106.061 97.346 97.521
1965	94.421 106.730 97.287	92.272 98.431 104.628	115.954 89.383 99.650	106.127 97.322 97.111
1966	94.000 107.290 99.082	94.322 96.547 105.071	116.367 89.310 99.636	104.879 97.326 95.771
1967	93.709 108.149 101.261	95.953 94.926 105.737	116.612 89.500 100.275	103.176 96.441 94.960
1968	93.639 108.519 102.937	97.153 94.190 107.208	115.392 90.478 100.932	101.245 95.154 94.607
1969	93.392 108.724 103.968	97.516 94.254 108.210	113.447 91.277 100.829	99.958 94.840 95.532
1970	92.894 107.657 103.734	97.582 95.124 109.457	111.006 92.562 100.808	99.599 94.887 96.679
1971	92.404 105.895 103.031	97.321 95.877 110.546	109.378 92.769 101.987	99.290 96.402 98.147
1972	91.238 103.261 102.264	96.930 96.220 112.020	106.173 93.380 103.812	98.817 97.809 98.651
1973	89.311 100.619 102.102	97.334 96.196 112.497	108.230 93.023 105.674	98.228 100.228 98.461
1974	87.011 98.172 102.755	97.970 96.663 112.019	108.603 93.106 106.979	98.318 101.605 96.892
1975	85.154 97.501 103.271	98.203 97.832 110.308	110.163 91.786 107.750	98.647 103.243 95.872
1976	83.848 98.875 103.302	97.247 98.519 107.930	111.444 90.850 107.045	99.568 104.440 95.291
1977	83.016 101.051 102.417	96.381 99.250 105.776	113.514 88.978 105.550	100.851 106.315 95.311
1978	82.871 103.396 101.184	95.507 99.259 104.181	114.812 87.705 104.587	102.044 107.732 95.112
1979	83.175 104.524 100.073	95.225 99.589 103.558	115.720 86.289	102.748 108.732

Source: Table 8-17

Table 8-19 Dry-van shipments, 1960–1979
(Seasonally adjusted)

Year	January May September	February June October	March July November	April August December	Annual Total
1960	4,063.131	4,151.623	3,359.175	3,436.039	
	3,023.300	3,112.907	2,721.098	2,645.743	
	2,506.342	2,092.642	2,026.187	1,896.479	35,034.665
1961	1,846.891	1,986.407	2,177.633	2,058.993	
	2,286.552	2,502.214	2,753.870	3,061.926	
	3,107.913	3,317.767	3,427.839	3,225.884	31,753.890
1962	3,713.396	3,713.202	4,075.322	3,962.677	
	3,972.328	3,571.779	3,483.387	3.225.310	
	3,488.621	3,763.226	3,781.393	3,896.775	44,647.415
1963	3,914.027	3,751.326	3,513.907	3,464.963	
	3,640.462	3,741.291	3,928.843	3,969.148	
	3,929.774	4,304.874	4,280.361	4,266.906	46,705.882
1964	4,095.718	4,021.162	3,728.010	4,514.368	
	4,311.543	4,615.518	5,057.742	4,485.041	
	5,054.236	3,970.136	3,552.817	4,624.646	52,030.938
1965	4,804.019	4,999.323	4,880.377	5,420.875	
	5,549.512	5,632.366	5,885.915	5,781.843	
	5,687.317	5,463.139	5,703.970	6,240.265	66,048.921
1966	6,036.169	5,929.682	6,506.992	6,691.543	
	6,219.596	7,175.774	5,829.138	6,403.240	
	6,661.171	6,155.819	5,982.803·	5,849.352	75,441.279
1967	5,629.102	5,474.529	5,410.264	4,680.362	
	4,970.922	4,212.768	4,116.202	4,496.031	
	4,561.473	5.247.940	5,146.827	5,009.500	58,955.920
1968	5,369.544	5,880.392	5,871.277	5,826.441	
	6,623.730	6,026.107	6,110.874	6,766.925	
	6,290.286	6,562.946	6,711.453	6,993.159	75,033.132
1969	7,215.795	7,593.617	7,563.862	7,913.285	
	7,298.316	9,487.081	8,699.911	7,965.002	
	8,396.804	8,096.260	7,690,277	6,862.610	94,782.819
1970	7,314.772	6,709.252	6,519.445	6,086.398	
	6,555.071	5,918.567	6,352.520	5,219.919	
	5,607.587	4,787.248	5,196.002	4,983.522	71,250.303
1971	4,531.189	4,373.139	4,340.897	4,932.028	
	4,169.230	5,469.488	5,669.988	5,567.291	
	6,166.111	6,617.127	6,356.683	7,397.032	65,590.203
1972	7,769.756	8,067.664	8,398.545	8,225.331	
	8,316.826	7,701.126	7,277.827	8,409.261	
	7,807.243	7,998,539	7,239.998	8,391.204	95,603.319
1973	8,424.454	8,847.839	8,869.063	9,111.468	
	9,165.287	9,357.954	9,451.383	8,670.232	
	8,267.232	9,230.446	9,737.468	9,581.474	108,714.303
1974	12,416.813	10,342.990	10,798.921	11,007.120	
	11,200.698	12,093.575	11,567.461	13,125.347	
	11,503.071	11,483.790	11,348.956	10,707.833	137.596.576
1975	5,648.582	4,026.364	3,108.119	3,732.494	
	3,820.485	2,914.172	3,405.750	2,788.565	
	3,323.289	4,481.990	2,751.749	3,967.788	43,969.347
1976	3,731.738	4,837.163	4,963.917	5,178.372	
	4,726.173	5,376.652	5,207.488	5,181.944	
	5,455.870	5,294.162	5,721.918	5,894.572	61,569.967
1977	6,644.486	7,268.053	7,368.266	8,130.840	
	8,078.064	8,571.295	8,186.314	8,962.019	
	9,426.213	9,068.238	8,822.398	8,630.652	99,156.839
1978	9,517.175	9,127.080	10,219.354	9,799,735	
	10,861.185	11,129.513	10,173.892	10,827.826	
	10,282.240	11,548.216	11,879.076	13,147.593	128,512.886
1979	12,408.791	11,453.953	11,953.830	11,996.285	
	12,620.037	10,737.143	12,195.002	12,459.977	
	11,435.683	11,380.115			118,640.816

Source: Table 8-17

Table 8-20 Trend-cycle series for dry-van shipments
(13-term moving average)

Year	January May September	February June October	March July November	April August December	Annual Total
1960	3,923.924	3,753.851	3,559.124	3,359.445	
	3,158.202	2,973.111	2,788.629	2,594.559	
	2,387.887	2,192.696	2,039.903	1,942.700	34,674.031
1961	1,910.968	1,938.122	2,023.809	2,156.192	
	2,326.341	2,519.319	2,743.037	2,950.068	
	3,129.905	3,279.143	3,410.281	3,548.178	31,945.363
1962	3,692.705	3,822.302	3,898.602	3,890.920	
	3,805.561	3,678.611	3,566.196	3,520.758	
	3,560.413	3,661.897	3,762.058	3,810.436	44,670.458
1963	3,786.108	3,715.139	3,644.790	3,612.463	
	3,636.665	3,717.285	3,841.894	3,979.153	
	4,093.242	4,159.816	4,186.509	4,186.351	46.559.415
1964	4,181.588	4,196.949	4,246.996	4,331.304	
	4,423.809	4,484.437	4,496.728	4,471.747	
	4,450.859	4,458.895	4,508.099	4,605.144	52,856.555
1965	4,749.130	4,925.392	5,124.159	5.330.940	
	5,515.779	5,642.560	5,704.747	5,724.769	
	5,724.513	5,735.278	5,801.112	5,917.606	65,895.984
1966	6,068.675	6,224.569	6,347.045	6,431.931	
	6,490.545	6,526.389	6,522.457	6,466.669	
	6,367.754	6,238.847	6,070.681	5,875.427	75,630.988
1967	5,663.562	5,417.994	5,143.182	4,850.591	
	4,581.644	4,408.523	4,365.621	4,441.878	
	4,607.081	4,823.605	5,044.538	5,261.183	58,609.401
1968	5,468.654	5,660.060	5,837.559	5,994.548	
	6,123.130	6,214.659	6,290.311	6,372.491	
	6,475.385	6,607.271	6,788.807	6,998.970	74,831.843
1969	7,204.268	7,419.834	7,630.892	7,822.657	
	8,006.982	8,179.283	8,290.153	8,298.212	
	8,184.752	7,961.728	7,654.081	7,322.068	93,974.909
1970	7,018.138	6,762.411	6,545.486	6,370.113	
	6,186.240	5,977.505	5,759.874	5,553.334	
	5,347.296	5,141.782	4,945.139	4,765.131	70,372.449
1971	4,614.895	4,549.407	4,590.825	4,739.797	
	4,975.205	5,260.747	5,543.970	5,821.457	
	6,121.004	6,472.155	6,876.006	7,309.308	66,874.777
1972	7,727.885	8,029.358	8,177.325	8,183.729	
	8,103.870	7,980.143	7,866.776	7,788.590	
	7,775.088	7,835.174	7,967.120	8,158.606	95,593.663
1973	8,392.980	8,672.184	8,956.863	9,140.607	
	9,185.446	9,124.767	9,026.032	8,948.862	
	8,967.228	9,119.535	9,402.922	9,756.465	108,693.891
1974	10,131.005	10,455.510	10,763.321	11,108.630	
	11,487.735	11,855.000	12,132.712	12,202.237	
	11,926.939	11,238.781	10,147.597	8,770.576	132,220.043
1975	7,280.894	5,878.217	4,719.153	3,868.202	
	3,352.179	3,088.862	3,004.297	3,040.428	
	3,153.031	3,331.564	3,587.104	3,897.404	48,201.334
1976	4,229.136	4,547.651	4,807.462	4,999.993	
	5,113.994	5,171.463	5,197.393	5,228.774	
	5,319.007	5,481.604	5,746.611	6,117.140	61,960.230
1977	6 582.213	7,064.880	7,500.776	7,867.100	
	8,175.400	8,449.722	8,672.477	8,844.107	
	8,938.989	8,983.124	9,009.262	9,059.699	99,148 149
1978	9,217.294	9,497.690	9,871.223	10,213.859	
	10,442.038	10,545.065	10,617.369	10,786.146	
	11,083.892	11,475.992	11,848.395	12,146.312	127,745.275
1979	12,268.562	12;203.810	12,064.688	11,950.234	
	11,911.986	11,915.728	11,890.982	11,818.246	
	11,723.444	11,625.895			119,373.573

Source: Table 8-17

Table 8-21 Irregular factors for dry-van shipments

Year	January May September	February June October	March July November	April August December
1960	103.548	110.596	94.382	102.280
	95.729	104.702	97.578	101.973
	104.961	95.437	99.328	97.621
1961	96.647	102.491	107.601	95.492
	98.290	98.928	100.395	103.792
	99.297	101.178	100.515	90.917
1962	100.560	97.146	104.533	101.844
	104.382	97.096	97.678	91.608
	97.984	102.767	100.514	102.266
1963	103.379	100.974	96.409	95.917
	100.104	100.646	102.263	99.749
	96.006	103.487	102.242	101.924
1964	97.946	95.812	87.780	104.227
	97.462	102.923	112.476	100.297
	113.556	89.039	78.810	100.423
1965	101.156	101.501	95.242	101.687
	100.612	99.819	103.176	100.997
	99.350	95.255	98.325	105.453
1966	99.464	95.263	102.520	104.036
	95.825	109.950	89.370	99.019
	104.608	98.669	98.552	99.556
1967	99.392	101.043	105.193	96.491
	108.496	95.560	94.287	101.219
	99.010	108.797	102.028	95.216
1968	98.188	103.893	100.578	97.196
	108.176	96.966	97.147	106.190
	97.141	99.329	98.861	99.917
1969	100.160	102.342	99.122	101.159
	91.149	115.989	104.943	95.985
	102.591	101.690	100.473	93.725
1970	104.227	99.214	99.602	95.546
	105.962	99.014	110.289	93.996
	104.868	93.105	105.073	104.583
1971	98.186	96.125	94.556	104.056
	83.800	103.968	102.273	95.634
	100.737	102.240	92.447	101.200
1972	100.542	100.477	102.705	100.508
	102.628	96.504	92.513	107.969
	100.414	102.085	90.873	102.851
1973	100.375	102.026	99.020	99.681
	99.781	102.556	104.712	96.886
	92.194	101.216	103.558	98.206
1974	122.563	98.924	100.331	99.086
	97.501	102.012	95.341	107.565
	96.446	102.180	111.839	122.088
1975	77.581	68.496	65.862	96.492
	113.970	94.345	113.363	91.716
	105.400	134.531	76.712	101.806
1976	88.239	106.366	103.254	103.568
	92.416	103.968	100.194	99.104
	102.573	96.581	99.570	96.362
1977	100.946	102.876	98.233	103.352
	98.809	101.439	94.390	101.333
	105.451	100.947	97.926	95.264
1978	103.253	96.098	103.527	95.945
	104.014	105.542	75.823	100.386
	92.767	100.629	100.259	108.243
1979	101.143	93.856	99.081	100.385
	105.944	90.109	102.557	105.430
	97.545	97.886		

Source: Table 8-17

Table 8-22 Dewald's monetarist model
(Quarterly, 1953:I to 1979:III)

Equations:

1. $\dot{Y}_t = 2.38 + \sum\limits_{i=0}^{4} m_i \dot{M}_{t-i} + \sum\limits_{i=0}^{6} e_i \dot{EF}_{t-i} + .04\dot{EX}_t$
   (3.28)   (2.34)

   $\sum m_i = 1.03 \quad \sum e_i = .02$
   (6.19)   (.22)

   $R^2 = .52$
   $SEE = 3.28$
   $DW = 1.90$

2. $D = ln(Y/p^a) - ln(XF)$

3. $\dot{p}_t^a = \sum\limits_{i=1}^{2} d_i D_{t-1} + \sum\limits_{i=1}^{12} p_i \dot{P}_{t-i} + \sum\limits_{i=1}^{7} w_i \dot{W}_{t-1}$

   $\sum d_i = .01 \quad \sum p_i = 1.00 \quad \sum w_i = .00$
   (.20)

   $R^2 = .81$
   $SEE = 1.33$
   $DW = 2.06$

4. $\dot{p}_t = \dot{p}_t^a + .04 D_t$
   (1.28)

   $R^2 = .81$
   $SEE = 1.20$
   $DW = 2.03$

5. $\dot{X} = \dot{Y} - \dot{P}$

6. $U_t = UF_t - .20 D_t - .16 D_{t-1}$
   (−7.82) (−6.38)

   $R^2 = .72$
   $SEE = .28$
   $DW = 2.05$
   $\rho = .73$

7. $R_t = 4.28 + \sum\limits_{i=1} b_i P_{t-1}$
   (.04)

   $\sum b_i = .37$
   (5.18)

   $R^2 = .26$
   $SEE = .18$
   $DW = 1.42$
   $\rho = 1.00$

Definitions of Symbols:

Y	= GNP	R	= Moody's corporate Aaa bond rate
M	= money stock (M1)	t	= quarter
EF	= high-employment federal government spending	ln	= natural logarithm
		·	= annual rate of change
EX	= exports	a	= anticipated
D	= demand pressure	lowercase letters	= coefficients
P	= GNP deflator	uppercase letters	= variables
XF	= high-employment real GNP	R^2	= coefficient of determination
W	= imports deflator	SEE	= standard error of estimate
X	= Y/P = real GNP	DW	= Durbin-Watson statistic
U	= unemployment rate	ρ	= serial correlation coefficient
UF	= high-employment unemployment rate	t values are in parentheses.	

Source: William G. Dewald, "Fast vs. Gradual Policies for Controlling Inflation," *Economic Review*, Federal Reserve Bank of Kansas City, January 1980, p. 25.

(Y), the GNP deflator (P), real GNP (X), the unemployment rate (U), and Moody's corporate Aaa bond rate (R), Professor Dewald assembled a system of seven equations based on these five endogenous variables and seven exogenous variables—money stock (Ml), high-employment federal government spending (EF), exports (EX), demand pressure (D), high-employment real GNP (XF), the anticipated GNP deflator (P^a), the imports deflator (W), and the high-employment unemployment rate (UF). The small size of this monetarist model is probably the characteristic that most vividly sets it apart from third-generation econometric models containing 800 or more equations. This substantial difference in size also symbolizes a theoretical dichotomy that exists between monetarist and nonmonetarist models.

Today's large-scale econometric models can no longer be accurately stereotyped as Keynesian or neo-Keynesian; it may be preferable to simply call them eclectic, since they have drawn upon many refinements and advances in theoretical analysis. Still, the monetarist model in Table 8-22 does embody a different theoretical view of the way the U.S. economy functions. First, Professor Dewald's model incorporates the fundamental proposition of the modern quantity theory of money, which states that "the rate of growth of the money stock is, in the long run, the most important determinant of the growth of nominal demand [GNP]."[21] In other words, the monetarist view emphasizes the linkage between total spending (GNP in current prices) and the stock of money (Ml, the public's holdings of demand deposits and currency, is used in Table 8-22). In contrast to the highly aggregative linkage between Ml and GNP, large-scale econometric models of the Keynesian variety emphasize the influence of autonomous shifts in such GNP components as consumer-durables purchases, capital-equipment expenditures, inventory investment, and government outlays for goods and services. The component approach leads to detailed studies of relative consumer optimism and pessimism, surveys of business capital-spending plans, questionnaires for purchasing agents in terms of planned inventory policy, and attempts to predict behavior quirks in the legislative and executive branches of the federal government that might lead to unexpected changes in government expenditures (for example, authorized monies not spent). In short, the expenditures approach focuses on the deter-minants of real demand in each of the key expenditure categories (consumption, investment, government, and net exports) in order to construct an estimate of real GNP. The monetarist approach does not dwell on the division of total demand into its individual components, arguing instead that a sudden jump in one sector—say, government expenditures—will, unless it is accompanied by the requisite monetary expansion, merely crowd out other private expendi-tures. It is total demand, therefore, that is at the center of monetarist analysis, not component analysis of the multiplier.[22]

The monetarist view on price-level changes is best labeled a demand theory. When current-dollar demand grows at a more rapid rate than high-employment real GNP, the aggregate price level will rise to accommodate the growth-rate differential. Although this relationship can be distorted in the short run, a nominal Ml growth rate of, say, 11 percent and a high-employ-ment real GNP growth rate of 3 percent should, according to the monetarist's view, yield an 8 percent rate of increase in the GNP deflator in the long run.

---

[21]William G. Dewald, "Fast vs. Gradual Policies for Controlling Inflation," *Economic Review*, Federal Reserve Bank of Kansas City, January 1980, p. 17.

[22]That is, the Keynesian multiplier concept is rejected by monetarists unless the source of the autonomous expenditure change is supported by a monetary expansion. In this instance, it is monetary expansion, not the expenditure increase, that is responsible for the growth in nominal GNP.

Compared to this demand theory of inflation, large-scale econometric models tend to place greater reliance on cost-push or supply-side theories of inflation, which center on markup pricing by large corporations, upward wage pressure by large unions, price manipulation by government, and other structural impediments to competitive markets. Given the eclectic nature of large-scale models, it cannot be said that these systems totally ignore the influence of money, only that they place relatively less emphasis on the monetary sector's impact on the price level. Although the monetarist model makes no attempt to explain relative prices of commodities, much of the advance in large-scale models has been devoted to predicting relative price ratios such as coal versus oil and steel versus plastic.

EMPIRICAL ANALYSIS
WITH A MONETARIST MODEL

After we examine the equations in Table 8-22, it is worthwhile to translate the information in the light of both business-cycle theories and experiences, and to investigate whether the model embodies an endogenous or exogenous theory of cyclical activity. In contrast to the endogenous theory of cycles espoused by Wesley Mitchell at the turn of the century, equation (1) in this monetarist model represents a completely exogenous view of movements in current-dollar GNP. The annual rate of change in quarterly GNP is, according to Professor Dewald's model, determined by the annualized rate of growth in the money supply (Ṁ1) for the current quarter and the prior four quarters, the annualized growth in high-employment federal spending ($E\dot{F}$) for the current and prior six quarters, and the growth in export demand ($E\dot{X}$).

The formulation in equation (1) of the monetarist model explicitly recognizes the lapse in time between changes in the independent variables (M_1 and EF) and the actual effect on the dependent variable (nominal GNP) by incorporating past values of Ml and EF. In its most general form, a distrubuted-lag model attempts to capture the influence of all past movements of an independent variable on the current value of the dependent variable:[23]

$$Y_t = \alpha + \beta_0 X_t + \beta_1 X_{t-1} + \ldots = \alpha + \sum_{i=0}^{\infty} \beta_i X_{t-i} + \epsilon_t \qquad (8\text{-}5)$$

where:

Y_t = value of the dependent variable in period t
X_{t-i} = value of independent variable in period $t - i$
ϵ_t = error term; $E(\epsilon_t) = 0$; $V(\epsilon_t) = \sigma^2$

In equation (1) in Table 8-22, a polynomial distributed-lag model has been used. In order to minimize the problem of multicollinearity, all the variables

---

[23]In equation 8-5, the dependent variable is linked to an infinite series of lagged observations for the independent variable.

in equation (1) are estimated on an annualized-percentage-change basis rather than in absolute magnitudes. Multicollinearity occurs when two or more independent variables are highly correlated, a situation quite likely to result if equation (1) included observed values of the money supply from consecutive quarters.

In equation (1) of Dewald's model, only the summations ($\sum m_i = 1.03$ and $\sum e_i = .02$) of the lagged regression coefficients are presented. If the growth rate of the money supply is increased by 1 percentage point for five consecutive quarters, then, according to this monetarist model, the growth rate of nominal GNP in the current period will be augmented by 1.03 percentage points. For high-employment federal expenditures (*EF*), however, a similar increase in expenditures maintained over seven quarters (the current quarter and the prior six quarters) adds only 0.02 percentage points to the growth rate of nominal GNP. Although nominal GNP is influenced in the short run by federal expenditures and export demand, it is, as expressed in this monetarist model, really the monetary sector that is the basic driving force behind nominal GNP. Taken literally, if the money supply moved along a steady growth path, a forecaster would expect nominal GNP to move in a parallel fashion. That is, if M1 grew at a steady rate of 8 percent over a sustained period, nominal GNP would also grow at 8 percent. Alternatively, a stop-and-go monetary policy that resulted in fluctuating growth rates for M1 would, according to the model embodied in equation 1, yield fluctuating (but not identical) growth rates for nominal GNP.

Before we look at the statistical and theoretical properties of the other equations in Table 8-22, it is interesting to consider some more general characteristics of polynomial distributed-lag models. Economic theory may provide the notion that present growth in nominal GNP is linked to both current and past growth rates in the money supply, but there is no corresponding insight concerning the length of the time lag. It is, of course, possible to pick the pragmatic strategy of running alternative lagged versions of the model and selecting that version with the highest $\bar{R}^2$. The best-fitting equation may not, however, turn out to be the best-predicting equation. For example, by simply a lengthening of the lag structure and an increase in the number of independent variables, the equation can be forced to have a high R^2. If the number of terms in the distributed lag is small, ordinary least-squares techniques can be used directly. If there are multiple variables and a lengthy lag structure, several alternative mathematical techniques exist for estimating what are known as lag weights—the specific numerical weights to be attached to current and lagged values of the independent variables.[24] One popular model is the polynomial-lag model. For example, consider a model that uses a third-degree polynomial-lag system to estimate the weight (w_i) to be assigned to each quarter:

$$w_i = d_0 + d_1 i + d_2 i^2 + d_3 i^3 \text{ for } i = 0, 1, 2, 3, 4 \qquad (8\text{-}6)$$

[24]See Pindyck and Rubinfeld, *Econometric Models*, Chap. 7.

where:

$$w_i = \text{lag weight for the } i\text{th quarter}$$
$$i = \text{number of the lagged quarter}$$
$$d = \text{lag coefficient to be estimated empirically}$$

Using this weighting system with a four-period lag, the lag model becomes:

$$Y_t = \alpha + w_0 X_t + w_1 X_{t-1} + \ldots + w_4 X_{t-4} + \epsilon_t \qquad (8\text{-}7)$$

Substituting equation (8-6) into equation (8-7) and combining terms, the model yields equation (8-8), which can be estimated using ordinary least squares:

$$
\begin{aligned}
Y_t = \alpha &+ d_0(X_t + X_{t-1} + X_{t-2} + X_{t-3} + X_{t-4}) \\
&+ d_1(X_{t-1} + 2X_{t-2} + 3X_{t-3} + 4X_{t-4}) \\
&+ d_2(X_{t-1} + 4X_{t-2} + 9X_{t-3} + 16X_{t-4}) \\
&+ d_3(X_{t-1} + 8X_{t-2} + 27X_{t-3} + 64X_{t-4}) + \epsilon_t \qquad (8\text{-}8)
\end{aligned}
$$

The empirical estimates of the ds from the regression equation are substituted in equation (8-6) to get the specific lag weights ws that appear in equation (8-7). Thus, polynomial distributed-lag models such as equation (1) in Dewald's model combine both the theoretical concept of time lags and the mathematical and statistical procedure of polynomial weighting.

Polynomial distributed-lag systems, although extremely useful analytically, are subject to the same problem of structural change that can plague any empirical model. For example, the effective money supply may be altered by such financial innovations as money-market funds and electronic transfer of funds in savings accounts. In addition, the responsiveness of the economy to injections of money may also change over time. The empirical estimates in Table 8-23 were carried out by Professor Dewald to deal with the structural issue of both alternative definitions of money and different lag structures.[25] At the top of Table 8-23, the general form of the polynomial distributed-lag model is presented. Across the top of each of the columns, a different money-supply measure is given (M2, M1, MA, and MF), with the definitions presented at the bottom of the table. The models in Table 8-23 were estimated for 100 quarterly observations stretching from 1953 through 1978, as compared to 103 observations in Dewald's other model in Table 8-22. Along the far left-hand column of Table 8-23 are the general coefficients or impulses linking lagged values of the independent variables to the dependent variables.

In fitting the models in Table 8-23, Professor Dewald alternatively tried a five-quarter lag for M2, a six-quarter lag for M1, a seven-quarter lag for MA, and a seven-quarter lag for MF. First, compare the six-quarter lag for

---

[25]See William G. Dewald, "Fast and Gradual Monetary Policies to Curb Inflation," *Bulletin of Business Research*, Volume LIV, No. 7 (July 1979), 5.

Table 8-23 A monetarist model of movements in GNP spending equations: 1953:Q1–1978:Q4

$$Y_t = \text{constant} + \sum_{i=0} m_i M_{t-1} + \sum_{i=-g} c_i EF_{t-1} + \sum_{i=0} x_i EX_{t-1}$$

Item	M2 Coefficient	M2 (t value)	M1 Coefficient	M1 (t value)	MA Coefficient	MA (t value)	MF Coefficient	MF (t value)
Constant	1.131	(1.24)	2.661	(3.49)	3.560	(4.66)	1.294	(1.15)
Monetary Impulse: M								
m_0	0.308	(1.97)	0.540	(3.63)	0.258	(1.14)	−0.081	(−146)
m_1	0.207	(1.83)	0.376	(4.75)	0.444	(3.85)	0.063	(2.02)
m_2	0.213	(2.35)	0.232	(2.62)	0.413	(2.96)	0.122	(3.63)
m_3	0.223	(2.49)	0.102	(1.63)	0.246	(2.17)	0.123	(4.48)
m_4	0.135	(1.19)	−0.016	(−0.18)	0.022	(0.20)	0.093	(3.70)
m_5	−0.155	(−1.00)	−0.128	(−1.55)	−0.175	(−1.25)	0.057	(1.85)
m_6	—		−0.235	(−1.55)	−0.266	(−2.31)	0.043	(1.42)
m_7	—		—		−0.168	(−0.77)	0.078	(1.70)
$\sum m_i$	0.931	(6.01)	0.871	(4.71)	0.774	(4.66)	0.499	(3.84)
Fiscal Impulse: $\dot{EF}$								
c_{-2}	—		—		—		0.018	(0.42)
c_{-1}	—		0.026	(0.68)	—		0.094	(3.66)
c_0	0.037	(0.89)	0.077	(3.74)	0.036	(0.82)	0.110	(3.87)
c_1	0.070	(2.70)	0.062	(2.59)	0.047	(1.62)	0.085	(3.67)
c_2	0.025	(0.91)	0.010	(0.51)	0.001	(0.03)	0.038	(1.63)
c_3	−0.051	(−2.41)	−0.047	(−2.48)	−0.061	(−2.67)	−0.014	(−0.50)
c_4	−0.105	(−3.93)	−0.078	(−3.57)	−0.100	(−3.53)	−0.052	(−2.10)
c_5	−0.088	(−3.44)	−0.052	(−2.55)	−0.075	(−2.68)	−0.058	(−1.37)
c_6	0.049	(1.35)	0.061	(1.88)	0.053	(1.41)	—	
$\sum c_i$	−0.063	(−0.80)	0.060	(0.79)	−0.099	(−1.13)	0.221	(2.63)
Trade Impulses: $\dot{EX}$								
x_0	0.048	(2.47)	0.038	(1.97)	0.037	(1.83)	0.044	(2.16)

Table 8-23 (continued)

Summary Statistics:	M2	M1	MA	MF
R^2	0.415	0.464	0.350	0.318
F	9.108	10.927	7.169	6.342
SEE	3.491	3.339	3.678	3.768
DW	1.83	2.05	1.76	1.66

Definitions:

M2 = money broadly defined to include currency and total bank deposits held by the public, other than large certificates of deposit

M1 = money narrowly defined to include currency and bank demand deposits held by the public

MA = monetary base adjusted: total currency plus member bank reserves with Federal Reserve Banks plus RAM (reserves absorbed or liberated by required reserve ratio changes)

MF = fiat monetary base 1: Federal Reserve holdings of U.S. government securities plus Treasury currency outstanding less Treasury deposits with Federal Reserve Banks plus RAM

Y = GNP (total spending)

EF = high-employment government spending

EX = exports

• = logarithm first differences

Source: William G. Dewald, "Fast and Gradual Monetary Policies to Curb Inflation," *Bulletin of Business Research*, Ohio State University, Vol. LIV, No. 7 (July 1979), 5.

M1 in Table 8-23 with the four-quarter lag for M1 in Table 8-22. In the original model in Table 8-22, the sum of the monetary impulses ($\sum_{i=0}^{4} m_i$) is 1.03, whereas in Table 8-23, the sum ($\sum_{i=0}^{6} m_i$) is 0.871. Note in Table 8-23, however, that the monetary impulses are negative for m_4, m_5, and m_6. If we drop the last two monetary impulses (m_5 and m_6) from the six-quarter lag model for M1 in Table 8-23, the sum becomes 1.23 as compared to 1.03 in Table 8-22. Looking at the impulse coefficients for M1 in Table 8-23, we see a steady decline from $m_0 = 0.540$ to $m_6 = -0.235$. Although the sum of the monetary impulses for M1 ($\sum m_i = 0.871$) is quite close to the sum for MA ($\sum m_i = 0.774$), the individual impulse coefficients for MA display a much different quarter-to-quarter pattern. MA, member bank reserves plus currency, represents the monetary base that is directly controlled by the Federal Reserve. M1, most of which is composed of demand deposits, is not directly controlled by the Federal Reserve, since demand deposits must be generated from bank reserves via the process of money creation. Theoretically, therefore, we would expect changes in M1 to have a quicker and more pronounced effect on the economy than MA, since it takes time for reserve injections to be transformed into demand deposits. Similarly, the effects of increases in MF, or the fiat monetary base, are even more drawn out, since changes in Federal Reserve holdings of government securities must be translated into changes in bank reserves and then into demand deposits.

Which of the money measures in Table 8-23 gives the best results? From the summary statistics at the bottom of the table, the M1 series yields the highest R^2 and F values, the lowest standard error, and the Durbin-Watson value closest to 2. Although the effects of government spending (EF) and export demand (EX) vary marginally from one money measure to the next, it is clearly the monetary impulses that propel nominal GNP. Although other measures of the money supply are possible, the breadth of the money measures in Table 8-23, the length of the period covered, and the statistical results suggest that no radical structural change has occurred and that the traditional reliance upon M1 is well founded. The empirical work in Table 8-23 represents the background analysis that had to be carried out before even the first equation in Dewald's monetarist model (Table 8-22) could be finalized.

USING A RECURSIVE MONETARIST MODEL

The remaining equations, (2) through (7), in Dewald's model form a recursive system "in so far as percentage changes in nominal demand affect inflation and/or output but not the other way around."[26] This recursive feature

---

[26]William G. Dewald, "Fast and Gradual Anti-Inflation Policies: Evidence for Germany, Italy and the United States," paper presented at the Eighth Brooklyn College Conference on Society in Change, March 10, 1980, p. 7.

can be seen in equations (1) to (5) of Table 8-22, since there is no method for real GNP to feed back or influence nominal GNP. In equation (5), real GNP growth is the residual or difference between growth in nominal demand and change in the price level.

In equation (2), demand pressure (D) is defined as the difference between high-employment real GNP and anticipated real GNP (nominal GNP divided by the anticipated deflator). The anticipated percentage change in the deflator ($\dot{P}_t^a$) is, in turn, based entirely on past values of demand pressure, a twelve-quarter lag for changes in domestic prices, and a seven-quarter lag for the imports deflator. In effect, the model assumes that price anticipations are a weighted average of past experience and gives no support to the hypothesis that inflation can be quickly truncated by controls or exhortation. Similarly, the polynomial distributed-lag model used for Moody's corporate Aaa bond rate (R_t) in equation (7) implies that interest rates will move downward permanently only when the rate of inflation has been reduced over a prolonged period.

Whereas it takes time for changes in the growth rate of M1 to affect nominal GNP, prices, and long-term interest rates, there appears to be a shorter response lag for unemployment, since it depends only on demand pressure for the current and prior quarter. If a particular company's sales were cyclically sensitive to long-term interest-rate movements, this model would be of immediate use. If, on the other hand, a company's sales volume is correlated with movements in steel production, then this monetarist model would have to be augmented by a system of satellite regression equations that link steel production to real GNP and other indicators. For detailed company-level forecasts, the projections generated by this monetarist model would have to be supplemented with estimates from a commercial forecast vendor. A forecaster would have to contrast the projections of nominal GNP, real GNP, unemployment, and interest rates generated by the small-scale monetarist model with similar variables from the large-scale commercial system. Radically different projections for inflation and real GNP could emanate from theoretical differences in the structures of the two models, or they could arise from discrepancies in underlying exogenous assumptions for monetary policy, fiscal policy, and so on. The advantages of the small-scale monetarist model are that it can be maintained and monitored at a relatively low cost and that it provides a cross-check against the more elaborate commercial forecasting systems.

If Dewald's monetarist model is to be used for policy simulations, specific assumptions must be made for each of the exogenous variables. The lower portion of Table 8-24 contains the parameter values used by Professor Dewald to explore the economy's sensitivity to a sustained policy of monetary restraint designed to slow the inflation rate. In particular, Dewald cites *The Budget of the United States Government, Fiscal Year,* 1980, prepared by the Carter administration, as the source for a 3 percent annual growth rate for high-employment output ($X\dot{F}$), a 5.1 percent high-employment unemployment rate (UF), and a 4 percent rate of increase in high-employment government spending ($E\dot{F}$). A

Table 8-24 Monetary impulses to reduce inflation fast and gradually: Simulated effects through 1988 (Constrained price anticipations)

		Simulated Value, Fourth Quarter, 1988							
		Ṁ2		Ṁ1		ṀA		ṀF	
Factor	1978 Average	Immediate Cut to 2 Percent	Gradual Cut from 7 Percent in 1979 to 2 Percent	Immediate Cut to Zero	Gradual Cut from 6 Percent in 1979 to Zero	Immediate Cut to Zero	Gradual Cut from 8 Percent in 1979 to Zero	Immediate Cut to Zero	Gradual Cut from 8 Percent in 1979 to 2 Percent
Inflation rate (P)—percent	7.8	-3.0	-2.0	-2.9	-1.7	-2.8	-0.6	-2.2	-1.0
Unemployment rate (U)—percent	5.8	8.8	10.2	8.5	10.4	7.9	10.4	9.3	9.9
Real GNP growth (X)—percent	6.9	6.5	5.5	6.4	5.2	6.6	4.3	6.0	4.9
Long-term interest rate (RL)—percent	9.0	5.6	6.1	5.6	6.3	5.5	6.7	5.9	6.5
Real GNP—billions of 1972 dollars	1,415	1,780	1,717	1,795	1,707	1,821	1,707	1,758	1,730

Simulation Assumptions:

From Carter administration projections:

$\dot{X}F$ = percentage change in high-employment output—falling to 3 percent annually

$\dot{E}F$ = percentage change in high-employment government spending—falling to 4 percent annually

UF = 5.1 percent-high-employment unemployment rate

From extrapolations of recent observations:

$\dot{F}X$ = percent change in exports = 15 percent a year

$\dot{W}$ = percentage change in import prices = 10 percent a year

From calculations based on estimated trends in monetary velocity and potential real growth assumptions of the monetary impulses that would be associated with approximately zero inflation in the long run:

$\dot{M}2$ = percentage change in currency plus bank deposits other than large certificates of deposit = 2 percent a year

$\dot{M}1$ = percentage change in currency plus demand deposits = 0

$\dot{M}A$ = percentage change in the monetary base adjusted = 0

$\dot{M}F$ = percentage change in fiat money adjusted = 2 percent a year

15 percent rate of change in exports $(E\dot{X})$ and a 10 percent change in import prices $(\dot{W})$ were obtained by historical extrapolation, a procedure that is somewhat controversial given the volatility of these trade-related concepts. Finally, the key monetary-policy measures $(M\dot{2}, M\dot{1}, M\dot{A}$, and $M\dot{F})$ were assumed to fall "to a level that would be associated with approximately zero inflation in the long run."[27]

Two simulations were performed for each monetary measure. For example, one simulation assumed an immediate reduction in M1's growth rate to 0 percent, and the alternative simulation posited a gradual decline in M1's growth rate. Feeding these assumptions into the alternative models listed in Table 8-23, Professor Dewald obtained the simulation results listed in the top half of Table 8-24. Focus on the column for $M\dot{1}$, where the model estimates two sets of projections for the fourth quarter of 1988. Viewed in isolation, these simulation results may appear puzzling, since they combine falling prices high unemployment, high real GNP growth, and a low long-term interest rate. The last row of Table 8-24 contains annualized real GNP estimates of $1,795 billion under the sharp cut for $M\dot{1}$ and $1,707 billion under the gradual cut. The projections in the $M\dot{1}$ column show only a single quarter from a ten-year simulation path.

The $M\dot{1}$ simulations in Table 8-24 were reestimated by Professor Dewald and published in graphical form in conjunction with his complete monetarist model in Table 8-22. Figure 8-1 presents the fast and gradual growth paths taken by $M\dot{1}$, and Figures 8-2 to 8-5 illustrate the resulting activity paths for inflation, real growth, and the unemployment rate. The comparison between Figures 8-2 and 8-5 dramatically illustrates the social cost (higher unemployment) of adopting a sustained antiinflationary monetary policy.

To a forecaster interested in the likelihood that the economy can be returned to a less inflationary environment, the graphs generated by Prof. Dewald's simulations are not a source of optimism. As seen in Figure 8-3, regardless of whether a fast or gradual monetary policy is pursued, unemployment rates far in excess of full employment (5.1 percent) would be experienced for roughly the entire decade following the implementation of an antiinflationary policy. These results reflect, of course, the polynomial distributed-lag model of inflation expectations discussed earlier. Even if a business forecaster felt that Prof. Dewald's model accurately captured the slowly changing nature of inflation expectations over the 1953–79 span, it does not necessarily follow that he or she would accept the simulation results. Both economic and psychological dimensions enter into the formulation of price expectations, and it is possible that the structural coefficients in equation (3) of Dewald's model could be altered by the presence of rising unemployment and falling inflation rates. That is, the process of implementing a new policy might independently modify the underlying economic structure.

[27]Dewald, "Fast and Gradual Monetary Policies," p. 5.

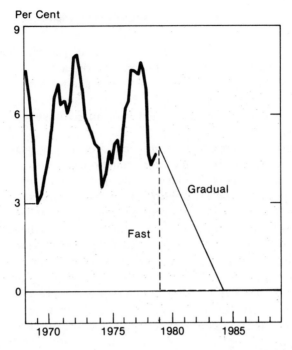

Figure 8-1 The Money Supply M1; Actual 1969–79, Model Assumptions 1980–89 (Percent change from year earlier)

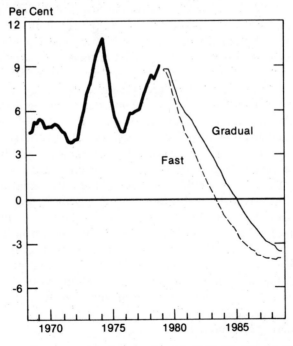

Figure 8-2 The Rate of Inflation; Actual 1969–79, Model Simulation 1980–89 (Change from year earlier in GNP price deflator)

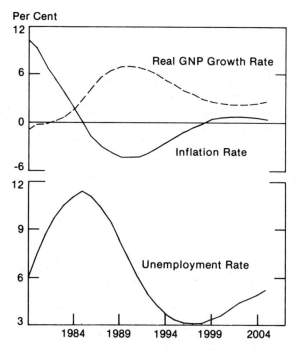

Figure 8-3   Inflation Rate, Real GNP Growth Rate, and Unemployment Rate, 1980–2005 (Model Simulation of Gradual Approach)

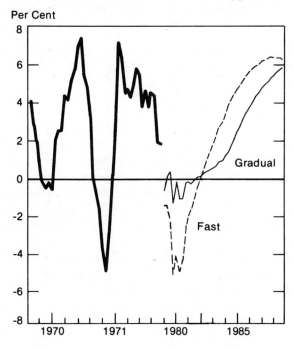

Figure 8-4   The Economic Growth Rate; Actual 1969–79, Model Simulation 1980–89 (Percent change from year earlier in real GNP)

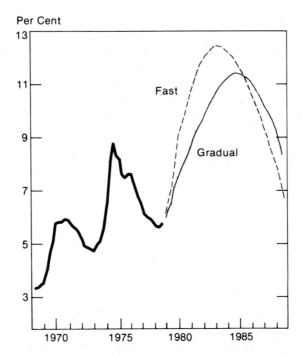

Figure 8-5 Unemployment Rate; Actual 1969–79, Model Simulation 1980–89

Source for Figures 8-1 through 8-5: William G. Dewald, "Fast vs. Gradual Policies for Controlling Inflation," *Economic Review*, Federal Reserve Bank of Kansas City, January 1980, pp. 19–21.

It is not necessary to accept literally each detail of the simulation in order to gain important insights concerning the functioning of the economy. At the macroeconomic level, the simulations in Figures 8-2 to 8-5 provide grounds for incorporating higher-than-average long-term inflation rates into a company's five- and ten-year plans. Because the results for unemployment are so dramatic, it becomes very unlikely that a politician or a political party would allow the Federal Reserve to carry out a policy of severe monetary restrictiveness. In addition, it may be felt that although a zero percent growth rate for $\dot{M}1$ is both unachievable and undesirable, a growth factor in the range from 3 to 5 percent would be more acceptable, since it would match or slightly exceed the 3 percent growth rate of high-employment real GNP. This would lead to a third simulation, which would necessarily involve a much longer period before the inflation rate was significantly reduced. Regardless of the specific steady-state growth rate assumption actually utilized for $\dot{M}1$, such a nondiscretionary monetary policy would represent a marked departure from the discretionary tradition of actively fine-tuning the economy by speeding up and slowing down the growth rate of M1 based on the perceived need for stimulus or restraint. Simulation of a discretionary monetary policy using Dewald's monetarist model would have to be confined to a shorter time horizon, since the focus would shift from selection of a steady M1 growth rate to actual predictions of shifts in the Federal Reserve's desired growth rate. Since the Federal Reserve keeps its cyclical analysis secret and does not explain policy shifts until after the fact, the problem of model error is compounded by the pitfalls of trying to guess the Federal Reserve's future course of action.

SUMMARY

Three separate cases were presented in this chapter as a way of illustrating both the technical steps to be followed in developing multiple regression demand models and the role theory and analysis play in formulating and interpreting the results. Although an appreciation of regression methods and technical formulations such as polynomial distributed-lag models is necessary in the model-building stage, an awareness of exogenous changes and the ability to quantify such shifts is equally important. Whether it is institutional guidelines such as SS 121 by NHTSA, alterations in M1's growth rate, or a government-induced boom in coal traffic, statistical models must be made to adapt to external factors.

Each of the cases contains general issues or problems that will be confronted in any statistical analysis. Dewald's monetarist model, for example, represents a general type of contingency analysis in which an economic structure or system of relationships is estimated, a policy assumption concerning exogenous forces is made, and a simulation is carried out. Before the simulation results are accepted, a critical appraisal has to be made of the model's historical fit, the likelihood that structural change will invalidate the model, and the appropriateness of both the theoretical structure and the exogenous assumptions. The same approach could be applied to a company-level model designed to estimate unit sales volume, dollar sales, production costs, labor demand, and profit based on a forecast of independent variables from a large-scale econometric model. Simulations could be generated based on both optimistic and pessimistic appraisals of the economy's performance, and a series of company-level scenarios could be presented in a manner analogous to that of Figures 8-2 to 8-5. The technique of *ex post* forecast evaluation, illustrated with the trailer-demand model, is also a general tool of statistical analysis, as were the *ad hoc*, nonstatistical procedures designed for a period of exogenous uncertainty. All the cases in this chapter should be viewed, therefore, in the context of general challenges facing the forecaster.

QUESTIONS FOR DISCUSSION AND ANALYSIS

1. Two possible explanations were given for the change in seasonality exhibited by the ton-miles data in Table 8-2—an alteration in the composition of freight traffic, and variable seasonality for the individual commodity categories. Evaluate these hypotheses by analyzing the aggregate rail data found in *Moody's Transportation Manual* in the reference section of the library. Compile a table that highlights the change in the percentage composition of annual freight tonnage over the last twenty years (select data at five-year intervals). Freight commodity data are provided in *Moody's* under the STCC (standard transportation commodity code) system on a quarterly basis. Based on the initial investigation of commodity composition, pick several major commodity categories (such as Farm Products—STCC 01) and statistically analyze whether the quarterly seasonal indexes are changing or are stable.

2. Table 8-6 summarizes the cyclical timing pattern of railroad ton-miles. The analysis in the chapter suggested that the two-quarter decline in ton-miles in 1959 might have been due to abnormal irregular movements, and the extra rail cycle in 1966–67 was thought to be tied to the credit crunch. Since neither of these episodes was matched by a reference cycle peak, it is important to understand where these declines in railroad tonnage were isolated. Using *Moody's* quarterly commodity data, isolate those commodities that experienced the most erratic tonnage movements during these periods. Was the 1966 rail-tonnage decline concentrated in construction-related commodities that are sensitive to monetary conditions, or did the downturn result from shortfalls in nonindustrial areas such as agriculture?

3. Suppose a commercial forecast vendor developed the rail-ton-mile model in Table 8-9 and is trying to persuade your company to subscribe to its forecasting service. To support the worth of the service, Tables 8-10 and 8-11 have been put forth as documentation of the model's accuracy. None of your immediate superiors is well versed in statistical procedures, so they have asked you to provide a critique of the model in Table 8-9 and to evaluate the error patterns presented in Tables 8-10 and 8-11.

4. After reading the critique of the rail-ton-mile model and considering the cost of the vendor's service, your company has decided to develop its own forecasting equation for seasonally adjusted quarterly rail ton-miles. Using the data in Table 8-3 for your dependent variable, formulate a different rail-ton-mile model. Begin by reviewing the study of rail commodity data that was carried out in problem 1. Next, examine publications such as the *Survey of Current Business* and the *Business Conditions Digest* to locate time series that could be used as independent variables in the demand formulation. For example, there are numerous production or output measures published in the *SCB*. You may want to try variable transformations or nonlinear formulations that can be linearized mathematically. Write a summary describing the model's statistical properties, its accuracy, and how it differs from the model in Table 8-9. (*Note:* It may seem ludicrous to prepare a second model, but it is a common practice among forecasters to develop alternative forecast systems in order to use one set of projections as a check against the other.)

5. Having examined the ten-year outlook for rail ton-miles contained in Table 8-13,

a senior executive of a major locomotive manufacturer asks what exogenous disturbances might cause the greatest deviation from this forecast path. The executive realizes that specific surprises are not forecastable, but she desires a general picture of the types of disturbances that would be most disruptive. How would the commodity data developed in problem 1 be of use in answering the executive's query? Describe the types of exogenous disturbances that would be linked to specific commodity sectors.

6. Two *ad hoc* forecasting equations were presented, equations (8-3) and (8-4), as a response to the exogenous disturbance to trailer shipments produced by SS 121. How else might a forecaster have responded to this sudden upsurge in trailer demand? What substitutes might be suggested for equations (8-3) and (8-4)? Compare the resulting projections with those in Table 8-16.

7. Tables 8-17 to 8-21 contain a complete set of time-series data for monthly shipments of dry-van truck trailers from 1960 through October 1979. Following the steps outlined in the case on rail ton-miles, carry out a full time-series analysis of the trailer data. That is, summarize the key characteristics for the trend, seasonal, cyclical, and irregular components over the 1960–79 period: Was there a stable seasonal pattern? Was there a linear or curvilinear trend path? What was the cyclical timing pattern?

8. Construct a multiple-regression demand model for dry-van trailer shipments. For background data and information on demand determinants for the trailer industry, consider the sources listed in Table 8-14; past issues of the *Transportation Journal*; *Freight Commodity Statistics*, published by the Interstate Commerce Commission; and publications by the American Trucking Association. In addition to the normal issues of model formulation and specification, the SS 121 effect will have to be explicitly considered, through either the use of dummy variables (see the discussion in Chapter 7) or other statistical techniques. (*Note:* The data can be aggregated from monthly to quarterly to reduce calculation time.)

9. Based on the model developed in problem 8, prepare a five-page report containing the following:
   a. An analysis of the statistical forecasting equation—variables used, historical fit, statistical significance of the coefficients, dummy variables, etc.
   b. An evaluation of the presence or absence of secondary SS 121 demand effects
   c. An *ex post* simulation for the last quarter of 1979 and all of 1980, based on actual values for the independent variables
   d. A five-year projection for sales, incorporating predicted values for the independent variables

10. Using quarterly data (seasonally adjusted) for the last ten years, taken from the *Federal Reserve Bulletin* and the *Survey of Current Business*, estimate the following simplified version of a monetarist model:

$$\dot{Y}_t = \alpha_1 + \beta_1 \dot{M}_t + \beta_2 \dot{M}_{t-1} + \beta_3 \dot{M}_{t-2} + \beta_4 \dot{M}_{t-3} + \beta_5 \dot{M}_{t-4} + \beta_t$$

where:

$\dot{Y}_t$ = percentage change in nominal GNP at an annual rate
$\dot{M}_t$ = percentage change in money supply (M1) at an annual rate

How well does this model track the growth rate of nominal GNP compared to Dewald's system (equation (1) in Table 8-22)? Is it likely that a high $\bar{R}^2$ can be obtained when the quarterly percentage change in nominal GNP is used as the dependent variable?

REFERENCES FOR FURTHER STUDY

Butler, William F., Robert A. Kavesh, and Robert B. Platt, eds., *Methods and Techniques of Business Forecasting*. Englewood Cliffs, N.J.: Prentice-Hall, 1976.

Friedman, Milton, "A Monetary Theory of Nominal Income," *Journal of Political Economy*, March/April 1971.

McLaughlin, R.L., "A New Five-Phase Economic Forecasting System," *Business Economics*, September 1975, pp. 49–60.

Nerlove, M., "Lags in Economic Behavior," *Econometrica*, Vol. 40 (1972), 221–51.

Thompson, H.E., and G.C. Tiao, "Analysis of Telephone Data: A Case Study of Forecasting Seasonal Time Series," *Bell Journal of Economics and Management Science*, Vol. 2, No. 2 (Autumn 1971).

TIME-SERIES MODELS

PART V

9

Time-Series Models

INTRODUCTION

The second general type of quantitative forecasting technique is the time-series model. In such models, historical data for the forecast variable are analyzed in an attempt to discern any underlying pattern. Once identified, this pattern is extrapolated into the future to produce the forecast values. A naive version of this technique forecasts the value of the variable in the next period to be the same as in the current period. Another simplistic technique is to use the mean value as the forecast value. In all time-series models, predictions are based entirely on the historical values and the pattern of the data. Time-series models are, therefore, most useful when economic conditions can be expected to remain relatively stable, and they can be misleading when conditions are changing. For example, a time-series model can be employed to estimate short-run company demand patterns as long as management expects to continue its present advertising strategy. However, this model will be futile in evaluating or predicting the probable change in sales resulting from a new advertising campaign, since the model reflects past, not future, decisions.

Time-series models are most applicable when the underlying data pattern can be extended into the future and near-term forecasts (next week or next month) are needed. In this chapter, we introduce moving-average and exponential-smoothing models. With both these models, forecasts can be quickly revised, and a relatively small number of computations are required to incorporate new information. Additionally, exponential smoothing permits the forecaster to place more weight on current observations and minimizes data-storage requirements. Furthermore, these models are capable of directly handling the autocorrelation problems generally associated with time-series data.

The principal disadvantage of time-series models is their reliance on the assumption that historical patterns will continue into the future. Because forecasters are frequently interested in turning points, intuitive judgments must supplement time-series models in the determination of cyclical highs and lows.

MOVING-AVERAGE MODELS

SIMPLE MOVING AVERAGES

The moving-average forecasting technique is one of the easiest time-series models to use and understand. With this technique, the analyst assumes that the pattern exhibited by the historical observations can best be represented by an arithmetic mean of past observations. In terms of the time-series model specified in Chapter 4, the presence or absence of seasonal, cyclical, and irregular forces in the moving average depends on the length of the moving average—three months, six months, twelve months, or longer.

The simple moving-average model is set forth in equation (9-1):

$$M_t = \frac{Y_t + Y_{t-1} + Y_{t-2} + \cdots + Y_{t-n+1}}{n} \qquad (9\text{-}1)$$

where:

M_t = moving average at time t
Y_t = actual value in period t
n = number of terms included in the moving average

For computational purposes, equation (9-1) can be restated as:

$$M_t = M_{t-1} + \frac{Y_t - Y_{t-n}}{n} \qquad (9\text{-}2)$$

In both equations, the moving average for time period t is the arithmetic mean of the n most recent observations.

Several characteristics of this model are noteworthy. First, equal weights are assigned to each of the n most recent observations, with zero weight to all other past observations. Second, as each new data point becomes available, it is included in the average and the data point for the nth period preceding the new data point is discarded. Thus, each *new* estimate of M_t is an updated version of the preceding estimate. Equation (9-2) highlights this characteristic. Third, the rate of response of the moving average to changes in the underlying data pattern depends on the number of periods included in the moving average. In general, the larger n is (that is, the more periods included), the less sensitive the moving average will be to changes in the pattern of the data. Conversely, a small value of n leads to a moving average that responds relatively rapidly to changes. Finally, to obtain forecasts for periods beyond the current period, t, equation (9-1) must be modified as follows:

$$\hat{Y}_{t+1} = M_t = \frac{Y_t + Y_{t-1} + Y_{t-2} + \cdots + Y_{t-n+1}}{n} \qquad (9\text{-}3)$$

or:

$$\hat{Y}_{t+3} = \frac{\hat{Y}_{t+2} + \hat{Y}_{t+1} + Y_t + Y_{t-1} + \cdots + Y_{t-n+3}}{n}$$

where the $\frown$'s refer to forecasted values.

To illustrate the computations and to help you understand the forecasting procedure, consider the weekly sales figures presented in Table 9-1. These weekly figures are used by a major department store to determine the need for temporary sales personnel. To show the effect of lengthening or shortening the number of periods included in the moving average, columns 2 and 3 present the moving averages for $n = 3$ and $n = 6$, respectively. To apply equation (9-3) for $n = 3$, the relevant values are substituted as follows:

$$
\begin{aligned}
\hat{Y}_4 = M_3 &= \frac{Y_3 + Y_2 + Y_1}{n} \\
&= \frac{5.4 + 4.4 + 5.3}{3} \\
&= 5.0 \qquad (9\text{-}4)
\end{aligned}
$$

Note that the moving average for $n = 6$ fluctuates much less than does the series for $n = 3$. Determining which of the two values of n provides better forecasts is a matter of comparing the mean square error (MSE), the mean absolute deviation (MAD), and the mean absolute percentage error (MAPE). These measures were introduced in Chapter 4 as tools to be employed in evaluating the reliability of alternative models. Based on the data in Table 9-1, an n value of 6 performs better according to all three criteria. As a matter of course, the analyst should check other values of n prior to making a final

Table 9-1 Moving-average computations, weekly department store sales (Millions of dollars)

Period	Sales (1)	M_t ($n = 3$) (2)	M_t ($n = 6$) (3)	M_t^w (4)	$\hat{M}_{t+1}^d$ (5)
1	5.3	—	—	—	—
2	4.4	—	—	—	—
3	5.4	5.0[a]	—	5.0[a]	—
4	5.8	5.2	—	5.4	—
5	5.6	5.6	—	5.6	—
6	4.8	5.4	5.2[a]	5.2	6.2[a]
7	5.6	5.3	5.3	5.3	5.4
8	5.6	5.3	5.5	5.5	5.1
9	5.4	5.5	5.5	5.5	5.3
10	6.5	5.8	5.6	6.0	5.7
11	5.1	5.7	5.5	5.6	6.4
12	5.8	5.8	5.7	5.7	5.7
13	5.0	5.3	5.6	5.3	5.8
14	6.2	5.7	5.7	5.7	4.7
15	5.6	5.6	5.7	5.7	5.9
16	6.7	6.2	5.7	6.3	5.8
17	5.2	5.8	5.8	5.8	7.0
18	5.5	5.8	5.9	5.6	5.6
19	5.8	5.5	5.8	5.6	5.6
20	5.1	5.5	5.7	5.4	5.1
21	5.8	5.6	5.7	5.6	5.3
22	6.7	5.9	5.7	6.1	5.8
23	5.2	5.9	5.7	5.8	6.3
24	6.0	6.0	5.8	5.9	6.1
25	5.8	5.7	5.8	5.8	6.2
MSE[b] ($)		0.40	0.30	0.43	0.74
MAD[b] ($)		0.52	0.45	0.55	0.68
MAPE[b] (%)		9.1	7.7	9.8	12.2

[a]M_t is the simple moving average generated by equation (9-1); n is sample size; M_t^w is the weighted moving average (3, 2, 1) given by equation (9-8); and $\hat{M}_{t+1}^d$ is the double moving forecast given by equation (9-12).
[b]The mean square error (MSE), the mean absolute deviation (MAD), and the mean absolute percentage error (MAPE) were defined in Chapter 4.

decision; the best moving-average model is the one that has the lowest MSE, MAD, and MAPE. Generally, one model performs better according to all three criteria. Should this not be the case, the analyst must use his or her own judgment in selecting the most appropriate model.

Forecasting with moving-average models is a straightforward application of equation (9-3). As an example, assume that $n = 3$ and that we want a forecast for period 27. Equation (9-3) is utilized as follows:

$$\hat{Y}_{27} = \frac{\hat{Y}_{26} + Y_{25} + Y_{24}}{3}$$

$$= \frac{\hat{Y}_{26} + 5.8 + 6.0}{3} \qquad (9\text{-}5)$$

To complete this computation, an intermediate step is required, because an actual value for period 26 (Y_{26}) is unavailable. The best estimate for this period is the moving average for period 26:

$$\hat{Y}_{26} = (Y_{25} + Y_{24} + Y_{23})/3$$
$$= (5.8 + 6.0 + 5.2)/3$$
$$= 5.7 \qquad (9\text{-}6)$$

This value is then substituted into equation (9-5), yielding the following:

$$\hat{Y}_{27} = (5.7 + 5.8 + 6.0)/3$$
$$= 5.8 \qquad (9\text{-}7)$$

as the forecasted value for period 27.

There are two major limitations of the moving-average technique. First and foremost, data-storage requirements, hence costs, are sometimes high. This follows from the fact that in computation of a moving average, the previous n values must be available. Second, a moving average is influenced only by those periods included in the average, and each period shares equally in the forecast. It would seem reasonable to argue that more recent observations are likely to contain more pertinent information, hence should have a greater effect on future forecast values. Catering to this likelihood, a modified system of moving averages has been developed.

WEIGHTED MOVING AVERAGES

Weighted moving averages attempt to correct the defects present in simple moving-average procedures by modifying observations based on their proximity to the current period. Specifically, the data for each period are multiplied by a weight, with the weights declining as the data observations recede into the past. The weighted observations are then divided by the sum of the weights. In its most generalized form, the weighted moving-average model is:

$$M_t^w = \frac{w_n Y_t + w_{n-1} Y_{t-1} + \cdots + w_1 Y_{t-n+1}}{w_n + w_{n-1} + \cdots + w_1} \qquad (9\text{-}8)$$

The ws are the appropriate weighting factors, with the specific weights depending on both the response rate desired by the analyst and the frequency of changes in the historical data.

Refer back to the weekly sales data in Table 9-1. Let us arbitrarily assign weights of 3, 2, and 1 to periods Y_t, Y_{t-1}, and Y_{t-2}, respectively. The weighted moving average for period 3 is 5.0, computed as follows:

$$M_3^w = \frac{3Y_3 + 2Y_2 + 1Y_1}{3 + 2 + 1}$$
$$= [3(5.4) + 2(4.4) + 1(5.3)]/6$$
$$= 5.0$$

The remainder of the historical weighted moving averages are detailed in column 4 of Table 9-1.

Forecasting with this type of model requires the same modifications made in equation (9-3) for use with equation (9-1). Thus, the weighted-moving-average forecast for period 26 is:

$$\hat{Y}_{26} = [3(Y_{25}) + 2(Y_{24}) + 1(Y_{23})]/6$$
$$= [3(5.8) + 2(6.0) + 1(5.2)]/6$$
$$= 5.8$$

The principal disadvantage of the weighted moving average is that future forecast values are sensitive to both the number of periods included in the moving average and the specification of the weights. Nevertheless, the advantage of greater reliance on current observations must not be overlooked. In fact, the weighted moving average performed poorly according to all three criteria listed at the bottom of Table 9-1 and less closely simulated the historical data pattern.

DOUBLE MOVING AVERAGES

If the data being analyzed have a linear or quadratic trend, then both the simple and weighted moving averages may be inappropriate. Specifically, if a trend is present in the data, simple moving averages will lag behind the actual data. In order to correct for this bias, a double moving average, M_t^d, should be computed. To calculate M_t^d, one treats the simple moving average, M_t, as an individual data point and derives a second moving average based on the M_t observations:

$$M_t^d = \frac{M_t + M_{t-1} + \cdots + M_{t-n+1}}{n} \tag{9-9}$$

The first M_t^d computation ($n = 3$) is:

$$M_t^d = \frac{M_5 + M_4 + M_3}{3}$$
$$= (5.6 + 5.2 + 5.0)/3$$
$$= 5.3$$

Double moving average forecasts are noted in column 5 of Table 9-1.

The difference between M_t^d and M_t serves as the starting point for the double moving-average forecast, and this projection is based upon the following system of equations:

$$a_t = 2M_t - M_t^d \tag{9-10}$$

$$b_t = \frac{2}{n-1}(M_t - M_t^d) \tag{9-11}$$

$$\hat{M}_{t+T}^d = a_t + b_t T \tag{9-12}$$

In using equation (9-12) to develop the one-period-ahead projections shown in column 5 of Table 9-1, T has a value of 1. Thus the forecast for period 6 (done at the end of period 5) would be estimated as follows:

$$a_5 = 2M_5 - M_5^d$$
$$a_5 = 2(5.6) - (5.3) = 5.9$$
$$b_5 = \frac{2}{3-1}(5.6 - 5.3) = 0.3$$
$$\hat{M}_{5+1}^d = a_5 + b_5(1)$$
$$\hat{M}_6^d = 5.9 + .3(1)$$
$$\hat{M}_6^d = 6.2 \text{ (as shown in Table 9-1)}$$

As each new observation becomes available, a_t and b_t are recalculated; these new coefficient values are substituted in equation (9-12), and a *rolling* one-period-ahead forecast is calculated.

EXPONENTIAL SMOOTHING

SINGLE EXPONENTIAL SMOOTHING

Exponential smoothing is perhaps the most widely used time-series model. Despite the awesome name, it is an extremely simple technique to understand and apply: New forecasts are derived by adjusting the prior forecast to reflect its forecast error. In this way, the forecaster can continually revise the forecast based on past experience. In addition to this feature, exponential smoothing offers several advantages vis-à-vis moving-average models. First, exponential-smoothing models mesh very easily with computer systems. Second, data-storage requirements are minimal when compared with other forecasting models—in spite of the fact that current forecasts with exponential-smoothing models are based on all previous historical observations. Finally, this type of model has all the advantages of a weighted moving average, in that current observations are assigned larger weights; however, an exponential-smoothing model reacts more quickly to changes in economic conditions than do moving-average models.

In simple exponential-smoothing models, the forecast for the next and all subsequent periods is determined by adjusting the current-period forecast by a portion of the difference between the forecast and the actual value. Intuitively, this is a very appealing characteristic for any forecasting system. If recent forecasts have proved accurate, it seems reasonable to base subsequent forecasts on these estimates. On the other hand, if recent predictions have been subject to large errors, new forecasts should take this into consideration.

The basic formula for computing the single-exponential-smoothing statistic is:

$$S_t^1 = \alpha Y_t + (1 - \alpha)S_{t-1}^1 \qquad (9\text{-}13)$$

S_t^1 is called the single-exponential-smoothing statistic; Y_t is the actual value in time period t; and α is the smoothing constant ($0 \leq \alpha \leq 1$) selected by the analyst. Equation (9-13) can be restated as:

$$\text{New estimate} = \alpha(\text{New data}) + (1 - \alpha)(\text{Previous estimate})$$

Exponential smoothing has the advantage of requiring retention of only a limited amount of data. There is no need to store data for many periods, because the historical profile is recorded in concise form in one number—the current smoothed statistic.

Equation (9-13) can be restated in terms of time period $t - 1$ as:

$$S_{t-1}^1 = \alpha Y_{t-1} + (1 - \alpha)S_{t-2}^1 \qquad (9\text{-}14)$$

Substituting equation (9-14) into equation (9-13), we get:

$$S_t^1 = \alpha Y_t + \alpha(1 - \alpha) Y_{t-1} + (1 - \alpha)^2 S_{t-2}^1 \qquad (9\text{-}15)$$

but:

$$S_{t-2}^1 = \alpha Y_{t-2} + (1 - \alpha)S_{t-3}^1 \qquad (9\text{-}16)$$

Substituting again, we obtain:

$$S_t^1 = \alpha Y_t + \alpha(1 - \alpha) Y_{t-1} + \alpha(1 - \alpha)^2 Y_{t-2} + (1 - \alpha)^3 S_{t-3}^1 \qquad (9\text{-}17)$$

Substituting recursively for S_{t-3}^1, S_{t-4}^1, and so on, we obtain:

$$S_t^1 = \alpha Y_t + \alpha(1 - \alpha) Y_{t-1} + \alpha(1 - \alpha)^2 Y_{t-2} + \cdots$$
$$+ \alpha(1 - \alpha)^{t-1} Y_1 + (1 - \alpha)^t S_0 \qquad (9\text{-}18)$$

In other words, S_t^1 is a weighted average of $Y_t, Y_{t-1}, Y_{t-2}, \ldots, Y_1$ and the initial estimate of S_0^1. The coefficients of the observations:

$$\alpha, \alpha(1-\alpha), \alpha(1-\alpha)^2, \ldots, \alpha(1-\alpha)^{t-1}$$

are the weights and measure the contribution each observation makes to the most recent estimate. Additionally, it can be seen that these coefficients decrease geometrically with the age of the observation. That is, the most recent observation, Y_t, makes the largest contribution to the current estimate, and past observations make successively smaller contributions to S_t^1. Thus, distant observations are dampened out with the passage of time. The rate at which this dampening occurs depends on the value of the smoothing constant, α. In particular, the larger α is, the more quickly the influence of distant observations is minimized. For example, when $\alpha = .8$, the weights are .8, .16, .032, and .0064 for Y_t, Y_{t-1}, Y_{t-2}, and Y_{t-3}, respectively, and periods past Y_{t-3} have almost no effect on the current estimate, S_t^1.

The preceding discussion also serves to highlight the critical role played by the smoothing constant in obtaining reliable forecasts. Indeed, from the analyst's viewpoint, the main input in any smoothing technique is the size of alpha. As noted in the preceding paragraph, the value of α determines the extent to which past observations influence forecasts. Since small values of the smoothing constant dampen previous observations slowly, a small α should be utilized with time-series data that are relatively stable. Conversely, if we are dealing with a series that changes rapidly, a large smoothing constant is desirable, because it assigns larger weights to more recent observations. Unfortunately, the rapid response rate of an exponential model with a large α value may place too much emphasis on irregular variations while ignoring the underlying data patterns. In practice, values of α from 0.1 to .4 usually work best. One way of selecting the smoothing constant is to simulate the historical data set using alternative values of α. That is, for each value of α, a set of forecasts is generated and compared with the actual observations. The value of α that yields the *best* forecasts thus becomes the appropriate smoothing constant to be employed in future analysis. The determination of the best forecast model is made by examining the forecast errors obtained in the simulation. Typically, the set of forecast that has the smallest sum of squared errors is judged to be the best. This corresponds to the mean-square-error criterion introduced in Chapter 4.

The principal difficulty with the preceding technique is that it involves a time-consuming and costly trial-and-error process. An alternative approach to selecting the smoothing constant is to investigate a plot of the variable over time. It can be shown that the appropriate value of α is fundamentally related to the data pattern. In general, if the data plot reveals a time series with a small irregular component (that is, little random variation), the smoothing constant should be relatively small. Alternatively, if there are large fluctuations in the actual data plot, a relatively large value for α should be employed. If a smoothing value greater than $\alpha = .4$ seems to provide the best fit, the values in the time series are likely to be autocorrelated. Although single-exponential-smoothing techniques are occasionally successful in such situations, other smoothing techniques, such as double exponential smoothing or the Winters's method, may be more appropriate.

Further, it can be shown that α is related approximately to the number of terms in a simple moving average by the relationship:

$$\alpha = \frac{2}{n+1} \tag{9-19}$$

Equation (9-19) implies that when α is close to zero, an exponential-smoothing model behaves like a mean forecast or a moving-average model with a large n (that is, when $\alpha = .1$, the results are similar to a moving-average model when $n = 19$). When α is close to 1, the exponential model responds quickly to changes in the data pattern and corresponds to a small value of n (that is, if $\alpha = .9$, $n = 1.2$).[1]

Using exponential smoothing, consider the monthly inventory data listed in Table 9-2 and graphed in Figure 9-1. In order to begin the smoothing process,

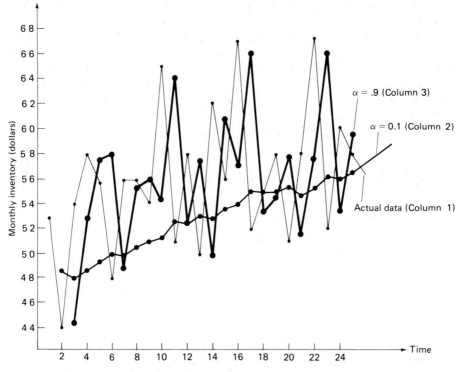

Figure 9-1 Monthly Inventory Forecasts Using Exponential Smoothing

Source: Table 9-2

[1]For example, if we assume that $\alpha = 1.00$, equation (9-13) becomes $S_t^1 = 1.00\ Y_t$; thus, the forecast for period $t + 1$ is simply Y_t.

Table 9-2 Single exponential smoothing: forecasting inventory levels

Date		Period	Inventory Level (1)	S_t^1 ($\alpha = .1$) (2)	S_t^1 ($\alpha = .9$) (3)	Exponential Forecast ($\alpha = .9$) (4)	Forecast Error ($\alpha = .9$) (5)
1978	Jan.	1	$53	53[a]	53[a]	—	—
	Feb.	2	44	52	45	53	9
	Mar.	3	54	52	53	45	-9
	April	4	58	53	58	53	-5
	May	5	56	53	56	58	2
	June	6	48	52	49	56	8
	July	7	56	53	55	49	-7
	Aug.	8	56	53	56	55	-1
	Sept.	9	54	53	54	56	2
	Oct.	10	65	54	64	54	-11
	Nov.	11	51	54	52	64	13
	Dec.	12	58	54	57	52	-6
1979	Jan.	13	50	54	46	57	7
	Feb.	14	62	55	60	46	-16
	Mar.	15	56	55	56	60	4
	April	16	67	56	66	56	-11
	May	17	52	56	53	66	14
	June	18	55	56	55	53	-2
	July	19	58	56	58	55	-3
	Aug.	20	51	55	52	58	7
	Sept.	21	58	56	57	52	-6
	Oct.	22	67	57	66	57	-10
	Nov.	23	52	57	53	66	14
	Dec.	24	60	57	59	53	-7
1980	Jan.	25	58	57	58	59	1
	MSE ($)						71

[a]This value is based on an assumed value for $S_0^1 = 53$.

the analyst must make an initial estimate of S_0^1 and select a value for α. The value for S_0^1 is needed to determine the smoothed statistic for S_1^1, as seen by:

$$S_1^1 = \alpha Y_1 + (1 - \alpha)S_0^1 \qquad (9\text{-}20)$$

The quickest way of determining a value for S_0^1 is to let $S_0^1 = Y_1$. (Alternative approaches for computing S_0^1 are noted in succeeding sections of this chapter.) To illustrate the effect of different smoothing constants, consider $\alpha = .1$ and $\alpha = .9$. Intuitively, it seems reasonable to base the smoothed statistic on recent observations rather than distant observations. This can be accomplished by starting with the initial estimate, S_0^1, and using equation (9-13) to recursively revise this smoothed statistic. Thus, at the end of the first period, the smoothed statistic is computed as follows:

$$S_1^1 = \alpha Y_1 + (1 - \alpha)S_0^1$$
$$= (.1)(53) + (1 - .1)(53)$$
$$= 53$$

The smoothed statistic for period 2 may now be computed as:

$$S_2^1 = \alpha Y_2 + (1 - \alpha)S_1^1$$
$$= (.1)(44) + (1 - .1)(53)$$
$$= 52 \qquad\qquad (9\text{-}21)$$

or, when $\alpha = .9$:

$$S_2^1 = (.9)(44) + (1 - .9)(53)$$
$$= 45 \qquad\qquad (9\text{-}22)$$

In a similar fashion, the single smoothed statistic is continually updated, using the remainder of the actual observations in column 1 of Table 9-2. The results for $\alpha = .1$ and $\alpha = .9$ are summarized in columns 2 and 3 and are plotted in Figure 9-1.

Selection of the most appropriate smoothing constant can be made by examining the plots in Figure 9-1. In this particular example, the model utilizing $\alpha = .9$ is more satisfactory. When $\alpha = .1$, the time series has been *oversmoothed;* that is, the turning points and data pattern have been missed and/or overlooked. Therefore, the model with $\alpha = .9$ as the smoothing constant will be used throughout the remainder of this example.

The quantities in Table 9-2 may now be used to generate forecasts of monthly inventory levels. Thus, at the end of period 1, the forecast for period 2 is 53. Furthermore, this would be the forecast for all future periods as long as the forecast is made in period 1. That is, $S_3^1 = S_4^1 = S_{26}^1 = 53$. However, when the actual data for period 2 become available, this forecast must be revised. For example, at the end of period 2, the actual inventory level is observed as 44. Now the forecast for period 3 is recomputed as 45:

$$S_2^1 = \alpha Y_2 + (1 - \alpha)S_1^1$$
$$= (.9)(44) + (.1)(53)$$
$$= 45$$

The remainder of the forecasts are prepared in a like manner and are presented in column 4. The errors associated with these forecasts are noted in column 5, with the mean square error (MSE) shown at the bottom of Table 9-2.

The preceding computations serve to highlight two of the more significant limitations of single-exponential-smoothing models. First, the model must be updated each time a new data point becomes available. This updating is useful in regression analysis, but it is critical in the case of exponential-smoothing models. Second, to be technically correct, this type of model will provide decision makers with forecasts for only one period into the future.

BROWN'S LINEAR EXPONENTIAL SMOOTHING

Whenever there is a growth pattern or trend in a time series, the single-exponential-smoothing model's statistics (and forecasts) will tend to lag behind movements in the actual time series. This occurs because the single-exponential-smoothing model is based on the assumption of a random variation around a constant value. If there is a linear trend, either positive or negative, in the data, Brown's linear-exponential-smoothing technique is apt to generate superior forecasts.

The underlying rationale for this linear-exponential-smoothing technique is relatively simple. Since both the single- and double-smoothed values lag the actual data whenever a trend exists, the difference between these two values can be added to the single-smoothed value and adjusted for trend. The basic equations employed in this process are:

$$S_t^1 = \alpha Y_t + (1 - \alpha)S_{t-1}^1 \qquad (9\text{-}23)$$

$$S_t^2 = \alpha S_t^1 + (1 - \alpha)S_{t-1}^2 \qquad (9\text{-}24)$$

where S_t^1 refers to the single-smoothed statistic and S_t^2 to the double-smoothed statistic. In order to apply equations (9-23) and (9-24), the analyst must have values for S_{t-1}^1 and S_{t-1}^2. However, when $t = 1$, these values are mathematically indeterminate and have to be specified at the outset of the smoothing process. This problem exists with all exponential-smoothing models, but it can be overcome with relative ease. The most common methods of assigning these initial values are either by letting $S_1^1 = S_1^2 = Y_1$, or by computing some type of average of the first few observations. This problem of arbitrarily fixing the initial value is not critical, because it can be shown that this value is quickly discounted, and the technique adjusts rapidly even if the initial estimate is grossly in error.

The figures shown in Table 9-3 are an example of applying Brown's technique for data with a significant trend component. These data represent monthly sales figures, beginning in January 1978, for a major department store in Memphis. Management would like to use these forecasts to plan for needed sales personnel in the near term. If the sales data in Table 9-3 are plotted against time, the series (see Figure 9-2) fluctuates around an average sales level that exhibits volatility over time.

To begin the process, assume that $S_1^1 = S_1^2 = (Y_1 + Y_2)/2 = 9{,}601$ and that $\alpha = .4$. Columns 2 and 3 of Table 9-3 provide the single- and double-

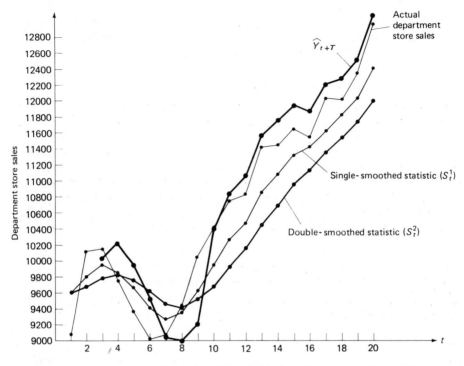

Figure 9-2 Alternative Smoothed Statistics for Department Store Sales

Source: Table 9-3

smoothed statistics that result from applying equations (9-23) and (9-24) to the sales data in column 1. For example, the computations for period 2 are:

$$S_t^1 = \alpha Y_t + (1 - \alpha)S_{t-1}^1 \tag{9-23}$$
$$S_2^1 = \alpha Y_2 + (1 - \alpha)S_1^1$$
$$= (.4)(10,128) + (.6)(9,601)$$
$$= 9,812 \tag{9-25}$$

and:

$$S_t^2 = \alpha S_t^1 + (1 - \alpha)S_{t-1}^2 \tag{9-24}$$
$$S_2^2 = \alpha S_2^1 + (1 - \alpha)S_1^2$$
$$= (.4)(9,812) + (.6)(9,601)$$
$$= 9,685 \tag{9-26}$$

The remaining figures in columns 2 and 3 are computed in an analogous manner. Additionally, the single- and double-smoothed statistics are plotted in Figure 9-2. Both the single- and double-smoothed statistics underestimate the trend

Table 9-3 Application of Brown's linear exponential smoothing to department store sales

Date		Period	Sales (1)	S_t^1 (2)	S_t^2 (3)	a_t (4)	b_t (5)	$\hat{Y}_{t+T}$ (6)	Error (7)
1978	Jan.	1	\$ 9,074	\$ 9,601[a]	\$ 9,601[a]				
	Feb.	2	10,128	9,812	9,685	\$ 9,939[b]	\$85[b]		
	March	3	10,155	9,949	9,791	10,107	105	\$10,024[c]	131[d]
	April	4	9,746	9,868	9,821	9,915	31	10,212	−466
	May	5	9,397	9,679	9,765	9,593	−57	9,946	−549
	June	6	9,012	9,412	9,624	9,200	−141	9,536	−524
	July	7	9,084	9,281	9,487	9,075	−137	9,059	25
	Aug.	8	9,447	9,347	9,431	9,263	−56	8,938	509
	Sept.	9	10,062	9,633	9,512	9,754	81	9,207	855
	Oct.	10	10,420	9,948	9,686	10,210	175	10,385	35
	Nov.	11	10,754	10,270	9,920	10,620	233	10,853	−99
	Dec.	12	10,826	10,493	10,149	10,837	229	11,066	−240
1979	Jan.	13	11,421	10,864	10,435	11,293	286	11,579	−158
	Feb.	14	11,442	11,095	10,699	11,491	264	11,755	−313
	March	15	11,665	11,323	10,949	11,697	249	11,946	−281
	April	16	11,559	11,417	11,136	11,698	187	11,885	−326
	May	17	12,046	11,619	11,349	11,989	213	12,202	−156
	June	18	12,024	11,811	11,534	12,088	185	12,273	−249
	July	19	12,350	12,026	11,731	12,321	197	12,518	−168
	Aug.	20	12,978	12,407	12,001	12,813	271	13,084	−106
MAD									288
MSE									121,243
MAPE (%)									2.65

[a]This value has been computed as $(9{,}074 + 10{,}128)/2 = 9{,}601$, which is the average of sales in periods 1 and 2. Also, we assume that $\alpha = .4$. S_t^1 and S_t^2 are defined in equations (9-23) and (9-24), respectively.
[b]The coefficients a_t and b_t are defined in equations (9-28) and (9-29), respectively.
[c]See equation (9-27). Results can be compared to Table 9-4.
[d]Column 1 less column 6.

pattern in Figure 9-2, and it is this defect that necessitates the use of Brown's linear-exponential technique.

Several additional formulas must be introduced in order to clarify the linkages between single and double exponential smoothing and Brown's technique:

$$\hat{Y}_{t+T} = a_t + b_t T \qquad (9\text{-}27)$$

T is the number of time periods from the present period, t, to the future period for which a forecast is desired, and a_t and b_t are defined as:

$$a_t = 2S_t^1 - S_t^2 \qquad (9\text{-}28)$$

$$b_t = \frac{\alpha}{1 - \alpha}(S_t^1 - S_t^2) \qquad (9\text{-}29)$$

As an example, suppose that we are currently in period 2 and want to develop a forecast for period 3. Based on the data in Table 9-3, the necessary calculations for equation (9-27) are:

$$a_2 = 2S_2^1 - S_2^2$$
$$= 2(9,812) - 9,685$$
$$= 9,939 \qquad (9\text{-}30)$$

$$b_2 = \frac{\alpha}{1-\alpha}(S_2^1 - S_2^2)$$
$$= \frac{.4}{.6}(9,812 - 9,685)$$
$$= 85 \qquad (9\text{-}31)$$

$$\hat{Y}_{t+T} = a_t + b_t T$$
$$\hat{Y}_{2+1} = a_2 + b_2(1)$$
$$= 9,939 + 85(1)$$
$$= 10,024$$

Thus, the forecast for period 3 made in period 2 is 10,024, as compared to the actual level of sales of 10,155, an error of $+131$, or $+1.3\%$. One-period-ahead forecasts for periods 3 through 20 are listed in column 6. The errors associated with these forecasts are presented in column 7, and MSE, MAD, and MAPE statistics are shown at the bottom of Table 9-3. The reliability of the forecasts can be seen by examining Figure 9-2.

Forecasting for time periods that extend beyond the data base involves virtually the same procedure. From the values of S_{20}^1 and S_{20}^2, the analyst can calculate the values of a_{20} and b_{20}:

$$a_{20} = 2(12,407) - 12,001$$
$$= 12,813 \qquad (9\text{-}32)$$

$$b_{20} = \frac{.4}{.6}(12,407 - 12,001)$$
$$= 271 \qquad (9\text{-}33)$$

Thus, forecasts for periods 21 to 25 *made in period* 20 are:

$$\hat{Y}_{21} = a_{20} + b_{20}(1) = 12,813 + (271)1 = 13,084$$
$$\hat{Y}_{22} = a_{20} + b_{20}(2) = 12,813 + (271)2 = 13,355$$
$$\hat{Y}_{23} = a_{20} + b_{20}(3) = 12,813 + (271)3 = 13,626$$
$$\hat{Y}_{24} = a_{20} + b_{20}(4) = 12,813 + (271)4 = 13,897$$
$$\hat{Y}_{25} = a_{20} + b_{20}(5) = 12,813 + (271)5 = 14,168$$

TRIPLE EXPONENTIAL SMOOTHING

Just as single-exponential-smoothing techniques fail when a linear trend is present in the data, Brown's linear exponential smoothing fails whenever the data exhibit a nonlinear trend pattern. Consider a situation in which the average level of the time series changes over time in a quadratic or curvilinear fashion. An appropriate model for such a time series is:

$$Y_t = \beta_0 + \beta_1 t + \beta_2 t^2 \tag{9-34}$$

Such a model implies that the time series being studied is either increasing at an increasing/decreasing rate or decreasing at an increasing/decreasing rate.

Triple exponential smoothing, sometimes called quadratic smoothing, involves the use of three smoothed statistics:

$$S_t^1 = \alpha Y_t + (1 - \alpha)S_{t-1}^1 \tag{9-35}$$

$$S_t^2 = \alpha S_t^1 + (1 - \alpha)S_{t-1}^2 \tag{9-36}$$

$$S_t^3 = \alpha S_t^2 + (1 - \alpha)S_{t-1}^3 \tag{9-37}$$

S_t^1 and S_t^2 are the single- and double-smoothed statistics used in Brown's linear exponential smoothing, and S_t^3 is the triple-smoothed statistic that is derived by smoothing the output of the double-smoothing equation (9-36).

Forecasts based on triple exponential smoothing require the estimation of three additional coefficients:

$$a_t = 3S_t^1 - 3S_t^2 + S_t^3 \tag{9-38}$$

$$b_t = \frac{\alpha}{2(1 - \alpha)^2}[(6 - 5\alpha)S_t^1 - (10 - 8\alpha)S_t^2 + (4 - 3\alpha)S_t^3] \tag{9-39}$$

$$c_t = \left[\frac{\alpha}{(1 - \alpha)}\right]^2 (S_t^1 - 2S_t^2 + S_t^3) \tag{9-40}$$

In turn, a_t, b_t, and c_t are used as follows:

$$\hat{Y}_{t+T} = a_t + b_t T + 1/2 c_t T^2 \tag{9-41}$$

The terms in equation (9-41) are defined as they were in equation (9-27).

To begin the triple-smoothing process, initial values for the smoothed statistics (S_t^1, S_t^2, and S_t^3) and α must be specified by the analyst. Based on $\alpha = .4$ and the initialization of S_1^1, S_1^2, and S_1^3, the smoothed statistics for the sales example are computed in columns 2, 3, and 4 of Table 9-4. Once these values have been determined, the forecasting procedure is similar to that presented in connection with linear exponential smoothing. In each time period, the relevant smoothed statistics are entered into equation (9-41) in order to produce the needed forecast. For example, in preparing a forecast for period 21, the initial step is to compute a_{20}, b_{20}, and c_{20}, based on values for S_{20}^1,

Table 9-4 Application of triple exponential smoothing to department store sales

Period	Sales (Millions) (1)	S_t^1 (2)	S_t^2 (3)	S_t^3 (4)	a_t (5)	b_t (6)	c_t (7)
1	$ 9,074	$ 9,601ᵃ	$ 9,601ᵃ	$ 9,601ᵃ			
2	10,128	9,812	9,685	9,635	$10,016ᵇ	$204ᵇ	$34ᵇ
3	10,155	9,949	9,791	9,697	10,171	205	28
4	9,746	9,868	9,821	9,747	9,888	−11	−12
5	9,397	9,679	9,765	9,754	9,496	−208	−43
6	9,012	9,412	9,624	9,702	9,066	−349	−60
7	9,084	9,281	9,487	9,616	8,998	−257	−34
8	9 447	9,347	9,431	9,542	9,290	−14	12
9	10,062	9,633	9,512	9,530	9,893	297	62
10	10,420	9,948	9,686	9,592	10,378	436	75
11	10,754	10,270	9,920	9,723	10 773	471	68
12	10,826	10,493	10,149	9,894	10,926	368	40
13	11,421	10,864	10,435	10,110	11,397	448	46
14	11,442	11,095	10,699	10,346	11,534	331	19
15	11,665	11,323	10,949	10,587	11,709	268	5
16	11,559	11,417	11,136	10,807	11,650	113	−21
17	12,046	11,619	11,349	11,024	11,834	94	−24
18	12,024	11,811	11,534	11,228	12,059	139	−13
19	12,350	12,026	11,731	11,429	12,314	186	−3
20	12,978	12,407	12,001	11,658	12,876	368	28

ᵃThe value of 9,601 is the average of actual sales in periods 1 and 2; that is, $9,601 = (9,074 + 10,128)/2$. Results of triple smoothing can be compared to Table 9-3.
ᵇThe coefficients a_t, b_t, and c_t are defined in equations (9-38), (9-39), and (9-40), respectively.

S_{20}^2, and S_{20}^3. Assuming $\alpha = .4$, these statistics can be calculated as:

$$S_{20}^1 = (.40)(12,978) + (.60)(12,026)$$
$$= 12,407$$
$$S_{20}^2 = (.40)(12,407) + (.60)(11,731)$$
$$= 12,001$$
$$S_{20}^3 = (.40)(12,001) + (.60)(11,429)$$
$$= 11,658 \qquad (9\text{-}42)$$

Substituting into the equations for a_{20}, b_{20}, and c_{20}, we get:

$$a_{20} = 3(12,407) - 3(12,001) + 11,658$$
$$= 12,876$$
$$b_{20} = \frac{.4}{2(1 - .4)^2}\{[6 - 5(.4)]12,407 - [10 - 8(.4)]12,001 + [4 - 3(.4)]11,658\}$$
$$= 368$$

$$c_{20} = \frac{(.4)^2}{(1-.4)^2}[12,407 - 2(12,001) + 11,658]$$

$$= 28 \tag{9-43}$$

Thus, the forecast for period 21 is:

$$\begin{aligned}
\hat{Y}_{20+1} &= a_{20} + b_{20}T + 1/2c_{20}T^2 \\
&= 12,876 + 368(1) + 1/2(28)(1^2) \\
&= 13,258
\end{aligned} \tag{9-44}$$

Similarly, the forecast for period 25 made in period 20 would be:

$$\begin{aligned}
\hat{Y}_{20+5} &= a_{20} + b_{20}(5) + 1/2c_{20}(5)^2 \\
&= 12,876 + 368(5) + 1/2(28)(5^2) \\
&= 15,066
\end{aligned} \tag{9-45}$$

EVALUATION OF SMOOTHING TECHNIQUES

The major advantages of the smoothing methods introduced here are their relative simplicity and low cost. This latter point cannot be overstated. For example, if a business has 5,000 items in inventory and wants forecasts of each, the fact that exponential smoothing requires only the latest smoothed statistics can lead to substantial cost savings when compared to other forecasting procedures. Although greater accuracy may be attainable with either regression models or the more advanced time-series models introduced in Chapter 10, the additional cost may outweigh the gain in accuracy.

The appropriate smoothing technique is dependent upon the data pattern exhibited by the data. If the data fluctuate around a relatively constant value, single exponential smoothing is preferable. Whenever a trend is present in the data, the analyst must determine whether the trend is linear or nonlinear. In addition to the smoothing techniques presented here, others are available that are applicable to data with a seasonal or cyclical pattern.

Despite the attractiveness of exponential smoothing, however, it has several limitations. First and foremost is the fact that the forecasts generated via exponential-smoothing techniques are sensitive to the specification of the smoothing constant. The decision as to the *correct* α value is pragmatic, in that it is based on a trial-and-error process. Second, exponential-smoothing techniques either miss or lag behind the turning points in actual time-series data. Finally, because these techniques are based on the assumption of constancy, they cannot be used to evaluate the effect of a managerial decision such as a price change or a modification in marketing strategies.

Example 9-1: Planning Flight-Attendant Requirements

The personnel manager for a major airline is responsible for ensuring that an adequate number of flight attendants have completed the four-week training program in time to fulfill the airline's demand. Specifically, his forecasting assignment involves development of a continuously updated forecast of next month's demand for flight attendants that can be used to determine how many trainees must be recruited for the current month's training program. The demand for this labor service is a derived demand, in the sense that the number of attendants required is directly related to the demand for the air passenger service. Thus, an estimate of next month's demand for passenger service can be utilized to derive an estimate of next month's demand for flight attendants and to determine the number of people needed in the training program in the current month. As a result, the immediate task is to construct a model that can be used to forecast the demand for air travel.

After a number of variables related to the company's traffic volume are analyzed, it is found that there is a stable relationship between the number of attendants required and the total number of air-miles flown. That is, the ratio of attendants per air-mile flown fluctuates very little. A regression model for air miles could be constructed (see, for example, the model in Chapter 5), but a time-series methodology is judged preferable in the present situation because the forecasts needed are very short term in nature and because the consequences of missing a turning point are minimal. Seasonally adjusted monthly data for the forecast variable, AMT (air-miles traveled), were collected for the period from October 1972 to December 1978. (The data employed in this problem are presented in Appendix I, Table I-1).

A visual inspection of the actual data indicates the presence of a trend component; thus, the appropriate time-series techniques are the double moving average, Brown's linear exponential smoothing, and triple exponential smoothing. S_1^1, S_1^2, and S_1^3 were initialized by setting them equal to Y_1's value, 7.00. Alternative values of α (the smoothing constant) and n (the number of periods in the double moving average) were tested by simulating the historical values. As a result of this trial-and-error process, a smoothing constant of $\alpha = .3$ was chosen and the two exponential-smoothing techniques were judged to perform better than the double moving average, according to the MSE and MAPE criteria.

Columns 2 through 7 of Table I-1 present the results of an *ex post* simulation for the entire historical data base for Brown's linear exponential smoothing (columns 2, 3, and 4) and triple exponential smoothing (columns 5, 6, and 7). A summary of these results is presented in Table 9-5. An examination of the statistics in that table indicates that the performance of both techniques is relatively similar. That is, on the basis of these summary statistics, a forecaster has no clear method of selecting one technique over the other. Since the airline is primarily interested in the model's ability to forecast accurately (as opposed to its ability to simulate historical data), it is necessary to carry out an *ex post* forecast in which the model is simulated beyond the estimation period but not beyond the last date for which actual observations are available. To perform this simulation, the two exponential-smoothing models were reestimated, with the last five monthly observations excluded from the data base. The results are presented in columns 2 through 7 of Table I-2 in Appendix I. In order to generate forecasts with the exponential-smoothing techniques, values for a_t, b_t, and c_t must be

Table 9-5 Time-series simulations for air miles traveled,
October 1972 to December 1978

	Brown's Linear Exponential Smoothing[a]	Triple Exponential Smoothing[a]
MSE (millions of miles)	1.09	1.08
MAPE (%)	3.5	3.7
Largest percentage error	26	31
Number of periods in which forecast error exceeded:		
5%	15	15
10%	4	4
Average percentage error over last 12 months	2.53	1.92

[a]$\alpha = .3, S_1^1 = S_1^2 = S_1^3 = Y_1 = 7.00$
Source: Table I-1 in Appendix I

computed, which, in turn, requires values for S_t^1, S_t^2, and S_t^3. Table I-3 of Appendix I presents the values of the smoothed statistics (S_t^1, S_t^2, and S_t^3) for all 70 months. The formulas utilized in forecasting with Brown's linear-exponential-smoothing technique are:

$$\hat{Y}_{t+T} = a_t + b_t T \tag{9-27}$$

and:

$$a_t = 2S_t^1 - S_t^2 \tag{9-28}$$

$$b_t = \frac{\alpha}{1-\alpha}(S_t^1 - S_t^2) \tag{9-29}$$

For example, the forecast for July 1978 (period 70) made in June 1978 (period 69) is based on the following computations:

$$\hat{Y}_{69+1} = a_{69} + b_{69}(1)$$
$$a_{69} = 2S_{69}^1 - S_{69}^2$$
$$= 2(39.85) - 37.68$$
$$= 42.01$$
$$b_{69} = \left(\frac{\alpha}{1-\alpha}\right)(S_{69}^1 - S_{69}^2)$$
$$= \frac{.3}{(1-.3)}(S_{69}^1 - S_{69}^2)$$
$$= (.42857)(39.85 - 37.68)$$
$$= 0.929997$$
$$\hat{Y}_{70} = 42.02 + 0.929997$$
$$= 42.94 \tag{9-46}$$

The remainder of the forecast values in column 2 of Table I-2 were prepared in a similar fashion. That is, the forecast for month 71 (August 1979) made in month 70 (July 1979) is:

$$a_{70} = 44$$
$$b_{70} = 1.11428 \qquad (9\text{-}47)$$

and:

$$\hat{Y}_{71} = a_{70} + b_{70}(1)$$
$$= 44 + 1.11428(1)$$
$$= 45.11 \qquad (9\text{-}48)$$

Alternatively, the forecast for December 1979 (period 75) made in July 1979 (period 70) would be:

$$\hat{Y}_{t+T} = a_t + b_t T \qquad (9\text{-}27)$$
$$\hat{Y}_{70+5} = a_{70} + b_{70}(5)$$
$$\hat{Y}_{75} = 44 + 1.11428(5)$$
$$= 49.57$$

Column 2 of Table 9-6 lists the *ex post* forecasts for periods 70–75 made with Brown's linear-exponential-smoothing technique.

Table 9-6 *Ex post* forecasts for air-miles traveled (Millions of miles)

Date	Actual Air-Miles Traveled Y_t	Brown's Linear Exponential Forecasts[a]			Triple Exponential Forecasts[b]		
		$\hat{Y}_t$	$e_t{}^c$	$e_{tp}{}^d$	$\hat{Y}_t$	$e_t{}^c$	$e_{tp}{}^d$
			(Absolute)	(Percent)		(Absolute)	(Percent)
(1978)	(1)	(2)	(3)	(4)	(5)	(6)	(7)
August	47.00	45.11	1.89	4.0	46.45	0.55	1.2
September	48.00	46.23	1.77	3.7	48.42	−0.42	−0.9
October	51.00	47.34	3.66	7.2	50.47	0.53	1.0
November	50.00	48.46	1.54	3.1	52.65	−2.65	−5.3
December	52.00	49.57	2.43	4.7	54.96	−2.96	−5.7

[a]These forecasts are based on $a_{70} = 44$ and $b_{70} = 1.11428$.
[b]These forecasts are based on $a_{70} = 44.67$, $b_{70} = 1.75$, and $c_{70} = 0.0615$.
[c]$e_t = (Y_t - \hat{Y}_t)$
[d]$e_{tp} = e_t/Y_t$

To forecast with the triple-exponential-smoothing technique, it is necessary to derive values for a_t, b_t, and c_t that can be substituted into:

$$\hat{Y}_{t+T} = a_t + b_t T + 1/2\, c_t T^2 \qquad (9\text{-}41)$$

For example, the forecast for August 1978 (period 71) is made in July 1978 (period 70) as follows:

$$a_t = 3S_t^1 - 3S_t^2 + S_t^3 \tag{9-38}$$
$$a_{70} = 3(41.4) - 3(38.8) + 36.87$$
$$= 44.67$$

$$b_t = \frac{\alpha}{2(1-\alpha)^2}[(6 - 5\alpha)S_t^1 - (10 - 8\alpha)S_t^2 + (4 - 3\alpha)S_t^3] \tag{9-39}$$
$$b_{70} = \frac{.3}{2(.7)^2}[(4.5)(41.4) - (7.6)(38.8) + (3.1)(36.87)]$$
$$= 1.75$$

$$c_t = \left[\frac{\alpha}{1-\alpha}\right]^2(S_t^1 - 2S_t^2 - S_t^3) \tag{9-40}$$
$$c_{70} = \frac{(.3)^2}{(.7)^2}[41.4 - 2(38.8) + 36.87]$$
$$= 0.0615$$

Therefore:

$$\hat{Y}_{70+1} = a_{70} + b_{70}(1) + 1/2\, c_{70}(1)^2$$
$$= 44.67 + (1.75)(1) + 1/2\,(0.0615)(1)$$
$$= 46.45 \tag{9-49}$$

The remainder of the *ex post* forecasts from the triple-exponential-smoothing model are listed in column 5 of Table 9-6.

Columns 3 and 6 in Table 9-6 present the absolute error of the two forecasting methods, and columns 4 and 7 illustrate the percentage errors. Brown's linear-exponential model consistently underestimates air miles traveled and would lead to underestimates in the demand for flight attendants. When demand for air passenger service is growing, underestimates are potentially more dangerous than overestimates. If too many attendants graduate this month, fewer need to be recruited next month. On the other hand, if sufficient attendants are not available, passenger service may suffer and the airline may receive bad publicity. Judged on the basis of these five periods, triple exponential smoothing is preferable, because the average error is less than for Brown's model. However, even this conclusion is tentative because of the results for the last two months (November and December 1978) in Table 9-6. As compared to errors of 3.1 and 4.7 percent via Brown's method, the triple-smoothing technique yields errors of −5.3 and −5.7 percent, respectively. In fact, a forecaster for an airline would rely on both models for monthly forecasts.

Thus, constant monitoring is required, since one or both methods might prove faulty owing to a variety of exogenous and endogenous factors. With the advantage of hindsight, we know that the economy peaked in January 1980, one year after the period outlined in Table 9-6. As the economy approaches such a turning point, all time-series models become suspect. The point to remember is that, since time-series models are extrapolations of the past, they are subject to relatively large errors when forecasts far into the future are needed. Indeed, one would probably find airline fore-casters combining the results of time-series analysis with regression models more closely attuned to cyclical forces in the economy. Once a projection for air miles has been prepared, it would be translated into an estimate of the demand for flight atten-dants and forwarded to the training-program manager, and would become part of the constantly updated information flows upon which decision makers must base their decisions.

Example 9-2: Combining Time-Series and Regression Models

In constructing regression models to be used for forecasting, the analyst must select independent variables for which future values can be obtained. Previous examples have illustrated the use of commercial-vendor forecasts of independent variables and incorporation of lagged independent variables. A third choice is to combine regression models with time-series techniques. This process can be illustrated by referring back to the installment-loan model for Memphis presented in Chapter 6 and reproduced below:

$$\widehat{INST}_t = -56.08784 + 0.9635235PINST_{t-1} - 1.249709U_t$$
$$t_e \qquad\qquad\qquad 58.07 \qquad\qquad 1.50$$
$$+ 0.6060539MEMIND_t \qquad (6\text{-}22)$$
$$3.01$$

$\bar{R}^2 = 0.995$ SEE = 3.44   DW = 2.02 $F_{3,56} = 3{,}892$ APE = 1.38

---

where:

$INST_t$ = installment-loan demand; monthly data in millions of dollars
$PINST_{t-1}$ = INST lagged one period
U_t = monthly unemployment rate in Memphis
$MEMIND_t$ = index of economic activity in Memphis

To make this equation operational, forecast values are needed for $PINST_{t-1}$, U_t, and $MEMIND_t$. Since $PINST_{t-1}$ is a lagged variable, this presents no particular difficulty. Additionally, commercial forecast vendors frequently provide forecasts of unemploy-ment rates for major metropolitan areas. However, we can be virtually certain that forecast values for $MEMIND_t$, the Memphis index of coincident economic indicators, will not be available from any source.

For the purpose of obtaining future values for $MEMIND_t$, a time-series model is developed based on the actual observations for $MEMIND_t$ presented in column 1 of Table 9-7. A cursory examination indicates that a linear-trend technique is apt to provide the best forecast values. A double moving average and Brown's linear exponen-tial smoothing were the alternative techniques tested, and the latter technique was deemed to be preferable. The forecasts and forecast errors associated with Brown's linear exponential smoothing are presented in columns 2 and 3 of Table 9-7. The sum-mary statistics noted at the bottom of the table indicate that this model performed

Table 9-7 *Ex post* analysis of time series forecasts of Memphis index of economic activity (1967 = 100.00)

Date		Period	MEMIND$_t$ (1)	$\widehat{\text{MEMIND}}_t^a$ (2)	ERROR Actual[b] (3)	ERROR Percentage[c] (4)
1975	Jan.	1	117.50			
	Feb.	2	118.20	117.90	.30	.25%
	March	3	116.90	118.06	−1.16	−.99%
	April	4	117.00	117.24	−.24	−.21%
	May	5	117.10	116.98	.12	.11%
	June	6	116.00	116.96	−.96	−.83%
	July	7	117.40	116.10	1.30	1.11%
	Aug.	8	117.20	116.89	.31	.26%
	Sept.	9	117.70	117.10	.60	.51%
	Oct.	10	116.90	117.59	−.69	−.59%
	Nov.	11	117.40	117.14	.26	.22%
	Dec.	12	117.70	117.34	.36	.30%
1976	Jan.	13	118.40	117.67	.73	.62%
	Feb.	14	117·30	118.35	−1.05	−.89%
	March	15	117.30	117.72	−.42	−.36%
	April	16	117.50	117.43	.07	.06%
	May	17	118.50	117.46	1.04	.88%
	June	18	118.30	118.28	.02	.02%
	July	19	118.50	118.45	.05	.04%
	Aug.	20	118.60	118.65	−.05	−.04%
	Sept.	21	120.40	118.77	1.63	1.35%
	Oct.	22	121.30	120.23	1.07	.88%
	Nov.	23	120.30	121.50	−1.20	−1.00%
	Dec.	24	122.80	121.13	1.67	1.36%
1977	Jan.	25	123.20	122.86	.34	.27%
	Feb.	26	122.40	123.80	−1.40	−1.14%
	March	27	122.70	123.40	−.70	−.57%
	April	28	123.00	123.33	−.33	−.27%
	May	29	123.30	123.45	−.15	−.12%
	June	30	123.40	123.66	−.26	−.21%
	July	31	123.60	123.76	−.16	−.13%
	Aug.	32	124.00	123.90	.10	.08%
	Sept.	33	124.20	124.22	−.02	−.01%
	Oct.	34	124.90	124.46	.44	.35%
	Nov.	35	125.00	125.06	−.06	−.05%
	Dec.	36	125.80	125.34	.46	.37%
1978	Jan.	37	125.60	126.02	−.42	−.33%
	Feb.	38	127.10	126.07	1.03	.81%
	March	39	127.40	127.21	.19	.15%
	April	40	128.40	127.85	.55	.43%
	May	41	128.60	128.80	−.20	−.16%
	June	42	129.20	129.24	−.04	−.03%
	July	43	129.10	129.78	−.68	−.53%
	Aug.	44	129.00	129.80	−.80	−.62%
	Sept.	45	128.40	129.61	−1.21	−.95%

Table 9-7 Continued

Date		Period	MEMIND$_t$ (1)	$\widehat{\text{MEMIND}}_t^a$ (2)	ERROR	
					Actual^b (3)	Precentage^c (4)
	Oct.	46	129.00	128.97	.03	.02%
	Nov.	47	130.00	129.13	.87	.67%
	Dec.	48	129.20	129.96	−.76	−.59%
1979	Jan.	49	129.10	129.63	−.53	−.41%
	Feb.	50	129.10	129.36	−.26	−.20%
	March	51	129.00	129.22	−.22	−.17%
	April	52	129.10	129.07	.03	.02%
	May	53	128.90	129.09	−.19	−.15%
	June	54	127.50	128.93	−1.43	−1.13%
	July	55	128.20	127.75	.45	.35%
	Aug.	56	127.20	127.85	−.65	−.51%
	Sept.	57	127.90	127.14	.76	.60%
	Oct.	58	127.30	127.45	−.15	−.12%
	Nov.	59	126.50	127.16	−.66	−.52%
	Dec.	60	126.20	126.43	−.23	−.19%

Mean Squared Error (MSE) = .49
Mean Absolute Precentage Error (MAPE) = .4%
^{a}These estimates were generated by applying Brown's linear-exponential-smoothing technique to the Memphis index of economic activity.
$^b e_t = \text{MEMIND}_t - \widehat{\text{MEMIND}}_t$
^{c}Percentage Error $= e_t/\text{MEMIND}_t$

admirably in the *ex post* (historical) simulation. The only potential difficulty is that the forecast values for the Memphis index tend to lag actual values by one period (month) at several of the turning points.

To test the effectiveness of combining time-series and regression models, we substituted the forecast values for $\widehat{\text{MEMIND}}_t$ (column 2 of Table 9-7) for the actual values of MEMIND$_t$ and reran the regression equation. That is, in estimating equation (6-22), actual values for the Memphis index (column 1 of Table 9-7) were utilized, whereas in the new equation, these values were replaced by the forecast values. (Note that this implies one less data point, because no forecast is available for the first period.) The new regression equation is:

$$\widehat{\text{INST}}_t = -56.851 + 0.9633114\text{PINST}_{t-1} - 1.199139\text{U}_t$$

$$t_e \qquad\qquad\quad 56.92 \qquad\qquad\qquad 1.42$$

$$+ 0.6087878\widehat{\text{MEMIND}}_t \qquad (9\text{-}50)$$

$$2.94$$

$\bar{R}^2 = 0.995$	SEE = 3.41	DW = 2.02	$F_{3,55} = 3{,}956$	APE = 1.50

All variables are defined as before except for $\widehat{\text{MEMIND}}_t$, which is now defined as the time-series estimate of MEMIND$_t$. A comparison of equations (9-50) and (6-22) is enlightening. The regression coefficients and the statistics are virtually identical. With the original regression model now modified and with equation (9-50) based on the estimated index of economic activity for Memphis, the model can be used to forecast installment-loan demand in Memphis. In this case, it was necessary to develop a secondary time-series model of economic activity in order to make the original regression usable.[2]

Example 9-3: Turning-Point Evaluations of Time-Series Models

Example 7-2 presented the details of the final regression equation developed for unit sales of automobiles. It is possible that a time-series model would perform as well or better in terms of providing one-period-ahead forecasts. If this turns out to be true, the time-series model would be preferable, because of its lower cost and ease of implementation. In this particular example, the model's turning-point performance is critical, since the forecasts are the major input in determining the availability of funds to finance inventories.

Actual values for unit sales of automobiles are listed in column 1 of Table 9-8. Since an examination of the data indicated the presence of a linear trend, the only two techniques tested were the double moving average and Brown's linear exponential smoothing. After a number of historical simulations, the latter technique was selected. Column 3 of Table 9-8 presents the forecasts of unit sales of automobiles generated by applying Brown's linear-exponential technique. The summary statistics are MSE = 0.64 and MAPE = 6.8 percent. The turning-point performance of Brown's linear-exponential model can be evaluated with the aid of Figure 9-3. The vertical axis measures actual changes in unit sales of automobiles ($\Delta Y_t = Y_t - Y_{t-1}$), and the horizontal axis measures predicted changes ($\Delta \hat{Y}_t = \hat{Y}_t - \hat{Y}_{t-1}$). The 45° line represents the line of perfect forecasts ($\Delta \hat{Y}_t = \Delta Y_t$). This simple graph can be used to quickly judge the turning-point reliability of a technique based on just a few considerations:

1. A clustering of points around the 45° line indicates that the model is forecasting accurately.
2. Quadrants IA and IIIA represent periods in which the technique overestimates changes: For point F, $\Delta \hat{Y} = .65$ and $\Delta Y = .23$; for point C, $\Delta \hat{Y} = -1.27$ and $\Delta Y = -.50$.
3. Quadrants IB and IIIB represent periods in which the technique underestimates changes: For point E, $\Delta \hat{Y} = .19$ and $\Delta Y = 1.04$; for point A, $\Delta \hat{Y} = -.08$ and $\Delta Y = -2.13$.

The remaining points in columns 2 and 4 are plotted in Figure 9-3. Of particular interest in this example are the points located in quadrants II and IV, since these represent periods in which turning-point errors occurred. In quadrant II, for example, at point D, actual unit sales of automobiles increased, but Brown's linear exponential model predicted a decline in sales. There were 19 quarters in which this type of turning-point error occurred. Conversely, quadrant IV represents periods in which actual unit sales decreased (ΔY_t at point B = -1.30), whereas the prediction was for an increase in sales ($\Delta \hat{Y}_t$ at point B = $+.81$). Twenty-one of these turning-point errors resulted

---

[2]Another technique employed by forecasters is to build a regression model, run the *ex post* simulation, measure the errors, and build a time-series model to estimate the error term.

Table 9-8 Turning-point analysis for unit car sales
(Millions of units, Quarterly, 1960: I to 1979: IV)

Period Number	Unit Sales of Automobiles (Y_t) (1)	Actual Change $(\Delta Y_t = Y_t - Y_{t-1})$ (2)	Forecast[a] $(\hat{Y}_t)$ (3)	Predicted Change $(\Delta\hat{Y}_t = \hat{Y}_t - \hat{Y}_{t-1})$ (4)	
1	6.13				
2	6.10		5.91		
3	6.33	.23	6.11	.20	
4	5.93	−.40	6.26	.15	
5	5.00	−.93	6.05	−.21	
6	5.43	.43	5.30	−.75	
7	5.63	.20	5.24	−.06	
8	6.17	.54	5.38	.14	
9	6.40	.23	5.85	.47	
10	6.67	.27	6.25	.40	
11	6.53	−.14	6.62	.37	
12	7.20	.67	6.69	.07	
13	7.23	.03	7.17	.48	
14	7.33	.10	7.39	.22	
15	7.10	−.23	7.54	.15	
16	7.60	.50	7.41	−.13	
17	7.63	.03	7.67	.26	
18	7.80	.17	7.79	.12	
19	8.13	.33	7.94	.15	
20	7.07	−1.06	8.22	.28	
21	9.20	2.13	7.59	−.63	
22	8.60	−.60	8.74	1.15	
23	8.67	.07	8.87	.13	
24	8.67	.00	8.94	.07	
25	9.87	1.20	8.93	−.01	
26	8.57	−1.30	9.74	.81	Point B
27	8.87	.30	9.19	−.55	
28	8.90	.03	9.09	−.10	
29	8.00	−.90	9.04	−.05	
30	8.90	.90	8.37	−.67	
31	8.50	−.40	8.68	.31	
32	8.07	−.43	8.55	−.13	
33	9.40	1.33	8.19	−.36	
34	9.37	−0.3	8.95	.76	
35	9.97	.60	9.31	.36	
36	9.80	−.17	9.89	.58	
37	9.67	−.13	10.02	.13	
38	9.60	−.07	9.96	−.06	
39	9.60	.00	9.85	−.11	
40	9.40	−.20	9.77	−.08	
41	8.77	−.63	9.58	−.19	
42	9.13	.36	9.03	−.55	

Table 9-8 Continued

Period Number	Unit Sales of Automobiles (Y_t) (1)	Actual Change ($\Delta Y_t = Y_t - Y_{t-1}$) (2)	Forecast[a] ($\hat{Y}_t$) (3)	Predicted Change ($\Delta \hat{Y}_t = \hat{Y}_t - \hat{Y}_{t-1}$) (4)	
43	9.00	−.13	9.02	−.01	
44	6.87	−2.13	8.94	−.08	Point A
45	10.03	3.16	7.42	−1.52	Point D
46	9.97	−.06	8.93	1.51	
47	10.40	.43	9.65	.72	
48	10.63	.23	10.30	.65	Point F
49	10.53	−.10	10.75	.45	
50	10.77	.24	10.85	.10	
51	10.93	.16	11.02	.17	
52	11.63	.70	11.18	.16	
53	12.37	.74	11.70	.52	
54	12.23	−.14	12.43	.73	
55	11.20	−1.03	12.64	.21	
56	9.93	−1.27	11.95	−.69	
57	9.43	−.50	10.68	−1.27	Point C
58	9.27	−.16	9.70	−.98	
59	9.63	.36	9.14	−.56	
60	7.53	−2.10	9.17	.03	
61	8.33	.80	7.77	−1.40	
62	7.85	−.48	7.71	−.06	
63	9.06	1.21	7.43	−.28	
64	9.38	.32	8.20	.77	
65	10.17	.79	8.86	.66	
66	10.08	−.09	9.76	.90	
67	9.96	−.12	10.12	.36	
68	10.24	.28	10.19	.07	
69	11.28	1.04	10.38	.19	Point E
70	11.54	.26	11.18	.80	
71	10.93	−.61	11.71	.53	
72	10.98	.05	11.48	−.23	
73	10.82	−.16	11.36	−.12	
74	12.04	1.22	11.14	−.22	
75	11.23	−.81	11.87	.73	
76	11.13	−.10	11.63	−.24	
77	11.63	.50	11.41	−.22	
78	10.53	−1.10	11.63	.22	
79	10.77	.24	10.96	−.67	
80	9.83	−.94	10.79	−.17	
MSE (millions)			0.64		
MAPE (%)			6.8%		

[a] $\alpha = .4$; forecasts generated via Brown's linear-exponential-smoothing technique; $S_1^1 = S_1^2 = Y_1 = 6.13$.

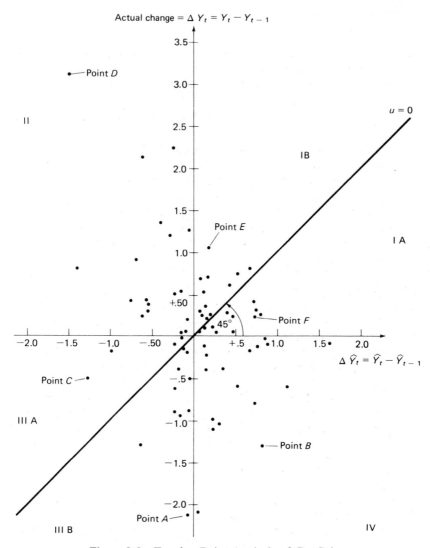

Figure 9-3 Turning-Point Analysis of Car Sales

from applying Brown's linear-exponential model to unit sales of automobiles. The overall result is that in fully 51 percent (40 out of 78 observations) of the quarters, the time-series model produced a forecast that involved a turning-point error. Even though the regression equation generated several turning-point errors, its performance is clearly superior in providing reliable forecasts for unit sales of automobiles in cyclically sensitive periods.

The purpose of Figure 9-3 is to emphasize the weakness of time-series models at upper and lower turning points. If the variable to be estimated is extremely sensitive to cyclical patterns in the economy (which is clearly true for automobile sales but not for air miles traveled), then exclusive reliance on a time-series model is unwise. It may still be worthwhile, however, to use a time-series model as a cross-check against an established regression model. When the two models give radically different signals, it is in the forecaster's best interest to diagnose the source of the discrepancy so that the decision maker is not forced into making choices at random.

QUESTIONS FOR DISCUSSION AND ANALYSIS

1. Table 8-19 in Chapter 8 contains data for monthly dry-van trailer shipments from 1960 to 1979.
   a. Using data from the period 1972 to 1973, calculate a six-month moving average (M_t), a weighted six-month moving average (M_t^w) with declining weights (6, 5, 4, 3, 2, 1), and a double moving average (M_t^d). See Table 9-1 for an example of these averages.
   b. Forecast shipments for January 1974 based on the three moving averages estimated above.
   c. Using $\alpha = .1$ and $\alpha = .9$, apply the single-exponential-smoothing model to the shipment data for 1972 to 1973. Carry out the forecast and error analysis as per columns 4 and 5 in Table 9-2. Does $\alpha = .1$ or $\alpha = .9$ work better?
   d. Forecast shipments for January 1974 based on the single-exponential-smoothing models.

2. Extend all the models estimated in problem 1 through 1974 and use them to predict shipments for January 1975. How did the models fare when compared to the forecasts for January 1974? What conclusions can you draw?

3. Apply Brown's linear-exponential-smoothing model to the shipments data from 1970 to 1973 and summarize the results as per columns 1 to 7 in Table 9-3. Use an α value of 0.4 and initialize S_1^1 and S_1^2 as was done in Table 9-3.

4. Based on the results from problem 3, forecast shipments for the first six months of 1974 and analyze the error pattern.

5. Extend the model in problem 3 through 1975 and make an analysis of the one-period-ahead forecasts for 1975 as was done in columns 6 and 7 in Table 9-3. How quickly did the model respond to the dramatic decline in shipments?

6. Apply the triple-exponential-smoothing model to the same shipments data for 1972 to 1973, and then use the model to forecast shipments for the first six months of 1974. Analyze the results.

7. Extend the triple-smoothing model through 1975 and analyze the error pattern generated by the one-period-ahead forecasts.

8. Apply the naive model $(\hat{Y}_t = Y_{t-1})$ to the shipments data for 1973 to 1975 and analyze the error pattern.

9. Did any of the time-series models forecast satisfactorily during 1973 and 1974? How was their performance altered in 1975?

10. What type of time-series data for businesses might lend themselves to the time-series models in this chapter?

REFERENCES FOR FURTHER STUDY

Brown, R.G., *Smoothing, Forecasting, and Prediction of Discrete Time Series.* Englewood Cliffs, N.J.: Prentice-Hall, 1962.

——, *Statistical Forecasting for Inventory Control.* New York: McGraw-Hill, 1959.

Chow, W.M., "Adaptive Control of the Exponential Smoothing Constant," *Journal of Industrial Engineering,* Vol. 16, No. 5 (1965), 315–17.

Crane, D.G., and J.R. Crotty, "A Two-Stage Forecasting Model: Exponential Smoothing and Multiple Regression," *Management Science,* Vol. 13, No. 8 (1967), 501–7.

Granger, C.W.J., and P. Newbold, *Forecasting Economic Time Series.* New York: Academic Press, 1977.

Makridakis, Spyros, and Steven C. Wheelwright, *Interactive Forecasting.* San Francisco: Holden-Day, 1977.

Trigg, D.W., and D.H. Leach, "Exponential Smoothing with an Adaptive Response Rate," *Operational Research Quarterly,* Vol. 18 (1967), 53–59.

Winters, P.R., "Forecasting Sales by Exponentially Weighted Moving Averages," *Management Science,* April 1960, pp. 324–42.

10

Advanced Time-Series Models

INTRODUCTION

The time-series models described in the preceding chapter are among the more common techniques applied by practicing forecasters. This popularity stems from their ease of application and their comprehensiveness. The objective of this chapter is to introduce several of the more advanced time-series models that have only recently been applied by practicing business forecasters. These techniques are not nearly as popular as the more basic techniques, because they are more difficult to understand, require extensive computational capabilities, and can be extremely expensive to estimate and monitor.

WINTERS'S SEASONAL EXPONENTIAL SMOOTHING

Exponential-smoothing techniques can be generalized so that both trend and seasonal patterns are incorporated in time-series forecasts. Winters's seasonal-exponential-smoothing technique applies the smoothing process three times:[1]

1. to estimate the average value of the time series;
2. to estimate the trend component; and
3. to estimate the seasonal index.

Each of the three stages has its own smoothing constant, which can be adjusted as the situation warrants, and these individual modifications can be made to any one of the constants without having to alter the others.

The flexibility and power of Winters's seasonal exponential smoothing is best illustrated through an actual application to a time series that has a trend and a seasonal component. Sample data for steel shipments are listed in Table 10-1 and illustrated in Figure 10-1. Several preliminary steps must be completed before applying Winters's model. These steps are designed to provide the initial estimates of trend and seasonality. The trend estimates can be generated via a simple linear regression line of the form:

$$\hat{Y}_t = a + bX_t \tag{10-1}$$

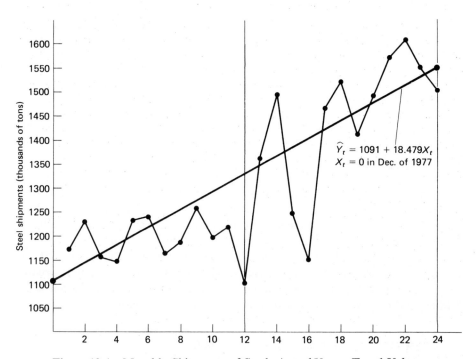

Figure 10-1   Monthly Shipments of Steel: Actual Versus Trend Values

[1]P.R. Winters, "Forecasting Sales by Exponentially Weighted Moving Averages," *Management Science*, Vol. 6, No. 3 (1960).

Table 10-1 Forecasts of monthly steel shipments based on Winters's seasonal exponential smoothing

Date		Period	Steel Shipments (Thousands of Tons) Y_t (1)	Trend[a] $\hat{Y}_t$ (2)	Ratio of Actual to Trend $Y_t/\hat{Y}_t$ (3)	Initial Estimates of Seasonal Factors[b] (4)
1978	Jan.	1	1,178	1,109	1.06	
	Feb.	2	1,239	1,127	1.10	
	March	3	1,158	1,145	1.01	
	April	4	1,150	1,164	0.99	
	May	5	1,231	1,182	1.04	
	June	6	1,236	1,201	1.03	
	July	7	1,173	1,219	0.96	
	Aug.	8	1,188	1,238	0.96	
	Sept.	9	1,266	1,256	1.01	
	Oct.	10	1,195	1,275	0.94	
	Nov.	11	1,224	1,293	0.95	
	Dec.	12	1,101	1,312	0.84	
1979	Jan.	13	1,369	1,330	1.03	1.045
	Feb.	14	1,494	1,349	1.11	1.105
	March	15	1,252	1,367	0.92	0.965
	April	16	1,150	1,386	0.83	0.910
	May	17	1,469	1,404	1.05	1.045
	June	18	1,521	1,423	1.07	1.050
	July	19	1,413	1,441	0.98	0.970
	Aug.	20	1,488	1,460	1.02	0.990
	Sept.	21	1,573	1,478	1.06	1.035
	Oct.	22	1,615	1,497	1.08	1.010
	Nov.	23	1,492	1,515	1.02	0.985
	Dec.	24	1,605	1,534	0.97	0.905
1980	Jan.	25	1,611			
	Feb.	26	1,512			
	March	27	1,402			
	April	28				

[a]These estimates are based on equation (10-2).
[b]This technique ignores the cyclicality present in column 1.

X_t is the trend variable measuring time, and it is incremented by one unit for each month beyond the beginning point. For the steel-shipment data in column 1 of Table 10-1, the estimated trend line is:[2]

$$\hat{Y}_t = 1,091 + 18.479 X_t \qquad (10\text{-}2)$$

$$X_t = 0 \text{ in December 1977}$$

This equation can be used to prepare trend estimates for any month by simply

[2]The derivation of least-squares estimators was illustrated in Chapter 5.

substituting the specific X_t value.[3] For example, the trend estimate for December 1979 (period 24) is:

$$\hat{Y}_t = 1{,}091 + 18.479\,X_t$$
$$= 1{,}091 + 18.479(24)$$
$$= 1{,}534 \text{ thousand tons} \tag{10-2}$$

Trend values for the historical period (January 1978 to December 1979) are derived in an identical fashion and are noted in column 2 of Table 10-1. Figure 10-1 provides a visual comparison of the actual and the trend magnitudes. The trend figures serve as the initial trend values in Winters's exponential technique, and they are also used in deriving the seasonal factors.

Seasonal factors are determined by dividing the actual values by the trend estimates and averaging these preliminary estimates. The first step in this process is to divide the actual values (Y_t) in column 1 of Table 10-1 by the trend estimates ($\hat{Y}_t$) in column 2. Thus, January 1978 steel shipments were 6 percent greater (1,178 versus 1,109) than the trend level. The ratios listed in column 3 must be averaged by month to determine the initial seasonal estimates utilized in Winters's exponential method. For example, the initial seasonal value for January is 1.045—(1.06 + 1.03)/2—and for February it is 1.105—(1.10 + 1.11)/2. Therefore, at time $t = 24$ (December 1979), the initial estimates of the multiplicative seasonal factors are: January, 1.045; February, 1.105; March, 0.965; April, 0.91; May, 1.045; June, 1.05; July, 0.97; August, 0.99; September, 1.035; October, 1.01; November, 0.985; December, 0.905. These values are listed in column 4 of Table 10-1.

Once these initial estimates of trend and seasonality are made, Winters's model incorporates them into an exponential-smoothing process, thereby permitting estimates of the intercept, the slope, and the seasonal factors to be continuously updated. The following four equations are utilized to derive the revisions prior to actually making a forecast:

1. The current estimate of the intercept of the trend line *at time t* is:

$$a_t = \alpha \frac{Y_t}{SF_{t-N}} + (1 - \alpha)(a_{t-1} + b_{t-1}) \tag{10-3}$$

2. The current estimate of the slope of the trend line *at time t* is:

$$b_t = \beta(a_t - a_{t-1}) + (1 - \beta)b_{t-1} \tag{10-4}$$

3. Seasonal factors are revised according to:

$$SF_t = \sigma \frac{Y_t}{a_t} + (1 - \sigma)SF_{t-N} \tag{10-5}$$

[3]The data for 1980 were excluded from the trend-line computations for reasons that will become apparent later in this section.

4. The forecast (made in period t) for a point T periods in the future is:

$$\hat{Y}_{t+T} = (a_t + b_t T) SF^*_{t+T} \qquad (10\text{-}6)$$

The terms in equations (10-3), (10-4), (10-5), and (10-6) are defined as:

Y_t = actual data value for period t

a_t = estimated intercept of the trend line at time t

b_t = estimated slope of the trend line at time t

N = number of periods in the seasonal pattern (12 in the case of monthly data, 4 with quarterly data, etc.)

SF_t = estimated seasonal factor for period t

SF^*_{t+T} = the best estimate of the seasonal factor in period $t + T$

α, β, σ = exponential smoothing constants, where $0 < \alpha, \beta, \sigma < 1$

$\hat{Y}_{t+T}$ = estimated value T periods in the future

The applicability of these equations can best be illustrated through the development of a one-period-ahead steel shipments forecast. Suppose that we are now at the end of December 1979 (period 24) and a forecast for January 1980 (period 25) is desired. Our best initial estimate of the intercept value of the trend level in period 24 is 1,534 as shown in equation (10-2). The best estimate for the slope of the trend line in period 24 is 18.479. The best estimate of the seasonal factor for January 1980 is the previous estimate of January's seasonality; that is, $SF^*_{24+1} = 1.045$. Our January estimate of steel shipments can then be computed as follows for January 1980:

$$\hat{Y}_{24+1} = \hat{Y}_{25} = [a_{24} + b_{24}(1)] \cdot SF^*_{25}$$
$$= (1{,}534 + 18.479) \cdot (1.045)$$
$$= 1{,}622 \qquad (10\text{-}7)$$

At the end of period 25, actual steel shipments are recorded as 1,611 thousand tons for January 1980. Once this latest observation is recorded we can develop revisions for the seasonal factors, intercept and slope values, based upon this latest information. To solve equations (10-3), (10-4), and (10-5), we must specify values for the smoothing constants α, β, and σ. For illustrative purposes, assume that $\alpha = \beta = \sigma = 0.4$.[4] The revisions are made as follows:

1. $\quad a_{25} = \alpha \dfrac{Y_{25}}{SF_{25-12}} + (1 - \alpha)(a_{24} + b_{24})$

$\qquad = .4\dfrac{1611}{1.045} + (.6)(1{,}534 + 18.479) = 1{,}548$

---

[4] The forecaster should experiment with alternative values of α, β, and σ.

2. $b_{25} = \beta(a_{25} - a_{24}) + (1 - \beta)b_{24}$

   $= (.4)(1,548 - 1,534) + (.6)(18.479)$

   $= 16.82$

3. $SF_{25} = \sigma\dfrac{Y_{25}}{a_{25}} + (1 - \sigma)SF_{25-12}$

   $= (.4)\dfrac{1,611}{1,548} + (.6)(1.045)$

   $= 1.043$

Note that the value used for a_{24} is 1,534, the predicted trend value from equation (10-2). This is the intercept of the trend equation when the origin is moved to period 24. SF_{25} becomes the new estimated seasonal factor for January, and SF_{13} is eliminated from future computations. This revised information can then be used to develop forecasts for future periods. For example, February's forecast (made in January) would be:

$$\hat{Y}_{t+T} = (a_t + b_t T)SF^*_{t+T}$$
$$\hat{Y}_{25+1} = (a_{25} + b_{25}T)SF^*_{t+T}$$
$$\hat{Y}_{26} = [1,548 + 16.82(1)]1.105$$
$$= 1,729 \text{ thousand tons (as opposed to the actual value}$$
$$\text{of 1,512 produced by the peak in the economy)}$$

Alternatively, the forecast for August 1980 (period 32) made in January 1980 is:

$$\hat{Y}_{t+T} = (a_t + b_t T)SF^*_{t+T}$$
$$\hat{Y}_{25+7} = [a_{25} + b_{25}(7)]SF^*_{25+7}$$
$$\hat{Y}_{32} = [1,548 + 16.82(7)]0.99$$
$$= 1,649 \text{ thousand tons}$$

By repeating this procedure of revising a_t, b_t, and SF^*_t each time an actual observation becomes available, we adapt the forecast values to changes in the activity being monitored. To see this, assume that period 26's observation of 1,512 thousand tons is recorded and a revised forecast for August 1980 is desired:

1. $a_{26} = \alpha\dfrac{Y_{26}}{SF_{26-12}} + (1 - \alpha)(a_{25} + b_{25})$

   $= (.4)\dfrac{1,512}{1.105} + (.6)(1,548 + 16.82)$

   $= 1,486$

2. $\quad b_{26} = \beta(a_{26} - a_{25}) + (1 - \beta)b_{25}$

$\qquad = (.4)(1{,}486 - 1{,}548) + (.6)(16.82)$

$\qquad = -14.61$

3. $\quad SF_{26} = \sigma \dfrac{Y_{26}}{a_{26}} + (1 - \sigma)SF_{26-12}$

$\qquad = (.4)\dfrac{1{,}512}{1{,}486} + (.6)(1.105)$

$\qquad = 1.070$

Therefore, the August 1980 forecast is revised downward from 1,649 to:

$$\hat{Y}_{26+6} = (a_{26} + b_{26}T)SF^*_{26+6}$$
$$\hat{Y}_{32} = [1{,}486 - 14.61(6)]0.99$$
$$= 1{,}384 \text{ thousand tons} \qquad (10\text{-}8)$$

There are two principal limitations associated with Winters's exponential smoothing. First, the existence of the cyclical component in economic time-series data is difficult to build into Winters's model. Second, the selection of the smoothing constants (α, β, and σ) is made through a trial-and-error process, which can become costly. In the illustration developed in this section, $\alpha = \beta = \sigma = 0.4$. Generally, higher values are assigned to the smoothing constants in order to place more emphasis on current observations, but the selection of parameter values remains highly judgmental.

ADAPTIVE-RESPONSE-RATE EXPONENTIAL SMOOTHING

Adaptive-response-rate exponential smoothing[5] is conceptually similar to single exponential smoothing, presented in the preceding chapter. The only difference, and it is an important one, is that with adaptive-response-rate exponential smoothing, the value of the smoothing constant varies. Specifically, the value of α changes (adapts) automatically whenever a change in the data pattern dictates that a change is desirable. The advantage is that the adaptive-response-rate exponential-smoothing technique is capable of representing almost all data patterns.

The basic equation for adaptive-response-rate exponential smoothing is:

$$\hat{Y}_{t+1} = \alpha_t Y_t + (1 - \alpha_t)\hat{Y}_t \qquad (10\text{-}9)$$

[5]S. Makridakis and S.C. Wheelwright, *Forecasting: Methods and Applications* (New York: John Wiley, 1978), pp. 53–55.

For preparation of forecasts employing this technique, several intermediate computations are required; using β as the error-smoothing parameter we get:

$$\alpha_t = \left| \frac{E_t}{AE_t} \right| \tag{10-10}$$

$$E_t = \beta e_t + (1 - \beta)E_{t-1}; \ 0 < \beta < 1 \tag{10-11}$$

$$AE_t = \beta|e_t| + (1 - \beta)AE_{t-1} \tag{10-12}$$

$$e_t = Y_t - \hat{Y}_t \tag{10-13}$$

E_t refers to the smoothed average error and AE_t to the smoothed absolute error. The following example illustrates the use of adaptive-response-rate exponential smoothing.

Juloy Incorporated, a small manufacturing firm, makes the Dalene doll. Management would like to develop a forecasting model that can be used to generate monthly point forecasts of the sales of the doll. If a reliable forecasting model can be developed, Juloy can more efficiently plan its production schedule and determine its inventory requirements. Since the company's policy is to ensure that retail outlets can be immediately supplied out of the existing stock of Dalene dolls, Juloy has to balance its inventory carefully against future demand. The marketing department has recorded monthly sales (in thousands of dollars) for the past two years. The sales history is presented in column 1 of Table 10-2. Using the data in Table 10-2 and assuming an initial value of $\alpha = .2$, the forecast for period 2 (made in period 1) is:

$$\hat{Y}_{t+1} = \alpha_t Y_t + (1 - \alpha_t)\hat{Y}_t$$
$$\hat{Y}_2 = (.2)(215) + (.8)(215)$$
$$= 215$$

This forecast value is recorded in column 2 of Table 10-2. The computations necessary to compute values for E_t, AE_t, and e_t are as follows, (using $\beta = 0.2$):

1. $e_t = Y_t - \hat{Y}_t$
   $e_2 = Y_2 - \hat{Y}_2$
   $= 216 - 215 = 1$; see column 3

2. $E_t = .2e_t + .8E_{t-1}$
   $E_2 = .2e_2 + .8E_1$
   $= (.2)(1) + (.8)(0)$
   $= .2$; see column 4

3. $AE_t = .2|e_t| + .8AE_{t-1}$

Table 10-2 Forecasting doll sales based on adaptive-response-rate exponential smoothing

Date		Period	Sales (Thousands) (1)	$\hat{Y}_t{}^a$ (2)	$e_t{}^b$ (3)	$E_t{}^c$ (4)	$AE_t{}^d$ (5)	$\alpha_t{}^e$ (6)
1978	Jan.	1	$215			0	0	.2
	Feb.	2	216	215	1	.2	.2	.2
	March	3	243	215	28	5.76	5.76	.2
	April	4	204	221	−17	1.21	8.01	.151
	May	5	212	218	−6	−0.23	7.61	.030
	June	6	240	218	22	4.38	10.49	.418
	July	7	238	227	11	5.70	10.59	.438
	Aug.	8	218	233	−15	1.56	11.47	.136
	Sept.	9	221	231	−10	−0.75	11.18	.067
	Oct.	10	260	230	30	5.40	14.94	.361
	Nov.	11	268	241	27	9.72	17.35	.560
	Dec.	12	296	256	40	15.78	21.88	.721
1979	Jan.	13	300	285	15	15.62	20.50	.762
	Feb.	14	280	296	−16	9.30	19.60	.474
	March	15	329	289	40	9.44	23.68	.399
	April	16	365	305	60	19.55	30.94	.632
	May	17	382	343	39	23.44	32.55	.720
	June	18	338	371	−33	12.15	32.64	.372
	July	19	332	359	−27	4.32	31.51	.137
	Aug.	20	328	355	−27	−1.94	30.61	.064
	Sept.	21	358	353	5	−0.55	25.49	.022
	Oct.	22	372	353	19	3.36	24.19	.139
	Nov.	23	384	356	28	8.29	24.95	.332
	Dec.	24	389	365	24	11.43	24.76	.462

^{a}See equation (10-9).
^{b}See equation (10-13).
^{c}See equation (10-11).
^{d}See equation (10-12).
^{e}See equation (10-10).

$$AE_2 = .2|e_2| + .8AE_1$$
$$= .2|1| + .8(0)$$
$$= .2; \text{ see column 5}$$

To allow the system to adjust to the initial value of α and the fact that we assumed $Y_1 = \hat{Y}_1 = 215$, let us further assume that $\alpha = .2$ for periods 2 and 3. Thus, the forecast for period 3 is:

$$\hat{Y}_{2+1} = \alpha_2 Y_2 + (1 - \alpha_2)\hat{Y}_2$$
$$= (.2)(216) + (.8)(215)$$
$$= 215.2$$
$$\approx 215 \qquad (10\text{-}14)$$

In order to revise α in period 4, the intermediate computations are:

1. $e_4 = Y_4 - \hat{Y}_4$
   $= 204 - 221$
   $= -17$

2. $E_4 = .2e_4 + .8E_3$
   $= (.2)(-17) + (.8)(5.76)$
   $= 1.21$

3. $AE_4 = .2|e_4| + .8AE_3$
   $= .2(17) + (.8)(5.76)$
   $= 8.01$

Steps 2 and 3 provide the final information needed to calculate α_4:

$$\alpha_4 = \left| \frac{E_4}{AE_4} \right|$$

$$= \frac{1.21}{8.01}$$

$$= 0.151; \text{ see column 6 of Table 10-2} \qquad (10\text{-}15)$$

This revised α value is now utilized to prepare the forecast for May 1978 (period 5) as follows:

$$\hat{Y}_5 = \alpha_4 Y_4 + (1 - \alpha_4)\hat{Y}_4$$

$$= (.151)(204) + (.849)(221)$$

$$= \$218 \text{ thousand} \qquad (10\text{-}16)$$

Equations (10-10), (10-11), (10-12), and (10-13) must be resolved for the values needed to compute α_5. Columns 2 through 6 contain the results of these computations for the entire historical data base. The information from period 24 (December 1979) can now be utilized to prepare a forecast for January 1980, as follows:

$$\hat{Y}_{25} = \alpha_{24} Y_{24} + (1 - \alpha_{24})\hat{Y}_{24}$$

$$= (.462)(389) + (.538)(365)$$

$$= \$376 \text{ thousand} \qquad (10\text{-}17)$$

A limitation of this technique is that it tends to generate forecasts that lag turning points by one time period; that is, it does not anticipate turning points in the forecasted time series.

HOLT'S TWO-PARAMETER EXPONENTIAL SMOOTHING

In Chapter 9, Brown's linear exponential smoothing was introduced as a means of dealing with a time series with a linear trend component. An alternative methodology is Holt's two-parameter exponential smoothing.[6] Conceptually, the two techniques are similar, except that with Holt's method, the trend present in the time series is dealt with by a smoothing constant that is different from the smoothing constant applied to the actual observations. Using Holt's technique, the analyst gains some flexibility, but the gain in flexibility requires that two smoothing parameters (as compared to one in Brown's model) be specified. Since two parameters must be quantified, the trial-and-error process of finding the best combination of parameters may be costly and time-consuming.

The basic equations in Holt's two-parameter exponential smoothing are:

$$S_t^h = \alpha Y_t + (1 - \alpha)(S_{t-1}^h + c_{t-1}) \qquad (10\text{-}18)$$

$$c_t = \beta(S_t^h - S_{t-1}^h) + (1 - \beta)c_{t-1} \qquad (10\text{-}19)$$

The terms in these equations parallel those given earlier for Brown's exponential-smoothing models. Equation (10-18) yields a smoothed statistic that adjusts for trend in order to eliminate the lag that occurs when a single-smoothed statistic is computed; this is similar to the double-smoothing process of Brown's model. Equation (10-19) revises the trend estimate from the previous period, and is similar to that of single-exponential-smoothing models. The forecasting equation for Holt's model is:

$$\hat{Y}_{t+T} = S_t^h + c_t T \qquad (10\text{-}20)$$

A direct comparison with Brown's technique can be made by referring back to the sales data and computations in Table 9-3. The actual sales data are reproduced in column 1 of Table 10-3. As is the case with all exponential-smoothing models, an initial value for the smoothed statistic, S_t^h, in period 1, is required. Assume that $S_1^h = 9,074 = Y_1$. With Holt's model, an initial value for c_1 is also required, and we will assume that:[7]

$$c_1 = \frac{Y_2 - Y_1}{2} + \frac{Y_4 - Y_3}{2} \qquad (10\text{-}21)$$

Finally, let the smoothing constants, α and β, equal 0.6. Generally, low values for α and β should be employed when there are frequent fluctuations in the data, whereas high values should be assigned when there is some pattern (that is, linear trend) in the data. High values of α and β also imply that recent

---

[6]Makridakis and Wheelwright, *Forecasting*, pp. 64–66 and 81.
[7]S. Makridakis and S.C. Wheelwright, *Interactive Forecasting*, 2nd ed. (San Francisco: Holden-Day, 1978), p. 87.

Table 10-3 Forecasting retail sales with Holt's two-parameter exponential-smoothing model (Millions of dollars)

Date		Period	Sales (Millions) (1)	S_t^{h}[a] (2)	c_t[b] (3)	$\hat{Y}_{t+T}$[c] (4)	Error Actual (5)	Error Per-centage (6)
1978	Jan.	1	$ 9,074	$ 9,074[d]	$ 322[e]			
	Feb.	2	10,128	9,835	586			
	March	3	10,155	10,261	490	$10,421	−266	−2.6
	April	4	9,746	10,148	128	10,751	−1005	−10.3
	May	5	9,397	9,749	−188	10,276	−879	−9.4
	June	6	9,012	9,232	−386	9,561	−548	−6.1
	July	7	9,084	8,989	−300	8,846	239	2.6
	Aug.	8	9,447	9,144	−27	8,689	758	8.0
	Sept.	9	10,062	9,684	313	9,117	945	9.4
	Oct.	10	10,420	10,251	465	9,997	423	4.1
	Nov.	11	10,754	10,739	479	10,716	38	0.4
	Dec.	12	10,826	10,983	338	11,218	−392	−3.6
1979	Jan.	13	11,421	11,381	374	11,321	100	0.9
	Feb.	14	11,442	11,567	261	11,755	−313	−2.7
	March	15	11,665	11,730	202	11,828	−164	−1.4
	April	16	11,559	11,709	68	11,933	−374	−3.2
	May	17	12,046	11,938	165	11,777	270	2.2
	June	18	12,024	12,056	137	12,103	−79	−0.7
	July	19	12,350	12,287	193	12,192	158	1.3
	Aug.	20	12,978	12,779	372	12,480	498	3.8
	Sept.	21	13,934	13,621	654	13,151	783	5.6
	Oct.	22	14,070	14,152	580	14,275	−205	−1.5
	Nov.	23	14,191	14,407	385	14,732	−541	−3.8
	Dec.	24	14,697	14,735	351	14,793	−96	−0.7

[a]Equation (10-18).
[b]Equation (10-19).
[c]Equation (10-20).
[d]Initial value of $S_1^{h} = Y_1$.
[e]Initial value of $c_1 = 322$; see equation (10-21).

observations of the forecast variables are weighted more heavily than are distant observations. Conceptually, the forecasting process can be illustrated by looking at the *ex post* forecast for period 3 made in period 2:

$$\hat{Y}_{t+T} = S_t^{h} + c_t T$$
$$\hat{Y}_{2+1} = S_2^{h} + c_2 \cdot 1$$
$$\hat{Y}_3 = S_2^{h} + c_2$$

where:

$$S_2^{h} = \alpha Y_2 + (1 - \alpha)(S_1^{h} + c_1)$$
$$= (.6)(10,128) + (.4)(9,074 + 322)$$
$$= 9,835 \tag{10-22}$$

and:

$$c_2 = \beta(S_2^h - S_1^h) + (1 - \beta)c_1$$
$$= (.6)(9{,}835 - 9{,}074) + (.4)(322)$$
$$= 586 \tag{10-23}$$

Therefore:

$$\hat{Y}_3 = 9{,}835 + 586$$
$$= \$10{,}421 \text{ million} \tag{10-24}$$

The remaining smoothed statistics (S_t^h), trend revisions (c_t), and forecasts $(\hat{Y}_{t+T})$ are listed in columns 2 through 4 in Table 10-3. The sales forecast for period 25, January 1980, is made as follows:

$$\hat{Y}_{24+1} = S_{24}^h + c_{24} \cdot 1$$
$$\hat{Y}_{25} = 14{,}735 + 351$$
$$= \$15{,}086 \text{ million} \tag{10-25}$$

Further, the sales forecast for April 1980 (period 28) made in December 1979 (period 24) is:

$$\hat{Y}_{24+4} = S_{24}^h + c_{24} \cdot 4$$
$$\hat{Y}_{28} = 14{,}735 + 351(4)$$
$$= \$16{,}139 \text{ million} \tag{10-26}$$

The performance of Holt's two-parameter exponential-smoothing model in simulating the historical sales observations can be seen in Table 10-3, where the average percentage error was 3.8 percent. Although the technique missed the turning points (as time-series models usually do), it did react to the basic changes in the data pattern. Finally, over the last twelve months, the average percentage error was only 2.3 percent. As with the other time-series models that we have studied, an extensive and ongoing process of empirical testing must be carried out in order to ensure that the model under study continues to track the data accurately.

CONFIDENCE INTERVALS
FOR EXPONENTIAL-SMOOTHING FORECASTS

Throughout this and the preceding chapter, we have explicitly chosen to present only the basic equations needed to develop point forecasts. In doing this, we have ignored the general statistical basis underlying these models. This statistical theory can be used to derive confidence intervals about a point forecast, $\hat{Y}_{t+T}(t)$, made at time t for T periods into the future:[8]

[8] B.L. Bowerman and R.T. O'Connell, *Forecasting and Time Series* (North Scituate, Mass.: Duxbury Press, 1979), p. 155.

$$Y_{t+T}(t) = \hat{Y}_{t+T}(t) \pm e_{t+T}^{\alpha}(t) \qquad (10\text{-}27)$$

The superscript, α, refers to the degree of confidence specified by the analyst, and (t) denotes that the confidence interval was computed in time period t. In turn, $e_{t+T}^{\alpha}(t)$ generates the interval about the point forecast:

$$e_{t+T}^{\alpha}(t) = zk_T\Delta(t) \qquad (10\text{-}28)$$

The symbol z is the number of standard deviations under the normal curve associated with the level of confidence, and:

$$k_T = 1.25 \qquad (10\text{-}29)$$

for single-exponential-smoothing forecasts.[9] For Brown's linear-exponential model, k_T is no longer a constant and is defined as:[10]

$$k_T = 1.25 \left[\frac{1 + \dfrac{\alpha}{(1+v)^3}[(1 + 4v + 5v^2) + 2\alpha(1 + 3v)T + 2\alpha^2 T^2]}{1 + \dfrac{\alpha}{(1+v)^3}[(1 + 4v + 5v^2) + 2\alpha(1 + 3v) + 2\alpha^2]} \right]^{1/2} \qquad (10\text{-}30)$$

Further, $\Delta(t)$ is computed by:

$$\Delta(t) = \frac{\sum_{t=1}^{n} |e_t|}{d} \qquad (10\text{-}31)$$

In equation (10-30), α refers to the smoothing constant and v equals $1 - \alpha$; the term d in equation (10-31) stands for number of terms in the numerator. In equation (10-28), α stands for level of significance.

To apply these formulas, refer back to the computations made in Table 9-3, in which Brown's linear exponential smoothing was applied to monthly sales data. In this example, the smoothing constant, α, was equal to .4. Further, let us assume we are interested in computing a 95 percent confidence interval for a one-period-ahead forecast made in period 20. As a first step, $\Delta(t)$ and the forecast errors must be computed. Table 10-4 contains the information needed to solve equation (10-31) in time period 20.[11]

$$\Delta(20) = \frac{\sum_{t=3}^{20} |e_t|}{18}$$

$$= \frac{5,189}{18} \text{ (see column 3 of Table 10-4)}$$

$$= 288 \qquad (10\text{-}32)$$

---

[9]Ibid., p. 157.
[10]Ibid., p. 158.
[11]Because we did not make forecasts for periods 1 and 2, $t = 18$.

Table 10-4 One-period-ahead forecasts of monthly
retail sales made with Brown's linear exponential smoothing

Period	Sales, Y_t (Millions) (1)	$\hat{Y}^a_{t+1}$ (2)	Forecast Error e_t (3)
1	$ 9,074		
2	10,128		
3	10,155	$10,024	−131
4	9,746	10,212	466
5	9,397	9,946	549
6	9,012	9,536	524
7	9,084	9,059	−25
8	9,447	8,939	−509
9	10,062	9,207	−855
10	10,420	10,385	−35
11	10,754	10,853	99
12	10,826	11,066	240
13	11,421	11,579	158
14	11,442	11,755	313
15	11,665	11,946	281
16	11,559	11,885	326
17	12,046	12,202	156
18	12,024	12,273	249
19	12,350	12,518	168
20	12,978	13,084	106

^{a}Table 9-3.

The next step in the process is to solve equation (10-28):

$$e^{.05}_{20+1}(20) = 1.96(k_T)\Delta(t) \tag{10-33}$$

If the forecast is made in period 20 for period 21, $k_T = 1.25$.[12] The coefficient value of 1.96 in equation (10-33) comes from a normal probability table, since 95 percent of the area under the normal curve falls within 1.96 standard deviations of the mean. Therefore:

$$e^{.05}_{21}(20) = (1.96)(1.25)(288)$$
$$e^{.05}_{21}(20) = 706 \tag{10-34}$$

Thus, given the forecast in Table 10-4 of 13,084 and the forecast error in equation (10-34), the 95 percent confidence interval for a one-period-ahead forecast made in period 20 is:[13]

[12]Equation (10-30) can be shown to be equal to 1.25 when $T = 1$.
[13]See equation (10-27).

$$\hat{Y}_{t+T}(t) - e^{\alpha}_{t+T}(t) \leq Y_{t+T}(t) \leq \hat{Y}_{t+T}(t) + e^{\alpha}_{t+T}(t)$$

$$13{,}084 - 706 \leq Y_{21}(20) \leq 13{,}084 + 706$$

$$12{,}378 \leq \quad Y_{21} \quad \leq 13{,}790 \qquad (10\text{-}35)$$

Confidence intervals for more than one period ahead can be determined by resolving equation (10-30) for the required value for k_T.

BOX-JENKINS METHODOLOGY

Throughout this text we have introduced many techniques for analyzing economic time series with the objective of actually developing forecasts. The Box-Jenkins methodology is regarded as one of the more powerful techniques for generating accurate and reliable forecasts; its strength lies in the fact that it generates information to guide the analyst in the selection of a particular model for his or her data.

This is significantly different from the alternative time-series models, where the analyst assumes a specific mathematical model and then proceeds to estimate the parameters that provide a good fit in the *ex ante* historical simulation. For example, the analyst may decide that linear exponential smoothing is the appropriate model for the data and estimate the necessary smoothing parameters. This approach has two deficiencies. First, there may be many models that seem to be equally good. Second, explicit algorithms for determining the best parameters are unavailable, and therefore, the forecaster must resort to a trial-and-error process. The Box-Jenkins model does not require an initial description of the data patterns, because it systematically eliminates inappropriate models and selects the most suitable one for the activity being studied. A three-step procedure of identification, estimation, and diagnostic checking is employed in arriving at the appropriate model, which is then used to forecast.

Our purpose is to present a discussion of the general features of the Box-Jenkins methodology. The Box-Jenkins approach is highly judgmental and extremely sensitive to the developer's level of expertise. Mastery of the methodology is very time-consuming. References are listed at the end of the chapter.

The first step in the Box-Jenkins methodology involves identification of a tentative model based on an analysis of the historical observations of the time series. This phase of the technique requires an understanding of the concepts of stationary versus nonstationary time series, differencing, and autocorrelation coefficients. Autocorrelation analysis can be explained through a brief example. Monthly inventory levels are presented in column 1 of Table 10-5. In column 2 and column 3, the same data are repeated, except that time lags of one and two months, respectively, are introduced. An autocorrelation coefficient can be computed as follows:

Table 10-5 Monthly inventory levels, time lags, and differences

Period t	Inventory Levels Y_t (1)	One-Month Time Lag Y_{t-1} (2)	Two-Month Time Lag Y_{t-2} (3)	Y'^a (4)	Y''^b (5)
1	26				
2	28	26		2	
3	22	28	26	−6	−8
4	29	22	28	7	13
5	30	29	22	1	−6
6	28	30	29	−2	−3
7	32	28	30	4	6
8	36	32	28	4	0
9	33	36	32	−3	−7
10	32	33	36	−1	2
11	36	32	33	4	5
12	30	36	32	−6	−10

$^a Y' = Y_t - Y_{t-1}$
$^b Y'' = Y'_t - Y'_{t-1}$

$$r_k = \frac{\sum\limits_{t=k+1}^{n} (Y_t - \bar{Y})(Y_{t-k} - \bar{Y})}{\sum\limits_{t=1}^{n} (Y_t - \bar{Y})^2} \tag{10-36}$$

where k is the number of time periods the individual observations are lagged, and n is the number of observations. For the data shown in column 2 of Table 10-5, the autocorrelation coefficient for a time lag of $k = 1$ is:

$$
\begin{aligned}
r_1 = &[(28 - 30)(26 - 30) + (22 - 30)(28 - 30) + (29 - 30)(22 - 30) + \\
&(30 - 30)(29 - 30) + (28 - 30)(30 - 30) + (32 - 30)(28 - 30) + \\
&(36 - 30)(32 - 30) + (33 - 30)(36 - 30) + (32 - 30)(33 - 30) + \\
&(36 - 30)(32 - 30) + (30 - 30)(36 - 30)] \div \\
&[(26 - 30)^2 + (28 - 30)^2 + (22 - 30)^2 + (29 - 30)^2 + (28 - 30)^2 + \\
&(32 - 30)^2 + (36 - 30)^2 + (33 - 30)^2 + (32 - 30)^2 + (36 - 30)^2] \\
= &\ 0.427
\end{aligned} \tag{10-37}
$$

Similarly, for time lags of two, three, and four periods, the autocorrelation coefficients are:

$$r_2 = 0.423$$
$$r_3 = 0.377$$
$$r_4 = -0.078 \tag{10-38}$$

By considering the autocorrelation coefficients of the various time lags, the analyst can frequently determine the underlying data pattern. Specifically, if the coefficients approach zero slowly, this implies that there is some pattern in the data (that is, the data are nonstationary). In this case, the data exhibit a trend. An alternative data pattern would be generated by the presence of seasonality; the autocorrelation coefficients for a twelve-period-lag with monthly data would be relatively high. Conversely, if the autocorrelation coefficient is relatively low for all time lags, the data are stationary. That is, there is no underlying pattern in the data.

The utility of the autocorrelation coefficients lies in identifying stationary or nonstationary patterns in the data. If a time series is stationary, the empirical observations fluctuate around a relatively constant mean, whereas nonstationary time series fluctuate about a trend path. The Box-Jenkins methodology assumes that the data being studied are stationary. The pattern of the auto-correlation coefficients of various time lags can be analyzed to check the validity of this assumption. This validation can be seen by examining the patterns illustrated in Figure 10-2. The vertical axis represents the computed value of the autocorrelation coefficient, and the horizontal axis represents the specific time lags. If the data are nonstationary, the autocorrelation coefficients will exhibit a pattern similar to that in Figure 10-2(a) or 10-2(b). The pattern in Figure 10-2(a) indicates a strong trend pattern, and Figure 10-2(b) indicates the presence of seasonality (that is, the autocorrelation coefficients of time lags 1, 5, 9, 13, and 17 are related). Stationarity is illustrated in Figures 10-2(c) and 10-2(d); the former illustrates random stationarity, and the latter shows a nonrandom pattern. In practice, the precise identification of these data patterns requires extensive experience.

If a study of the autocorrelation coefficients indicates that the data are nonstationary, they must be transformed. Seasonality can be eliminated by adjusting the data via the Census X-11 technique. Whenever the autocorrelation pattern indicates the presence of a linear trend, the data can be transformed by taking the first differences of the original time series. Thus, to achieve stationarity, a new series is created by applying equation (10-39) to each observation in the original time series:

$$Y'_t = Y_t - Y_{t-1} \tag{10-39}$$

As an illustration, the first difference for period 2 in Table 10-5 is computed as:

$$
\begin{aligned}
Y'_2 &= Y_t - Y_{t-1} \\
&= Y_2 - Y_1 \\
&= 28 - 26 \\
&= 2
\end{aligned}
\tag{10-40}
$$

The remaining first differences are listed in column 4 of Table 10-5.

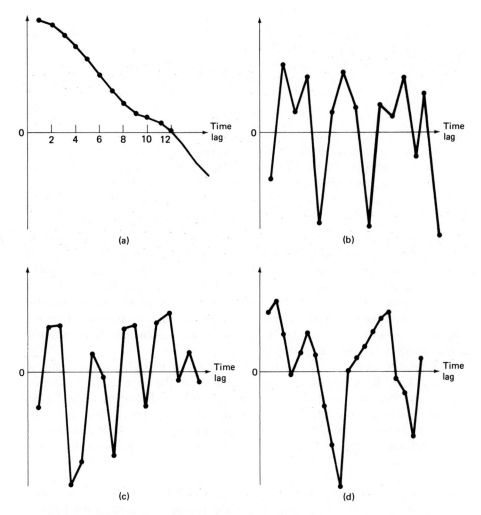

Figure 10-2 Analysis of Autocorrelation Coefficients: Stationary Versus Nonstationary Data Patterns

In many business and economic situations, first-differencing will generate a stationary time series. As was the case with the original data, stationarity in the first differences can be verified by analyzing the autocorrelation coefficients of the transformed data. However, if the autocorrelation coefficients of the first differences indicate nonstationarity, second differences can be derived by applying equation (10-41):

$$Y_t'' = Y_t' - Y_{t-1}' \tag{10-41}$$

The second differences of the monthly inventory levels are listed in column 5 of Table 10-5. In actual practice, it is seldom necessary to go beyond first differences.

These beginning steps allow the analyst to decide which time lags should be considered for inclusion into the model. The specification of the time lags implies the initial model to be estimated. One of the more popular Box-Jenkins models is the autoregressive model, which in general form is:

$$\hat{Y}_t = \gamma_1 Y_{t-1} + \gamma_2 Y_{t-2} + \gamma_3 Y_{t-3} + \cdots + \gamma_k Y_{t-k} + e_t \qquad (10\text{-}42)$$

This kth-order autoregressive scheme is generally simplified to match the time lags the analyst deems relevant. For example, if first-order observations are highly correlated (have a high autocorrelation coefficient) and if the data are stationary, then the first-order autoregressive model may be most applicable:

$$\hat{Y}_t = \gamma_0 + \gamma_1 Y_{t-1} \qquad (10\text{-}43)$$

The specific estimates for the unknown parameters (γ_i's) are determined by applying the least-squares methodology to either equation (10-42) or (10-43). The majority of the Box-Jenkins computer packages require that the analyst provide preliminary estimates of the unknown parameters. Preliminary estimates are generally based on the relationships between the autocorrelation coefficients and the model parameters. These preliminary estimates are then run through a series of iterative steps in which revisions occur and final estimates of the model parameters are determined.

After the final model has been estimated, it must be checked for its accuracy. This check is made through an analysis of the error terms. In particular, the Box-Jenkins computer packages rely on the Box-Pierce Chi Square statistic to indicate the adequacy of the model. This statistic focuses on the autocorrelations of the residuals and in general indicates whether or not the model estimated accounts for the observed relationship between the observations. If the model is inadequate, it must be reestimated by returning to an analysis of the autocorrelation coefficients. If the model is valid and reliable, it can be used to generate forecasts for the activity being modeled. Generally, the Box-Jenkins methodology generates these forecasts in a recursive fashion. That is, the forecast for period $t + T$ must be constructed from forecasts for periods $t + 1$, $t + 2$, and so on.

Despite the power of the Box-Jenkins methodology, it has several important limitations. First, in order to build a reliable Box-Jenkins model, the analyst must have at least fifty (and preferably more) data points at his disposal. For this reason, Box-Jenkins techniques are commonly utilized in conjunction with immediate-term forecast needs. Thus, like all time-series models, Box-Jenkins cannot be applied to long-term forecast problems. Second, Box-Jenkins procedures require that the analyst have a sound theoretical background in mathematics and have access to sophisticated computer facilities. Third, each time a new data point is observed, the entire model must be reestimated, since there are currently no automatic procedures to revise the parameters or to adapt to changes in the data pattern. Finally, the complexity and data requirements of the Box-Jenkins methodology imply that it can be very time-consuming and costly. This becomes especially critical when we note that the model must be completely revised each time a new data point is recorded.

COMPARISON OF REGRESSION
AND AUTOREGRESSIVE TECHNIQUES

Prof. Ronald Cooper recently compared the regression forecasts of 33 endogenous variables from seven macroeconomic models with autoregressive forecasts of these same variables. He found that the autoregressive models performed better in 18 of 33 cases. In another study, J. Phillip Cooper and Charles Nelson reached similar conclusions when they compared autoregressive forecasts of six variables with projections from the regression model of the Federal Reserve Bank of St. Louis. Nariman Behravesh found that inflation forecasts derived from regression equations were superior to those generated by autoregressive schemes.[14] Further clouding the picture is the fact that not all regression models perform equally well. Stephen McNees compared the results from the macroeconometric models of Chase Econometrics Associates (Chase), Data Resources Inc. (DRI), the MAPCAST model of General Electric, the Wharton Econometric Forecasting Model (Wharton), and the median forecast derived by the American Statistical Association National Bureau of Economic Research (ASA). This study focused on a subset of 17 variables, with the following general conclusions:

1. ASA was the most accurate for the unemployment rate, the change in business inventories, and housing starts.
2. Chase was the most accurate for the money stock.
3. DRI's model performed better for federal government purchases and short-term interest rates.
4. Wharton's model estimated the GNP price deflator, employment, final sales, consumer purchases of nondurable goods and services, business fixed investment, and net exports more accurately.
5. In many cases, no forecaster's model was most accurate for both level and change forecasts. That is, one model performed better on a quarter-to-quarter basis, while another, whose quarter-to-quarter errors were larger, produced more reliable level forecasts owing to error offsets.[15]

[14]The articles cited herein are: Ronald L. Cooper, "The Predictive Performance of Quarterly Econometric Models of the United States," *Econometric Models of Cyclical Behavior*, Vol. 2. Bert G. Hickman, ed., *Studies in Income and Wealth*, no. 36, (1972). Charles R. Nelson, "The Prediction Performance of the FRB-MIT Model of the U.S. Economy," *American Economic Review*, 72, no. 5, (December 1972), 902–17. J. Phillip Cooper and Charles R. Nelson, "The ExAnte Prediction Performance of the St. Louis and FRB-MIT-PENN Econometric Models and Some Results on Composite Predictions," *Journal of Money, Credit, and Banking*, 7, no. 1, (February 1975), 2–32. Nariman Bahravesh, "Forecasting Inflation: Does the Method Make a Difference?" *Monthly Review*, (September/October 1976).

[15]Stephen S. McNees, "The Forecasting Record for the 1970's," Federal Reserve Bank of Boston, *New England Economic Review* (September/October 1979), pp. 33–53.

The significance of these conclusions is that there is no *best* forecasting technique or model for all forecasting situations. Rather, it is necessary to weigh the strengths and weaknesses of alternative methods before making a technique selection.

Example 10-1: Forecasting Sales Tax Receipts: Box-Jenkins and Regression Models

A forecast analyst has received a request from the mayor to develop a model that can be used to generate monthly forecasts of the city's sales tax receipts. These projections will be used by various city departments to quantify monthly cash-flow requirements from banks, personnel needs, and potential budgetary problems. The sales tax data listed in Table 10-6 covers the period from July 1971 to November 1980. In order to test the accuracy of the estimated models, it was decided to fit the forecast equations over the period from July 1971 to June 1980 and to use the last five observations for comparative *ex post* simulations. In addition to estimating a Box-Jenkins model, a multiple regression equation was developed using a trend variable and a series of seasonal dummy variables.

Figure 10-3 depicts the autocorrelation coefficients for sales tax receipts, while Figure 10-4 illustrates comparable coefficients for the tax series after it has been transformed using first differences. In Figure 10-3, for example, the autocorrelation coefficient was 0.58 for a 12-month lag in tax receipts. Several conclusions can be drawn from these figures:

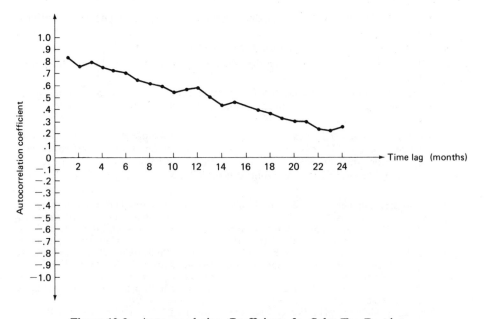

Figure 10-3   Autocorrelation Coefficients for Sales Tax Receipts

Table 10-6 Monthly sales tax receipts: July 1971–November 1980
(Thousand of dollars)

Date		Sales Tax Receipts	Date		Sales Tax Receipts
1971	July	91.1	1976	April	103.5
	Aug.	96.0		May	135.0
	Sept.	95.9		June	145.2
	Oct.	101.0		July	142.3
	Nov.	94.5		Aug.	147.5
	Dec.	97.4		Sept.	142.5
1972	Jan.	99.9		Oct.	142.6
	Feb.	100 5		Nov.	145.4
	March	123.0		Dec.	141.6
	April	91.6	1977	Jan.	147.8
	May	90.0		Feb.	188.4
	June	101.7		March	116.9
	July	101.9		April	120.2
	Aug.	103.5		May	161.1
	Sept.	108.6		June	148.8
	Oct.	102.3		July	149.1
	Nov.	107.1		Aug.	158.1
	Dec.	107.3		Sept.	156.4
1973	Jan.	107.3		Oct.	160.1
	Feb.	108.3		Nov.	155.0
	March	135.4		Dec.	161.7
	April	102.1	1978	Jan.	152.9
	May	98.9		Feb.	158.0
	June	109.2		March	189.7
	July	114.9		April	141.0
	Aug.	122.2		May	170.1
	Sept.	126.0		June	172.5
	Oct.	118.9		July	171.3
	Nov.	128.3		Aug.	184.0
	Dec.	126.4		Sept.	169.9
1974	Jan.	117.5		Oct.	178.2
	Feb.	126.4		Nov.	178.7
	March	146.3		Dec.	176.9
	April	121.1	1979	Jan.	182.5
	May	112.2		Feb.	224.9
	June	129.5		March	163.0
	July	129.5		April	152.0
	Aug.	131.3		May	186.0
	Sept.	134.2		June	187.0
	Oct.	134.8		July	188.4
	Nov.	140.0		Aug.	198.4
	Dec.	134.3		Sept.	185.8
1975	Jan.	155.2		Oct.	192.4
	Feb.	168.4		Nov.	190.1
	March	167.5		Dec.	190.2
	April	140.2	1980	Jan.	208.4
	May	148.1		Feb.	213.0
	June	128.1		March	195.8
	July	137.6		April	169.4
	Aug.	135.7		May	192.0
	Sept.	134.9		June	188.2
	Oct.	139.9		July	200.0
	Nov.	141.0		Aug.	202.4
	Dec.	131.6		Sept.	190.8
1976	Jan.	141.8		Oct.	207.2
	Feb.	163.3		Nov.	190.1
	March	146.8			

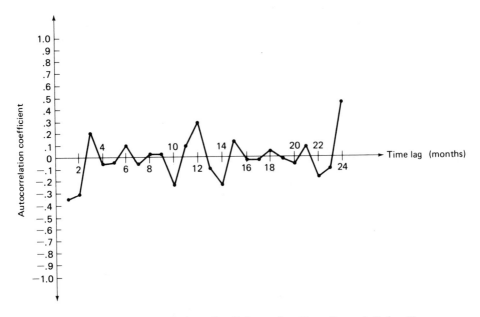

Figure 10-4 Autocorrelation Coefficients for Transformed Sales Tax Receipts

1. Since the autocorrelation coefficients for the original data contain a positive trend component, the series is not stationary. The coefficients in Figure 10-3 are positive, and when graphed, they resemble a trend line. Further, all of the autocorrelation coefficients are statistically significant, because their absolute values exceed 0.2.
2. The values of the autocorrelation coefficients in Figure 10-4 indicate that the trend in the original data has been eliminated and the transformed series is stationary.
3. Because the autocorrelation coefficients in periods 24, 12, 14, and 2 of Figure 10-4 are statistically significant, the transformed data exhibit monthly seasonality. This pattern can be removed by seasonally adjusting the data or by computing long-term differences that are greater than twelve months in duration.

Having identified the level of stationarity and the length of seasonality, we can proceed to estimate and test the two models of interest. The multiple regression model can be represented by:

$$\widehat{STR_t} = \hat{\beta}_0 + \hat{\beta}_6 T + \sum_{i=1}^{5} \hat{\beta}_i M_i + \sum_{i=7}^{12} \hat{\beta}_i M_i \qquad (10\text{-}44)$$

where

STR = monthly sales tax receipts in period t
T = trend value; 1 in July 1971 and augmented by 1 for each succeeding month
M_i = monthly seasonal dummy variable which takes a value of 0 or 1

The results of estimating the ordinary least squares regression were:

$$\widehat{STR_t} = 89.968 + 0.927T + 0.860M_7 + 5.552M_8$$
$$+ 2.130M_9 + 2.976M_{10} + 3.136M_{11} + 0.806M_{12}$$
$$+ 4.986M_1 + 19.373M_2 + 11.015M_3 - 16.933M_4$$
$$- 0.916M_5 \tag{10-45}$$

Only eleven seasonal coefficients need to be estimated. We have selected June as the reference month; this implies that all other seasonal factors are stated relative to June. If we are interested in deriving a forecast for July 1980, period 109, equation (10-45) becomes:

$$\widehat{STR_t} = 89.968 + 0.927T + 0.860M_7 \tag{10-46}$$

Since July is the seventh month of the year, all other months have M values of zero. Substituting into equation (10-46), we obtain:

$$\widehat{STR_{109}} = 89.968 + 0.927(109) + 0.860(1)$$
$$= 89.968 + 101.043 + 0.860$$
$$= 191.871 \tag{10-47}$$

The regression forecasts for periods 110 through 113, August 1980 to November 1980, are calculated below and summarized in column 2 of Table 10-7:

$$\widehat{STR_{110}} = 89.968 + 0.927(110) + 5.552(1)$$
$$= 197.490$$

$$\widehat{STR_{111}} = 89.968 + 0.927(111) + 2.130(1)$$
$$= 194.995$$

$$\widehat{STR_{112}} = 89.968 + 0.927(112) + 2.976(1)$$
$$= 196.768$$

$$\widehat{STR_{113}} = 89.968 + 0.927(113) + 3.136(1)$$
$$= 197.860 \tag{10-48}$$

The information provided in Figures 10-3 and 10-4 can be utilized to estimate a series of Box-Jenkins models with different time-lag structures. The general model chosen for the sales tax example is a mixed autoregressive-moving-average (ARMA) model of the form:

$$\hat{Y}_t = \hat{\beta}_1 Y_{t-1} + \hat{\beta}_2 Y_{t-2} + \cdots + \hat{\beta}_k Y_{t-k} + MA_t + \hat{\alpha}_1 MA_{t-1}$$
$$+ \hat{\alpha}_2 MA_{t-2} + \cdots + \hat{\alpha}_j MA_{t-j} \quad (10\text{-}49)$$

where

$$\sum_{n=1}^{k} \hat{\beta}_n Y_{t-n} = \text{autoregressive component}$$

$$\sum_{n=1}^{j} \hat{\alpha}_n MA_{t-n} = \text{moving average component}$$

Empirical identification of the best equation requires judgmental analysis of the autocorrelation coefficients, trial-and-error testing, and experience with the Box-Jenkins methodology.

The sales tax forecasts generated by the ARMA model are noted in column 4 of Table 10-7. The monthly Box-Jenkins estimates have an average absolute

Table 10-7 *Ex post* evaluation of multiple regression and Box-Jenkins forecasting models

Month	Sales Tax Receipts (Thousands) (1)	Estimated Sales Tax Receipts from Multiple Regression Model[a] (Thousands) (2)	Absolute Regression Error (%) (3)	Estimated Sales Tax Receipts from Box-Jenkins Model[b] (Thousands) (4)	Absolute Box-Jenkins Error (%) (5)
July 1980	$200.0	191.9	4.1	194.8	2.6
August 1980	202.4	197.5	2.4	199.9	1.2
September 1980	190.8	195.0	2.2	197.3	3.4
October 1980	207.2	196.8	5.0	199.8	3.6
November 1980	190.1	197.9	4.1	200.3	5.4

[a]Equations (10-47) and (10-48).
[b]Equation (10-49).

percentage error of 3.2 percent. In comparing the accuracy of the *ex post* simulations in Table 10-7, the average absolute regression error of 3.6 percent is slightly higher than that of the Box-Jenkins model. Both techniques capture the directional changes up to October 1980, but neither method anticipated the sharp drop in tax receipts in November 1980.

Given the much higher cost of constructing and maintaining the Box-Jenkins model, it is likely that the regression equation would be chosen if the decision were based solely on the results in Table 10-7. However, it would be up to the mayor and the city department heads to determine whether the benefits of either model outweighed the added costs. If, for example, the mayor had relied upon a naive forecasting system ($\hat{Y}_t = Y_{t-1}$) to forecast sales tax receipts, it is a simple matter to calculate the monthly error pattern of the naive system and compare it to similar figures for the regression and Box-Jenkins models. Given the month-to-month volatility of actual tax receipts exhibited in column 1 of Table 10-7, it can quickly be seen that the naive model would have had the highest average absolute percentage error during the period from July to November 1980. Still, the mayor might decide to stick with the naive system because of its relative simplicity and low cost.

CONCLUSION

In Chapters 9 and 10 we have introduced and studied the most common time-series techniques that are used in modeling economic activity. Time-series models range from the naive model that $\hat{Y}_{t+1}$ is equal to Y_t, to the extremely complex Box-Jenkins methodology. These models are primarily applicable when immediate term forecasts are desired. When compared to regression models, time-series models are apt to perform better in cases where the trend and seasonal components are dominant. They will generally perform poorly when the activity being studied has a strong cyclical component.

QUESTIONS FOR DISCUSSION AND ANALYSIS

1. Apply Winters's exponential smoothing to the air-miles-traveled data listed in column 1 in Table 4-2.
2. Construct a 90 percent confidence interval for the period 49 forecast prepared in problem 3 in Chapter 9.
3. Apply the adaptive-response-rate exponential-smoothing technique to the air-miles-traveled data presented in Example 9-1.
4. Apply Holt's exponential smoothing to the automobile data presented in Example 9-3.
5. Construct a confidence interval for the forecast developed in problem 1c in Chapter 9.
6. If you have access to a Box-Jenkins software package, estimate alternative ARMA models for the tax data in Table 10-6 and perform *ex post* simulations similar to those in Table 10-7.

REFERENCES FOR FURTHER STUDY

Box, G.E.P., and G.M. Jenkins, *Time Series Analysis: Forecasting and Control,* rev. ed. San Francisco: Holden-Day, 1976.

Brown, R.G., *Smoothing, Forecasting, and Prediction of Discrete Time Series.* Englewood Cliffs, N.J.: Prentice-Hall, 1962.

Harris, L., "A Decision-Theoretic Approach on Deciding When a Sophisticated Forecasting Technique Is Needed," *Management Science*, Vol. 13, No. 2 (1966), 66–69.

Hausman, W.H., and R.S.G. Sides, "Mail Order Demands for Style Goods: Theory and Data Analysis," *Management Science*, Vol. 20, No. 2 (October 1973), 191–202.

Naylor, T.H., and T.G. Seaks, "Box-Jenkins Methods: An Alternative to Econometric Models," *International Statistical Review*, Vol. 40, No. 2 (1972), 123–37.

Wade, J.B., "Determining Reorder Points When Demand Is Lumpy," *Management Science*, Vol. 24, No. 6 (February 1978), 623–32.

TRANSLATING THE FORECAST FOR MANAGEMENT

———

PART VI

11

Communicating Forecasts to Management

INTRODUCTION

The focus in the first ten chapters has been on the technical and judgmental facets of preparing a forecast, with little attention given to the equally important skill of presenting the forecast to management in a form that will most effectively facilitate the task of decision making. In Chapter 1, we outlined the forecast needs of management, but a complete appreciation of the more subtle aspects of translating a forecast is not possible until one has grappled with the job of data analysis and model development.

In some cases, management may present the forecaster with a very precise mandate that leaves little room for speculation concerning either the variable to be forecasted or the manner in which the results are to be reported. In the majority of instances, however, the forecaster must expend considerable effort interacting with forecast users in order to determine how forecast output can become a part of a firm's information and control system. The forecaster needs to present GNP-related statistics, but management is increasingly disenchanted with general economic summaries that are devoid of specific policy recommendations concerning company-level operations. There is, however, a constant need for updated forecasts that "limit the range of uncertainty within which management decision making is exercised."[1]

The task of the present chapter is to examine how a company's forecast needs can be evaluated and how the output can be communicated in a format that facilitates decision making.

DETERMINING MANAGEMENT'S
FORECAST NEEDS

People who engage in forecasting often view their activity as conforming to Say's Law—supply creates its own demand. Just as surveys of potential demand for in-house copying services often produce demand estimates that are far below the level actually experienced once the copier is procured, so the demand for in-house forecasting services frequently outstrips the forecast unit's effective capacity. In some cases, this is a matter of a poor pricing strategy for internal services; that is, the disparity between the quantity of forecast services supplied and the quantity demanded disappears once the internal price is raised high enough. In part, however, the surge in internal demand for forecast services reflects a recognition of the vast number of decisions that are directly or tangentially related to projections of company-level activity measures.

Table 1-1, in Chapter 1, contains a survey of potential corporate forecast users that helps to illuminate the problem of evaluating management's forecast needs. As pointed out in a study of corporate economists completed in the early 1970s by The Conference Board, forecasters are also called upon to provide:

Economic advice for management
Assignments in public relations
Counsel on management-science techniques
Analysis of industry competition
Acquisition studies
Responses to government agency requests
Service on executive committees[2]

The categories of service provided by forecasters are amplified in Table 1-1 by the list of potential users in various functional areas within the corporation. For example, the personnel department is apt to have manpower-planning and fringe-benefit responsibilities that necessitate forecasts spanning

[1]Walter E. Hoadley, "Reporting Forecasts to Management and the Use of Forecasts as a Management Tool," in *Methods and Techniques of Business Forecasting*, William Butler et al., eds. (Englewood Cliffs, N.J.: Prentice-Hall, 1974), p. 619.

[2]David I. Fisher, *The Corporate Economist*, Report No. 655 (New York: The Conference Board, 1975), p. 13.

periods from one month to five years. Similarly, the marketing and sales departments need projections of economic conditions, product demand, and inventory levels, both nationally and regionally. The finance department, on the other hand, must have a multitude of dollar and volume forecasts in order to monitor net income, cash-flow, short-term loan requirements, budgeted performance standards, and long-term capital-expenditure plans. These and the other functional forecast requirements listed in Table 1-1 are general in nature and can be found in varying degrees in any business organization. Although a forecaster needs to have the overall forecast profile of Table 1-1 firmly in mind, the table provides little insight into the specific variables that must be analyzed and projected into the future. To arrive at a precise menu of forecast variables, therefore, an in-depth assessment of forecast needs for each particular subunit within the major functional areas must be prepared.

QUANTIFYING MANPOWER REQUIREMENTS: SUPPORT-STAFF PROJECTIONS FOR PERSONNEL

It would seem to be a straightforward task to estimate the needed secretarial staff and the number of computer support personnel required for data entry. A small company can operate effectively with a rule of thumb such as one secretary per office manager, but a major corporation employing hundreds of secretaries is forced to engage in detailed planning. A request to a forecaster in a large corporation from the personnel department might be initiated in the following fashion:

> Dear Mr. Forecaster:
>   As you know, both the annual budget and the five-year company plan will be finalized this coming October. We have been asked to provide a monthly projection of labor-hours and average wage rates for the secretarial staff and for the keypunch support personnel over the next ten years. We have attached monthly data for labor requirements and wage rates over the last five years. Would you please provide us with the requested forecast magnitudes no later than the end of next week so that we can complete our report.
>   I.M. Labor
>   Vice-President of Personnel

Although this letter may appear farfetched, many business situations occur in which a forecast request is passed along from manager to manager until it finally reaches someone who can generate the needed set of numbers. The attachment of historical data by the forecast user is a rare practice; users typically are not oriented to time-series data collection.

After the arrival of such a request, there are two separate paths the forecaster may follow. First, a simple trend line or moving average might be applied to the data and extrapolated over the five-year horizon. This procedure would require no more than a couple of hours, and the numbers could be returned to personnel far in advance of the two-week deadline. Alternatively, the forecaster might initiate a round of meetings with personnel officials in order to better understand their needs and to determine whether a more elaborate manpower-demand study is warranted. The scope of such a study is, however, constrained by both users' and preparers' perceptions of the importance of the forecast to management and by resources available to the forecast unit. An admittedly worthwhile study may be supplanted by a two-hour trend analysis if budgeted funds are inadequate to support the cost of developing a causal model.

Assume that resources are available and that the forecaster has sent the following response:

> Dear Mr. Labor:
>
> In response to your recent letter requesting a forecast of man-hours and wage rates for secretarial staff and keypunch personnel, we have carried out a preliminary analysis that suggests that these two labor categories made up 28 percent of our operating costs during the current fiscal year, as compared to 21 percent only five years ago. Present indications are that this upward trend will continue, and a meeting is needed to clarify the specific factors causing the rise in this labor-expense category. As a way of focusing the discussion, here are some initial questions and comments:
>
> 1. Are there historical data available on the departmental breakdown of hours worked by the secretarial staff?
>
> 2. Have any major labor-saving equipment purchases been made for either the secretarial or keypunch staff? For example, has word-processing equipment been installed in place of traditional, single-typewriter installations? Are such purchases contemplated in the five-year plan?
>
> 3. What is the company's position concerning the use of part-time workers and overtime as a means of meeting peak-period demand?
>
> 4. Is keypunch work mainly related to data entry from standard invoices? If so, is it possible to substitute optical machine readers for keypunch operators?
>
> 5. Is the company willing to implement labor-saving programs that will reduce the labor force or keep its size constant?
>
> 6. By industry norms, is the company currently over- or understaffed with secretaries and keypunch workers relative to the volume of production and total employment?
>
> 7. Are wage rates currently tied to a cost-of-living escalator? If not, are workers likely to secure such a benefit in the next five years?
>
> 8. Have any studies been done on worker productivity? For example, are there historical data on the number of invoices keypunched per hour?
>
> 9. Does the company purposely maintain excess secretarial and keypunch capacity in order to meet recurring intramonth peaks such as record keeping during the first ten days of the month? If so, is it possible to smooth out these peaks and reduce this excess?
>
> 10. Other than the stated need to meet budgetary and planning requirements, would a monthly update of this forecast be of use in internal personnel-planning activities?
>
> Sincerely,
> Mr. Forecaster

Although the list appears to be voluminous, it is a necessary first step in attempting to project hours worked and wage rates paid. The preparer needs to develop a clear perception of how the forecasted figures mesh with the decisions and constraints faced by management. For example, several of the questions listed by the forecaster dealt with potential discretionary actions by management to substitute machinery for labor. In some companies, such a strategy would be viewed as progressive, but in others, the desire not to agitate union leaders might preclude introduction of any labor-saving technology. Alternatively, a company might be reluctant to change past procedures unless the potential rise in cost from following traditional techniques begins to seriously erode profitability. In effect, issues such as capital–labor substitution form the basic parameters of the forecaster's analysis. If radical innovations are precluded because of management constraints, then the forecaster need not worry so seriously about structural changes altering the firm's demand function for secretarial or keypunch labor.

A user's response to this list of questions will reveal whether he has any serious appreciation of how a manpower forecast could be used by the personnel department. At one extreme, the user may disclaim any responsibility for the request, arguing instead that the projections are just meaningless numbers that he has been requested to include as part of personnel's contribution to the company budget and five-year plan. In this case, the user becomes merely an intermediary, with no commitment to the forecast and probably little interest in exploring related issues such as worker productivity and capital–labor substitution. Alternatively, the user may have a clear perception of why the forecast is needed, how the manpower projections fit into the budget and five-year plan, and the degree to which management is willing to introduce labor-saving technology.

In the situation where a knowledgable and cooperative forecast user exists, a quick and productive interchange will expose the time-series data available for analysis and the forecast package needed to meet the requirements of management for decision making. In the case of a forecast user who is merely serving as an intermediary or conduit for information, the forecaster can either revert to the initial strategy of producing a simple trend projection for manpower or seek out the ultimate user of the forecast (perhaps the vice-president of finance) and solicit the same detailed information about the need for a manpower projection.

Ultimately, the forecast preparer must be willing to keep probing until the exact nature of a user's request can be pieced together. It may, in fact, turn out to be a rather whimsical, spur-of-the-moment request intended to fill a page in the five-year plan and serve no other apparent purpose. In this case, the forecast merits no more than an afternoon's work. Suppose, however, that there is a critical need for the manpower estimate. It is then up to the forecaster to help the vice-president of personnel translate the request into a usable forecast. For example, a linear-trend extrapolation of the past five year's growth in monthly labor-hours for secretarial and keypunch support might serve to illuminate a possible path for the company's labor needs over the next five years. Such a trend outlook would ignore, however, the company's own forecast of monthly sales volume. Thus, the second stage of the forecast analysis would call for two or more multiple-regression demand models linking the dependent variables (demand for secretarial and keypunch services) to independent variables such as unit sales volume, hours of production labor, or thousands of sales invoices processed. For example, a forecast for secretarial services could be generated by inserting predictions of future company sales into a simple regression equation that measured the historical fit between unit sales (X) and hours of secretarial labor (Y).

Although the regression approach utilizes more information than the trend forecast, the regression model still assumes an absence of structural change over the forecast period. Just as the amount of labor needed to produce an automobile changes over time, so the amount of secretarial or keypunch labor per unit of output may be altered by technological changes. If these alterations are continuous and steady over time, they may be adequately incorporated in a trend model or multiple-regression equation. In many cases, however, the demand for labor is modified in a lumpy fashion by factors such as major capital purchases. Management's goal is to maximize profits (given certain societal and company-level constraints), and it must therefore be concerned with productivity improvements. Based on trend extrapolations and multiple-regression estimates, management may become convinced that it faces labor-cost increases that will outpace revenue growth and damage profitability. As an aid to decision making, management may ask for a study incorporating a major labor-saving expenditure for word-processing equipment and computers in the second year of the five-year plan. A forecast can provide insights into a broad spectrum of decision alternatives, but these options may be inadequately explored if management is not prodded and compelled to articulate clearly both the underlying reasons for a manpower forecast and how it plans to use the projections.

Table 11-1 suggests one way in which the original, terse request for a trend extrapolation may actually be fulfilled. Really useful forecast formats are not apt to spring directly from the user, and it is equally unlikely that the forecaster will be able to produce a format that communicates effectively without going through the arduous process of questioning and prodding outlined above. The hypothetical forecast in Table 11-1 contains the annualized precentage rate of change for the company's unit sales, dollar sales, secretarial hours, keypunch hours, and wage rates, as well as a summary ratio for secretarial and keypunch salaries as a percentage of operating costs. The high and low projections for unit sales and dollar sales correspond to alternative assumptions for variables such as cyclical growth in the economy and market share. Similarly, the high and low projections for labor requirements are partially linked to variability in sales growth. Since decision makers are apt to

Table 11-1 Format for a hypothetical five-year manpower forecast
(Annual percentage change)

Forecast Category	Year 1	Year 2	Year 3	Year 4	Year 5
Unit sales: High	7%	6%	6%	5%	5%
Low	3	3	4	4	4
Dollar sales: High	15	14	14	9	9
Low	11	11	11	7	7
Manpower trend (hours worked)[a]					
Secretarial	8.5	8.5	8.5	8.5	8.5
Keypunch	9	9	9	9	9
Regression estimate (hours worked)[b]					
Secretarial: High	12	11	11	10	10
Low	8	8	9	9	9
Keypunch: High	13	12	12	11	11
Low	9	9	10	10	10
New technology (hours worked)[c]					
Secretarial: High	12	8	7	2	0
Low	8	5	5	2	2
Keypunch: High	13	9	9	5	2
Low	9	6	7	7	6
Wage rates ($/hour)[d]					
Secretarial: High	8	8	8	6	6
Low	6	6	6	4	4
Keypunch: High	7	7	7	5	5
Low	5	5	5	3	3
Secretarial and keypunch expense as a percentage of sales revenue[e]					
Trend	28	29	30	31	32
Regression: High	29	31	33	34	35
New technology: High	28	28	25	22	20
Regression: Low	28	30	32	33	34
New technology: Low	28	28	26	24	22

[a]Based on trend extrapolation of last five years.
[b]Uses statistical demand models for both labor categories.
[c]Assumes capital expenditures for word-processing equipment and computers beginning in second year.
[d]Based on forecast of consumer price index.
[e]Total dollar expenditures for secretarial and keypunch labor as a percent of total sales revenue.

be more familiar with sales forecasts than with labor-demand projections, the first two sets of estimates for unit and dollar sales provide an understandable reference base. For example, trend growth rates of 8.5 and 9.0 percent for secretarial and keypunch labor, respectively, may appear incongruous to management when they exceed even the high growth rate for unit sales. This dichotomy would have to be documented by another table detailing past growth trends for manpower and unit sales, as well as by analysis explaining the specific historical factors that have caused secretarial and keypunch labor-hours to outpace unit sales. The regression model yields growth factors for secretarial and keypunch labor that are even higher than the trend estimates. Again, supplementary tables would outline the regression model and describe why the high-growth scenario caused demand for secretarial and keypunch labor to climb at such a high level. For example, the predicted growth in unit sales might be concentrated in high-service commodities that require more voluminous customer contact (including written correspondence) and record keeping (warranty and complaint records stored on the computer).

The third set of manpower projections, labeled *new technology*, assumes that major capital expenditures for word-processing equipment and computers are begun in the second year of the five-year plan. In this instance, supplementary tables would describe how the regression estimates have been modified to reflect the substitution of capital equipment for labor. At the very bottom of Table 11-1, ratios summarize the percentage of annual revenue that would be absorbed by secretarial and keypunch salary expenses. Since the company hires secretaries and keypunchers from a large and competitive metropolitan labor market, the competitive setting of market wage rates would not be affected by company hiring policies. Even under the new-technology scenario, the secretarial-keypunch expense ratio does not start to fall until the third year. This decline results not from a smaller secretarial-keypunch work force (hourly growth factors are nonnegative) but from revenue outpacing salary expenses for secretarial and keypunch manpower.

Table 11-1, together with the support tables and text, is the forecaster's response to the cryptic request originally sent by the personnel department. The utility of such a manpower presentation to decision makers is dependent on whether management is able to interpret the information and draw policy conclusions that lead to specific decisions pertaining to secretarial and keypunch labor.

OPERATING A RAILROAD: TON-MILE PROJECTIONS

The case in Chapter 8 detailing the regression model for rail ton-miles highlighted the statistical procedures of time-series analysis and regression formulation and outlined how ton-mile estimates might be used by a locomotive manufacturer to make decisions concerning capital expenditures for plant expansion during the 1980s. The ton-mile projections in Chapter 8 can also be expanded to serve as the basis for operating decisions internal to an individual railroad company. In the manufacturing sector of the economy, decisions concerning inventory scheduling and output planning are usually handled in the production department. The analogous function of scheduling trains and maintaining system capacity is carried out by the operating department of the individual railroad. Just as production decisions are geared to the volume of output, so operating decisions are geared to the volume of ton-miles of traffic handled on the rail system.

Suppose a railroad's operations department has asked the company forecaster to provide a monthly estimate of ton-miles of traffic. Upon further questioning, the operations department's managers reveal that on the first of each month the department quantifies the total locomotive horsepower available and the amount of horsepower demanded in order to answer the following questions:

1. Is there a surplus (supply greater than demand) or a deficit (demand in excess of available supply) of locomotive horsepower?
2. If there is a surplus, is the margin great enough that the company can lease part of the fleet to other railroads in a deficit horsepower position?
3. If there is a deficit, can the quality of service (average speed and frequency) be reduced as a temporary means of handling traffic demand? If not, can horsepower be leased from other railroads?
4. Does the surplus (deficit) appear to be temporary (a seasonal fluctuation), cyclical (a business phenomenon that may stretch out for a number of months), or long run (a permanent situation stretching out over the planning horizon)?
5. Is the surplus (deficit) geographically uniform? That is, are all regions of the rail system likely to experience the same pattern, or does the aggregate projection mask large regional surpluses and deficits in different parts of the system?
6. Are particular freight commodities experiencing unusual surges or declines in demand owing to irregular or cyclical factors, as opposed to normal seasonal fluctuations?

This preliminary list of questions can be viewed as the forecaster's interpretation of the operating department's planning parameters. In effect, the operations department makes a collection of interrelated decisions spanning a planning period from the current month to five years hence. In the most immediate time span, the current month, operations analysts must assess the capability of the locomotive fleet to meet system demand. In the period stretching beyond the present month, they must update past judgments concerning system capacity for current and future years. The initial request for a monthly rail-ton-mile projection by the railroad's operations department was, therefore, a small fraction of the total information that could be utilized productively for system-capacity planning.

After a study of the initial list of six questions concerning the supply of and demand for locomotive horsepower, the next step would be to ask the operations department to clarify the procedures it follows in using a ton-mile projection for the current month's locomotive plan. Suppose the system is as follows: Each month (for example, in April), the seasonally adjusted annualized rate (SAAR) for projected ton-miles (102 billion in April) is divided by the railroad's average ratio of ton-miles hauled per unit of horsepower (14,000 ton-miles per unit of horsepower) in order to derive horsepower demand of 7.286 million (as shown in the second column of Table 11-2).[3] This horsepower demand

---

[3]In 1978, Class I U.S. railroads used 61.2 million horsepower to handle 858.1 billion ton-miles of traffic, or roughly 14,000 ton-miles per unit of horsepower. See Association of American Railroads, *Yearbook of Railroad Facts*, 1979 edition.

is spread across the five subregions of the system according to the percentage of total ton-miles hauled in each region for the same month in the prior year. That is, if region 4 handled 17.6 percent of the total ton-miles last April, this region would be expected to produce approximately 18 billion ton-miles (0.176 · 102 billion) this April. Regional-demand projections are then matched against a proportional spreading (again, using last year's percentage ratios) of the available daily supply of horsepower in order to produce an initial regional projection of locomotive surpluses and deficits that can be presented to a high-level management committee for interpretation and follow-up decisions.

The procedures outlined above for the monthly analysis of horsepower needs illustrate both how a ton-mile projection can be converted into a micro-economic planning parameter and how the information might finally arrive before management in a decision-making situation. In effect, decisions concerning regional horsepower allocation are too important to be left to a single department. For example, based just on operating considerations, there might evolve a policy of uniformly spreading deficits across all regions. The consequences of a 10 percent horsepower shortage in region 1 may be much less severe than even a 5 percent shortage in region 2. Traffic in region 1 may be primarily low-valued construction materials, which have a relatively modest profit margin and are not highly sensitive to an increase in transit time. Traffic in region 2, however, may be predominantly high-valued manufactured products that are very profitable, extremely time-sensitive, and easily divertible to other modes such as trucks. Thus, once the ton-mile forecast has been converted into a preliminary projection of regional horsepower demand and supply, management must explicitly consider the profit implications of alternative horsepower-allocation schemes.

Systems such as the operations department's are pragmatic in nature and not likely to be criticized by management if they work reasonably well. The procedures of the operations department, however, do raise fundamental issues: When does the forecaster lose control of his projection? Stated differently, is the forecaster responsible for the accuracy of the regional horsepower analysis when he or she has provided the initial ton-mile number but has not been involved in the intermediate steps that converted ton-miles to horsepower? In the case of personnel's request for a manpower forecast, this issue did not arise, because no existing procedure had been formulated. The forecaster could (as was illustrated in Table 11-1) put together a forecast package that provided all the information desired by management for decisions related to secretarial and keypunch staff. In the instance of the operations department's request, however, there is already an established procedure for the conversion of ton-miles to horsepower, and the forecaster is only being asked to provide an external estimate of ton-miles. The management committee that meets monthly to decide on locomotive allocation is interested in regional horsepower surpluses and deficits, not in total ton-miles. If the forecaster provides just the requested ton-mile projection, he may be blamed for errors in the regional horsepower-demand projections when, in fact, the operations department's conversion process from ton-miles to horsepower is at fault.

Although it is clearly in the best interests of the company to have the regional horsepower-demand projections be as accurate as possible, control of the preliminary numbers that go to the management committee may be a source of political power within the company and may not be easily relinquished by the operations department. How deeply the forecaster becomes involved in the ton-mile-to-horsepower conversion process is as much a question of politics as it is of salesmanship. There are numerous gray areas of overlap between the forecaster's domain of expertise and the responsibility of functional departments such as operations, personnel, finance, and marketing. How far the forecaster will be allowed to intrude into a functional responsibility is largely determined by his or her credibility in the company—the ability to analyze correctly management's information needs, put together a complete forecast package, argue persuasively the merit of projections, and explain precisely the reasons for past errors.

Having developed a clear understanding of how the ton-mile projection is actually converted by the operating department, and having analyzed management's decision-making process relative to monthly horsepower needs, the railroad forecaster might put together the summary report presented in Table 11-2 as a means of selling both the operations department and management on the desirability of having the forecaster complete the horsepower analysis. Table 11-2 is a top-down system that allows management to view company horsepower needs in the context of traffic volume in the entire railroad industry. Each month, this report would start (row 1 of Table 11-2) with an assessment of predicted national ton-miles of traffic. The work for this forecast was illustrated earlier by the quarterly rail-ton-mile model in Chapter 8, and these projections could easily be converted to a monthly forecast.

Next, in rows 2 to 4 of Table 11-2, the national rail-ton-mile projections are broken into major regional subcomponents using the Interstate Commerce Commission's breakdown of Eastern, Southern, and Western regions. The historical regional figures were illustrated in Chapter 8, and it would be necessary to develop regression models to predict the percentage composition of regional rail ton-miles of traffic. Next, in row 5, the company's ton-mile estimate is illustrated. In addition to a single number for monthly company ton-miles, the full report would contain a supplementary table decomposing the total ton-mile projection into the twenty major commodity categories used in budgetary analysis. This decomposition is important for two reasons. First, the regional allocation of ton-miles shown in rows 6 to 10 is mainly linked to the composition of the commodities transported in each region. The commodity mix determines ton-miles, which in turn affects horsepower demand. Second, the management review committee making decisions concerning horsepower allocation is apt to be composed of many of the same people who occupy seats on the budget committee. Familiarity with the budget means more rapid ac-

Table 11-2 Rail disaggregation schema: Ton-miles to monthly horsepower demand (Hypothetical monthly projections)

	Regression Estimates	Operation's Estimates	Autoregression Projections
(1) National ton-miles[a] (billions, SAAR)	975.0		
(2) Eastern	224.5		
(3) Western	566.0		
(4) Southern	184.5		
(5) Company ton-miles[b] (billions, SAAR)	105.0	102.0	100.0
(6) Region 1	15.5	14.1	13.3
(7) Region 2	28.3	27.0	26.5
(8) Region 3	22.6	23.0	20.6
(9) Region 4	17.1	18.0	18.5
(10) Region 5	21.5	19.9	21.1
(11) Company horsepower demand[c] (thousands, SAAR)	8,057	7,286	7,372
(12) Region 1	1,309	1,006	1,092
(13) Region 2	1,947	1,930	1,941
(14) Region 3	2,080	1,646	1,657
(15) Region 4	1,063	1,286	1,315
(16) Region 5	1,658	1,418	1,367
(17) Company horsepower surplus or deficit[d] (thousands, SAAR)	−557	214	128
(18) Region 1	−273	60	−56
(19) Region 2	40	57	46
(20) Region 3	−386	48	37
(21) Region 4	260	38	9
(22) Region 5	−198	41	92

[a]The national figures could be derived from the quarterly rail-ton-mile model developed in Chapter 8. The Interstate Commerce Commission divides the U.S. mainline into three broad regions. The actual report would supplement this regional breakdown with historical analyses. All data presented as seasonally adjusted annualized rates (SAAR).

[b]Reading across rows 5 to 10, the first set of projections is generated via regression techniques, the second incorporates the operations department's assumption that this month's business will equal last month's, and the third uses autoregressive methods.

[c]Reading across rows 11 to 16, the first set of projections is generated via regression techniques and utilizes the corresponding estimates in rows 5 to 10, the second uses prior ton-mile-to-horsepower ratios, and the last is based upon autoregressive methods. See footnote 3 in text.

[d]The three sets of estimates in rows 17 to 22 were derived by substracting available horsepower from the demand estimates in rows 11 to 16. The regional supply of total horsepower is assumed to match the percentage distribution for horsepower demand. Total supply is 7.5 million horsepower.

ceptance of the ton-mile projections in Table 11-2, which is linked (via supplementary tables) to the same commodity base. Thus, established credibility in one forecast activity (the budget) can be used to extend credibility to a new area such as horsepower analysis.

The breakdown of ton-miles in rows 5 to 10 in Table 11-2 is then used to derive the regional horsepower-demand figures in rows 11 to 16. Three sets of projections are provided. The first utilizes regression equations to link ton-miles in each region to horsepower demand. The second is based on the operations department's procedures, which use a historical ratio to convert ton-miles to horsepower, and the third set is based on an autoregressive system that uses historical regional horsepower data to estimate demand for the next month. Rows 17 to 22 contain three corresponding sets of surplus/deficit horsepower projections, which were estimated under the assumption that the available supply would be allocated in proportion to the percentage of total horsepower demanded in each region. This may appear to be a weak initial assumption to make for the distribution of horsepower, but railroad management operates under the decision-making constraints of the Interstate Commerce Commission (ICC). A basic tenet of ICC regulation has been the railroad's obligation to serve all customers fairly, and a distribution of horsepower in proportion to demand is, therefore, a reasonable starting point for management decision making.

Rather than the single number for rail ton-miles in row 5 of Table 11-2 that was requested by the operations department, the forecaster has supplied all the data in Table 11-2, together with backup tables and analysis. This could be described as an unreasonably voluminous response to a rather simple request. In actuality, many forecast requests would be supplied by the forecaster in the perfunctory and succinct manner requested by the user. This example was meant to illustrate, however, a situation in which management was making important decisions based on inadequate forecasting information. In this situation, the forecaster has already done a substantial amount of research on the national ton-mile model, and conversion into the standard budgetary format had already been completed. The horsepower-demand figures represent a spinoff of the commodity data already estimated for the budget rather than a completely new project. From the standpoint of management, such a spinoff has the advantage of integrating decision-making activities that were formerly disjointed.

If we look in more detail at the projections in Table 11-2, several interesting comparisons can be drawn. First, the regression estimates for national ton-miles in rows 1 to 4 are not matched by comparable operations or autoregression estimates. The concept of top-down disaggregation implies a logical and direct connection between aggregate and company-level forecasts. The operating estimates are devoid of such connections and merely reflect the assumption that this month's ton-miles equal last month's ($\hat{Y}_t = Y_{t-1}$). The autoregressive projections forecast the company's current ton-miles based upon statistical analysis of the company's historical experience, but autoregressive systems do not provide any causal linkage to determinants of future ton-mile movements. In effect, the operations and autoregression estimates are based entirely on past series movements. The regression projections, however, indicate (as was the case for the rail model in Chapter 8) how future movements in the independent variables are expected to influence the coming month's freight ton-miles.

Between the three estimates of company ton-miles in row 5 of Table 11-2 there appears to be little difference, but the regional company ton-mile totals in rows 6 to 10 display substantial differences, and these are amplified in the company horsepower-demand figures in rows 12 to 16. It is not uncommon for alternative forecasting approaches to yield aggregates (for example, the projections in row 11) that are similar and subcomponents that vary widely (see rows 12 to 16). In this case, total company demand for horsepower differs by about 10 percent, whereas regional demand varies by as much as 30 percent. Although these figures are hypothetical, they are a realistic reflection of anomalies that the forecaster must be prepared to explain to management. In this case, the horsepower-demand differentials were constructed so as to mirror differences in techniques as well as unique cyclical characteristics. In situations where the economy is declining slowly, growing steadily, or moving along a plateau, the assumption of continuity between next month's horsepower demand and the past month's may not produce large forecast errors. If the economy is at an upper or lower turning point, however, the continuity assumption is likely to produce projections that are misleading. The ton-mile and horsepower-demand figures generated via regression techniques were prepared under the assumption that the railroad would experience a rebound following a lower turning point in the economy, and that resurgence would be concentrated in a select group of commodities. For example, a railroad that was a major transporter of lumber could have used a top-down regression model to incorporate a forecasted surge in housing starts and lumber traffic as the basis for region 1's predicted horsepower deficit in row 18. Even though the economy was expected to rebound and to buoy the derived demand for lumber and other cyclically sensitive commodities, the projected horsepower surplus in region 4 (see row 21) mirrors the forecaster's prediction that record crop production would deflate grain prices, increase grain storage, and actually inhibit grain shipments. Again, these are unique factors that will be overlooked in an autoregressive system.

The horsepower surplus and deficit numbers in row 17 of Table 11-2 are based upon a total supply of 7.5 million horsepower (7,500 thousand). This supply is spread across the regions by using the percentage distribution projected for horsepower demand. Thus, if 14.2 percent of the horsepower is demanded in region 1 under operation's estimates, the initial supply assumption of 1,066 thousand horsepower in region 1 (0.142 • 7,500) yields a surplus of 60 thousand horsepower in row 18—demand of 1,006 less supply of 1,066.

The text material accompanying a summary such as Table 11-2 would have to contain an expanded description of the commodities in each region that are likely to experience the most substantial horsepower surpluses or deficits. It is important to have such detailed commodity data as backup information, since the effect on profitability is, as explained earlier, commodity-sensitive. The horsepower projections in rows 17 to 22 become, therefore, the initial input for management decision makers concerned with the coming month's allocation of horsepower. Although there are really no significant horsepower deficits under the operations or autoregression scenarios, the regression estimates include substantial deficits and surpluses. We have shown only one set of regression estimates in Table 11-2, but support tables might include contingency analysis of alternative forecast assumptions such as a continued recession or an even stronger rebound. The number of demand and supply combinations is, of course, innumerable, and the forecaster may wish to stick with the regression estimates in Table 11-2 as the best guess.

The short-run nature of the monthly estimates in Table 11-2 precludes answers to longer-run questions concerning the adequacy of horsepower for the next year or the next five years. Quarterly forecasts of ton-miles such as those presented in Chapter 8 can also serve as the starting point for long-run capital expenditures for locomotives. In this instance, the problem becomes similar to the case of the locomotive builder in Chapter 8 who was trying to anticipate the railroad industry's long-run demand for locomotives. The summary in Table 11-2, as well as the relevant support information, grew out of the operations department's initial request for a monthly ton-mile projection to incorporate within the existing system of horsepower analysis. Political and budgetary constraints may prevent the fruition of the complete system outlined in Table 11-2, but the most critical variable is likely to be the forecaster's willingness to prepare a system that responds to management's decision-making needs.

FORMULATING THE BUDGET: THE ROLE OF THE FORECASTER

INTRODUCTION

Of all the uses and applications of forecasts, none is more directly tied to the company's daily functioning and its financial-control systems than the company budget. A mystique often surrounds the budgetary process and keeps a host of issues intertwined in a seemingly insoluble maze. Consider these questions:

1. How does a forecast become part of a budget?
2. What is a company budget? a fixed budget? a variable budget?
3. What is the level of regional disaggregation in the budget? the level of product disaggregation?
4. How does the budget reconcile the field sales (bottom-up) forecast with the statistical (top-down) forecast?
5. How are budgeted dollar magnitudes decomposed into volume and price subcomponents?
6. How are actual company results analyzed and compared to the budget? What is budgetary variance analysis, and how is this process related to *ex post* forecast evaluation?

7. When is the old budget thrown out in favor of a new set of numbers?
8. How do the forecast and budget fit into the management information system?
9. How can time-series concepts such as seasonality be adapted to fit into the framework?
10. How can contingency forecasts and probabilistic assessments be incorporated within a budget?

These general issues can best be discussed and illuminated by reference to the budgetary situation faced by the lamp manufacturer whose sales history and budget for the past three years are summarized in Tables 11-3 and 11-4, respectively. As shown in Table 11-3, four basic lamp styles are sold in the four major regional markets; the individual lamp designations correspond to price categories from high to low. The first row of Table 11-4 reproduces the total sales figures from Table 11-3 and shows the linkages from dollar sales to gross profit, operating profit, profit before taxes, and profit after taxes. The regional sales totals in Table 11-3 are accompanied by market penetration or

Table 11-3 Lamp sales by product category and region
(Millions of dollars)

Region and Lamp Category	Last Year Sales	Last Year Market Share	2 Years Ago Sales	2 Years Ago Market Share	3 Years Ago Sales	3 Years Ago Market Share
Region 1	$18.0	16.0%	$18.9	17.0%	$21.0	18.5%
Lamp grade:						
A	6.5		7.0		9.0	
B	4.5		4.8		4.5	
C	3.6		3.9		4.1	
D	3.4		3.2		3.1	
Region 2	$25.0	19.0%	$23.0	18.5%	$20.0	17.0%
Lamp grade:						
A	8.0		7.5		7.0	
B	6.2		5.7		5.2	
C	3.8		3.3		2.8	
D	7.0		6.5		5.0	
Region 3	$26.8	23.0%	$23.9	21.0%	$21.2	20.0%
Lamp grade:						
A	4.7		4.0		3.3	
B	8.1		7.4		6.7	
C	9.1		8.4		7.7	
D	4.9		4.1		4.5	
Region 4	$22.2	19.0%	$23.6	21.0%	$22.9	22.0%
Lamp grade:						
A	7.0		7.8		7.2	
B	6.5		7.1		7.1	
C	5.4		5.4		5.2	
D	3.3		3.3		3.4	
Total	$92.0	19.6%	$89.4	19.5%	$85.1	19.5%

Table 11-4 Income statement of lamp manufacturer for three previous years (Millions of dollars)

	Last Year	2 Years Ago	3 Years Ago
Net sales[a]	$92.0	$89.4	$85.1
Cost of sales	69.4	66.6	62.1
Gross profit	22.6	22.8	23.0
% of sales	24.6%	25.5%	27.0%
Selling expenses	10.4	9.9	9.0
General and administrative	5.8	5.6	6.5
Operating profit	6.4	7.3	7.5
% of sales	6.9%	8.2%	8.8%
Other income	0.2	0.1	0.1
Other expense	0.1	0.1	0.1
Net profit before income taxes	6.5	7.3	7.5
Provision for taxes	3.3	3.7	3.8
Net profit	$ 3.2	$ 3.6	$ 3.7
% of sales	3.5%	4.0%	4.4%
Return on investment	11.3%	12.3%	12.8%

[a]As explained in the text, it is company revenue, or net sales, that will serve as the main forecast variable in the present example on budgeting.

share figures, which illustrate an overall deterioration in the market share of regions 1 and 4 and an improvement in that of regions 2 and 3. As seen in Table 11-4, net profit after taxes has not been growing; it has actually been falling as a percent of sales. In addition, the company's return on average investment has been declining over the same three-year period.

In anticipation of the October budget meeting, the vice-president of finance, who is in charge of the budget, has sent around the schematic in Figure 11-1 to illustrate the planning inputs needed from all departments and the logical flow of information during the preparation of the budget. Figure 11-1 helps to clarify the second question of those listed earlier in this section, concerning the logical relationship of the forecast to the budget. Literally all functional divisions in the lamp manufacturing company are represented in Figure 11-1, but the sales forecast marks the logical starting point for the planning information that flows throughout the company. The budget is a planning system designed to control and monitor all the functional activities within the company. In regard to the income statement in Table 11-4, forecasting activity will be defined as involving only the projection of total sales; the remainder of the activities related to the entries in the table have to do with cost and financial analysis and will be viewed as outside the purview of forecasting. Although the forecaster is frequently called upon to offer assumptions for inflation that can be used to estimate future materials costs and to provide interest-rate projections needed in computing the cost of borrowed funds, the bulk of his or her budgetary activity is tied up with the job of estimating unit

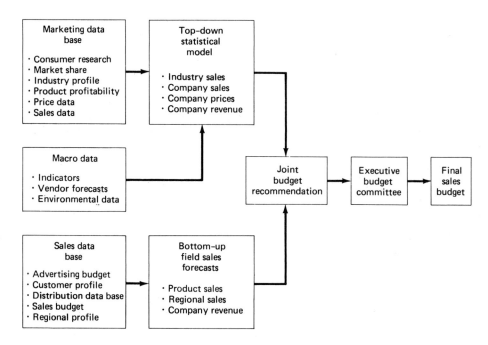

Figure 11-1 Budgetary Schema: Integration of Top-Down and Bottom-Up Forecasts of Sales Revenue

and dollar sales for the company, utilizing the time-series techniques outlined in the text. It is revenue projections, not cost or net-income estimates, that will serve as the focus of this case on budgeting.[4]

STAGE ONE: SYNTHESIZING TOP-DOWN AND BOTTOM-UP PROJECTIONS

The budgetary schematic in Figure 11-1 is general enough to apply to almost any manufacturing organization, and it permits an overview that helps to integrate the specific examples listed below for the lamp manufacturer. The first stage, as shown in Figure 11-1, involves the integration of statistical or top-down projections emanating from the marketing department with field sales or bottom-up estimates produced by the sales department. The statistical, or top-down, approach involves the following general steps:

1. Develop the outlook for GNP and other key macroeconomic indicators, such as disposable income, that are closely related to lamp sales.
2. Prepare an industry-level forecast for lamp sales in physical units and dollars, and decompose these figures into the four main product subcategories.

[4]Fisher, *Corporate Economist*, pp. 6–12. This allocation makes sense, since there is much greater uncertainty surrounding the level of sales revenue than there is around projected cost and net income once the value of forecasted revenue has been specified.

3. Regionalize the national sales figures to match the four major markets served by the company.
4. Making use of external information concerning the competitive environment and internal market research related to consumer preferences and company capacity, develop market-share projections for the company.
5. Produce a forecast of total company sales in dollars and physical units for the coming budgetary year, and disaggregate by region and by product line (so as to match the historical detail in Table 11-3).

The procedures followed in linking GNP to company lamp sales will be an amalgam of the many techniques outlined in the previous chapters of this text. Some statistical forecasters may jump from GNP to total lamp sales in one equation, and may never make an explicit market-share assumption. Other business analysts might spend thousands of dollars to develop a disaggregated statistical model of industry lamp sales and then utilize nonstatistical or judgmental assessments of the company's market share for each major industry product line. There are literally hundreds of ways the top-down forecaster could arrive at a set of projections for lamp sales by region and product line that matched the format of Table 11-3; however, they would all share a common analytical view in which company sales were linked to an explicit set of numerical assumptions for aggregate economic performance.

There is equal, or perhaps even greater, diversity in the approaches followed by sales departments in order to generate the field sales projections for next year's budget. The underlying procedure of bottom-up forecasting is one of pyramiding sales estimates from individual salespeople in order to reach a grand total. For example, in the case of the lamp manufacturer, each of the four regions might be staffed by ten salespeople. The head of company sales would request each of the forty salespeople to project lamp sales by price category for the coming year, and then these projections would be totaled by region and by product category to match the categories in Table 11-3. On the one hand, each of the forty salespeople would have privileged access to information about sales characteristics in his or her region that would permit incorporation of factors not available to top-down forecasters in the company's headquarters. For instance, the opening or closing of a major furniture store in a salesperson's territory might swamp cyclical forces that normally dominate lamp sales.

On the other hand, it is unlikely that the entire sales staff is operating with the same set of macroeconomic assumptions for the economy. Many salespeople will make no explicit assumptions at all about next year's real GNP growth, and even if the head of the sales department provides them with a baseline projection for the economy, it is unlikely that the sales force will be capable of interpreting and applying the information uniformly.[5] Field sales forecasts are nevertheless important, because they are compiled from internal

---

[5]This is not meant to disparage the talent of sales personnel, who are, in fact, quite knowledgeable about the customer-to-company environment.

or ground-level information about prospects in each of the company's sub-regions. The statistical projections are necessary because they build upon the broader economic and sociopolitical environment surrounding the company.

Table 11-5 outlines a first-stage comparison between field sales and statistical projections of lamp sales for the coming year. These are, of course, hypothetical numbers, but they serve to point out a number of questions that typically arise when the two groups get together to synthesize their projections:

1. Are the field sales estimates used to set quotas for the salespeople? If so, will they not tend to be biased downward?
2. If quotas or targets are independent of the budget, will the field sales estimates merely be wild guesses devoid of any serious thought?
3. Are salespeople in each region using the same set of assumptions for the prices of next year's lamps? Do they mesh with the top-down assumptions?
4. Are sales estimates affected by differentials in lamp profitability? That is, have salespeople inflated estimates for high-priced lamps because they yield higher commissions?
5. How can statistical projections incorporate unique regional influences such as sales promotions by competitors?
6. Is it legitimate to assume that the company's promotional and advertising expenses will continue to absorb the same percentage of the sales dollar?

As shown in the first two columns of Table 11-5, the field sales and statistical forecasts differ substantially. For some users of the budget, the key characteristic is the level of total dollar sales; for others, it may be the composition of the physical units sold. For example, the marketing department, based on historical and industry norms, may always allocate 2.5 percent of total budgeted sales revenue for advertising and product promotion. The actual distribution of advertising dollars for particular lamp product lines may be viewed as more important than the dollar value of budgeted total revenue. The purchasing department, however, needs to order materials and supplies for four physically distinct lamp styles, and it must also plan for the distribution of the finished products to four regional warehouses, depending on the regional sales volume incorporated in the budget.

The third column of Table 11-5 presents a recommended budget for the coming year, which the head forecaster prepared. Again, the numbers are hypothetical, but the steps used to arrive at the numbers are suggestive of compromises that often occur. The process of arriving at a synthesis of sales and statistical forecasts involves a step-by-step discussion for each of the sixteen lamp/region combinations (four regions multiplied by four products). For example, the sales forecast of $4 million of grade D lamp sales in region 1 is higher than the statistical projection of $3.5 million. In turn, both those projections exceed the corresponding historical figures for past sales shown in Table 11-3. Whereas the statistical projection for grade D lamp sales in region 1 envisions a continuation of the historical trend (see Table 11-3), the sales forecast of a substantial jump in sales of low-priced lamps was based on the assumed opening of a major new company employing low-wage laborers in

Table 11-5 Comparative estimates of budgeted lamp revenue
(Millions of dollars)

Region	Field Sales Forecast (1)	Statis- tical Projection (2)	Recom- mended Budget (3)	Opti- mistic Outlook (4)	Pessi- mistic Outlook (5)	Final Budget (6)
Region 1	$23.0	$19.0	$20.2	$23.0	$19.0	$21.0
Lamp grade:						
A	8.0	6.5	6.7	8.0	6.5	6.9
B	6.0	4.7	5.2	6.0	4.7	5.4
C	5.0	4.3	4.3	5.0	4.3	4.5
D	4.0	3.5	4.0	4.0	3.5	4.2
Region 2	$27.0	$24.0	$25.2	$27.0	$24.0	$26.0
Lamp grade:						
A	8.0	6.7	6.8	8.0	6.7	7.0
B	6.8	5.7	6.8	6.8	5.7	7.0
C	4.2	3.6	3.6	4.2	3.6	3.8
D	8.0	8.0	8.0	8.0	8.0	8.2
Region 3	$30.8	$26.8	$26.9	$30.8	$26.8	$27.7
Lamp grade:						
A	4.7	3.7	3.7	4.7	3.7	3.9
B	9.1	9.1	9.1	9.1	9.1	9.3
C	10.5	9.1	9.1	10.5	9.1	9.3
D	6.5	4.9	5.0	6.5	4.9	5.2
Region 4	$27.2	$24.0	$24.5	$27.7	$23.5	$25.3
Lamp grade:						
A	8.0	7.0	7.0	8.0	7.0	7.2
B	7.5	8.0	7.5	8.0	7.5	7.7
C	6.4	5.7	6.0	6.4	5.7	6.2
D	5.3	3.3	4.0	5.3	3.3	4.2
Total	$108.0	$93.8	$96.8	$108.5	$93.5	$100.0

region 1. Although there is substantial variance in the two forecasts, only a follow-up phone call is necessary to check the legitimacy of the salesperson's assumption. In this case, it was decided to accept the higher sales number. However, in region 3, just the opposite occurred for forecasted sales of high-priced, grade A lamps. In this case, the sales numbers called for no growth, but the statistical projections yielded a substantial drop resulting from a predicted regional decline in disposable income. Of course, a phone call cannot be made to confirm a future decline in regional income, but the underlying reasons can be articulated and discussed.

The act of merging the forecasts in the first two columns of Table 11-5 into the proposed budget in the third column involves compromise, analysis, and persuasion. In some unreconcilable cases, the proposed number may merely split the difference between the original bottom-up and top-down numbers. In addition to the proposed budget in column 3, optimistic and pessimistic projections were generated in columns 4 and 5 by summing the highest and lowest regional sales figures, respectively. The data in the first five columns of Table 11-5, together with an analysis of the key underlying controversies, would be forwarded to the vice-president of finance.

Budgets are not decided upon unilaterally, and the importance of the annual budget necessitates a meeting of the vice-president of finance with his counterparts throughout the company. Since all activity levels within the company will be geared to the budgeted figures for the coming year, all functional areas of the company must be able to respond to the proposed budgeted numbers in terms of the implications for the financial and physical operations of the company. For example, the forecasted jump in grade D lamp sales in region 2 may cause warehouse demand to exceed local warehouse capacity, and the drop in grade A lamp sales in region 3 may introduce inventory problems at the main factory. The company forecaster is likely to be called upon to repeat many of the explanations presented earlier to the sales staff, as well as to discuss contingencies in the general economic outlook. The forecaster's persuasiveness will be one of the key factors shaping the final budget, shown in column 6 of Table 11-5, but the ultimate decision rests in the hands of the vice-president of finance. The final budget in column 6 is closest to the recommended budget presented in column 3. The statistical forecaster may feel that the budget in column 6 is too high, but the vice-president of finance is the person faced with the ultimate responsibility of achieving the targeted magnitudes for net income implied by the budget. The difference between the forecaster's original recommendation in column 2 and the final budget in column 6 may reflect a relative difference in optimism between a conservative forecaster and an optimistic finance officer, or it may be due to substantive issues such as the predicted success of a planned advertising campaign, or the effect of lamp imports on domestic sales. The process of formulating the revenue portion of the budget requires the skills of diplomacy and salesmanship; the task of explaining the variance between actual and budgeted figures is objective, analytical, and full of potential pitfalls.

MONITORING THE BUDGET
AND FORECAST

In many companies, the top-down, or statistical, forecaster is also given the job of monitoring the monthly sales figures, writing explanations to reconcile the difference between actual and budgeted figures, and preparing analytical updates to management that can be used to determine when significant budget revisions are required. Part of the advantage of having an ongoing forecasting staff prepare preliminary budget figures is that the volume, price, and dollar magnitudes will be internally consistent. That is, when the forecasted dollar figures are deflated by prices, they should yield the original volume numbers projected by the forecast models. That is only true, however, of the preliminary forecast in column 2 of Table 11-5, which is directly under the control of the forecaster. The final budget in column 6 becomes a hybrid prediction that incorporates suggestions from many groups. The final budget of $100 million in column 6 may, for example, be a revised version of an earlier budget that was sent to the president and rejected because budgeted revenue and net income were inadequate to support capital expenditures to which the president was already emotionally committed. The vice-president of finance may simply have been forced to inflate all recommended budgeted revenue categories in column 3 in order to reach total revenue of $100 million. Thus, on top of compromises between alternative forecast figures, there are frequently unilateral additions to or subtractions from the consensus forecast that may partially or completely distort volume-price-revenue relationships. Ultimately, actual sales results must be explained and the budget critically appraised. The task of the forecaster becomes one of candidly analyzing the changing forces in the economy and bringing them to bear on management's monthly budget decisions.

Suppose that total revenue was below budgeted revenue by $2.1 million in January and February, and that corporate headquarters is seriously questioning the company's ability to achieve either the targeted revenue for the remainder of the year or the full-year projections. In effect, the forecaster's original set of statistical projections serves as a measuring stick for a host of interrelated questions:

1. How accurately did the original statistical projections for volume and the assumptions for lamp prices measure up against actual volume and prices?
2. Did the national and industrial assumptions vary significantly from actual economic conditions?
3. Using the original forecast models and the actual values for the independent variables in January and February, would the *ex post* forecasts have differed significantly from the forecaster's initial assessment in column 2 of Table 11-5?
4. In those cases where there was a significant difference between the forecaster's projections and the final budget, what part of the error (final budget less actual sales) was due to the forecaster's error (forecast less actual sales), and what part was due to managerial fiat (final budget less forecast)?
5. What unanticipated internal company-level events occurred? Will they lead to secondary repercussions during the remainder of the year?
6. What level of sales would be needed in each of the remaining months to achieve the final budget? the original forecast?

These and other questions must be answered before the forecaster responds to management's request for an explanation of actual results during January and February. Unless the forecaster saves information such as Table 11-5 for future comparisons, he or she may be falsely labeled the originator of the final budget. It is hard enough to explain one's own errors, but it is folly to assume the responsibility for budgetary adjustments made by others.

Question 4 above can be used to set up a simple error-analysis model:

$$(\text{Final budget} - \text{Actual sales}) = (\text{Forecast} - \text{Actual sales})$$
$$+ (\text{Final budget} - \text{Forecast}) \quad (11\text{-}1)$$

or:

$$\text{Actual error} = \text{Forecast error} + \text{Managerial error} \qquad (11\text{-}2)$$

This error model decomposes the difference between actual and budgeted results into one portion that is the forecaster's direct responsibility and the residual that represents a discretionary adjustment by management. As a starting point, the forecaster may use such an error model to gain some perspective on the primary sources of error.

Questions 2 and 5 above focus on the external and internal framework of assumptions that can be used to highlight both forecast error and managerial error. That is, was the gap between the forecaster's recommended budget and the budget adopted by management due to differences in opinion about the economy and industry, or was it due to differing assessments of internal company programs? For example, at a prior budgetary meeting, management might have disavowed the forecaster's prediction of a severe decline in aggregate economic activity in January and February. Alternatively, management might have been more confident than the forecaster that a new advertising campaign would boost lamp sales and offset cyclical forces. Ideally, both the forecaster and management would have explicitly articulated their assumptions. Realistically, only the forecaster will have listed his or her assumptions explicitly, and the forecaster will have only general impressions of management's assumptions, based on terse comments made at budgetary meetings.

Although the process of assessing management's reasons for altering the budget is highly subjective, feedback to management is necessary if past mistakes are to be avoided in the future. As necessary to the forecaster as the evaluation of errors in managerial judgment related to the budget is the attempt to quantify the impact of the forecaster's own erroneous assumptions. With a statistical forecasting model, it is a simple matter to incorporate actual values of the independent variables during January and February in order to produce an *ex post* forecast of lamp sales for these two months. The difference between the *ex post* forecast and the forecaster's original recommended budget becomes a precise measure of the forecast error arising from incorrect external assumptions about the economy. If the *ex post* forecast still differs significantly from the actual level of lamp sales in January and February, then the problem may lie within the structure of the forecasting model rather than with the assumed values of the independent variables. The analysis of the variance between actual and budgeted sales combines, therefore, traditional statistical error evaluation with a more subjective interpretation of the effect of managerial actions on budgetary levels.

A sample response to management's request for an explanation is given below:

> Lamp sales in both January and February were below budgeted levels, owing to the unexpected severity of the economic downturn in regions 2 and 3, the intense

competition from off-brand lamps in region 1, the minimal success of the new advertising program in region 4, and the generally overoptimistic assessment of our field sales force. Although the forecast department had foreseen a softening in lamp demand in regions 2 and 3 because of a predicted economic slowdown, the decline in regional employment has been unprecedented based on past economic downturns. Two of the major employers in regions 2 and 3, plywood and automobile manufacturers, respectively, are extremely sensitive to interest-rate movements, and the record interest rates recently experienced have devastated plywood and automobile sales. The subsequent decline in employment has undermined lamp sales in regions 2 and 3 by 3,000 units. The bad experience in region 1 can be ascribed to the appearance of off-brand lamps, which have made serious inroads into our market share of low-priced lamps and reduced region 1 lamp sales by 1,500 units. The new advertising campaign in region 4 has not been successful in taking away lamp sales from the established competition in this region. Based on marketing data collected from our retail distributors, the advertising campaign produced new sales of only 1,000 units. Finally, field sales estimates have been overoptimistic for practically all lamp categories in January and February. Although the following are only crude indicators of the relative contribution to budgetary error, it appears that incorrect cyclical assumptions by the forecast department were responsible for 20 percent of the budgetary error, off-brand lamp sales 10 percent, the advertising campaign 20 percent, field sales projections 15 percent, and independent adjustments by management 35 percent. Of these factors, none are viewed as temporary phenomena that will affect sales only in January and February. A revised forecast is attached.

An *ex post* budgetary analysis such as the one summarized above is an attempt to weave statistical and company-level institutional factors into a coherent fabric that is readily understood by decision makers faced with the task of reevaluating the budget. The next step is to move from an evaluation of past results to a reappraisal of the budget during the remaining portion of the budgetary year.

REASSESSING THE BUDGET

The springboard for budgetary changes is the error analysis carried out for lamp sales in January and February. Major changes in the budget are unsettling to all segments of a corporation, since an extensive web of plans has been built around the existing budget. Many of the participants in the budgetary reassessment have a vested interest in keeping the budget at its present size, since a host of maintenance, personnel, and production programs will be curtailed if the budget is significantly reduced. The forecaster is faced with the task of moving from a description of what has happened to cause sales to fall below the budget in January and February to the preparation of a new recommended budget. According to the summary given in the preceding section, roughly 20 percent of the budgetary error in January was due to the forecaster's model, with the remainder largely due to discretionary additions by management.

An attempt to reach the existing budget by offsetting the decline in the first two months with higher sales in the last ten months might be the first method suggested by those unfamiliar with seasonally adjusted annualized rates (SAAR), but this analytical tool can help to cast aside what might otherwise appear to be a reasonable forecast revision. Although budget numbers have traditionally been presented to management on the basis of expected actual monthly magnitudes, it is important for management to be conversant with SAAR presentations, since forecasts are most often prepared on a seasonally adjusted annualized basis and then converted to a monthly rate and deseasonalized. Suppose, for example, that a company had budgeted sales of $200 million for the full year and actual sales of $50 million for the first quarter. It does not necessarily follow that the company is achieving a level of sales consistent with the budget. If the first-quarter seasonal index for sales is 80, then sales are running at an SAAR of $250 million. If, however, the seasonal index for the first quarter is 110, then the SAAR is $181.8 million. In both cases, the results could be consistent with the quarterly budget, but budgetary data need to be annualized and seasonally adjusted before conclusions are reached about the achievability of the budget.

In Table 11-6, the monthly lamp sales figures have been seasonally adjusted and annualized. The actual sales results can be analyzed in several ways. First, as shown in column 3, if full-year sales maintain the SAAR of the first two months, then total lamp sales will be $91.9 million, or $8.1 million less than the original budget in column 1. Since total sales were below the budget by $2.1 million in January and February, this projection of continuity in the SAAR implies an actual worsening in terms of absolute deviation from the budget. Second, the sales data can be analyzed by asking what SAAR for sales would have to be maintained from March through December to hit the targeted budget of $100 million. As shown in column 4, lamp sales must attain a SAAR of $105 million during the last ten months to reach the original budget forecast of $100 million. When compared to the year-to-date's SAAR of $91.9 million, the annualized sales rate would have to increase roughly 14 percent.

At this point, the logical question is whether there is any reason to expect a budgetary turnaround. The analysis in the previous section suggested that much of management's past overoptimism was due to inflated field sales projections, misplaced confidence in the new advertising program, and lack of awareness concerning new regional competitors. The forecaster's original recommended budget in Table 11-5 called for sales of $93.8 million, with the new recommendation slightly lower at $91.0 million. In effect, the forecaster is saying that business conditions will degenerate, since the SAAR during the first two months was $91.9 million. In column 2, the actual sales results in the first two months are substituted for the original budgeted figures. The presentation of seasonally adjusted annualized data can help to move management away from a budget that it might otherwise cling to until too late in the

Table 11-6 Budgetary revenue analysis (Millions of dollars)

Lamp Category	Original Budget[a] (1)	Original Budget Less Year to Date[b] (2)	Year to Date[c] (SAAR) (3)	Needed Budget[d] (SAAR) (4)	Recom- mended Budget (5)
A	$25.0	$24.5	$23.0	$26.0	$22.7
B	29.4	28.9	26.8	30.5	26.6
C	23.8	23.1	21.6	25.1	21.5
D	21.8	21.4	20.5	23.4	20.2
Total	$100.0	$97.9	$91.9	$105.0	$91.0

[a]Column 6 in Table 11-5.
[b]January and February lamp sales were $2.1 million below the budget. These numbers are substituted into the budget, with all other monthly figures kept at their budgeted levels.
[c]Rate for the first two months of the year.
[d]Sales rate needed for the last ten months of the budget in order to achieve original budget target of $100 million.

year. That is, since actual sales were below the budget by $2.1 million in January and February (see column 2), it may not seem too unrealistic to simply add $210,000 to each of the original revenue projections for the remaining ten months and stick with the original budget total of $100 million. When actual sales data are converted to a seasonally adjusted annualized rate (column 3), compared to the SAAR of sales needed to keep the budget, and contrasted with current business conditions, the likelihood of being able to make up for past budgetary shortfalls can be more objectively appraised.

The budget is fixed only insofar as tradition and institutional rigidity keep it so, and the use of analytical tools such as SAAR, contingency forecasts, and subjective probability distributions provide additional information upon which management can base budgetary decisions. The use of seasonally adjusted annualized data in the example above helped to clarify the actual results for lamp sales in January and February and to place the existing budget in sharper contrast. Before an existing budget is abandoned, however, management may request a contingency forecast that gives low, medium, and high sales prospects for lamp sales in the remainder of the year and attaches a subjective probability to each occurrence. Table 11-7 contains such a forecast assessment, and each sales scenario can be compared to the existing budget. Only under the high-growth, or optimistic, scenario does sales revenue reach $100 million, and this outcome is given a subjective probability of only 10 percent. The control, or medium-growth, outlook calls for a 60 percent chance that revenue will reach $91 million, and the low-growth scenario attaches a 30 percent probability that sales will hit $88 million. This set of contingency projections would be accompanied by text material outlining the presumed economic environment and detailing the requisite assumptions. No comparable

Table 11-7 A contingency forecast for lamp sales
(Millions of dollars)

Lamp Category	Original Budget (1)	Pessimistic, or Low, Sales[a] (2)	Control, or Medium, Sales[a] (3)	Optimistic, or High, Sales[a] (4)
A	$25.0	$22.0	$22.7	$25.3
B	29.4	26.1	26.6	30.0
C	23.8	20.8	21.5	23.9
D	21.8	19.1	20.2	21.8
Total	$100.0	$88.0	$91.0	$101.0

[a]Columns 2, 3, and 4 have subjective probabilities of 30, 60, and 10 percent, respectively. The expected sales level is, therefore, $91.1 million.

set of projections is likely to be available from the field sales force, since the rapid turnaround time required for a monthly budgetary review is more amenable to computerized modeling than is the time-consuming process of multiple contacts with the field sales force. Given the analysis of sales in January and February, the SAAR data, and the contingency projections in Table 11-7, management might still elect to stay with the existing budget for another month, but it is unlikely that it would do so without a sense of foreboding. The credibility of the forecaster affects management's willingness to abandon the old budget in favor of a new version that means lower profitability and greater stockholder discontent.

THE POLITICS OF FORECASTING

Diagnosing the needs of forecast users is an important task, but the analyst must never forget that business forecasts are inherently political. Having devoted considerable time and effort to the technical task of preparing a forecast and to the equally arduous job of translating the projections into a report, the business forecaster may make the mistake of naively offering up a forecast and waiting for universal acclaim. Since control of the forecast implies, to a large extent, control over major expenditure and resource allocation decisions within the company, a politically naïve forecaster may become a pawn in a struggle for power within the company. Unfortunately, many forecasters, while superbly trained and skilled in the techniques of statistical model building, are unprepared for the hostile political environment in which they operate. Forecasters, who may have purposely chosen to work in a quantitative area as a way of escaping political in-fighting, suddenly find themselves in the midst of a power struggle among vice-presidents who wish to control the forecast.

Political and human-relations skills are likely to be much more important than technical expertise when it comes to determining the success or failure of a company's forecasting department. In many cases, a forecast is not only perceived as a threat but is in fact a threat to the job security of those individuals whose department is placed in the spotlight by what the forecaster views as an objective projection. A forecast can be a threat regardless of its accuracy; the following case serves to highlight the nature of this conflict.

Several years ago a large and profitable financial consulting company undertook to upgrade its marketing and forecasting functions simultaneously. The marketing organization had been reorganized, and market development managers were made responsible for creating business opportunities within major sectors such as the banking, automotive, lumber, and chemical industries. Since the company was mainly serving the western and midwestern sections of the country, it was the forecaster's responsibility to develop statistical models that would link national activity to these two regions. It immediately became apparent that a market development manager would be able to get more resources if he could demonstrate high profit potential in his industrial sector. For example, the manager of market development for lumber products touted his area, arguing that the pent-up demand for housing and, therefore, lumber products meant increased demand for consulting services. The forecaster, however, correctly projected that the bulk of the increase in lumber activity would be confined to the southeastern and southwestern portions of the country, regions not served by the consulting company. Unfortunately, the forecaster did not anticipate the devastating impact his projection would have on the lumber manager's credibility, and he unveiled his findings after the vice-president of marketing had publicly proclaimed a glowing outlook for consulting services in the lumber industry. Rather than discuss his preliminary findings with the market manager of lumber products and the vice-president of marketing so as to discover in advance any potential areas of controversy, the forecaster inadvertently placed himself in an adversary position and caused a permanent rift between the marketing and forecasting departments.

The inherently political dimension of forecasting can logically be traced to the independent nature of the functional areas which comprise the modern corporation. A seemingly minor forecast change in the company's annual budget can lead to major revisions in production plans, estimated cash-flow patterns, and projected inventory requirements. Thus, in a sense, the powerful political tremors generated by a forecast are merely a reflection of the important role economic forecasts play in the overall planning process of a business. Forecasts are an integral part of the overall information system which continuously feeds new data into the company's strategic planning process. Professor Thomas H. Naylor of Duke University has cogently analyzed the political nature of forecasting and planning in a monograph entitled *The Politics of Corporate Planning and Modeling.*[6] While the threads of his analysis

---

[6]Thomas H. Naylor, ed., *The Politics of Corporate Planning and Modeling* (Oxford, Ohio: Planning Executives Institute, 1978).

are too varied to be briefly summarized, Prof. Naylor attempts to describe the political pitfalls of business strategic planning and outlines methods of circumventing these hazards. Much of his discussion is equally applicable to forecasting and is must reading for analysts just entering the politically charged environment of forecasting.

FORECAST COMMUNICATION:
SUMMARY AND OVERVIEW

The task of conveying economic forecast information to management cannot be separated from the job of analyzing management's forecast needs. It is not the responsibility of management to present the forecaster with a predetermined information format into which the economic projections are merely entered and passed back to management. The quality and quantity of prepared forecast information is not constrained just by the technical skills of the forecaster and the resources at his or her disposal; rather, the ultimate constraints may be found in the ability of management to articulate the general steps followed in making key business decisions. If, in fact, no coherent or logical process is followed in deciding whether to build a new regional plant or expand an existing factory, a forecaster will be hard pressed to provide information that enhances the decision-making process. If, however, an established decision-making framework for capital expenditures is in existence, the forecaster can analyze the needed information flows and determine where forecast information can be best utilized. It could be argued that the forecaster could initiate and design an entire decision-making system in the instance where no logical system exists; however, this is not likely to occur unless the forecaster enjoys a senior management position and, in effect, is both decision maker and forecaster.

Literally all companies have formalized budgeting systems, so it would seem that this would be one activity where the forecaster would always be able to make productive use of his or her skills. Even here, however, the forecaster remains at the mercy of company traditions, as well as the technical and economic literacy possessed by management. If decision makers do not wish to deal with contingency forecasts, subjective probabilities, and seasonally adjusted data, the breadth of the forecaster's potential contribution will be correspondingly reduced.

Even if the forecaster has a clear mandate and a willing executive audience, the ability to communicate effectively with top management may be muted if he or she is misplaced in the organization. Many times the forecaster is the bearer of bad, or at least unpopular, news, and the farther that position is removed from key decision makers by organizational roadblocks, the less likely the forecaster is to be able to present forecast data in the most appropriate format. A manager of forecasting who successively reports to a director, an assistant vice-president, and a vice-president may find that the budgetary report has been reformulated and watered down by the time it reaches the vice-president. In the end, therefore, effective forecasting is as much bound up with institutional considerations as it is with quantitative forecasting techniques.

QUESTIONS FOR DISCUSSION AND ANALYSIS

1. Table 1-1 presents a list of corporate forecast users that is delineated by functional responsibility. One important forecasting dimension that is not explicitly considered is the time horizon of the user. Making use of Table 1-1 and the time frames discussed earlier (immediate, short run, intermediate, and long run), select any two functional areas and discuss how the forecast needs of each department are affected by the time horizon.

2. The last column of Table 1-1 specifies that top management is interested in social trends and new-product technology. Discuss these two concepts in the context of top management's forecast needs in the following settings:
   a. A major New York city bank
   b. A rural bank in Kansas
   c. A California-based manufacturer of transistors
   d. A major railroad in the Southeast
   e. A regional brewery in Colorado
   f. A leading lumber-products company
   g. A small furniture manufacturer in North Carolina
   h. A major producer of baby food
   i. A toy manufacturer

3. Suppose that the model for loan demand in Memphis (Table 6-5) was developed by a major Memphis bank and that the forecast was part of a top-down disaggregation schema. Using the regression system for rail ton-miles in Table 11-2 as a guide, construct an analogous top-down schema for loan demand that could be used by bank management to estimate its monthly need for external funds (either borrowing to meet expected shortages or lending projected surpluses).

4. The five-year manpower forecast in Table 11-1 focused on a financial parameter of particular interest to managers concerned with the growth of labor cost— specifically, secretarial and keypunch staff expense as a percent of total sales revenue. If the time horizon is altered from five years to six months, what might become the major forecast needs in the personnel department of the lamp manufacturer described in Tables 11-3 to 11-7? Put together a replacement for Table 11-1 that is based on personnel's monthly forecast needs.

5. List the sequence of forecast variables that would be needed to provide the top-down projections required for next month's production schedule at an automobile-manufacturing plant in the United States.

6. As explained in the footnote to Table 11-4, the forecaster's budgetary role has been restricted in the present chapter to revenue forecasting. Given the forecaster's knowledge of statistical and time-series techniques, what other entries in Table

11-4 might logically fall within the forecaster's domain. For example, could the forecaster project the cost of sales as well as lamp sales revenue? What information would the forecaster have had in preparing the projections in column 2 of Table 11-4 that would be particularly helpful in projecting the cost of goods sold? What other data would be needed to make a cost projection?

7. The footnote to Table 1-1 states that the law department might be a user of manpower projections if a new pension law was being analyzed. Explain. What particular types of manpower projections would be useful? Are there other categories in Table 1-1 that might also be used by the law department? What about projections of new-product technology?

8. Interview the budget director of a local company, and prepare a two-page paper summarizing the role of the forecaster in the budgeting process and the use of such analytical techniques as contingency forecasts, subjective probability analysis, and seasonalized rates.

9. Select a local government unit and carry out the steps suggested in question 8. In addition, contrast the unique forecast problems of government units.

10. Contact a publicly managed business such as the local utility, obtain historical data on monthly sales volume, and prepare a sales revenue forecast that can be compared to the company's. Analyze the actual year-to-date results and prepare tables similar to 11-6 and 11-7. Does the company (or your own colleagues) agree with your budgetary analysis? Why, or why not? If you are unable to secure current-year budgetary data, use historical data, cut off the last twelve months of data, fit your model, and carry out the project for a historical rather than a current forecast period.

REFERENCES FOR FURTHER STUDY

Armstrong, J. Scott, *Long-Range Forecasting, from Crystal Ball to Computer.* New York: Columbia University Press, 1978.

Ascher, William, *Forecasting: An Appraisal for Policy Makers and Planners.* Baltimore: The Johns Hopkins University Press, 1979.

Bell, Daniel, "Twelve Modes of Prediction," in *Penguin Survey of the Social Sciences,* J. Gould, ed. Baltimore: Penguin Books, 1966.

Lendblom, Charles, "The Science of Muddling Through," *Public Administration Review,* Vol. 19 (Spring 1959), 79–88.

Milne, Thomas E., *Business Forecasting: A Managerial Approach.* New York: Longman Group, 1975.

Naylor, Thomas, *Corporate Planning Models.* Reading, Mass.: Addison-Wesley, 1978.

Naylor, Thomas, and Horst Schouland, "A Survey of Users of Corporate Planning Models," *Management Science,* Vol. 22, No. 9 (May 1976), 927–37.

Strauch, Ralph E., " 'Squishy' Problems and Quantitative Methods," *Policy Sciences,* Vol. 6, No. 2 (June 1975), 175–84.

APPENDICES

APPENDIX A

Census X-11 Seasonal Adjustment Program Applied to Memphis Retail Sales

Beginning with the original series for Quarterly Retail Sales in Memphis, the X-11 program carries out a complete time series analysis by decomposing the sales series into its trend, seasonal, cyclical, and irregular components. For applications, see:

Chapter 4, pp. 109–26
Chapter 7, pp. 233–36
Chapter 8, pp. 276–83, 308–12

Table A-1 Original series, Memphis retail sales (thousands of $)

Year	1st Quarter	2nd Quarter	3rd Quarter	4th Quarter	Total
1965	220,042	257,366	258,083	294,946	1,030,437
1966	247,497	291,641	286,270	323,113	1,148,521
1967	283,961	307,188	318,003	342,979	1,252,131
1968	299,388	351,013	359,353	383,750	1,393,504
1969	341,613	388,040	385,235	413,320	1,528,208
1970	336,631	398,551	412,105	447,740	1,595,027
1971	419,089	471,831	489,506	540,687	1,921,113
1972	484,097	542,971	542,163	594,706	2,163,937
1973	545,714	606,860	615,529	643,119	2,411,222
1974	593,731	666,389	661,525	670,057	2,591,702
1975	606,090	673,974	704,782	749,458	2,734,304
1976	703,142	709,194	728,018	806,882	2,947,236
1977	691,595	796,586	825,619	889,356	3,203,156
1978	757,851	908,940	920,399	991,309	3,578,499
1979	875,830	997,521	—	—	1,873,351
Avg.	—	—	—	—	—
Table total	31,372,320	Mean	540,902	Std. deviation	212,886

Table A-2 Irregular series

Year	1st Quarter	2nd Quarter	3rd Quarter	4th Quarter	S.D.
1965	99.1	100.3	98.7	101.7	1.2
1966	98.5	100.9	98.8	100.2	1.0
1967	101.8	96.8	100.8	99.7	1.9
1968	99.6	100.2	100.8	99.1	.6
1969	100.1	100.3	100.0	102.3	1.2
1970	96.1	100.2	100.3	99.2	2.0
1971	101.3	99.1	99.6	100.8	.9
1972	99.8	100.6	98.9	100.3	.7
1973	100.4	100.0	100.5	98.9	.6
1974	100.3	100.6	100.5	98.6	.8
1975	100.9	99.3	100.5	98.5	1.0
1976	104.8	96.8	99.0	101.7	3.1
1977	99.0	99.8	100.4	100.7	.7
1978	98.2	101.2	100.2	95.3	1.1
1979	100.2	100.0	—	—	.1
S.D.	1.8	1.3	.8	1.2	
Table total	5796.8	Mean	99.9	Std. deviation	1.3

Table A-3 Final weights for irregular series, graduation range from 1.5 to 2.5 sigmas

Year	1st Quarter	2nd Quarter	3rd Quarter	4th Quarter	S.D.
1965	100.0	100.0	100.0	85.5	1.0
1966	100.0	100.0	100.0	100.0	1.0
1967	77.9	.0	100.0	100.0	1.0
1968	100.0	100.0	100.0	100.0	.9
1969	100.0	100.0	100.0	.0	.9
1970	.0	100.0	100.0	100.0	.7
1971	49.7	100.0	100.0	100.0	.7
1972	100.0	100.0	93.5	100.0	.7
1973	100.0	100.0	100.0	100.0	.8
1974	100.0	100.0	100.0	100.0	1.1
1975	100.0	100.0	100.0	100.0	1.1
1976	.0	.0	100.0	100.0	1.2
1977	100.0	100.0	100.0	100.0	1.2
1978	96.9	100.0	100.0	100.0	1.2
1979	100.0	100.0	—	—	1.2

Table A-4 Final unmodified SI ratios

Year	1st Quarter	2nd Quarter	3rd Quarter	4th Quarter	Avg.
1965	89.8	102.6	98.4	109.4	100.1
1966	89.6	103.2	98.6	107.6	99.8
1967	91.9	98.2	100.5	106.6	99.3
1968	90.7	102.2	101.1	105.4	99.8
1969	91.5	102.1	100.8	108.4	100.7
1970	87.9	101.5	101.1	104.9	98.9
1971	93.8	101.0	100.1	106.1	100.2
1972	92.5	102.1	99.5	105.3	99.8
1973	93.3	101.4	101.2	103.8	99.9
1974	93.2	101.8	101.4	103.8	100.1
1975	93.3	100.6	101.5	104.5	99.9
1976	96.7	98.0	99.9	108.0	100.6
1977	90.3	101.2	101.4	107.4	100.1
1978	89.1	102.7	101.1	106.1	99.8
1979	90.7	101.7	—	—	96.2
Avg.	91.6	101.3	100.5	106.2	
Table total	5788.3				

Stable Seasonality Test				
	Sum of Squares	Degrees of Freedom	Mean Square	F
Between quarters	1,626.282	3	542.094	192.808[a]
Residual	151.825	54	2.812	
Total	1,778.107	57		

[a]Stable seasonality present at the 1 percent level

431

Table A-5 Final replacement values for extreme SI ratios

Year	1st Quarter	2nd Quarter	3rd Quarter	4th Quarter	Avg.
1965	—	—	—	109.2	—
1966	—	—	—	—	—
1967	91.5	101.4	—	—	—
1968	—	—	—	—	—
1969	—	—	—	105.9	—
1970	91.5	—	—	—	—
1971	93.1	—	—	—	—
1972	—	—	99.5	—	—
1973	—	—	—	—	—
1974	—	—	—	—	—
1975	—	—	—	105.6	—
1976	92.3	101.2	—	—	—
1977	—	—	—	—	—
1978	89.2	—	—	—	—
1979	—	—	—	—	—

Table A-6a Final seasonal factors, 3 × 5 moving average

Year	1st Quarter	2nd Quarter	3rd Quarter	4th Quarter	Avg.
1965	90.4	102.4	99.6	107.5	100.0
1966	90.5	102.4	99.7	107.3	100.0
1967	90.7	102.3	100.0	106.7	99.9
1968	91.1	102.0	100.4	106.3	99.9
1969	91.5	101.8	100.6	105.8	99.9
1970	92.0	101.7	100.6	105.5	99.9
1971	92.3	101.7	100.6	105.2	99.9
1972	92.7	101.5	100.7	105.0	100.0
1973	92.9	101.4	100.7	105.0	100.0
1974	92.8	101.3	100.8	105.4	100.1
1975	92.4	101.3	100.9	105.8	100.1
1976	91.8	101.4	101.0	106.3	100.1
1977	91.2	101.5	100.5	106.7	100.1
1978	90.7	101.7	100.9	106.9	100.0
1979	90.4	101.8	—	—	96.1
Table total	5792.2				

Table A-6b Seasonal factors one year ahead

Year	1st Quarter	2nd Quarter	3rd Quarter	4th Quarter	Avg.
1979	—	—	100.9	107.1	104.0
1980	90.3	101.5	—	—	96.1

Table A-7   Final seasonally adjusted series, Memphis retail sales

Year	1st Quarter	2nd Quarter	3rd Quarter	4th Quarter	Total
1965	243,282	251,224	259,246	274,366	1,028,118
1966	273,426	284,827	287,120	301,225	1,146,597
1967	313,127	300,387	317,887	321,300	1,252,701
1968	328,658	344,087	358,012	361,160	1,391,916
1969	373,390	380,994	382,999	390,749	1,528,161
1970	366,027	391,883	409,550	424,508	1,591,967
1971	454,014	464,023	486,590	514,205	1,918,830
1972	522,102	534,795	538,601	566,557	2,162,052
1973	587,420	598,223	611,277	612,355	2,409,273
1974	639,561	657,815	656,154	636,026	2,589,554
1975	656,249	665,060	698,414	708,519	2,728,239
1976	766,097	699,633	720,784	759,397	2,945,909
1977	758,719	784,467	817,929	833,750	3,194,864
1978	835,575	894,076	912,265	927,008	3,568,924
1979	968,752	979,915	—	—	1,948,666
Avg.	—	—	—	—	—
Table total	31,405,728	Mean	541,478	Std. deviation	211,088

Table A-8   Final trend-cycle, 5-term Henderson curve, Memphis retail sales

Year	1st Quarter	2nd Quarter	3rd Quarter	4th Quarter	Total
1965	245,317	249,900	261,267	270,199	1,206,683
1966	276,894	281,764	289,782	300,762	1,149,201
1967	309,652	312,825	316,288	321,605	1,260,369
1968	329,674	344,062	355,863	363,628	1,393,227
1969	372,451	380,734	382,918	381,238	1,517,341
1970	382,177	392,210	407,812	427,414	1,609,613
1971	447,502	466,068	488,075	510,568	1,912,212
1972	524,871	531,480	543,558	564,593	2,164,500
1973	586,256	600,165	607,433	617,749	2,411,602
1974	637,782	656,869	651,929	644,179	2,590,757
1975	649,822	670,698	694,412	718,201	2,733,132
1976	727,027	722,353	729,228	748,689	2,927,295
1977	764,935	784,967	815,740	828,974	3,194,616
1978	848,203	884,369	912,691	933,488	3,578,749
1979	963,471	979,278	—	—	1,942,749
Avg.	—	—	—	—	—
Table total	31,411,984	Mean	541,586	Std. deviation	210,536

Table A-9 Final irregular series

Year	1st Quarter	2nd Quarter	3rd Quarter	4th Quarter	S.D.
1965	99.2	100.5	99.2	101.5	1.0
1966	98.7	101.1	99.1	100.2	1.0
1967	101.1	96.0	100.5	99.9	2.1
1968	99.7	100.0	100.6	99.3	.5
1969	100.3	100.1	100.0	102.5	1.3
1970	95.8	99.9	100.4	99.3	2.2
1971	101.5	99.6	99.7	100.7	.9
1972	99.5	100.6	99.1	100.3	.6
1973	100.2	99.7	100.6	99.1	.6
1974	100.3	100.1	100.6	98.7	.7
1975	101.0	99.2	100.6	98.7	1.0
1976	105.4	96.9	98.8	101.4	3.2
1977	99.2	99.9	100.3	100.6	.5
1978	98.5	101.1	100.0	99.3	1.0
1979	100.5	100.1	—	—	.4
S.D.	2.0	1.4	.6	1.1	
Table total	5,796.7	Mean	99.5	Std. deviation	1.4

Table A-10 Original series modified for extremes

Year	1st Quarter	2nd Quarter	3rd Quarter	4th Quarter	Total
1965	220,042	257,366	258,083	294,946	1,030,437
1966	247,497	291,641	286,270	323,113	1,148,521
1967	283,961	319,908	318,003	342,959	1,264,850
1968	299,388	351,013	359,353	383,750	1,393,504
1969	341,613	388,040	385,235	403,229	1,518,116
1970	351,484	398,551	412,105	447,740	1,603,880
1971	419,089	471,831	489,506	540,687	1,921,113
1972	484,097	542,971	542,163	594,706	2,163,937
1973	545,714	606,860	615,529	643,119	2,411,222
1974	593,731	666,389	661,525	670,057	2,591,702
1975	606,090	673,974	704,782	749,458	2,734,304
1976	667,283	732,225	728,018	806,882	2,934,407
1977	691,595	796,586	825,619	889,356	3,203,156
1978	757,851	908,940	920,399	991,309	3,578,499
1979	875,830	997,521	—	—	1,873,351
Avg.	—	—	—	—	—
Table total	31,376,976	Mean	540,982	Std. deviation	212,439

Table A-11 Modified seasonally adjusted series, Memphis retail sales

Year	1st Quarter	2nd Quarter	3rd Quarter	4th Quarter	Total
1965	243,283	251,224	259,246	274,366	1 028,118
1966	273,426	284,827	287,120	301,225	1,146,597
1967	313,127	312,825	317,887	321,300	1,265,140
1968	328,658	344,087	358,012	361,160	1,391,916
1969	373,390	380,994	382,999	381,238	1,518,620
1970	382,177	391,883	409,550	424,508	1,608,118
1971	454,014	464,023	486,590	514,205	1,918,830
1972	522,102	534,795	538,601	566,557	2,162,052
1973	587,420	598,223	611,277	612,355	2,409,273
1974	639,561	657,815	656,154	636,026	2,589,554
1975	656,249	665,060	698,414	708,519	2,728,239
1976	727,027	722,353	720,784	759,397	2,929,559
1977	758,719	784,467	817,929	833,750	3,194,864
1978	835,575	894,076	912,265	927,008	3,568,924
1979	968,752	979,915	—	—	1,948,666
Avg.	—	—	—	—	—
Table total	31,408,416	Mean	541,524	Std. deviation	210,409

Table A-12 Modified irregular series

Year	1st Quarter	2nd Quarter	3rd Quarter	4th Quarter	S.D.
1965	99.2	100.5	99.2	101.5	1.0
1966	98.7	101.1	99.1	100.2	1.0
1967	101.1	100.0	100.5	99.9	.6
1968	99.7	100.0	100.6	99.3	.5
1969	100.3	100.1	100.0	100.0	.1
1970	100.0	99.9	100.4	99.3	.4
1971	101.5	99.6	99.7	100.7	.9
1972	99.5	100.6	99.1	100.3	.6
1973	100.2	99.7	100.6	99.1	.6
1974	100.3	100.1	100.6	98.7	.7
1975	101.0	99.2	100.6	98.7	1.0
1976	100.0	100.0	98.8	101.4	.9
1977	99.2	99.9	100.3	100.6	.5
1978	98.5	101.1	100.0	99.3	1.0
1979	100.5	100.1	—	—	.4
S.D.	.8	.5	.6	.9	
Table total 5,800.2	Mean	100.0	Std. deviation	.7	

Table A-13 Quarter-to-quarter changes in original series

Year	1st Quarter	2nd Quarter	3rd Quarter	4th Quarter	Avg.
1965	—	17.0	.3	14.3	10.5
1966	−16.1	17.8	−1.8	12.9	3.2
1967	−12.1	8.2	3.5	7.9	1.9
1968	−12.7	17.2	2.4	6.8	3.4
1969	−11.0	13.6	−.7	7.3	2.3
1970	−18.6	18.4	3.4	8.6	3.0
1971	−6.4	12.6	3.7	10.5	5.1
1972	−10.5	12.2	−.1	9.7	2.8
1973	−8.2	11.2	1.4	4.5	2.2
1974	−7.7	12.2	−.7	1.3	1.3
1975	−9.5	11.2	4.6	6.3	3.1
1976	−6.2	.9	2.7	10.8	2.0
1977	−14.3	15.2	3.6	7.7	3.1
1978	−14.8	19.9	1.3	7.7	3.5
1979	−11.6	13.9	—	—	1.1
Avg.	−11.4	13.4	1.7	8.3	
Table total	181.5				

Table A-14 Quarter-to-quarter changes in final seasonally adjusted series

Year	1st Quarter	2nd Quarter	3rd Quarter	4th Quarter	Avg.
1965	—	3.3	3.2	5.8	4.1
1966	−.3	4.2	.8	4.9	2.4
1967	4.0	−4.1	5.8	1.1	1.7
1968	2.3	4.7	4.0	.9	3.0
1969	3.4	2.0	.5	2.0	2.0
1970	−6.3	7.1	4.5	3.7	2.2
1971	7.0	2.2	4.9	5.7	4.9
1972	1.5	2.4	.7	5.2	2.5
1973	3.7	1.8	2.2	.2	2.0
1974	4.4	2.9	−.3	−3.1	1.0
1975	3.2	1.3	5.0	1.4	2.7
1976	8.1	−8.7	3.0	5.4	2.0
1977	−.1	3.4	4.3	1.9	2.4
1978	.2	7.0	2.0	1.6	2.7
1979	4.5	1.2	—	—	2.8
Avg.	2.5	2.0	2.9	2.6	
Table total	143.7				

APPENDIX B

Student *t* Distribution

For applications, see:

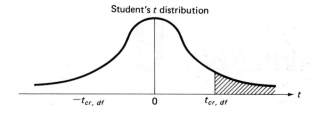

Student's t distribution

$-t_{cr, \, df}$ 　 0 　 $t_{cr, \, df}$ 　 t

Degrees of Freedom	Probability of a Value Greater in Value than the Table Entry					
	0.005	0.01	0.025	0.05	0.1	0.15
1	63.657	31.821	12.706	6.314	3.078	1.963
2	9.925	6.965	4.303	2.920	1.886	1.386
3	5.841	4.541	3.182	2.353	1.638	1.250
4	4.604	3.747	2.776	2.132	1.533	1.190
5	4.032	3.365	2.571	2.015	1.476	1.156
6	3.707	3.143	2.447	1.943	1.440	1.134
7	3.499	2.998	2.365	1.895	1.415	1.119
8	3.355	2.896	2.306	1.860	1.397	1.108
9	3.250	2.821	2.262	1.833	1.383	1.100
10	3.169	2.764	2.228	1.812	1.372	1.093
11	3.106	2.718	2.201	1.796	1.363	1.088
12	3.055	2.681	2.179	1.782	1.356	1.083
13	3.012	2.650	2.160	1.771	1.350	1.079
14	2.977	2.624	2.145	1.761	1.345	1.076
15	2.947	2.602	2.131	1.753	1.341	1.074
16	2.921	2.583	2.120	1.746	1.337	1.071
17	2.898	2.567	2.110	1.740	1.333	1.069
18	2.878	2.552	2.101	1.734	1.330	1.067
19	2.861	2.539	2.093	1.729	1.328	1.066
20	2.845	2.528	2.086	1.725	1.325	1.064
21	2.831	2.518	2.080	1.721	1.323	1.063
22	2.819	2.508	2.074	1.717	1.321	1.061
23	2.807	2.500	2.069	1.714	1.319	1.060
24	2.797	2.492	2.064	1.711	1.318	1.059
25	2.787	2.485	2.060	1.708	1.316	1.058
26	2.779	2.479	2.056	1.706	1.315	1.058
27	2.771	2.473	2.052	1.703	1.314	1.057
28	2.763	2.467	2.048	1.701	1.313	1.056
29	2.756	2.462	2.045	1.699	1.311	1.055
30	2.750	2.457	2.042	1.697	1.310	1.055
∞	2.576	2.326	1.960	1.645	1.282	1.036

Source: Reprinted from Table IV in Sir Ronald A. Fisher, *Statistical Methods for Research Workers*, 13th ed. (Edinburgh: Oliver & Boyd Ltd. 1963), with the permission of the publisher and the late Sir Ronald Fisher's literary executor.

APPENDIX C

Critical Values for the *F* Distribution

For applications, see:

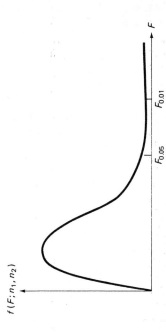

$f(F; n_1, n_2)$

$F_{0.05}$ $F_{0.01}$ F

Table C-1 5% (Roman type) and 1% (boldface type) points for the distribution of F

n_1 Degrees of Freedom in the Numerator

n_2	1	2	3	4	5	6	7	8	9	10	11	12	14	16	20	24	30	40	50	75	100	200	500	∞	n_2
1	161	200	216	225	230	234	237	239	241	242	243	244	245	246	248	249	250	251	252	253	253	254	254	254	1
	4,052	**4,999**	**5,403**	**5,625**	**5,764**	**5,859**	**5,928**	**5,981**	**6,022**	**6,056**	**6,082**	**6,106**	**6,142**	**6,169**	**6,208**	**6,234**	**6,258**	**6,286**	**6,302**	**6,323**	**6,334**	**6,352**	**6,361**	**6,366**	
2	18.51	19.00	19.16	19.25	19.30	19.33	19.36	19.37	19.38	19.39	19.40	19.41	19.42	19.43	19.44	19.45	19.46	19.47	19.47	19.48	19.49	19.49	19.50	19.50	2
	98.49	**99.00**	**99.17**	**99.25**	**99.30**	**99.33**	**99.34**	**99.36**	**99.38**	**99.40**	**99.41**	**99.42**	**99.43**	**99.44**	**99.45**	**99.46**	**99.47**	**99.48**	**99.48**	**99.49**	**99.49**	**99.49**	**99.50**	**99.50**	
3	10.13	9.55	9.28	9.12	9.01	8.94	8.88	8.84	8.81	8.78	8.76	8.74	8.71	8.69	8.66	8.64	8.62	8.60	8.58	8.57	8.56	8.54	8.54	8.53	3
	34.12	**30.82**	**29.46**	**28.71**	**28.24**	**27.91**	**27.67**	**27.49**	**27.34**	**27.23**	**27.13**	**27.05**	**26.92**	**26.83**	**26.69**	**26.60**	**26.50**	**26.41**	**26.35**	**26.27**	**26.23**	**26.18**	**26.14**	**26.12**	
4	7.71	6.94	6.59	6.39	6.26	6.16	6.09	6.04	6.00	5.96	5.93	5.91	5.87	5.84	5.80	5.77	5.74	5.71	5.70	5.68	5.66	5.65	5.64	5.63	4
	21.20	**18.00**	**16.69**	**15.98**	**15.52**	**15.21**	**14.98**	**14.80**	**14.66**	**14.54**	**14.45**	**14.37**	**14.24**	**14.15**	**14.02**	**13.93**	**13.83**	**13.74**	**13.69**	**13.61**	**13.57**	**13.52**	**13.48**	**13.46**	
5	6.61	5.79	5.41	5.19	5.05	4.95	4.88	4.82	4.78	4.74	4.70	4.68	4.64	4.60	4.56	4.53	4.50	4.46	4.44	4.42	4.40	4.38	4.37	4.36	5
	16.26	**13.27**	**12.06**	**11.39**	**10.97**	**10.67**	**10.45**	**10.27**	**10.15**	**10.05**	**9.96**	**9.89**	**9.77**	**9.68**	**9.55**	**9.47**	**9.38**	**9.29**	**9.24**	**9.17**	**9.13**	**9.07**	**9.04**	**9.02**	
6	5.99	5.14	4.76	4.53	4.39	4.28	4.21	4.15	4.10	4.06	4.03	4.00	3.96	3.92	3.87	3.84	3.81	3.77	3.75	3.72	3.71	3.69	3.68	3.67	6
	13.74	**10.92**	**9.78**	**9.15**	**8.75**	**8.47**	**8.26**	**8.10**	**7.98**	**7.87**	**7.79**	**7.72**	**7.60**	**7.52**	**7.39**	**7.31**	**7.23**	**7.14**	**7.09**	**7.02**	**6.99**	**6.94**	**6.90**	**6.88**	
7	5.59	4.74	4.35	4.12	3.97	3.87	3.79	3.73	3.68	3.63	3.60	3.57	3.52	3.49	3.44	3.41	3.38	3.34	3.32	3.29	3.28	3.25	3.24	3.23	7
	12.25	**9.55**	**8.45**	**7.85**	**7.46**	**7.19**	**7.00**	**6.84**	**6.71**	**6.62**	**6.54**	**6.47**	**6.35**	**6.27**	**6.15**	**6.07**	**5.98**	**5.90**	**5.85**	**5.78**	**5.75**	**5.70**	**5.67**	**5.65**	
8	5.32	4.46	4.07	3.84	3.69	3.58	3.50	3.44	3.39	3.34	3.31	3.28	3.23	3.20	3.15	3.12	3.08	3.05	3.03	3.00	2.98	2.96	2.94	2.93	8
	11.26	**8.65**	**7.59**	**7.01**	**6.63**	**6.37**	**6.19**	**6.03**	**5.91**	**5.82**	**5.74**	**5.67**	**5.56**	**5.48**	**5.36**	**5.28**	**5.20**	**5.11**	**5.06**	**5.00**	**4.96**	**4.91**	**4.88**	**4.86**	

n_2 Degrees of Freedom in the Denominator.

Table C-1 (Continued)

n_1 Degrees of Freedom in the Numerator

n_2	1	2	3	4	5	6	7	8	9	10	11	12	14	16	20	24	30	40	50	75	100	200	500	∞	n_2
9	5.12	4.26	3.86	3.63	3.48	3.37	3.29	3.23	3.18	3.13	3.10	3.07	3.02	2.98	2.93	2.90	2.86	2.82	2.80	2.77	2.76	2.73	2.72	2.71	9
	10.56	**8.02**	**6.99**	**6.42**	**6.06**	**5.80**	**5.62**	**5.47**	**5.35**	**5.26**	**5.18**	**5.11**	**5.00**	**4.92**	**4.80**	**4.73**	**4.64**	**4.56**	**4.51**	**4.45**	**4.41**	**4.36**	**4.33**	**4.31**	
10	4.96	4.10	3.71	3.48	3.33	3.22	3.14	3.07	3.02	2.97	2.94	2.91	2.86	2.82	2.77	2.74	2.70	2.67	2.64	2.61	2.59	2.56	2.55	2.54	10
	10.04	**7.56**	**6.55**	**5.99**	**5.64**	**5.39**	**5.21**	**5.06**	**4.95**	**4.85**	**4.78**	**4.71**	**4.60**	**4.52**	**4.41**	**4.33**	**4.25**	**4.17**	**4.12**	**4.05**	**4.01**	**3.96**	**3.93**	**3.91**	
11	4.84	3.98	3.59	3.36	3.20	3.09	3.01	2.95	2.90	2.86	2.82	2.79	2.74	2.70	2.65	2.61	2.57	2.53	2.50	2.47	2.45	2.42	2.41	2.40	11
	9.65	**7.20**	**6.22**	**5.67**	**5.32**	**5.07**	**4.88**	**4.74**	**4.63**	**4.54**	**4.46**	**4.40**	**4.29**	**4.21**	**4.10**	**4.02**	**3.94**	**3.86**	**3.80**	**3.74**	**3.70**	**3.66**	**3.62**	**3.60**	
12	4.75	3.88	3.49	3.26	3.11	3.00	2.92	2.85	2.80	2.76	2.72	2.69	2.64	2.60	2.54	2.50	2.46	2.42	2.40	2.36	2.35	2.32	2.31	2.30	12
	9.33	**6.93**	**5.95**	**5.41**	**5.06**	**4.82**	**4.65**	**4.50**	**4.39**	**4.30**	**4.22**	**4.16**	**4.05**	**3.98**	**3.86**	**3.78**	**3.70**	**3.61**	**3.56**	**3.49**	**3.46**	**3.41**	**3.38**	**3.36**	
13	4.67	3.80	3.41	3.18	3.02	2.92	2.84	2.77	2.72	2.67	2.63	2.60	2.55	2.51	2.46	2.42	2.38	2.34	2.32	2.28	2.26	2.24	2.22	2.21	13
	9.07	**6.70**	**5.74**	**5.20**	**4.86**	**4.62**	**4.44**	**4.30**	**4.19**	**4.10**	**4.02**	**3.96**	**3.85**	**3.78**	**3.67**	**3.59**	**3.51**	**3.42**	**3.37**	**3.30**	**3.27**	**3.21**	**3.18**	**3.16**	
14	4.60	3.74	3.34	3.11	2.96	2.85	2.77	2.70	2.65	2.60	2.56	2.53	2.48	2.44	2.39	2.35	2.31	2.27	2.24	2.21	2.19	2.16	2.14	2.13	14
	8.86	**6.51**	**5.56**	**5.03**	**4.69**	**4.46**	**4.28**	**4.14**	**4.03**	**3.94**	**3.86**	**3.80**	**3.70**	**3.62**	**3.51**	**3.43**	**3.34**	**3.26**	**3.21**	**3.14**	**3.11**	**3.06**	**3.02**	**3.00**	
15	4.54	3.68	3.29	3.06	2.90	2.79	2.70	2.64	2.59	2.55	2.51	2.48	2.43	2.39	2.33	2.29	2.25	2.21	2.18	2.15	2.12	2.10	2.08	2.07	15
	8.68	**6.36**	**5.42**	**4.89**	**4.56**	**4.32**	**4.14**	**4.00**	**3.89**	**3.80**	**3.73**	**3.67**	**3.56**	**3.48**	**3.36**	**3.29**	**3.20**	**3.12**	**3.07**	**3.00**	**2.97**	**2.92**	**2.89**	**2.87**	
16	4.49	3.63	3.24	3.01	2.85	2.74	2.66	2.59	2.54	2.49	2.45	2.42	2.37	2.33	2.28	2.24	2.20	2.16	2.13	2.09	2.07	2.04	2.02	2.01	16
	8.53	**6.23**	**5.29**	**4.77**	**4.44**	**4.20**	**4.03**	**3.89**	**3.78**	**3.69**	**3.61**	**3.55**	**3.45**	**3.37**	**3.25**	**3.18**	**3.10**	**3.01**	**2.96**	**2.89**	**2.86**	**2.80**	**2.77**	**2.75**	
17	4.45	3.59	3.20	2.96	2.81	2.70	2.62	2.55	2.50	2.45	2.41	2.38	2.33	2.29	2.23	2.19	2.15	2.11	2.08	2.04	2.02	1.99	1.97	1.96	17
	8.40	**6.11**	**5.18**	**4.67**	**4.34**	**4.10**	**3.93**	**3.79**	**3.68**	**3.59**	**3.52**	**3.45**	**3.35**	**3.27**	**3.16**	**3.08**	**3.00**	**2.92**	**2.86**	**2.79**	**2.76**	**2.70**	**2.67**	**2.65**	
18	4.41	3.55	3.16	2.93	2.77	2.66	2.58	2.51	2.46	2.41	2.37	2.34	2.29	2.25	2.19	2.15	2.11	2.07	2.04	2.00	1.98	1.95	1.93	1.92	18
	8.28	**6.01**	**5.09**	**4.58**	**4.25**	**4.01**	**3.85**	**3.71**	**3.60**	**3.51**	**3.44**	**3.37**	**3.27**	**3.19**	**3.07**	**3.00**	**2.91**	**2.83**	**2.78**	**2.71**	**2.68**	**2.62**	**2.59**	**2.57**	
19	4.38	3.52	3.13	2.90	2.74	2.63	2.55	2.48	2.43	2.38	2.34	2.31	2.26	2.21	2.15	2.11	2.07	2.02	2.00	1.96	1.94	1.91	1.90	1.88	19
	8.18	**5.93**	**5.01**	**4.50**	**4.17**	**3.94**	**3.77**	**3.63**	**3.52**	**3.43**	**3.36**	**3.30**	**3.19**	**3.12**	**3.00**	**2.92**	**2.84**	**2.76**	**2.70**	**2.63**	**2.60**	**2.54**	**2.51**	**2.49**	
20	4.35	3.49	3.10	2.87	2.71	2.60	2.52	2.45	2.40	2.35	2.31	2.28	2.23	2.18	2.12	2.08	2.04	1.99	1.96	1.92	1.90	1.87	1.85	1.84	20
	8.10	**5.85**	**4.94**	**4.43**	**4.10**	**3.87**	**3.71**	**3.56**	**3.45**	**3.37**	**3.30**	**3.23**	**3.13**	**3.05**	**2.94**	**2.86**	**2.77**	**2.69**	**2.63**	**2.56**	**2.53**	**2.47**	**2.44**	**2.42**	
21	4.32	3.47	3.07	2.84	2.68	2.57	2.49	2.42	2.37	2.32	2.28	2.25	2.20	2.15	2.09	2.05	2.00	1.96	1.93	1.89	1.87	1.84	1.82	1.81	21
	8.02	**5.78**	**4.87**	**4.37**	**4.04**	**3.81**	**3.65**	**3.51**	**3.40**	**3.31**	**3.24**	**3.17**	**3.07**	**2.99**	**2.88**	**2.80**	**2.72**	**2.63**	**2.58**	**2.51**	**2.47**	**2.42**	**2.38**	**2.36**	
22	4.30	3.44	3.05	2.82	2.66	2.55	2.47	2.40	2.35	2.30	2.26	2.23	2.18	2.13	2.07	2.03	1.98	1.93	1.91	1.87	1.84	1.81	1.80	1.78	22
	7.94	**5.72**	**4.82**	**4.31**	**3.99**	**3.76**	**3.59**	**3.45**	**3.35**	**3.26**	**3.18**	**3.12**	**3.02**	**2.94**	**2.83**	**2.75**	**2.67**	**2.58**	**2.53**	**2.46**	**2.42**	**2.37**	**2.33**	**2.31**	
23	4.28	3.42	3.03	2.80	2.64	2.53	2.45	2.38	2.32	2.28	2.24	2.20	2.14	2.10	2.04	2.00	1.96	1.91	1.88	1.84	1.82	1.79	1.77	1.76	23
	7.88	**5.66**	**4.76**	**4.26**	**3.94**	**3.71**	**3.54**	**3.41**	**3.30**	**3.21**	**3.14**	**3.07**	**2.97**	**2.89**	**2.78**	**2.70**	**2.62**	**2.53**	**2.48**	**2.41**	**2.37**	**2.32**	**2.28**	**2.26**	

n_2 Degrees of Freedom in the Denominator.

Table C-1 (Continued)

n_1 Degrees of Freedom in the Numerator

n_2	1	2	3	4	5	6	7	8	9	10	11	12	14	16	20	24	30	40	50	75	100	200	500	∞	n_2
24	4.26	3.40	3.01	2.78	2.62	2.51	2.43	2.36	2.30	2.26	2.22	2.18	2.13	2.09	2.02	1.98	1.94	1.89	1.86	1.82	1.80	1.76	1.74	1.73	24
	7.82	**5.61**	**4.72**	**4.22**	**3.90**	**3.67**	**3.50**	**3.36**	**3.25**	**3.17**	**3.09**	**3.03**	**2.93**	**2.85**	**2.74**	**2.66**	**2.58**	**2.49**	**2.44**	**2.36**	**2.33**	**2.27**	**2.23**	**2.21**	
25	4.24	3.38	2.99	2.76	2.60	2.49	2.41	2.34	2.28	2.24	2.20	2.16	2.11	2.06	2.00	1.96	1.92	1.87	1.84	1.80	1.77	1.74	1.72	1.71	25
	7.77	**5.57**	**4.68**	**4.18**	**3.86**	**3.63**	**3.46**	**3.32**	**3.21**	**3.13**	**3.05**	**2.99**	**2.89**	**2.81**	**2.70**	**2.62**	**2.54**	**2.45**	**2.40**	**2.32**	**2.29**	**2.23**	**2.19**	**2.17**	
26	4.22	3.37	2.98	2.74	2.59	2.47	2.39	2.32	2.27	2.22	2.18	2.15	2.10	2.05	1.99	1.95	1.90	1.85	1.82	1.78	1.76	1.72	1.70	1.69	26
	7.72	**5.53**	**4.64**	**4.14**	**3.82**	**3.59**	**3.42**	**3.29**	**3.17**	**3.09**	**3.02**	**2.96**	**2.86**	**2.77**	**2.66**	**2.58**	**2.50**	**2.41**	**2.36**	**2.28**	**2.25**	**2.19**	**2.15**	**2.13**	
27	4.21	3.35	2.96	2.73	2.57	2.46	2.37	2.30	2.25	2.20	2.16	2.13	2.08	2.03	1.97	1.93	1.88	1.84	1.80	1.76	1.74	1.71	1.68	1.67	27
	7.68	**5.49**	**4.60**	**4.11**	**3.79**	**3.56**	**3.39**	**3.26**	**3.14**	**3.06**	**2.98**	**2.93**	**2.83**	**2.74**	**2.63**	**2.55**	**2.47**	**2.38**	**2.33**	**2.25**	**2.21**	**2.16**	**2.12**	**2.10**	
28	4.20	3.34	2.95	2.71	2.56	2.44	2.36	2.29	2.24	2.19	2.15	2.12	2.06	2.02	1.96	1.91	1.87	1.81	1.78	1.75	1.72	1.69	1.67	1.65	28
	7.64	**5.45**	**4.57**	**4.07**	**3.76**	**3.53**	**3.36**	**3.23**	**3.11**	**3.03**	**2.95**	**2.90**	**2.80**	**2.71**	**2.60**	**2.52**	**2.44**	**2.35**	**2.30**	**2.22**	**2.18**	**2.13**	**2.09**	**2.06**	
29	4.18	3.33	2.93	2.70	2.54	2.43	2.35	2.28	2.22	2.18	2.14	2.10	2.05	2.00	1.94	1.90	1.85	1.80	1.77	1.73	1.71	1.68	1.65	1.64	29
	7.60	**5.42**	**4.54**	**4.04**	**3.73**	**3.50**	**3.33**	**3.20**	**3.08**	**3.00**	**2.92**	**2.87**	**2.77**	**2.68**	**2.57**	**2.49**	**2.41**	**2.32**	**2.27**	**2.19**	**2.15**	**2.10**	**2.06**	**2.03**	
30	4.17	3.32	2.92	2.69	2.53	2.42	2.34	2.27	2.21	2.16	2.12	2.09	2.04	1.99	1.93	1.89	1.84	1.79	1.76	1.72	1.69	1.66	1.64	1.62	30
	7.56	**5.39**	**4.51**	**4.02**	**3.70**	**3.47**	**3.30**	**3.17**	**3.06**	**2.98**	**2.90**	**2.84**	**2.74**	**2.66**	**2.55**	**2.47**	**2.38**	**2.29**	**2.24**	**2.16**	**2.13**	**2.07**	**2.03**	**2.01**	
32	4.15	3.30	2.90	2.67	2.51	2.40	2.32	2.25	2.19	2.14	2.10	2.07	2.02	1.97	1.91	1.86	1.82	1.76	1.74	1.69	1.67	1.64	1.61	1.59	32
	7.50	**5.34**	**4.46**	**3.97**	**3.66**	**3.42**	**3.25**	**3.12**	**3.01**	**2.94**	**2.86**	**2.80**	**2.70**	**2.62**	**2.51**	**2.42**	**2.34**	**2.25**	**2.20**	**2.12**	**2.08**	**2.02**	**1.98**	**1.96**	
34	4.13	3.28	2.88	2.65	2.49	2.38	2.30	2.23	2.17	2.12	2.08	2.05	2.00	1.95	1.89	1.84	1.80	1.74	1.71	1.67	1.64	1.61	1.59	1.57	34
	7.44	**5.29**	**4.42**	**3.93**	**3.61**	**3.38**	**3.21**	**3.03**	**2.97**	**2.89**	**2.82**	**2.76**	**2.66**	**2.58**	**2.47**	**2.38**	**2.30**	**2.21**	**2.15**	**2.08**	**2.04**	**1.98**	**1.94**	**1.91**	
36	4.11	3.26	2.86	2.63	2.48	2.36	2.28	2.21	2.15	2.10	2.06	2.03	1.98	1.93	1.87	1.82	1.78	1.72	1.69	1.65	1.62	1.59	1.56	1.55	36
	7.39	**5.25**	**4.38**	**3.89**	**3.58**	**3.35**	**3.18**	**3.04**	**2.94**	**2.86**	**2.78**	**2.72**	**2.62**	**2.54**	**2.43**	**2.35**	**2.26**	**2.17**	**2.12**	**2.04**	**2.00**	**1.94**	**1.90**	**1.87**	
38	4.10	3.25	2.85	2.62	2.46	2.35	2.26	2.19	2.14	2.09	2.05	2.02	1.96	1.92	1.85	1.80	1.76	1.71	1.67	1.63	1.60	1.57	1.54	1.53	38
	7.35	**5.21**	**4.34**	**3.86**	**3.54**	**3.32**	**3.15**	**3.02**	**2.91**	**2.82**	**2.75**	**2.69**	**2.59**	**2.51**	**2.40**	**2.32**	**2.22**	**2.14**	**2.08**	**2.00**	**1.97**	**1.90**	**1.86**	**1.84**	
40	4.08	3.23	2.84	2.61	2.45	2.34	2.25	2.18	2.12	2.07	2.04	2.00	1.95	1.90	1.84	1.79	1.74	1.69	1.66	1.61	1.59	1.55	1.53	1.51	40
	7.31	**5.18**	**4.31**	**3.83**	**3.51**	**3.29**	**3.12**	**2.99**	**2.88**	**2.80**	**2.73**	**2.66**	**2.56**	**2.49**	**2.37**	**2.29**	**2.20**	**2.11**	**2.05**	**1.97**	**1.94**	**1.88**	**1.84**	**1.81**	
42	4.07	3.22	2.83	2.59	2.44	2.32	2.24	2.17	2.11	2.06	2.02	1.99	1.94	1.89	1.82	1.78	1.73	1.68	1.64	1.60	1.57	1.54	1.51	1.49	42
	7.27	**5.15**	**4.29**	**3.80**	**3.49**	**3.26**	**3.10**	**2.96**	**2.86**	**2.77**	**2.70**	**2.64**	**2.54**	**2.46**	**2.35**	**2.26**	**2.17**	**2.08**	**2.02**	**1.94**	**1.91**	**1.85**	**1.80**	**1.78**	
44	4.06	3.21	2.82	2.58	2.43	2.31	2.23	2.16	2.10	2.05	2.01	1.98	1.92	1.88	1.81	1.76	1.72	1.66	1.63	1.58	1.56	1.52	1.50	1.48	44
	7.24	**5.12**	**4.26**	**3.78**	**3.46**	**3.24**	**3.07**	**2.94**	**2.84**	**2.75**	**2.68**	**2.62**	**2.52**	**2.44**	**2.32**	**2.24**	**2.15**	**2.06**	**2.00**	**1.92**	**1.88**	**1.82**	**1.78**	**1.75**	
46	4.05	3.20	2.81	2.57	2.42	2.30	2.22	2.14	2.09	2.04	2.00	1.97	1.91	1.87	1.80	1.75	1.71	1.65	1.62	1.57	1.54	1.51	1.48	1.46	46
	7.21	**5.10**	**4.24**	**3.76**	**3.44**	**3.22**	**3.05**	**2.92**	**2.82**	**2.73**	**2.66**	**2.60**	**2.50**	**2.42**	**2.30**	**2.22**	**2.13**	**2.04**	**1.98**	**1.90**	**1.86**	**1.80**	**1.76**	**1.72**	

n_2 Degrees of Freedom in the Denominator.

Table C-1 (Continued)

n_1 Degrees of Freedom in the Numerator

n_2	1	2	3	4	5	6	7	8	9	10	11	12	14	16	20	24	30	40	50	75	100	200	500	∞	n_2
48	4.04	3.19	2.80	2.56	2.41	2.30	2.21	2.14	2.08	2.03	1.99	1.96	1.90	1.86	1.79	1.74	1.70	1.64	1.61	1.56	1.53	1.50	1.47	1.45	48
	7.19	5.08	4.22	3.74	3.42	3.20	3.04	2.90	2.80	2.71	2.64	2.58	2.48	2.40	2.28	2.20	2.11	2.02	1.96	1.88	1.84	1.78	1.73	1.70	
50	4.03	3.18	2.79	2.56	2.40	2.29	2.20	2.13	2.07	2.02	1.98	1.95	1.90	1.85	1.78	1.74	1.69	1.63	1.60	1.55	1.52	1.48	1.46	1.44	50
	7.17	5.06	4.20	3.72	3.41	3.18	3.02	2.88	2.78	2.70	2.62	2.56	2.46	2.39	2.26	2.18	2.10	2.00	1.94	1.86	1.82	1.76	1.71	1.68	
55	4.02	3.17	2.78	2.54	2.38	2.27	2.18	2.11	2.05	2.00	1.97	1.93	1.88	1.83	1.76	1.72	1.67	1.61	1.58	1.52	1.50	1.46	1.43	1.41	55
	7.12	5.01	4.16	3.68	3.37	3.15	2.98	2.85	2.75	2.66	2.59	2.53	2.43	2.35	2.23	2.15	2.06	1.96	1.90	1.82	1.78	1.71	1.66	1.64	
60	4.00	3.15	2.76	2.52	2.37	2.25	2.17	2.10	2.04	1.99	1.95	1.92	1.86	1.81	1.75	1.70	1.65	1.59	1.56	1.50	1.48	1.44	1.41	1.39	60
	7.08	4.98	4.13	3.65	3.34	3.12	2.95	2.82	2.72	2.63	2.56	2.50	2.40	2.32	2.20	2.12	2.03	1.93	1.87	1.79	1.74	1.68	1.63	1.60	
65	3.99	3.14	2.75	2.51	2.36	2.24	2.15	2.08	2.02	1.98	1.94	1.90	1.85	1.80	1.73	1.68	1.63	1.57	1.54	1.49	1.46	1.42	1.39	1.37	65
	7.04	4.95	4.10	3.62	3.31	3.09	2.93	2.79	2.70	2.61	2.54	2.47	2.37	2.30	2.18	2.09	2.00	1.90	1.84	1.76	1.71	1.64	1.60	1.56	
70	3.98	3.13	2.74	2.50	2.35	2.23	2.14	2.07	2.01	1.97	1.93	1.89	1.84	1.79	1.72	1.67	1.62	1.56	1.53	1.47	1.45	1.40	1.37	1.35	70
	7.01	4.92	4.08	3.60	3.29	3.07	2.91	2.77	2.67	2.59	2.51	2.45	2.35	2.28	2.15	2.07	1.98	1.88	1.82	1.74	1.69	1.62	1.56	1.53	
80	3.96	3.11	2.72	2.48	2.33	2.21	2.12	2.05	1.99	1.95	1.91	1.88	1.82	1.77	1.70	1.65	1.60	1.54	1.51	1.45	1.42	1.38	1.35	1.32	80
	6.96	4.88	4.04	3.56	3.25	3.04	2.87	2.74	2.64	2.55	2.48	2.41	2.32	2.24	2.11	2.03	1.94	1.84	1.78	1.70	1.65	1.57	1.52	1.49	
100	3.94	3.09	2.70	2.46	2.30	2.19	2.10	2.03	1.97	1.92	1.88	1.85	1.79	1.75	1.68	1.63	1.57	1.51	1.48	1.42	1.39	1.34	1.30	1.28	100
	6.90	4.82	3.98	3.51	3.20	2.99	2.82	2.69	2.59	2.51	2.43	2.36	2.26	2.19	2.06	1.98	1.89	1.79	1.73	1.64	1.59	1.51	1.46	1.43	
125	3.92	3.07	2.68	2.44	2.29	2.17	2.08	2.01	1.95	1.90	1.86	1.83	1.77	1.72	1.65	1.60	1.55	1.49	1.45	1.39	1.36	1.31	1.27	1.25	125
	6.84	4.78	3.94	3.47	3.17	2.95	2.79	2.65	2.56	2.47	2.40	2.33	2.23	2.15	2.03	1.94	1.85	1.75	1.68	1.59	1.54	1.46	1.40	1.37	
150	3.91	3.06	2.67	2.43	2.27	2.16	2.07	2.00	1.94	1.89	1.85	1.82	1.76	1.71	1.64	1.59	1.54	1.47	1.44	1.37	1.34	1.29	1.25	1.22	150
	6.81	4.75	3.91	3.44	3.14	2.92	2.76	2.62	2.53	2.44	2.37	2.30	2.20	2.12	2.00	1.91	1.83	1.72	1.66	1.56	1.51	1.43	1.37	1.33	
200	3.89	3.04	2.65	2.41	2.26	2.14	2.05	1.98	1.92	1.87	1.83	1.80	1.74	1.69	1.62	1.57	1.52	1.45	1.42	1.35	1.32	1.26	1.22	1.19	200
	6.76	4.71	3.88	3.41	3.11	2.90	2.73	2.60	2.50	2.41	2.34	2.28	2.17	2.09	1.97	1.88	1.79	1.69	1.62	1.53	1.48	1.39	1.33	1.28	
400	3.86	3.02	2.62	2.39	2.23	2.12	2.03	1.96	1.90	1.85	1.81	1.78	1.72	1.67	1.60	1.54	1.49	1.42	1.38	1.32	1.28	1.22	1.16	1.13	400
	6.70	4.66	3.83	3.36	3.06	2.85	2.69	2.55	2.46	2.37	2.29	2.23	2.12	2.04	1.92	1.84	1.74	1.64	1.57	1.47	1.42	1.32	1.24	1.19	
1000	3.85	3.00	2.61	2.38	2.22	2.10	2.02	1.95	1.89	1.84	1.80	1.76	1.70	1.65	1.58	1.53	1.47	1.41	1.36	1.30	1.26	1.19	1.13	1.08	1000
	6.66	4.62	3.80	3.34	3.04	2.82	2.66	2.53	2.43	2.34	2.26	2.20	2.09	2.01	1.89	1.81	1.71	1.61	1.54	1.44	1.38	1.28	1.19	1.11	
∞	3.84	2.99	2.60	2.37	2.21	2.09	2.01	1.94	1.88	1.83	1.79	1.75	1.69	1.64	1.57	1.52	1.46	1.40	1.35	1.28	1.24	1.17	1.11	1.00	∞
	6.64	4.60	3.78	3.32	3.02	2.80	2.64	2.51	2.41	2.32	2.24	2.18	2.07	1.99	1.87	1.79	1.69	1.59	1.52	1.41	1.36	1.25	1.15	1.00	

n_2 Degrees of Freedom in the Denominator.
Source: George W. Snedecor and William G. Cochran, *Statistical Methods*, 6th ed. (Ames, Iowa: The Iowa State University Press, 1967). Copyright © 1967 by the Iowa State University Press; reprinted by permission.

APPENDIX D

Data for Air-Miles Traveled and Retail Sales of New Automobiles

Table D-1 Air-miles traveled: sample data[a]

Date	Quarterly Air-Miles Traveled (Seasonally Adjusted, Billions of Miles)[b]	Gross National Product in 1972 Dollars (Seasonally Adjusted Annual Rate, Billions of Dollars)[c]	Disposable Personal Income in 1972 Dollars (Seasonally Adjusted Annual Rate, Billions of Dollars)[c]	Quarterly Air-Miles Traveled, Lagged One Year (Seasonally Adjusted, Billions of Miles)
1961:I	7	737	491	7
II	7	749	498	7
III	8	759	503	7
IV	8	777	512	7
1962:I	8	788	516	7
II	8	798	521	7
III	8	804	524	8
IV	8	806	526	8
1963:I	9	814	531	8
II	9	824	536	8
III	9	839	541	8
IV	10	847	549	8
1964:I	10	861	560	9
II	10	872	576	9
III	11	880	583	9
IV	11	884	590	10
1965:I	11	903	596	10
II	12	916	603	10
III	13	932	620	11
IV	13	952	631	11
1966:I	14	970	636	11
II	15	976	639	12
III	12	985	646	13
IV	16	993	653	13
1967:I	18	994	662	14
II	18	1,001	668	15
III	20	1,014	673	12
IV	20	1,021	678	16
1968:I	21	1,031	686	18
II	22	1,049	697	18
III	22	1,062	697	20
IV	23	1,065	701	20
1969:I	24	1,075	702	21
II	25	1,080	707	22
III	26	1,083	719	22
IV	26	1,078	723	23

[a]See Examples 5-1 and 5-3.
[b]Civil Aeronautics Board, *Air Carrier Traffic Statistics*.
[c]Taken from *Business Conditions Digest*.

Date	Quarterly Air-Miles Traveled (Seasonally Adjusted, Billions of Miles)[b]	Gross National Product in 1972 Dollars (Seasonally Adjusted Annual Rate, Billions of Dollars)[c]	Disposable Personal Income in 1972 Dollars (Seasonally Adjusted Annual Rate, Billions of Dollars)[c]	Quarterly Air-Miles Traveled, Lagged One Year (Seasonally Adjusted, Billions of Miles)
1970:I	26	1,074	727	24
II	25	1,074	743	25
III	27	1,082	750	26
IV	26	1,071	746	26
1971:I	25	1,095	761	26
II	26	1,103	770	25
III	27	1,111	770	27
IV	28	1,120	776	26
1972:I	29	1,141	784	25
II	29	1,163	791	26
III	30	1,178	804	27
IV	31	1,202	827	28
1973:I	31	1,230	845	29
II	31	1,231	853	29
III	32	1,236	858	30
IV	32	1,243	862	31
1974:I	33	1,230	847	31
II	33	1,224	843	31
III	32	1,217	843	32
IV	32	1,200	835	32
1975:I	32	1,172	830	33
II	32	1,190	874	33
III	34	1,220	863	32
IV	34	1,228	872	32
1976:I	35	1,256	883	32
II	36	1,268	888	32
III	36	1,276	893	34
IV	37	1,284	903	34
1977:I	38	1,307	908	35
II	38	1,326	922	36
III	39	1,344	936	36
IV	41	1,355	952	37
1978:I	43	1,368	957	38
II	45	1,395	966	38
III	47	1,407	976	39
IV	48	1,427	992	41
1979:I	51	1,431	997	43
II	50	1,422	993	45
III	52	1,433	993	47

Table D-2 Retail sales of new passenger cars: sample data[a]

Date	Retail Sales of Automobiles (Seasonally Adjusted, Millions of Dollars)[b]	Personal Income Less Transfer Payments in 1972 Dollars (Seasonally Adjusted Annual Rate, Billions of Dollars)[c]	Date	Retail Sales of Automobiles (Seasonally Adjusted, Millions of Dollars)[b]	Personal Income Less Transfer Payments in 1972 Dollars (Seasonally Adjusted Annual Rate, Billions of Dollars)[c]
1956:I	8,920	470	1967:I	13,028	698
II	8,939	475	II	13,530	702
III	8,888	476	III	13,562	709
IV	9,268	485	IV	13,810	715
1957:I	9,769	484	1968:I	14,804	725
II	9,767	486	II	15,091	734
III	9,691	488	III	15,309	745
IV	9,329	484	IV	16,500	751
1958:I	8,606	476	1969:I	16,384	758
II	8,335	474	II	16,141	765
III	8,518	486	III	16,118	773
IV	8,726	493	IV	16,863	777
1959:I	9,816	498	1970:I	15,922	778
II	10,155	507	II	16,265	782
III	10,374	504	III	16,220	783
IV	9,074	509	IV	14,632	776
1960:I	10,128	516	1971:I	18,242	786
II	10,155	519	II	18,995	789
III	9,746	518	III	19,722	792
IV	9,397	515	IV	21,348	802
1961:I	9,012	517	1972:I	20,747	822
II	9,084	523	II	21,573	831
III	9,447	529	III	22,005	843
IV	10,062	540	IV	24,506	859
1962:I	10,420	545	1973:I	26,236	874
II	10,754	552	II	25,210	881
III	10,826	556	III	25,135	887
IV	11,421	560	IV	24,843	893
1963:I	11,442	563	1974:I	22,949	874
II	11,655	569	II	23,897	869
III	11,559	575	III	25,360	868
IV	12,046	582	IV	22,982	857
1964:I	12,024	590	1975:I	24,140	842
II	12,350	601	II	25,367	846
III	12,978	611	III	27,109	859
IV	11,995	619	IV	28,890	867
1965:I	14,191	628	1976:I	30,113	877
II	13,934	638	II	31,476	889
III	14,070	649	III	31,265	894
IV	14,697	663	IV	32,868	908
1966:I	14,898	670	1977:I	35,596	919
II	13,972	678	II	35,489	932
III	14,685	685	III	35,326	941
IV	14,590	690	IV	37,302	962

[a]See Examples 5-2 and 5-4.
[b]*Survey of Current Business.*
[c]*Business Conditions Digest.*

APPENDIX E

Data for Auto Sales and Installment Loans

Table E-1 Unit sales of automobiles: sample data[a]

Date	Unit Sales of Automobiles (SAAR, Millions)[b]	Personal Income Less Transfer Payments (SAAR, Billions of Dollars)[b]	Index of Consumer Sentiment (1966:1 = 100)[b]	Unemployment Rate, Total (Percent)[b]
1960:I	6.13	516	99	5.1
II	6.10	519	93	5.2
III	6.33	518	92	5.5
IV	5.93	515	90	6.3
1961:I	5.00	517	91	6.8
II	5.43	523	92	7.0
III	5.63	529	93	6.8
IV	6.17	540	94	6.2
1962:I	6.40	545	97	5.6
II	6.67	552	95	5.5
III	6.53	556	92	5.6
IV	7.20	560	95	5.5
1963:I	7.23	563	95	5.8
II	7.33	569	91	5.7
III	7.10	574	96	5.5
IV	7.60	582	97	5.6
1964:I	7.63	589	99	5.5
II	7.80	601	98	5.2
III	8.13	611	100	5.0
IV	7.07	619	99	5.0
1965:I	9.20	628	102	4.9
II	8.60	638	102	4.7
III	8.67	648	103	4.4
IV	8.67	663	103	4.1
1966:I	9.87	670	100	3.9
II	8.57	678	96	3.8
III	8.87	685	91	3.8
IV	8.90	691	88	3.7
1967:I	8.00	698	92	3.8
II	8.90	702	95	3.8
III	8.50	709	97	3.8
IV	8.07	715	93	3.9
1968:I	9.40	724	95	3.7
II	9.37	735	92	3.6
III	9.97	746	93	3.5
IV	9.80	752	92	3.4
1969:I	9.67	758	95	3.4
II	9.60	765	92	3.4
III	9.60	772	86	3.6
IV	9.40	776	80	3.6

[a]See Examples 6-1 and 6-3.
[b]Taken from *Survey of Current Business* and *Business Conditions Digest*.

Table E-1 (Continued)

Date	Unit Sales of Automobiles (SAAR, Millions)[b]	Personal Income Less Transfer Payments (SAAR, Billions of Dollars)[b]	Index of Consumer Sentiment (1966:I = 100)[b]	Unemployment Rate, Total (Percent)[b]
1970:I	8.77	777	78	4.2
II	9.13	783	75	4.7
III	9.00	784	77	5.2
IV	6.87	776	75	5.9
1971:I	10.03	787	78	5.9
II	9.97	790	82	5.9
III	10.40	791	82	6.0
IV	10.63	801	82	6.0
1972:I	10.53	821	88	5.8
II	10.77	830	89	5.6
III	10.93	843	94	5.6
IV	11.63	859	91	5.3
1973:I	12.37	874	81	4.9
II	12.23	882	76	4.9
III	11.20	889	72	4.8
IV	9.93	894	76	5.0
1974:I	9.43	874	61	5.1
II	9.27	869	72	5.2
III	9.63	868	64	5.6
IV	7.53	857	58	6.6
1975:I	8.33	842	58	8.2
II	7.85	845	73	8.9
III	9.06	856	76	8.5
IV	9.38	867	75	8.3
1976:I	10.17	879	85	7.7
II	10.08	891	82	7.5
III	9.96	897	89	7.7
IV	10.24	911	86	7.8
1977:I	11.28	922	88	7.4
II	11.54	935	89	7.1
III	10.93	946	88	6.9
IV	10.98	966	83	6.6
1978:I	10.82	972	78	6.2
II	12.04	988	84	6.0
III	11.23	1,001	79	6.0
IV	11.13	1,022	82	5.8
1979:I	11.63	1,024	83	5.7
II	10.53	1,022	80	5.8
III	10.77	1,021	82	5.8
IV	9.83	1,029	78	5.9

Table E-2 Installment loans: sample data[a]

Date		Installment Loans in Memphis (Millions of Dollars)	Installment Loans in Memphis, Lagged One Month	Unemployment Rate in Memphis (Percent)	Memphis Index of Economic Activity (1967 = 100)
1975:	January	235	228	6.36	117.5
	February	227	235	6.83	118.2
	March	221	227	6.89	116.9
	April	214	221	7.37	117.0
	May	210	214	7.10	117.1
	June	208	210	7.67	116.0
	July	205	208	7.79	117.4
	August	205	205	7.85	117.2
	September	198	205	8.10	117.7
	October	203	198	7.71	116.9
	November	198	203	7.79	117.4
	December	197	198	7.96	117.7
1976:	January	199	197	7.88	118.4
	February	196	199	6.75	117.3
	March	197	196	6.58	117.3
	April	195	197	6.53	117.5
	May	198	195	6.57	118.5
	June	201	198	5.58	118.3
	July	203	201	6.00	118.5
	August	204	203	5.97	118.6
	September	209	204	7.10	120.4
	October	209	209	5.88	121.3
	November	209	209	5.53	120.3
	December	214	209	5.68	122.8
1977:	January	212	214	6.48	123.2
	February	210	212	6.36	122.4
	March	212	210	6.71	122.7
	April	214	212	6.52	123.0
	May	217	214	6.60	123.3
	June	223	217	6.78	123.4
	July	226	223	6.71	123.6
	August	234	226	6.44	124.0
	September	237	234	6.32	124.2
	October	241	237	6.22	124.9
	November	245	241	5.52	125.0
	December	251	245	5.72	125.8

[a]See Example 6-2.

Table E-2 (Continued)

Date		Installment Loans in Memphis (Millions of Dollars)	Installment Loans in Memphis, Lagged One Month	Unemployment Rate in Memphis (Percent)	Memphis Index of Economic Activity (1967 = 100)
1978:	January	251	251	5.57	125.6
	February	254	251	5.64	127.1
	March	262	254	5.60	127.4
	April	266	262	5.44	128.4
	May	269	266	5.36	128.6
	June	272	269	5.20	129.2
	July	275	272	5.19	129.1
	August	278	275	5.88	129.0
	September	281	278	5.56	128.4
	October	285	281	5.44	129.0
	November	301	285	5.43	130.0
	December	308	301	5.44	129.2
1979:	January	308	308	6.33	129.1
	February	310	308	5.22	129.1
	March	308	310	5.10	129.0
	April	317	308	4.50	129.1
	May	322	317	4.81	128.9
	June	327	322	4.88	127.5
	July	328	327	5.19	128.2
	August	334	328	5.16	127.2
	September	338	334	5.56	127.9
	October	340	338	5.60	127.3
	November	340	340	5.98	126.5
	December	343	340	5.88	126.2

Table E-3   Correcting for multicollinearity: sample data[a]

Date	Final Sales in 1972 Dollars[b] (Billions)	Population (Millions)	Disposable Personal Income in 1972 Dollars[c] (Billions)	Per Capita Disposable Income in 1972 Dollars	Per Capita Final Sales in 1972 Dollars
1958	681	174	459	2,636	3,914
1959	714	177	477	2,696	4,034
1960	732	181	487	2,697	4,044
1961	752	184	501	2,725	4,087
1962	791	187	522	2,796	4,230
1963	823	189	539	2,849	4,354
1964	867	192	577	3,009	4,516
1965	915	194	612	3,152	4,716
1966	964	197	644	3,274	4,893
1967	996	199	670	3,371	5,005
1968	1,043	201	695	3,464	5,189
1969	1,068	203	712	3,515	5,261
1970	1,071	205	742	3,619	5,224
1971	1,101	207	769	3,714	5,319
1972	1,162	209	801	3,837	5,560
1973	1,218	210	855	4,062	5,800
1974	1,210	212	842	3,973	5,708
1975	1,212	214	860	4,025	5,664
1976	1,264	215	891	4,136	5,879
1977	1,324	217	926	4,271	6,101
1978					

[a]See Chapter 6 under "Multicollinearity" and equations (6-27), (6-28), and (6-31).
[b]*Business Conditions Digest*, Series No. 213.
[c]*Business Conditions Digest*, Series No. 225.

The Durbin-Watson
d Statistic

For applications, see:

Table F-1

Level of Significance $\alpha = .025$

n	$k^a = 1$ d_l	d_u	$k = 2$ d_l	d_u	$k = 3$ d_l	d_u	$k = 4$ d_l	d_u	$k = 5$ d_l	d_u
15	0.95	1.23	0.83	1.40	0.71	1.61	0.59	1.84	0.48	2.09
16	0.98	1.24	0.86	1.40	0.75	1.59	0.64	1.80	0.53	2.03
17	1.01	1.25	0.90	1.40	0.79	1.58	0.68	1.77	0.57	1.98
18	1.03	1.26	0.93	1.40	0.82	1.56	0.72	1.74	0.62	1.93
19	1.06	1.28	0.96	1.41	0.86	1.55	0.76	1.73	0.66	1.90
20	1.08	1.28	0.99	1.41	0.89	1.55	0.79	1.72	0.70	1.87
21	1.10	1.30	1.01	1.41	0.92	1.54	0.83	1.69	0.73	1.84
22	1.12	1.31	1.04	1.42	0.95	1.54	0.86	1.68	0.77	1.82
23	1.14	1.32	1.06	1.42	0.97	1.54	0.89	1.67	0.80	1.80
24	1.16	1.33	1.08	1.43	1.00	1.54	0.91	1.66	0.83	1.79
25	1.18	1.34	1.10	1.43	1.02	1.54	0.94	1.65	0.86	1.77
26	1.19	1.35	1.12	1.44	1.04	1.54	0.96	1.65	0.88	1.76
27	1.21	1.36	1.13	1.44	1.06	1.54	0.99	1.64	0.91	1.75
28	1.22	1.37	1.15	1.45	1.08	1.54	1.01	1.64	0.93	1.74
29	1.24	1.38	1.17	1.45	1.10	1.54	1.03	1.63	0.96	1.73
30	1.25	1.38	1.18	1.46	1.12	1.54	1.05	1.63	0.98	1.73
31	1.26	1.39	1.20	1.47	1.13	1.55	1.07	1.63	1.00	1.72
32	1.27	1.40	1.21	1.47	1.15	1.55	1.08	1.63	1.02	1.71
33	1.28	1.41	1.22	1.48	1.16	1.55	1.10	1.63	1.04	1.71
34	1.29	1.41	1.24	1.48	1.17	1.55	1.12	1.63	1.06	1.70
35	1.30	1.42	1.25	1.48	1.19	1.55	1.13	1.63	1.07	1.70
36	1.31	1.43	1.26	1.49	1.20	1.56	1.15	1.63	1.09	1.70
37	1.32	1.43	1.27	1.49	1.21	1.56	1.16	1.62	1.10	1.70
38	1.33	1.44	1.28	1.50	1.23	1.56	1.17	1.62	1.12	1.70
39	1.34	1.44	1.29	1.50	1.24	1.56	1.19	1.63	1.13	1.69
40	1.35	1.45	1.30	1.51	1.25	1.57	1.20	1.63	1.15	1.69
45	1.39	1.48	1.34	1.53	1.30	1.58	1.25	1.63	1.21	1.69
50	1.42	1.50	1.38	1.54	1.34	1.59	1.30	1.64	1.26	1.69
55	1.45	1.52	1.41	1.56	1.37	1.60	1.33	1.64	1.30	1.69
60	1.47	1.54	1.44	1.57	1.40	1.61	1.37	1.65	1.33	1.69
65	1.49	1.55	1.46	1.59	1.43	1.63	1.40	1.66	1.36	1.69
70	1.51	1.57	1.48	1.60	1.45	1.63	1.42	1.66	1.39	1.70
75	1.53	1.58	1.50	1.61	1.47	1.64	1.45	1.67	1.42	1.70
80	1.54	1.59	1.52	1.63	1.49	1.65	1.47	1.67	1.44	1.70
85	1.56	1.60	1.53	1.63	1.51	1.66	1.49	1.68	1.46	1.71
90	1.57	1.61	1.55	1.64	1.53	1.66	1.50	1.69	1.48	1.71
95	1.58	1.62	1.56	1.65	1.54	1.67	1.52	1.69	1.50	1.71
100	1.59	1.63	1.57	1.65	1.55	1.67	1.53	1.70	1.51	1.72

$^a k$ = number of regressors, excluding the constant.
Source: Reprinted, with permission, from J. Durbin and G. S. Watson, "Testing for Serial Correlation in Least Squares Regression, II," *Biometrika*, Vol. 38 (1951), 159–78.

Tabe F-2

Level of Significance $\alpha = .01$

	$k^a = 1$		$k = 2$		$k = 3$		$k = 4$		$k = 5$	
n	d_l	d_u	d_l	d_u	d_l	d_u	d_l	d_u	d_l	d_u
15	0.81	1.07	0.70	1.25	0.59	1.46	0.49	1.70	0.39	1.96
16	0.84	1.09	0.74	1.25	0.63	1.44	0.53	1.66	0.44	1.90
17	0.87	1.10	0.77	1.25	0.67	1.43	0.57	1.63	0.48	1.85
18	0.90	1.12	0.80	1.26	0.71	1.42	0.61	1.60	0.52	1.80
19	0.93	1.13	0.83	1.26	0.74	1.41	0.65	1.58	0.56	1.77
20	0.95	1.15	0.86	1.27	0.77	1.41	0.68	1.57	0.60	1.74
21	0.97	1.16	0.89	1.27	0.80	1.41	0.72	1.55	0.63	1.71
22	1.00	1.17	0.91	1.28	0.83	1.40	0.75	1.54	0.66	1.69
23	1.02	1.19	0.94	1.29	0.86	1.40	0.77	1.53	0.70	1.67
24	1.04	1.20	0.96	1.30	0.88	1.41	0.80	1.53	0.72	1.66
25	1.05	1.21	0.98	1.30	0.90	1.41	0.83	1.52	0.75	1.65
26	1.07	1.22	1.00	1.31	0.93	1.41	0.85	1.52	0.78	1.64
27	1.09	1.23	1.02	1.32	0.95	1.41	0.88	1.51	0.81	1.63
28	1.10	1.24	1.04	1.32	0.97	1.41	0.90	1.51	0.83	1.62
29	1.12	1.25	1.05	1.33	0.99	1.42	0.92	1.51	0.85	1.61
30	1.13	1.26	1.07	1.34	1.01	1.42	0.94	1.51	0.88	1.61
31	1.15	1.27	1.08	1.34	1.02	1.42	0.96	1.51	0.90	1.60
32	1.16	1.28	1.10	1.35	1.04	1.43	0.98	1.51	0.92	1.60
33	1.17	1.29	1.11	1.36	1.05	1.43	1.00	1.51	0.94	1.59
34	1.18	1.30	1.13	1.36	1.07	1.43	1.01	1.51	0.95	1.59
35	1.19	1.31	1.14	1.37	1.08	1.44	1.03	1.51	0.97	1.59
36	1.21	1.32	1.15	1.38	1.10	1.44	1.04	1.51	0.99	1.59
37	1.22	1.32	1.16	1.38	1.11	1.45	1.06	1.51	1.00	1.59
38	1.23	1.33	1.18	1.39	1.12	1.45	1.07	1.52	1.02	1.58
39	1.24	1.34	1.19	1.39	1.14	1.45	1.09	1.52	1.03	1.58
40	1.25	1.34	1.20	1.40	1.15	1.46	1.10	1.52	1.05	1.58
45	1.29	1.38	1.24	1.42	1.20	1.48	1.16	1.53	1.11	1.58
50	1.32	1.40	1.28	1.45	1.24	1.49	1.20	1.54	1.16	1.59
55	1.36	1.43	1.32	1.47	1.28	1.51	1.25	1.55	1.21	1.59
60	1.38	1.45	1.35	1.48	1.32	1.52	1.28	1.56	1.25	1.60
65	1.41	1.47	1.38	1.50	1.35	1.53	1.31	1.57	1.28	1.61
70	1.43	1.49	1.40	1.52	1.37	1.55	1.34	1.58	1.31	1.61
75	1.45	1.50	1.42	1.53	1.39	1.56	1.37	1.59	1.34	1.62
80	1.47	1.52	1.44	1.54	1.42	1.57	1.39	1.60	1.36	1.62
85	1.48	1.53	1.46	1.55	1.43	1.58	1.41	1.60	1.39	1.63
90	1.50	1.54	1.47	1.56	1.45	1.59	1.43	1.61	1.41	1.64
95	1.51	1.55	1.49	1.57	1.47	1.60	1.45	1.62	1.42	1.64
100	1.52	1.56	1.50	1.58	1.48	1.60	1.46	1.63	1.44	1.65

[a]k = number of regressors, excluding the constant.

Source: Reprinted, with permission, from J. Durbin and G.S. Watson, "Testing for Serial Correlation in Least Squares Regression, II," *Biometrika*, Vol. 38 (1951), 159–78.

Unit Sales of Automobiles: Sample Data

Table G-1

Date	Unit Sales of Automobiles[a] (SAAR, Millions)	Personal Income Less Transfer Payments (SAAR, Billions of Dollars)	Index of Consumer Sentiment (1966:I = 100)	Unemployment Rate, Total (Percent)	Index of Cost of Car Ownership[b] (1972 = 1.000)	Average Miles per Gallon of Current Model Year Cars[b]	Dummy Variable for Automobile Strikes[b]	Depreciation Rate-Stock of Cars[b]	Index of the Average Price of a New Car[b]	Stock of Cars[b] (Millions)	Finance Rate on Automobile Loans[b] (Percent)
1965: I	9.20	628	102	4.9	0.782	14.1	0	0.022	3.003	68.2	8.09
II	8.60	638	102	4.7	0.780	14.1	0	0.023	3.006	68.9	8.02
III	8.67	648	103	4.4	0.778	14.1	220	0.024	2.954	69.6	8.02
IV	8.67	663	103	4.1	0.778	13.9	0	0.025	2.991	70.2	8.10
1966: I	9.87	670	100	3.9	0.783	13.9	0	0.025	3.002	70.9	8.21
II	8.57	678	96	3.8	0.795	13.9	0	0.025	3.044	71.3	8.50
III	8.87	685	91	3.8	0.812	13.9	0	0.025	3.057	71.7	8.88
IV	8.90	691	88	3.7	0.827	13.5	0	0.024	3.091	72.2	9.13
1967:I	8.00	698	92	3.8	0.817	13.5	0	0.024	3.109	72.5	8.99
II	8.90	702	95	3.8	0.816	13.5	0	0.024	3.142	73.0	8.69
III	8.50	709	97	3.8	0.830	13.5	3,816	0.022	3.208	73.5	8.73
IV	8.07	715	93	3.9	0.846	13.6	7,261	0.022	3.282	73.9	8.89
1968: I	9.40	724	95	3.7	0.862	13.6	22	0.022	3.333	74.6	9.08
II	9.37	735	92	3.6	0.876	13.6	0	0.022	3.391	75.4	9.40
III	9.97	746	93	3.5	0.895	13.6	0	0.022	3.385	76.2	9.81
IV	9.80	752	92	3.4	0.900	13.5	234	0.021	3.472	77.0	9.77
1969: I	9.67	758	95	3.4	0.916	13.5	0	0.022	3.528	77.8	10.03
II	9.60	765	92	3.4	0.940	13.5	1,792	0.022	3.540	78.5	10.41
III	9.60	772	86	3.6	0.958	13.5	664	0.023	3.573	79.1	10.86
IV	9.40	776	80	3.6	0.972	13.0	0	0.023	3.564	79.6	11.06
1970: I	8.77	777	78	4.2	0.984	13.0	0	0.023	3.513	79.9	11.34
II	9.13	783	77	5.2	1.001	13.0	0	0.022	3.511	80.4	11.30
III	9.00	784	77	5.2	1.001	13.0	5,120	0.020	3.549	81.1	11.37
IV	6.87	776	75	5.9	1.024	12.6	16,320	0.019	3.448	81.3	11.25
1971:I	10.03	787	78	5.9	1.025	12.6	0	0.019	3.754	82.2	10.59
II	9.97	790	82	5.9	0.999	12.6	0	0.019	3.738	83.1	10.12
III	10.40	791	82	6.0	1.005	12.6	0	0.021	3.694	84.0	10.42
IV	10.63	801	82	6.0	0.996	12.6	0	0.021	3.708	84.9	10.41
1972:I	10.53	821	88	5.8	1.001	12.6	0	0.022	3.777	85.7	10.20
II	10.77	830	89	5.6	0.995	12.6	0	0.022	3.862	86.4	9.96

[a]See Example 7-2 and equations (7-7), (7-8), and (7-23).
[b]Data Resources Incorporated, Lexington, Mass., Historical Data Bank.

Table G-1 (Continued)

Date	Unit Sales of Automobiles[a] (SAAR, Millions)	Personal Income Less Transfer Payments (SAAR, Billions of Dollars)	Index of Consumer Sentiment (1966:I = 100)	Unemployment Rate, Total (Percent)	Index of Cost of Car Ownership[b] (1972 = 1.000)	Average Miles per Gallon of Current Model Year Cars[b]	Dummy Variable for Automobile Strikes[b]	Depreciation Rate-Stock of Cars[b]	Index of the Average Price of a New Car[b]	Stock of Cars[b] (Millions)	Finance Rate on Automobile Loans[b] (Percent)
III	10.93	843	94	5.6	1.004	12.6	0	0.024	3.938	87.1	10.02
IV	11.63	859	91	5.3	1.000	13.3	0	0.025	3.937	87.9	10.02
1973:I	12.37	874	81	4.9	1.009	13.3	0	0.024	4.019	88.8	10.05
II	12.23	882	76	4.9	1.023	13.3	0	0.023	4.005	89.8	10.05
III	11.20	889	72	4.8	1.042	13.3	0	0.021	4.139	90.7	10.25
IV	9.93	894	76	5.0	1.080	12.1	0	0.020	4.076	91.3	10.49
1974:I	9.43	874	61	5.1	1.131	12.1	0	0.019	4.111	92.0	10.53
II	9.27	869	72	5.2	1.194	12.1	0	0.018	4.231	92.6	10.65
III	9.63	868	64	5.6	1.261	12.1	0	0.016	4.526	93.5	11.14
IV	7.53	857	58	6.6	1.310	13.6	0	0.015	4.632	94.0	11.57
1975:I	8.33	842	58	8.2	1.315	13.6	0	0.015	4.564	94.7	11.53
II	7.85	845	73	8.9	1.336	13.6	0	0.015	4.982	95.2	11.36
III	9.06	856	76	8.5	1.369	13.6	0	0.017	5.010	95.9	11.31
IV	9.38	867	75	8.3	1.389	14.3	0	0.018	5.166	96.5	11.24
1976:I	10.17	879	85	7.7	1.396	14.3	0	0.019	5.341	97.2	11.17
II	10.08	891	82	7.5	1.407	14.3	0	0.020	5.459	97.8	11.04
III	9.96	897	89	7.7	1.441	14.3	2.000	0.021	5.462	98.2	11.07
IV	10.24	911	86	7.8	1.470	15.3	1.537	0.022	5.558	98.6	11.03
1977:I	11.28	922	88	7.4	1.492	15.3	0	0.022	5.749	99.2	11.03
II	11.54	935	89	7.1	1.489	15.3	0	0.022	5.749	99.9	10.82
III	10.93	946	88	6.9	1.498	15.3	0	0.020	5.873	100.6	10.85
IV	10.98	966	83	6.6	1.522	15.8	0	0.020	5.999	101.4	10.87
1978:I	10.82	972	78	6.2	1.550	15.8	0	0.020	6.161	102.1	10.86
II	12.04	988	84	6.0	1.571	15.8	0	0.021	6.329	103.0	10.84
III	11.23	1,001	79	6.0	1.629	15.8	0	0.022	6.503	103.6	11.09
IV	11.13	1,022	82	5.8	1.666	16.4	0	0.022	6.611	104.0	11.29
1979:I	11.63	1,024	83	5.7	1.745	16.4	0	0.023	6.825	104.5	11.60
II	10.53	1,022	80	5.8	1.854	16.4	0	0.024	6.742	104.7	11.73
III	10.77	1,021	82	5.8	1.958	16.4	0	0.023	6.999	105.0	11.88
IV	9.83	1,029	78	5.9	2.083	17.0	0	0.023	7.063	105.0	12.85

APPENDIX H

Clothing Sales: Sample Data

Table H-1

Date	Sales[a] (Millions)	Average Price Level of the Company's Product, Lagged One Quarter	Income, Lagged Two Quarters (Millions)	New Credit Extended, Lagged One Quarter (Thousands)	Advertising Expenditures, Lagged One Quarter (Thousands)	Advertising Expenditures of Competitors, Lagged One Quarter (Thousands)
1970:III	6.039	61.26	434	54.4	84	106
IV	5.929	64.36	402	18.1	97	243
1971:I	4.676	61.83	292	97.2	56	284
II	5.998	63.07	528	116.3	43	347
III	5.310	64.44	429	155.4	56	440
IV	5.132	65.52	362	66.8	22	267
1972:I	5.044	65.23	366	-33.1	44	354
II	4.481	65.46	417	-48.6	34	323
III	4.494	68.82	311	-30.9	14	235
IV	5.278	67.91	302	82.5	74	444
1973:I	6.257	70.76	497	157.0	57	100
II	5.553	70.69	387	123.1	84	332
III	5.868	69.32	397	139.9	105	116
IV	5.329	71.52	349	11.0	52	329
1974:I	4.396	73.05	339	-27.0	30	64
II	5.387	72.93	395	127.3	79	258
III	5.791	72.14	445	131.2	68	152
IV	5.602	73.97	472	132.8	27	314
1975:I	4.793	75.09	392	77.5	81	447
II	5.613	77.85	519	-4.6	69	223
III	5.614	75.51	452	-51.2	31	86
IV	5.438	76.01	458	8.3	100	463
1976:I	6.461	79.75	584	139.0	81	295
II	5.127	79.97	471	54.0	18	334
III	5.848	79.63	475	109.1	47	302
IV	5.047	81.65	452	-43.8	45	340

[a]See Example 7-3 and equation (7-28).

Table H-1 (Continued)

Date	Sales[a] (Millions)	Average Price Level of the Company's Product, Lagged One Quarter	Income, Lagged Two Quarters (Millions)	New Credit Extended, Lagged One Quarter (Thousands)	Advertising Expenditures, Lagged One Quarter (Thousands)	Advertising Expenditures of Competitors, Lagged One Quarter (Thousands)
1977: I	6.226	79.79	504	74.3	101	229
II	5.554	80.84	468	95.9	91	127
III	6.676	80.97	564	29.5	82	373
IV	5.218	84.08	358	64.7	96	152
1978: I	5.489	85.66	456	154.7	81	90
II	5.765	84.03	561	137.8	23	430
III	5.065	85.27	449	32.2	29	134
IV	5.794	84.94	496	19.6	103	127
1979: I	6.736	88.33	604	46.2	101	174
II	5.233	87.03	481	−23.5	55	437
III	6.008	87.90	454	161.8	91	120
IV	5.747	89.69	503	−19.2	99	184

APPENDIX I

Smoothed Statistics

Table I-1 The historical performance of Brown's linear exponential smoothing and triple exponential smoothing: simulating air-miles traveled, 1972:10—1978:12.[a]

Date	Period	Air-Miles Traveled (1)	Brown's Linear Exponential-Smoothing Forecasts[b] (2)	Brown's Exponential Error		Triple Exponential-Smoothing Forecasts[c] (5)	Triple Exponential Error	
				Actual (3)	Percentage (4)		Actual (6)	Percentage (7)
1972: 10	1	7.00						
11	2	7.00	7.00	.00	.00	7.00	.00	.00
12	3	8.00	7.00	1.00	12.50	7.00	1.00	12.50
1973: 1	4	8.00	7.60	.40	5.00	7.90	.10	1.25
2	5	8.00	7.93	.07	.87	8.26	-.26	-3.25
3	6	8.00	8.10	-.10	-1.22	8.35	-.35	-4.38
4	7	8.00	8.17	-.17	-2.14	8.32	-.32	-3.98
5	8	8.00	8.19	-.19	-2.40	8.24	-.24	-3.04
6	9	9.00	8.18	.82	9.06	8.16	.84	9.30
7	10	9.00	8.76	.24	2.61	8.99	.01	.07
8	11	9.00	9.07	-.07	-.78	9.30	-.30	-3.35
9	12	10.00	9.21	.79	7.87	9.35	.65	6.46
10	13	10.00	9.86	.14	1.36	10.20	-.20	-1.99
11	14	10.00	10.20	-.20	-1.96	10.47	-.47	-4.70
12	15	11.00	10.34	.66	6.00	10.47	.53	4.78
1974: 1	16	11.00	10.98	.02	.18	11.27	-.27	-2.47
2	17	11.00	11.30	-.30	-2.69	11.51	-.51	-4.60
3	18	12.00	11.42	.58	4.80	11.48	.52	4.32
4	19	13.00	12.05	.95	7.32	12.26	.74	5.68
5	20	13.00	12.95	.05	.38	13.39	-.39	-2.96
6	21	14.00	13.40	.60	4.31	13.72	.28	2.03
7	22	15.00	14.18	.82	5.47	14.58	.42	2.77

[a]Example 9-1.
[b]Equations (9-27), (9-28), and (9-29).
[c]Equations (9-35) through (9-41).

Table I-1 (Continued)

Date	Period	Air-Miles Traveled (1)	Brown's Linear Exponential-Smoothing Forecasts[b] (2)	Brown's Exponential Error		Triple Exponential-Smoothing Forecasts[c] (5)	Triple Exponential Error	
				Actual (3)	Percentage (4)		Actual (6)	Percentage (7)
8	23	12.00	15.15	-3.15	-26.22	15.68	-3.68	-30.64
9	24	16.00	13.81	2.19	13.70	13.23	2.77	17.29
10	25	18.00	15.39	2.61	14.51	15.65	2.35	13.08
11	26	18.00	17.42	.58	3.23	18.38	-.38	-2.12
12	27	20.00	18.47	1.53	7.67	19.31	.69	3.43
1975: 1	28	20.00	20.14	-.14	-.68	21.19	-1.19	-5.95
2	29	21.00	20.94	.06	.27	21.64	-.64	-3.05
3	30	22.00	21.85	.15	.67	22.36	-.36	-1.63
4	31	22.00	22.82	-.82	-3.74	23.22	-1.22	-5.55
5	32	23.00	23.22	-.22	-.97	23.25	-.25	-1.11
6	33	24.00	23.91	.09	.38	23.86	.14	.56
7	34	25.00	24.76	.24	.94	24.76	.24	.96
8	35	26.00	25.71	.29	1.10	25.78	.22	.84
9	36	26.00	26.72	-.72	-2.75	26.85	-.85	-3.26
10	37	26.00	27.14	-1.14	-4.39	27.02	-1.02	-3.92
11	38	25.00	27.25	-2.25	-8.99	26.82	-1.82	-7.28
12	39	27.00	26.59	.41	1.53	25.61	1.39	5.13
1976: 1	40	26.00	27.32	-1.32	-5.08	26.76	-.76	-2.94
2	41	25.00	27.05	-2.05	-8.21	26.26	-1.26	-5.06
3	42	26.00	26.22	-.22	-.86	25.06	.94	3.62
4	43	27.00	26.31	.69	2.56	25.43	1.57	5.83
5	44	28.00	26.92	1.08	3.85	26.51	1.49	5.32
6	45	29.00	27.83	1.17	4.03	27.87	1.13	3.91
7	46	29.00	28.89	.11	.38	29.27	-.27	-.92
8	47	30.00	29.42	.58	1.93	29.72	.28	.95
9	48	31.00	30.24	.76	2.45	30.62	.38	1.22
10	49	31.00	31.22	-.22	-.72	31.72	-.72	-2.31

Table I-1 (Continued)

Date	Period	Air-Miles Traveled	Brown's Linear Exponential-Smoothing Forecasts[b]	Brown's Exponential Error Actual	Brown's Exponential Error Percentage	Triple Exponential-Smoothing Forecasts[c]	Triple Exponential Error Actual	Triple Exponential Error Percentage
11	50	31.00	31.68	-.68	-2.20	31.96	-.96	-3.10
12	51	32.00	31.85	.15	.48	31.84	.16	.51
1977: 1	52	32.00	32.45	-.45	-1.41	32.49	-.49	-1.53
2	53	33.00	32.71	.29	.89	32.60	.40	1.22
3	54	33.00	33.37	-.37	-1.12	33.38	-.38	-1.15
4	55	32.00	33.66	-1.66	-5.19	33.56	-1.56	-4.87
5	56	32.00	33.14	-1.14	-3.57	32.57	-.57	-1.79
6	57	32.00	32.79	-.79	-2.46	32.05	-.05	-.14
7	58	32.00	32.54	-.54	-1.69	31.79	.21	.67
8	59	34.00	32.37	1.63	4.79	31.68	2.32	6.82
9	60	34.00	33.46	.54	1.60	33.46	.54	1.59
10	61	35.00	34.04	.96	2.75	34.20	.80	2.28
11	62	36.00	34.92	1.08	3.01	35.32	.68	1.88
12	63	36.00	35.96	.04	.12	36.57	-.57	-1.57
1978: 1	64	37.00	36.47	.53	1.43	36.91	.09	.25
2	65	38.00	37.28	.72	1.90	37.75	.25	.67
3	66	38.00	38.25	-.25	-.66	38.79	-.79	-2.09
4	67	39.00	38.70	.30	.76	39.01	-.01	-.02
5	68	41.00	39.46	1.54	3.75	39.77	1.23	3.01
6	69	43.00	40.99	2.01	4.67	41.67	1.33	3.10
7	70	45.00	42.94	2.06	4.57	44.02	.98	2.19
8	71	47.00	45.10	1.90	4.03	46.47	.53	1.12
9	72	48.00	47.35	.65	1.35	48.88	-.88	-1.83
10	73	51.00	49.02	1.98	3.87	50.29	.71	1.40
11	74	50.00	51.55	-1.55	-3.10	53.03	-3.03	-6.05
12	75	52.00	52.14	-.14	-.27	52.71	-.71	-1.36
Mean squared error (MSE)				1.09			1.08	
Mean absolute PC error (percentage)					3.5%			3.7%

Table I-2 The historical performance of Brown's linear exponential smoothing and triple exponential smoothing: simulating air-miles traveled, 1972: 10—1978: 7.[a]

Date	Period	Air-Miles Traveled	Brown's Linear Exponential-Smoothing Forecasts[a]	Brown's Exponential Error Actual	Brown's Exponential Error Percentage	Triple Exponential-Smoothing Forecasts[c]	Triple Exponential Error Actual	Triple Exponential Error Percentage
1972:10	1	7.00						
11	2	7.00	7.00	.00	.00	7.00	.00	.00
12	3	8.00	7.00	1.00	12.50	7.00	1.00	12.50
1973:1	4	8.00	7.60	.40	5.00	7.90	.10	1.25
2	5	8.00	7.93	.07	.87	8.26	-.26	-3.25
3	6	8.00	8.10	-.10	-1.22	8.35	-.35	-4.38
4	7	8.00	8.17	-.17	-2.14	8.32	-.32	-3.98
5	8	8.00	8.19	-.19	-2.40	8.24	-.24	-3.04
6	9	9.00	8.18	.82	9.06	8.16	.84	9.30
7	10	9.00	8.76	.24	2.61	8.99	.01	.07
8	11	9.00	9.07	-.07	-.78	9.30	-.30	-3.35
9	12	10.00	9.21	.79	7.87	9.35	.65	6.46
10	13	10.00	9.86	.14	1.36	10.20	-.20	-1.99
11	14	10.00	10.20	-.20	-1.96	10.47	-.47	-4.70
12	15	11.00	10.34	.66	6.00	10.47	.53	4.78
1974:1	16	11.00	10.98	.02	.18	11.27	-.27	-2.47
2	17	11.00	11.30	-.30	-2.69	11.51	-.51	-4.60
3	18	12.00	11.42	.58	4.80	11.48	.52	4.32
4	19	13.00	12.05	.95	7.32	12.26	.74	5.68
5	20	13.00	12.95	.05	.38	13.39	-.39	-2.96
6	21	14.00	13.40	.60	4.31	13.72	.28	2.03
7	22	15.00	14.18	.82	5.47	14.58	.42	2.77

[a]Example 9-1
[b]Equations (9-27), (9-28), and (9-29).
[c]Equations (9-35) through (9-41).

Table I-2 (Continued)

Date	Period	Air-Miles Traveled	Brown's Linear Exponential-Smoothing Forecasts[b]	Brown's Exponential Error		Triple Exponential-Smoothing Forecasts[c]	Triple Exponential Error	
				Actual	Percentage		Actual	Percentage
8	23	12.00	15.15	-3.15	-26.22	15.68	-3.68	-30.64
9	24	16.00	13.81	2.19	13.70	13.23	2.77	17.29
10	25	18.00	15.39	2.61	14.51	15.65	2.35	13.08
11	26	18.00	17.42	.58	3.23	18.38	-.38	-2.12
12	27	20.00	18.47	1.53	7.67	19.31	.69	3.43
1975: 1	28	20.00	20.14	-.14	-.68	21.19	-1.19	-5.95
2	29	21.00	20.94	.06	.27	21.64	-.64	-3.05
3	30	22.00	21.85	.15	.67	22.36	-.36	-1.63
4	31	22.00	22.82	-.82	-3.74	23.22	-1.22	-5.55
5	32	23.00	23.22	-.22	-.97	23.25	-.25	-1.11
6	33	24.00	23.91	.09	.38	23.86	.14	.56
7	34	25.00	24.76	.24	.94	24.76	.24	.96
8	35	26.00	25.71	.29	1.10	25.78	.22	.84
9	36	26.00	26.72	-.72	-2.75	26.85	-.85	-3.26
10	37	26.00	27.14	-1.14	-4.39	27.02	-1.02	-3.92
11	38	25.00	27.25	-2.25	-8.99	26.82	-1.82	-7.28
12	39	27.00	26.59	.41	1.53	25.61	1.39	5.13
1976: 1	40	26.00	27.32	-1.32	-5.08	26.76	-.76	-2.94
2	41	25.00	27.05	-2.05	-8.21	26.26	-1.26	-5.06
3	42	26.00	26.22	-.22	-.86	25.06	.94	3.62
4	43	27.00	26.31	.69	2.56	25.43	1.57	5.83
5	44	28.00	26.92	1.08	3.85	26.51	1.49	5.32
6	45	29.00	27.83	1.17	4.03	27.87	1.13	3.91
7	46	29.00	28.89	.11	.38	29.27	-.27	-.92
8	47	30.00	29.42	.58	1.93	29.72	.28	.95
9	48	31.00	30.24	.76	2.45	30.62	.38	1.22

Table I-2 (Continued)

Date	Period	Air-Miles Traveled	Brown's Linear Exponential-Smoothing Forecasts[b]	Brown's Exponential Error		Triple Exponential-Smoothing Forecasts[c]	Triple Exponential Error	
				Actual	Percentage		Actual	Percentage
10	49	31.00	31.22	-.22	-.72	31.72	-.72	-2.31
11	50	31.00	31.68	-.68	-2.20	31.96	-.96	-3.10
12	51	32.00	31.85	.15	.48	31.84	.16	.51
1977: 1	52	32.00	32.45	-.45	-1.41	32.49	-.49	-1.53
2	53	33.00	32.71	.29	.89	32.60	.40	1.22
3	54	33.00	33.37	-.37	-1.12	33.38	-.38	-1.15
4	55	32.00	33.66	-1.66	-5.19	33.56	-1.56	-4.87
5	56	32.00	33.14	-1.14	-3.57	32.57	-.57	-1.79
6	57	32.00	32.79	-.79	-2.46	32.05	-.05	-.14
7	58	32.00	32.54	-.54	-1.69	31.79	.21	.67
8	59	34.00	32.37	1.63	4.79	31.68	2.32	6.82
9	60	34.00	33.46	.54	1.60	33.46	.54	1.59
10	61	35.00	34.04	.96	2.75	34.20	.80	2.28
11	62	36.00	34.92	1.08	3.01	35.32	.68	1.88
12	63	36.00	35.96	.04	.12	36.57	-.57	-1.57
1978: 1	64	37.00	36.47	.53	1.43	36.91	.09	.25
2	65	38.00	37.28	.72	1.90	37.75	.25	.67
3	66	38.00	38.25	-.25	-.66	38.79	-.79	-2.09
4	67	39.00	38.70	.30	.76	39.01	-.01	-.02
5	68	41.00	39.46	1.54	3.75	39.77	1.23	3.01
6	69	43.00	40.99	2.01	4.67	41.67	1.33	3.10
7	70	45.00	42.94	2.06	4.57	44.02	.98	2.19
Mean squared error (MSE)				1.02			1.00	
Mean absolute PC error (percentage)					3.6%			3.8%

Table I-3 Smoothed statistics for air-miles traveled[a]

Period	Actual Air-Miles Traveled	$S_t^{1\,b}$	$S_t^{2\,c}$	$S_t^{3\,d}$
1	7	7.00	7.00	7.00
2	7	7.00	7.00	7.00
3	8	7.30	7.09	7.03
4	8	7.51	7.22	7.08
5	8	7.89	7.42	7.19
6	8	7.92	7.57	7.30
7	8	7.94	7.68	7.41
8	8	7.96	7.76	7.52
9	9	8.27	7.92	7.64
10	9	8.49	8.09	7.78
11	9	8.64	8.25	7.92
12	10	9.05	8.49	8.09
13	10	9.34	8.75	8.29
14	10	9.53	8.98	8.50
15	11	9.97	9.28	8.73
16	11	10.28	9.58	8.99
17	11	10.50	9.86	9.25
18	12	10.95	10.18	9.53
19	13	11.56	10.60	9.85
20	13	11.99	11.01	10.20
21	14	12.60	11.49	10.59
22	15	13.32	12.04	11.02
23	12	12.92	12.30	11.41
24	16	13.85	12.77	11.81
25	18	15.09	13.46	12.31
26	18	15.96	14.21	12.88
27	20	17.17	15.10	13.55
28	20	18.02	15.98	14.28
29	21	18.92	16.86	15.05
30	22	19.84	17.75	15.86
31	22	20.49	18.57	16.67
32	23	21.24	19.37	17.48
33	24	22.07	20.18	18.29
34	25	22.95	21.01	19.11
35	26	23.87	21.87	19.94
36	26	24.51	22.66	20.75
37	26	24.95	23.35	21.53
38	25	24.97	23.83	22.22
39	27	25.58	24.36	22.86
40	26	25.70	24.76	23.43
41	25	25.49	24.98	23.90
42	26	25.65	25.18	24.28
43	27	26.06	25.44	24.63

[a]Example 9-1.
[b]Equation (9-13).
[c]Equations (9-23) and (9-24).
[d]Equations (9-23), (9-36), and (9-37).

Table I-3 (Continued)

Period	Actual Air-Miles Traveled	$S_t^{1\,b}$	$S_t^{2\,c}$	$S_t^{3\,d}$
44	28	26.64	25.80	24.98
45	29	27.35	26.27	25.37
46	29	27.84	26.74	25.78
47	30	28.49	27.26	26.22
48	31	29.24	27.86	26.71
49	31	29.77	28.43	27.23
50	31	30.14	28.94	27.74
51	32	30.70	29.47	28.26
52	32	31.09	29.96	28.77
53	33	31.66	30.47	29.28
54	33	32.06	30.95	29.78
55	32	32.04	31.27	30.23
56	32	32.03	31.50	30.61
57	32	32.02	31.66	30.92
58	32	32.01	31.76	31.17
59	34	32.61	32.02	31.43
60	34	33.02	32.32	31.69
61	35	33.62	32.71	32.00
62	36	34.33	33.19	32.36
63	36	34.83	33.69	32.76
64	37	35.48	34.22	33.20
65	38	36.24	34.83	33.69
66	38	36.77	35.41	34.20
67	39	37.44	36.01	34.75
68	41	38.50	36.76	35.35
69	43	39.85	37.68	36.05
70	45	41.40	38.80	36.87

Brown's Linear Exponential Smoothing	Triple Exponential Smoothing
$a_{70} = 44$	$a_{70} = 44.67$
$b_{70} = 1.11428$	$b_{70} = 1.75$
	$c_{70} = .0615$
$\hat{Y}_{71} = 45.11$	$\hat{Y}_{71} = 46.48$
$\hat{Y}_{72} = 42.23$	$\hat{Y}_{72} = 48.42$
$\hat{Y}_{73} = 47.34$	$\hat{Y}_{73} = 50.47$
$\hat{Y}_{74} = 48.46$	$\hat{Y}_{74} = 52.65$
$\hat{Y}_{75} = 49.57$	$\hat{Y}_{75} = 54.96$

Author Index

Subject Index